A HISTORY OF THE EARLY CHURCH

Volume I, *The Beginnings of the Christian Church,* and Volume II, *The Founding of the Church Universal,* of this work are available in a companion paperbound volume   (Meridian Books, MG26A).

A HISTORY OF THE EARLY CHURCH

III: From Constantine to Julian
IV: The Era of the Church Fathers

HANS LIETZMANN

translated by Bertram Lee Woolf

N 106

Meridian Books
THE WORLD PUBLISHING COMPANY
Cleveland and New York

From Constantine to Julian: first published in 1950, translation revised 1953.

The Era of the Church Fathers: first published in 1951, translation revised 1953.

A MERIDIAN BOOK

Published by The World Publishing Company
2231 West 110th Street, Cleveland 2, Ohio
First Meridian printing August 1961
Second printing February 1964
Library of Congress Catalog Card Number: 61-15602
Printed in the United States of America   2MWP264

From Constantine to Julian

Volume III of

A HISTORY OF THE EARLY CHURCH

*For
Rosalind, Rosalie, Elizabeth,
Jasper, and Philip*

CONTENTS

Attacks by Germans and Persians, 17. Empire of Postumus on the Rhine, 18. Empire of Palmyra, 19. Claudius the Conqueror of the Goths, and Aurelian, 19. New Cult of the Sun, 20. Diocletian, 21. The Tetrarchy, 22. Court Ceremonial, 25. New Divisions of the Empire, 26. Tax Reform, 27. Coinage, 27. Price-fixing, 27. Army reform, 28. Buildings, 29. Sculpture, 30. Literature, 32. Plotinus, 32. Porphyry, 38. His Asceticism, 42. Against the Christians, 44. Chaldean Oracles and Theurgy, 47. Hermetic Writings, 48. Jewish Influence, 52. Magical Papyri, 53.

Increasing extension of Christianity, 57. Church Buildings, 58. Isolated Conflicts, 59. Edict of Diocletian, 61: its background, 62. Galerius, 62. Edicts against the Marriage of Relatives, and against Manicheans; ancient Roman Motives, 63. Fire in the Palace; Disturbances; second and third Edicts, 64. Bloody Persecution, 65. Fourth Edict, 67. Renunciation of Empire by Diocletian and Maximian, 67. Rise of Constantine and Maxentius, 68. The second tetrarchy, 69. Persecution under Maximinus, 70. Edict of Tolerance, and death of Galerius, 71. Further persecution under Maximinus, 72. Constantine against Maxentius, 74. Battle at Ponte Molle, 74. Legends, 75. Measures of tolerance decided at Milan, 77. Victory of Licinius in Campus Serenus, 78. Death of Maximinus, 78. Licinius's revenge, 78. Diocletian's death, 78. Licinius against the Christians, 79. His downfall; Constantine sole ruler, 80.

TRANSLATOR'S NOTE

THE PRESENT VOLUME CONTINUES THE HISTORY OF THE EARLY CHURCH which Professor Lietzmann projected in five volumes. The first two volumes, *The Beginnings of the Christian Church* and *The Founding of the Church Universal*, carried the record as far as the death of Origen, and have now been completely revised for the new issue. The present volume tells the story of the Christian Church to the death of Julian; it covers the Arian controversy and shows the links between that issue and imperial policy.

Owing to the war of 1939-45, the present translation of Professor Lietzmann's *Reichskirche* has not had the benefit of his revision, especially valuable as it would have been in the difficult issues discussed in the following pages. But I hope I have not done serious injustice to the meaning of what he wrote so lucidly.

The Select Bibliography for students beginning work on this fascinating, complex, and important period, has been prepared by the Rev. H. Chadwick, M.A., Fellow of Queens' College, Cambridge, who has also greatly enriched the footnotes throughout, especially by references to works more readily accessible to English readers; my obligations to him on behalf of the readers of this volume are beyond computation.

I am also deeply indebted and grateful to Mr. Harry Cowlishaw of Beaconsfield and to my wife for numberless suggestions, and for their willing help in reading the proofs and preparing the Index; and to the Rev. Gordon Hewitt, Editor of the Lutterworth Press, for his unfailing kindness and patience.

While *From Constantine to Julian* was in the Press, news was received, after much delay, that my honoured and learned friend, Hans Lietzmann, had died on June 25, 1942. He had been seriously ill for nearly twelve months, and unable to complete his great *History of the Early Church*, originally planned for publication in five volumes. He had seen three volumes in print in Germany before the outbreak of the war in 1939, and had done much work on the fourth, *The Era of the Church Fathers*, before he was finally laid low. The MS. was in a condition so nearly complete that it was possible for Dr. W. Eltester, with certain assistants, to arrange to publish most of what had been written. An English translation is already in the course of preparation, and will show, in due time, that Hans Lietzmann retained all his brilliance of exposition to the last.

> *Danke dem Herrn denn er ist freundlich,*
> *Und seine Güte währet ewiglich.*

BERTRAM LEE WOOLF.

BEACONSFIELD,
Christmas, 1949.

Chronological Table

268–270 *Claudius II*

270 Death of Plotinus

270–275 *Aurelian*

284–305 *Diocletian*

after 285, with Maximian

293 Constantius and Galerius, Cæsars

West		East	
293 Constantius	Maximian	Galerius	Diocletian
	305 Severus		305 Maximinus
306 Constantine	306 Maxentius		
	308 Licinius		

312 Constantine

311 Maximinus

313 Licinius

324 Constantine

323–337 *Constantine sole Emperor*

303 Beginning of Persecution of Christians

311 Edict of Tolerance by Galerius

313 Ordinance of Tolerance at Milan

315 Royal Verdict in Milan *re* Donatists

325 Council of Nicea

328 Athanasius Bishop of Alexandria

335 Athanasius banished to Trèves.

337–340 *Constantine II   Constans   Constantius*

340 Constans

350 Constantius

350–361 *Constantius sole Emperor*

339 Athanasius flees to Rome: Gregory in Alexandria

341 Church Consecration Synod in Antioch

342 Synod at Serdika

346 Return of Athanasius

350 Catechisms of Cyril of Jerusalem

355 Synod at Milan

356 Athanasius expelled: George in Alexandria

358 Synod of the *Homoiousians* at Ancyra

359 Duplicate Synod at Rimini and Seleucia

361–363 *Julian*

362 Synod of Athanasius in Alexandria

Chapter One

THE DOWNFALL AND RECONSTRUCTION
OF THE ROMAN EMPIRE

IN THE COURSE OF A.D. 260, THE EMPEROR VALERIAN WAS TAKEN
prisoner by the Persians, and his son Gallienus had to
defend himself against foes within and without. It may be said
that the Roman empire collapsed round about this time, a
terrible catastrophe which had long been feared, and which
had been prevented several times only by the greatest efforts.

The historical records have been preserved only piecemeal.
There are no surviving self-consistent sources of information,
and no person of outstanding ability wrote a complete account
of all the numberless phases of the disastrous events. All that
reaches our ears from this tempestuous era are cries of woe
coming from every quarter of the world, leaving us largely to
guess the appalling extent of the distress.

Frankish armies marched up the Rhine, crossed into Gaul,
and penetrated into Spain; Tarragona was conquered and
plundered. The invaders remained for twelve years in that
unfortunate country, and some of them took the opportunity of
crossing into Africa. From that point all trace of them is lost.
For 200 years the right-angle between the eastern bank of the
upper Rhine and the upper Danube had been protected by the
mighty bulwark of the *limes*. Now, however, the Alemanni
poured like a flood over this breakwater, and settled in the
region of the Black Forest: from that time onwards, the *limes*
was entirely lost to the Empire. On the other hand, the
Alemanni did not remain peacefully on the Rhine. An army
penetrated into the valley of the Rhône, and plundered its way
to the sea; another army marched over the Alps and wandered
to and fro in upper Italy, threatening Ravenna, and being
at last conquered by Gallienus near Milan. Goths, in alliance
with other Germanic tribes and with Sarmatians, laid waste
the northern regions of the Balkans; they also crossed the Black
Sea and plundered Trebizond. Shortly afterwards, they laid
waste the cities on the Bosphorus, and in the seventh decade of
the third century they continued these attacks in ever increasing

measure. All regions bordering on the sea suffered dreadfully, and the burning of the Temple of Artemis in Ephesus (A.D. 262) was a fiery signal giving warning of the collapse of the ancient Mediterranean civilization. Hosts of Goths poured ever afresh through wide breaches in the frontier into Greece itself and encamped before Athens. During the same period the eastern frontiers of the Empire were overrun by the Persians; and swarms of oriental horsemen conquered the important metropolis of Antioch and penetrated far into the eastern parts of Asia Minor.

In spite of his great courage, Gallienus was in no position to overcome the numerous dangers which crowded upon him from every side.[1] Thus it came about that the regions which were most severely threatened took measures for their own defence and, as a consequence, shortly came to constitute independent bodies within the state, even to the extent of hostility toward the imperial Government. This was especially the case in those regions which seemed to be in a position to defend themselves. In the west, the legions situated on the Rhine proclaimed as emperor the veteran warrior Postumus, and he was recognized as such by the armies in Gaul, Britain, and Spain. He made Trèves his headquarters, and defended the town by a surrounding wall. The most beautiful of the gates in this wall, the *Porta Nigra*, even to-day, furnishes an impressive testimony to Rome's conquering will in those times. No matter what might happen to the Empire elsewhere, there was every intention in the west that the Roman civilization should at least be maintained. Postumus was successful in this respect, during the ten years of his rule (A.D. 258–68), and over a fairly broad region he maintained outer security and inner order. His successors, Victorinus and Tetricus, were never equal to their problems.

In the east, after Valerian's defeat, the desert town of Palmyra, which had become rich and powerful, constituted the centre of a new state. In the first instance, it acted with the formal consent of Rome; later, by virtue of its own authority, it organized the defences of Mediterranean civilization on the Euphrates frontier. A kingdom was founded and ruled by the patrician Odaenath, of Palmyra, as the recognized vicegerent;

[1] cf. The panegyric 8 addressed to Constantius; ed. Baehrens (2nd ed.) Chap. 10

and after his death by his consort Zenobia. She called herself Augusta, and arranged that her son, Waballeth, should be proclaimed emperor while still a minor. This empire was able to hold the Persians in check and drive their military rule out of Syria, Asia Minor, and Egypt. But its glory did not last longer than a single decade.

At this point the incredible took place, and the miraculous happened; although the Roman empire was bleeding from a thousand wounds, it gathered together its last resources, flung back its worst enemies, and joined its separated members once more into a single body. In the year 268, the Emperor Claudius destroyed an Alemannic army near Lake Garda, and in the next year won an overwhelming victory over the Gothic army, consisting of more than 800,000 men, who were laying waste Greece and the North Balkan districts. Not until one hundred years later were the Goths again able to take any significant part in the tribal migrations. The Emperor Aurelian made the Danube the boundary of his empire, and granted to the Germanic tribes the privilege of settling in the province of Dacia, the scene of Trajan's famous victory. He flung the Alemanni out of northern Italy, and then turned toward the orient. Zenobia's power gave way with astonishing rapidity before Aurelian's attack. The queen was taken prisoner and her city was destroyed, because it was not willing to acknowledge the victor (A.D. 273). The mighty ruins give us some idea as to the glory of the city: the chief temple with its spacious court, the long colonnaded streets with numerous crossings, the small temples, the burial vaults, the numerous monuments of an indigenous sculpture; the ruins of all these things are found far in the wilderness, surrounded by palms, and appearing like visions seen in a dream.

Aurelian now turned to the western Empire. The Emperor Tetricus handed it over to his doughty opponent with scarcely any opposition. As a consequence, Aurelian was able to celebrate a double triumph in the year 274, and rightly to boast that he was the *restitutor imperii*: in the truest sense of the word, he had "restituted" the Empire.

The sun god had been his heavenly helper in doing this work. He it was who had appeared in the crucial battle of

Emesa, confirmed the ranks at the moment when they were giving way, and had led them to victory. In recognition and thanks, Aurelian made princely donations to the temple of Elagabal in Emesa, the ancient city of the sun: moreover, in Rome he built a glorious temple to the sun on the *campus Agrippae*, i.e., near the *corso*, close to the Via Friattina. It was true that the statues of the Palmyrenian Baals were to be found in the temple amongst others which had been taken as booty, nevertheless Aurelian was not doing honour to the god of Elagabal and his fellow nationals. The statue of *Sol Invictus*, the "Unconquerable Sun God", was Roman, and it was this god whose image Aurelian stamped on his coins. The pontifical college which was responsible for the cultus was also Roman, as well as the games which it was decreed should take place on the feast of midwinter's day.[1] The sun god illuminated all the peoples with his rays, and brought them into subjection to the power of the Roman Imperium, and it was he, as the divine protector of the Empire, whom Aurelian worshipped in the most public manner. Worship was offered, not to some divine being limited in one way or another, but to the one and only god who, although seen in a thousand different forms, nevertheless gave the highest revelation of himself in the essential nature of the sun. Ancient Monotheism in the form of the national Roman worship of the sun, created the idea of a new imperial god.[2] One god, one empire, one emperor—that was the goal which Aurelian sought.

His next work, after his decisive military successes, was to attack the defects in the economic structure of the Empire. He took the first steps towards improving the coinage; he promoted agriculture, and did away with the oppressive practices of the provincial bureaucracies. These were promising beginnings, and they were conjoined with plans for the further security of the frontiers. But at this moment, August, A.D. 275, all hopes were dashed to the ground by the assassin's dagger of a group of malcontents. An impressive memorial to his labours has been preserved in Rome to the present day, in the form of the city walls which he erected for repelling future attacks against

[1] G. Wissowa, *Relig. u. Kult. d. Römer*, 2nd ed. p. 367. F. Cumont, *Orient. Relig.*, 3rd ed. p. 104   [2] cf. Vol. 2, 42ff.

a city which, up to that time, had been open. The walls offered an impressive sign of the times: previously, the walls of Rome were found in the *limes* on the Rhine and the Danube, and in the fortresses built in the Syrian wilderness.

After Aurelian's death, there was a period of nine years when seven emperors and rival emperors appeared on the scene. They were years full of restlessness and distress, marked also to a painful extent by frontier battles and by inroads on the part of foreign brigands. Nevertheless, there was no great national invasion. The troubles which had marked the sixties of the third century were not repeated. Hence, the unity of the Empire was maintained in spite of everything. After Numerianus had been assassinated on November 17, A.D. 284, a man who belonged to the eastern army, was proclaimed emperor. He possessed both the will and the power to continue Aurelian's work, and in addition, he managed to rule for a period of twenty years. This man was Gaius Aurelius Valerius Diocletianus. At the time when he was made emperor he was in command of the imperial body-guard. He was born in Dalmatia, and was originally called Diocles. He had fought as a private soldier on various fronts, and had earned the rank of officer. He then succeeded in obtaining higher posts of command, until finally he received the above mentioned confidential position in the immediate entourage of the Emperor Carus and his son Numerianus.[1] Carinus, the brother of the murdered man, ruled in the west as Augustus. He advanced with his troops against the new ruler, and was on the very point of overthrowing him when he was slain by an assassin. Now for the first time, was Diocletian's rule unchallenged: he reconciled the adherents of the overthrown dynasty by permitting them to retain their posts. Carinus, anxious for his throne, had left unfinished certain military tasks in the west, and these tasks Diocletian confided to Maximian, who was a Pannonian from Illyria, and a younger comrade of Diocletian. Under the name of Marcus Aurelius Valerius Maximianus, he was raised to the position of the new emperor's brother, and given the title of Cæsar.

Since neither of these two men possessed a family tree on

[1] *Prosop. Imp. Rom.*, 1 (2nd ed.), 332. No. 1627

earth, one was found in heaven, and Diocletian called himself "Jovius", the descendant of Jupiter, whereas Maximian had to be content with calling himself "Herculius". Thus the relationship between the two men was described unmistakably, and, indeed, quite in accordance with the facts. It is true that, soon afterwards, Maximian assumed the title of Augustus, although we do not know precisely what method he used; and in this way he became legally the equal of the elder man. Being originally a rustic boor, he had always felt himself to be the subordinate, and had recognized the personal superiority of Diocletian. He was successful in throwing back the Germanic tribes on the upper reaches of the Rhine, and in suppressing an extremely dangerous insurrection of the peasantry in the so-called *bagaude* in Gaul. But he was not able to prevent Carausius, the Celtic officer in command of the Rhine fleet, from making himself independent, and from setting up a rulership of his own based on England after the pattern of Postumus. For a while Maximian attempted to render this rulership harmless by apparently giving it recognition.

On March 1, A.D. 293, the government of the Empire developed into its final form, in a way that corresponded to the prevailing military requirements and Diocletian's statesmanlike ideas. He and Maximian were the reigning emperors; they divided the rule between them, in fact although not in law, on a geographical basis: Diocletian reigned in the east, and Maximian in the west. In order to assure the succession, each Augustus sought for his own crown prince who would carry the title of Cæsar, and who would be entrusted with a special sphere in the commission of his emperor. In addition, both Cæsars were the adopted sons and the sons-in-law of their respective Augusti. Diocletian again chose an Illyrian, C. Galerius Valerius Maximianus, and appointed him ruler of the Danubian province. It would appear that the Cæsar chosen by Maximian was also an Illyrian of unknown origin, M. Flavius Valerius Constantius by name. Only later, when he was known to history as the father of Constantine the Great, was he said to be of noble birth. Gaul and Britain constituted the region assigned to him.[1]

[1] cf. C. Stein, *Gesch. d. spätröm. Reiches*, I, 99

Constantius's first task was to overthrow Carausius. He began by re-conquering Boulogne and the surrounding district, together with the region round about the delta of the Rhine. He then spent two years in building a fleet with which he regained control over Britain. He had considerable successes also against the Franks and the Alemanni, with the result that by the end of the century he had firm hold of that part of the empire which had been assigned to him. Meanwhile Maximian had fought in Africa, and Galerius had guarded the Danube frontier in a war which lasted for years. Between the Danube, the Drava, and Lake Balaton, he added an extensive colony or settlement. This he colonized by means of the frontier tribes and made it a new province under the name of Valeria.

Diocletian was accustomed to entrust his colleagues with most of the military expeditions, but in A.D. 295 he had to march into Egypt, where a dangerous rebellion had gone to such lengths that an opposition emperor was proclaimed in the person of Achilleus. The war lasted for eight months before Alexandria was conquered and Achilleus killed. Diocletian punished the rebellious country and its capital with terrible severity, but then contented it by wise measures in regard to governmental authority and protection of the frontiers. Meanwhile, danger was threatening from the Persians, and Diocletian sent Galerius into Mesopotamia, where he suffered a severe defeat. In the next year (A.D. 297) he brought veteran troops drawn from the Danubian states and defeated the Persians decisively in the mountains of Armenia. In the settlement which followed, the Empire was extended on the upper Euphrates and Tigris almost as far as the Caspian Sea; for a long time it exercised a decisive influence on northern Armenia and ensured respite from Persian attacks. A triumphal arch was erected in Salonika, and it still stands, with its carved figures, proclaiming the glory of this successful war.

All these military expeditions meant that the really important objective had been attained: the boundaries of the Empire were again rendered secure, a fact which guaranteed a considerable sense of assurance. The security must indeed be regarded everywhere as effective, especially if one compares the situation about the middle of the century. But, in order to gain this success, it had been necessary to increase the size of the army very considerably, and this could only be carried out by increasing the imperial taxation. Appropriate measures had been needed for making sure of peace within the Empire, and this had been brought about by means of a stern, well-planned, and practical action on the part of the administrators. Civil wars and the proclamations of opposition emperors had to be ended once for all. This, however, was only possible when the entire constitution was completely rebuilt. Diocletian saw what was required, and acted accordingly.

He divided the imperial rulership, the primary reason probably being that he required a general who would conduct his wars: and this general would otherwise have been proclaimed an opposition emperor by the army as soon as he made good. Hence, he gave him the position voluntarily and at once, knowing that only by force of arms would he have been able to deny it to him at a later date. Diocletian's personal supremacy, which the other readily recognized, guaranteed the unity of the regime. As a consequence, although it was contrary to the old Roman principle of joint responsibility, there was no danger in assigning to the second Cæsar one half of the Empire as his special province. Similarly, the appointing of two crown princes arose from concern about the stability of the new Imperium. As the Augustus had no son, it was not difficult for him to reject the idea of a hereditary monarchy, and to leave the choice of successors to be dealt with on the basis of proved capacity. But to Maximianus, whose son Maxentius at that time was thirteen years old, such an arrangement would have been unacceptable. The military and administrative functions of these "Cæsars" was not due to their status—a crown prince as such had no official duties—but was the consequence of the commission which Augustus himself gave, or was due to their capacity as Augustus's representatives. On the other hand, Diocletian had cleverly increased the status of the *Imperium* by outer means, and raised it above that of the rulers chosen by the army during the preceding decades. The mythological glory which attached to the earlier divine kingship had faded, if only because too many military and civil contemporaries were alive who had been glad to see such "gods" beheaded.

As a consequence, Diocletian, who understood human nature quite thoroughly, made use of ceremonial in a manner that was always genuinely effective. He wore gorgeous eastern garments made of silk, with decorations of purple and gold, shoes to correspond, and also a great number of pearl ornaments. Anyone who was granted an audience had to perform the Persian style of obeisance, viz., kneel and kiss the imperial purple:[1] the official description of this ceremonial was "petition". This brought out the significance of the inscription, which had been usual on the coinage since Aurelian: "To our Lord and God". This phrase embodies the hyperbole of an obsequious people. It would be untrue to say that Diocletian raised himself to the status of deity: apart from other considerations he was a man of too much common sense in his methods of thought to do so. On the other hand, just as in the case of Aurelian, he felt that he had been chosen by the godhead to occupy the imperial position; and, therefore, that he stood under divine protection and exercised a divine commission:[2] and this fact endowed him with moral authority. He completely transformed the administration of the Empire, and based the new divisions on geographical considerations. He divided up the provinces of an earlier date into considerably smaller regions; a list has come down to us from A.D. 297,[3] which mentions ninety-six of these new provinces; even Italy was no longer an exception, but was carved up into at least nine provinces. A number of such provinces were combined together to form "dioceses" under a higher authority: there were twelve dioceses in the Roman empire covering the ninety-six provinces already mentioned. At the head of the provinces there were pro-consuls, consuls or "correctors" of senatorial rank, or presidents of equestorial standing: the diocese was governed by the vicar, i.e., the "representative of the imperial chancellor". This last bore the title of *Praefectus Praetorio*, i.e., Commander of the Guard, and under Diocletian this person still exercised actual military authority; Constantine was the

[1] Gothofredus, *zu Cod. Theod.*, 6, 8   Alföldi, *Röm. Mitteilungen*, 1934, 6ff.

[2] A. D. Nock in *Harv. Theol. Rev.* 1930, 264. Norman H. Baynes in *JRS.*, 1935, 83f.

[3] *Laterculus Veronensis*, ed. Seeck in *Notitia Dignitatum*, 1876, 247–253. Mommsen, *Ges. Schriften*, 5, 561–588

first to make him a purely civil officer.[1] Each emperor installed a chancellor as the head of his administration, and the extent of the region governed by this highest of the officials, coincided with that of his imperial lord.[2]

The new delimitations of provincial boundaries always kept in view the matter of taxation; and at the same time a new principle of taxation was worked out, which was intended to combine the objects of the taxation with the simplest means of collecting the taxes.[3] The greater part of the taxes was paid in goods, and as a consequence the entire productive soil of the Empire was divided up according to a plan in which the areas subject to taxation were roughly of equal value if one also took into account the peasant labour which was available: the soil and the inhabitants together constituted a single datum for taxation purposes: *jugum* and *caput*. In this way, the annual budget could be quickly divided up according to the number of taxable units in the dioceses and provinces, and then passed on by the administrators of the different towns. Here, the details of the taxable units of the different regions were known, and it could be immediately calculated what each landed proprietor had to pay. Here were also to be found the members of the common council, the *Decuriones*, whose families inherited the dignities of their office, and along with that also the duty of personal responsibility for collecting all the required taxes. In this way the entire Empire was covered by a net, with a very small mesh, out of which it was extremely difficult to escape. Diocletian achieved his object and raised far higher sums than his predecessors; but because the impost was on the whole equally divided, and was not introduced retrospectively, the new methods were regarded by the subject-people as essentially an improvement:[4] a view with which we must agree when we take into account the confusion and distress of the preceding decades.

Diocletian was not so successful in attempting to raise the level of economic life, and hence the productivity of the Empire. He made serious efforts to improve the wholly depreciated

[1] Mommsen, *op. cit.* 6, 266   [2] *ibid.* 6, 284ff.
[3] Seeck in *Pauly-W.* 3, 1513–21   Rostovtzeff, *Gesells. u. Wirtsch.*, 2, 225ff.
[4] Wilcken in *Archiv f. Papyrusforschung*, 11, 1935, 312f.

currency; he attempted to give a definite weight to the gold coinage, whose changing value had hitherto been determined by weighing: but he himself made mistakes in his decrees, and constantly changed them. As distinct from the *denarii* which had lost all value, owing to debasement, he made a new coinage of pure silver, the *miliarense*, which corresponded approximately to the old value of a Swiss franc; and a new coin of alloy, the *follis*, worth about a farthing or rather more. This new system of coinage, however, was frequently revised, a fact which shows that it had not attained its purpose; and there are certain indications that false coinage in many regions increased the confusion still more. The Emperor then attempted to use legal means to control the increase of prices together with all the accompanying phenomena of a period of inflation, and in A.D. 301 he proclaimed the famous edict[1] for regulating market prices.

The preamble severely rebukes the greed of the people as responsible for the rise in prices due to numerous small increases; then it goes on to threaten the death penalty to anyone who asked or paid more than the maximum prices contained in the given list. The merchant who withheld his goods would be liable to the same penalty. Certain of the costs of transport did not justify any increase in the prices as proclaimed, for the tariff held good without exception throughout the empire. Then came a long list of goods in alphabetical order, beginning with leguminous produce, wine, oil, and meat: then traversing all departments of human requirements and desires. Not only were the maximum prices fixed for the different articles, but also the maximum value of gold and silver; all of which implied a certain stabilization of value. There followed quite logically, and in accordance with the requirements of economics, the question of wages. Shaving cost a halfpenny; a donkey driver received about fourpence a day in addition to his bread and olives. A senior teacher of languages or geometry received 3s. 6d. a month from each pupil; and a lawyer, about 18s. for a case. If we reckon in addition the cost of a hundredweight of wheat at about 6s. 4d.; beef at 2d. per pound; a quart of olive

---

[1] *CIL.*, 3, 801. cf. Dessau, *Inscr. latin.*, 642   Mommsen u. Blümner, *D. Maximaltarif d. Diocletian*, 1893   Blümner in *Pauly-W.*, 5, 1948–57

oil 3*d.* or more; a pound of butter 4*d.* or 5*d.*, we shall gain a fairly accurate idea of the cost of living at that time, and we can calculate how much a working man, an ordinary citizen, or a scholar, would be able to buy of the remaining desirable items in the list; and how much a bishop would have to place at the disposal of his deacons in order to support a hundred poor people each day. It seems clear that, as a matter of fact, the edict was only put into effect in the east; and that, even there, in spite of the severity which was exercised in applying its penalties, it was not successful.[1]

Diocletian is not to be blamed on this account: he was neither the first, nor the last, honestly to believe that he could make an unsound economy sound by means of severe legal penalties. Nevertheless, he was successful to the extent of bringing about peace and tranquillity within the Empire itself, and he collected so many of the taxes regularly that he was able to effect a definite increase of the military forces at his disposal, and to maintain them permanently.

The oversight of the army was now withdrawn from the provincial governors, and the army itself was reorganized:[2] each frontier province received two legions under the command of a brigadier-general (*dux*) as a permanent protection; and although it is true that the new legions were smaller than before, nevertheless, when these measures were brought into effect, it meant, if not a doubling, at least a considerable increase of the man-power. Moreover, the frontier troops were made so strong that mobile corps of troops could be detached from them and combined with the active armies which were specially organized for each campaign, and united with the allied troops belonging to the imperial camp. It was only in course of time that these field armies attained a permanent footing, and that their members were distinguished as guards (*comitatenses*) from the frontier troops (*limitanei*). The necessity and the value of strengthening the military striking power in this way, were justified by their obvious success, and this also nullified the objections raised against Diocletian by

---

[1] Lactant. *mort.* 7, 6f.

[2] Ritterling in *Pauly-W.* 12, 1348–67   E. Stein, *Gesch. d. spätröm. Reiches,* 1, 106ff.

unfriendly critics when they spoke of pointless militarism.[1]

Similarly also, the known facts do not support the objections raised by the same parties against Diocletian's "boundless passion for building". He loved to build, and to build magnificently, but he always did so after careful consideration, and with a definite purpose. Since he had chosen his special sphere of rule in the east, it was quite reasonable on his part not to take up his residence either in the metropolis of Antioch, or, even Alexandria, but that he should search for a situation near to the Bosphorus. Once his choice had fallen on Nicomedia, he provided this city with all the buildings which were essential to the seat of an emperor: these included not only palaces for the ruler and his family, but also such public buildings as basilicas, baths, and theatres. It is certain that he never attempted the impossible, by trying to make Nicomedia equal to Rome; some such dream came indeed to Constantine when building his capital, and the Christian historians did not regard it as wrong on his part. We must bear in mind also that in the great *thermae* on the Viminal, Rome possesses a monument founded by Diocletian, the mighty ruins of which Michel Angelo restored and made into a church. Moreover, the Emperor was more frequently a visitor to Antioch on military and political grounds than he cared to be; and, even though it was never more than a temporary stay, yet he had to live there, and as a consequence, he erected a large number of state buildings in the town.[2]

The ruins of two of his palace buildings have survived: one was a magnificent establishment, a military centre in Palmyra, with rooms to accommodate subordinates of the commander-in-chief, apparently the Emperor himself, for he spent A.D. 296–97 with the troops on the Euphrates, while Galerius conducted the attack from Armenia.[3] The other was a place of seclusion, and this too was built on the plan of a Roman camp, which Diocletian erected on the Adriatic. The magnificent palace was an oblong, measuring about 650 by 575 feet;

[1] Lactant. *mort.* 7, 2. 3, 8. 9

[2] Malalas. *Chron.* 12, 306–8 *Paneg. Eumenii pro inst. schol.* 18, 1. 4   Zosim. *Hist,* 2, 34, 2

[3] The date of building was between A.D. 293 and A.D. 303: J. Cantineau, *Inventaire des Inscr. de Palmyre,* 6, 2

the cloisters were decorated with pillars, and they looked out over the sea. Behind it lay the imperial apartments and the state rooms, approached from the main street by an extremely ornamental forecourt, with porticoes. To-day, the houses of the city of Spalato fill the entire space, and a circular building surmounted by a dome, intended by the Emperor for his mausoleum, was transformed during the middle ages into a cathedral, and dedicated to the Virgin Mary.

We hear also of munition factories, of city fortresses, and of the building of numerous frontier castles. In particular, an imposing road on the eastern *limes* bears Diocletian's name (*Strata Diocletiana*); it starts from the Euphrates and goes to Sura in a southerly direction, touches Palmyra, and then proceeds to Damascus. Half way, another road branches off and turns southward to Basra.[1] At regular distances, frontier castles were erected or restored, and were connected with one another by the road: here, for Diocletian, lay the eastern frontier of the Empire, face to face with the desert and the Persian danger beyond.

When Diocletian came into power it again became the fashion to build on a colossal scale, after a century when nothing had been done. The increasing stabilization of economic life, together with the growing strength of the frontiers, gave opportunities for work on majestic lines, the most splendid memorial being the basilica on the forum at Rome, begun by Maxentius and finished by Constantine. The immense vaults which still tower to the skies represent only a third of the original building. Nevertheless, it is of overpowering majesty. Bramente drew his inspiration from it when building St. Peter's.

Moreover, the art of carving historical reliefs again came to life, although it had lain dormant since the time when Septimius Severus built his arch on the Forum Romanum (A.D. 203). Galerius built a triumphal arch in Salonika, and made use of rows of figures in high relief to describe the Persian war of A.D. 297. These figures continue the best tradition of this style of art, and in a certain way bring it to perfection. At any rate,

---

[1] Dunand in *Revue biblique*, 1931, 227–248 416–434 A. Poidebard, *La trace de Rome dans le désert de Syrie*, 1934 Fabricius in *Pauly-W.* 13, 654ff.

the next edifice of this kind, Constantine's arch in Rome, reveals a wealth of creative power in a work whose art is quite naïve and popular, and which does not attempt to follow any traditional forms and ideas.

The public and private practice of the art found a broad field of activity, throughout the whole of the century, in the decoration of sarcophagi. In Attica and Asia Minor, especially in Ephesus and on the Black Sea, magnificent marble tombs were produced, which were decorated on all four sides, and sent to Italy and even beyond: but the economic collapse in the second half of the century brought this activity to an end.[1] During this period, the city of Rome increased its production of this kind of work, and developed a rich type of sarcophagus decoration; it exported examples, sent sculptors themselves abroad, and so came to dominate the entire west in the following period. In this case also, the ruling tradition continued the classical principles of the late Antonine era, and frequently took the form of magnificent lion hunts and battle pieces with a medley of men and horses. Towards the middle of the third century, however, a baroque style became fashionable, an intoxication of wild, restless movements, flapping garments, and hair like tongues of flame.[2] Its effects can be traced in all directions, and is perhaps as noticeable in the strange little round temple in Baalbek as in the structure and ornamentation of the monuments on the Rhine at Neumagen.

On the other hand, the reliefs at Neumagen are extremely creditable examples of provincial art. On the Rhine and Moselle, this exhibits astonishing freshness and maturity; the sculptors obviously enjoyed carving representations of such subjects as paying the rent, unloading corn, learning Latin, and drinking Moselle wine.[3] Moreover, in the Roman portrait-heads, we can perceive the attitude normal to Roman character during the third century, and examples exhibit a variety of forceful styles. Instead of the mode usual during the Antonine period, when the head is represented with a full beard, curly

[1] G. Rodenwalt, *D. Klinensark. v. S. Lorenzo* in *Jarhb. d. Arch. Inst.*, 1930, 183–189
[2] G. Rodenwalt, *Zur Kunstgesch. d. Jahre 220–270* in *Jarhb. d. Arch. Inst.*, 1936, 82–113
[3] W. v. Massow, *D. Grabm. v. Neumagen*, 1932

hair, and idealized facial traits, we find a plain naturalism as early as Caracalla (A.D. 211–217); and after Severus Alexander (A.D. 222–235) a plain simplicity.[1] This was continued under his successors until Valerian (A.D. 253–260), and was taken up again impressively, after a short interval, by Diocletian and his co-regents. In the time of Gallienus (A.D. 260–268), there was a reaction, and the philosopher's beard again became the mode. The decoration of sarcophagi took the form of divine muses, or earthly men and women grouped round a philosopher in the act of teaching.[2] Nevertheless, the spirit prevalent in late antiquity forced its way through the classic style, and was recognizable in the decay of plastic expression as seen in the representation of the full face of the main person, and in the symmetrical arrangement of the entire work. Sculpture lost its ancient tradition, and a new period began.

The economic distress of the second half of the third century also spoiled the spirit of literature. For a long time there had been no poets, but even the writers of doggerel were now rare. Very little history was written, and what was produced has been happily lost sight of: the best historian seems to have been Dexippos, the commandant of Athens, who was successful in defending his native city when it was attacked by the Goths. Oratory, of course, survived, but was of a mediocre quality, and showed nothing to compare with the preceding period. The best that one can say is that in this period a few erotic romances were produced, which might enable the reader to while away weary hours. Longinus, the orator, philosopher, and philologist, is interesting on account of his importance as one of Zenobia's councillors, and because he had to pay with his life for having abandoned his success as a scholar. Similarly, the sciences were at a standstill with the exception of mathematics, in which field at that time the important persons were Pappos and Diophantos, both of Alexandria.

The spiritual qualities of this period were concentrated in the philosophy of Plotinus: he was the last thinker of the ancient world who dominated thought as the recognized head of a school. His influence was extremely great, and its effects can

---

[1] L'Orange, *Studien z. Gesch. d. spätant. Porträts*, 1933, Plate 1
[2] Rodenwalt, *ibid.*, 1936, Plates 5 & 6

still be felt in our own day. Nevertheless, a greater than he speaks through his lips: the "divine Plato", whom Plotinus regarded as his master, and whose disciple and expounder he was in fact. The ancient tradition had been fading away now for more than a century, and the vital elements which had descended from Plato came together in Plotinus. He brought them to a focus, and passed them on to succeeding ages. He extracted a dogmatic philosophy from Plato's writings, and this became a living faith. It exalted its disciples, whether men or women, from the dark earth to the shining stars, and indeed beyond, until it enabled them to enjoy ineffable communion with God.

His Neoplatonism was the religion of educated persons in the silver age of antiquity, and, as such, it came into opposition even with Christianity. If we compare the graphic quality and the artistic perfection of Plato's *Dialogues* with the abstract language of Plotinus's *Enneads*, which were quickly forgotten, we shall obtain a clear idea of the difference between the cultures of the two periods. Plotinus was well aware that he was no *littérateur*, and, indeed, he never tried to be such. In fact, he was no more a writer than Epictetus. It was only the insistence of his disciples and the requirements of actual teaching which compelled him to attempt to write; and the difficulty which he found in this sort of work is expressed frankly enough in the introduction which Porphyry wrote as the editor of his collected works. The value of these tractates is similarly not to be found in the first instance in the words used, the proofs offered, or even the rarefied atmosphere which characterizes the movements of his thought: but rather in Plotinus's personality as a man, which shines out clearly enough through the motley confusion, in spite of all his shy reticence. Only on rare occasions is it seen completely, although then it is very attractive. His quality of mind is clearly revealed in his tractate against the Christian gnostics.[1]

He holds that it is not true that this world is essentially evil, nor that it owes its existence to the creative activity of a secondary demi-urge. In any case, it was not created at one particular time, but was constantly coming into being from

[1] Plotinus, *Enn.* 2, 9

above with diminishing degrees of radiance. It was good, beautiful, and glorious, and could not possibly be improved. One ought not to fix one's attention on details, but ought to keep the whole in view, the fullness of beauty in nature on earth, the majesty of the starry skies, the harmony which rules everywhere; and allow these to exercise their effect upon one's mind. Then we should be able to recognize that the world is the revelation of a Supreme Being, who penetrates the whole, although inevitably in diminishing degree from stage to stage; yet, even in the deepest depths, He still awakens the soul's desire to mount from darkness into the light. No one who knows this, imagines to himself a new earth beyond the present world, nor speaks of the sinful fall of the entire cosmos, nor of repentance and the punishments of hell; nor does he fear demons or recognize the validity of magic formulas.

In this way, Plotinus expresses his opposition to every type of dualism, and to all pessimistic conceptions about the creation of the world. Plotinus was a monist, i.e., he understood the whole as an organism controlled by a single principle; and he was a philosophical optimist, i.e., he regarded this world as the best among all that might otherwise have been possible.

The ultimate source of the world was the One, the First, the highest Good, whose origin was in its own will; it was that from which everything issued, and towards which everything strove to move, the "Father of Cause" as Plato named the Godhead.[1] From it flowed existence, and this was at the same time thought, i.e., genuine reality on the highest level, the "intelligible world"; it combined in itself the whole of what originally existed, i.e., the Ideas. Put in more personal terms, it was the *nous*, the "royal creator of the world"[2] and this is what we described as the *logos* when discussing Philo's Platonism.[3] The third stage of existence was constituted by the soul of the world, which received its splendour from the world of ideas and passed it on to the world of matter. The phenomenal world round about us gains form from matter by means of the *logoi* which themselves originated in *nous*.[4] As the *nous* comprises

[1] *Enn.* 1, 7, 1   1, 8, 2   6, 8, 13   5, 1, 8; cf. Plato, *Letters* 6, p. 323d   *Tim*, 28c
[2] *Enn.* 5, 1, 4.8   [3] *vide*, Vol. 1. p. 95f.
[4] *Enn.* 1, 8, 2   3, 5, 3   3, 2, 2

in itself the various ideas, so, too, all the separate souls find their organic unity in the soul of the world.[1] These have important distinctions amongst themselves, partly because the very idea of a universal harmony necessarily implies differences, and partly because the free will of souls urges them to go their own way, and causes many to forget their divine origin.[2] In this way, the world of our senses contains an immeasurable variety of appearances, beginning with the gods which, existing as the shining stars in the sky, give the purest reflection of the light of the intelligible world; through the crowds of dæmonic beings, down to animals and plants—for they also share in reason and soul and life.

Man stands between God and the animals; he is endowed with heavenly beauty, and filled with spiritual power, a power which liberates him from the fetters of his material body, and which is able to lead him to the highest goals.[3] What then is matter? It is the necessary final phase of the series of beings descending from the First One; the last, which cannot be followed by anything else: hence, it is the antithesis to what exists, it is the non-existent. It would be equally true to say that matter is the antithesis to the good, and is therefore absolute evil. Both these, however, are negative conceptions, and can be understood only by contrast with existence, i.e., the good. Matter "is" where real existence ceases, and evil "is" where good fails.[4]

Having said this, we are now in a position to discuss the question of the origin of evil, as well as the problem of providence and of theodicy.[5] The "original evil" is, as we have just seen, a cosmic necessity; but, in virtue of her origin, every soul can escape the dominance of evil as incarnate in matter. If the soul does not do so, but succumbs to earthly passions, her free will is responsible.[6] The suffering and struggle which arise as a consequence are the result of the retributive righteousness which obtains in the world; and "providence" is only another name for the harmony of the whole, the harmony which implies that the numerous separate disturbing elements cancel one another out, and which serves the immanent pur-

[1] *Enn.* 3, 5, 4   4, 4, 32   [2] *ibid.* 3, 2, 18   5, 1, 1   [3] *ibid.* 3, 2, 7–9
[4] *ibid.* 1, 8, 7.11   [5] *ibid.* 3, 2 & 3   [6] *ibid.* 3, 2, 7.9   3, 3, 3

poses of the creator of the world.[1] Even to our eyes, it is obvious that many things which appear evil prove to be good from a standpoint which takes account of the whole. This is particularly true in the bloody struggles of the battle for existence;[2] although at the same time we must bear in mind that no earthly suffering touches the inner life of a philosopher's soul, and that no physical need can prevent his striving towards the highest good. This solves the problem of the suffering of the righteous, and of the apparent good fortune of the wicked: in each case, their lot is an outer thing which has nothing to do with true happiness—and, in addition, we must take into account the fact that men's lot in life is dependent on their deeds and omissions in a previous existence, i.e., conduct and recompense are spread over past, present, and future.[3]

Plotinus's Neoplatonism derived from Plato the truth that all genuine systematic knowledge is, at bottom, religious in character: hence, to the men of his time who were called upon to endure sufferings of every kind, and were tortured by oppression, Plotinus proclaimed a religion of redemption by means of philosophy. The human soul originated from above, and bore in herself the reflection and the powers of the world of ideas; but the soul was condemned to the fetters of the body, and had grown accustomed to give all her attention to the restless variety of "becoming", and to the varied forces of the world of sense: she was submerged in matter.[4] She must be made to strive in the opposite direction, viz., toward that which was above, to the good, and to what really existed. The starting-points varied according to the circumstances of the individual, but the method of mounting upwards was always the same: it took place by means of a clarification of our everyday understanding, a correction of our desires, followed by the dialectic of thought in accordance with the philosophy of the school: and this thought is also the goal, the final One beyond the intelligible world, God.[5]

A heavenly Eros dwells in every soul, delivers her from the chains of sense, gives her control of the body, leads her upwards

[1] *Enn.* 2, 9, 9   3, 2, 11–13   [2] *ibid.* 3, 2, 15
[3] *ibid.* 2, 9, 8–9 3, 2, 5–6. 13   [4]*ibid.* 1, 8, 4.14   [5] *ibid.* 1, 3

from stage to stage,[1] until she becomes similar to God, as Plato also taught; for the human soul, when she permits herself to be guided by *nous*, can become divine.[2] How seriously all this is intended, is shown by the fact that the ascent of the soul to ever purer understanding is described in a variety of ways. If she were to go beyond the limits of the region proper to the soul, a region in which discursive thought leads to understanding, she enters the realm of the intelligible, where she can perceive, by intuitive insight, that she herself is of superhuman nature.[3] Nor even there does she finally rest. The goal of her desire is the vision of God, the becoming divine in union with the Highest Being, embraced by which the ego feels itself to be only a part of the divine light, and abandons in blessed ecstasy all forms of thought and being.[4] Nevertheless, this ecstatic enjoyment of the Highest is only rarely granted to men who are still imprisoned on the present earth: Plotinus experienced it four times in five years. Porphyry, at 68, had attained this height only once,[5] a height which, both before and after Plotinus, was the goal of the desires of Platonists. The ancient Greek hymn about the beauty of the present world was still to be heard on the lips of Stoic philosophers of religion in praise of the omnipotent Godhead, and resounding in clear tones. This hymn was transformed amongst the Neoplatonists into the form of a pleasant song, which, like a comforting heavenly voice, was to be heard throughout a world; to abandon this world brought the highest blessedness. Plotinus inherited this idea from ancient Greece, and passionately defended it against the barbarous Christian idea that the world was a foe: nevertheless, it did not provide him with a foundation for his sense of the value of earthly life; it had become only a dogmatic element, and was required by his system of philosophy.

While Gallienus was emperor, the favour shown by himself and his consort Salonina cheered Plotinus, who dreamed of building in Campania a philosophers' city on Plato's model; perhaps even of educating statesmen in Plato's spirit;[6]

---

[1] *ibid.* 3, 5, 1.4   6, 9, 9   3, 3, 17   2, 9, 18   cf. 3, 9, 2   5, 5, 9   2, 9, 17
[2] *ibid.* 1, 2, 3   2, 9, 9   [3] *ibid.* 5, 3, 4
[4] *ibid.* 6, 9, 4.9   5, 5, 4–8   4, 8, 1   6, 7, 35–36
[5] Porph., *Vita Plotini*, 23   [6] *ibid.* 12   cf. M. Wundt, *Plotin*, 1, ff.39

but it remained a dream. The blaze of a pure will, ignited by the inspiration and example of the master, might have become a really creative force in the world, but Plotinus was bitterly disillusioned, and inevitably so. He directed the main lines of his life and thought insistently toward the inner life, and so toward heaven and apart from the phenomenal world. He preserved the Greek gospel of beauty and harmony, and placed it in the supramundane fields of pure spirituality, where it possessed the proud privilege of being associated with powers which abide eternally while everything below fell to pieces; powers which alone were also able to create and to reconstruct world after world in ever new forms.

It was only a small circle of choice spirits who associated with Plotinus in Rome. This circle consisted of Romans and Greeks, and also of "eastern" Arabs and Egyptians. The most important of them was Porphyry, a Semite of Phoenicia, and originally called Malchos. He has given us a hastily written but impressive description of the life of this group of philosophers. The leader Plotinus had the fewest possible physical requirements, but was also without any means; he lived as a guest in the house of his friends, whether in Rome or in Campania, where he died on the estate of an Arab called Zethas.[1] "His appearance was as of one who was ashamed of his body"; he never spoke of himself or his circumstances; only by means of a device did a painter succeed in sketching his portrait from memory. He suffered from indigestion, but never attempted to cure it, nor to change his preference for vegetarianism. He lived for his work as a teacher. He read and explained Plato, and also dealt systematically with Aristotle: this constituted the foundation.[2] He then discussed the Stoics, the Peripatetics, and later, the moderns.[3] The material was dealt with in the same manner as in our seminars. The teacher proposed the problems, indicated the literature, dealt with incidental questions, and was not content until he had reached complete clarity; he himself, however, took an active part and lectured, or concluded a lengthy debate with a critique which brought the various points together. He paid no attention to style when speaking, and he frequently made mistakes. But his naturally

---

[1] *Vita.* 9, 2   [2] J. Bidez, *Vie de Porphyre*, 45f.   [3] *Vita*, 14

agreeable temper increased in charm in the course of his
address until he became most attractive, and his forehead,
bedewed with beads of perspiration, seemed to be illumined
with the brillance of his spirit.[1] It is obvious that Porphyry
liked to recount his reminiscences of hours in Plotinus's class-
room, and he lets us feel how proud he was whenever he earned
the master's praise. The gatherings enjoyed red letter days
when they celebrated Plato's anniversary on May 7. On these
occasions the more intimate pupils met with their master for a
Platonic banquet, and did homage to their hero with newly
composed hymns; it was on one of these festive occasions that
Porphyry sang of the "heavenly marriage", and won recognition as poet, philosopher, and priest. In fact, here in Rome,
Plotinus was surrounded by the odour of sanctity belonging
properly to Attica; whereas in Athens, on Plato's anniversary,
the pedants, presided over by Longinus, amused themselves
with plagiarisms of famous men.[2]

Porphyry never forgot his debt to Plotinus, and a critical
edition of his writings fully confirms this. The very introduction
reveals his spiritual unity with his master. The other members
of the circle were in the same case. We hear of women who
followed his manner of life; of parents on their deathbeds who
confided the education of their children to Plotinus; and, in
fact, he took these boys and girls into his house, administered
their property, and introduced them to philosophy. He was
trustee and umpire in numerous cases, keeper of conscience
even for senators and politicians. When he left Rome, after
twenty-six years, he had not a single enemy among the political
leaders in the capital.[3] He was very ill, and he could scarcely
speak: but he lived rather more than a year out in the country,
and died in A.D. 270.

His place in the history of Neoplatonism was taken by
Porphyry, a man quite different from Plotinus in natural gifts
and attitude of mind. A holy calm had surrounded Plotinus,
but as soon as we approach Porphyry, we hear unmistakable
echoes of contemporary movements.[4] He was born in Tyre of an
eminent family; and, at an early date, felt himself in sympathy

---

[1] *ibid.* 13   [2] *Vita,* 15; cf. Porph. in Eus. *Praep.,* 10, 3   [3] *Vita,* 9
[4] J. Bidez, *op. cit.,* is of primary importance

with the manifold religious life of his surroundings. Nor did Christianity remain foreign to him, and it would appear that he attended lectures by Origen, whom he always respected as a scholar,[1] but he was particularly attracted by the esoteric art of magic. He listened to orators and, indeed, while still a young man, he exorcized a dæmon.

In his book, *Oracular Philosophy*, a youthful work, he published a collection of oracular sayings, which he edited from the philological standpoint and explained on a philological basis. These oracles were not, e.g., sayings of the ancient Pythia with an historical foundation, but examples drawn from the most recent period. Here we find the practices of soothsayers and exorcists mingled in quite a strange manner with all kinds of astrological lore and isolated portions of religious philosophy. Porphyry felt very much at home in this region, and persuaded his readers that they would find themselves here on the direct road to the salvation of their souls, and able to purify their manner of life. He liked to mingle the occult with fragments of all sorts of religion, and he supported the view that Christ was acknowledged by the divine oracles: but he upbraided the Christians unsparingly for their erroneous faith.[2]

However, Porphyry soon abandoned these lower regions. In his work entitled *Images of the Gods*,[3] all the ghostly magic has disappeared, and we find the gods modelled according to Stoic ideas, as symbols of the powers which operate in nature; e.g., Zeus is the supreme god, the living essence of the universe, which he had created by virtue of his being intellect in action.[4] The heavenly constellations are revelations of gods, and the images made by men of insight give graphic expression, in form and ornament, to a manifold acquaintance with the invisible: they are like books from which those who can read obtain information about the gods.[5] Porphyry received his first lessons in strict academic method from Longinus in Athens, a man whom Plotinus esteemed as a philologue, but not as a philosopher.[6]

It was only when he joined the circle round about Plotinus,

---

[1] Eus. *H.E.*, 6, 19, 5
[2] Wolff, 180ff.
[3] Fragments given in Bidez, p. 1*–23*
[4] *ibid.* 3*–7*
[5] *ibid.* p. 1*
[6] *Vita Plotini*, 14. Bidez, pp. 29–36

that the influence which proved decisive was exercised upon his inner life; by this time, A.D. 262, he was thirty years old. During his six years' stay in Rome, he not only came to attack the gnostic apocalypses,[1] and grew to be a trained philosopher; but he also learned how to follow the road that eventually led him to become a famous exegete of Aristotle; in particular, he deepened his religion by means of philosophy, developed his ascetic freedom from the world, and brought it to maturity. All these features are revealed in his writings.

He accepted without question everything which had been passed on to him by the far superior spirit of his master, but he worked it all out and put it in a simplified form which corresponded more closely to his own nature, and enabled him to set it down in a way which could be more easily understood. Porphyry wished to make his influence felt by the general public, even though he still frequently asserted that his words were only for the elect. He knew well enough that amongst the educated classes round about himself there were hundreds and thousands who longed for this kind of instruction, and that it was impossible to exclude them from access to the truths that would set them free.

His writings lack the strenuous earnestness of Plotinus's tractates. They were written with an easier pen, graphically, in a simple style which could be easily understood, and with as much rhetoric as the taste of his public was justified in expecting. In addition, it is quite clear that he strove to preserve the traditional forms of religion; and he used allegory and symbolism to prove that their existence was justified to some extent. Naturally, the hocus-pocus of magic now played no part with him as a thinker, and popular ideas belonging to nature religions were subjected by him to sharp criticism. The criticism brought out innumerable problems and difficulties in every single case.[2] The study of his version of Plotinus's philosophy was of course intended to provide the relevant answers.

The sort of thing Porphyry had in mind is made plain in Augustine's polemic: *The Return Home of the Soul*.[3] Here we are

[1] *Vita Plotini*, 16

[2] *Epist. ad Anebonem* in Iamblichos, *de Mysteriis*, ed. Parthey, 29–45

[3] For Fragments *vide* Bidez, 27–44

told of a "pneumatic" vehicle of the soul, an astral body which can be combined with matter according to the particular inclinations of the soul. Then it crystallizes out, receives a small airy part, and thereby comes under the influence of evil dæmons which live in the air. Such an astral body drags the soul downwards, with the result that, after death, it must always enter into new bodies and bear much suffering in order to atone for its guilt.

There are two ways along which freedom can be obtained. The first is familiar to everybody, and consists of the mystical and magical rites of the "theurgi", particularly the "Chaldæans". These purify the astral body by means of symbolic practices, and gain for it a good dæmon as a friend, who will lift it up above the earth together with the soul that dwells within, and carry it out to the heavenly sphere of the planets. This way is uncertain and dangerous, however, because the envy and ill will of earthly magicians, and the vengeance of evil dæmons, oppose such liberating magic vigorously.

The second way consists of self-redemption by means of philosophy. Here everything of a bodily character is abnegated, and the spirit strives to reach God: moreover, this way alone leads to a final liberation from every form of reincarnation, and to a union with God and His Son, i.e., Nous, who is similar in essence to the human soul. Those who are not strong enough to climb the philosophic steeps must follow the lower way, along with the great masses. There is no such thing as a way of redemption accessible to all. Strict asceticism characterizes the philosopher's upward way, and vegetarianism is an indispensable foundation; when a group of Plotinus's disciples wished to abrogate this prescription, Porphyry sharply repudiated such heresy.[1]

The *Letter to Marcella* gives a most graphic account of the significance of asceticism for liberating man from earthly affairs.[2] Marcella was the wife of one of his philosopher friends who, by the death of her husband, lost everything that supported her outer and inner life: she found herself suddenly

[1] Porph., *de abstinentia* in A. Nauck, *Porphyrii Opuscula Selecta*, 2nd ed., 85–270
[2] *ibid.* 273–297

cast entirely on her own resources, with seven children. Then Porphyry married her in order to help, although he was already approaching old age. This act appeared, however, both to the world and also to many friends, as a betrayal of his ascetic principles, and he felt compelled to justify himself. While away on a journey, he therefore addressed an open letter to his wife, who had remained at home. He presented her with a kind of philosophical looking-glass, ornamented with a good deal of traditional proverbial wisdom, and dedicated both himself and her to the ideal of a life apart from the world, and directed toward God.

The aim of this life was the redemption of the soul as seen in its similarity to God, while dutifully recognizing the traditional forms of religion. The four elements of this philosophical religion are faith, truth, love, and hope;[1]—there is an unmistakable echo here of Paul's triad of faith, hope, and love; another passage reflects the words of Jesus in Mark 9: 43, 45, when Porphyry requires us not only to cut off a limb, but to abnegate the entire body for the sake of salvation. As a philosopher, Porphyry felt himself exalted above the illusion of the senses, and he did not regard his life's companion as a wife, nor she him as a husband: only a virgin soul could bring forth to pure Nous the children of salvation.[2]

A comparison of Origen's theory of the universe and his philosophical system with the conceptions of Plotinus and Porphyry shows the great similarity between the thought of a Christian and two pagans. Every step they take shows their mental kinship, and that they were the pupils of a single teacher, Ammonios Sakkas. The first Christian systematic thinker, and the last man to follow the tradition of pagan Greece, really belonged to the same school; both pursued knowledge by the same strict methods, and this constituted a part of their religion; both sought God along the same road, and found Him as the highest good; and both enjoined sheer asceticism as the means by which men could escape this world and enter into a better one beyond. Nevertheless, they belonged to two hostile camps.

How great the hostility was, is shown by Porphyry's polemic

[1] *Epist. ad. Marcellam*, 24   [2] *ibid.* 33, 34

against the Christians; written in fifteen books, it is the most comprehensive, and also the most penetrating and acute controversial work of a philosophical character written in the first millennium of Christian history. Unfortunately, it has not been preserved in its entirety, and the numerous works written by the most eminent Christian scholars against it were destroyed in order that every trace of this dangerous poison should be removed from the world. Nevertheless, a few quotations have been preserved, and a fictitious dialogue of Makarios of Magnesia contains numerous excerpts from a writing hostile to Christianity, a writing which may be regarded with all probability as that of Porphyry.[1] Hence it is possible to form some sort of estimate of the attitude and method of Porphyry's polemical work, even if his position as a whole, and his line of thought, still escape us.

We have already seen how highly Porphyry valued a pious attitude towards the "religion of the fathers", and this in spite of all his philosophical insight and education. He regarded the Christians as altogether contemptible because they contemned their ancestral traditions and accepted the foreign and despicable myths of the Jews. Nor had that been sufficient for them, rather they had chosen a new and unique way which had no national basis, but which required blind faith.[2] As a consequence, it was impossible for the new religion to be the truth, because it neglected men of the pre-Christian era, and had to do only with moral invalids.[3] In addition there were impossible doctrines about a suffering Son of God, a destruction of the sky, and a resurrection of the body, doctrines which contradicted a true conception of God.[4] But Porphyry was not content with these general objections, which are similar to those in Celsus's polemic.[5] In his case, the significant thing is that his criticism attacked the Bible, proved its untrustworthiness and the self-contradictions of its doctrines. This fact of itself led him to deny the person of Jesus, whom he had honoured at an earlier date.

[1] The fragments collected by Harnack, *Porph. Geg. die Christen* (*Abh. Akad.* 1916, No. 1); cf. also A. B. Hulen, *Porph. Work against the Christians* (*Yale Studies in Religion*, No. 1), 1933

[2] Harnack, *Fragm.*, 1, 52, 73

[3] *ibid.* 81. 82. 87

[4] *ibid.* 84, 85, 89, 92, 94

[5] Vol. 2, 173, 175f.

He spoke sharply against an allegorical explanation of the Old Testament on the part of such a scholar as Origen, forgetting that he had employed the same method, without hesitation, in regard to Homer.[1] He examined the Old Testament chronology on the basis of his own knowledge and, as an expert chronographer, he proved that the book of Daniel was undoubtedly written in the time of Antiochus Epiphanes—an assertion which, of course, was indignantly repudiated at the time by the Christians.[2] But his hatred only came to full expression against writers of the Gospels and the Epistles, whom he frequently describes as ignorant and clumsy deceivers. He uses a biting criticism, in a style to be found again in the heyday of the period of the Enlightenment. Thus he makes great play with the contradictions in their writings, the historical impossibility of some of the records or legendary narratives, and sets them one against another. Nor is he ever weary of depicting the faults in the character, or describing the foolish acts, of the two chief apostles, Peter and Paul.[3]

Even Jesus Himself finds no grace in his eyes. His parables are trivial and even incomprehensible; and if His secrets are hidden from the wise, but revealed to the babes (Matthew 11: 25) then it is advisable to strive for ignorance and unreasonableness. This is not to be marvelled at, because Jesus never had any real schooling. His beatitudes on the poor and His repudiation of the rich make serious moral effort impossible; and anyone who sells all he has and gives to the poor (Matthew 19: 21) abandons freedom, and voluntarily becomes a beggar, and a burden on others.[4]

Moreover, Jesus by no means followed His own teaching. He preached fearlessness, but when He was arrested He trembled and shrank in Gethsemane; and neither before the High Priest, nor before Pilate, did He speak in a manner worthy of the wise and godly man. How differently Apollonios of Tyana stood before Domitian, and then disappeared miraculously from the audience-chamber, to be found a few hours later, visible to all, in Puteoli.[5] Jesus had not been able to

---

[1] *Fragm.*, 39; cf. *de antro Nympharum*   [2] *ibid.* 40, 41, 68, 43

[3] *Fragm.*, 2–18, 49, 55, 19–37   [4] *ibid.* 54, 52, 56, 58

[5] *ibid.* 62, 63; cf. Philostrat., *Life*, 8, 8–10

perform real miracles. Why, otherwise, should He have refused to leap from the parapet of the temple? Why, after His death, did He not appear to Pilate, to Herod, to the High Priest, or, in particular, to the senate and people of Rome, as one who had risen from the dead? In that case, all the world would have believed on Him; and His adherents, who had been led astray by false prophecies, would not have needed to be punished on His account and even executed as deceivers. Thus, this pretended saviour of the world was, in reality, responsible for the outpouring of much blood.[1]

It is obvious that this type of criticism of the Bible and of Christianity is based on a thoroughgoing rationalism and cuts down to the bone; it reveals all the pride of a thinker who has received a genuine academic training, and feels contempt for a despicable superstition. Nevertheless, the dynamic and the active principle of his polemic are not to be found in these characteristics of the philosopher. We have already seen with what understanding and reasonableness this rationalist can treat the conceptions found in Greek religion, deriving originally from the religion of nature; and how he can deal with the wizardry of theurgics and magicians; how he pays homage to Hellenistic redemptive mysticism, and longs for an ecstasy which he regards as the most blessed goal of his life, leaving far behind everything of a merely rational character; indeed, how his entire philosophy coincides to a large extent with that of the Christian scholar Origen. It follows that the burning hatred against Christianity, shown in Porphyry's polemical writing, is not grounded in philosophical points of contrast, nor even in religious attitudes; rather it is due to the active cross-currents of the period. It arises by an inner necessity out of an ancient and proud culture endeavouring to assert itself and come to vital spiritual expression for the last time. It is a culture which finds itself faced with a powerful, new, and growing phenomenon which, for its part, rightly feels itself as something entirely different, and which, in spite of all attempts at accommodation, is really of a completely different nature. The only thing possible in those circumstances was a life and death struggle; and it was because he recognized these facts that

[1] *Fragm.* 48. 64. 65. 66. 60. 61

Porphyry wielded his pen, and became, for us, a typical representative of the attitude to life found in the silver age of the ancient world.

We see how true this is, not only by virtue of his hatred, but more positively by virtue of the things towards which he feels himself attracted. Here, oracles and theurgic miracles play a significant part, and it is possible to prove that the Neoplatonists of the succeeding generations adhered even more warmly to these strange speculations. The movement which appeared in the second century as Gnosticism, and which was fed by a thousand sources,[1] grew in the third century considerably, and was frequently combined with the religious endeavours of those who adhered to a modernized form of Pythagoreanism and Platonism. Naturally, this type of Gnosticism, which was outside the Christian church, was not that attacked by the Church when defending herself. We may assert confidently that most of the documents dealing with these conflicts have disappeared without a trace, and, consequently, the few fragments that have been preserved are all the more precious.

Porphyry mentions several collections of the oracles of gnostic theurgists.[2] One of these is quoted so often by him, and still oftener by his followers, that we are able to gain a fairly clear picture of their contents: it was a collection of Chaldæan oracles.[3] In accordance with the title, these sayings are given in hexameters, and the metre is more exactly maintained than is the case in the Sibylline oracles, a Jewish piece of writing; nevertheless, the poet's difficulties frequently call for sympathy on the part of the reader. The sayings speak of One, the highest Being, Nous, who dwells in unattainable exaltation above the world and everything else that can be comprehended by rational thought. This Being created the world by a mediator, the "second Nous". We also hear about the divine Silence (*Sigē*),[4] and about a Trinity of a certain kind. The world is constructed in three grades or storeys; these are the fiery empyrean, the realm of the aether in which move the seven

[1] Vol. 1, 264ff.   [2] *Supra*, 39f.

[3] Ed. with commentary by W. Kroll, *de oraculis Chaldaicis*, 1894 (*Bresl. philolog. Abh.* Vol. 7, Part 1). Also Kroll in *Rhein. Mus. f. Philol.*, Vol. 50, 1895, 636–639

[4] cf. Vol. 1, 288; Kroll, p. 16

planetary spheres, and the material region which is beneath the moon.[1]

Moreover, this entire universe is inhabited by innumerable divine and dæmonic beings, whose influences largely determine the fate of man. If a man gives himself to the servitude of the flesh, he surrenders to the wicked dæmons of the earth, and to the appropriate consequences or fate, to *Heimarmene*.[2] If, however, the divine spark in the human soul, the Nous, is reminded of its heavenly origin by the symbols which are scattered about in the world, the help of the friendly gods will open up the way by which it may return to the highest god. And, since God's nature is expressed in terms of fire, fire worship is a ritual which leads to salvation. Unfortunately, the philosophical exegetes dealing with this side of the oracular religion have not given further details: but it is highly probable that the readers were introduced to a magic based upon fire, which put them in a position to call up the dead and make gods appear.[3] Hence, this oracular philosophy, in spite of its high-sounding phrases, issues finally in a cultus of symbolism, and this provides bridges giving access to the lower regions of superstition.

One stage higher are the numerous writings which bear the name of Hermes Trismegistos, and which are therefore put forward as divine revelations in a sense similar to that of the oracles which we have just discussed. For the "three times great Hermes" is identical with Thot, the ancient Egyptian god of wisdom.[4] Up till quite recently, it was genuinely believed that these writings gave us the Greek version of Egyptian religion, affected afterwards by certain Iranian influences.[5] Nevertheless, if the ancient orient exercised any influence here, it did so, in any case, only very indirectly: on the whole, as well as in detail, these revelations exhibit the character of the philosophical mysticism of the second or third centuries. A collection of tractates of this kind has been preserved in certain manuscripts, and numerous other fragments are contained in an encyclopædic symposium belonging to the fifth

---

[1] Kroll, p. 31   [2] *Op. cit.* 48f., 52–54, 62f.   [3] *ibid.* 54–58
[4] A. Erman, *D. Religion d. Aegypter*, 3rd ed., 407, 343ff.
[5] R. Reitzenstein, *Poimandres*, 1904. R. Reitzenstein, u. H. H. Schaeder, *Stud. z. antiken Synkretismus*, 1926 (*Stud. d. Bibl. Warburg*, Vol. 7)

century. In addition, our knowledge is extended by translations and by occasional quotations preserved in Christian writers.[1]

The individual writings are of considerable length, and mostly in the form of instructions given by Hermes to his son Tat, or to Asklepios; but once, as if by Isis, to Horos. Their content consists of items of information giving a more profound knowledge of God, the world, and mankind, knowledge which consists of a redemptive gnosis in a sense with which we are already quite familiar. By means of this perfected insight, man would be placed in a position to rise above his earthly form of existence, and become divine.[2] Nevertheless, the reader is not presented with a system of philosophy and no effort is made to maintain a consistency between the different pronouncements on the most important problems: if the contradictions were all brought together, their number would be seen to be impressive. Writing of this kind is not used for systematic discussions, a fact that makes it impossible to discover a criterion for separating the different strata and placing them in a chronological sequence.[3] Quite in accordance with the capricious character of gnosticism, and with their own conscious lack of concern, the different writers give rein to a fantasy which is inspired by religious impulses, and in this way construct their world.

We can trace the Stoic doctrine of the knowledge of God based on the observation of nature and of the teleological structure of the human body; and we are told that God pervades the entire universe and is in everything: "Everything is full of God".[4] Nevertheless, this type of pantheism is unhesitatingly combined with a conception of God deriving from the Platonic tradition, and conceived in terms of the most extreme transcendence. God can be described neither by the predicates of *nous*, light, spirit, nor even by the idea of existence: rather He is the cause of all these entities.[5] Sometimes He is

---

[1] Collected and provided with an English translation by Walter Scott, *Hermetica*. 4 Vols. 1924–36
[2] *Hermetica*, 4, 7 10, 6. *Asklepios*, 376, 1f. gr. Scott, *Kore Kosmou* in Stobaeus, *Ecl.* 1, 408, 14 (=p. 496, 22 Scott)
[3] Joseph Kroll, *D. Lehren d. Hermes Trismegistos*, 1914 W. Kroll in *Pauly-W.* 8, 804–820 W. Bousset in *Göttingen Gel. Anz.* 1914, 748ff.
[4] *Hermetica*, 5, 4–6 9 11, 6   [5] *Herm.* 2, 12–14 12, 1

described and worshipped as the final unity (*Monas*) which is the cause of all; elsewhere we read that He is the One, and at the same time, the source of the One.[1] A positive account of His nature would describe Him as the Will from which originate all existence and all development.[2]

As is the case with the conception of God, so also Stoic and Platonic elements mingle in the conception of the universe. There is an antithesis between the intelligible world of ideas, and the tangible, sensible cosmos of matter which is hostile to God.[3] We are told of the creative activity of the demiurge who had been sent out by the highest God, who was the Logos or the Nous, and who, on one occasion, is even described as the sun god Helios,[4] and there are planetary spheres as well as innumerable dæmonic beings in the space between heaven and earth.

Interest centres on man, who, being imprisoned in an earthly body, is the victim of every kind of evil, threatened by a relentless fate,[5] and, as a consequence, to his own hurt, he carries everywhere a body which is a garment of ignorance and a living death.[6] At bottom, however, he is of a divine origin, and Nous, which created the world, discovers everywhere the scattered seed-corns of divine existence.[7] It calls and awakens mankind, who is endowed with Nous—although this is not always the case! It rouses him out of the sleep due to the drugging effect of the senses,[8] and teaches him the way of gnosis, how the soul ascends[9] to God when freed from the fetters of the body. A most impressive tractate[10] makes use of expressions parallel to those employed by Hermes, and describes the mystery of a spiritual second birth which takes place in the case of his son and disciple Tat as an example for every reader.

Sin is ignorance, gnosis is piety:[11] such is the phraseology that meets us continually, and that urges the disciple to deny his body and its passions. Various vices are ascribed to the operation of dæmons: adultery, murder, doing violence to parents, sacrilege, impious deeds, suicide; and in another passage twelve

---

[1] *Herm.* 4, 10   5, 2
[2] *ibid.* 10, 2–4
[3] *ibid.* 1, 7   16, 12. 17
[4] *ibid.* 16, 5   [5] *ibid.* 12, 5
[6] *ibid.* 7, 2. 3
[7] *ibid.* 9, 3–4. 6
[8] *ibid.* 1, 27   7, 1–3
[9] *ibid.* 1, 25   4, 11
[10] *ibid.* 13
[11] *ibid.* 1, 20   11, 21   6, 5   9, 4

sins of the flesh are enumerated as dominating the sentient soul.[1] Nevertheless, the antithesis between the soul and the body does not appear to have led to asceticism in any real sense. The writings must have contained other traces of this feature in addition to the isolated remark at the conclusion of the Latin version of Asklepios's speech according to which the hearers, after prayer, were to partake of a "pure and vegetarian meal". Nothing at all is said about sexual asceticism; on the contrary, we are told on one occasion[2] that childlessness is the greatest misfortune and evil. On every hand, we gain the impression that the ethical requirements of this mystic move essentially along the lines of Stoic morality; and that it is left to the individual, whether he will or will not adopt definite means for fighting against his body.

Moreover, prescriptions for conducting worship are entirely lacking. The way to apotheosis is by means of contemplation, by the concentration of all the powers of the soul on the forms of knowledge which conduce to salvation and which are mediated by reading the Hermetic writings.[3] We may therefore say that, in contrast to the known magical and theurgic practices, and similarly also to the gnostic organizations for the purposes of worship, we are dealing with a "bookish" mysticism, which has become entirely literary in character. Nevertheless, it aims at the same goals as the others: the ascent of the soul after death through the heavenly spheres[4] is prepared for already here on earth. Particularly gifted persons are successful in liberating the soul for a time from the body, and, in ecstasy, seeing visions and experiencing the sense of being equal with God.[5]

There is scarcely a trace of the syncretism which occurs frequently elsewhere in gnostic · spheres. The Greek and Roman gods have disappeared, and, if they are ever mentioned,[6] they appear as cosmic powers, or else as beings belonging to the world of stars. The outstanding significance of the sun god, Helios,[7] reflects the views of Stoic theologians, and perhaps also the official religion of the period. The Egyptian gods

---

[1] *ibid.* 9, 3   13, 7   [2] *ibid.* 2, 17   [3] cf. in particular *Herm.*, 13
[4] *ibid.* 1, 24–26   [5] *ibid.* 6, 1   10, 5   11, 20   13, 3
[6] *Asclepius*, 19. 27   [7] *Herm.* 5, 3   10, 2   16, 5. 12

appear as persons and speak their messages; they are regarded as vehicles of the highest forms of revelation, but are no longer felt to be national godheads who ought to be worshipped. It may well be asserted that the Hermetic writings are not only cool, but perhaps even hostile, towards contemporary "paganism".

They adopt an essentially different attitude toward Judaism. The Judaistic type of conceptions exercised a strong influence on the imagination and the phraseology of the writers.[1] Some significance must attach to the fact that the two accounts of the creation of the world, in tractates one and three, are constructed on the basis of the Mosaic records in the Septuagint; and, indeed, a large number of detailed explanations of a strange kind are closely parallel to what is found in Philo's writings. The celebrated concluding prayer of Poimandres, with its "Holy, Holy" repeated nine times, sounds so Biblical that, at a later date, it was adopted without hesitation in a Christian liturgical volume.[2] Nor are these points of contact with Hellenistic and Judaistic wisdom confined to the two tractates just mentioned, but are to be found in other passages of the Hermetic writings.

Such facts prove that the propaganda of the Judaism of the dispersion which we have already described[3] had made contact with these mystic philosophers, and had influenced them profoundly: and this again possibly explains how they came to abandon current forms of paganism. The period when the Hermetic books were written is still a matter of uncertainty: possibly they were begun in the second century, but the further we penetrate into the third century, the more comprehensible all this literature becomes as a whole; one could readily place them in the period between Numenios[4] and Porphyry.

In this connection, we ought also to comment on the magical papyri. There have been magical books probably in every age, and their significance increased as the world became more literary. By his preaching in Ephesus, Paul brought it about

---

[1] Of prime importance is C. H. Dodd, *The Bible and the Greeks*, 1935, 99–248

[2] *Herm., ibid.* 1, 31f.; in addition, cf. Reitzenstein and Wendland, *Gött. Nachr.* 1910, 324–329. The papyrus comes from the fourth, or the end of the third, century (Schubert).

[3] Vol. 1, 90ff.   [4] Vol. 2, 298

that magical books to the value of 50,000 drachmas were collected and burnt:[1] a fact which was a characteristic sign of the times. By their remarks, both serious and scoffing, Apuleius and Lucian show us what was the part played by magic in the second century: Hippolytus[2] is full of a Christian teacher's indignation, as he assembles numerous details to justify his attitude.

In the days when spiritual culture existed in fixed forms, magic ruled among the lower classes, and on good grounds avoided the light of publicity in every form. Nevertheless, side by side with the other phenomena accompanying religious decay, its power continually increased, spread ever further, and even penetrated the higher cultural levels. These facts can be readily studied during the centuries of the Roman emperors, and, Iamblichos, Porphyry's pupil, recounts an astounding plenitude of empty magical tricks in his work on the mysteries.

The magical books which have survived[3]—and their number is very considerable—come for the most part from the fourth, although a few are probably from the fifth, century; while the first and third centuries are also represented. The two most important, the *Papyrus Mimaut* and the *Great Parisian Book of Magic*, were written during Constantine's reign, and others a little later. Hence we may be confident of finding reflected in these texts the evolution followed to the time of Diocletian.[4] Naturally the foremost place is occupied by the principal concerns of magic: the conjuring of gods and demons for the purpose of glimpsing the future; means of protection from and cure of diseases and other forms of evil; how to damage the body and soul of hated persons with the aid of demons; and, especially, love magic in every form, and the creation of a familiar spirit (*Paredros*) to give assistance in all cases of need. But the religious conceptions of this late age have affected the primordial practices of nature religion, given form and content to prayers and exorcisms, and invented secret names and

[1] Acts 19:19
[2] *Refut.* 4, 28–42
[3] All the Greek texts together with the German translation have been edited by Preisendanz, *Papyri Graecae Magicae*, 2 Vols. 1928–31
[4] On the whole subject cf. Th. Hopfner in *Pauly-W.*, 14, 301–393; E. Masson-neau, *La magie dans l' antiquité romaine*, Paris, 1934

incomprehensible sayings, all of which give the characteristic flavour to this type of activity. Here we find the same phenomena as we have already observed in loftier spheres.

The Olympic gods have almost disappeared, and only Apollo, as a god who gives oracles, comes to our notice, but in complete isolation: if the others are named, as a rule their names apply to the planets. The old goddess of witchcraft, Hecate, has preserved, as we should expect, her power and prestige; but side by side with her, and even as a rule in front of her, we find the Egyptian gods, Hermes-Thot, Anubis, Osiris, Typhon, Harpocrates, Bes, together with the sacred animals found in Egyptian worship.

We have already discussed the *Leyden Cosmogony*,[1] a compilation of Egyptian ideas, popular Greek philosophy, and Jewish elements—a typical example of syncretistic gnosis. This was formerly a religious work in the higher sense, but it had now deteriorated, and was made to serve magical purposes. In the *Papyrus Mimaut*,[2] we find at the conclusion of a conjuring of the sun god that a prayer is appended which derives from the Hermetic tractate of Asklepios. This prayer offers thanks for the apotheosis of the pious by means of gnosis. And in the great Parisian papyrus[3] instructions are given for reaching immortality by mystical rebirth; this is attributed to Mithras. It also tells how the god, clothed in Persian garments, and holding in his hand the constellation of the Great Bear, revealed himself to a mystic who had ascended to heaven. What appears in broad outline in these cases is continually repeated in detail.

These magical papyri are like the ancient rubbish heaps in which the antiquarian finds potsherds belonging to a past civilization, neatly arranged in separate strata. No one will be surprised that Egyptian influence is predominant in books which originated in Egypt, nor that other oriental gods are to be met there with Mithra at their head. The astonishing thing is the strength of the Jewish influence; as early as in a papyrus of the first century the divine name Adonai Sabaoth is invoked; and the name Yahweh, in the form Yao, constitutes almost

---

[1] Vol. 1, 267ff. Preisendanz, *Pap. Mag.*, 2, 93–97 and 109–114

[2] Preisendanz, *op. cit.* 1, 56–58

[3] *ibid.* 1, 88–100. A. Dieterich, *Eine Mithrasliturgie*, 3rd ed. 1923

everywhere a constant feature in the magical formulas. The papyrus containing the *Leyden Cosmogony* is described as the "Eighth Book of Moses", and at the end we are told of a "Tenth Book of Moses".[1] Both Zoroasta and Moses are cited as authorities, and "the Great Name in Jerusalem" is mentioned as possessing a magic power.[2] The sun is invoked in a prayer full of names and formulas drawn from the Old Testament; and in another passage, but in a similar context, first Mithras is mentioned, and then the magic power of the Hebrew language is emphasized: a text follows in which the magician describes himself as Adam, the first-born, and then as Yao Sabaoth, Adonai; and he conjures the archangels Suriel, Gabriel, and Raphael.[3] A leaf of papyrus in Berlin, belonging to the fourth century, contains two magic dreams and a "prayer of Jacob" full of Jewish formulas.[4] But of more importance than such isolated phenomena is the observation, which holds good in general, that the divine names and angel-names used by the Jews occur ever and again among the magic words.

These facts confirm the point of view which we gained from the Hermetic writings, in regard to the influential propaganda exercised by Judaism on the syncretistic type of religion during the period of the Empire.[5] Traces of Christianity are rare: the name of Jesus occurs twice in interpolated Coptic phrases; in Greek, we find the Holy Spirit and the strange phrase "I adjure thee by the God of Jesus the Hebrew", which may have originated at an earlier date, since the pagan magician still makes no distinction between Christians and Jews.[6] But probably this inference is drawn without sufficient warrant, and it is more likely that these people who belonged to the syncretistic movement in the larger sense were entirely unaware of such differences. At any rate, all these Christian names are found in a Jewish context; and, in the case of more general

[1] Preisendanz, *op. cit.* 2, 87. 105. 120. 131 Dieterich, *Abraxas*, 1891, 155ff.

[2] Preisendanz, *op. cit.* 1, 128f. cf. 184 v. 109

[3] *op. cit.* 1, 12 v. 196ff. 38 v. 119. 144ff. Similarly 1, 112 v. 1173ff. 1204ff. Jerusalem v. 1222

[4] *op. cit.* 2, 148f.

[5] cf. also Vol. 1, p. 161. The "Hypsistos Theos" occurs also in Preisendanz, *op. cit.* 1, 108 v. 1069 182 v. 46 2, 62 v. 71

[6] *op. cit.* 1, 50 v. 420 1, 114 v. 1233 1, 48 v. 393 1, 170 v. 3019

formulas, even we to-day would not be able to determine whether they were Jewish or Christian.[1] Christianity played practically no part in this magic literature, not even in its gnostic forms. On the other hand, Judaism had roused the liveliest curiosity in men who were eager for secret lore.

[1] *op. cit.* 2, 12 v. 270

Chapter Two

THE FINAL VICTORY OF THE CHRISTIAN CHURCH

THE CHURCH ENJOYED UNDISTURBED PEACE FOR MORE THAN forty years after the time when Gallienus's edict of partial tolerance[1] put an end to the decade of persecution, A.D. 250–260. By being able to maintain itself in spite of persecution, the Church gained in prestige and self-confidence; it survived as an organized institution, and outgrew the severest tests of the times of oppression. The leaders showed both shrewdness and caution towards the weakness of the average Christians in a way that won back the majority of those who had recanted, and at the same time doubled the renown of the numbers of braver souls who had borne witness with their blood. Among these last, however, were to be found by this time many persons who belonged to the upper classes of society; and a man like Origen proved to the Roman world by his death that there were by now a few people of the highest education who not only confessed the Christian faith, but also exhibited a well-balanced and noble character. The years when the Church was left in peace, came as an unexpected blessing, and the number of Christian believers increased not only among the masses but also among the cultured classes. As a consequence, the practical life of the Church was no longer hampered by many a prejudice which had seemed well-founded at the beginning of the century. The more that persons of higher rank became Christian, the less practicable was it to prohibit Christians from sharing in the work of the administration of city or state.[2] By the year 200, Christians no longer felt it quite reasonable to refuse to be soldiers, and by the middle of the century the custom fell into desuetude.

The Church, however, was not alone in being faced by new circumstances, for the state did not insist on requirements which were impossible for a Christian. It shut its eyes and released Christian officials from the obligation to offer sacrifice.[3] This condition of affairs no longer offered so great a

[1] Vol. 2, 172   [2] Vol. 2, 152   [3] Eus. *H.E.* 8, 1, 2

legal difficulty once Gallienus had recognized the right of the Church to possess property, although in theory the Church was still a forbidden institution. The Emperor Aurelian was actually called in to help in the dispute about the bishopric of Antioch (A.D. 272), and without hesitation he declared that the see should belong to that person who was in association with the Italian bishops and the bishop of Rome.[1] Naturally this was not to be understood as a fundamental principle with a legal basis. Nevertheless, it showed that the Church, now an institution found everywhere in the Empire, had gained the respect of the authorities. It would appear that, at a later date, Aurelian intended to carry out a persecution of the Christians, but his death intervened.[2]

Therefore we have every ground for believing Eusebius to be trustworthy when he gives a rhetorical description of the happy situation of the Church c. A.D. 300.[3] Christians were to be found at court[4] and in the army, and might freely confess their faith; the bishops enjoyed respect in their contact with the provincial governors, and, indeed, occasionally Christians reached the highest posts in the administration.[5] The Empress Prisca, Diocletian's consort, and his daughter Valeria, were won over to Christianity.[6]

No wonder that the old meeting places were now not big enough for the public worship of the increasing multitudes, and everywhere new and larger churches were built. Nor is it surprising that scarcely a trace of this building activity has survived to the present day. For, once a piece of ground had been used for a church, it remained consecrated even when the edifice itself disappeared. When such took place, a new building was erected on the old site, and so a new church developed out of the previous one, a process frequently repeated throughout the centuries until the present day. To dig down to the earliest foundations, an archaeologist would have to destroy more than he would be permitted. Nevertheless, in Aquileia, under the great mediaeval cathedral, there has been discovered the complete foundations of a church, still decorated richly with

---

[1] Eus. *H.E.* 7, 30, 19
[2] *Op. cit.* 7, 30, 20f. Lactant. *mort.* 6, 1f. Const. *or. ad. s. Coetum.* 24, 3 190 Heikel.
[3] Eus. *H.E.* 8, 1, 1–6. army, *Acta Maximil.* 2, 9 (Knopf, 86f.)
[4] Eus. *H.E.* 8, 6, 1. 4. 5   [5] *Op. cit.* 8, 9, 7 8, 11, 2   [6] Lactant. *mort.* 15, 1

mosaic. This church was built at the beginning of the fourth century,[1] but of course it cannot be determined whether before or after the persecution. The same was the case with many churches in Rome,[2] which numbered, by the way, at this time probably more than forty.[3]

Hence it cannot be doubted that Christianity was making very great progress and enjoyed peace. If, on religious grounds, a conscript obstinately refused to perform his military service, he had to pay the penalty of death[4]—much the same as in modern times, and in "Christian" states, when Quakers, Adventists, and people of similar views adopt a comparable attitude. Such cases were rare: an incident of which we have record, took place in Africa, the seat of extreme tendencies, and where persecutions were frequent on other counts. The execution on this occasion cannot be regarded as a Christian persecution, any more than the death of the centurion Marcellus, who belonged to a Spanish troop. During the celebration of the Emperor's birthday, he suddenly threw away his weapons and badges of rank, and, in front of the standards of the legion, shouted out that he was a Christian and that he retracted his oath of loyalty as a soldier. He was sent to the then representative of the Prefect of the Pretorium at Tangiers, and there executed. This event must have been of the same general character as that recorded by the *Acts of Marcellus*.[5] Nevertheless, an appendix to this story is of very doubtful authenticity. It says that Cassianus, the clerk to the court, declared the judgment against the law and flung the records, together with his pen, to the ground.[6] On the other hand it may only have been an attempt to seek martyrdom, and therefore an act such as the church had for a long time deprecated.

Eusebius records the instance of Marinos, a non-commissioned officer, who sought to obtain the position of centurion.[7] He was denounced by a rival, and this fact, together with the resentment occasioned by what had been said against him, brought about a conflict between his military obedience

[1] Anton Gnirs, *D. christl. Kultanlege in Aquileia* (*J. d. Kunsthist. inst.* Vienna, 1915 140ff.), cf. *ZNW.*, 1921, 249–252

[2] Vol. 2, 250

[3] Optat. Milev. 2, 4 (39, 4. ed. Ziwsa)

[4] *Acta Maximil.* (Knopf, 86f.)

[5] *Acta Marcelli* (Knopf, 87–89)

[6] *Acta Cassiani.* (Knopf, 89f.)

[7] Eus. *H.E.* 7, 15, 1–5 (Knopf, 85f.)

and his faith in Christ which led to a tragic conclusion. Such isolated, but unfortunate cases, were almost unavoidable in view of the legal position, and do not affect the general favourable view taken of the Christian status as such. Lactantius alone included Aurelian in his gallery of rogues, and ascribed to him blood-thirsty schemes against the Christians, which, however, on account of his sudden death, were never carried out.[1] It is impossible for us to subject the details· to criticism in a systematic manner.

All Christendom was taken completely by surprise when, on February 23, 303, in the city of Nicomedia, where the governor had his residence, a church was destroyed by the Emperor's orders, and on the following day, an edict was published hostile to the Christians. Nor is it surprising that an eminent citizen, moved by great indignation, tore down the placard. He was immediately arrested, tortured, and "roasted alive in accordance with the law". In this manner, what is known as "Diocletian's persecution", was begun.[2]

It is not easy to discover how matters had come to this issue. No surviving pagan writings have anything to say about such a persecution. Two Christian authors furnish detailed descriptions of the course of events. The first is Lactantius, who lived about this time in Nicomedia, as a teacher of rhetoric[3] and who, as a consequence, may be assumed to have been an eyewitness. Shortly after A.D. 316, he wrote a work entitled *The Death of Persecutors of Christians*. Here he puts forward the thesis that ever since the days of Nero, all the emperors who were enemies of Christians had come to an evil end and, as a consequence, a divine judgment was to be seen in the final lot of Maximian, Galerius, Maxentius, Maximinus Daia, and Diocletian, together with their families. His fierce hatred for the emperors is expressed vigorously; but in describing the facts, he plays fair everywhere: He tells what he believes to be true, and the only question is whether in every case he had received reliable information.

The second authority is Eusebius, who lived at this time in Cæsarea in Palestine, as expert assistant to Pamphilos, the

---

[1] Lactant. *mort.* 6   [2] *Op. cit.* 12, 13   Eus. *H.E.* 8, 2, 4   8, 5
[3] Lactant. *Instit.* 5, 2, 2

learned presbyter. He evinced the scientific spirit and skill of a genuine historian in describing the history of the persecution as far as his horizon extended: the eighth book of his *Church History*, tells of the events in the east, up to A.D. 311, when Galerius published his edict of tolerance. Eusebius's *History* was published about the same time; in other words, it was written almost contemporaneously with the last persecutions. Probably during the same months there was published a special work dealing with the Palestinian martyrs, and added to the *Church History* as an appendix at a later date. Here Eusebius gives many details of what he had seen with his own eyes, either in the city, or in the course of his journeys. In addition to these two writers describing what they had seen, several *Acts of the Martyrs* of differing values have survived.[1]

Lactantius is the only one who tells what led up to the edict of A.D. 303.[2] It may well be that he includes some of the gossip of the court, such as was current in the royal residence. Nevertheless, his account seems highly probable on the whole. It would appear, therefore, that during a journey which he made in the east, Diocletian could obtain no divine answer to his customary sacrifice to the oracle, the reason being given that certain Christians were present when the rite was performed, and they had crossed themselves as a protection against the demons who were being invoked. The Emperor thereupon decreed that all the servants of the court were to make the sacrifices; and whoever refused was to be flogged. At the same time, he gave orders to all the military commands that every Christian was to be dismissed from the army. In the following winter, A.D. 302–303, he was visited in Nicomedia by Galerius, who had long desired to attack the Christians, and who had been incensed by his mother, who was a devotee of Cybele. The old man kept himself in hand for a long time, and wanted to be satisfied with dismissing the Christians from service in the court or in the army. In the end, however, he gave way to Galerius's insistence, and called a privy council of jurists and officers, who advised a Christian persecution. Thereon, the

---

[1] Ed. by R. Knopf, *Ausgew. Märtyrerakten*, 3rd ed. by G. Krüger, 1929. Crit. account in Harnack, *Chronol.* 2, 473–482. Also H. Delehaye, *Les passions des martyrs, etc.*, 1921, together with his *Origines du culte des martyrs*, 2nd ed., 1933
[2] Lactant. *mort.*, 10f. *Instit.* 4, 27, 4

question was put to the oracle of Apollo in Didyma[1] and, since this oracle agreed, Diocletian decided to proceed while still desirous of avoiding bloodshed. Moreover, Eusebius bears witness[2] to the fact that, previous to the persecution properly so-called, there had been a purging of the court and the army, and Eusebius regards Galerius as alone responsible for this general order.

It is in accordance with the facts of the case to hold that Galerius was of such a nature that he felt a passionate hatred against the Christians, and that he was called upon to avenge himself on those who despised Mars, his physical father,[3] and the rest of the Roman gods. Diocletian was very cautious and far more intelligent than Cæsar, and preferred to ignore the sudden attack; and this can scarcely be doubted. On the other hand, it may also be taken as assured that it was part of Diocletian's programme to give definite protection to the ancient Roman State religion, at least after A.D. 290.

The edict of the year 295 forbidding marriages among blood relatives had often led to immorality, although it made frequent reference to the prescriptions of the good old law which must be observed with religious respect. If the immortal gods saw that all the inhabitants of the Empire lived a devout, religious, quiet, and modest life, then, as in the past, so in the future, they would be propitious and gracious to the Roman name.[4]

Shortly afterwards, another edict was promulgated,[5] which ordered a war of religion in accordance with the law and for the protection of the ancient gods—in particular it was directed against the Manichæans "who had penetrated into the Roman world from amongst the hostile Persians"; Julianus, pro-consul of Africa, had made a report about the disorder which they occasioned. The Emperor ascribed the religion and manner of life, which had been fixed by the sages of ancient times, to the providence of the immortal gods; and he declared that no

[1] Lactant. *mort.* 11, 7   and Eus., *Vita. Const.* 2, 50. 54

[2] Eus. *H.E.* 8, 1, 7f. p. 796, Schwartz

[3] Aurelius Victor, *Epitome*, 40, par. 17. Lactant. *mort.* 9, 9

[4] *Collatio*, 6, 4, 1 in Mommsen. *Collectio librorum juris antejustiniani*, 3, 157. K. Stade, *Der Politiker Diokletian* (Diss. 1926), 78ff.

[5] *Collatio*, 15, 3, 1 p. 187. Mommsen. Stade, 86ff.

criticism of these ancient and accustomed views on the part of new religions was in any way permissible. For it was well-known that the Manichæans had already caused much unrest in Persia, and there were reasons to fear that they would poison the peaceful Roman people with their detestable Persian customs; this at least was what the pro-consul's report had already declared in regard to all sorts of evils practised by them. Hence their leaders and their holy books must be burned, stubborn adherents beheaded, or, if they belonged to the upper class, they were to be sent to work in the quarries—and this meant that their possessions would be confiscated.

We see that this edict breathed all the hatred of a Roman general against the enemies of the State on the eastern frontier, and it was obviously caused by an army of Persian Manichæan propagandists who, on account of persecution in their own country, had fled to Africa. But the reason for the measures of punishment was held to be so nearly universal and so much in accordance with the customs of ancient Rome, that it would have been possible on the same basis to order a persecution of the Christians. It was only to be expected that in some places the Christians would be felt in certain respects at least as dangerous as these Manichæans; the feeling preparatory for persecution was already present as the edict shows. From this standpoint we can understand how Galerius oppressed the Church as Lactantius records, and also how he finally triumphed over Diocletian's doubts from the standpoint of state policy; for, fundamentally, Augustus agreed with his Cæsar.

In February, A.D. 303, matters had gone so far that Diocletian gave way, although on the understanding that no blood must be shed. At the *Terminalia* of February 23, the Prefect of police, with his constables, appeared at dawn before the church of Nicomedia. The doors were broken in, the Bibles burned, and the furnishings plundered. Then pioneers appeared and razed the building to the ground.[1] On the following day an edict was promulgated which declared war in every form against the Christians. It drew attention to the Emperor's efforts to reform the State in accordance with ancient Roman ideas of law and order, and to make Christians who had abandoned the faith

[1] Lactant. *mort.* 12

of their fathers return to reason; it would not be permissible that they should any longer order their lives in accordance with their own capricious ideas, nor that they should institute churches here and there composed of all and sundry. For this reason orders were given that all persons of the upper classes who adhered to Christianity should lose their privileges, and that those who belonged to the Imperial Court, the majority of whom were freed men, should return to slavery if they maintained a similar attitude. Moreover all Christians were deprived of the legal protection which the state gave to its recognized citizens. The church buildings were to be razed and the sacred books burned.[1]

Naturally there was great excitement among the Christian population, and when, with a brief interval, fire broke out twice in the Imperial Palace, this was regarded as an act of vengeance on the part of the Christians. Immediately, there was a cruel persecution carried out with the shedding of blood, which, first at the Court, but afterwards also in the city, led to many being martyred. The Empress Prisca and her daughter Valeria were compelled to offer sacrifices; Bishop Anthimus of Nicomedia was beheaded and numerous clergy and laymen were executed both singly and in groups.[2] About this time unfortunately there were in Antioch and in Melitene of Cappadocia minor persecutions for ridiculous reasons; but Diocletian had become wrath. He punished persons in Antioch beyond all measure, and thundered in the background about Christian intrigues.[3]

A second edict was promulgated ordering the incarceration of all clerics, followed quickly by a third which ordered that the prisoners were to be compelled to sacrifice or pay the penalty on the gallows.[4] At this point bloody persecution began in full force, a persecution which remains indelibly impressed on the memory of the Church as its most terrible testing-time, and which branded Diocletian's name beyond that of all his predecessors. In the legends which came to be written down

---

[1] Lactant. *mort.* 13, and Eus. *H.E.* 8, 2, 4. = *Mart. Palaest. pr.* 1, 1. Lactant. 34, 1–2 gives the motives
[2] Lactant. *mort.* 14. Eus. *H.E.* 8, 6, 1–9
[3] Eus. *H.E.* 8, 6, 8. Libanius, *Oratio*, 11, 159   19, 45   20, 18, ed. Förster
[4] Eus. *H.E.* 8, 6, 3–10

afterwards, he is regarded as nothing more nor less than the typical persecutor.

However, those records which are historically reliable are dreadful enough. All the cruelties of the earlier periods were multiplied, and were added to and exceeded by the new inventions due to the devilish imagination of the executioners. Violence was now exercised even on corpses; they were refused burial and were handed over as food to the beasts; in certain cases indeed, they were disinterred and thrown into the sea.[1] But even in this instance, the purpose was not to eradicate but to convert the Christians, as is seen from a strange proceeding which was occasionally followed: the unfortunates' hands were chained or crippled by fire and then the powerless limbs were made to throw incense on the sacrificial flame. The same result might be reached by taking the unconscious bodies of those who had been tortured, and compelling them to perform the sacrificial act; but in the end it was enough to set the person concerned free, and to declare that he had yielded. Who was in a position to test that statement? Not the person concerned who, of course, only remembered his conscious acts. The purpose was to make the number of recanting clergy as large as possible, and thereby to create indifference among the rank and file of the churches.

As a matter of fact, the weak were not inconsiderable in number; but the Church nevertheless dealt effectively with this false show.[2] The number of those who paid the death penalty, apart from those in Nicomedia, was not large in the first year of the persecution. Eusebius gives exact details about it, and mentions four persons killed altogether in Palestine and Antioch. In the second year, according to the same author, the number was increased, although he seems to be dealing in essence with a single extended process in which voluntary provocation played a considerable part.[3] The edict of persecution naturally held good for the entire Empire; it bore the name of both Emperors and both Cæsars at the head, and Lactantius expressly assures us that Diocletian wrote to

[1] *ibid.* 8, 6, 7
[2] Eus. *Mart. Pal.* 1, 4. Petrus Alex. *Can.*, 14. (Lagarde, *Reliq. iur. eccl. antiqu. Graece*, 73). *Conc. Ancyranum, can.* 3
[3] Eus. *Mart. Pal.* 3, 1–4

Maximian and Constantius impressing on them that it should be carried out. Constantius contented himself with destroying the churches, whereas Maximian acted energetically in the Italian province.[1]

It is probable that not a few of the martyrs, revered in Rome and in the rest of Italy, suffered under Diocletian's persecution; nevertheless, no reliable records have been preserved. We are better informed about the case in Africa. Here we learn from the *Acta* that the proconsul Anulinus not only proceeded against the clerics and compelled them to hand over their Bibles, but also in February, 304, executed a small church of forty-nine persons in Carthage who had celebrated the forbidden Lord's Supper.[2] In December, 304, Crispina, an eminent lady, was beheaded in Theveste, and several other ladies had preceded her. It was probably in the year 304 also, that Maxima was executed with two women companions, an event which took place under Anulinus on the 29th of a certain July.[3]

Similarly it would appear that in Africa as early as the beginning of A.D. 304, the bloody persecution was extended also to the laity. In any case, the number of those who paid the sacrifice of death was not small. This follows from the numerous names of martyrs found in inscriptions and in liturgical texts, which can be traced back with a fairly high degree of probability to Diocletian's persecution; but we must be careful to distinguish them from the long lists of martyrs belonging to the later periods of controversy.[4]

We have very little information about Spain under Maximian's rule. Our knowledge is derived essentially from the not very informative verses of the Spanish poet, Prudentius, who wrote about A.D. 400. He mentions an imposing number of martyrs of his native land, and describes in full detail the martyrdom of the revered Vincentius of Saragossa:[5] but it is

---

[1] Lactant. *mort.* 15, 6–7

[2] *Acta Felicis* (Knopf, 90); von Soden, *Urkunden z. Entstehungsgeschichte des Donatismus*, 39–41; *Acta Saturnini* (Ruinart, 414–422)

[3] *Acta Crispinae* (Knopf, 109), cf. Diehl, *Inscr. lat. christ*, n. 2042, 2043. *Acta Maximae*, (*Analecta Bollandiana* 9, 107)

[4] Delehaye, *Les Origines du culte des Martyrs*, 2nd ed. 1933, 386–400. The inscriptions are conveniently reproduced by Diehl, *op. cit.* 2031–2104. 1911. 1931

[5] Prudentius, *Peristephanon*, 4 and 5; 6 is quite uncertain

by no means sure that all these saints belong to Diocletian's persecution. Most of the legends from Spain are unreliable. We remain dependent upon general considerations, as most of the inscriptions coming from a later date afford us no further help. Bishop Ossius of Cordova is the only one who tells us that he himself bore witness as a "confessor" at that time.[1]

It can be affirmed confidently that, as early as the beginning of the year 304, the laity were made to undergo bloody persecution in Africa. The same facts hold good in regard to the provinces governed by Galerius and Diocletian. On April 1, 304, in Thessalonica, five women and one boy were accused of hiding Christian writings, and of having refused to sacrifice after they were arrested; three of them were burned, the other three being permitted to suffer imprisonment only, on account of their youth.[2]

Hence it appears that the notorious fourth edict which gave a general order that all Christians throughout the Empire should offer sacrifices, was promulgated as early as the beginning of A.D. 304: Eusebius is not clear about the exact date,[3] but the increase of severity must be connected with the general political situation. In November, 303, Diocletian came to Rome, and there entered upon the celebration of the twentieth year of his reign, the *Vicennalia*. During his hurried journey back, he caught a severe cold of which he was unable to rid himself throughout the whole of the following year; and during December, 304, it was even rumoured that he had died. It is obvious that Galerius and Maximian exercised a free hand against the Christians all this time.

Diocletian had felt broken and ill, and had therefore decided to renounce the crown: he was successful in inducing Maximian to make a similar renunciation although he was still full of vigour.[4] On May 1, 305, the two Augusti solemnly completed their act of renunciation on a parade ground in Nicomedia. Constantius and Galerius, who had hitherto been crown princes, now became Augusti. In the west, a superior officer, Severus by name, and in the east, a nephew of Galerius, called

---

[1] Ossius's letter in Athanasius, *Hist. Ar.* 44, 1   [2] *Acta Agapes* (Knopf, 95)
[3] Eus, *Mart. Pal.* 3, 1=4, 8. Also N. Baynes in *The Classical Quarterly* 18 (1924), 189–193. Lactantius does not mention this edict
[4] *Panegyrici lat.* 7 (6), 9, 5

Maximinus Daia, became Cæsars. At the same time, the provinces of the four rulers were defined afresh. As the senior in rank, Galerius became the head of the imperial college.

The sons of the Emperors were left without appointment; these were Maxentius, Maximian's son, and the young Constantine, who was still in attendance for the time being at Galerius's court. A few months later, however, Constantine departed in a hurry that seemed like a flight, and paid a visit to his father who was seriously ill.[1] He met him in Boulogne and accompanied him to York, where he died on July 25, 306. The son was immediately hailed as Augustus by his troops. Galerius had no alternative to accepting the facts, and recognized him at any rate as Cæsar; he raised Severus to the rank of Augustus in the place of Constantius.[2]

About the same time[3] Maxentius in Rome, the other son who had been passed over, allowed himself to be proclaimed a leader by the dissatisfied pretorian guard. Galerius wished to proceed against him with military force, and sent Severus in advance. But the latter's troops changed sides, and adhered to the son of their old general; and when the old man himself appeared on the field, and once more put on the purple of Augustus, Severus's situation had become hopeless: he died in Ravenna. The date was April, 307.

At this point, Maximian went to Trèves, came to an arrangement with Constantine, and raised him to the rank of Augustus: he stood in urgent need of the young man to protect his rear during his war in the orient. The political alliance was sealed by Constantine's marriage with Maximian's daughter, Fausta, to whom he had been engaged since a youth. The official ceremonial speech at the marriage of the young couple has survived.[4] Anyone who knows the circumstances, finds this speech particularly interesting. It is also noteworthy that not a word is said about his dear brother-in-law, Maxentius. It is obvious that, even at that time, the relation between father and son was lacking in due cordiality. As was to be expected, Galerius marched to Italy as the avenger of Severus and the

[1] *Zosimos*, 2, 8. Lactant. *mort.* 24   [2] Lactant. *mort.* 25, 5. *Paneg. lat.* 7 (6), **5, 3**

[3] These events are described in Lactant. *mort.* 26–30 and *Zosimos*, 2, 9–11

[4] *Paneg. lat.* 7 (6)

protector of his authority as senior regent. But the troops refused to obey him in the march toward Rome; he was compelled to turn back, and he saw to it that the Italians should remember him as an incendiary. Peace now came to the west. Maxentius reigned as Augustus in Italy, Africa, and Spain, while Constantine held a similar position in Gaul ·and Britain.

The aged Maximian, deposed by his son, fled to his son-in-law. He even went to Carnuntum (on the Danube frontier in Pannonia, near Pressburg), where he met Galerius and Diocletian. Here on November 11, 308, Licinius, one of the generals belonging to Galerius's circle of friends, was entitled Augustus of the West. No amount of persuasion could move Diocletian to abandon his retirement, and to risk the fame of his twenty years' reign: that he was proclaimed consul for the year 309, must be regarded as a last move in accordance with these dubious doings. Scarcely anything was altered in the actual situation. The new ruler had to content himself with the administration of Pannonia. Maximian returned to Constantine, brought about a further amount of unrest and, finally, in A.D. 310, had to disappear from history as an impossible figure. Maxentius asserted himself everywhere, even against the rebellious prefect Alexander in Africa. The persecution of Christians had ceased since A.D. 306 in the western half of the Empire, and not only Constantine, but also Maxentius are celebrated expressly as having restored freedom of worship.[1]

The situation was different in the east. Granted it is only possible to say, in regard to the provinces of Licinius and Galerius, that no change was made in the circumstances. The few *Acta* that can be dated, appear to belong to the year 304, and most of the remaining material shows no sign of date. Here, as elsewhere, we can only make the general inference that most of the martyrs who are mentioned in the tradition of the sacred liturgies, are ascribed to this persecution which was both the last and the greatest. Only by accident do we hear that under Galerius the entire Christian population, together

---

[1] Optatus Milev. 1, 18. Eus. *H.E.* 8, 14, 1. *Re* Constantine, *vide* Lactant. *mort.* 24, 9

with other inhabitants of a township in Phrygia, were consigned to the flames; and that in Cappadocia and Pontos, Christians were terribly persecuted.[1]

On the other hand, Eusebius supplies detailed information about the circumstances in Maximinus's province. When the new Cæsar entered on his office, he first of all increased the severity of the persecution. Later, however, he ordered a halt in the shedding of blood, and decreed as the normal punishment the blinding of one eye, and the laming of one leg: in addition, by way of a rounding off, there was compulsory labour in the quarries in Palestine, or in Silesia.[2] These methods were applied from A.D. 307, and Eusebius gives an impressive description of the way in which the cripples of both sexes and every age, were sent from Egypt to Palestine. Naturally, punishment by death was retained in special cases, in particular if the person seemed to thrust himself forward as a Christian. On the whole, however, the Christians experienced an easing of their situation, until all at once the obligation to make the sacrifices was again brought to the front.

In this instance, concrete things were done side by side with the requirement to observe the official cultus: ruined temples were rebuilt, and the priesthood was definitely reinstituted.[3] Pamphilus, Eusebius's learned patron, died in this new wave of hatred on February 16, 309, after he had lain in prison without charge for two years; admittedly his imprisonment had allowed him the possibility of carrying on literary work.[4] Eleven others died with him; Eusebius gives a list of twenty-three martyrs who died during the increased severity of the compulsion to sacrifice in Palestine. In the next year, 310–311, the unfortunate workers in the quarry, who had already formed themselves into churches, and had built themselves meeting-rooms, suffered an unexpected deterioration of their case by being transferred to other places. An entire church of thirty-nine cripples who were incapable of performing any work were killed off, obviously because they had incensed their

[1] Eus. *op. cit.* 8, 11, 1   12, 1. 6. Lactant. *Inst.*   5, 11, 10
[2] Eus. *Mart. Pal.* 4, 1   *H.E.* 8, 12, 9–10   Lactant. *mort.* 36, 6f.
[3] Eus. *Mart. Pal.* 9, 2   *H.E.*, 8, 14, 9   Lactant. *mort.* 36, 5
[4] Eus. *Mart. Pal.* 7, 4   11, 1–28 Photios, *Bibl. cod.* 118, p. 92 *b*, ed. Bekker. Appendix to *Esther* in the *cod. sinaiticus* in the Septuagint

enemies by continually practising religious exercises in the place to which they had been deported.[1]

It is impossible not to be moved to the depths by the severity of their struggle; and their courage in face of death rivets our attention when we read the accounts of the sufferings through which all these martyrs passed. The records rest to a large extent upon the testimony of eye-witnesses, and their testimony is silently supported by the long lists of names which have been preserved in the calendars of the saints in the different provinces. Far and wide, the churches were completely broken up: many, far too many, of the clergy recanted, and became "traitors", i.e., they saved their lives by surrendering their copies of the Holy Scriptures, or by cleverly deceiving the authorities. In Africa as well as in Palestine, a cleric who had lived through the period of persecution with a whole skin was therefore regarded with contempt—and often rightly so.[2] Some fell on account of their weakness, others by envy or because they were busy-bodies.[3] We must also take account of the fact that the hard times fostered a rank growth of evil motives on every hand.

Nevertheless, in spite of the fact that all these great evils were widespread amongst the masses, they did not settle the fate of the Church; rather, the heroism of the few won the victory. State policy prepared the way. Galerius became seriously ill, and his case hopeless. On April 30, 311, while in Nicomedia, he promulgated an edict putting an end to the persecution of the Christians.[4] This edict declared that the object which had been sought in the earlier decrees, viz., to force the Christians to return to the state cult, had not been successful. The great majority had proved obstinate, and now worshipped neither the gods of the State nor served the God of the Christians. Consequently the Emperor had decided with the clemency which was traditional, to license Christianity and church worship, naturally within the limits prescribed for public order. Regulations for carrying the edict out would be given later to the governing authorities. For the present, the

[1] Eus. *Mart. Pal.* 13, 4–10
[2] Gathering in Cirta cf. Von Soden, *Urkunden zur Geschichte des Donatismus* n. 5, 7f. Epiphan., *haer.*, 68, 8, 4
[3] Eus. *Mart. Pal.* 12   [4] Lactant. *mort.* 33, 11 34. Eus. *H.E.* 8, 17, 1–11

Christians were permitted to pray to their own God for the well-being of the Emperor, the Empire, and their own selves.

Five days later, on May 5, 311, Galerius died. It is obvious from the wording that his "edict of tolerance" was by no means the repentant confession of a remorseful sinner, as it was said to be by the Christians; rather it was an act decided upon on grounds of state policy. There is indeed some reason for believing[1] that Constantine had compelled the dying Augustus to stop the Christian persecution because of its lack of success on the whole. Maximinus, who was now the senior Augustus, then issued the promised orders for carrying out the details under the charge of his *praefectus praetorio* Sabinus:[2] but the tart phraseology plainly reveals that the Emperor disliked making this concession.

A transport of joy passed through the whole of the east, the prisons opened, hosts of crippled and ill-treated confessors streamed out of the quarries; and those who were liberated united with those who had retained their freedom in services of thanks to God. This period of peace lasted not quite six months, i.e., till October, 311. Then Maximinus gave orders for new restrictions in the freedom of worship. In the first instance, ceremonials were forbidden in the cemeteries. Then there were further martyrs: on November 24, 311, Bishop Peter of Alexandria died, and on January 7, 312, a presbyter, Lucian of Antioch, who was very eminent as a scholar, was executed in Nicomedia, during the time that Maximinus was himself in residence in the city. Nor were these the only two who paid the penalty during this period. In the autumn of A.D. 312, a zealous official caused a flood of petitions to rush in from different cities to the Emperor.[3] He wished to prohibit Christians from remaining in the cities. Nicomedia and Antioch made a beginning, numerous others followed, and it is easy to see that Maximinus always gave a favourable answer to the petitioners. Cities honoured in this way put their request and the imperial decision in permanent form on an inscription.[4]

[1] E. Schwartz, *Konstantin*, 58f.   [2] Eus. *op. cit.* 9, 1, 3–6

[3] Eus. *op. cit.* 9, 2–4   Maximinus in Eus. *op. cit.* 9, 9a, 4. For the date, cf. 9, 10, 12

[4] Eus. *op. cit.* 9, 7, 1–14   Inscription at Arykanda in Dittenberger, *Or. Insc.* n. 569. Schwartz, *Gött. Nachr.* 1904, 529f.

Eusebius quotes the text of the imperial permission as he copied it from a tablet in Tyre, and his reliability is confirmed by the fact that a similar inscription has actually been found in the little Lycaonian town of Arykanda, the text of which agrees *verbatim* with Eusebius. Here also is preserved the rhetorical bombast of city records.

Nevertheless, the imperial decision was only a *beau geste* and was not followed by any orders for carrying it out—in practice it was impossible to bring into effect a ban which would expel all Christians from the main towns. In the following year (A.D. 313), a communication sent to the prefect Sabinus[1] admits the facts fairly plainly, and renews the earlier order that violent measures against Christians were to be avoided, and that they were to be won over by kindly persuasion. It is clear that the replies quoted as given to the cities, left the way open for spiteful tricks of all sorts; and in order to create the necessary atmosphere amongst the people, the malicious and spurious *Acts of Pilate* were distributed by the civic authorities.[2] It follows that when Maximinus is said to have once more insisted on clemency on the part of the officials, there must have been some special reason; in all probability this reason was provided by the foreign politics of the Empire in the winter of A.D. 312–313.

When Galerius died, the problems connected with the sharing of authority in the Empire, now became urgent. Maximinus took possession of Asia Minor, which was part of Licinius's province, and claimed it as his share of the Empire. Licinius had to agree. At this stage, he entered into a compact with Constantine and became engaged to his daughter Constantia: this fact gave him a certain expectancy in regard to the future. For the time being, Constantine gained the assurance of his benevolent neutrality in the crucial struggle for the west. In particular, whereas the three Augusti, Maximinus, Constantine, and Licinius recognized one another, and appeared with due formality as the heirs of Diocletian's tetrarchy, Maxentius was regarded as a usurper.[3]

Constantine emphasized his own legitimacy as against

---

[1] Eus. *op. cit.* 9, 9A, 1–9   [2] Eus. *H.E.* 9, 5, 1   7, 1
[3] Dessau, *inscr. lat. sel.* n. 663, 664

Maxentius:[1] his father had been the honoured Augustus Constantius, whereas Maxentius derived from the deposed Maximinian, whose memory was accursed and despised.[2] Moreover Constantius was the son of Claudius, who had been legally instituted as emperor, and who had conquered the Goths in A.D. 269–270. No one hitherto had been aware of this, but from A.D. 310, the glad news was published officially. It followed that Constantine was the third in succession to wear the crown of a glorious dynasty.[3] In this way, he appeared by right of birth as the guardian of the most honourable Roman traditions, the liberator of Rome and the supreme senate from unworthy servitude to a tyrant.[4]

As far as Maxentius was concerned, he saw the danger and sought security by an alliance with Maximinus: the honourable obligation to avenge his father's death afforded him the necessary appearance of moral backing if it came to a question of war.[5]

Hence the two opponents watched one another for a while like beasts of prey ready to spring. Suddenly, and to the surprise even of his entourage, Constantine marched over the Alps with troops well schooled to war in Germany. He conquered Susa, Turin, Milan, and Verona; even Aquileia fell to him; and he appeared before Rome unexpectedly early. Maxentius had provisioned the city thoroughly and had gathered a very large army in it. Then a Sibylline oracle of the usual ambiguity encouraged him to meet his enemy before the gates. On the place occupied to-day by the Ponte Molle, he rebuilt the bridge over the Tiber and marched across with his troops. A large number of owls perched on the city walls watched the march out, a fact over which Constantine appears to have rejoiced; for he attacked, and smote his opponent. Maxentius had the misfortune to be torn from the bridge in the course of his flight, and drowned. The war was over. Constantine entered Rome as sole ruler of the western Empire, and was greeted as supreme

---

[1] *Paneg. lat.* 6 (7), 2 and 4, 1; cf. the coins mentioned on 146

[2] Lactant. *mort.* 42, 1   Dessau, *op. cit.* 627, 630–633, 644

[3] *Paneg. lat.* 6 (7), 2, 4

[4] "Liberation of Rome" as catchword. Lact. *mort.* 44, 11   *Paneg. lat.* 12 (9) 3, 2   Eus. *H.E.* 9, 9, 2   Dessau, *op. cit.* 694

[5] Lactant. *mort.* 43, 4   Zosimos, 2, 14, 1

Augustus by the Senate.[1] The date was October 28, 312.

All the world regarded the astonishingly fortunate issue which followed Constantine's enterprise as a judgment pronounced by the Higher Powers. The story of the owls is a reflection of this belief: the gathering of the unlucky birds appeared to be an omen, a prodigy of the kind recorded in Livy's History. When the Senate erected a triumphal arch to his honour in A.D. 315, Constantine, in the dedication thereon, ascribed his victory not only to the greatness of his imperial genius, but also to the "inspiration of the godhead".[2] The same view is expressed in various phrases in a contemporary panegyric, but a few years later (A.D. 321), it was no longer regarded as satisfactory. Nazarius, the imperial court orator, now belauded the fact that Constantine had enjoyed divine protection in all his undertakings, but that in the battle with Maxentius, Constantius of blessed memory had come to his son's assistance personally at the head of a heavenly army.[3]

Nor did the Christians think otherwise. In the ninth book of his *Church History*, which he began in A.D. 315, Eusebius describes Constantine's triumphant march as under God's miraculous protection, a protection for which the Emperor had petitioned in the course of prayer to the God of Heaven and to His logos, Jesus Christ.[4] He asserts that after the victory, the Emperor caused a statue of himself, cross in hand, to be erected in Rome, the inscription declaring that he owed his victory to this symbol. Lactantius, who wrote at about the same time, gives further details: Constantine had been advised in a dream to put the divine sign of the monogram of Christ, ☧, on his soldiers' shields. He had acted accordingly and thus won the victory.[5] But more than twenty years later, when the Emperor died on May 22, 337, Eusebius delivered a memorial oration, and added many details to the record contained in his *Church History*. He declared that at the time of the crucial war, Constantine had come to a knowledge of Christian truth,

---

[1] Lactant. *mort.* 44 Eus. *H.E.* 9, 9, 1–9 Zosimos, 2, 16 *Paneg. lat.* 12, (9), 16–20

[2] Dessau, *op. cit.* 694

[3] *Paneg. lat.*, 12 (9), 2, 4 4, 1 11, 4 13, 2 16, 2 22, 1 25, 4 and *Paneg. lat.* 4 (10), 14, 1–7 29, 1

[4] Eus. *H.E.* 9, 9, 1f.   [5] Lactant. *mort.* 44, 5f.

and had prayed God for a revelation of His being and for His help. He then received a sign: early in the afternoon, a cross of light shone above the sun with an accompanying inscription, "Conquer by this". The Emperor, together with the whole army, looked at it in astonishment. During the following night, Christ appeared to Constantine with that cross of light in his hand, and urged him to prepare a copy of the heavenly symbol as a means of protection. Thereupon the standard of the imperial bodyguard was created in the form known as the *Labarum*. This standard copied the cross with its horizontal transom and carried the monogram of Christ, ☧, in a crown. It appeared that the Emperor had himself told his biographer the facts in later years, and had affirmed their truth by an oath.[1]

In this instance, the process of legend-building is open to the day on both the pagan and the Christian sides. As time went on, the ideas of what had happened, gathered head in proportion to the eagerness with which they were accepted. The Christians busied themselves in making the Emperor even at that date into a protagonist of their faith: and in the later years of his life, which Eusebius recorded, this tendency suited Constantine so well, that he himself helped it forward. In A.D. 313, he still hung back; but the whole matter is one which must be examined in its larger setting.

Certainly, the war with Maxentius was not a war of religion: that was a fact which even the Christian writers of the time did not venture to assert, much as it would have suited them to do so. Maxentius had been tolerant towards Christianity, and although he had intervened roughly in the disputes about the Roman bishopric, he observed due formality when he caused the church property which had been confiscated in the period of persecution, to be given back to Miltiades, who had been consecrated on July 2, 310.[2] This was more than had been done hitherto by any other ruler. Now, however, it was exceeded by Constantine.

Constantine went to Milan, where he passed the winter, and where Licinius was also staying. The projected marriage was

[1] Eus. *Vita Const*, 1, 28. All the relevant texts are given in Aufhauser *Konstantins Kreuzesvision* (*K. Texte 108*)

[2] Eus., *H.E.* 8, 14, 1   Optat. Milev, 1, 18   Augustine, *Brev. Coll.* 3, 34   Schwartz, *Gött. Nachr.* 1904, 530–533

celebrated here, and the two emperors were now brothers-in-law. At the same time, they reached an agreement about dealing with the Christians. They decided to give them complete freedom of worship, and equality with all other religions, in order that "the godhead on the heavenly throne, whoever he may be, might be propitious and merciful to us and our subjects". They abrogated the restrictive regulations which had held good hitherto, and gave back the confiscated buildings and plots of ground used for divine worship, even in cases where meanwhile these had become private property. Owners who had been dispossessed by this order, were compensated from the state treasury. In this way, members of the Church were explicitly recognized as legal persons in the eyes of the law. The emperors hoped by taking these measures to obtain "the eternal perpetuation of the divine grace which had been experienced in the great events of the most recent past". That is the content of the decisions taken at Milan, which it has become the custom to describe, not quite correctly, as "the Edict of Tolerance at Milan". The exact wording has not been preserved, but the essence can be deduced from the edict which Licinius decreed, and which we shall discuss immediately.[1]

The regulations made at Milan were sent as usual to Maximinus, but he refused publication. Instead, he issued the communication addressed to Sabinus, which we have already mentioned,[2] and which prohibited violent measures: he was not in a mood to do anything more. He had no alternative to regarding Constantine as his enemy, seeing that the latter had allowed the Roman Senate to give him the title of Senior Augustus, a title which belonged to Maximinus himself. Constantine had departed immediately after the marriage in Milan, and gone again to Gaul in order to continue his interrupted work of defending the frontier on the Rhine.[3]

Licinius was left to his own resources, and Maximinus hoped he might be able to proceed with his victorious march,[4] which had stopped short at the Bosphorus in A.D. 308, and at the same time obtain stronger means of defence against Constantine.

---

[1] Eus. *H.E.* 9, 9, 12   Lactant. *mort.* 45, 1   cf. 48, 2   Wording as given by Lactant. 48 and Eus. *H.E.* 10, 5, 2–14

[2] *supra*, 73   [3] Zosimos, 2, 17. *Paneg. lat.* 12 (9), 21, 5   [4] *supra*, 73

He brought troops from Syria by forced marches, and invaded Thrace. He captured Byzantium, and then besieged Perinth, but this took up valuable time. Licinius had broken up camp and come to the rescue with surprising speed. He was already in Adrianople. On April 30, 313, the forces engaged in battle on the *Campus Serenus*, after the two Emperors had conferred to no purpose. Maximinus was completely defeated, and was only able to save his own person by rapid flight disguised as a slave. His first halt was made in Cappadocia, where he again gathered his soldiers about him. Licinius crossed the Bosphorus and marched into Nicomedia, the capital. Here, on June 13, he promulgated immediate tolerance for the Christians, and thus made the settlement reached at Milan effective in the east.[1] There were various battles in Asia Minor throughout the summer. Maximinus retreated over the Taurus, and settled in Tarsus. In the autumn, for reasons which we cannot discover, he himself promulgated an edict of tolerance which recognized Licinius's concessions.[2] Shortly afterwards he was overtaken by death.

The imperial ladies belonging to Diocletian's family had sought the protection of Maximinus, when Galerius died; but they found no peace: dissensions soon took place, and Valeria, Galerius's widow, as well as her mother Prisca, were banished to various places, and their trusted companions were put to death. Diocletian was helpless in the matter. Licinius's victory handed the unhappy women over into the hands of the new ruler, whose blood lust raged against others besides officials among the adherents of Maximinus. He therefore executed the consort and the daughter of the former Emperor, together with Maximinus's family.[3] The lonely man, at the glorious palace at Spalato, was compelled to drink the cup of suffering to the dregs. He saw the collapse of a life's work which he had built up so carefully; and now in addition he saw the bloody end of his family. Fate had no mercy, either on the Emperor or the man. He was never of a gentle nature, but now he was indeed embittered and gradually his heart was eaten out; Diocletian died on December 3, 316.[4]

[1] *supra*, 77, n. 1   [2] Eus. *H.E.* 9, 10, 7–11
[3] Lactant. *mort.* 40 41 50 51 Eus. *H.E.* 9, 11, 3–8
[4] Lactant. *mort.* 42. *Chron. Minora*, 1, 231

The Christians had every reason for regarding Maximinus's downfall as a divine judgment, for now the victory of the Church was settled publicly and obviously throughout the Empire. Licinius himself had no inclination towards Christianity, and the act of tolerance was for him nothing more than a political move. Nevertheless, Lactantius has it on record[1] that before the crucial battle of *Campus Serenus*, an angel had appeared to the Emperor during his sleep and had dictated a prayer which he then passed on to the troops, and which was audibly uttered by the entire army at the moment of making their attack. There is nothing specifically Christian in the wording, but it is capable of a Christian interpretation—and that satisfied the Church. The parallel to the legend about Constantine is unmistakable. The prayer for use on Sundays,[2] which at a later date was prescribed by Constantine to the pagan soldiers of his army, is only another form of the wording first used by Licinius.

The relationship between Constantine and Licinius was never really cordial, nor could it be, since it was the unmistakable goal of Constantine's policy to do away with all rivals. There is therefore nothing surprising in the fact that the two brothers-in-law stood face to face, weapons in hand, on the lower Danube as early as October, 314. Although Constantine's luck in victory seemed to hold, his power was not sufficient to obtain a decision, and they finally agreed to renew the double rulership; Licinius received only Thrace and the adjoining territories up to the mouth of the Danube as his share of the European part of the Empire. It should be said at once that the peace lasted just about seven years. Then the tension between the two Emperors became acute, and a number of oppressive regulations[3] brought the facts home to the Christians in the east of the Empire.

Licinius might rightly assume that in case of war, their sympathies would not be with him but with Constantine who was emphatically on the side of the Christians. First of all Licinius expelled the Christians who occupied high positions in the Court and the Army. This was followed by various

[1] Lactant. *mort.* 46   [2] Eus. *Vita Const.* 4, 20
[3] Eus. *H.E.* 10, 8, 10f., 14–19. *Vita Const.* 1, 51–54

cunning prohibitions; women and men were not permitted to attend divine worship together, and women might not be instructed by male clerics. The concern for morals shown by the authorities gave rise to mirth far and wide, and this led to their forbidding church-going altogether. The Christians were now ordered to hold their meetings in the open air in a space on the outskirts of the city. The bishops were forbidden to meet together, and particularly to hold synods, a blow against the large-scale organization of the Church which was severely felt. Naturally, there was much opposition, and the prisons were filled with Christians. The prisoners might not be comforted by Christian charity under heavy penalty. In a few provinces over-zealous officials used the sword, and in the district of Pontos church buildings were damaged. Nevertheless, on the whole Licinius remained content with measures which prevented certain kinds of activity among Christians.

At length, Gothic troops crossed the lower Danube and invaded Licinius's province: Constantine immediately intervened, and defeated the enemy. Licinius took it wrongly, and matters came to a breach in the spring of A.D. 324. Constantine manœuvred cautiously. He ordered his son, the Cæsar Crispus, to blockade the entrance to the Dardanelles with a strong fleet, forcing Licinius to retire toward Byzantium. When Crispus had destroyed the enemy fleet near Gallipoli, Licinius was compelled to abandon Byzantium. He fled to Chalcedon, but shortly afterwards came to the end of his resources even on Asiatic soil. He therefore sent his consort, Constantia, to her brother to beg for peace and personal security. His request was granted, and he was told he might take up his residence in Thessalonica; here he died a death which was almost unavoidable in such circumstances, and in fact was well deserved.[1] His memory was proscribed like that of Galerius, Maxentius, and the aged Maximian.

In the autumn of A.D. 324, Constantine was the sole ruler of the entire Roman Empire: he had attained his ambition. He built a palace for himself six years later on the most beautiful site in the newly founded city of Constantinople, and an inscription placed over a gateway that looked out across the sea,

[1] *Anon. Valesilanus* 21–29 in *Chron. Minora*, 1, 9f.

said that Christ had helped him on account of his constant and devout reverence for the "divine"; Christ had quenched the fire of the tyrant, and granted him the rulership of the entire world.[1] This was a plainer statement than the inscription on Constantine's arch in Rome. Christianity had gained final victory.

[1] E. Mamboury and Th. Wiegand, *Kaiser Paläste von Constantinopel,* 1934, 7f.

Chapter Three

THE DONATIST CONTROVERSY

CONSTANTINE'S CHRISTIAN CONVICTIONS MAY BE REGARDED as highly questionable, and correspondingly of little value: nevertheless, it is indubitable that his policy was to set a positive value on the Church, and to weave it into the texture of the Roman Empire as a dominant element and a political bond. By this policy, he reached a success which went far beyond everything he could have hoped. At the same time, he was confronted with a new type of problem, one having to do with the relation between Church and State, a problem which has continually occasioned political disturbances right up to the most recent times.

When he had defeated Maxentius, he was in a position to take up his enemy's church policy in the sphere which he had newly won.[1] Even before the edict of Milan, Anulinus, the Proconsul of Africa, of whom we heard during the period of persecution, was ordered to return to the Christian churches all confiscated property, particularly buildings and plots of land, even in those cases where they had meanwhile come into private possession.[2] Moreover, the clerics of the church catholic were granted freedom from public burdens, i.e., they were relieved of the obligations of the propertied classes, who could be distrained upon for all the municipal expenses.[3] This privilege was much sought after, but was only granted to those people who were already in public service like the economically indispensable merchants and ship-owners, firemen, tax-collectors, and estate stewards. Pagan priests never possessed this privilege *ex officio*, and only occasionally were civic obligations modified in their case.[4] This valuable concession was now granted to Christian clerics as such, because their influence with the God of Heaven was desired, and because it brought

---

[1] *supra*, 70, 76f.

[2] Eus. *H.E.* 10, 5, 15–17   Von Soden, *Donatismus*, No. 7   [3] Vol. 2, 22f.

[4] M. Rostovtzeff, *Gesells. und Wirtsch. im Röm. Kaiserreich*, 2, 120–122. U. Wilcken, *Gründz. d. Papyruskunde*, 1a, 129, 344f.

luck and happiness to the Roman Empire; i.e., they were regarded as public servants.[1] In all this, the will of Constantine was plainly operative.

It must be regarded as a special kind of favour, when the Emperor caused a sum of £15,000 to be given to Caecilian, bishop of Carthage, in collaboration with Ossius, bishop of Cordova, for distribution among deserving clergy of Africa, and if necessary, further sums would be available. In the same communication, the Emperor invited the bishop to ask for the help of the state in case of further disturbances of the peace of the Church by misled people.[2] This suggestion and the special mention of the church catholic in all the communications, shows us that everything was not in good order in regard to church affairs in Africa. The answer sent by the proconsul gives us further details.[3]

A few days after the Emperor's attitude became known, a deputation accompanied by a great multitude appeared before the government buildings. It protested against the recognition of Caecilian, and handed in two documents of accusation with the request that they should be given to the Emperor: this was done. The head of the opposition party responsible for this act, was named Maiorinus, and the date is given as April 15, 313.[4]

What was the reason? A variety of opposing views had disturbed the life of the Church in Africa from the beginning. In the shape of Montanism and Novatianism, they had given rise to forms of organized opposition against the normal Christianity of the church catholic. These opposition movements had by no means disappeared in the second half of the third century. In addition, there appear to have been dissensions based on local loyalties, in particular between Numidia (Algiers) and Proconsular Africa (Tunis). In Carthage,[5] the house of a rich and bigoted lady, Lucilla by name, constituted the centre at

---

[1] Eus. *H.E.* 10, 7, 1f. *Cod. Theod.*, 16, 2, 2. The same question in regard to the Jews received a variety of answers: *Cod. Theod.* 16, 8, 2–4 F. Juster, *Les Juifs dans L'Empire Romain*, 2, 259

[2] Eus. *H.E.* 10, 6, 1–5 = Von Soden, *op. cit.* n. 8

[3] The decrees are conveniently given by H. von Soden, *Urkunden zur Entstehungsgeschichte d. Donatismus (Kleine Texte* 122); important discussion by L. Duchesne, *Le Dossier du Donatisme* in *Melanges d'Archéol. et d'Histoire*, 10 (1890), 589ff.

[4] Von Soden, *op. cit.* n. 10   [5] Optat. 1, 16–19 describes the beginnings

which the malcontents gathered. She had formerly been rebuked by Cæcilian when Archdeacon, and threatened with ecclesiastical punishment because, before partaking of the elements of the Eucharist, she had been accustomed to kiss some bones which were the relics of a martyr not recognized by the Church. She did not forget this insult, and she waited for an opportunity to retaliate. There was the persecution of A.D. 303–304, and there was the following peace. Mensurius, bishop of Carthage, did not return home alive from a journey to the Court. As usual, the archdeacon, i.e. Cæcilian, was chosen as his successor.

Then war broke loose. Lucilla and her adherents, a few unattractive busy-bodies, and the Numidian party, came into action. A Numidian bishop, Donatus, of Casae Nigrae, organized a split in the Church, even before the new bishop was chosen.[1] The senior bishop of Numidia, Secundus of Tigisis, was sent to Carthage; and he assembled under his presidency a council of about seventy bishops.[2] This council objected to the choice of Cæcilian, firstly because he had been consecrated by "traitors", secondly because he had put hindrances in the way of caring for the martyrs while in prison. This last point might have been a matter of shrewd foresight after the fashion of Cyprian, but perhaps was unavoidable on account of police regulations;[3] in any case, it was only a venal offence. Crucial importance, however, attached to the claim that consecration by traitors was invalid. The names of three bishops were mentioned who had taken part in Cæcilian's ordination, and who were held as traitors:[4] Felix of Aptunga, Novellus of Tyzicum, and Faustinus of Tuburbo. The last two names were soon left out of account, obviously because the accusation was nonsense,[5] but afterwards, the objection to Felix was all the more stubbornly maintained.

Cæcilian interposed in a friendly manner, and made an offer unheard of in church law, to allow himself to be consecrated again by the Numidian party. This offer was rejected with contempt, and Lucilla's private chaplain, Maiorinus, was

---

[1] August., *Brev. Col.* 3, 12, 24. p. 72. 27. Petschenig
[2] Von Soden, *op. cit.* n. 6
[3] Cypr. *Epist.* 5, 2. cf. Eus. *H.E.* 10, 8, 11
[4] *supra*, 70   [5] August., *c. partem Donati post gesta*, 22, 38

elected opposition bishop in Carthage. This lady made a largesse of 400 *folles*, i.e., £2,000, a gift which exercised much influence.[1] The opposition in the capital naturally had its effect upon the hinterland, and the African Christians, together with their bishops, divided into two sharply opposed camps: the "Cæcilian party" and the "Maiorinus, or Donatus party", as they called themselves after the spiritual leader of the movement.

That was the situation which faced Constantine in A.D. 312, and which compelled him to intervene. Even if the Church had appeared to him less important than in fact it was, he would not have been able to avoid giving a decision. For the local authorities would have had to be instructed in regard to the matter of returning church property, as to which of the two parties was to be the legally recognized Christian organization capable of receiving it: both parties laid claim to sole competency. In this way, a new kind of problem in regard to the relation between church and state began to bud forth from the edict of tolerance.

At first, Cæcilian appeared to the Emperor as indubitably the legal bishop of Carthage, but the report made by his proconsul, and the documents of accusation which were handed to him, convinced him of the necessity of closer examination. It may indeed be the case that the "bishops of the Donatus party" expressly requested him to appoint a tribunal of Gallic bishops, Gaul being unaffected by the persecution, and therefore its bishops were inclined to neither party.[2] But the genuineness of this document is not altogether free from doubt. At any rate, in writing to Miltiades, bishop of Rome,[3] Constantine ordered him to institute an inquiry, and to do so in formal association with three leading bishops of Gaul, Reticius of Autun, Maternus of Cologne, and Marinus of Arles, who were to travel to Rome by imperial command. At the same time, Cæcilian was to be present in Rome along with ten friendly and ten opposing bishops. The synod met at the end of September, A.D. 313. The Emperor appointed for the purpose of the sittings, a palace which had once belonged

[1] Von Soden, *op. cit.* n. 38 p. 42, 139
[2] *op. cit.* n. 11   [3] *op. cit.* n. 12

to the Lateran family, and which was now in possession of the crown, as belonging to the Empress Fausta. It was this same palace which he afterwards presented to the Church, and on whose foundations the complex of buildings called the Lateran stands to-day.[1] Fifteen Italian bishops were present in addition to Constantine's three confidential advisers from Gaul. The Italians included the bishops of Milan, Rimini, Florence, Pisa, Capua, Benevento, and Terracina. It was therefore a genuinely representative gathering of the heads of the Italian church that assembled in Rome, and that was presided over by Miltiades.

On the very first day of the trial Donatus was unexpectedly placed in the role of defendant, and the charges upon which his accusers depended proved ineffectual. The accusers referred to witnesses whom they intended to call in the succeeding days. But the favourable witnesses who had been mentioned could not be found, and this on good grounds; the result being that the Donatists did not appear again before the synod. Instead of this, a new list of accusations against Cæcilian was propounded. After several useless discussions, the bishops paid no further attention to this obvious attempt at obstruction, but gave their verdict on the third day of the trial, Friday, October 2, 313. One after the other declared Cæcilian innocent, and Donatus's accusation groundless. Miltiades, as president, spoke last and he summed up the verdicts of innocence pronounced by the members of the synod, and gave them final form; and he promised Cæcilian full communion with the Church.[2] Donatus was excommunicated on account of practices not recognized by the Church, viz., rebaptism, and the ordination of back-sliding bishops. But in order to bring about an honourable peace in Africa, the synod proposed that in every place where there were now two opposing bishops, the one who had been ordained first should be recognized, while the second should receive another see when opportunity offered.[3] It was a reasonable suggestion, and it would have

[1] *Lib. Pontif.* 34, 9   also Duchesne, *op. cit.*, 191; Cabrol-Leclercq, *Dictionnaire* 8, 1545

[2] Von Soden, n. 13   and also Gerwin Roethe, *Zur Geschichte d. Röm. Synoden* (in *Forsch. zur Kirchen und Geistesgesch.*, 11, 2,) 51–81

[3] Von Soden, *op. cit.* n. 13 D

been practicable, if the real issue in Africa had been purely and simply the legal problems with which the decree had dealt; but the opposing opinions had roots which pierced deeper, and therefore the opponents remained unappeased.

Nor did it help matters when Donatus was forbidden to return immediately to Carthage, and when Cæcilian was compelled to remain in Brescia on account of Donatist representations. A commission, under two leaders, which was intended to carry out the decisions of the council in Africa, mismanaged affairs for forty days in Carthage, without reaching the desired results. Finally, the heads of the two parties returned to Africa, and the struggle blazed up with increased bitterness.[1] The Donatists had been quick to recognize that the Roman synod had not been a very propitious court for them; they therefore demanded that the case should be transferred to Carthage where the Church itself could present its accusation— the result being that the council was held under the pressure exerted by an excited populace.[2] For these reasons, they kept the witnesses away, and did not even themselves attend any further sittings. Moreover, they refused, quite logically, to recognize either the verdict that was reached, or the proposals for peace. Rather, they immediately protested to the Emperor against the over hasty verdict which had been reached without sufficient examination, and behind closed doors, by "a handful of people",[3] as they contemptuously called the synod. Constantine's first attempt to unite the African church by means of an ecclesiastical pronouncement had failed.

The Emperor was disappointed with this failure, and expressed his dissatisfaction vigorously. The exhibition of Christian disunity in the presence of paganism seemed to him very disgraceful,[4] and he regarded it as his duty toward God, to whose heavenly authority he owed his position as ruler, to bring back all the persons concerned to brotherly unity within the church catholic.[5] But he drew back, although raging inwardly, on account of the Donatists' manœuvre to obstruct

---

[1] *Optat.* 1, 26   cf. Constantine in Von Soden, *op. cit.* n. 14, p. 16, 20f. Unfortunately, the date of these proceedings in Africa cannot be precisely determined.

[2] August., *epist.* 43, 5, 14.   Roethe, *op. cit.*, 70. Note 67 explains it rightly

[3] Von Soden, *op. cit.* n. 14. p. 17, 39: n. 15. p. 19, 19

[4] *ibid.* n. 14. p. 67. 22–32. n. 15 p. 19. 24–27   [5] *ibid.* n. 14   toward the end

proceedings, and ordered a new ecclesiastical trial; this was not to take place in Carthage again, but in Arles. The letter has survived in which he ordered the *vicar* of Africa to send Cæcilian with certain adherents, and also representatives, of the Donatist party, by the imperial post, and at the responsibility of the State, through Spain to Arles before August 1, 314.[1] Eusebius also gives the Emperor's letter in which he invited Bishop Chrestos of Syracuse.[2]

A list of members of the council has been preserved among the records of the church law.[3] This list mentions eight African bishops who accompanied Cæcilian, besides representatives of thirty-five bishoprics in Gaul, Britain, Spain, Italy, Sicily, Sardinia, and Dalmatia. What had actually assembled was a delegation representative of the west of the Empire ruled by Constantine. They felt themselves to be such in fact, and they discussed not only the Donatist controversy but, in addition, a number of problems in the life of the Church which were of general significance. The results reached by them are to be found in the twenty-two canons, special importance attaching to the desire for a uniform rule for the date of Easter, and the repudiation of heretical baptism, which Cæcilian's churches would have been compelled to recognize in these circumstances. The Donatists were condemned "according to the judgment of God and the Mother Church", and repudiated together with their demands. Moreover, the synod decided, as against the unruly complaints which were arising, that the Church could take action in a case of "*traditio*" only when officially requested to do so by the civil authorities (who, of course, could now be approached by the Church); the oral testimonies of miscellaneous persons were not sufficient. False witness in such cases, would be punishable with excommunication and even with death. Finally, persons consecrated by the *traditores* were held to be duly recognized.[4]

The council sent a report of its conclusions to Silvester, bishop of Rome, whose absence it deeply regretted. At the same time, it requested that he would make these conclusions

---

[1] *ibid.* n. 14   [2] *ibid.* n. 15   = Eus. *H.E.* 10, 5, 21-24
[3] Labbe, *Concilia*, 1, 1429f. Routh, *Reliquiae Sacrae*, 2nd ed. 4, 312-314
[4] Canon 13. 14

universally known, especially as he "was the head of the largest province": obviously he was regarded with honour as one of the western presidents. The authority of the council was strongly emphasized; its decisions had been reached in the presence of the Holy Spirit and His angels.[1] The presence of the Holy Spirit was conceived quite in the manner of the early church:[2] similarly in the manner of the early church was the freedom with which the Donatists repudiated the verdict. On the other hand, it was a novel feature that they should appeal to the court of the Emperor from the pronouncement promulgated by this ecclesiastical synod. The communication with which Constantine informed the synod of this fact, expresses vigorously the disagreeable astonishment which the ruler felt at this step. In the first heat of his wrath, he ordered that the appellants from Arles as well as the Donatist ringleaders from Africa should be sent to him at the Court. He intended to incarcerate them there, and if necessary to enforce the finding of the synod with the death penalty.[3] But he quickly learnt that he could do nothing in this way, indeed that the opposition were numerous and powerful enough to make him change his view.

He earnestly desired to set the Donatists aside, and to restore unity in the "catholic" sense. Nevertheless, he was remote from the idea that the state should intervene in church affairs. The Church ought to settle its own controversies with its own means. He himself was unwilling to do more than to give assistance; this was indeed a necessity of state for him. But now the unruly behaviour of the Donatists compelled him to go beyond his self-imposed limits and to issue an imperial decree.

The Donatists had already been diligently making preparations. Scarcely two weeks after the pronouncement of Arles on August 19, 314, a Donatist lawyer presented a protocol to the civic authorities in Carthage. This document proved that Felix, bishop of Aptunga, was a "traitor", as shown by a letter and by the spoken word of the person who had been mayor of

---

[1] Letter to Silvester, cf. Von Soden, *op. cit.* n. 16; the writing breaks off suddenly at Canon 8.

[2] *vide* Vol. 2; 67   [3] Von Soden, *op. cit.* n. 18, 24, 62–69p.

the town in the year of the persecution.[1] The accuser had no scruple about asking that this document should be brought before the imperial court against both Cæcilian, and Felix who had ordained him.[2] Before very long, the Emperor found himself compelled to order official trials. At least, fragments have survived of the report of a trial held before the proconsul of Africa on February 15, 315, when the accusations which were found in the documents were proved to be lies, and the letter itself to be a forgery.[3] A few months later, the forger was compelled to make the dangerous journey to the imperial court, in order to have his case tried afresh.

The parties were sent to Rome, where Constantine was staying from the end of July to the end of September, 315, celebrating the festival of his ten years as Emperor. Cæcilian did not appear—why we do not know—and in this connection the Emperor seriously thought of acceding to the Donatists' desire, by permitting the affair to be settled in Africa. But he soon changed his mind, for even he shrank from the power of the Donatists over the populace.[4] Cæcilian came to the court in Milan, and his accusers were present, if not in full numbers: some had dropped out on the way, whereupon the rest received an honourable convoy of official persons. The trial followed its expected course, and Cæcilian was declared innocent with all due form by the Emperor: an official document informed everyone of the verdict.[5]

But it would appear that this last decision was purposely postponed by the Emperor. A letter which Constantine wrote to Celsus, the *vicar* of Africa, has been preserved. It refers to the culpable flight of the Donatist accusers as a clear confession that they were in the wrong; on the other hand, the letter presupposes that both parties had already returned home. The Emperor takes up an entirely different attitude from that which he had adopted hitherto, when he allowed matters to take their course; and he now threatens to adopt the severest measures against, and indeed impose the death penalty on, disturbers of the peace. Moreover, he pronounces a clear and definite

---

[1] Von Soden, *op. cit.* n. 19. Enclosure p. 26, 37–38, 98
[2] *ibid.* p. 26, 41–44   [3] *ibid.* n. 19. Also Optat. 1, 27 and n. 20
[4] Von Soden, *op. cit.* n. 21   [5] August., *epist.*2043,

judgment about the true worship of God, and the appropriate ceremonial should he shortly come personally to Africa.[1] This projected journey came to nought, and therefore, after considerable delay, the official communication declaring that Cæcilian was to be set free, was sent on November 10, 316, to the *vicar*, Eumelius.[2]

Never for a moment is it likely that Constantine deceived himself by hoping that he had put an end to the controversy by these measures: but he was well aware that it must now be dealt with in some way or another, if the authority of the Supreme Court was to be maintained after the Donatists themselves had appealed to it. Unfortunately, at this point documentary evidence fails us. We learn of a law promulgated by Constantine ordering the Donatist places of worship to be confiscated.[3] But we do not know its date. It is certain too, that, probably in Numidia, severe disturbances on the part of unruly bands of Donatists broke out during this period, and had to be suppressed by military force: the names of Dux Leontius, and after him Ursacius, are mentioned in this connection,[4] and we may infer from a letter of Constantine,[5] that the Donatists were able to stir up the old fanaticism of the martyrs amongst their protagonists, and to make it respected. Moreover, some of the leading spirits were sent into exile. There was also a consular by the name of Zenophilus, who was regarded as one of the persecutors of the Donatists.[6] In the course of a trial at which he was present, and the record of which has survived,[7] he proved that Silvanus, bishop of Cirta, had been one of the zealous protagonists of Donatism, that he had also been a *traditor*, and accessible to bribery; Zenophilus had deposed the unmasked humbug from office.[8] At the same time, six other leaders of this party were exposed; fifteen years earlier they had confessed themselves *traditores*, but now they pretended to lead the upright into battle against Cæcilian. It

[1] Von Soden, *op. cit.* n. 23   [2] *ibid.* n. 25

[3] August., *epist.* 88, 3 (p. 409, 12 Goldbacher); Von Soden, *op. cit.* n. 26

[4] cf. Optat. 3, 4. 10; cf. Seeck, *Untergang d. ant. Welt*, 3, 514

[5] Von Soden, *op. cit.* n. 23. p. 35, 28–33

[6] August., *c. Cresc.* 3, 30, 34. p. 441, 23 ed. Petschenig; Optat. 2, 15. p. 50, 14. Ziwsa

[7] Von Soden, *op. cit.* n. 28   Also n. 5   [8] August., *op. cit.* 3, 30, 34

is impossible to determine whether Zenophilus punished any
of these persons with exile, because no further details have
survived, and the fewness of the notices makes it impossible to
be certain of the chronology.[1]

At any rate, on May 5, 321, the Emperor promulgated a
decree addressed to the *vicar* of Africa, raising the ban against
the Donatists who had come under the regulations; it uses
expressions of contempt in consigning them to the divine
condemnation.[2] It must have been about the same time that
Constantine wrote, and exhorted all the orthodox bishops of
Africa, together with their faithful people,[3] to look for the
conversion of the Donatists by God's saving influence; and
meanwhile, patiently to bear their acts of arrogance and
violence, as God would certainly reckon such sufferings as the
equivalent of martyrdom. This was nothing more nor less than
a confession that the Emperor was powerless against the
fanatical multitudes of the countryside of Numidia, and the
comforting language blinded no one to the fact that Constantine
regarded his church policy as a failure. The means at the
disposal of the Church had not been successful, and when
the State employed force, it threatened to provoke the entire
province into open rebellion. This could not be permitted on
any account, and so there was no alternative to tolerating
a split in the Church. The Donatists had no qualms about
the matter, but they caused much further unpleasantness to
the Emperor.

The Emperor had built a church for the orthodox in the city
of Cirta, which had been rechristened Constantia, but the
Donatists had taken possession of it. The orthodox could not
exercise force against them, and therefore the bishops of the
province applied to Constantine with a request for help. Help
came, although of a different kind from what they might have
expected. The Emperor heaved a sigh, put his hand deeply
into his purse, and built a second church for the orthodox of
Cirta. He praised the bishops because they had borne their
opponents' sacrilege with Christian patience, and had left
the vengeance with God. He also bade them hope that all

---

[1] Seeck, *op. cit.* 3, 326–332, has attempted to restore a practicable sequence
[2] Von Soden, *op. cit.* n. 30   [3] *ibid.* n. 31

persons of this kind, who had been instigated by the Devil, would receive a dreadful punishment in the next world.[1] This document re-echoes that of A.D. 321, although now it was A.D. 330: plainly the Emperor had not altered his attitude to the question of the African church, although meanwhile, slipping and sliding, he had entered on a further and very much more important controversy elsewhere. Donatism was confined to Africa alone, and left the rest of the Church untouched. Hence the Emperor could act with restraint here because to do so seemed the lesser evil.

[1] Von Soden, *op. cit.* n. 36

Chapter Four

BY HIS VICTORY OVER LICINIUS, CONSTANTINE ADDED THE east to his sphere of rule, and thereby became the master of the entire Roman empire. The whole Christian church regarded this elevation of its patron with hope and thankfulness. Moreover, he himself might now rightly expect to gather the fruits of his friendship toward the Christians, for these fruits were already ripe and others might be anticipated in the future. But events turned out similarly to those during the ten preceding years when he was conquering the west: the cancer of dissension was eating into the heart of the Church so recently won over. During the previous period it had been the Donatist split; this had rested upon earlier antagonisms, and had acted like an open sore in the African church. It had been nourished ever afresh by wild fanaticism, by class antagonisms, and perhaps race hatreds. But the malady remained confined to this one province, and in a certain sense the oppositions had even helped to strengthen the consciousness of unity in western Catholicism. In the regions where theology was discussed systematically, the malady had not yet shown its head.

At this point, Constantine found a split in the eastern Church, which ran through every province. It affected the leading bishops, was conducted with a great show of theological learning, claimed ecclesiastical authority, and was combined with provincial rivalries; it threatened the unity of the Church to a most alarming extent. The Emperor intervened once more. On this occasion, however, he did so with greater authority and effect than in Africa, and in such a way that the consequences following upon his action may be traced to the present day.

In order to understand the whole of the Arian controversy, we must discuss one or two further considerations; there was a prelude in the second half of the third century. In Alexandria a pupil of Origen's, Dionysius by name, successor to Heraklas, while head of the catechumen school, was raised in A.D. 247

to the status of bishop;[1] until his death in A.D. 264, he exercised far-reaching influence in this position. We have already discussed his various sufferings during the persecutions under Decius and Valerian,[2] and showed reason for regarding him as a trustworthy friend of Rome, and as an impressive mediator in cases of ecclesiastical controversy.[3] His spiritual quality, which he owed largely to Origen, brought him into opposition to the plebeian and uncouth chiliasm of Nepos of Arsinoë, and made him a critic of the Revelation of John.[4] Toward the end of his rule, he became involved in a theological dispute, the importance of which only became clear at a much later date.

In the late fifties of the third century theological battles had broken out in the city of Ptolemais in the Pentapolis of Libya. The reason was that a teaching had been preached there, which our documentary authorities describe as "Sabellian", and which therefore belonged to the same general sphere as the earlier popular Monarchianism.[5] The "Sabellians" refused to have anything to do with the philosophical speculations of the Logos theology. Rather, they held that the fundamental Christian dogma was the doctrine that there was only one God, that He had appeared on earth physically in Jesus Christ, and had redeemed mankind by His death on the Cross and His resurrection. Against this point of view, those men who had been influenced by Alexandrine learning, defended the doctrine of the proper personality (*hypostasis*) of the divine Logos. Both sides appealed to Dionysius, and he replied to them in scholarly epistles. Incidentally, he informed Xystus, the bishop of Rome, of this dispute, and sent him copies of his writings.[6]

But that was not the end of the difficulty. The "Sabellians" sought to justify themselves, and Dionysius wrote once more to Ammon, bishop of Berenice, and to a certain Euphranor who is otherwise unknown to us: on this occasion, it is obvious that he formulated the differences in the clearest possible manner.

[1] Vol. 2, 300 [2] Vol. 2, 167f. 170
[3] Vol. 2, 66f., 237, 254f. [4] Vol. 2, 103 [5] Vol. 2, 243f. cf. 190
[6] Karl Müller, *ZNW.*, 24, 1925, 278–285 cf. C. L. Feltoe, *The Letters and other remains of Dionysius of Alexandria*, 1904; cf. especially pages 165–198. Eus. *H.E.* 7, 6 7, 26, 1

The Son of God was not identical with the Father, but was another being as different from the Father as the vine from the vine-dresser, and the boat from the boat-builder. The Son was created, i.e., He came into being only by the Father's creative act.

We have no record of the exact wording which Dionysius employed in these formulas, but this is what the Arians at a later date read out of the communication, and Athanasius did not hesitate to regard the doctrines as dubious.[1] Moreover, the immediate contemporaries took offence at this document, and certain faithful brethren of the Church—probably belonging to the Alexandrian community[2]—turned without more ado to Rome, and accused their own bishop to his Roman namesake. The latter dealt with the problem at a Roman synod,[3] issued a pronouncement against the Sabellians, and informed his colleague in Alexandria of the complaint made against him; whereupon this last answered in an apology written in four books.[4]

Only one of the doctrinal writings of Dionysius of Rome has survived, and in this he sets aside the division of the godhead into three "powers" (*dynameis*), or three "essences" (*hypostaseis*), and laid great emphasis upon the exalted doctrine of the divine "monarchy". He did so against Dionysius of Alexandria who had used the formula after the example of his own teacher, Origen.[5] But even as early as this instance, we can see the unfortunate consequence of the ambiguity in the meaning of the word *hypostasis*. The Roman Dionysius understood it in the sense of "essence" or "substance", whereas the Alexandrine Dionysius used it in the sense of "person": in fact it may mean both. Moreover, Dionysius of Rome controverted the description of the Son as a "creature" who had "come into being in time", and this even when Proverbs 8: 22 was quoted in support.

[1] Athan., *sentent. Dion.* 4, 2–4 (2, 48f. ed. Opitz)   14, 4 p. 56; cf. Dionysius, *op. cit.* 18, 1 p. 59 (p. 188 Feltoe). Also Opitz in *Quantulacumque* (Essays in honour of Kirsopp Lake, 1937)   50–53

[2] Athan., *op. cit.*   13, 1   p. 55, 13 Opitz; cf. Dion. Rom. in Athan. *decr. Nic.* 26, 5 p. 22, 4. 25 Opitz. Feltoe p. 177, 5   180, 6–8

[3] Athan., *de synod.*   43. 45

[4] Athan., *sentent. Dion.*   13, 1–3

[5] Dion. p. 196, 1 ed. Feltoe   Orig. *in Joh.*, Tome 2, 10, 75; cf. *contra Celsum*, 8, 12, p. 229, 22 (ed. Koetschau)

Against this view, he held that the Son was begotten, and also that he was eternal. Finally, Dionysius of Rome ended his doctrines with a simple confession of the Father, Son, and Holy Ghost, adding the clause: "but the Logos is united with the God of the universe":[1] which did not follow logically from the learned arguments which he had adduced. This Roman document did not in fact provide a positive formula for deciding the actual question in dispute: it did no more than refute the formulas which had been put forward in Alexandria.

Dionysius of Alexandria admitted without more ado in his Apology, which by the way, was written in exile in A.D. 259–260,[2] that he had expressed himself unfortunately more than once. He withdrew his clumsy metaphors of vine and boat, as being of a superficial character, and explained his appellation of God's Son as "creature" by means of the Greek idiom which describes the production of spiritual entities (*logoi*) by means of the word "create".[3] As to the objections which had been made, he replied with the following propositions: he must hold firmly to the doctrine of three hypostases (=persons) against all criticism; anyone who held the contrary view could not hold a doctrine of the Trinity.[4] He then went on to acknowledge that the Son was eternal: He was the eternal radiance of the Eternal Light, and light can never be conceived as without radiance. The analogy held good of the Holy Spirit.[5] Origen had taught precisely the same.

Dionysius of Alexandria has been criticized because he did not declare that Christ was one in essence (*homousios*) with God. He admitted this was the case; but objected that this word did not occur in the Bible. On the other hand, he asserted that he had in fact expressed the substance of the matter. Parents and children were different persons, but "of the same nature", and plants were different from the roots from which they sprang, but nevertheless, "came from the same seeds". Again, the river differed in form and name from the spring which was its source: both had a separate existence, but both consisted of

---

[1] Dion. in Athan., *decr. Nic. synod.* 26 p. 21–23 Feltoe 176–82
[2] Dion. in Athan., *sentent. Dion.* 18, 3 (Feltoe, p. 189, 8)
[3] *ibid.* 18, 1 (Feltoe 188, 4) 21, 3 cf. 20, 3 (Feltoe 195, 2 cf. 194, 3)
[4] Dion. in Basilius, *de Spiritu Sancto* 29, 72 (t.3 p. 61a, ed. Garnier) Feltoe p. 196, 1
[5] Dion. in Athan., *sentent. Dion.* 15, 1–5 Feltoe p. 186f.

water. In the case of human beings, the spirit living in man was
one thing, and thoughts born of the spirit and flowing from the
lips were another thing, viz., the formulated words. Nevertheless, the two formed a unity. The same was the case with God,
Father and Son. Moreover the Holy Spirit belonged to them in
an inseparable communion. Dionysius would acknowledge and
support the formula proposed by his colleague in Rome, when
understood in this way. The divine unity must be understood
in the enlarged sense of an indivisible Trinity, and the undiminished Trinity as combined in a unity.[1]

In all essentials, Origen's conception had been reaffirmed, and
we may suppose that Dionysius of Alexandria had honestly
expressed his view and not masked it by some sort of diplomatic subterfuge. The readiness with which he acknowledged
the clumsiness of his earlier pronouncement, a readiness which
is only too rare among eminent princes of the Church, justifies
our drawing this conclusion. It is also possible that meanwhile
he had read Tertullian's writing *Against Praxeas*, and had made
use of some of its phraseology, which agreed with his general
standpoint, and which he might reasonably expect the Roman
Church would understand.[2] This was the end of the discussion,
but the Egyptians kept it well in mind.

Certain points are noteworthy: (a) The natural and obvious
manner with which the malcontents in Alexandria had complained to Rome against their own bishop; (b) the self-conscious
and explicit manner with which Rome sat in judgment on this
Egyptian affair; and (c) the lack of any record that Dionysius
of Alexandria had resented either of these actions. On the
contrary, the impression is that he accepted the verdict of
Rome without offence. The entire circumstances are so unusual,
and so sharply in opposition to the attitude that we find
elsewhere amongst the heads of the Eastern Church, that it
can only be explained if we assume that there must have been
longstanding respect on the part of the bishops of Alexandria
towards those of Rome. Other considerations have already led
us to make the same inference.[3]

[1] *ibid.* 182–185 23, 2–4 17, 2 Feltoe, p. 188–193 196–198 cf. Dion. of
Rome, in Athan., *decret. Nic.* 26, 3 p. 22, 10–12 Opitz (Feltoe, p. 178, 7–9)
[2] cf. K. Müller, *ZNW.*, 24 (1925), 282–285; cf. vol. 2, 224
[3] Vol 2, 66 256f.

Moreover, there occurs the ominous word *homousios*, "one in essence", as the watchword of true orthodoxy in the Church, a term which he was required to accept, and to which Dionysius regarded it as essential to agree. As far as substance goes, Tertullian had long before taught the *homousia* of the Father and the Logos at the time when he spoke of "one substance".[1] Probably the same view is to be found occasionally in the writings of Origen, but here the term, *homousios* with God, is extended and applied to all other rational beings,[2] as was usual among Neoplatonists and Gnostics—a state of affairs which naturally robbed the formula of any value when applied to Christ.

Those who complained against Dionysius were trying to use this word in such a way as to express the full equality of Christ (i.e. the Logos) with God, in the most exalted philosophical sense, as against any and every attempt to describe Christ as a "second God" of a subordinate sort—the very thing which Origen,[3] and Dionysius after him, had done. The ready concessions which Dionysius made in his Apology, rather subtly avoided this very point. We shall see how it came into the foreground once again.

Meanwhile the question of *homousios* was being discussed in other quarters. A foreigner, Paul by name, who was born in Samosata on the Upper Euphrates, had become bishop of Antioch about A.D. 260. He came of a poverty-stricken family, and had risen by his own ability. His skill in handling material things brought him wealth, and earned him the title of an imperial *ducenarius*, i.e., a sort of privy councillor, an honour of which he seems to have been proud. Moreover, even his status as bishop did not prevent him from advising and actively helping the prisoners under his charge in the civil prisons. He kept his own secretariat for this purpose, and when extremely pressed by his work, he sometimes dictated letters to his stenographer while walking along the street. All these facts are known to us from his enemies, who did not forget to besmirch him. They also faithfully recorded that he built himself a lofty

[1] Vol. 2, 224
[2] Orig. *de princ*. Koetschau, 33. *Footnote to 2f*. Rufinus, *vide* Vol. 2, 305. 307 For the language employed, cf. Loofs in *Essays presented to Karl Müller*, 1922, 69–71
[3] Vol. 2, 306

bishop's throne, that when he was preaching, he smacked his thighs with his hands, and when he came to important passages, stamped with his feet. But if dealing with matters that concerned the Church, he was true to established custom, and this is the point of special importance for our purpose. He supported the custom of "spiritual marriages"—known as *Syneisaktos*—a phenomenon which had appeared in the earliest period of the Church,[1] and had advised, and even practised it himself. He wrote hymns of a modern kind, and had scoffed at the learning of "dead commentators on the Bible", using high-sounding phrases in the presence of his congregation: in other words, he warned them against Origen, with whom he would have nothing to do even on other matters.

Alexandria and Antioch had always been rival cities, hating and envying one another, and matters had not changed in the Christian era. Hence we find them also as the rallying points of two antagonistic types of theology; the opposition between them now became plain as the day; and it shaped the theology of the next century or two. The leading bishops of the East, the majority of whom owed their theological education to Origen, soon found that they had so much to discuss concerning Bishop Paul's doctrines that they considered common action, although indeed, Dionysius of Alexandria was aged and in ill-health, and could only take part by writing. The others included Helenos of Tarsus, Hymenæus of Jerusalem, Theoteknos of Cæsarea in Palestine, Maximus of Bostra, and Nikomas of Iconium, and also Firmilian of Cappadocia, who died shortly afterward. They were together in Antioch and discussed matters with one another, and with Bishop Paul.

They expounded Scripture, held discussions, and issued summary reports; thus matters continued for several years. Finally, about A.D. 268, the opponents assembled for a last synod, when they deposed Paul on account of heresy, and instituted Domnus, the son of Paul's predecessor Demetrian, as bishop of Antioch. This action was officially published to the world in a document which the council addressed to Dionysius of Rome and Maximus of Alexandria: Eusebius has preserved a large part of it, and this is our principal source of

[1] Vol. 1, 136   Vol. 2, 197

information about the whole matter.[1] We learn, a little later on, that the deposition was ineffectual as long as Antioch was under the rule of Zenobia, Queen of Palmyra; and that only when Aurelian conquered the city, A.D. 272, did he depose Paul. The reason he did so was, according to Eusebius,[2] that he desired a bishop who would be recognized by Italy and Rome.

Ever since his own time, Paul of Samosata has been regarded as a typical heretic. Century after century, up to the credal pronouncements of the Reformation, it has been regarded as justifiable to treat him with disdain. Nevertheless, it is not easy to describe his teaching precisely. We possess very few fragments with reliable accounts of his teachings; he never appears to have put anything into writing himself, and most of the records appear suspiciously as if they presented his teaching one-sidedly. Indeed, the earliest sources give the impression that Paul did not think at all in theological terms, and that his opponents in the discussions really put theological formulas into his mouth: many contradictions in the records could be explained on this supposition.

But this much can at least be said, that Origen's system of theology appeared repellent to him, and he felt it ought to be attacked; in fact, he would have nothing at all to do with movements dominated by philosophy. The Biblical account of Jesus occupied the centre of his thought; and he regarded Jesus as the Son of God, because according to Luke 1: 35, he was begotten of the Holy Spirit and the Virgin Mary. The divine Logos dwelt and operated in this Son of God as if in a temple, the Logos appearing as another being clearly distinct from the man Jesus Christ. Previously the Logos had acted in the prophets, particularly in Moses, and now he revealed himself with the highest degree of fullness in Jesus. Paul did not regard this Logos or *Sophia* as an independent person after the fashion conceived by Greek speculation; he did not sit at the side of God the Father; or, to put it otherwise, the Logos was not God's Son. This latter title applies only to the miraculously

---

[1] Eus. *H.E.* 7, 27–30 A critical examination and reproduction of all the records are to be found in F. Loofs, *Paulus von Samosata* (T.U. 44, 5), 1924 G. Bardy, *Paul de Samosate*, 2nd ed., 1929
[2] Eus. *H.E.* 7, 30, 19 Loofs, *op. cit.* 59 is sceptical about the motive

begotten "historical" Jesus Christ during His earthly life and after His ascension. Rather, the Logos was a form of God's operation, a manifestation of His being; in short, not a self-subsistent being (*ousia*) to be separated from God, but rather "one in essence", i.e., *homousios*.

Consequently, when Paul of Samosata followed the custom of the Church, and spoke about the Trinity, what he had in mind was neither the clearly defined doctrine of hypostases as found in Origen, or even in the Apologists,[1] but a Trinity which depended upon revelation, which had a Biblical foundation, but which was not clearly conceived. Yet it could be understood as one divine person in three-fold operation. Paul as a theologian, insisted on an unconditional monotheism as fundamental, and he was quite willing to pass over the problems and difficulties of the Trinity. If, therefore, the Logos had no independent personality, but was only a term for a divine mode of activity, the way in which he dwelt in the man Jesus Christ, could only be conceived, on closer inspection, as a kind of exalted inspiration. The difference between Jesus and the prophets in this regard was to be conceived only quantitatively and not qualitatively. Nevertheless, there was a qualitative difference. It was to be found in the miraculously begotten human nature, i.e., in Jesus' divine sonship, as distinct from the ordinary human nature of the prophets.

In some such way is it possible to state Paul's system of thought. His opponents belonged to Origen's school, and they regarded the denial of independent personality to the Logos as an unforgivable heresy. Since Paul had used the word *homousios* in order to give expression to this teaching of his, they emphatically repudiated this very word,[2] and branded it with the stigma of heresy. The fact that the term *homousios* had been supported in Egypt by Dionysius's opponents, and that Dionysius himself had partially agreed to it, was forgotten; moreover, Dionysius was dead.

The Arian controversy brought all these matters to life again, and opened up wounds which had scarcely healed over. The controversy was particularly violent in Egypt, because dissensions of another kind had already come to the light of day

[1] *vide* Vol. 2, 180   306   [2] Loofs, *op. cit.* 147–153

during the persecution under Diocletian, and these oppositions combined only too easily with the new theological points of dispute. What is known as the "Meletian" schism was the rallying point.[1] Peter, bishop of Alexandria, had been taken into custody in the first years of Diocletian's persecution, and had administered his church from his prison. As little as anywhere else were there lacking in Egypt excited fanatics who voluntarily sought martyrdom, who also wished this defiant attitude to be regarded as a sign of genuine Christian faith, and who were actually extolled as heroes worthy of admiration. In these circumstances, it is easy to surmise that the flight of the leading bishop in Egypt was frequently criticized in as unfriendly a manner as had formerly been the case with Cyprian in Africa.

A South Egyptian bishop, Meletius, of Lykopolis, in the Thebaid (present-day Assiut), drew a strange conclusion, the deeper reasons for which are now incomprehensible. He travelled to and fro in the countryside, and voluntarily took over the visitations of Peter when he was in prison. In particular, he consecrated new presbyters and deacons in the leaderless churches, and this, not only in the Thebaid, but also further north; finally, in towns on the Delta. A letter of expostulation written by four bishops of this region has survived. These bishops were in prison in the capital, and they had heard the incredible news: they urgently requested Meletius to put an end to this undesirable action. But he took no notice; rather he went to Alexandria itself, and was not altogether unsuccessful in gaining to his side the presbyters commissioned to represent Peter. Moreover, he received assistance from two men named Isidoros and Arius.

He was imprisoned while in the very midst of this activity, and afterwards banished to the quarries at Pheno in Palestine.[2] While in prison, he consecrated two other adherents to officiate in Alexandria: it is possible they were the two assistants, just mentioned, whom he had made presbyters. Now that he was taken prisoner, it seemed that the danger to the unity of the

[1] cf. F. Kettler in *ZNW*. 35 (1936), 155–193   Schwartz, *Gött. Nachr.* 1905, 164–187   K. Müller, *Abhandlung berl. Akad.* 1922, n. 3   *Beiträge z. Gesch. d. Verf. d. Alten Kirche*, 12–17
[2] *supra*, 70

Church was at an end, and Bishop Peter, in a letter which has survived, warned the Church against further fellowship with Meletius, until he himself, together with a few persons of understanding, had examined the matter more thoroughly. All this took place toward the end of A.D. 305.

About this time, there was a certain abatement in the severity of the persecution, and large numbers of the backsliders urgently sought a decision as to the possibility, and the conditions, of their being re-accepted into the Church: in many instances, the Confessors revived an earlier custom[1] and gave absolution to the penitents.[2] Soon after Easter, A.D. 306, i.e., probably toward the end of April, Peter sent a circular letter from his cell, and gave fundamental and comprehensive regulations for dealing with the problem.[3] He specified different dates for the various classes of backsliders, according to the seriousness of their sin. They were to do their penances in accordance with the regulations of the Church before they could be readmitted to the Communion. As for those who had made the state sacrifices without resistance, they were to undergo one year's probation before qualifying to do the penances proper. He said nothing about any rights which the Confessors might possess. He sharply rebuked all forms of provocation on the ground that martyrdoms, gained in this easy fashion, endangered the Church, as they could only embitter the State time after time. Clerics who had once played false, but who had later given themselves up voluntarily to the civic authorities, could be regarded in a certain sense as having regained their Christian standing; but they were not to be allowed to continue in office. He discussed in great detail the example of the Apostles to show that it was permissible to flee from persecution, and indeed, that this was the duty of office bearers in the Church.

Taken as a whole, the way in which he had settled the problem was entirely in accordance with the facts of the case, and in agreement with the course of the Church's development, as was clearly to be seen on every hand. In so doing, he had

---

[1] Vol. 2, 228, 251   [2] *Petrus epist. can.* 5, p. 65, 22 (Lagarde)
[3] Lagarde, *Reliq. iuris Eccl. antiq. Graece,* 1856, 63–73. Syriac in Lagarde, *Rel. iuris Eccl. antiq. Syriace,* 1856, 99–166 and XLVI–LIV E. Schwartz, *loc. cit.* 166–175

put an end, in good catholic fashion, to the radicalism of the primitive church, and to the privileges claimed by and granted to Confessors as men of special spiritual quality. It is not to be wondered at that the opposition of the fanatics who were in prison, was expressed vigorously, because they felt they were not receiving their deserts, and because they regarded the pastoral and studied mildness of the bishop as weakness to be condemned. Epiphanius preserves a story containing various legendary traits and a confused combination of details, but which reveals a geniune historical reminiscence.[1] He says that even in the quarries at Pheno, the extreme protagonists of enthusiasm called themselves the "Church of the Martyrs", and separated from the orthodox Church, who were faithful to the bishop. Meletius, who might rightly have felt himself attacked by Peter when the latter was repudiating criticism of his flight, joined the "Church of the Martyrs". This action seemed likely to bring an influential ideology to the aid of his own ambitions to be a leader.

At this stage, it was possible to raise the battle-cry of a relentless radicalism against the Alexandrian bishop, and to establish an independent church under this standard. That, indeed, is what took place. Further persons were ordained in addition to those of A.D. 305/6. The prisons were opened after the edict of tolerance in A.D. 311, and the convict workers in the quarries were allowed to return home. Meletius was now in a position to raise a vigorous agitation, on account of his fame as a Confessor, and since he was projecting the building of a new church, bishops might and must be consecrated. No details have survived in regard to the founding and growth of Meletius's church; our only information is that, about A.D. 325, it already possessed twenty-eight bishoprics of its own.[2]

Of course, Peter excommunicated Meletius, and according to calculations that we can make, the synod[3] which pronounced the condemnation met in A.D. 306. Athanasius asserts that it was regarded as proved that Meletius was guilty of making the state sacrifices: but this is scarcely credible in view of Meletius's attitude as a whole. It shows how embittered was the hatred of

---

[1] Epiph. *Haer.* 68, 1–3   [2] Athan. *apol. contra Arian.*, 71
[3] *op. cit.* 59   Opitz, *ZNW.* 33 (1934), 143

the official church against the Meletians when Peter decided that the baptisms which they had administered could not be regarded as valid. In itself, this corresponded to the custom of the ancient Church, and had been maintained by the eastern churches in common with those of Africa as against Rome. Yet at an early date, Dionysius of Alexandria had adopted an intermediate attitude,[1] and had recognized Montanist baptisms.[2] This was in accordance with the tendency of the times, as is shown by the council of Arles, and also very clearly by the sharp distinctions made at the council of Nicea. It is noticeable that nothing was said at the latter about the rebaptism of any who came over from the Meletian church.[3] It is true that when the persecution flared up for the last time, Peter died as a martyr on November 24, 311, and thus far outshone his enemies; but the schism was already complete and could not be undone. Egypt and Africa lost their outer unity at about the same time.

The name of Arius occurs in the earliest records[4] of the Meletian schism. He is described as one of the ambitious persons who opened the door for Meletius to the Alexandrine priesthood. And he also appears to have been one of the two men who were consecrated as presbyters in the capital. But when Peter returned, Arius soon came to terms, and permitted Peter to ordain him as deacon; this happy relationship only lasted, however, until Peter refused to recognize Meletian baptism. This act threw him into the arms of the opposition, and meant that he was excommunicated. He made his reconciliation with Achillas, Peter's successor, was again appointed deacon, and indeed became presbyter[5] and pastor of the Baukalis church;[6] he was also in good standing with Bishop Alexander, who was installed in the summer of A.D. 312, and was able to pursue his inclination for theological speculation without let or hindrance.

It is easy to understand that the Meletians hated the turncoat, and eagerly sought an opportunity to cast doubts against his

---

[1] Vol. 2, 237

[2] Basil, *epist. Canon.* 1, ad Amphilochium=*epist.* 188 can. 1   (3, 268 d. ed. Bened.)

[3] Athan. *Opera*, Doc., 23, 6–10   (3, 49f. Opitz). Hinschius, *Kirchenrecht*, 4, 44

[4] Kettler in *ZNW*. 35 (1936), 162, 1. 8

[5] Sozom. 1, 15, 2–7   [6] Epiph. *Haer*. 68, 4, 2   69, 1, 2

orthodoxy when he ventured too far in the contest with Sabel-lianism. For good or ill, Bishop Alexander was compelled to follow a line along which he would avoid appearing as the patron of a heresy, and, in the end, Arius was condemned for false doctrine. Those who thought like him among the Alex-andrian clergy, five presbyters and six deacons, were con-demned at the same time.[1] The natural consequence was great excitement in the Church, among Arius's numerous adherents, but the controversy quickly spread beyond the boundaries of the city, for the men who had been condemned felt themselves dealt with unjustly, and looked elsewhere for help.[2]

Arius was not a person of minor importance, but one well-known in the theological world. He was of special importance for Alexandria, because he had not been brought up in the indigenous tradition, but had come from the school at Antioch, which was diametrically opposed to it. In this latter city, a presbyter held in high repute, Lucian by name, had laboured as a teacher until his martyrdom in A.D. 306. A considerable number of students were drawn to him, and these, in the course of time, occupied the most eminent dioceses in the east; these men felt united in faithful fellowship by the memory of their teacher. Arius belonged to this circle, and as he had only given expression in accentuated form to Antiochene points of view, he might well reckon on support from his fellow students who had sat under Lucian. Nor was he mistaken. Eusebius, bishop of Nicomedia, which had lately become the royal residence, took his side, and asked the other friends to write in support.[3]

At this point, we may ask what was the subject of the dispute which in the end stirred up the entire Church? Once more, it had to do with the theological understanding of the divine nature of Christ. The Meletians are said to have pronounced the divine Logos, which had become incarnate in Jesus, to be co-eternal with the Father, and that they had required con-fession of the *homousia* of the Son with God the Father.[4] What this amounted to in effect was to set aside the idea that the Son was subordinate to the Father, and this again was a sign that those who belonged to the Meletian way of thinking originated

---

[1] cf. *Doc.* 14, 60 (3, 29, 24 Opitz)
[3] cf. *Doc.* 2, 8

[2] Sozom. 1, 15, 8f.
[4] Sozom. 1, 15, 5

in the very circles which had raised complaints against Bishop Dionysius, two generations earlier, in Rome.

There was a religious requirement behind this theory, viz., the need of retaining, even in altered circumstances, the simple article, "God Himself became man for our salvation". The naïve form of the earlier Monarchianism was no longer satisfactory in saying that God the Father had Himself appeared on earth as Son. This was now Sabellian heresy. Somehow or other, the Logos which had become incarnate in Jesus Christ, had to be confessed as the Son of God, but in some way different from the Father. Every effort was now made to minimize this distinction, and to restrict it as much as possible to a question of names and vague formulas.

If now, the redemption of mankind consisted in the miracle of the deification of man's substance, it followed that the full Godhead must have combined in Jesus Christ with human nature, and so raised it to a divine status. In this way, it inevitably followed that this theory of redemption required the recognition of the complete substantial deity of the Logos. In the last analysis, this is what is meant when the Logos Son is declared to be *homousios*, i.e., the "same substance" as the Father. It meant to say that God's nature as present in Christ, the nature which was recognized as Son or Logos, possessed everything which belonged to the full, divine, miraculous operation. To put it otherwise, our human bodily form represented in Jesus' bodily form, was combined with the entire and most exalted nature of God, without any sort of diminution, and was thereby withdrawn from the perishableness of the earthly.

For this reason, any attempt to maintain degrees of the divine essence in the case of Father and Son must be repudiated. Whether, in these circumstances, the Son could be conceived as a person in his own right, whether closer inspection would reveal that the name of Son, and the conception of the Logos were only masks which hid the person of God the Father, and therefore, whether at bottom, this theory was only another name for Sabellianism; all such were questions which attracted no attention. It was sufficient to have found formulas which seemed to assure the deeper religious facts in the case.

This rough and ready fashion of dealing with the immense

problem was naturally acceptable to the theologically inclined among the laity, and to the bulk of the half-educated clergy, but it could not be acceptable amongst those of serious theological attainments: their most eminent representative was Origen. His influence, however, had become less effective in the sixty years since his death, and had given rise to many other lines of inquiry. In Antioch, his speculations and his allegory had been taken up by men of a certain insipidity of thought, and of a Biblicism which held fast to the simple word-sense; the mixture which resulted, bore a new kind of theological fruit in the above-mentioned school of Lucian. Here were to be found, as distinct from the earlier theories of Origen, closer definitions of the idea of the Son of God, as different from the Father. This was the problem of which Arius laid hold in the different atmosphere of Alexandria. He attempted to solve it in a manner which unavoidably landed him in controversies.

His presupposition was the superiority of the Father to the Son, as also taught by Origen, although slightly veiled by him. He took quite seriously the doctrine of the divine unity and monarchy. God in the full sense of the word, the "genuine God", is alone the Father; and there once was a time, even if only logically conceivable, in which God existed for Himself alone. He then created or begot the Son out of nothing, by His own will and counsel. The words "create" and "beget" mean the same in this connection. Time then began to exist, and the Aeons to run their course; the Son was not only the first-born and the beginning, but now also the architect of the universe, a being with his own free will, who in Himself might have been capable of sin; hence the Son owed His heavenly status to the virtue which He had preserved on earth, but which had already been foreseen by the Father.[1] Arius utterly repudiated any and every attempt to make the Son equal to the Father, to declare Him eternal, or to regard Him as God in substance. This repudiation naturally included the *homousia* which Arius condemned as Manichæan heresy. Nor would he have anything to do with a theory that the Logos was first of all hidden

[1] Documents in Athan. *Opera,* ed. Opitz, vol. 3   *Doc.* 1 and 6, also *Doc.* 3 and 4b, 7–10

in the Father as a property and had proceeded from Him as a separate person. On the contrary, he expressly separated the being described as "Logos" from the divine property bearing that name, and denied to the Son perfect knowledge of the Father: for He was limited, and could not fully comprehend the Father's infinity. The Trinity could be described by the formula of "three hypostases", i.e., in this case, three independent beings and persons, of whom only one, viz., the Father, was substantially and truly God from all eternity.[1]

From this standpoint, the redemption of man did not consist in an essential deification, but in spiritual elevation and instruction on the part of the Logos after the fashion of the teaching of the Apologists, whose doctrines frequently come to life once more in this connection. Nor did the Logos need to be of divine substance in order to fill the world with a true knowledge of God, and to impart a correct doctrine of virtue.

This point of view seemed impossible to Bishop Alexander, who was accustomed to keeping more closely to Origen. He would have preferred to avoid raising an alarm, and to leave Arius alone; but he was compelled by the charges of the Meletians to defend his own orthodoxy against the suspicion of sympathy with Arius. This took place at a synod consisting only of the clergy of the city and of the immediate neighbourhood, the province of Mareotis; but soon afterwards, A.D. 318, at a synod of nearly a hundred Egyptian bishops,[2] Arius and all his adherents were condemned and deposed.

Alexander set Origen's thesis of the eternal begetting of the Logos, against Arius's doctrine: since the Father was eternally the Father, He could never be without Son, and consequently, the Son too was eternal;[3] and this Son, the Logos, is in every respect equal to the Father in nature and therefore in substance (*ousia*):[4] He was by no means created out of nothing as Arius taught, but proceeded from the bosom of the Father;[5] this He did as a special person, and therefore it was correct to speak of Father and Son as two "*hypostases*", i.e., persons.[6] Anyone

---

[1] Arius Thalia in Athan. *oration* 1. c. *Arian.*, 5f. *Doc.* 14, 12

[2] *Doc.* 4a, 1,   4b, 11; for the date, Opitz *ZNW*. 33, (1934), 146   [3] *Doc.* 14, 26

[4] *ibid.* 4b, 13   p. 9, 3   *ibid.* 14, 38   p. 25, 24, 47   p. 27, 14   52 p. 28, 5

[5] *ibid.* 4b, 12 p. 9, 1. *ibid.* 14, 46 p. 27, 5

[6] *ibid.* 14, 19 p. 22, 24   20, p. 23, 4   38 p. 25, 23

who attempted to formulate the difference between the two, would find there was none apart from the fact that the Son was not "unbegotten": this predicate applied to the Father alone.[1]

In this way, the Logos, who was conceived as an independent personality of divine substance, was brought so near to the Father, and made so like Him in fact, that we cannot hold it against the opposite party if they objected that Alexander[2] was teaching a doctrine of two "unbegotten beings"; nor was he able to avoid this objection except by referring to the "ineffable" secret of the divine genesis,[3] an argumentative device with which one can defend a great deal.

Alexander's theology expressed Origen's ideas in a less refined form, and it omitted to subordinate the Son in the way which the great teacher had himself made perfectly clear. As a consequence, the indispensable safeguards of the system were set aside, and it now amounted to a complete ditheism. The Logos was now presented side by side with the Father as a second and entirely similar God. On account of the essential equality of the status of the Logos, this guaranteed the essential deification of redeemed mankind, in accordance with the needs of popular religion. Alexander declared "we become the adopted sons of God by benefit of Him who is God's Son by nature".[4] Alexander therefore solved the problem of redemption with the same assurance as popular Monarchianism or the non-philosophical Meletians had done, but he had to surrender far more logic for the privilege.

It is easy to understand that Arius's friends immediately discovered this vulnerable place, making it light for them to defend the men who had been condemned. Both Eusebius of Nicomedia, and also his namesake of Cæsarea, the church historian, repudiated vigorously the terms "equal status", and "genuine godhead"; the latter in addition particularly emphasized the subordination of the Son to the Father, and the impossibility of deriving the Son in any way from the substance of the Father.[5]

[1] ibid. 14, 47   p. 27, 14   cf. 18   p. 22, 16   [2] ibid. 14, 44 p. 26, 23
[3] ibid. 14, 21   p. 23, 9   46 p. 27, 7   [4] ibid. 14, 21 p. 24, 24
[5] ibid. 3, 1. 2   8. 5–7

Arius wrote numerous letters in all directions, and made a journey to Palestine in order to defend his view practically and personally.[1] Letters of protest came from all parts of the compass to Alexander, and a synod met in Bithynia, either in or near Nicomedia. The synod agreed with Arius, and advised Alexander to withdraw his verdict.[2] The step would be rendered all the easier for him by a confession of faith which Arius would make in polite and restrained terms.[3] The conclusion reached by a synod in Palestine was not so favourable, the persons taking part in it being, among others, Paulinus of Tyre, Eusebius of Cæsarea, and Patrophilus of Scythopolis. Here, Arius and his adherents were confirmed in their clerical status and offices. This fact alone was a tremendous invasion of the rights of another diocese, although the synod recognized their subordination under Bishop Alexander and urged them to maintain the peace, and to cultivate his friendship diligently;[4] yet in view of the actual circumstances, this advice must have appeared as seriously lacking in consideration for him.

The presbyters in Alexandria had always enjoyed a peculiarly independent position,[5] and as Arius was obviously being supported by his church and congregation, the bishop was unable to prevent his continuing to officiate, nor could he even send him away from the city. Moreover, the condemned clergy now received additional support from the outside. There were disturbances in the city itself, which broke out even in the streets, and which seriously threatened the bishop.[6] At this point, the Arian party combined with the party of a certain presbyter, Kolluthos, the reasons for whose opposition are unknown; in the end, Kolluthos got himself instituted as an opposition bishop.[7] If we also take account of the activity of the Meletians, we shall realize the disorder in the Egyptian church: it became a public scandal, and provided material for jokes in the pagan theatres.[8]

Alexander defended himself by sending an open letter to

---

[1] Epiph. *Haer.* 69, 4, 1
[2] Sozom. 1, 15, 10=*Doc.* 5   cf. the documents in *Doc.* 2. 3. 7. 8. 9
[3] *Doc.* 6   [4] Sozom. 1, 15, 11=*Doc.* 10
[5] Vol. 2, 64   cf. Epiph. *Haer.* 69, 2, 4–6   [6] *Doc.* 14, 3–5
[7] *Doc.* 14, 3   Epiph. *Haer.* 69, 2, 7 Athan. *apol. c. Arian.* 12. 74. 76
[8] Eus. *vita Const.* 2, 61

bishops in other regions,[1] and was no less diligent than his opponents in seeking support from important persons; but he could make no real headway, and the split only deepened and widened in the entire eastern church. It must have been about seven years[2] from the first beginnings of this dispute that it reached its greatest intensity. The bitterest extremes were reached about the beginning of the third decade of the century, at a time when Licinius was pressing his anti-Christian policy.[3] Alexander's great encyclical was written perhaps at a time when Constantine's victory was still hoped for, and his intervention desired.[4]

In September, A.D. 324, Licinius capitulated, and the new ruler set to work without loss of time to weave the unity of the Church into the political unity of the Empire, which he had so happily won. He gives clear expression to this objective in a document which he sent to Alexandria in October, 324, addressed "To Alexander and Arius". He referred to the Donatist controversy in Africa which, after conquering Maxentius, he had found a means of resolving by sending bishops to lay a foundation for peace. This reference is astonishing because we know that Constantine's intervention had failed, and that at this very time, complete confusion reigned in Africa: the facts, however, do not appear to have weakened his optimism, which was based on his good fortune in war. At any rate, in the preamble of the document, he offers himself to the Alexandrians as a peacemaker, and advises them to bear with one another, especially as the dispute was by no means concerned with important points of faith, but with learned hair-splitting, which had been unnecessarily discussed in public. Both parties were agreed in all essentials, and thus they might well enter again into fellowship with one another, and, by their unity, add to the glory of the journey which the Emperor planned to make in the east.[5] This letter was delivered in Alexandria[6] by Bishop Ossius of Cordova, who, as we have already said, was in Constantine's confidence during the Donatist controversy.[7]

---

[1] Doc. 4b. 14. 15. 16
[2] H. G. Opitz, ZNW. 33 (1934), 131–159
[3] supra, 79f.
[4] Opitz, ZNW., 1934, 150
[5] Doc. 17
[6] supra, 83
[7] Eus. vita Const. 2, 63. 73   Socrates, 1, 7, 1   1, 8, 1

It is not surprising that the enterprise was unsuccessful, for Alexander felt that Arius ought not to be dealt with as his equal and rival. Moreover, both parties must have felt hurt by the disrespectful manner in which the Emperor dealt with the point at issue in his letter. As far as they were concerned, they were not dealing with secondary matters, but with the basis of the entire Christian faith. Constantine, as a man of the west, did not yet know the Christianity of the east.

But Alexandria was not the only city in which the Emperor found it needful to intervene. Antioch, too, had suffered severely during the persecution, and in Licinius's last years, its church organization had fallen to pieces. The Emperor possibly sent an encouraging communication to it, similar to the one addressed to Alexandria, and the city was honoured by a visit from Ossius. This visit probably took place while on the way to Alexandria. Moreover, Ossius may well have decided, in view of the difficulties already in existence, to call a synod consisting of the bishops of Antioch and the surrounding regions. Meanwhile, he journeyed on to Alexandria, but saw that his intermediation was futile; thereupon he returned to Antioch, where the invited bishops were already beginning to gather. He naturally sent a report post-haste to the Emperor, about his failure in Alexandria. Then Constantine decided to use again in the east the means which had proved successful in regard to Africa, and call a great synod together. It was decided that the place of meeting should be Ancyra in Galatia, the modern Turkish capital, Ankara.

Bishop Philogonius died, December 20, 324, in the city of Antioch, and was succeeded by Eustathios. With the New Year, work was begun by the synod which had been called together by Ossius[1] and was presided over by him. Unfortunately, we know practically nothing about what took place in Antioch. The 16 canons[2] decided on by the synod show how it defined the regulations for punishments for all kinds of sexual offences, for witchcraft, for pagan superstitions, and for denying Christ. Incidentally we may notice the permission to remit some of the

[1] The name of Ossius is miswritten in the best source, and here restored only conjecturally, though with the greatest probability; cf..*Doc.* 18, p. 36, 3

[2] cf. E. Schwartz, *Gött. Nach.* 1908, 322ff. and E. Seeberg, *D. Synode von Antioch*, 1913, 13–56

sentences in the interest of spiritual welfare. But quite special use was made of this gathering to take action in regard to the Arian controversy.

The majority of those present stood outside the struggle, and indeed were scarcely in a position to follow the academic discussion. No one from Egypt was present; instead there were three bishops who were of similar views to the Lucianist group, Theodotos of Laodicea, Narcissos of Neronias in Cilicia, and Eusebius the church historian. Out of high esteem for "a few brethren of sound technical understanding in matters of the church's faith",[1] the decision went against Arius; and a creed was established which closely followed Alexander's confessional formula, but was still more cautious in its positive statements. It asserted emphatically that the genesis of the Son far excelled all human understanding, and then went on to say of the Son: He was not created, but begotten; He did not come into being out of nothing, but is a copy of the paternal nature (*hypostasis*). The Arian theses were condemned, which asserted that He was a creature; that there had been a time when He was not; and that He possessed freedom of the will in the human sense, i.e., including freedom to do evil. Not a word was said about *homousios* and similar terms: colourless formulas sufficed, and a united front was turned against Arius. The three Lucianists, strongly though they were inclined to peace, could not agree and so were excommunicated. However, they were granted more time for consideration—until the great council at Ancyra. A circular letter, now extant only in a Syriac translation,[2] informed the other churches of their conclusions.

The direction that the Emperor's peace moves would take was now plain. The gesture of writing to both Alexander and Arius was just as much a pose as the similar attitude at the beginning of the Donatist controversy. Ossius had plainly been ordered to abandon Arius, but also to support Alexander only to a certain degree. The restraint of the synod in regard to making positive pronouncements corresponded throughout to the Emperor's disinclination towards introducing academic

---

[1] *Doc.* 18, 7   p. 38, 5

[2] *Doc.* 18   Discovered by E. Schwartz, *op. cit.*, 1905, 305–374 and also 1908, 305–374   cf. E. Seeberg, *op. cit.*

speculations into the broad stream of the Church's life. The synod of Antioch was a good preparation and a sort of preliminary test, in view of the approaching synod properly so-called.

Meantime Constantine had decided that it was to be organized on the very largest scale; the west was to be included and, most important of all, he himself would take part personally in the proceedings. He therefore transferred it from Ancyra to Nicea,[1] a city which lay only thirty miles south of the capital, Nicomedia, and which possessed, in the imperial palace, a suitable building for the council meetings. Thus by the Emperor's interest, the Church acquired a most important precedent for decrees of universal application—in the form of the general council. She could not have called such a council into being through her own authority. And at the beginning of the fourth century, she was far from the path that could have led to such a centralization of authority. Hence the State, itself driven by the need for political unity, had compelled the Church to move in the same direction.

The bishops and their trains, travelling by imperial post, came from everywhere in the east. According to Eusebius, they numbered over 250; Constantine himself speaks of more than 300. The names of 220 of those taking part are known,[2] and the list is incomplete. Of the few delegates from the west, the first to be mentioned is Ossius of Cordova; then two presbyters from Rome representing its bishop, who never liked going to councils in other countries: Cæcilian of Carthage, and further, one bishop each from Pannonia, Calabria, and Gaul: that is all. On the other hand, the eastern churches were represented right to the farthest corners of Armenia, Mesopotamia, and Persia. And let it be remembered, the sun of the Emperor's grace shed its beams over these men, all of whom had lively memories in their hearts of the last bloody persecutions, many also bearing marks on their bodies. These men were transported by the state to Nicea; here they lived as guests of the Emperor, and were surrounded on all sides by glittering pomp. Constantine, with his shrewd insight into human nature, did not forget to calculate on the working of the impressions they would

[1] *Doc.* 20
[2] Eus. *vita Const.* 3, 8   *Doc.* 25, 5   Eustathius in Theod. *H.E.* 1, 8, 1 names 270

receive, increased by the respect he paid at every opportunity to the bishops as "priests of God and servants of our Lord and Saviour". There is a credible rumour that when the old ascetic Paphnutios visited him, he kissed that eye of his that had been blinded during the persecution under Maximin.[1] Thus the leaders of the Church sensed in every direction that a new era had begun, and that their own dignity had been publicly enhanced. On the other hand, they perceived that, thereby, and at the same time, a new responsibility had been laid on their shoulders. Moreover, the Emperor, who had so successfully created the new order, presented them with a difficulty and also showed them the way towards overcoming it, viz., that they ought to respond to him with gratitude and trust.

The day came for the opening of the synod[2] in the high central chamber of the royal palace. Here the bishops were seated in silence in rows parallel to the two long walls. A chamberlain entered, followed by a second, and a third; but the otherwise customary military guard was lacking. Only the closest attendants of the Ruler, so far as they belonged to the Christian faith, entered the hall. The master of ceremonies gave a sign and all rose. The Emperor appeared in full state, "resplendent as one of God's angels in heaven". He shone in the radiance of his purple mantle, and in the gleaming shimmer of golden and bejewelled ornaments. With downcast eyes but majestic dignity he stepped slowly to his place at the front, marked by a small golden armchair, but he did not take his seat until the bishops requested him to do so by a sign, when he seated himself, together with the whole assembly.

The leader of the section sitting on the right, Eusebius, bishop of Nicomedia the capital, now arose and addressed a speech of gratitude to the Emperor. He replied in a few words and in carefully chosen phrases: He hoped that the victory achieved by military success over the tyrants would now be followed by victory over the much more serious matters of dissensions within the Church. He greeted the assembly with joy and in the hope that it might reach unity, become of one heart and soul, and bestow upon the whole world peace and

---

[1] Rufinus, *H.E.* 10, 4 Socrates, 1,11, 2   [2] Eus. *vita Const.* 3, 10–14

concord. He spoke in Latin in order to stress that this was a solemn occasion of state; a Greek version, given by a translator, followed.

Business began with charges and countercharges. The delegates soon noted that the Emperor spoke Greek. He not only listened attentively and gave signs of his agreement or disagreement, but took part in the discussion in order to guide them to the desired goal of peace.[1] But no record is extant giving a strictly historical account of the proceedings. Nobody described this very important occasion. There were either no official reports at all, which may have been due to considerations of state,[2] or else, because of sound political sense in the Church, they may have been allowed to fall into oblivion. Thus the few fragments extant in tradition must suffice us.

The three men who had been provisionally excommunicated in Antioch were readmitted; Eusebius has recorded the details:[3] As his own confession of faith, Eusebius placed before the assembly the ancient baptismal formula used by his church at Cæsarea. The Emperor declared it unobjectionable; of course the synod agreed, and the issue was settled. Similarly with the other two excommunicants, for the Emperor was averse to their being excommunicated; rather he desired the greatest possible unity. It would have accorded with this aim if the synod had solemnly recognized one of the ancient, traditional baptismal creeds as the expression of the true faith, had gone on to set aside Arius's negations, and finally declared impious and vain all attempts to penetrate into the ineffable mystery of the genesis of the Son from the Father as incomprehensible to the human understanding. It would have been only a question of phraseology to make such a declaration acceptable even to theological circles; and there can be no doubt that the synod would thus have met the corresponding desires of the Emperor. More than once afterwards a solution of that kind was attempted, but it was no longer possible to do what could have been easily accomplished at Nicea.

It is quite astonishing that the Emperor should have placed great emphasis on introducing into the creed a term that hitherto neither of the parties had put forward: the term

[1] Eus. *op. cit.* 3, 13   [2] Schwartz, *Constantine,* 2nd ed. 127   [3] *Doc.* 22

homousios. He instructed a commission to carry out a corresponding redaction of the creed. The result[1] was that clause in the Nicene Creed which confesses the genesis of the Son "from the substance (*ousia*) of the Father" and describes Him as "of one nature with the Father", the condemnation of the Arian articles following at the end.

As to the reason why the Emperor should have taken this step, there is no light at all; nor has any hint survived as to the theological writing or passage that had suggested the term to him—it was certainly not derived from his own personal studies and thought. At one time, it was held to be due to occidental influence mediated, say, through Ossius; but the difficulty attaching to such an explanation is that, even in its Latin translation, the word was not used as a theological term. Even during the Dionysios dispute,[2] it was not used by the Roman protagonists. On the other hand, it was employed by the Alexandrians in their complaints against their bishop, and it occurs again among the Meletian denunciations of Arius. Nor must it be forgotten that Paul of Samosata[3] also had employed the term. Again, wherever it does occur in these times, it is an omnibus word frequently on the lips of the unlettered, but eager and quick-witted, members of the laity when seeking to refute the logos-speculations of Origen and his school. It was a kind of protest against any thought-out doctrine of an *hypostasis*. By using this philosophical term, they asserted the unity and monarchy of God, and rebutted any further attempt to think out the Trinity. Such may have been the reasons which moved someone to commend the word to the Emperor, and it may have been palatable to him because it suited equally the Lucianists and the disciples of Origen. Its introduction into the creed was therefore ordered and carried through.

Thus the amateurish theology of the Emperor, supported by the immeasurable prestige due to his status, became interwoven with the modes of thought which were responsible for the furthering of learned speculation. This speculation ought to have gone forward according to the rules which were

[1] *Doc.* 24 and remarks by Lietzmann thereon in *ZNW.* 24 (1925), 193–202
[2] *vide supra*, 95ff.
[3] *vide supra*, 102

germane to the matter concerned, but now it had suffered a great disturbance; and this disturbance told as heavily against the State whose interests the Emperor believed he had guarded, as against the Church which bowed to his will.

Nevertheless, at first the outlook promised fair weather. The delegates discussed the proposed credal formula, let themselves be won over by assuring phraseology, and, finally, gave the Emperor the pleasure of agreeing to his proposition. How hard that was for the more learned delegates may be gathered from the letter which Eusebius sent to his church at Cæsarea by way of justifying his action. The explanations are tortuous, but it is clear that he had a great sense of obligation to the Emperor who had patronized the Church and brought it into union; and only this sense had induced him to renounce views that hitherto he had openly stood for. It must have been much the same with other scholarly men. They could not help what they did, and they hoped that the achievement of peace within the Church would justify the dubious means.[1]

Only two men remained in opposition, but even these did so on other than theological grounds. Eusebius of Nicomedia and the local bishop, Theognios of Nicea, subscribed indeed to the Confession of Faith, but refused to agree to the condemnation of Arius, because they held that the official phrases distorted their doctrine.[2] Both bishops knew exactly what they were doing. In contradistinction from their fellow-delegates, they were used to life at court, and were not over-awed by the splendour and pomp of ceremonies of state; they also knew how rapidly the wind could change in the most exalted station. At first, their abstention was regarded as an offence, but they were given a time-limit within which to add their signatures.

Those who had been definitely condemned, Arius and the two bishops, Secundus of Ptolemaïs and Theonas of Marmarika, were immediately exiled from Egypt.[3] They arrived in Bithynia, and were given a friendly reception by the two bishops of the opposition. They were also welcomed by the Church. This was more than the Emperor could tolerate. Without waiting for the

---

[1] Compare the angry outburst of Eustathius in Theod. *H.E.* 1, 8, 1–5
[2] *Doc.* 31, 2 and K. Müller *ZNW.*, 1925, 290   [3] *Doc.* 23, 5

time-limit set by the council, he banished the two delinquents
to Gaul.[1] Towards Eusebius (of Nicomedia) who supported
Licinius till the last moment, he was extremely angry,
and now required the church at Nicomedia to choose a new
bishop.[2] A special warning[3] was written to Bishop Theodotos of
Laodicea, drawing his attention to the lot of the two exiles, and
thus warning him against similar folly.

When the disagreement about the faith had been ended in
accordance with the Emperor's ideas, and in his presence, the
synod passed on to smoother and more humdrum work in
discussing questions of the organization and discipline of the
Church; the result being extant in several epistles and twenty
canons. The Meletians were promised—in sheer opposition to
Alexander's views—that their ordination would be recognized
when they returned to the Church, the only conditions being
that their bishops must cease to exercise their functions in
favour of those consecrated by Alexander. Meletius himself must
withdraw to Lycopolis, content himself with his title of bishop,
and discontinue further ordinations.[4] The same solution of the
problem was prescribed for returning Novatianists.[5] Bishop
Alexander demanded, too, that Meletius should provide him
with a list of the clergy he had ordained. When he actually
received the list,[6] it was found to enumerate 29 bishops, 5
presbyters, and 3 deacons; but further proceedings soon came
to a standstill, and made it necessary for the Emperor to
intervene again.

The synod of Arles[7] had already made it obligatory for
Easter to be celebrated at the same time throughout Christendom. This prescription was accepted at Nicea, and now given
special emphasis. Particularly in Antioch's sphere of influence
did the old custom continue of observing Easter on the Sunday
after the Jewish Passover, whereas Alexandria and Rome had
long reckoned Eastertide after its own cycle, and had not
adhered to the Jewish mode. It was now forbidden to "celebrate
with the Jews", the idea being that Easter was an independent
foundation; and it was decreed that it should be observed

---

[1] *Philostorgius*, 2, 1b   p. 12, 26   ed. *Bidez*   [2] *Doc.* 27   [3] *ibid.* 28
[4] *Doc.* 23, 6–7   [5] *Can.* 8   cf. *Doc.* 23, 6. 7
[6] Athan. *Apol. c. Ar.* 71   [7] *Can.* 1, Arles

universally at the same time. In the heat engendered by the worthy cause, the fact was overlooked that different Christian traditions often led to different results[1]—with the consequence that, in spite of all the conclusions reached by councils, the Christian church is not even yet in a position to put into practice the ideal of one date everywhere for Easter. But in those days, everybody believed that the objective was virtually attained, and Constantine prepared an epistle[2] in which he expressed his satisfaction with the achievement.

The creed and the canons were officially signed on June 19, 325. Before the synod dispersed, the Emperor once more caused the delegates to be assembled, and he addressed them in moving terms. He pressed them to keep the peace and urged them to personal friendliness among themselves; he also suggested that not everyone could be a scholar. Finally he asked them to remember him always in their prayers. It is indeed possible that he believed he had attained unity in the Church, and thus could celebrate the twentieth anniversary of his reign in a happy atmosphere. On July 25, he gave a great banquet to the bishops, the day being observed as a public holiday throughout the Empire.[3] Perhaps he thought he had laid down the essential principles necessary to regulate the relations between Church and state; and that it was only a matter of handling these two great interests tactfully enough for them to mesh together without friction.

The Emperor was moved by the state interest of political unity when he created the supreme ecclesiastical court of the General Council. The Church, from purely ecclesiastical considerations, was glad to avail itself of this instrument, especially because, in many ways, it was only the extension and completion of a provision already to be found in the Church. In the council, problems of the Church were discussed and decided according to the customs of the Church. Of course it was an innovation that the Emperor, a catechumen, should be present, and should take part in the discussions. But this was regarded favourably as a sign that the state was positively promoting the interests of the Church. Moreover, the con-

1 cf. E. Schwartz, *Christl. u. Jud. Ostertafeln* (*Gött. Abh.* NF. Vol. 8, 1905)   118f.
2 *Doc.* 26   3 Eus. *vita Const.* 3, 15. 16. 21–22

clusions reached by the council were accepted by the Emperor and passed on as imperial edicts to the persons concerned. Indeed, the very number of such edicts issuing from the imperial chancellery[1] shows that the Emperor took a lively interest in the carrying out of the council's work. The Church had also the further advantage that when she passed verdicts of condemnation, certain political consequences followed. Thus the Arians and the opposing bishops, Eusebius (of Nicomedia) and Theognios, were not only excommunicated from the Church, but also removed from their offices by the power of the state, and sent into exile.[2] Was it possible to conceive a seemlier harmony between Church and state? Yet in the deepest depths of many a bishop's soul, there stirred an uncomfortable feeling that all was not well, and that, just to please the Emperor, a great mistake had in fact been made on the question of the faith. Ah well, one must hope it would all come right some day.

Meantime, among the Meletians in Egypt, difficulties appeared which were to increase in the next few years. Again, the Arian movement did not seem to have been suppressed by excommunicating the Arians and sending the leaders into exile; on the contrary their opposition became more active. The Emperor felt that it would be well to call the synod together again in Nicea in the late autumn of A.D. 327 in order to reach a final settlement. Arius and his fellow-sufferer in exile, Euzoïos, had prayed for clemency,[3] and the petition had been supported by a lady of the royal house. In compliance with the Emperor's orders, Arius had presented a confession of faith; this was a creed in the ancient style, omitting, however, each of the disputed expressions, but retaining the concluding phrase which desired peace with the Church, and deprecated hair-splitting. When given an audience, Arius assured the Emperor that he assented to the Nicene creed; and it was thought appropriate to accept his word.[4] The synod readmitted Arius to their fellowship.[5] Thereupon, Eusebius (of Nicomedia) and Theognios wrote and asked the synod for a revision of their own condemnation, and for intercession with the Emperor.[6] They, too

---

[1] *Doc.* 25. 26. 27. 28 cf. Eus. *vita Const.* 3, 24 [2] *Doc.* 27, 16
[3] *Doc.* 30 [4] *ibid.* 32, 2
[5] *ibid.* 31, 4 p. 65, 16–17 [6] *ibid.* 31, followed by Socr. 1, 14, 1

were granted their plea, and indeed were once more installed in their sees, their *locos tenentes*, Amphion and Chrestos, disappearing again without a sound into (what is for us) the obscurity from which they had appeared. The Emperor wrote[1] personally on behalf of Arius to Bishop Alexander; he recommended as emphatically as possible that Arius be readmitted to the clerical status, and most deferentially invited him to the court before he left.

The dispute with the Meletians, too, was brought to an end during this second assembly of the synod, and their readmission was decreed under the conditions previously laid down. In other words, the deliberations of the council of A.D. 327, achieved a considerable amelioration and, broadly speaking, a revocation of many of the decisions of A.D. 325; and, it must be granted, in quite an unobjectionable form. The revisions were made at the expense of the views of the bishop of Alexandria. When at a later date, Athanasius came to write his version of the events, it is not difficult to understand why he consigned the second assembly at Nicea to oblivion. Only if we combine unimpeachable fragments of extant information, can the history of the actual course of events be approximately traced.

The view of historians, generally accepted hitherto, regards the further course of things as essentially a struggle for or against the Nicene Creed, or as Goethe vividly put it:

> *Two enemies there are who ceaselessly box:*
> *The Arians fighting the Orthodox.*[2]

But that is not a remark that can be properly applied to the early period when foundations were being laid, because then there were really no Nicene theologians and, in accordance with what has been said above[3] about the term *homousios*, there could have been none. All, including Arius, accepted the Nicene Creed, and each read his own theology into it. What is more, the Emperor was content that it should be so. When, on occasion, he chose to give his own theological hobby horse— for he had such—an airing,[4] he was at least statesman enough

---

[1] *Doc.* 32, 29   [2] Goethe, *Zahme Xenien*, 9 (4, 124 Jubilee Ausg.)   [3] *supra*, 118f
[4] *Doc.* 27, 1–5   *Doc.* 34 in many passages. Address to the Synod: Gelas. *H.E.* 2, 7

not to demand that these performances should be accepted; and that was his way till his death.

It was older rivalries that really disturbed the Church, and especially those affecting power and prestige. These acquired quite a new importance once the leading churchmen perceived that state support could present the protagonist who enjoyed the royal favour with unlimited means of defeating his opponent. Of course, one had to be wary, for all could see that Constantine could not exactly be led like a child.

In the autumn of A.D. 324, Eustathios, who had hitherto been bishop of Beroea, took his seat on the episcopal throne at Antioch, but a storm rose against him towards the end of the same decade. A synod met in the city and deposed him; thereupon, the Emperor banished him to Thrace, where a few years later, he died.[1] He had been strongly against Origen, and a tractate is extant in which he deplores and condemns Origen's allegorical method of expounding scripture. He bases his criticisms on the case of the witch of Endor, and shows what he believes to be a sound exegesis. In doing so he tries to keep close to the actual wording and literal meaning of the passage; and it must be granted, he reaches a fairly reasonable result. No wonder, therefore, that he crossed literary swords with Eusebius of Cæsarea, and also that he wrote polemically against the Arians. His main point was the sheer separation of the full humanity of Jesus from the divine nature which dwelt in this "man" as in a temple. This divine nature was the Logos or Sophia, the infinite and incomprehensible One who was Son of God "by nature", who, during the time that He dwelt in Jesus's body, swayed all heaven and earth; He searched the souls of men, and embraced the universe "as a divine and ineffable power".[2] This view approximated fairly closely to that of Paul of Samosata, who held that the Logos was a function of God the Father. It is easy to see that Origen's school would accuse Eustathios of Sabellianism. But that was not why he was deposed; nor was it because he intervened on behalf of the Nicene Creed—if in fact he did so. All the evidence

[1] Socrates 1, 23, 8   24, 1–9   Sozom. 2, 18, 4   19, 1–7   Jer. *vir. inl.* 85
[2] cf. the fragments in F. Cavallera, *S. Eustathii in Lazarum homilia*, Paris, 1905
Also the tractate on the *Hexe von Endor*, ed. Klostermann (Kleine Texte 83)

agrees that his conduct was stigmatized as unworthy of a priest, and Athanasius also mentions a charge of insulting Helena, the queen-mother.[1]

The verdict, however, roused violent opposition in Antioch. There were even street demonstrations and riots which the military had to be called out to suppress. Constantine sent a general to the city with orders to use all vigour, short of bloodshed, in allaying the unrest. He seems to have been successful. The synod chose Eusebius of Cæsarea as successor to the deposed bishop, but he was too wary. He declined the dangerous post by appealing to the regulation issued at Nicea forbidding a bishop to transfer from one see to another. The Emperor praised him for taking this course, and recommended two other candidates to the synod; these elected from themselves Euphronius, a presbyter from Cappadocia.[2] But half the congregation at Antioch remained faithful to Eustathios, and separated. It would appear that the former adherents of Bishop Paul,[3] who had only recently been reconciled, and that with difficulty, were to be found among the schismatics. From that time, the Antiochene nucleus in the east was crippled in the part it took in the wider life of the Church. Each of those who came to occupy the episcopal chair at Antioch, was only halfmaster in his own house, and must reckon with the hostility of the bishop of the Eustathian sect in ways that caused irritation. This state of affairs lasted eighty long years, and quite markedly affected the whole history of the Church in the east.

The same synod at Antioch which deposed Eustathios may have drawn up the twenty-five canons which acquired universal authority in the Church. These canons have been wrongly believed from ancient times to have been issued by the "Church Consecration" synod of A.D. 341.[4] The extant list of delegates to the synod shows that the Council of Nicea was still recent, and Eusebius of Cæsarea heads the list of names, the Emperor having prevailed upon him, after declining the see, to take part in the Synod of Antioch.[5]

---

[1] E. Schwartz, *Gött. Nach.* 1908, 356   *ZNW.* 34 (1935), 159   Athan. *Hist. Ar.* 4
[2] Eus., *vita Const.* 3, 60. 61. 62   [3] *vide supra,* p. 100f.
[4] E. Schwartz, *op. cit.* 1911, 389–400   [5] Eus. *vita Const.* 3, 61 p. 109, 22 Heikel

As regards content, the canons represent a further development of the regulations drawn up at Nicea; and it was now seen to be necessary to have a defence against the organization of schismatic congregations. The independence of provincial areas was carried further; provincial synods were to be held at regular intervals, and their competence was defined and regulated. The problem of Church and state again first came to light here in the prohibition against referring church matters to the Emperor without permission of the Metropolitan; or to appeal to him against the judgment of the Church.[1]

It may be added that the see of Antioch suffered the further misfortune that Bishop Euphronius, and also his immediate successors, only exercised office for a short time before being called away by death. But in regard to all the concerns of Antioch, very little exact and reliable information has survived, and it should be clearly understood that it is therefore impossible to describe properly the most important subject-matters of the history of the Church in the fourth century. In addition, many individual events of this period remain obscure. We hear incidentally, at a later date,[2] with some surprise, that not only Marcellus, bishop of Ancyra, but also a great number of other bishops, including one as important as Paul of Constantinople, had to go into exile; they were called upon to make these sacrifices by the Emperor's policy of preserving the peace. The Emperor, who was very gracious to bishops who complied with his policy, suppressed all serious opponents with ruthless force.

In regard to the happenings in the Alexandrine patriarchate, better information is available. Alexander in spite of being on the losing side as described earlier, nevertheless gained valuable advantages from Nicea. In its sixth canon the Council gave formal recognition to the contention, as a custom obtaining from ancient times, that the bishop of Alexandria was the supreme pastor of all Egypt including Libya and the Pentapolis. This was the final ratification of an overlordship which had been shrewdly and systematically built up. This overlordship extended far beyond the borders of the province as existing in Diocletian's time, and was only paralleled by the dominion

[1] *Can. Antioch*, 11. 12   [2] Athan. *Hist. Ar.* 5–8

exercised by the Roman bishop over central and southern Italy. The similarity can scarcely be accidental, but was rather the result of the spiritual relation of the two cities in regard to church policy, as frequently remarked in the foregoing pages. The Nicene canon proceeds: "similarly in Antioch and the remaining provinces, the privileges of the Church ought to be maintained"; but this had little significance for the time being; and, in particular, Alexandria had little to fear from Antioch—we have seen why.

The Meletian movement, however, must have caused Alexander serious concern when it refused to acknowledge the Peace of Nicea. Then again, there was a question of the readmission of Arius during the second session, together with the requirement which the Emperor based thereon. Granted, to all appearances, this did not encroach upon Alexander's free spiritual judgment,[1] but it was clear that the request conveyed a command in a politer form. Alexander might have delayed answering the letter; but it must have arrived when he was already on his death-bed, for he died on April 17, 328.

The new mode of choice which had been decreed by Alexander, was tested in the election of his successor. This test also published abroad the fact that Alexander had succeeded in breaking through the privileges hitherto enjoyed by the presbyters of his city. No longer were they allowed to make the election themselves, and raise one of their own number to the episcopate; instead of this the bishops of Egypt, as many as so wished, now came together in the capital and exercised a free choice. In this instance, as was customary elsewhere, they elected the late bishop's confidential deacon, Athanasius by name, a man in his early thirties. He was consecrated bishop on June 8, 328.[2] He had accompanied his bishop to the Nicene Council, and it is quite likely that the latter had desired him to be his successor.[3] But the election surely cannot have been entirely plain-sailing. Fifty-four bishops came together in Alexandria and, in view of the significance of the impending

[1] *Doc.* 32, 4

[2] Athan., *ep.* preface; *hist. aceph.* 17   p. 83, ed. Fromen. But the Syriac text asserts that it was a Sunday; and this is in accordance with liturgical custom. If so, the date must have been June 9

[3] Athan., *apol. c. Ar.* 6, 2   Sozom. 2, 17, 1. 3

choice, they met with jealous looks from each other. Before the election, they carefully tested any objections brought against the candidates. This appears to imply—as also does the long interval, nearly two months, between the death of Alexander and the choice of his successor—that considerable difficulties were being encountered. Indeed, finally, seven bishops lost patience, gathered themselves together, elected Athanasius and consecrated him. The Emperor granted him recognition.[1]

In this way, Athanasius became a bishop, but he found himself at once in serious difficulties. The Meletians shrewdly united with the other bishops for the purposes of the election, presumably because they expected practical advantages for themselves by doing so. But they must now have felt cheated. and they immediately opened hostilities against the new bishop, He defended himself and bade his bishops do the same. In many localities there were serious clashes, and when at last the Meletians appealed to the Emperor with charges against Athanasius, they had a long list of outrages to present. Athanasius defended himself by attack, and accused his opponents of departing from the Nicene faith.[2] His counsels were two Egyptian presbyters who lodged for the time being at the Court, but the Emperor cited Athanasius himself in order to hear him personally.

About the turn of the years A.D. 331–332, he appeared in the royal Villa Psamathia near Nicomedia. The main charges brought by the Meletians were (a) bribery of a king's messenger, and (b) sacrilege in the matter of a certain Ischyras. The latter was a presbyter in association with Kolluthos, and had been denounced to Athanasius for having made a visitation in Mareotis. The bishop sent the presbyter, Makarios, to fetch Ischyras. The former must have had an unpleasant reception in the village, during which Makarios overturned a bishop's throne and the altar-table. In addition, a communion chalice was broken to fragments. Athanasius was held responsible for the sacrilege in defiling the sacred building.[3]

[1] Sozom. 2, 17, 4 25, 6 Athan. *op. cit.* 6, 4 Philostorg. 2, 11 p. 23. *Re* mode of election, *vide* Eutychius *Annals* in Schwartz, *op. cit.* 1908, 350

[2] Sozom. 2, 22, 1–3 Athan. *apol. c. Ar.* 59–60 p. 139–141, ed. Opitz; and see footnote

[3] Athan. *apol. c. Ar.* 63 p. 142f. Opitz. Schwartz, *op. cit.* 1911, 373, footnote 4

Athanasius succeeded in fully justifying himself before he returned to Egypt at the end of March, 332, in the middle of Holy Week.[1] He brought with him, for the benefit of the Alexandrines, a royal document which castigated them thoroughly for their stupidity, their unruliness, and their hostility to the bishop. It went on to declare that Athanasius was innocent of the charges brought by his wicked enemies, and extolled him as a godly man.[2] Ischyras himself had put it solemnly on record that the whole of the charges were untrue.[3] Athanasius had achieved a brilliant success by his personal intervention, and he is to be held in the higher esteem, as he had to be prepared for an unfriendly reception.

To particularize: a short time earlier, the Emperor, acting through Eusebius of Nicomedia, had been obliged to remind Athanasius that he had not yet admitted Arius, and Eusebius had clearly indicated the dubious consequences of refusing. Then came a communication from the Emperor to the effect that Athanasius must be prepared for instant deposition and banishment if he did not admit Arius. Athanasius's answer was that a heretic could not be received into the church catholic. Constantine let himself be content for the time being, and did not make the overbearing fellow suffer for his temerity in asserting himself to the contrary.[4] There is nothing available to show that this subject was discussed in Psamathia, but it is not unlikely that Athanasius referred to facts which testified that Arius had again brought to life the heresies condemned at Nicea. In this way, Athanasius may have justified his refusal.

Against this view, however, Arius would appear to have regarded his position as safer than it would then have been on the above supposition. He knew that the Emperor could not avoid sending him back, if only to support the authority of the council which had pardoned him on recantation. He even thought himself in a position to admonish the Emperor, and wrote him a spirited letter. The masses stood behind him, he said, and, like him, expected immediate fulfilment of the promises. If the bishop should again refuse to admit him, then he should

---

[1] *ep.* 4 p. 77. 80 Larsow; cf. p. 27 mistakenly ascribed to epistle 3
[2] Athan. *op. cit.* 61–62   [3] *ibid.* 64   [4] *ibid.* 59, 3–6

be granted liberty, together with his adherents, to build a legally recognized church of his own.[1]

The answer[2] was conveyed by two king's messengers, and read aloud publicly in the palace of the governor. It was a forceful and even rough-toned denunciation of Arius and his proposals, intermingled with theological corrections of his heresies. It held out the prospect of considerable increases of land-taxes and other public dues to any schismatic church. Then, finally, and quite surprisingly, there came an invitation to come to the court, and prove before the Emperor, "that man of God", the correctness of his faith. The strange document concluded with a greeting written in Constantine's own hand. At the same time, however, a royal edict[3] was given the widest publicity in the Church. This put Arius's adherents in the same position as the followers of Porphyry the enemy of the Christians, ordered Arius's writings to be burned, and threatened the death penalty on any who kept them in secret. Arius journeyed to the Emperor, and once more convinced him of his orthodoxy by a personal confession during an audience.[4]

As a consequence, it seemed for a while in A.D. 333 as if the sun of the royal favour shone equally on both opponents. The Meletians were deceived by this state of affairs, and took to dubious means in order to disturb the influence of Athanasius: their leader, John Archaphos, successor to Meletius, accused him of the murder of a certain bishop, Arsenios by name. They said he had been lashed to a pillar in his house, and the house set on fire by a Bishop Plusianos acting on the orders of his superior.[5] The Emperor immediately ordered his half-brother, Dalmatius,[6] who resided in Antioch and bore the title, strange for the time, of Censor,[7] to inquire into the circumstances; moreover, a synod was called together there for the same purpose.

Meantime, Athanasius was not idle. He set his sharpest-witted deacon on the track of the vanished Arsenios. In a very

---

[1] *Doc.* 34, 5. 8–11
[2] *ibid.* 34, with the date A.D. 333 (cf. p. 75, 7 Opitz)
[3] *Doc.* 33
[4] Athan. *apol. c. Ar.* 84, 4 = *de synod.* 21
[5] Sozom. 2, 25, 12
[6] *Pauly-W.* 4, 2455
[7] On this point, cf. O. Seeck, *Regesten,* 127

short time he discovered the bishop in a monastery in Upper Egypt. While the brothers of the monastery managed to ship their guest down the Nile, two of the chief of those concerned were arrested, brought to Alexandria, compelled to confess before the military commander that Arsenios was alive, and therefore had not been put to death. The monks immediately sent a warning to John Archaphos not to bring forward the charge against Athanasius, but the messenger came too late.[1] Athanasius also discovered his pretended victim in his new hiding-place in Tyre, and caused him to be brought before Paul, the local bishop. His identity was established in Paul's presence in spite of many initial denials. The charge of murder was thus finally proved groundless.

Athanasius immediately communicated the outcome to the Emperor, who stopped Dalmatius's inquiry, dismissed the synod, and wrote a warm letter of congratulation to the men who had once more been so brilliantly exculpated. The letter concluded with the threat that, if the Meletians should again contrive such charges, proceedings would no longer be taken against them according to the Church's law, but as intriguers dangerous to the state.[2] John Archaphos acknowledged his defeat and wrote a letter to Constantine, in which he also spoke of having reached agreement and harmonious fellowship with Athanasius. The Emperor was pleased and invited him in gracious words to come to the court.[3] Arsenios at once rejoined the "catholic" church, and submitted to Athanasius.[4] It seemed as if Egypt would now be at peace.

However, the Emperor's friendliness towards Arius, the repentant sinner, and John Archaphos was uneasy. Suddenly in the spring of A.D. 334, Constantine assembled a synod at Cæsarea to inquire into the accusations against Athanasius. Naturally Eusebius, as the local bishop, presided over this court of justice, and his namesake from Nicomedia was his most influential colleague. Athanasius refused to appear before judges who were outspokenly hostile to him, and they had to pocket the rebuff for the time being. In Alexandria, he had the

---

[1] For the monks' letter cf. Athan. *apol. c. Ar.* 67
[2] The record is in Athan. *op. cit.* 65   Constantine's letter, *ibid.* 68
[3] *Op. cit.* 70, 2   [4] *Op. cit.* 69, 2–4

authorities on his side, and he attacked the Meletians with rough violence.[1]

The thirtieth anniversary of the reign was now approaching, and Constantine wished to observe this jubilee, among other ways, by consecrating the Church of the Holy Sepulchre which he had built in Jerusalem. It was also to be an opportunity for a great representative synod modelled on that held ten years before at Nicea.[2] But it would be needful previously to bring the Church into good order, which meant, however, settling the problem of Athanasius. The Eusebians, as it had become customary to call the members of the eastern Church after their leader, Eusebius of Nicomedia, had mooted to the Emperor a sort of preparatory synod at Tyre. They submitted suggestions for the choice of delegates, and asked for an imperial commissioner as chairman and guarantor of good order. Constantine granted every request, sent Dionysius the Consular to represent the state, and promised, if it came about that any who were indicted should prove difficult—Athanasius was meant—that such should be forcibly held under arrest to await imperial orders.[3]

The proceedings began as early as July, 335.[4] The charges were made by Ischyras who bore the fragments of the communion chalice. He was surrounded by a circle of Meletian bishops who swore they had suffered violence. To strengthen the case for the accusation, attention was drawn to the irregularity of Athanasius's election. In addition, Arsenios, back again to life, put in an appearance; for if he had not been actually murdered, he could make justifiable charges of serious assault.[5] After some hesitation Athanasius attended, accompanied by a group of loyal bishops, a list of whom contains forty-eight names.[6] They first protested against the presence of the Eusebians as hostile to their Patriarch. Then Athanasius refused to answer the charges of Ischyras, because he was not

[1] Sozom. 2, 25, 1   Athan. *ep.* Pref. 6   p. 28 Larsow   Also Schwartz, *op. cit.* 1911, 376   Holl., *Ges. Schr.* 2, 283

[2] Eus. *vita Const.* 4, 47

[3] *ibid.* 4, 42, 3–4   cf. Athan. *apol.* 71, 2   The records have been collected by Schwartz, *op. cit.* 1911, 413–416

[4] Athan. *ep.* Pref. 8   p. 28 Larsow   [5] Sozom. 2, 25, 3–7. 12

[6] Athan. *apol.* 78, 7.   Idris Bell, *Jews and Christians in Egypt*, 1924, 60, 38ff.
Holl., *Ges. Schr.* 2, 288

even a cleric. Scenes of considerable uproar ensued until Athanasius was taken into custody by the Consular.[1]

The synod decided to send a fact-finding commission to Mareotis; but they proceeded with the arrangements in such a partisan way, that not only did the Athanasians protest, but even such a realistic man as Alexander of Thessalonika drew Dionysius's attention to it. The result was that he sent a written warning to them,[2] but to no purpose. Shortly afterwards, loud protests were echoed against the methods of the commission in Egypt, accompanied by complaints on the part of the imperial officials.[3] At this point we are told that the loyal Athanasians demanded that the charges against Athanasius should be brought before the imperial Court of Justice.[4] This corresponded with the wish of Athanasius himself.

Athanasius left the synod secretly, and took a roundabout way to Constantinople; latterly he had not been sure even of his life in Tyre, and the officials had facilitated his departure.[5] He arrived in the capital on October 30,[6] the verdict being issued against him in Tyre in his absence. This deposed and banished him from Alexandria, because at one time, in disobedience to the royal command, he had not put in his appearance in Cæsarea; had behaved in an unseemly manner at Tyre; and, in regard to the Ischyras affair, the result of the fact-finding commission was that he was held guilty of the whole charge. The Meletians, with officials and dignitaries, were readmitted to the fellowship of the Church.[7] Once again the delegates set forth, urged by royal command to hurry, and journeyed to Jerusalem. On September 17, 335, they consecrated, with due ceremonial, the splendid basilica on the rock of Golgotha.[8] As Constantine desired them to reinstate Arius in his office in Alexandria, they did his pleasure without reluctance, and wrote the Egyptians accordingly.[9]

The Emperor returned to Constantinople, followed quickly

---

[1] Sozom. 2, 25, 18   Athan. *apol.* 71, 5   [2] Athan. *apol.* 81
[3] *ibid.* 73. 74–75. 76 (dated September 8, 335)   [4] *ibid.* 79, 1 (160, 6 Opitz)
[5] Sozom. 2, 25, 13. 14
[6] Athan., *ep.* pref. 8 (28 Larsow, who gives the wrong year, 336 instead of 335)
[7] Sozom. 2, 25, 15–19
[8] *Chronicon paschale*, p. 531, 11 ed. Dindorf   But the date of the consecration of the church (Holy Cross Day) according to the liturgy is September 14.
[9] Athan. *de synod.* 21

by the chief Eusebians, because, it seems, they wished to take part in further jubilee celebrations, perhaps also because they were aware of Athanasius's excursion. The latter cleverly presented himself to the Emperor *en route*, and was greeted by the royal train; yet only with difficulty did he obtain an audience. But once there Athanasius demonstrated the charm of his personality. Constantine immediately called together the delegates, who had acted as judges at Tyre, to a new synod in Constantinople; but the summons had scarcely been issued when the Eusebians succeeded in approaching the Emperor, telling him that Athanasius had threatened to prevent the transport of corn to the capital. It was actually within the power of the Patriarch of Alexandria to do this and the non-arrival of the freight-ships would mean famine for the masses who were accustomed to be issued with 80,000 bushels of corn daily.[1] The Emperor blazed up in furious anger, and immediately banished Athanasius to Trèves without a hearing. The condemned man set out on his journey that self-same day, November 7, 335.[2] Thus, Eusebius of Cæsarea was able to read his Jubilee address with a lighter heart, and take his seat with the rest of his brother office-bearers at the banquet spread on the royal tables,[3] for their enemy had been finally overthrown.

Loud cries rose in Alexandria over the loss of their chief shepherd, and the clergy, together with the "consecrated virgins", set on foot petitions beseeching his return. But the Emperor bade them be silent and roughly refused to show clemency to an insurgent who had been legally condemned. Even the saintly Antonius, the miracle-working ascetic of the wilderness, received only the cold answer to his letter that the Emperor was in no position to ignore the verdict of the Church; and it was scarcely credible that such a large assembly of respected and able bishops had pronounced a judgment inspired by hatred and bias.

The Meletian bishop, John Archaphos, seems to have regarded the fact that the see of Alexandria was vacant, as a good opportunity of extending his power; but his demeanour roused

---

[1] Socrates, 2, 13, 5

[2] Athan., *apol.* 87, 1–2   *ep.* pref. 8 p. 28 Larsow (by mistake assigned to A.D. 336)

[3] Eus. *vita Const.* 4, 46

vigorous opposition, and the alarm penetrated to the Emperor's ears. As a result, John also had to go into exile.[1] Arius, it would appear, died about this time. When all was said and done, he had been ineffective in Alexandria; so he remained in Constantinople where he died suddenly in the street. Athanasius, twenty years later, concocted out of the event a scarcely edifying miracle-story[2] which has since constituted the sure standby of popular propaganda; but to the critical reader, it appears to be at most a story of murder by poison.

The Emperor Constantine, shortly after Easter, 337, was overcome by an indisposition which rapidly grew worse. He then arranged to be baptized, lay in the white robes of the "new-born" on his death-bed, and died on Whit-Sunday, May 22, in Ankyrona near Nicomedia.[3] He does not seem to have been more than sixty years of age in spite of all the assertions of historians to the contrary.[4] His son, Constantius, laid him in the rotunda of the Church of the Apostles built by the Emperor for that purpose in the capital. The coffin stood in the centre of twelve sarcophagi dedicated to the Apostles.[5]

---

[1] Sozom. 2, 31

[2] Athan. *ep. ad Serap. de morte Arii*; this was copied by Rufinus and other historical writers

[3] Eus. *vita Const.* 61–64   Jerome, *chron. ol.* 279, 1 p. 234, 8 (ed. Helm). Aurelius Victor Caes. 41, 15

[4] Seeck, *Untergang*, 1, 407   [5] Eus. *ibid.* 4, 60. 71

Chapter Five

CONSTANTINE

CONSTANTINE LAID ASIDE HIS FIELD-MARSHAL'S BATON AFTER his victory over Licinius. His prestige was so secure and exalted that he could leave to his sons whatever fame was still to be gained from war. The eldest surviving son, Constantinus, while still in his twelfth year, was made supreme commander of an army, which defeated the Alemanni: but his father stood prudently in the background, having led out the forces from Trèves to begin the campaign.[1] Three years later, in the spring of A.D. 332, the young prince overcame the Goths with shattering consequences. The victory over the Sarmatians which followed soon afterwards, appears to have been won by his half-brother, Constantius, who was almost of the same age.[2] The sequel to these events was that 300,000 Sarmatians settled in the border districts which had been laid waste on the north of the Danube.

But the military frontier on the Euphrates also required increased vigilance. At first, Constantius was entrusted with the safety of this region. As the situation grew more serious, the Emperor, in view of the size of the problem, decided to take the field himself against the Persians; but death overtook him while in the midst of the preparations.

In the year 335, the Controller of the Royal Camel-droves, Calocaeros of Cyprus, conceived the really mad idea of making himself independent king of the island. The younger Dalmatius, son of the censor of Antioch, and therefore nephew of the Emperor, received the commission to suppress the insurrection: he burned the unfortunate man alive in Tarsus.

Constantine's eldest son Crispus[3] had been similarly entrusted at an earlier date with warlike enterprises which earned him fame in the title of Conqueror of the Franks and the Alemanni; and he had shared in the struggle against Licinius as com-

---

[1] Seeck, *Untergang*, 4, 370f.   [2] *ibid.* 4, 382
[3] Seeck, in *Pauly-W.* 4, 1722 n. 9 and *Untergang* 3, 558f.

mander of the fleet.[1] He had filled his father with the highest hopes; but it was this very son that Constantine put to death by poison in Pola in A.D. 326. It is still uncertain whether he had an adulterous relation with his step-mother, Fausta, who tried to save herself by playing the part of Potiphar's wife. But soon after Crispus's death, she was drowned in a hot bath on Constantine's orders.

Into the room of Crispus, according to the Emperor's plan of succession, Dalmatius was promoted. He was Constantine's brother's son, and was made Cæsar in A.D. 335. The other nephew, Hannibalian, was given the prospect of being the ruler of a Greater Armenian empire which was to be founded beyond the Euphrates. Thus Diocletian's ideas continued to guide the further development of the Empire, although this principle had not held in the case of the strong personality of Constantine. He had rightly been able to regard himself as an exception and, therefore, when arranging the succession, he could turn back to the previous rule.

The further development of the administration also moved in the direction initiated by Diocletian. The *praefecti praetorio* were now deprived of their last remaining military functions, and in this way the civil administration was completely freed from military elements. Instead of the earlier arrangement that such a prefect was attached to the person of the emperor as his chancellor, it seemed appropriate to divide the Empire into praefectural districts, which, independent of the number of emperors or cæsars, would possess their supreme authority in the person of their own *praefectus praetorio*.[2] Moreover, within these districts, the administration was more closely unified, and the leaders of the dioceses and provinces, although their outward honours were carefully preserved, became increasingly the organs for carrying out orders issued by the prefect. The power of the chancellors was systematically raised until their jurisdiction was explicitly protected from appeals to the Emperor.[3] They exercised unlimited rule in their districts, and could even legislate within the framework of the general imperial constitution.

[1] *supra*, 80   [2] Seeck, *Regesten*, 141–149
[3] *Cod. Theod.* 11, 30, 16   cf. E. Stein, *Gesch. d. spätröm. Reiches*, 1, 179f.

Besides this, new organs of the royal administration and legislation were developed at court. The imperial council, the *consistorium*, was an authority of predominantly permanent members, the highest rank (*comites*) among those attached to the imperial court. The preparation and elaboration of the laws, as well as the attention required by petitions, were the concern of the *quaestor sacri palatii*, who, in the eastern empire, had also to make out the patents of a certain number of staff-officers.[1] The whole of the others employed in the military and civil services were under the *primicerius notariorum*,[2] who was the chief of the cabinet secretaries of state. These are often found, bearing the title of *tribunus et notarius*, also on special missions. The *notitia dignitatum*, the army list of the Empire, was kept up to date in his office: the extant copy of a portion of it is the basis of our knowledge of the body of officials of this century.[3] The *magister officiorum* was responsible for the arsenals, and was the head of the security and police service;[4] in particular, he was the head of the frequently mentioned *agentes in rebus*, i.e., king's messengers.

The finance-minister was called *comes sacrarum largitionum*, literally, minister of the royal charities, viz., the gifts of money or goods (which had become a right by custom) made to the troops and populace of the capital. As, in the last analysis, every imperial payment was regarded as an outflow of His Majesty's grace, i.e., a charity, so the stage-exchequer was called simply the "Charity" (*largitio*). Naturally the mint came under this ministry also.[5]

The *comes rerum privatarum*[6] administered the Emperor's private property, the huge domains scattered over the entire empire and providing his main income. These two finance ministers, together with the *quaestor* and the *magister officiorum*, constituted the permanent members of the *consistorium*.

Further, amongst the highest officials of the court was the

---

[1] *Notitia dignitatum, Or.* 12, *Oc.* 10   Mommsen, *Ges. Schr.* 6, 392

[2] *Not. dignit. Or.* 18, *Oc.* 16

[3] *Not. dignit.* ed. O. Seeck, 1876; E. Böcking, 1839–53, gives a full commentary

[4] *Not. dignit. Or.* 11, *Oc.* 9

[5] *Not. dignit. Or.* 13, *Oc.* 11 Seeck, in *Pauly-W.* 4, 671–675

[6] *Not. dignit. Or.* 14, *Oc.* 12 Seeck, *op. cit.* 4, 664–670

general commanding the bodyguard, the *comes domesticorum* and the High Chamberlain, the *praepositus sacri cubiculi*, who gradually rose to ever higher eminence; according to oriental custom he was always a eunuch; in the extant *notitia dignitatum*, he ranks among the highest ministers of state, the *viri inlustres*, and chiefs-of-staff, and before the consistorial ministers. He was over the First of the Gentlemen of the Chamber, *primicerius sacri cubiculi*, with his court officers, including the Masters of the Ceremonies and the Gentlemen of the Wardrobe (*sacra vestis*).

Contemporaneously with the growth of the centre of government, and in a way which was to be fundamental for the next centuries, there took place a reform of the army in which the development begun by Diocletian[1] was carried logically further. The highest places in the army were those assigned to the two generals-in-chief (*magistri militum*), one in command of the infantry, and the other in command of the cavalry. After Constantine, these positions were increased in numbers, and those appointed to them were distinguished, not by the branch of the service they commanded, but geographically, by the military commands which they controlled. They commanded directly the mobile field armies, the *comitatenses*, and the *élite* troops of the *palatini*, who according to requirement could be thrown on to any front, and who really bore the brunt of the war. These formations of first-class soldiers were kept up to strength with all emphasis on numbers and quality, and the best elements of the frontier troops were drafted into them. These elements were withdrawn from the frontier troops, and concentrated in the city garrisons in the interior.[2] The divisions of the standing army of the home-command guard were under the command of the generals (*duces*) of the different provinces; they gave security to the cities, and especially to the frontier fortresses in which they lived as colonists with wife and children. In an ever-increasing degree "barbarians" penetrated into both classes of soldiers, and the Germanic element proved, even under Constantine, indispensable for battle in the field. The historian, Ammianus, with a resentment which we cannot but respect,[3] deplores that Constantine as a rule allowed

---

[1] *vide supra*, 28 and Vol. 2, 23f.   [2] Zosim. 2, 34, 2   Stein, *Gesch.* 1, 189
[3] Ammian. Marcell. 21, 10, 8

barbarians to rise to the highest imperial dignities. It had become an unavoidable necessity.

Less than ever was it possible to think of a diminution of expenses on the army, and face to face with this fact was the impossibility of any serious increase of the burden of the taxes. Constantine imposed on the senators a class-tax graduated according to their landed property[1] to be paid, not in goods, but in gold. And from all wage-earners, servant-maids down to hawking beggars, every five years and sometimes oftener, a money payment was exacted according to the amount of working capital.[2] In this way, the last possibilities of direct taxation were exhausted.

Diocletian had attempted to improve the economic situation by stabilizing values, but with uncertain success. Constantine used the same means as he had employed, but none with enduring results in a certain sense. He created a gold standard whose basis was the gold *solidus* of $\frac{1}{7}$ oz. fine metal, and thus of a value of about 20s. by the gold standard. This coin was used during the entire Byzantine period (in round figures about 1,000 years) as the basis of international trade. The silver coin, the *miliarense*, was given a new value, and a new copper coin replaced the *follis*.[3] These were brought into an appropriate relation to the gold; but they soon began to fluctuate. The copper coinage minted on the occasion of the founding of Constantinople were already considerably lighter in weight.[4] But the gold money, which was plentifully minted, held good, and furthered the nascent beginnings of a strengthening economy based on gold, whereas the small coinage was continually divided up afresh.[5]

Unfortunately there was not a single sign of improvement in the economic outlook. The weight of the taxes called for by the situation due to military policy, a situation which was aggravated incidentally by the Emperor's ostentatiousness, rendered it scarcely possible to make a living by honourable labour, and thus poisoned all commercial activity. The general uncertainty of the law favoured violence on the part of the

---

[1] *Collatio glebalis,* cf. Seeck, in *Pauly-W.* 4, 365
[2] *Collatio lustralis, ibid.* 4, 370
[3] *vide supra,* 27
[4] Bernhart, *Handbuch,* 1, 24f.
[5] Rostovtzeff, *Gesellschaft u. Wirtschaft,* 2, 230

eminent and the rich. Corruption was a normal road to wealth, and raised many men of little worth to be powerful landlords.

The unconditional character of the royal absolutism pressed with the weight of iron on the whole population and, in consequence of the traditional system of espionage by the secret police, was sometimes felt directly by the middle and lower classes. Whoever, as a master, was in the position to do so, passed this weight on to those under him, and so enjoyed the tawdry privilege of being an absolute ruler in a small way. That such a general atmosphere should strangle the courage and freshness of vitality, without which any creative commercial activity is impossible, can be readily understood.[1] It came to be a case of snatching with all one's power at what was there and holding on to it, and not of producing anything new.

The new spirit, which Christianity brought into this sick world, was able to produce healthy consequences within its own community and among the class that came under its influences; but it did not rescue public life as a whole out of the conditions which had already persisted for several generations. For that to happen, a much longer time would have been needed; and we shall take the opportunity later on to discuss the question whether Christianity proved itself to be a revitalizing power adequate to the Roman empire as a whole. At this point, we can only test the steps which were taken by the government to improve the situation.

Hence the point must first be made that Constantine was lacking in the much vaunted faithfulness to the traditional laws of Rome, although this quality had been a characteristic of Diocletian's legislation. Constantine was conscious of being an innovator. He wanted to give due validity to the folk-laws and customs of the east. This often meant giving a certain legality to the sense of fairness characteristic of a healthy human appreciation of the nature of a case, as distinct from reaching a verdict on the basis of abstract interpretations of the law.[2] That alone must have had an encouraging effect on the people, and awakened their confidence. But numerous new laws brought about the amelioration of previous hardships,

[1] *ibid.* 2, 233–238. 351f.
[2] e.g., his will; cf. Eus. *vita Const.* 4, 26, 5–6

furthered humanitarian sensibility, and supported an earnest morality at the same time as it strengthened the Church's influence on public life.[1]

As early as A.D. 321, a law decreed Sunday rest for the cities.[2] That may have appeared to be a "neutral" measure because the "day of the sun" was also sacred to the old Imperial god. Among soldiers, Christians were freely allowed to attend church, while it was prescribed that pagans should recite a general monotheistic prayer. But when this law was introduced is not known. It is significant, however, that from A.D. 317 at latest, the Christian banner with the device of the *labarum* was carried in front of the army. There was a similar restraint shown in tacitly retaining the Greek custom of manumitting slaves in the temple; the corresponding ceremony carried out in the Christian churches was recognized as quite legal.[3] The legal disadvantages suffered by unmarried or childless persons were abolished or modified,[4] a change unmistakably due to the influence of the high esteem in which celibacy was held by the Church. An attempt was made to increase the sense of the sacredness of marriage by severely reducing the number of divorces, which indeed might incur punishment by exile.[5] The same aim was the object of laws to the disadvantage of illegitimate children,[6] to facilitate legitimization by the marriage of the father with the free-born mother,[7] and to abolish concubinage among married men.[8] The union of a lady with her slave, to which formerly Callistus, bishop of Rome, had given the Church's sanction, was forbidden by the strict-minded Constantine under penalty of death to both parties.[9] Still more fearful threats were made against abductors and their companions in guilt.[10]

On the other hand, the state gave assistance to poverty-stricken parents in order that they need not sell their children, or, as by ancient custom, "set them out" and so let them die;[11] this barbarity was prohibited to converts at an early date by

---

[1] Stein, *Gesch.* 1, 190–193   [2] *Cod. Just.* 3, 12, 2   cf. *Cod. Theod.* 2, 8, 1
[3] *Cod. Theod.* 4, 7, 1   cf. L. Mitteis, *Reichsrecht*, 375, 548–552
[4] *Cod. Theod.* 8, 16, 1   [5] *ibid.* 3, 16, 1   [6] *ibid.* 4, 6, 2. 3
[7] Cited in *Cod. Just.* 5, 27, 5, pre.   [8] *Cod. Just.* 5, 26, 1
[9] *Cod. Theod.* 9, 9, 1   cf. also Vol. 2, 248   [10] *ibid.* 9, 24, 1
[11] *ibid.* 11, 27, 1. 2   Gothofredus compares Lactantius, *div. inst.* 6, 20, 18–25

Christians, and harmonized with the principles of any sound population-policy. Constantine, perhaps to honour the Nicene Fathers, forbade bloody spectacles and dismissed the gladiators on October 1, 325; but it was only a fine gesture, because it stands well enough on record that this popular form of entertainment continued undisturbed.[1] The populace of the great cities were still not converted to Christianity to the extent of allowing themselves to be deprived of the amphitheatre and the chief pleasures it gave them. But the beginning of progress in this direction must be acknowledged.

The Emperor's intention to make the standpoint of the Christian religion binding also on the state is seen in the extant fragments of his legislation with sufficient clarity; which means it was more than a freakish opportunism.

Constantine was clearly conscious that he had to grapple with a problem of world-wide significance for the coming centuries in founding the Roman empire afresh, now that it had become all disjointed. He was aware that the same requirements were demanded of him, though in totally different circumstances, as those to which Augustus long before had so brilliantly responded. Hence it is nothing to marvel at if he had similar lines of thought.

Even to Augustus in his earliest beginnings it was a question whether the new imperium could be bound up with a city like Rome which was burdened with overwhelming traditions, and he had thought of building a new capital of the Empire in the east. Indeed he gave consideration to Troy as the site of the future residency, for this was the legendary tribal home of the Julian house according to the epic story of Æneas. Horace made an impassioned protest, still extant,[2] against such intentions, and he fought them with arguments based on mythology. Others must have brought forward more realistic considerations and so the project was allowed to drop.

When Constantine took it up again, his action was determined in the first place by the fact that the centre of gravity of the Empire had moved eastwards—even Diocletian had drawn inferences from that fact. To extend the ground covered

[1] *Cod. Theod.* 15, 12, 1   with notes by Gothofredus
[2] Horace, *Odes* 3, 3, 17ff.   Suetonius, *Cæsar*, 79

by Nicomedia would not have been enough to meet Constantine's purposes. He felt that his empire, being a monarchy, was a new foundation. Hence the projected imperial city ought to be something new and yet be bound up with the revered origin of the imperium by linking it with the ideas of Augustus. Consequently, he decided on the plain of Troy as the site of the new city, and shortly the walls and portal towers rose from the ground.[1]

Then God appeared to him in a dream and commanded him to chose another site, viz., Byzantium at the entrance to the Bosphorus.[2] Its outstandingly suitable situation must have been patent to Constantine even when he awoke. Thus it came about that the lines of the walls at Troy were abandoned—they could still be seen standing there in the fifth century—and a start was made to extend Byzantium and make it beautiful. After building activities had been going on for a few years, the ceremonial founding of the city was carried out on May 11, 330; at the same time a gilded statue of Constantine was erected, holding the *Tychē* of the city in his right hand. The Emperor named it Anthusa, and marked the occasion by offering to God a "bloodless sacrifice"; meaning, probably, he made the ancient ceremonial harmless, and even sacred, by observing the communion of the Christian Lord's Supper in connection with it.

Many details have been handed down about the site of the city,[3] including the fact that Constantine drew the required inhabitants from other cities with more or less gentle compulsion in order to fill the vastly extended space. He contrived a "senate" out of Roman and other aristocratic families whom he made to come to his new city, and he put the populace on the same footing as that of Rome by providing for bread and games in Constantinople. A multitude of new public buildings, squares, pillared halls, baths, hippodromes, and palaces were erected, and ornamented with works of art plundered and gathered here from every quarter—a few remains may still be seen to-day. The frontage of the royal residence was along the

[1] Zosim. 2, 30, 1   Sozom. 2, 3, 2
[2] Sozom. 2, 3, 3   cf. *Cod. Theod.* 13, 5, 7; the city was founded "by God's command"
[3] Especially Malalas 13, p. 319–322   Sozom. 2, 3, 1–7   and Zosim. 2, 30–31

shore of the Sea of Marmora, and over the sea-gate was an inscription which proclaimed that Constantine had always worshipped the Godhead and had therefore been able to quench the fire lighted by his foes. Consequently Christ had made him lord of the whole world, and heartfelt praise was therefore due to Him.[1]

The Emperor undoubtedly wished that this city of his should be founded as a Christian city, and church historians are right, by and large, in asserting that he did not allow pagan sacrifices in Constantinople; instead, he built numerous houses of prayer and martyrs' chapels. The sites of public wells were graced with bronze statues of the Good Shepherd and Daniel in the Lions' Den. A pagan critic of Constantine bitterly deplores the transformation of a statue of Cybele into the figure of a woman engaged in prayer.[2]

The Emperor founded two large churches in his city. One was consecrated to the honour of the Holy Apostles, and he wished to be buried in the centre of this church;[3] the other was consecrated to "Holy Peace"—*Irene*. Augustus in Rome had dedicated a famous altar (*ara pacis*) to the Imperial Peace: and this was surely the model which Constantine followed in naming his Christian foundation. Both rulers knew that they had won peace for a distracted world, and consciously wished to bring that fact home to the people's understanding. Besides the two churches just mentioned numerous martyrs' chapels were erected both inside and outside the city, and a sanctuary dedicated to the Archangel Michael was built at the mouth of the Bosphorus.[4]

A resplendent church was also built in Nicomedia; and in Antioch there was erected a unique octagonal building in the centre of the city which was praised as a marvel of beauty.[5] Recently a small place of similar form has been excavated, and the influence of this style of architecture is unmistakable in the Cloister of Symeon at Djebel Sem'an.[6] Building activity became

[1] Mamboury and Wiegand, *Kaiserpaläste von Konstantinopel* 1934, 6–9
[2] Eus. *vita Const.* 3, 48. 49. 54　Sozom. 2, 3, 7　Zosim. 2, 31, 3
[3] Eus. *op. cit.* 4, 58–60
[4] *ibid.* 3, 48　Sozom. 2, 3, 8　also L. Deubner, *de incubatione*, p. 65
[5] Eus. *op. cit.* 3, 50　cf. the *Thirtieth Ann. Address*, 9, 14, 15
[6] Leclerq, *Dict.* 1, 2381　following Vogüé

particularly vigorous in the Holy Land. Not only did Count Josephus of Tiberias receive permission to build a church in his native city and to do the same in other places in Palestine[1]— the Emperor himself also intervened, and built basilicas on many sites held in special honour by Christians. A general instruction was issued to all bishops in every province diligently to restore in a worthy manner churches which had been destroyed, and to erect churches in places where they were needed; and to charge the necessary expenses to the government. Then came a special instruction to Makarios of Jerusalem with detailed directions for building a magnificent church over the site of Christ's sepulchre. A shrine of Aphrodite there was pulled down, and the cave beneath it in which Christ had been buried was opened to the air. A rotunda was then erected over the sacred site, and connected by a court with the rock of Golgotha and the basilica. Eusebius gives a detailed description of the whole, the traces of which can to-day only be followed with the greatest difficulty in the maze of the present Church of the Holy Sepulchre of which no summary account is possible.[2]

Whereas this building was directly due to Constantine's initiative, the ladies of the royal house gave the impetus to others. The queen-mother, Helena, travelled throughout the Holy Land when advanced in her seventies, and brought about the building of a church in Bethlehem over the cave in which Jesus was born: a short time ago its foundations were laid bare under the church of the present day which goes back to Justinian.[3] Helena had a church built also on the Mount of Olives, a basilica with a square forecourt surrounded by pillars as proved by the remains which have been rediscovered.[4] The oak of Mamre, where Moses long ago had entertained the Lord,[5] was regarded as a sacred place by pagans also, and when Constantine's mother-in-law, Eutropia, visited it, she recorded excitedly that idol images stood there and that bloody sacrifices were made. On receiving this news from her, the

---

[1] Epiph. *haer.* 30, 4, 1

[2] Eus. *vita Const.* 2, 46   3, 30–32   for description of the building, see 3, 33–40; cf. Heisenberg, *Grabeskirche und Apostelkirche,* and remarks thereon by G. Dalman, *Palästinajahrbuch,* 9 (1913), 98–123   Leclerq, *op. cit.* 7, 2312–2320

[3] P. Vincent, *Revue Biblique,* 45 (1936), 544–574   46 (1937), 93–121   Also A. Rücker, *Das Heilige Land,* 81 (1937), 41–52   See also *infra,* 315, n.2

[4] Leclerq, *op. cit.* 7, 2321   [5] Gen. 18: 1

Emperor commanded that the cult-structures be destroyed
and a Christian church erected; considerable remains of both
these buildings have lately come to light.[1]

Eusebius's list of the Constantine church-buildings is far
from being exhaustive. This fact is made plain not only by an
incidental remark that even in Heliopolis (Baalbek) a church
was built and provided, too, with the appropriate clergy by
the Emperor, but also the latter himself says that the accession
of crowds of new believers in Constantinople made it necessary
to build a larger number of churches, for use in which he
ordered from Eusebius fifty manuscript copies of the Bible.[2]
Not all these new buildings were paid for out of the royal
treasury; nevertheless it is indubitable that Constantine took
an active part in their erection.

If our extant records regarding the history of the Church in
the west were better than they are, we should probably find
plenty of evidence of Constantine's activity in forwarding the
building of churches in the west also. In any case, he founded
the Church of St. Peter in Rome, although it was only completed by his son Constans; and there is a certain degree of
probability that the oldest church of St. Paul there was built
at the same time.[3] The Roman *Book of the Popes* ascribes the
origin of several other basilicas to Constantine, viz., the Lateran
and St. Croce close by, St. Agnese Fuori, St. Lorenzo Fuori,
and finally the Church of the Martyrs, Peter and Marcellinus.
These still exist as ruins together with the mausoleum of
Helena on the Via Labicana near the Tor Pignattara in the
Campagna. Several churches outside Rome must be added: in
Ostia, Albano, Capua, and Naples.[4]

Archeological discovery has already shown that several of
these records are trustworthy, although many others have still
to be confirmed by modern methods. But even if it should be
necessary to make deletions here and there, the fact is beyond
doubt that Constantine, with his zeal for establishing and

---

[1] Eus. *vita Const.* 3, 51–53   cf. P. Rader in *Revue Biblique* 39 (1930), 84–117 199–
225   *Rivista di Archeologia Cristiana* 6 (1929), 249–312

[2] Eus. *vita Const.* 3, 58   4, 36

[3] Diehl, *Inscr. lat. christ. vet.* 1, n. 1752. 1753 and remarks thereon by Lietzmann,
Petrus u. Paulus, 2nd ed. 190. 218

[4] *Lib. pont.* 34, 9.   11. 21.   22–26.   28. 30.   31. 32.; cf. Duchesne, *Commentary*

uniting the Church from within, combined with it a concern for erecting worthy church buildings. The consecration of the Church of the Holy Sepulchre, as a worthy way of celebrating the thirtieth anniversary of his reign, and simultaneously as the occasion of a great synod of bishops on the model of Nicea, expresses symbolically what his efforts on behalf of the Church meant in relation to his policy for the Empire.

There is no need to discuss in any special way the weakness of the underlying paganism. As soon as state aid was no longer available, collapse followed immediately and of its own accord. The temples were not purposely destroyed, but the state did not prevent their ruin.[1] When it was appropriate to do so, the government stepped in, and took possession of roofing tiles or the valuable metal of bronze statues. Images of gods were brought from the provinces to Constantinople to ornament the public squares of the new capital with works of art. Nowhere was this a new proceeding, and many an earlier emperor had done it to a gross extent with the same object.[2] But now such conduct was agreeable to the Christians, who described what was done and added edifying comments.[3] Only a few shrines which had become the lurking-places of immoral cults were closed by the police or destroyed; e.g., in Jerusalem, Mamre, Aphaka in Phoenicea, and in Baalbek. There is no explanation why the temple of Asklepios on Aegaeae in Cilicia was razed to the ground.[4]

Any soothsayer who entered a private house for the purpose of divining the future by sacrifices was threatened with the penalty of death by fire. Nevertheless he was permitted to use divination in his official residence, and such a "consultation" was expressly ordained to take place, "according to ancient custom", in a state-building in the case of a stroke of lightning.[5] Otherwise, no trustworthy records are extant claiming that pagan cultus suffered in general any hindrance. When Eusebius asserts that the Emperor forbade sacrifices altogether, he is

---

[1] *Cod. Theod.* 15, 1, 3 must not be cited in this connection, as this law comes from Julian; cf. Mommsen, *a. l.*

[2] e.g., Nero cf. *Dio Chrys.* 31, 148   Pausanias 10, 7, 1   Rostovtzeff, *op. cit.* 2, 161. 164

[3] Eus. *vita Const.* 3, 54

[4] *ibid.* 3, 25. 52. 55. 56. 58   cf. the dedication of the Nile, 4, 25

[5] *Cod. Theod.* 9, 16, 1. 2 (A.D. 319) 16, 10, 1 (A.D. 320)   cf. 16, 10. 2

making an unjustifiable generalization, but it is certain that
he disliked all forms of witchcraft and the accompanying
sacrifices, and, on occasion, he was not afraid to intermit
customs sanctified by ancient usage.[1]

It was not permitted to hang any picture of him in a pagan
temple.[2] When the city of Hispellum, near Assisi, expressed a
desire to be recognized as the capital of Umbria and to be
allowed to institute its own games, Constantine granted the
request and gave the name "Flavia Constans" to it. Now, to
institute games it was necessary to have a temple and to
celebrate its day of dedication: this was indeed a deeply-rooted
custom. Accordingly, the Emperor decreed the erection and
dedication of a temple in honour of his, the Flavian, family.
So far everything followed the usual course. At this point,
however, he added the condition that the temple dedicated to
his name must "not be defiled with any fraudulent superstition",
i.e., he forbade the customary priestly ceremonies and sacrifices.
He seems to have set down similar conditions when the name
of the city of Cirta was changed to Constantine.[3]

In these ways it becomes plain once more—and inscriptions
in stone bear out what the extant epistles of Constantine have
to say—that although he did much to spare the traditional
pagan customs, nevertheless he gave official expression, and
this in forthright terms, to his disapproval of these outworn
religions. Conversely, towns with an explicitly Christian
population could reckon on official recognition just on this
account.[4] Granted that at the dedication of Constantinople, he
had set up his statue with the nimbus of the sun god round its
head, and placed it on top of a porphyry pillar; but this statue
had been erected earlier in Ilion, and therefore dated from an
older period. Similarly, the ceremony in honour of the "Tyche"
of Constantinople was a concession to ancient usage which,
however, was weakened by using a Christian form of dedica-

---

[1] See the preceding note, and Eus. *vita Const.* 4, 25, 1   Zosim. 2, 29, 5; further
notes in J. Geffcken, *Ausgang d. Heidentums*, 94f.

[2] Eus., *vita Const.* 4, 16

[3] Dessau, *Inscr. lat. sel.* n. 705. Aurelius Victor Cæsar, 40, 28   together with
Mommsen, *Ges. Schriften*, 8, 24ff.

[4] Dessau, *op. cit.* 6091: Orcistus in Phrygia. Eus. *vita Const.* 4, 37–38   Sozom.
2, 5, 7–8   Maiumas in Palestine

tion.[1] Eusebius tells of a statue of Constantine[2] in Rome bearing a crucifix on its lance and with an inscription to the effect that he had freed the city from tyrants by virtue of this sign of salvation. The data afforded by Eusebius of Cæsarea in regard to such matters can be tested to-day to a large extent, and they have always proved trustworthy; but in the above instance Eusebius was not speaking from first-hand knowledge for he never visited Rome, and mistakes have always to be reckoned with.

This item of information, however, gives us the opportunity of discussing the Emperor's public statements about his attitude to religion. The earliest panegyrists always make it appear quite frankly that the ancient gods were friendly to Constantine, and gave him their blessing. Apollo crowned him with the laurel which promised him a long reign; and when Constantine visited Autun, all the images of the gods were brought in procession to meet him.[3] That was in the last few years before the battle of the Milvian Bridge: it follows that homage could be done to him freely at that time in pagan forms. Then came the great occasion which decided the rulership of the west, agreed upon by both pagans and Christians as due to divine aid, as we have already seen.[4] Is there any truth at the bottom of these legends? In particular, is it right to declare that, before the battle of Ponte Molle, Constantine had already inscribed on his soldiers' shields the monogram of Christ?

In the year 315, on the occasion of celebrating the tenth anniversary of the reign, the Roman senate erected the Arch of Constantine. The inscription[5] ascribes the victory over Maxentius to the "inspiration of the godhead", and the figures in relief depict the army marching forward under the protection of the sun god, the *Sol Invictus*, who had been the protecting deity of the Empire since the time of Aurelian. Nowhere is there the monogram of Christ on the soldiers' shields,[6] not even in the scene of the battle of Ponte Molle. This triumphal arch is

[1] Malalas, 13, p. 320, ed. Dindorf and *supra*, p. 145

[2] Eus. *vita Const.* 1, 40   *H.E.* 9, 9, 10–11

[3] *Panegyrici*, 6 (7), 21, 4   and 5 (8), 8, 4   [4] *vide supra*, 74

[5] Dessau, *op. cit.* 694

[6] L'Orange, *Spätantike Reliefs des Constantinsbogens* (*Studien zur spätantiken Kunstgeschichte* 10) 1938

an official monument, not erected by Constantine, but by the senate; it reproduced therefore the pagan conception of the miraculous happening. It used the language of art to express the same ideas as the official panegyrists poured forth in echoing phrases in A.D. 312 and 321. But whereas these latter spoke, in agreement with the inscription or in general terms, of the "godhead", i.e., the god of the pale monotheism of late antiquity, the sculptors calmly made reliefs of the sun god, and he was to be found depicted on contemporary coins minted in workshops operating in Constantine's sphere.

Hence the conclusion has been drawn that the Emperor stood above party, and that he was indifferent whether the godhead in which he himself believed, was worshipped under the name of the pagan sun god or under that of the God of the Christians, i.e., that he held back from publicly intervening on either side.[1] In this case what Lactantius says about the monogram on the soldiers' shields would be a legend contradicted by the plain facts. But Constantine's own pronouncements during this critical period completely destroy the theories of his religious neutrality.[2]

It is true that in the Settlement of Milan, made in common with Licinius, the record speaks only of tolerance towards Christians and equal freedom for all, in order that "upon His heavenly throne" "the highest godhead, to whose worship we dedicate ourselves in freedom of soul", may be gracious unto us, and the "divine favour which we have experienced in such high matters", may also continue to abide with us to the welfare of the state.[3] But already, in writing to the bishop of Carthage, Constantine had spoken of the "lawful and most holy 'catholic' worship, and had praised him in the name of the godhead of the great God". He laid it down to the proconsul of Africa in A.D. 312–313, that "the worship in which the profoundest awe is felt towards the holiest heavenly Power" must be protected in lawful ways, for He had bestowed exceptional well-being on the whole Roman empire; and he

[1] M. Schiller, *Gesch. d. röm. Kaiserzeit*, 2, 204ff.   Geffcken, *Ausgang des Heiden tums*, 92. 96, is more cautious
[2] cf. Lietzmann, *Der Glaube Konstant. d. Grosse* in Berliner Sitzungsb., 1937, 263–275
F. Stähelin, *Konst. d. Gr. u. d. Christent.* in Zeitschr. f. schweiz. Gesch., 1937, 385–417
[3] Lactant. *mort.* 48, 2. 3. 11

named the "catholic" clergy as responsible for this worship.[1]

To reach greater clarity, it is necessary to read the letter sent to the African governor Ablabius in A.D. 314, which contains instructions for the synod of Arles. It concludes by saying: "For as I am convinced that you also are a worshipper of the most high God (Ablabius was in fact a Christian), I therefore acknowledge frankly to Your Excellency that I consider it wrong to regard lightly quarrels and strifes of that kind (i.e., re Donatism), for, on account of these matters, the most high God may be wrath not only with mankind in general, but also with me to whom He has entrusted by His divine will the rule of the whole world (including the eastern region once ruled by Licinius) in order that I should watch over it; and He will threaten us with calamity if He be provoked. Nay, I shall not be really and fully secure and able to trust in God Almighty's goodness which freely dispenses happiness and salvation until all men offer worship in harmony and brotherliness to the all-holy God in the prescribed forms of the 'catholic' religion. Amen."

That is quite unambiguous. Constantine confesses himself a Christian to a Christian official; he knows that it was the Christian God who had granted him the victory over Maxentius, and was giving him now the prospect of conquering Licinius; but requiring in return watchfulness for the well-being of the church catholic. Writing on another occasion,[2] he deplored that these disputes "give those men (i.e., pagans) reason to scoff whose souls are strangers to this all-holy worship". In August, 314, he reminded the Donatists who were making their appeal to the royal court that "you are asking me to pronounce judgment, who myself await the judgment of Christ". These are plain confessions of Christian faith reaching back quite closely in time to the battle with Maxentius, which battle was itself regarded as proving the favouring grace of the Christian God. In view of these declarations of the Emperor's, the story recorded by Lactantius cannot be held impossible. Something of the sort must have happened. We know to-day how Constantine himself thought. Nor is it surprising in itself,

[1] Eus. *H.E.* 10, 6, 1. 5 7, 1–2 Letter to Ælasius (=Aflasius=Ablabius) in Optat. appendix, 204–206 Ziwsa. v. Soden, *Donatismus*, n. 8. 9. 14. *Pauly-W.* I, 103

[2] Eus. *H.E.* 10, 5, 22 Optat. appendix, 209, 22 Ziwsa (v. Soden, n. 15. 18)

for in any case Christianity was not strange to his father's house, as one of his half-sisters bore the indubitably Christian name of Anastasia. It follows that he may have been inclined towards the new faith at quite an early age, and his successes taught him to worship Christ as his protector.

But he did not force on others his own form of belief in God and providence, and he even tolerated the ideas of the Roman senate with a breadth of mind which he maintained till his death. This spirit breathes in the great encyclical which he sent to all the provinces[1] after conquering Licinius; here he depicts his own religious evolution, confesses himself a Christian, recommends this faith to all, but is very emphatic that no one should be compelled; each might live without restraint in accordance with his own convictions. It is in this temper of mind that we find the clue to understanding conduct which sometimes seems self-contradictory.

The stampings on his coins also are to be evaluated from the same standpoint, though this has often been wrongly done. At first, they remained in the usual forms, and the figures of *Sol Invictus* as well as that of *Juppiter Conservator* recur continually; indeed as late as A.D. 317, when Crispus and the young Constantine were named Cæsars, the coins minted for the occasion bore the sun god both in the figure and the superscript. In A.D. 315 a signet-cutter in Pavia placed a cross beside the figure of the god,[2] but that was only his personal confession of faith to which he ventured to give expression, trusting that Constantine would not object; but he did not repeat it in the next issue of the same coins. More significance attaches to the fact that after A.D. 319 in Constantine's sphere of authority, coins were issued simultaneously from several minting places bearing a cross on the altar of victory instead of the usual signs; or else (A.D. 321–327) the monogram of Christ was placed near the military standard.[3] On rare occasions, the cross is found on the Emperor's helmet, and Eusebius declares that that is what he wore in fact.[4]

---

[1] Eus. *vita Const.* 2, 48–60　cf. especially 56 and 60

[2] J. Maurice, *Numismatique Constantinienne*, 2, 248f. plate 7, 17

[3] e.g., Maurice, *op. cit.* 2　plate 8, 2 (259)　8, 7–10 (264)

[4] Eus. *vita Const.* 1, 31　Maurice, *op. cit.* 2, plate 10, 4. 5 (287, 336)　Delbrück, *Kaiserporträts*, plate 1, 11. 12. p. 72

Nothing of this, however, proves that orders were received from the Emperor, but only suggests encouragement in high places of what masters of the mint in different centres adopted according to their own judgment, and in very varying degrees. The figures themselves at this date were religiously neutral; the ancient gods disappeared. Only in Licinius's sphere do we still find, even after A.D. 319, a *Juppiter Conservator*, and a sacrifice figured in the year 322. As against this, the known western series occur without Christian counter-marks.[1] The continually growing antagonism between the two rulers was expressed on the coinage less by means of the symbols of religion than in the fact that Constantine, as formerly, before the war against Maxentius, once more displayed his gallery of legalized ancestors: Constantius, Maximianus, Herculius, and Claudius the conqueror of the Goths.[2] After his victory, and to mark the twentieth anniversary of his reign, coins were issued bearing the idealized head of the Emperor (and the princes) with eyes raised to heaven in prayer: here the prototype was the figure of Alexander apotheosized by the Diadochi.[3] Eusebius describes this "attitude of prayer", and says that Constantine caused representations of himself with uplifted eyes and hands to be placed over many town-gates.[4] Naturally, he was praying to the Christian God—but that was not explicit, and a pagan observer could interpret the figure in his own way.

Only once in minting coins did Constantine abandon his reticence: in the year 326/327 he had coins stamped with an abbreviated form of a triumph approaching his palace. These coins were minted in the capital. The *labarum*, decorated with the sign of Christ and the figures of the Emperor and the two princes, stand victoriously over a dragon writhing on the ground.[5] But this stamp was not adopted by the other mints, and throughout the following years we find again only the cross and monogram as the voluntary additions of the masters of the mint. The founding of Constantinople

---

[1] H. v. Schoenebeck, *Beiheft der Klio*, 1938, prints the material

[2] Maurice, *op. cit.* 1, 211ff. 313ff. 325. 406. 444

[3] K. Regling, *Die antiken Münzen*, 1922, 39

[4] Maurice, *op. cit.* vol. 2, plate, 17, 18 (599); vol. 3, plate 3. 3. 10. 11. 21. 23. 24 (59–77) Eus. *vita Const.* 4, 15

[5] Maurice, *op. cit.* 2, plate 15, 7 (506) Eus. *vita Const.* 3, 3

never gave rise to a Christian transformation of the figures on coins.

A change was made only after the Emperor had passed away. As custom required, his sons "consecrated" him, i.e., caused him to be elevated towards heaven. Coins were minted commemorating the ceremony. The obverse depicts him with head veiled, and the reverse shows him on a bier drawn by horses climbing up to heaven; and the hand of God is stretched out through the clouds to receive him. The meaning was clear to both pagan and Christian, and shortly afterwards the imagery was copied on Christian sarcophagi as a representation of Elijah's ascent to heaven.[1] About the same time, i.e., shortly before or after Constantine's death, coins were issued with the monogram of Christ upon the battle-standard, and this design was then favoured by his sons, and later became normal.[2] The end which was put in this way to Constantine's self-restraint went hand in hand with a change of the entire policy in regard to religion.

From all these facts it is plain that, while the coinage gives valuable particulars about Constantine's policy, it cannot be regarded as revealing his personal attitude and feeling. To study these, we must keep to what he put down in writing, and this bears its witness with a welcome clarity. The time is past when these important documents could be thrust aside as forgeries; their complete genuineness has been proved by critical examination of both form and content; and Eusebius, who has preserved the majority of them, has been shown to be a reliable witness, writing with a faithful hand.

He tells us that Constantine in his later years composed exhortations of a theological character, sometimes during sleepless nights. They were written by him in Latin, and put into Greek by skilled translators. Then he read them, sometimes before large assemblies, sometimes before smaller circles of people of the court; and gained dutiful, but hardly sincere, approbation.[3] Eusebius, in his biography of Constantine, gives,

[1] Maurice, *op. cit.* 2   plate 17, 26 (607f.)   3. plate 3, 26 (82)   8, 27 (217) 10, 28 (282).   Eus., *vita Const.* 4, 73

[2] Maurice, *op. cit.* 2. plate 6, 26 (193ff.)   Gnecchi, *Medaglioni romani*, Vol. 1 plates 9, 12   13, 11   14, 1. 9   19, 8. 12   30, 9–11   32, 12   33, 2. 3 and oft.

[3] Eus. *vita Const.* 4, 29. 32. 55

as an example of the Emperor's writing in this sphere, a discourse delivered on a Good Friday and entitled "An Address to the Congregation of the Saints". Elsewhere a discourse to the synod of Nicea[1] has been preserved, and this bears equally the stamp of authenticity.[2] If we add the numerous statements of a religious and theological nature in his letters and edicts, we shall have a considerable body of material from which to draw when seeking to understand his thoughts about God and Christ, about the world and the Church.

The key to Constantine's general bearing was the consciousness, beginning from early years, that God had destined him for high things, and therefore granted him special protection. It is scarcely credible that, while he was a youth, the God who directed his ways and granted him aid, was regarded by him as Apollo or the *Sol Invictus* of the Empire;[3] although the pagan orators at festivals, and the artists who worked on the Arch of Constantine, held this belief. To him, even in those days, such names were scarcely other than references to the one divine Being of whom he had learned in his parents' home as the God of the Christians. For we have already seen that his parents gave one of his half-sisters the name of Anastasia,[4] a fact which shows that a Christian atmosphere prevailed in the house. But he was also aware that a genuinely Christian understanding was lacking to him in his youth, nor had it been acquired through his education; God Himself had granted it to him in mature manhood,[5] and this means nothing else than that he had received a revelation. When he set out to conquer the entire Roman world, he already felt himself to be fighting on behalf of the God of the Christians, and he was true to this belief till the end of his life.

In statements made in his later·years, he explains precisely how the error of polytheism led the peoples into darkness and moral chaos, and perverted the idea of a just retribution into poetic mythology. From this error sprang the wrong-doings of

[1] Gelasius, *H.E.* 2, 7. pp. 46–53. ed. Heinemann
[2] Loeschcke in *Rhein. Museum f. Philologie*, 61 (1906), 57–61   E. Schwartz, in *Pauly-W.* 6, 1412   1427
[3] A. Piganiol, *L'empereur Constantin*, 50 and remarks thereon by H. Grégoire in *Byzantion*, 7 (1932), 645–652
[4] *Amm. Marc.* 26, 6, 14   *Chron. min.*, 1, 8, 29 ed. Mommsen
[5] *Good Friday Ad.* 11, 1. 2   p. 166, 10–15 Heikel

princes and evil for the entire world. The coming of Christ brought justice and peace on earth when he founded the Church as the temple of sublime virtue. But the world rose up against it till there was civil war and persecution of Christians.[1] At length Constantine received a divine commission to carry out God's judgment[2] by liberating the peoples from servitude to the Devil, by uniting them in the worship of the Christians' God, and so healing the whole world of the severe wounds suffered earlier;[3] indeed, converting it.

His attacks on polytheism and his reference to the Sibyl as a witness to Christian truth are hints that he had actually read Lactantius's *Institutes*,[4] the theological *magnum opus* dedicated to him. Constantine's proof of the existence of God, based on the teleological order of the world and of the human organism,[5] like his polemic against the idea of fate and of chance,[6] followed the familiar lines of Stoic thought. He continually repeated his confession of unshakable faith in divine "providence" (*pronoia*) which ruled over everything, and by which he himself had been chosen as an instrument in God's hands: he knew himself the "servant of God"—a term which he was never tired of using, and which consequently Eusebius felt it possible to use in his jubilee address.[7]

By virtue of his divine commission, he felt himself bound to exercise concern for the Church. To strengthen it and give it peace seemed to him necessary to complete the security and unity of the Roman empire as won by military and political means. As a consequence, he felt it was legitimate that he should take an active part in the discussions at the synod of Nicea;[8] and for the same reason he felt justified in intervening yet further in church disputes. From this standpoint also, we can understand that strangely interesting document[9] which

[1] *ibid.* 1, 3   3, 2–4   4, 1–3   10, 1–2. 22–26
[2] *ibid.* 25, 5   p. 191, 28 Heikel
[3] Address given in Gelasius 2, 7, 38   *Doc.* 17, 1 (Athan. 3, 32 Opitz)   *Doc.* 27, 6. 7   (Athan. 3, 59)   Letter in Eus. *vita Const.* 4, 9 (p. 121 Heikel)
[4] Lactant. *Instit.* 1, 1, 13   7, 27, 11
[5] *Good Friday Ad.* 8   Letter in Eus. *vita Const.* 2, 48, 58   Speech in Gelasius, 2, 7, 33
[6] *Good Friday Ad.* 6–7   [7] Eus. *Thirtieth Ann. Ad.* 7, 12 p. 215, 17 Heikel
[8] Speech in Eus. *vita Const.* 3, 12   Speech in Gelasius, 2, 7, 3–41   *Doc.* 27, 7 (in Athan. 3, 59 ed. Opitz)
[9] Eus. *ibid.* 4, 9–13

he wrote to the Persian king, Shapur II, and in which he both extolled the excellences of Christianity and also urgently commended to him the Christians living in Persia. Church policy was for him an inseparable part of State policy and the latter, once again, was a divinely ordained responsibility. At a banquet on a certain occasion he said to the bishops who had been invited:[1] "You have been installed bishops for the inner affairs of the Church, and I have been installed bishop by God for its outer affairs." That describes his view exactly; and he spent no precious time trying to draw a precise line between inner and outer.

The royal bishop was by no means unwilling to go beyond general discussions. He commended the glory of the Church eloquently, instructed Arius in the unity of the divine essence (*ousia*), and explained exactly how the begetting of the Son implied no lessening of the being of the Father. Father and Son were related as cause and effect (but when he said this, the debarred description of the Son as a second God slipped in).[2] The Logos who had proceeded from the Father according to His providential will was the ruler of the world, and the cause of all existence and life in it. For our sakes He had accepted "from a virgin the abode of a pure body", and become man. He had gathered round Himself the "wisest of all men", viz., the twelve apostles, and had preached the law of divine righteousness, proving its heavenly authority by miracles. The Church preserved this law, and to obey it meant salvation for all men.[3] Christianity was life by faith in God, sympathy with the unfortunate, unalloyed uprightness, purity and holiness: in short, the exercise of every virtue, Christ having taught and exemplified them. Christ was our Saviour on account of His teaching,[4] and Christianity was the moral life keeping always in view the retributive righteousness of God.[5]

[1] ibid. 4, 24 cf. 1. 44, 1

[2] Speech in Gelasius 2, 7, 6   Good Friday Ad. 1, 4   Eus. vita Const. 2, 55, 2 Doc. 27, 3. 8   34, 14 (Athan. 3, 58. 59. 71 Opitz)   Good Friday Ad. 9, 3; 11, 8 (163, 20; 168, 17 Heikel)

[3] Good Friday Ad. 11, 3–5   Gelasius, ibid. 2, 7, 13

[4] Good Friday Ad. 15. 23. Gelasius, ibid. 2, 7, 4   13. 21. 25   Letters in Eus. vita Const. 2, 59   4, 10, 2–3   Doc. 27, 5   (Athan. 3, 59 Opitz)

[5] Good Friday Ad. 23, 3   Gelasius, ibid. 2, 7, 1. 21. 25

It was a theology of a fairly amateurish sort,[1] and can be re-garded as a kind of dilute apologetics. Its principles are derived from the spiritual tone of the silver age of antiquity, and its Christian character is given mainly by its outer form of words. It may well be that Constantine had read his Bible, but he read it with the spectacles of the general ethic of his age, and did not understand it. He says, for example, that Jesus raised Lazarus "by using a small staff",[2] but we remark that Constantine did not derive his information from the wording of the Gospel, but from pictorial representations of the incident which never failed to show the miracle-working staff in the Lord's hand. But he took pleasure in his knowledge of theology, and was plainly proud of it. Further, it is unquestionable that he was quite serious about these matters, for they laid bare to him the secret of his own life, the divine origin of his mission. It is perfectly credible that he instituted divine service in his palace, and prayed daily at set times. Similarly at an earlier date, he was accustomed to beseech God's help in prayer before he took his stand in front of his tent and gave the order to attack. His sermon on Good Friday ends with an inspiring hymn on prayer made strong by faith.[3]

Of course he was a despot, a man of political affairs without softness when it was a matter of attaining his purpose; nor did he shrink from imposing a harsh death-penalty. Maximianus, Herculius and Licinius left him no alternative to ordering their execution. Valens, considered by Licinius in the final battle to be worthy of the part of a Cæsar, had to die like his successor Martinian at the fall of his master. There appears to-day no point in the killing of Licinius's son whom he had already degraded to slavery;[4] the death of Crispus and of Fausta is unrelieved tragedy, and these bloody doings were followed by a long series of nameless persons deprived of life by the Emperor's command.[5] Is it possible for a Christian to act like this?

[1] The self-consistency of theology in all Constantine's utterances shows that the various passages really go back to him and not to theological secretaries; cf. also note 2 below on Lazarus.

[2] Eus. *vita Const.* 1, 32, 3   4, 17   Gelasius, *ibid.* 2, 7, 41   For story of Lazarus vide *ibid.* 2, 7, 15

[3] Eus. *vita Const.* 4, 14. 17. 22   2, 12   *Good Friday Ad.* 26

[4] Seeck, in *Pauly-W.* 13, 231

[5] Eutrop. 10, 6, 3 "and many friends"

There is no need to go to Philip of Spain or to Calvin to obtain the affirmative answer of history to this and similar questions. An ambitious man, who knows himself dedicated to a work given him by God, sees good and evil in the light of his goal. He is easily seized by a dæmonism which drags his conscience from the straight path. It has been so in every age, and, it may be added, other breaches of the propriety and ethics proper to the Church prove nothing against the sincerity of a Christian conviction. Works and faith have gone separate ways even in the case of more devout Christians, and Constantine could rely upon pardon at a time when, already, the Church had had to grant it ever more widely; indeed he could look forward to receiving baptism and with it the forgiveness of all his sins. His enemies, in any case, have never accused him of hypocrisy, but of a conscience genuinely troubled by sin.[1] Hence the logical inference, however reluctantly drawn, is that he was a genuinely religious person.

A quick change of mood was characteristic of him as a man, and appears as an irrational element in his statecraft; the documents at times speak frankly of his sudden outbursts of blazing anger.[2] That is why Athanasius, shortly after he had been received with all respect, had to go the following morning, unheard, into exile; and why Crispus and, soon after, Fausta were put to death. But he was no bloodthirsty savage. Rather it is quite likely that he afterwards regretted his orders; and it is certain that in the last years of his life, he had a definite dislike of the death sentence. Eusebius ventures even to blame him slightly on this account,[3] believing it was for this reason that governors no longer dared to deal sternly with law breakers, and that this led to many perplexities. In the same connection, we hear complaints that the Emperor did not exercise the necessary caution towards the swarm of opportunist Christians who pressed round him, and that, as a consequence, he was led to issue many wrong regulations.

All this may be quite true, similarly to the edifying details which Eusebius records out of his personal intercourse with His Majesty; at least we gain some idea of what the Emperor

[1] Zosim. 2, 29, 3 Sozom. 1, 5 Julian Cæsares, 336 a b
[2] Athan. *apol.* 87, 2   [3] Eus. *vita Const.* 4, 31. 54

wished to look like to his Christian subjects. An estimate of
his character does not depend on that sort of thing; much more
to the point is the passage at the end of Eusebius's *Jubilee
Address*.[1] The passage may sound like unworthy flattery, but
here the writer grasps firmly the consciousness that pervaded
the Emperor's life. In this passage Eusebius summons the
whole world to give praise with one voice to Almighty God, to
the only-begotten Son and Saviour, and to the Emperor as
His vicegerent on earth; yes, the peace on earth that Jesus had
brought from heaven[2] in the days of Augustus, Constantine
intended to bring to full perfection in the Roman empire.

[1] Eus. *Thirtieth Ann. Ad.* 10, p. 223, 9–11 Heikel
[2] Eus. *Praepar. Evang.* 1, 4, 3. 4   5, 1, 5   *Dem. Evang.* 7, 2, 22   8, 4, 13   9, 17, 18

Chapter Six

THE SPIRIT OF THE AGE OF CONSTANTINE

CONSTANTINE WAS BORN IN THE WESTERN HALF OF THE Empire, and it was in the Rhineland that he spent the years of crucial importance to him as a statesman and a soldier. The impressive basilica at Trèves still stands as a vivid reminder of his fertile genius as a young man. But it was in the east that he developed into one of the greatest emperors in the history of the world. He first went to the orient while still a growing youth, and there he made his home when he had become a victorious ruler. In the west, panegyrics were |addressed to him only on ceremonial occasions; but the Greek east produced a Christian biographer, who dutifully presented his records in the literary form of an appreciation, but in doing so never forgot that he was a scientific historian.

That biographer was Eusebius, bishop of Cæsarea, a man who may be regarded, in a certain sense, as representative of the era of Constantine. The changes that were taking place in those days are faithfully reflected in the writings which were his main life's work. His words re-echo both the joys which then filled successful men and the high hopes with which his contemporaries looked forward into the future. We must start from this general position to gain a true estimate of him. In this way, it will be easy to avoid the temptation of judging Eusebius, as one attractive but not impartial critic has done[1] as "the first, thoroughly dishonest and unfair historian of ancient times". No greater wrong could be done to this honourable man.[2]

He came from humble parentage, and grew up in and along with the library which Pamphilus, his rich patron, was building up in Cæsarea out of the ruins of the collection founded by Origen and destroyed in the persecution under Decius. He was trained here in philology, and, together with his master, collated and corrected manuscripts of the Bible: documents

[1] J. Burckhardt, *Die Zeit Constantins* (Krönersche Ausg.) 362
[2] Of fundamental importance is E. Schwartz's article in *Pauly-W.* 6, 1370–1439

still survive bearing witness to this activity of his.[1] Also it was while librarian here that he learned the value of writings coming down from the early church, and this led him to undertake his own labours. Here also he lived continually surrounded by the spirit of Origen, in appreciation and defence of whom he wrote his first work (in common with Pamphilus), the *Apology* for the great scholar.

When his spiritual father, after whom he called himself "the son of Pamphilus", had suffered death by martyrdom on February 6, 310, Eusebius became heir of the tradition of solid learning which had been embodied in him. He published a collection of Origen's letters and wrote a biography of Pamphilus. At the same time, he published the first of the two works which have made his name world-famous, viz., the *Chronicon* (a history of the world to A.D. 328). Hippolytus of Rome had already published a chronological sketch of general history in the year 234,[2] and still earlier, in A.D. 221, Julius Africanus of Alexandria had brought out a similar book which served as pattern to all future works of the same character, and to a large extent as their basis. Unfortunately it has perished, and can only be partially and with difficulty recovered from citations and parallels.[3] But these show that it put the numerous historical dates of the various peoples in a continuous series of years, beginning with the creation of the world, the incarnation of Christ in the year 5500 of that era. Following Daniel 9: 24 he therefore expected the Last Day in the 6000th year after the Creation i.e. A.D. 500.[4] Thus he retained the apocalyptic hope, but in a form that ceased to be a drag on the Church as it developed. That was an advantage as against the chronography worked out by a certain Judas,[5] of whom nothing else is now known, but whose reckoning of time was based on the same passage in Daniel. According to this scheme, the advent of the Anti-Christ and therefore the beginning of the Last Age, was calculated to take place shortly after A.D. 202.

Eusebius deserves applause for having liberated Christian

[1] Signatures on Codices Q, Sinaiticus, Patmensis, and Syro-Hexaplar; cf. Harnack, *Altchristl. Litt.* 1, 543–545
[2] See Vol. 2, 245
[3] Fragments in Routh, *Reliquiae Sacrae*, 2nd ed. 2, 238–309
[4] *ibid.* 306 and Georgios Syncellos, 614, ed. Bonn   [5] Eus. *H.E.* 6, 7

chronography from the bonds of apocalypticism, and for basing it on purely logical foundations. He refused any traffic with calculations having an arbitrary bias, and also proved that the creation of the world could not be fixed to the year. He criticized other suggestions of Africanus,[1] and based his system on an era beginning with Abraham (2016 B.C.), his argument being that only from the time of this patriarch was Biblical chronology assured and free from the inconsistency of the textual tradition. As distinct from Africanus, he dismissed the fateful passage in Daniel; and calculations as to the Last Day had no place in his system of chronology.[2] Naturally, he was not lacking in a theological teleology, but this was confined to a proof based on prophecy appealing to what critical readers would accept as reasonable, and, by a comparison with familiar works of secular writers, he made plain to such readers the age in which the predictions of Moses and the other prophets were spoken.

In carrying out his purpose, Eusebius used a keen eye in searching out the best sources, and was especially wary of admitting and dating without proof matters otherwise unknown. In this way, he handed down to future ages, including our own, much valuable material in trustworthy form. The *Chronicon* has survived only in an Armenian translation and one in Latin prepared by Jerome, both going back to an edition revised probably after Eusebius's death. In this edition the substance is left unchanged, but it is re-arranged to fit into a conventional series in which the rulers are divided up into neat tables of names. In this way, history was given a spurious exactness which was altogether remote from Eusebius himself. Nevertheless these translations preserve valuable sources for historians to-day.

Eusebius always showed a strong liking for the method of proof from prophecy. He lived in an era when the Church had to defend itself from Porphyry's criticism, and when it expected to win the day by expounding the text of the Bible philologically and by using a scholarly chronology. With this end in view, Eusebius wrote a *General Elementary Introduction*, of which the

---

[1] Eus. *chron. armen.* 36, 47, ed. Karst
[2] Eus. *Dem. evang.* 8, 2, 55–66   *chron. armen.* 2, 3, ed. Karst

second part is extant.[1] We see here, how, in comparison with Jewish exegesis, the Christian way of expounding the message of the prophets was applied to the text. Eusebius expanded these preliminary studies at a later date into a great work in two parts, viz., *The Preparation for the Gospel*, and *The Proof of the Gospel*. The form of apologetics found in the ancient Greek church reached its highest point in Eusebius. Those ideas which had been full of vital energy in the past were now combined by this resourceful and learned man into a whole in a practical way, and given a scholarly basis on which facts and arguments were brought forward that overwhelmed by their very plenitude. It is obvious on every side that the author of this work had access to an incomparable library, and that he had made use of it with outstanding skill.

Eusebius provided in these writings the reply to the anti-christian work of Porphyry, and did so in a form which presented the case objectively. It is quite amusing on occasion to see how Eusebius takes his opponent's explanations, and turns them to his own advantage. Eusebius describes the self-con-tradictory character of polytheism, and goes on to give the theological explanation of the plan whose basis he had demon-strated in the *Chronicon*. The proof was that the best Greek philosophers, Plato in particular, had borrowed their pro-foundest thought from Moses and the prophets. The *Demon-stratio* is directed against Jewish objections to the Gospel. He wrests the Old Testament from the Jews and proves its universal significance. This significance validates the use of prophecy to prove the main heads of Christian doctrine, and to sub-stantiate the earthly life of the incarnate Logos. Eusebius used the Old Testament to develop the idea of a world-wide religion before Moses. The idea had been misconstrued by the Jews, but was brought to its fullness by Christianity. It consisted in the true worship of God brought about by the Logos. That worship, on the one hand, was seen in a manner of life which freed men from the dominance of the passions by ascetic training; in this life also, overflowing heavenly love lifted them out of the world and all its bonds; such men were raised to

[1] Known as "*Eclogae Propheticae*" (ed. Gaisford) 1842   For the following remarks, cf. H. G. Opitz. *Eus. v. Caes. als. Theologe, ZNW.*, 1935, 1–19

Christian perfection as supermen dedicated to God. On the other hand, there was the case of the great mass of Christians, in whom every earthly relationship and activity was penetrated with a devout spirit, whose influence was seen at given days and hours in asceticism and in listening to the word of God.[1]

A comparison of the Christian ideal of life with that of contemporary philosophers shows to a large extent the same fundamental principles; but what according to Plotinus and Porphyry was the privilege of a small circle of spiritual aristocrats,[2] was to be found amongst the Christians as a mode of life for the great masses, indeed as a means needed to transform the whole world. Even the perfection of an ascetic recluse was not reserved for the spiritually *élite*, but could be reached by the most unpretentious of men—as the facts proved. The apologists of the second century had directed attention to this difference.[3] An apologetic polemic written by Eusebius is extant, in which he demolishes the apotheosis of Apollonius of Tyana by Hierokles of Bithynia, a governor who was hostile to Christianity. The great polemic against Porphyry would have been of greater value to us, but it has been lost, like everything else bearing this name.[4]

The extant fragments of a discussion between Eusebius and Porphyry are concerned with inquiries into the differences between the gospel writers, especially *re* the genealogies of Jesus, and the story of the Resurrection. Here we find the beginnings of the problem of harmonizing the Gospels, of explaining all their inconsistencies; everything was brought to bear that keen minds and scholarship could levy. "Harmonistics" enjoyed in the fourth century a success which was partly justified, and the nineteenth century would probably have been better advised if it had been willing to leave well alone.

There is no extant continuous commentary on any gospel, nor is it likely that Eusebius expounded any document in the New Testament. But he had worked through the Psalms and Isaiah, perhaps also Jeremiah and Ezekiel, adding copious explanations. These, however, have only survived in small pieces and still await editing by scholars. On the other hand,

---

[1] Eus. *Dem. Evang.* 1, 8, 1–4   [2] *vide supra*, 38f., 42, 27
[3] *vide* Vol. 2, 184   [4] *vide supra*, 44

a gazetteer of Biblical sites has come down to our day; it rests on knowledge of the best quality and is of the greatest service. The gospels were intelligently divided into chapters by the school of scribes in Cæsarea, and the system spread. When used in combination with paragraphs giving summaries, it became easily possible to find parallel passages in the gospels. The system passed over into Syriac and Latin manuscripts, and was known as the Eusebian canons, and when they came to be decorated by artists, they won their place in the general history of art. Nevertheless, these are labours of only secondary importance.

The other principal work of world-wide renown existing alongside of, and arising from, the labour which Eusebius gave to the *Chronicon*, is his *Church History*. This is not a history in the same sense as those of the major and minor historians of the ancient world who used the art of writing history in order to exhibit their literary skill; rather it is of a new genus, its nearest relatives being among the learned and widely published collective works on the history of physics or philosophy such as were written by Pliny, Aelian, and Diogenes Laertius.[1] Eusebius made his purpose quite plain in the very preface to his book, viz., he would make it plain who succeeded the Apostles in lists of bishops, accompanied with chronological and historical notes; those who proclaimed Christian doctrine, in the order of generations; and, side by side with them, he would describe the heretics whom they opposed. All this would be followed by a description of the divine punishment of the Jewish people, and finally a sketch of the Christian persecutions, the martyrdoms, and the final deliverance by the Saviour's help.[2] The programme was carried out to the last detail in the first seven books, and this in such a way that he amplified the results of his researches to a large extent by quoting his sources word for word; his library had placed these sources at his disposal in a unique manner. The eighth book tells of the persecution under Diolectian and of the end which God put to it; the book concludes with the edict of tolerance issued by

[1] E. Schwartz, *Über Kirchengeschichte*, in *Gött. Nachr.* 1908 111f.=*Ges. Schriften*, 1, 116
[2] Eus. *H.E.* 1, 1, 1

Galerius in the year 311. The first edition appeared in the next twelve months.

Only three years later Eusebius published a new edition. This time, the eighth book was expanded by a description of the tyrannies exercised by Maxentius and Maximin;[1] and a further book, the ninth, records the downfall of both these persecutors of the Christians. An appendix gives a list of the sources Eusebius had used.[2] The third edition came out in A.D. 317; the work had been extended by a few passages including the address which Eusebius had delivered at the ceremony when the basilica at Tyre was consecrated.[3] Finally, at the time of the Council of Nicea in A.D. 325, the definitive edition was published. The notices of Licinius, appreciative in character, in A.D. 324, were deleted, being replaced by an addition giving an account of his downfall (10, 8–9). Similarly, the list of sources found in the second edition and several of the expansions in the third, had had to go.

The work immediately achieved such success, and was so often re-copied, that the extant codices still reveal traces of their earliest history, and the skill of Ed. Schwartz, a literary critic of genius, has disentangled the story of the various editions.[4] Naturally, such an impressive collection of historical material was made for a theological purpose, viz., to deliver the proof showing how the Church had been guided by God; and this is the reason why this work concludes triumphantly with the battles fought by the martyrs down to the most recent times, and now crowned with success. Eusebius took special pains in describing Dionysius of Alexandria and, above all, Origen, and in showing the reader that the victory of Christianity did not imply a loss of culture, but, rather, smoothed the way towards the elevation of the entire life of the spirit.

Eusebius's personality, taken on the whole, is an incarnation of the idea of a world-conquering Christian civilization, and therefore Constantine's polity appeared to him as the fulfilment of his highest hopes. Quite logically he placed himself and his pen unconditionally at the Emperor's service, and the Emperor

[1] *ibid.* 8, 13, 12–15, 2   [2] *ibid.* 10, 5–7
[3] *H.E.* 8 pp. 796f., Schwartz, and *H.E.* 10, 1–4 foll[d]. by 5–7
[4] Ed. Schwartz, in his larger edition, vol 3, pp. XLVII–LXI

in turn regarded him as really and truly commissioned by God. Constantine's monarchy, he felt, was the earthly copy of the divine rule over the world, the refutation of every polytheistic error; it spread and defended the lordship of the Logos on earth against all the resistance of barbarians and demons.[1] These are the terms of praise which Eusebius solemnly used of him on the thirtieth anniversary of his reign, and again after his death, when Eusebius described his life's work in four books, books which constituted a single impassioned tribute to the ideal of a world-wide Christian monarchy.

Everything of less importance seemed a matter of indifference in face of this great conception. Hence the Arian controversies were only touched upon in passing; he found no inner necessity for them, no clash of genuine opposites—as he had judged to be the case in many a controversy in the past—rather they were ineffective attempts of the Devil and his demons to sow hatred and envy at the eleventh hour into the growing unity of state and church, and so to destroy the labours of the great Emperor on behalf of peace.[2]

He took a literary share in the disputes of his times by means of two writings directed against Marcellus of Ancyra, a man whom we shall discuss in the sequel. Eusebius, as was proper in one of Origen's school, defended the doctrine of two hypostases as against the "Sabellians", although sometimes he declared that the mystery of Christ's sonship was beyond human comprehension.[3] He also wrote against Eustathios of Antioch,[4] but the work quickly fell into oblivion. His *Theophany* made a deeper impression, although it contains clear evidences of a receding tide of theological ability. He composed a compendium of Christian theology in five books for converting educated laymen. He took most of the material from his two great works, and wrote with the ultimate purpose of awakening men to understand God's work in renewing the world as revealed in Constantine,[5] thus leading the undecided into the church. A small writing of the year A.D. 335, and dedicated to Constantine, brought his fundamental ideas together once

[1] Eus. *Th. Ann. Ad.*, 1. 2. 5. 7. 10   N. H. Baynes in *Mélanges Bidez*, 1933, 13–18
[2] Eus. *vita Const.* 2, 61, 3   2, 73   3, 1, 1   3, 4   4, 41, 1
[3] Eus. *eccl. theol.* 1, 20   2, 7 (85f. 104 ed. Klostermann)
[4] *vide supra*, 125   [5] e.g., *Theophany* 134 f. ed. Gressmann

more, expressing his opinion that the buildings composing the Church of the Holy Sepulchre in Jerusalem symbolized the Emperor's God-given mission.

All the works written by Eusebius in his old age had the same centre: Constantine. He did not live more than three years after the great Emperor's death, but it was long enough to discover that their father's heritage weighed heavily on the sons of Constantine. When Eusebius died, the ecclesiastical and spiritual voice of the Constantine era became silent, and with that its most important theologian. Eusebius was the heir and master of the tradition of Origen in this age, and he fulfilled his duties outstandingly. Compared with him, the earlier disciples of the great Alexandrian were only of minor importance. This judgment applies also to Gregory "the miracle-worker", who was bishop of Neocaesarea on the Black Sea, whose literary remains, apart from a thanksgiving speech addressed to Origen,[1] are insignificant and uncertain, but who wrought great benefit in his diocese as an energetic bishop and a pastor who understood human nature.[2]

Similarly Methodius, bishop of Olympos in Lycia, wrote a fairly large number of books, which are extant partly in the original, and partly in a Slavonic translation; but their literary and theological value is modest.[3] "Banquets" had been a popular form of literature since Plato's time, and accordingly Methodius imagined ten maidens discussing chastity at a banquet. And why not? Plato had described his guests discussing *eros* and surely Christian girls might discuss chastity. But unfortunately Methodius imitates Plato so obviously that a reader who has read the latter's work has it always before his eyes. The original is constantly "improved" upon by allegorical fantasies; e.g., the girls are made first to climb the familiar steep hill from the Stoa, in order to reach the garden of their hostess, *Arete* (i.e., Virtue), daughter of Philosophy, and then they take their seats at the feast intentionally spread under a Chaste Tree (*Vitex agnus castus*).

What then follows is naturally not a discussion with speech

---

[1] *vide* Vol 2, 303f.
[2] cf. his *Epistula Canonica*, ed. Lagarde, in *Reliq. iur. eccl. ant. graece*, 60–63
[3] N. Bonwetsch, *Die Theologie des Methodius* (Gött. Abh., N.F., Vol. 7, 1). Bonwetsch published the Works in 1917

and genuine counter speech; rather all are of one view, and they sing the praise of virginity with a plenteous citation of Biblical proofs, and no lack of allegory. In the end, all unite in singing a hymn interesting to us more for its form than its content.

The Platonic form reappears in other writings of his, the best being the Dialogue on the resurrection of the flesh. Here Origen's spiritual doctrine is attacked, and the physical views of popular belief are brought forward and supported on Biblical and philosophical grounds. Methodius swore to the witch of Endor, in opposition to Origen's interpretation, and so prepared the way for Eustathios.[1] Nevertheless he lived on the feast of good things Origen had provided, even when attacking him. His purpose was only to help the tradition of the Church to obtain its due, and according to this view to fit the theology traditional to Alexandria to the average faith, a feat which could not be accomplished without mutilation. But the majority of the bishops of that time, as far as they were at all capable of scholarly methods of thought, must have felt the same need. Just for this reason, Methodius is a typical representative of the tendencies of those days, tendencies which, on closer inspection, Eusebius also exhibits. Both men had it at heart to effect a similar union between Christianity and the kind of spiritual outlook which Plato had greatly enriched; but Methodius was in advance of most of his contemporaries in that he really had studied Plato for himself. His work a as writer—he died as a martyr in A.D. 311—was overshadowed by that of Eusebius, who is the sole representative of Greek literature in Constantine's period. Porphyry had already died in A.D. 304, and his successor, Iamblichos,[2] was primarily the spiritual leader and pastor of the men of the next generation. In the period after Constantine, the non-Christian Greek writers reached considerable heights, although there was brisk competition with the Christians who were pouring out their writings far and wide.

The lead established by Christians was not less evident where Latin was spoken. A series of biographies of Roman emperors from Hadrian to Numerian (A.D. 117–284) appears to have been written under Diocletian and Constantine on the far-famed model of Suetonius; but in fact their more or less doughty authors used pseudonyms, and in Julian's time their derogatory passages were put on the debit side against them.[1] The "Panegyrists" are of much greater value, and their extant speeches on festive occasions in honour of the emperors, afford many invaluable items of information; but when we compare their writing with the grand style used by Eusebius to depict and extol Constantine, it becomes obvious that they were of minor quality.

Arnobius of Africa was a very characteristic figure belonging to the same period. He was a skilled teacher of rhetoric and a convinced pagan until he was converted by a dream. But the bishop distrusted the sudden change in a well-known enemy of Christianity,[2] and so the candidate hastened to write, as testimony to his seriousness, seven books *Against Pagans*. Here we find only very foggy ideas of Christianity. He was still entirely unacquainted with the Bible, and all he tells of Christ are hearsay reports of His miracles. But these very miracles were regarded by him as proving the Lord's divinity, for He worked them without material aids, whereas the pagan gods effected their miraculous cures by using medicine, being therefore, in the last analysis, no different from human physicians.[3] Over and above all this, Jesus had transmitted His miraculous powers to His disciples. Arnobius looked back with shame to the time when he was lost in pagan errors, when he used to worship divine beings in pictures and statues, in sacred trees and anointed stones; but now, in all gratitude, he did homage to Jesus the great Teacher who had led him into the pathways of truth. Of course he did not leave out the scandalous stories with which mythology was replete, and the present-day student of Comparative Religion is happy in being able to extract from Arnobius the scholarly knowledge acquired by Cornelius Labeo, the Platonist, regarding Roman and Etruscan religion.

Everywhere in the midst of his rude polemic, it is apparent that Arnobius was thankful that he had been freed from the

[1] N. H. Baynes, *The Historia Augusta*, 1926
[2] Jerome, *chron. Olymp.* 276, 3, p. 231 (ed. Helm)
[3] Arnobius, *adv. gentes*, 1, 48–50   1, 39

burden of a primitive nature-religion, strangely linked up with an allegorizing philosophy, and that now he breathed a purer air as a man who has been saved. Immortality, the "Health of the Soul", for which men search along so many strange paths, he found established with greater certitude in the proven power of hope in Christ than in the speculations of philosophers and the performances of theurgics. Arnobius's writing is a valuable witness to the inner character of a man who had only just then been converted to Christianity. The standpoint of old-time religion was still real to him, with its unsatisfying answer to man's quest; and we learn exactly why he became a Christian.[1] The proof from miracle convinced him that Christ was really God; sent into the world by the Most-High God, He had assumed the outer form of humanity, and, as man, had promised immortality to all who followed His teaching.[2] That was the sum total of Arnobius's theology.

Lactantius, though somewhat younger, laboured and wrote contemporaneously with him, after having benefited by him as a teacher of rhetoric, but only to rise far above his teacher. Throughout his life a poverty-stricken school-teacher,[3] he had his Cicero in both his head and his heart, and was able to write better Latin than the average litterateur of the time of the Empire. Diocletian made him transfer his home to Nicomedia, but even there he earned little, for in this Greek city only a few wished to be taught Latin. Diocletian's persecution caused him to be driven back to the west, where at last a dilatory good fortune smiled on him. Constantine, to whom Lactantius dedicated his chief work, entrusted him with training his young son Crispus in Latin—and, it may be gathered that, at the same time, he ensured him his livelihood.

Here is another instance of a man who became Christian in his later years, and his experience of the spiritual change is what gives his writing its force. To no lesser degree than Arnobius was he typical of the outlook of his times, but he was far more cultured both in literary style and in content of thought. Moreover, he became a Christian because this religion

---

[1] A. D. Nock, *Conversion*, Oxford, 1933, 257–259
[2] Arnobius, 1, 42   53, 60. 62   2, 32–34   60. 65. 66. 78
[3] Jerome, *vir. inl.* 80   *chron. Olymp.* 274, 2. p. 230 ed. Helm

guaranteed him the highest good, i.e., immortality, which was in no way a quality proper to the soul, but had to be earned as the reward of a virtuous life.[1]

Two ways, he held, lay open to men, the one leading through earthly pleasure and comforts of all sorts, to Hell; the other, through continual struggle and much self-denial, to Heaven.[2] The cultivation of the virtues as the only true service of God could be set over against the sacrificial cultus amongst pagans; and the Christian virtues were more suitable than those taught by the philosophers. The first commandment was to know God rightly, obey Him alone, worship Him alone. The second directed our attention to our fellow-men and required mercy or "humanity", i.e., the kind of righteousness that maintained human society.[3] It was to be seen particularly in the form of hospitality, redemption of prisoners, support of widows and orphans, care of the sick, and concern for the interment of dead and indigent strangers.[4] Almsgiving was also worthy, and served to annul sins, for no one could be free from sin as long as he wore the garment of flesh. Hence there was a threefold graduation of righteousness: the "satisfactory" was free from evil deeds; the "complete" also from evil words; but he who could also keep free from evil thoughts, had reached the highest peak, being like God.[5]

No one should hang back because the demands were so high; at bottom it was quite easy to be a good man and lay hold on righteousness; it was all a matter of the will. Of course, there was an unavoidable presupposition, and that was in being set free from polytheism. As long as men remained in the bonds of disbelief and therefore of the Devil and his demons, they could not attain to true virtue.[6] The attitude of the virtuous towards the world was altogether of a negative character, denial of the present temporal life in expectation of the eternal; despising the body as compared with the soul; joyous surrender of earthly good which after all only loads the heart with chains. Out of his own experience, he wrote that poverty and destitution gave men steel, and made them ready to exercise virtue.[7]

[1] Lactant. *inst.* 7, 5, 20   7, 6, 1   7, 8, 1   [2] *ibid.* 6, 3–4
[3] *ibid.* 6, 9, 1   6, 10, 1–2,   6, 12, 1   [4] *ibid.* 6, 12, 5. 15. 21. 24. 25
[5] *ibid.* 6, 13   [6] *ibid.* 5, 8, 1–6
[7] *ibid.* 4, 28, 1   6, 12, 36   7, 5, 25   7, 27, 1   7, 1, 17

Again, man was like Adam, a mixture of good and evil; were that not so, there would be no real virtue, since it could only be authenticated by an ethical struggle.[1]

As a consequence, and before the creation of the world, God had caused "a spirit similar to Himself" to proceed from Himself as His Son; a second spirit, however, did not preserve the divine status but, turning to wickedness, became the Devil; the first was God's right hand, and the second His left. The same separation of good and evil was repeated among the hosts of angels and demons.[2] Then, by the agency of His first-born Son, God created the world out of nothing, and this Son, the Logos, was called upon to intervene in its antagonisms as teacher and herald of the divine secrets.[3] To effect this purpose, He was born a second time, but now in flesh and human form, from a virgin. Indeed He was burdened with sinful flesh which He first washed clean at the hands of John in the Jordan.[4] Thus He appeared among men as a "teacher of virtue and righteousness"—Lactantius made continual use of this terminology for Him—outwardly like them. He overcame sin as a mortal man, in order that mankind might learn from His example that sin could be conquered. He, being at once God and man, had opened and pointed out to mankind the way to virtue, and thereby to immortality.[5]

Lactantius found the essence of Christianity in ethical redemption through a divinely-sent teacher, and he went into the greatest detail in explaining these matters to the pagan readers for whom he was writing. He proved his theses by preference from ancient writers with Cicero at their head, and Virgil at his side; but the Sibyls and Hermes Trismegistos were frequently quoted for their testimonies. He used the elegant style of a rhetorician in arranging his series of quotations from Greek and Roman writers, and placed them alongside the evidence of the Biblical prophets whose predictions occupied much of his space.

He was well aware that Minucius Felix, Tertullian, and

---

[1] ibid. 7, 5   Appendix 602f. ed. Brandt   2, 8   Appendix 130f.
[2] ibid. 2, 8, 3–8   4, 8, 7–8   [3] ibid. 4, 11, 14   12, 1   15, 2
[4] e.g., 4, 8, 8   4, 11, 14   4, 13, 1   4, 16, 4   4, 24, 12. 15
[5] ibid. 4, 24, 10–25, 10

Cyprian had written on behalf of Christianity, and he praised them discreetly in nicely formulated phrases. But it was painful to him that an educated pagan should have been able to scoff at Cyprian laughingly, and say it was a pity that such a superior mind should have gone astray over nursery-tales. But it appeared to Lactantius to be only the inevitable consequence of the fact that the men just mentioned had really written in a way which Christians alone could understand. He himself would do otherwise. Immediately at the beginning of the persecution under Diocletian, two antichristian writers had arisen, one an unknown philosopher, and Hierokles the governor familiar to us. Lactantius intended to answer them in such a way as to deal with every other opponent of Christianity at the same time, because the answer would not be negative defence, but an objective exposition on the basis of clear and logical proof.[1]

At this point we might halt, and we should have in front of us a not entirely strange picture of a Christian who had found his former ideal of culture actualized in the new faith—but the conclusion of his chief work opens a door admitting us into a secret chamber of the soul. He had just employed the usual arguments to substantiate faith in immortality as did Cicero and Hermes Trismegistos, but very different from Lucretius. Lactantius continued that he must now explain how and when immortality was granted to men.[2] He then entered upon a description of the End, painted with all the colours of the Johannine apocalyptic, and enriched by a few elements drawn from the Sibylline Oracles, Daniel, Hystaspes,[3] and other apocalyptic writers. Lactantius reproduces the calculation of the Daniel year-week as 6000 years, a millennial sabbath-year with Christ ruling over an earth which blossoms into a miraculous Garden of Eden; and then the last and decisive battle in which all evil is destroyed and heaven and earth are made new. He tells his pagan readers all this as certain truth, but reserved for Christians to know.

Lactantius linked himself up with historical experience in quite a jejune manner. He pointed to the then present day

[1] *ibid.* 5, 1, 22–28 5, 2, 1–3 5, 4, 1–7
[2] *ibid.* 7, 14, 1ff. [3] *vide* Vol I, 82

in which, he said, injustice and evil had reached their acme,[1] and proceeded to reckon that, after about 200 years,[2] the point of time would come when the moral deterioration of mankind would have gone still further and reached its absolute end. Then the Roman empire—dreadful to think—would disappear from the earth, and an Asiatic tyrant would bring about the rule of the orient over the enslaved occident, using barbaric cruelty. It was only needful to carry Seneca's interpretation[3] of history further to see that the Roman empire had reached old age when it became a monarchy; what cause was there for astonishment if death should one day put an end to old age?

Here is the attitude towards the end of the world characteristic of apocalyptic writers, and it comes now from a man hitherto clear and reasonable. It shows that he was no mere cool rational thinker as he had seemed. The terrors of the times of persecution still reverberated in his heart, and laid his soul open to accept ideas born of an unlimited yearning for a bright future not of this world. Yet a pleasant period was to be his lot in life, and when Constantine brought peace to western Christianity, Lactantius dedicated a new edition of the *Institutes* to him as the divinely nominated "servant" of God on High.[3] Then in writing of the death of those who had persecuted the Christians, he changed over to write the story of the collapse of the times. The passion of his language grew with the loftiness of his subject, for Lactantius felt himself to be a witness to a world-shattering divine judgment; and he did real justice to his task as he conceived it.

Speculations about the millennium at the close of history, such as we find in the last book of the *Institutes*, were by no means a rarity confined to Lactantius, but were among the traits characteristic of western Christianity, faithfully preserved for centuries as part of the fund of ideas coming down from the first ages. On the other hand, the east had come under the influence of Greek academic scholarship with its clarity of thought. Then having fought and won its contest with Montanism, eastern thinkers had vanquished "Chiliasm" at an early date. In harmony with this, is the fact that the book of the

---

[1] *Inst.* 7, 15, 7   [2] *ibid.* 7, 25, 5   [3] *ibid.* 7, 15, 16–17
[4] *ibid.* p. 4 and p. 668n., ed. Brandt; 95, 13   177, 3   274, 3   485, 6

Revelation of John was not favoured by eastern theologians, and was not to be found in the canon of the Church far and wide; whereas it was used everywhere in the west. It is quite significant that out of the whole of the writings of the first Latin Biblical exegete, namely Victorinus, bishop of Poêtovium (Pettau) in Styria, martyred in A.D. 304, the only surviving work is a commentary on the book of Revelation, issuing in, and leading to, chiliastic ideas. We may remark, by the way, that the book is of meagre quality, and shows that the world has not lost greatly by the disappearance of the others. Its real value consists, not in its wealth of theological material, but in the form of ancient Christianity that receives expression here.

Lactantius[1] and other writers much later than he used to complain that the books of the Bible could scarcely be made acceptable to educated people on account of their inelegant language, a fact which explains the attempts made to abolish the difficulty by improving the style. Among the phenomena characteristic of the Constantine period is that Juvencus, a Spanish presbyter, turned the gospels of Luke and Matthew into verse; those who liked this sort of thing could now read the gospel of Jesus in polished Virgilian hexameters. The age and number of the extant manuscripts show that there were many readers, century after century, who were delighted with this, the earliest great achievement of a Christian Latin poet.

Constantine, unlike Alexander the Great, had no Homer; instead, fate provided him with a poetical Court-fool, whom Constantine, in harmony with contemporary taste, took fairly seriously. The gracious letter is still extant in which the Emperor thanks Optatianus Porphyrius for dedicating to him some poems he had written.[2]

He must have been an eminent person of high rank, for the Emperor honoured him with the unusually intimate address of "Dear Brother", and he is also known actually occupying the office of city prefect in Rome A.D. 329 and 333. Round about A.D. 325, he fell into disfavour and was banished; but he seems to have been saved by a poem which he wrote ending

[1] *Inst.* 5, 1, 15
[2] R. Optatiani Porfyrii, *carmina*, ed. E. Kluge, 1926

in a prayer for forgiveness.[1] It was only just, for no poet before him had done what he could do.

He was skilled in making verses having the same number of letters, and the verses could be placed under one another to form a square or an oblong. Then the initial and final letters of the lines were made to stand out in red ink, when they were seen to make another verse. Sometimes the words of a line could be read backwards with equal effect. Yet again, the poems were written on purple, probably with silver ink, many letters being brought out in gold. If the gold series were now read by themselves, they made a verse once more, or even a whole poem; and the lines in gold set forth among themselves figures as on a carpet, e.g. the monogram of Christ, a ship, or else a formula of homage; at their best, the gold letters formed a Greek poem.

Poets of Alexandria had formerly, in a playful spirit, shaped shepherds' pipes and the wings of Eros out of verses, but now they were far excelled by a manipulator of verse who could make actual what seemed impossible. The art of poetry had become a matter of clever manual dexterity, but without soul. It is quite astonishing that such poems retained any meaning at all, even when it was a case of wordy homage addressed to the Emperor, to Cæsar Crispus, and to Bassus, an unknown patron. These men exhibited a taste for what the Muses of the fourth century were still capable of offering them. Optatianus was long marvelled at in the succeeding ages, and those who had sufficient self-confidence gave much pains to imitating him. That fact must also be taken into account in attempting to assess this period.

[1] cf. *carm.* I, 15   2, 21

Chapter Seven

CONSTANTINE'S SUCCESSORS

CONSTANTINE HAD SHATTERED DIOCLETIAN'S SYSTEM OF rulerships, since it was his intention to be the sole master of the entire imperium. He had attained his goal because, in addition to an iron will, he was gifted with very great ability and good luck and then more good luck. That is what made him one of the great men in the history of mankind. He was always conscious of being divinely led along the lofty road of his life, and it was in this light that he judged himself and others. A further consequence was that he was under no illusion that his own exceptional place could be handed down; he therefore felt it advisable that the question of his successors should be settled again by the rules drawn up by Diocletian's astuteness.

But the experiences through which he had passed had taught him that the system could only be maintained, and the Empire could only be ruled as a united whole, as was indispensable, by means of a dynasty all of the same blood. Hence, on March 1, 317, he appointed, in the first instance exclusively, his sons to be Cæsars; Crispus was then ten years old, and Constantinus one month, both having been born of concubines. His legal wife, Fausta, bore him a son, Constantius, only in the late summer of the same year, and he was raised to the rank of Cæsar in A.D. 324; followed, six years later by Constans, the last in the number of his sons. He was made Cæsar in A.D. 333, and the same exalted rank was given, in A.D. 335, to his nephew Dalmatius, son of the "Censor" of Antioch to whom reference has already been made;[1] Crispus had been put to death in A.D. 326.[2]

The Cæsars were entrusted with military commands even while they were still boys, and appointed rulers of parts of the Empire, with the result that their place as rulers in both the military and civil spheres was regarded as self-evident from an early date, and it was rightly expected that this would be regarded as an established custom in the future. Nor was the

[1] *vide supra,* 131   [2] Seeck, *Untergang,* 4, 1–7 with the footnotes

expectation falsified, for, soon, a sense of dynasty developed which issued unexpectedly in dire effects. When Constantine died, the Empire was to be divided into four parts; besides the positions assigned to his three surviving sons, the Emperor had placed Dalmatius as regent of the Balkan peninsula;[1] and another nephew, Hannibalianus, was to be king of Armenia, with Cæsarea in Cappadocia as his capital.

The extension of the idea of dynasty was distasteful in military circles where only the Emperor's sons were regarded as rightful heirs. On September 9, 337, these were proclaimed *Augusti*, and installed by the Roman senate with due ceremony. The other heirs apparent to thrones were made harmless in accordance with oriental custom; they were murdered, and a considerable train of important personages died with them. In this way, all Constantine's brothers and nephews were done away with except two boys, Gallus, aged twelve, and Julian, aged seven; their father, Julius Constantius, brother to the Emperor, was murdered. Constantius witnessed all these events unable, perhaps also unwilling, to interfere. He made active use of his momentary advantage, but later suffered severely from remorse.[2]

The Empire was then divided into three parts: Constantine II ruled over the west; Constans at twelve years of age received Italy, Africa, and Greece; Constantius was the lord of the east together with the Danubian region.[3] Constantius, besides succeeding to the crown of the east, inherited also the Persian war, for which his father had been preparing for a few months before his death. Constantius was heavily engaged here without break for the next thirteen years, and even afterwards was frequently tied up there. He could therefore be only a helpless spectator of events in the west.

There the boy, Constans, in no way played a subordinate part to his elder half-brother, Constantine II, as had been expected; but on the contrary so irritated him that the latter invaded the Po valley and pressed forward to Aquileia. Constans was taken completely by surprise, and advanced out of

---

[1] *Anon. Valesianus* 35 in *chron. minora*, I, p. 11   Vict. *ep.* 41, 20   *Consularia Epolitana chron. min.* I, 235
[2] Seeck, *op. cit.* 4, 29   Julian, *ep. ad Athen.* 271a (I, 349 ed. Hertlein)
[3] Zonaras, 13, 5   p. 11, b, c.

the region of Serbia against his enemy brother. But the war was soon settled. Attempting to storm a barricaded Alpine pass, Constantine was ambushed and killed on a spring day in A.D. 340. Constans added his share of the Empire to his own. The boy, who had been somewhat underestimated by his elder brother, had grown into a youth who knew exactly what he wanted, and who was now far more powerful than Constantius who was wearing himself out on the Euphrates frontier. His military ability had been put to the proof in battles with the Sarmatians, and he was successful in the following years on the Rhine, the Danube, and in Britain.

But he did not retain the goodwill of his soldiers, and the civilian population had the more to endure the longer his harsh régime lasted. His homosexuality, to which he gave free rein, made him despised, and surrounded him with vile associates. Hence those hopes which at first had been raised by the young prince rapidly wilted: in a decade he had wasted the rich heritage of dynastic authority which had come to him from his father.

In the meantime, the war on the eastern frontier swung to and fro. Nisibis was besieged thrice for months at a time by the Persians, but in vain. The enemy was severely defeated on one occasion near Singara in northern Mesopotamia; Armenia came again under Roman influence; and, finally the Persians were so busily engaged on their own northern frontier, that they left Constantius in peace for many years. Thereby he was set free to take an interest in the internal necessities of the Empire.

He is the only one of the royal brothers of whom some detailed personal information has come down, as not a few contemporaries wrote of him from their own acquaintance.[1] He took over from his father the consciousness of being under special divine protection, and felt he owed his success to this happy circumstance. At times he saw with his own eyes his guardian angel, even if not clearly. But neither in spirit nor physique was his personality sufficiently outstanding to cause

[1] Records given by Seeck, *Untergang*, 4, 393f. cf. also *ibid.* 29–39 H. Schiller, *Röm. Kaiserzeit*, 2, 245–249 Amm. Marc. 21, 16 gives a detailed sketch of Constantius

an imperial influence, equal in majesty to his father's, to stream spontaneously from himself. Hence he adopted a stiff and formal inaccessibility of attitude in his personal contacts, and his educated contemporaries found delight in "taking him off". A further consequence was also that the Emperor became fenced in by a ring of Court attendants who were his confidants, and who made ruthless use of their position as favourites. His Court was under the administration of eunuchs, and this ominous fact was deplored with one consent.

He remained well-intentioned throughout, and in his own way took the injunctions of the Church seriously, for he confessed himself a Christian. Even those who criticize him adversely[1] admit that he was morally conscientious, and faithful in marriage; that he lived simply and kept his body in subjection. He was at pains to appear as a mild and upright ruler, even when his position as a despot led to cruelty and violent bloodshed. He possessed a certain rhetorical and literary ambition, and although what he himself accomplished was modest, yet this predilection smoothed the path of gifted contemporaries and graced it with kindliness. But he did not develop and become equal to the great demands which his position as Emperor made upon him more and more as time went on. This was the case both in the east, where his original share of the Empire lay, and also at a later time when fate called upon him to rule the world-empire that had been his father's.

As long as Constantine the Great held the reins, no serious effects could arise from the discords due to the legal position of the Church as recognized by the Empire, and to the increased sense of authority felt by the heads of the Church. The inconvenient bishops, of whom Athanasius was chief, were dispatched into exile by the temporal arm, and so rendered innocuous. The Emperor's death immediately changed the situation and relieved the burden pressing on the Church: the Empire fell apart into three regions whose rulers felt only the urgency of what concerned their own third of it, and therefore regarded the problems of the Empire as a whole from an unduly restricted standpoint. This state of affairs gave rise to

[1] *Amm. Marc.* 21, 16, 5–7. 18   Aur. Vict. *ep.* 42, 18. 19

a possibility which was dangerous for the Church to use. It might seek to overcome internal differences by making sectional appeals, each to the political interests of its own province of the Empire, and it might strive to make use of the element of State authority for settling church affairs. The emperors and the bishops were equally subject to this seductive temptation.

Hardly had the news of the Emperor's death arrived in Trèves, when the Crown Prince, Constantine, raised the ban on Athanasius, and sent him with an official letter,[1] dated June 17, A.D. 337, back to his church. It may be quite true, as Constantine explained, that he was only doing what his father had already intended. We are quite familiar with the caprice of Constantine's personal politics. But under the rule of the three sons, the effect of the act of grace was necessarily different from what it would have been in their father's lifetime. And not only might Athanasius now return, but also the rest of the bishops banished by Constantine. Maximin of Trèves appears to have given the prince that advice,[2] and Athanasius was not without reason in rejoicing at the magnanimity of the amnesty.

Constantius had to be patient for a while when the return of these men of the opposite camp was demanded of him by his brother. Perhaps he also hoped to come to agreement with them. At any rate he twice gave audience to Athanasius on his homeward journey, in Viminacium (Vrastolatz near Semendria) and—in Cæsarea in Cappadocia.[3]

It is striking that Athanasius should have touched the centre of Asia Minor on his journey from Trèves to Alexandria, but we also learn that he only arrived home on November 23, and therefore had been on his way fully five months. The conclusion to be drawn is that he used the opportunity of consolidating personal relationships in various places, and the correctness of this inference is proved by the complaints made later by his foes.[3] The road to Cappadocia probably took him through Ancyra, to which the deposed Bishop Marcellus had now

[1] Athan. apol. 87, 4–7

[2] Athan. hist. Ar. 8   cf. Philostorg. 2, 18   ep. synod. or. Sardic. 27, 7 in Hilarius 4, 66 ed. Feder

[3] Athan. apol. ad Const. 5   ep. synod. or. Sardic. 8, in Hilarius 4, 54 f. Feder

ventured to return. Thus, very quietly, but with skilled sedulousness, an Athanasian party had been built up in the orient without Constantius's being able to hinder it. The consequences of the Emperor's indulgence soon came to light.

Everywhere the return of the exiles caused lively unrest among the populace.[1] Contrary efforts developed on the other side, and Athanasius's old counterpart, Eusebius of Nicomedia, immediately took over the leadership in the contest. Paul of Constantinople was deposed by a synod. Weighty accusations must have been brought forward against him, for he was removed in chains and banished to Singara in Mesopotamia (west of Nineveh).[2] Eusebius of Nicomedia succeeded and so at last obtained the ruling position which was his due; he was not reluctant to leave Nicomedia, for it had become of insignificant importance.[3] Further, Marcellus of Ancyra, Lucius of Adrianople, and Asklepas of Gaza were again banished from the country, and this by imperial decree and without a pronouncement by the Church. The Athanasian party of the east was robbed of its leader before it had become at all aware of its own existence.

Very extensive preparations had been made for the attack on Athanasius himself. Naturally he had immediately taken the administration of his church firmly in hand, without first troubling about being restituted by that church through a synod; he had refused to recognize the deposition pronounced at Tyre, but had replied to it by appealing to Constantine. Eusebius had taken advantage of this circumstance by maintaining that the Church's condemnation of Athanasius still held good. Then he drew the conclusion which had been long deferred, that the vacant see at Alexandria must now be filled. The "Eusebians" chose a certain Pistos for the position,[4] a man who had formerly belonged to the adherents of Arius, for which cause he had been excommunicated together with Arius by Bishop Alexander. Secundus of Ptolemaïs later installed him somewhere as bishop.[5] Naturally all the elements of the

---

[1] *ep. synod. or. Sardic.* 9, in Hilarius 4, 55f. Feder

[2] Athan. *hist. Ar.* 7 cf. Schwartz, *Gött. Nachr.* 1911, 476f.   [3] Socrates, 2, 7

[4] Doc. of Egypt. Syn. in Athan. *apol.* 19, 2 *Julii ep. ibid.* 24, 1–3 Athan. *encycl.* 6

[5] *Doc.* 4a in Athan. 3, p. 6, 12 ed. Opitz *Doc. ibid.* p. 13, 23

opposition rallied round this man, and the schism in Alexandria became an organized movement.

The bishops who recognized Eusebius met together with a certain regularity at Antioch from now on. Here no metropolitan with his own claims to authority threatened Eusebius's leadership and, on the other hand, the Emperor was frequently present. He could get from here more rapidly than from Constantinople to the Persian frontier, which was always under hostile pressure; and these circumstances afforded the essential presupposition for the Church's power-politics. A document of charges against Athanasius was drawn up in Antioch during the winter of A.D. 337–338, and was sent to all three Emperors with the idea of making the situation impossible for so dangerous a man no less in the west than in the east. It pointed to the undeniable cases of restlessness which had been caused by his return to Alexandria; complained about the contempt of church rules of which Athanasius had become guilty in taking up office again on his own authority though he was still legally deposed; and in conclusion raised a charge of irregularities in connection with the sharing out of the imperial issues of corn.[1]

It had not been kept hidden from the bishops in Antioch that Athanasius had won great respect for himself during his exile in the west, and that between Alexandria and Rome, there was an ancient relation of mutual regard. So they wrote also to Julius, bishop of Rome,[2] and told him that the regular bishop of Alexandria was Pistos, and that Athanasius had lost his position for sound ecclesiastical reasons. The document was taken to Rome by a special delegation consisting of Makarios, a presbyter, and two deacons, Martyrios and Hesychios. As proof, the minutes of the synod of Tyre, and an announcement by the opposition bishops of Egypt, were put in.

But Athanasius had heard what was taking place. He called a synod at Alexandria; eighty bishops gathered there, and bore testimony to their leader. The document produced by the synod is a defence, full of very rhetorical phrases, against

---

[1] The charge sheet can be reconstructed from Athan. *apol.* 3–19 and Sozom. 3, 2, 8 cf. Schwartz, *ibid.* 480f.

[2] Inferred from *Julii ep.* in Athan. *ibid.* 22–27

every charge, and supported by an immense number of relevant records.[1] A delegation of Alexandrian presbyters brought this material to Rome where they found that the Eusebian messengers had already arrived.

There was then a dramatic scene in which the Eusebians played a very base part, which enabled the Athanasians to gain an impressive victory. When, to avoid further painful controversy, the former therefore left Rome on a foggy night, they completed their diplomatic defeat.[2] Driven into a corner, they had obviously concocted something that required examination by a synod, and that provided Julius with a convenient handle for continuing the action. He requested both parties to let the matter come up for decision at another synod, and to choose a suitable place for it.[3]

Meanwhile, the eastern party had converted Constantius completely to their side, and pushed forward vigorously to their goal. They gathered in Antioch in order to make a new appointment to the see of Alexandria; Pistos had plainly become impossible, and disappeared without trace.[4] After Eusebius of Emesa had prudently declined,[5] they chose a Cappadocian named Gregory who had known Alexandria since his student days.[6] Philagrios was appointed prefect of Egypt.[7] Hence Gregory could go to Alexandria under military protection. Weeks earlier, wild scenes had taken place when Athanasius's supporters defended themselves against the transfer of the churches, and they must have been dispersed with bloodshed by the authorities. The church of Dionysius with the adjoining baptistry was set on fire.[8]

Athanasius succeeded in remaining hidden for a while, and so escaping arrest; but on March 18 his hiding-place was discovered in the church of Theonas, and the next day he had

---

[1] Document of the synod preserved in Athan. *ibid.* 3–19   On the records, cf. Schwartz. *ibid.* 482f.

[2] *Julii ep. ibid.* 22, 3   24, 1–3

[3] Athan. *hist. Ar.* 9. *encycl.* 7. *Julii ep. op. cit.* 30, 1

[4] Athan. *encycl,* 6   [5] Socr. **2, 9**

[6] Gregor. Naz. *or.* 21, 15. (1, 394 d. Bened.)

[7] Schwartz. *ibid.* 1904, 347

[8] *Julii ep.* in Athan. *apol.* 29, 3   30, 1   cf. Soc. 2, 8 (who, however, gives the wrong date for the synod at Antioch)   Athan. *encycl.* 2f., *hist. Ar.* 10   Preface to the *Syepr.* . 11, p. 30, ed. Larsow

to flee. Four days later, i.e., March 22, 339, Gregory made a ceremonial entry into Alexandria. From then until Easter (April 15) there followed a further series of violent disturbances. Athanasius remained in hiding near-by, and had full reports brought to him. Then he compiled a moving encyclical giving an affecting account of all that had happened, and sent it as a blazing protest everywhere against such unheard-of enormities.

This "encyclical" was the first of his writings on church polity, issued contemporaneously with the events; it has thrown out a light which, from that day to this, has blinded scholars who were trying to discover the naked facts—a powerful testimony to the force of the outstanding personality whose skill could produce such an effect. Even this first brochure of his strikes the key-note which was perceptible thereafter throughout his entire writings, viz., Athanasius is the protagonist of the true faith, and his opponents are corroded by Arius's poison; they fight as blind heretics against the Christian truth. The interest of the Patriarch of Alexandria was God's interest, and must therefore be an object of hatred to the wicked Arians. This meant in effect that Athanasius branded every opponent, no matter what his motive, as an Arian, and so regarded him as altogether in the wrong.

It has already been shown, on an earlier page, how far removed were the Eusebians from agreeing with the theology of Arius, and on what excellent grounds they were opposed to the Nicene term *homousios*. It can also be proved, even at that stage of the struggle, that their objections to Athanasius belonged entirely to the sphere of church polity, and that they carefully avoided any invasion of the sphere of theological discussion. Every step forwards made it clearer that the wrestling between Eusebius and Athanasius had to do, in the last analysis, with a question of the hierarchy, viz., whether the bishop of Alexandria or of Constantinople was to be pope of the eastern church.

At one time Eusebius succeeded in harnessing Constantius, his own emperor, into his team—which would have been quite impossible with the great Constantine. When the latter removed troublesome bishops from their sees, it was in the interest of his own peace policy, which was altogether antipathetic to every hierarchical claim. His son Constantius, without noticing what he was doing, allowed himself to become the instrument for carrying out the wishes of Eusebius, and only became aware of the consequences some little time afterwards.

Athanasius decided to go to Rome, where he might hope for trustworthy support. He did not hurry, and took many round-about ways if they offered him the chance of agitation about church polity.[1] He may have reached the end of his journey about the close of the year, to find that another exile, Marcellus of Ancyra, had arrived before him as a fellow-sufferer. Marcellus was one of the few who could claim that they had stood up in Nicea on behalf of the faith,[2] a fact which made him suspect to the other theologians of the east. When he issued a polemic, in A.D. 335, declaring war against the Eusebian school of theology and those of Origen's way of thinking, Eusebius of Cæsarea came into the arena as a literary antagonist. The challenged bishops met in synod at Constantinople and decided that Marcellus's teaching was heretical. They deposed him from his see;[3] the amnesty granted him by the younger Constantine had afforded him only a short time back at home.

Marcellus accused his enemies of supporting the doctrine of two or three gods, i.e., that they ascribed independent being to the Logos and the Holy Spirit; they placed both beside God the Father, each with His own personality. In rebutting this doctrine, he laid stress repeatedly on God's oneness, which in the course of the work of redemption, i.e., in the sphere of time, had unfolded into a trinity, and subsequently returned to the original unity. St. Paul had borne the same testimony (1 Cor. 15: 25) when he said that Christ's lordship would come to an end.[4] The Trinity, Marcellus held, was not three in essence, and it was not possible to speak of three hypostases or beings or persons; but it must always be kept in mind that, in the absolute sense, the Logos and God were one and the same

[1] ep. synod. or. Sardic. 10, in Hilarius 4, 55f. Feder   Athan. hist. Ar. 11   apol. ad Const. 4

[2] Fragm. 129   Julii, ep. in Athan. apol. 23, 3   32, 2

[3] Sozom. 2, 33   Fragments of Marcellus in Eus. gegen Marcell., ed. E. Klostermann, 185–215

[4] Fragm. 66. 67. 76. 77. 80. 81; 112–114. 121

person. He regarded Son and Spirit as the operative forms of the one godhead, who alone existed and usually was called the Father.[1] Marcellus it was who used the illustration, sometimes ascribed to Paul of Samosata and to Sabellius, viz., that the relation between God and the Logos was like that of a man and his logos, i.e., reason or speech: this logos was only a function of man; and so was it with God.[2] Further, the human nature received by the Logos from Mary, could be described, as by the Apostle (Col. 1: 15) also, as the "image of the invisible God", because it was precisely through the body which Jesus had, that the godhead became visible to men; and also that mankind was given the possibility of becoming divine.[3]

If we pass over all the learned details of his argument, and inquire into the fundamental ideas of his doctrine, we see plainly that he was defending the traditional monarchianism. The Eusebians acted quite logically in condemning him as a heretic, for he stood in the same position as Sabellius and Paul of Samosata in disputing that the Logos was an independent person. That is why he could also so readily agree to the Nicene term *homousios*—although he never used the word in the surviving fragments. On the other hand, his condemnation afforded a welcome opportunity to prove that the Nicene formula was in fact dubious.

Julius of Rome at once adopted an unambiguous attitude by dealing with the two refugees as in no way legally condemned; rather he wrote a second time to the eastern bishops demanding that the charges should be re-examined at a synod. He named Rome as the meeting-place and mentioned a definite period within which those invited should appear. This treatment of the two outcasts was declared wrong, and, quite in accordance with Athanasius's view, was held to be an intolerable attack on the Nicene creed. Two Roman presbyters, Elpidius and Philoxenus, journeyed in the first months of the year 340 to Antioch.[4]

There, however, they went through an annoying testing time, for they had to wait till January A.D. 341 for an answer.

---

[1] Fragm. 81–84 and 67; 71. 73   [2] *ibid.* 61   cf. Epiph. *haer.* 62, 1, 4   65, 1, 5
[3] Fragm. 94. 111   cf. 96
[4] Sozom. 3, 8, 3   Athan. *apol.* 20   *hist. Ar.* 11

Eusebius had no cause for haste. The tone of the Roman document offered no prospect of advantage when the matter was dealt with, and meanwhile everything in the east was on the way to a settlement which his own party could not but regard as desirable. The Emperor Constantius remained still in the field against the Persians, and the eastern bishops could maintain, with every appearance of being right, that the situation on the frontier did not allow them to leave their churches, and undertake distant journeys by sea. Further, it might be to the purpose to await the issue of the war in the west between the brothers[1] and afterwards very calmly to make sure whether the victory of Constans, and his immense growth of power, would not have consequences for church policy.

At length, Eusebius decided on an answer that in form and substance corresponded precisely with the atmosphere arising from the circumstances.[2] He objected to the outer form of the communication as inappropriate, and declared the time set for the answer was too brief. With all due respect for the apostolic origin of the Roman church, he reminded them that their apostles had come from the east, and that the standing of a church could not be determined by the size of the city, or the numbers belonging to the church; on the contrary, all bishops were of equal importance. But Julius had ventured to undervalue the verdict of the synods which had deposed Athanasius and Marcellus, and received both into the fellowship of his church: that was an attack on the principles of canon law.

Athanasius had been a notorious agitator, and now, once he had been expelled, peace prevailed in Alexandria and Egypt; Marcellus had been deposed largely on account of his intolerable and impious doctrine concerning Christ. Then came the sharply-pointed concluding issue: in his day, the Roman bishop had excommunicated Novatian and the act had been recognized unconditionally in the east, in spite of sympathy with the man who had been lawfully sentenced. The same restraint was now required from Rome towards the judgment pronounced by the eastern bishops. Julius would have to choose

---

[1] *vide supra*, 182f.
[2] The extant fragments of the letters have been assembled by Schwartz, *Gött. Nachr.* 1911, 494–496

between communion with the east, and the recognition of the two refugees—together with schism between east and west. The charge of hostility to the Nicene creed was described as not worth discussion.

A considerable pause in the military relations between the share of the Empire belonging to Constans, which had by now become overwhelmingly large, and the eastern quarter of it, ruled by Constantius, would have made it easier for Julius to decide on peace or war with the Eusebians. He convoked the fifty Italian bishops; they met in the church named after the Presbyter Vito, and gave their assent to Julius's statements.[1] Athanasius and Marcellus were declared innocent, and church-fellowship with them confirmed. The synod having agreed, Julius passed these results on to the east in a striking document which has been preserved for us verbatim through Athanasius.[2]

He deplored the arrogance of the answer which had been sent him to his friendly letter; and, notwithstanding the principle that a synod's verdicts were sacrosanct, claimed the support of the fifth canon of Nicea—which does not help us much. Then he defended Athanasius by a constant reference to the minutes which had been sent to himself, found fault with the installation of Gregory, and took Marcellus under his protection as having shown himself at Nicea an authentic protagonist of the true faith. He made an effective reference to the increasing number of deposed bishops fleeing to Rome from the east, and the manifold violent acts accompanying their expulsion. He then sharply retorted to the eastern bishops' charge of breaking the peace. He himself was acting straight-forwardly, and in accordance with the canon, whereas the opposite side were working towards schism. This was not true of all, but rather of a few intriguers who were to blame for the whole trouble. He protested sharply against the threat of schism as made by these men, and uttered a warning against such a step in high tones: "for Christ's sake". Once more, he invited a renewed examination of the charges brought forward, and pointed out that when such accusations were made against

---

[1] Gerwin Roethe, *Röm. Synode im 3 und 4 Jahrhundert*, 85 (=*Forschungen zur Kirchen und Geistesgeschichte* 11, 1937, 2) Athan. *apol.* 20 *hist. Ar.* 15
[2] Anath. *apol.* 21–35

bishops of churches founded by Apostles, the judgment ought to have been pronounced, according to canon law, "by us all", i.e., the west should have been included.

It was possible to hold that the metropolitan church of Ancyra in Galatia had been founded by an Apostle, but that in Alexandria only indirectly through St. Mark. Hence in regard to this bishopric, another argument[1] was brought to bear, viz., that Rome had, from ancient times, been competent in a special way to deal with the affairs of the church at Alexandria, and must be called in when a charge was made against its bishop. There is no doubt that in making this claim, Julius was referring to the close connection between the two churches, on which we have already often laid stress.[2] He was aware that he was standing for the teachings of St. Paul and the tradition of St. Peter when he again required the eastern bishops to revise their attitude, for it was this and nothing less that was his purpose in writing, and he had no intention of modifying it. The letter began rather feebly, but grew noticeably more forceful, and ended on a high note. The detailed explanations at the close signify an increase of the Roman claims. These were concealed under the reference to the canon law, although the term "canon law" lacked precision in use.

The Eusebians had been quite right from their own point of view in saying that Rome had deposed Novatian, and Antioch Paul of Samosata, and that these actions had been recognized by the other side without discussion: that was therefore "church law", i.e., the law of custom. But Rome seized on the principle involved, and could reply that the reason these instances had been "recognized", without more ado, was because the verdicts were correct. The west had always had the right, as such, to re-examine the case of Paul of Samosata, since no one synod was superior to another; each came to its own conclusions, as prompted by the Holy Spirit. So far all was in conformity with the style of the ancient Church.[3]

But a new epoch began when the demand was made that important decisions of the Church must be universally accepted, for it was intolerable to affirm and deny in answer to the same question: the Church as recognized by the Empire made greater

---

[1] *Julii ep.* in Athan. *apol.* 35, 4   [2] Vol. 2, 66   [3] Vol. 2, 67

claims than the free Church of earlier times, which tolerated differences even in important matters, and which was content with unresolved contradictions. Constantine had given the Church a central organ when he called a synod of the whole Empire, and carried out its resolutions with the authority of the state. The east had already felt the consequences of a compulsory unity so strongly, that it desired at least to maintain the independence of the eastern synods. But in the situation in which the Eusebians were placed, the manner of thought belonging to the ancient Church was no longer practised. The draught from the flagon of the power of the state tasted so sweet that it could never be dispensed with. So the east fought the west under the banner of the ancient Church on behalf of the independence of the eastern synods, and at the same time, it used the powers of the state to force the conclusions reached at Antioch on the completely independent Egyptian church.

Julius of Rome was in the fortunate position of being able to harmonize the ancient tradition with what he required in developing the law of the Church. He explained that, in the case under discussion, the Roman synod first of all refused its assent to the eastern pronouncements—and this was well within her rights from the standpoint of the ancient Church. He drew the inference from the present circumstances and from the new status of the Church in the Empire, that, in such important matters, unity must be reached; and consequently that the Church should set up a court of appeal composed of bishops representing every district. The point was that the Church would voluntarily recognize a council called together, not by the Emperor, but by itself. It would have been more politic in raising such an important point, if he had first of all written to all the leading bishops, and so reached a common opinion. And in regard to the affairs of the Alexandrian church, Rome asserted her special right, based on a lengthy relationship, to take part in all actions against its bishop.

Everything he said had been carefully weighed, and well conceived in accord with Church tradition. In addition, in the prevailing circumstances, it was well adapted to increase the Roman bishop's authority in the east. But it was this final point in particular that the eastern bishops wished to prevent. Nor was it theologically unimportant that the Roman synod should have declared Marcellus orthodox,, and that Julius had explicitly said so when he wrote, although only with reference to what the accused himself had set forth.[1]

It is still possible to re-examine the bases of this decision, because they are to be found in a document[2] which Marcellus sent to Julius on leaving Rome before the synod reached its verdict. He laid stress on his longstanding hostility against Arian doctrines, and then artfully quoted the ancient symbol of the Roman church, surrounding it with theological phrases which reveal his anti-Arian standpoint, but not the peculiarities of his doctrine of the Trinity for which he had been condemned. Julius was satisfied with it, and saw no need to inquire further, for he had let himself be convinced by Athanasius that the whole outlook of the Eusebians, and all their individual actions, were conditioned by their dislike of the Nicene creed and their secret inclination for Arianism.

The eastern bishops answered Julius's letter when they came together in the summer of A.D. 341 in Antioch to consecrate the "Great Church" that Constantine had founded ten years earlier.[3] Ninety-seven bishops arrived for the ceremony, and the Emperor Constantius was also present;[4] whether he followed his father's example and took part in the synod is not definitely certain. Moreover, the records of the synod are quite inadequate, and it is therefore not possible to say what was really the purpose of the transactions. In any case, the assembly defended itself against the charge of Arianism, and maintained its orthodox faith in a writing partly preserved by Athanasius, including its credal formula. The formula contains nothing striking, but corresponds to the familiar eastern type, except that it includes an attack on Marcellus.

Other doctrinal problems were dealt with at this synod. Theophronios, bishop of Tyana, had raised suspicion of his heresy. He therefore put in a statement of his belief.[5] Here he

---

[1] *Julii ep.* in Athan. *apol.* 32, 1–3
[2] Preserved in Epiph. *haer.* 72, 2, 1–3, 5 = *Marcell. Fragm.* 129, ed. Klostermann
[3] Theodoret. *H.E.* 3, 12, 1 Malalas 13, p. 326, 7 ed. Dindorf
[4] Athan. *de synod.* 25. Socrates, 2, 8–10   Sozom. 3, 5   Hilarius, *de synodis*, 28ff. The formulas are given by Athan. *de synod.* 22–25, and reprinted in Lietzmann's *Symbole* (*Kleine Texte* 17/18)
[5] Known as the "Third Formula"

said, as regards the Son, that He was with God as a person (hence not merely a function), and that He was eternal. Paul of Samosata and Marcellus denied this, and both were in the end declared accursed along with Sabellius. It was in this connection that the synod also put forward its own creed,[1] which interpolated theological additions into a lengthy formula of the usual type. The theological passages which were added describe Christ as the unchangeable likeness of the divine Being (*ousia*), and speak of three Beings (*hypostaseis*) bound together into a unity by Their harmony of will. Each had His own personality (*hypostasis*), rank, and glory. These expressions gave the idea of a divine Trinity composed of individual persons standing in superior and inferior relation to each other. Strictly speaking, here was the direct opposite of the Monarchianism represented by Marcellus and now supported in Rome.

Thus the synod took its stand, without being explicit, on the ground laid out by Origen. When it described Christ as the likeness of the divine *ousia*, it was much nearer Arius than was any possible exposition of the Nicene *homousios*. It is a characteristic of the controversies of this period, that the Nicene term never appears, a fact which bears out the view, discussed earlier (p. 119), of the unserviceable character of its theology. Nobody, not even Julius or Athanasius, used it as a test of orthodoxy, and nobody quoted the Nicene creed or required opponents to subscribe to it. The content of the Nicene declaration of faith exhausts its purpose in condemning Arius, and the relevant condemnatory sentences were regularly repeated. The Antiochene formula now under discussion ends with anathematizing those who confine the Logos to time, describe Him as a creature, or otherwise make Him like others who have come into existence; but meanwhile these propositions disposed of Arius and his adherents.[2] The synod also gave assurances that the creed now put forth went back to the martyr Lucian, a claim which paid respect to the celebrated teacher, and guaranteed the theological correctness of the symbol.

---

[1] The "second" formula is given in Athan. *de synod*. 23   Hilarius, *de synod*. 29 (Lietzmann, *Symbole*, 28ff.)   Sozom. 3, 5, 9
[2] *Doc*. 6 in Athan. 3, 12f. Opitz

Thus the "Eusebians" calmly asserted their former, pre-Nicene, position, paid due reverence to the Nicene synod by recognizing its condemnatory clauses, but refused to be forced into new and strange paths by the term *homousios*. Athanasius, again, was equally unable to make use of this ponderous term. When he was not tired by pillorying the Eusebians as Arians, his thesis was not some theological discussion of *homousios*, but some question of their conduct of church policy. Even Marcellus of Ancyra, though he had no need to do so, avoided using *homousios*, and, compared with Julius, used the Roman more frequently than the Nicene creed. By the fact that Marcellus had been recognized by Rome, and that the Antiochene symbol was directed against that recognition, there was a change in the nature of the opposition which had hitherto obtained between the east and the Romans who intervened on behalf of Athanasius. Whereas hitherto it had been concerned with the policy of the Church, it now turned to the sphere of theology, and so was deepened.

It was a hard blow for the assembly centred on Antioch that at that moment they were robbed of their leader. Eusebius, bishop of Constantinople, died shortly after the Church Consecration synod. The eastern Church was thus deprived of its only outstanding personality, a man clever in giving a tactful lead, one who, also, through his excellent, indeed family, relation with the ruling dynasty[1] was a born mediator between the régime of the Church and the administrators of the state. The deposed Paul felt that his opportunity had now come; he returned to Constantinople accompanied by Asklepas of Gaza, and found a considerable number of adherents among the populace. But the "Eusebian" bishops chose Makedonios as bishop of the capital; and the result of these contradictory actions was quickly seen in bloody struggles between partisans in the streets. Hermogenes, the general in command of the cavalry, was ordered to quell the disturbance, but was unable to resist the mob. His house was stormed and set on fire; he himself was chased through the streets by the raging masses, and killed.

Constantius had to intervene personally; he came back in all

[1] Amm. Marc. 22, 9, 4   Athan. *hist. Ar.* 5. 6

haste from Antioch, and his sudden presence immediately brought the tumult to an end. He threw Paul out of the city, yet did not confirm Makedonios, because he felt he was partly to blame for the uproar. Still, he allowed him to conduct service unhindered at a church in the city. In other respects, he imposed very mild penalties, the harshest being that he stiffened the regulations governing the issue of bread to the insolent mob, and reduced the corn-ration from 80,000, as fixed by Constantine for public support, to 40,000 bushels. These events took place in A.D. 342,[1] possibly in the spring.

About the same time, a deputation from the east, consisting of the bishops Narcissos of Neronias-Irenopolis (in Cilicia), Maris of Chalcedon, Theodoros of Heraklea, Marcus of Syrian Arethusa (Restan, near Hama), brought to the Emperor Constans in Trèves a confession of faith of the Antiochene synod. This creed repeated the articles of the old type, and only referred to the present-day problems by lightly touching on the deposition of Marcellus, and deprecating the terms employed by the Arians.[2] Afterwards this was called the fourth formula of Antioch, and it was to play an important part.

There is little certainty as to why it was sent, and none at all why the eastern bishops made their surprising journey to the Court in the west. The source[3] asserts that Constans had himself expressed desire for a personal report about the problems of the eastern church. It is unquestioned that the bishop of Trèves went unpunished for denying the fellowship of his church to his own Emperor's guests[4] and that Athanasius was soon afterwards respectfully received in Milan by the Emperor; he then went on to Trèves there to meet the aged Ossius of Cordova.[5]

It was useless to delay the synod desired by Rome, but completely refused by Eusebius. The old leader was dead, and the two Emperors now agreed to Constans's wish to bring together a synod, normative for the whole Empire, either on the common frontier, or else in the western part, at Serdika (Sophia). It took place in autumn of the same year, A.D. 342,

[1] Soc. 2, 12. 13 Sozom. 3, 7 Libanius, or. 59, 94–98; document from the ep. synod. or. Sardic. 20 in Hilarius, 4, 61, 23ff. Feder
[2] Athan. de synod. 25 (Lietzmann, Symbole, 30f.)   [3] Socrates, 2, 18
[4] ep. synod. or. Sardic. 27, 7 in Hilarius 4, 66, 30 Feder   [5] Athan. apol. ad Const. 4

though in a different way from that which Constans had expected.[1] For the eastern bishops never thought of submitting to the judgment which Rome threatened to pronounce. Only 76 of them altogether took part in the synod, whereas the west sent almost 300 delegates.

Both parties gathered at the prescribed date in Serdika, but did not agree as to the common business. The eastern bishops asked for recognition of their former decisions made in synod, and this in a material form for all to see, viz., that the deposed bishops, Athanasius, Marcellus, and their associates, be not allowed to attend the sittings; for they were prepared to circulate their contentions in the synod. The bishops of the west refused, the discussions went to and fro, and at length, the eastern bishops left Serdika, and published their protestation in Philippopolis.[2]

The others held meetings with Ossius of Cordova and the local bishop, Protogenes, as chairmen, and without further disturbance. They issued an encyclical proving the complete innocence and orthodoxy of all the accused; turning the "flight" of the eastern bishops to good account as proof of their bad conscience, deposing and excommunicating the leaders of the hostile party as guilty of Arian heresy and actual crime. The persons named were Gregory of Alexandria, Basil of Ancyra, Quintianus of Gaza, Theodoros of Heraklea, Narcissos of Neronias, Acacius of Cæsarea in Palestine, Stephanos of Antioch, Ursacius of Singidunum (Belgrade), Valens of Mursa (Esseg at the mouth of the Drava), Menophantos of Ephesus, and George of Laodicea in Syria; and also the western bishops thought bitterly of the "two Eusebiuses" who had died in the interim.[3]

Theological reasons[4] were then brought to bear in support of the charge of Arianism, but, strangely enough, not based on documentary statements of individual opponents, still less on their professions of faith made in synod. Only once, and that

---

[1] The date is confirmed by Athan. *apol. ad Const.* 4, and the compilation of Theodosius Diaconus, in Schwartz, *op. cit.* 1911, 516   Athan. *ep.* preface (31, Larsow) gives the date A.D. 343   Socrates, 2, 20, 4, says A.D. 347

[2] Letter of the east. bishops, 14f. in Hilarius, 4, 58f. ed. Feder; letter of the west. bishops, *ibid.* 107   Socrates 2, 20, 7–9   Athan. *ep.* Pref. 343 (31 ed. Larsow)

[3] 123f. and 119. Feder   [4] Preserved by Theodoret *H.E.* 2, 8, 37–52

without mentioning any name, did they attack Marcellus's enemy, Asterius. The remainder of the encyclical was occupied, in quite general terms, with the doctrine of three distinct hypostases of the Trinity as taught by Valens and Ursacius; it was described as Arian snake-poison; and the doctrine of the one substance, "which they call *ousia*", was put forward against it. There was only one God, one godhead of Father and Son, one divine substance (*hypostasis*); and the Son, as Logos, was the Power (*dynamis* as in 1 Cor. 1: 24) of the Father; granted the Father was greater than the Son (John 14: 28), yet not in the sense of an essential difference, but because the name of Father expressed a pre-eminence.

Nothing of all this can in fact be clearly understood. The theses contained in this document cannot be brought together to form an intelligible conception as a whole; rather they oscillate to and fro between a doctrine of the Logos and the Trinity as required by many Biblical passages on the one hand, and traditional Monarchianism, the doctrine of the one incarnate God on the other. But the theses reveal a certain hesitation to accept the awkwardly clear formulas of Marcellus, however nearly they were approached, and, by preference, to take refuge in shielding the indefiniteness of their own position behind high-sounding phraseology.

The significance of this considered opinion of the theologians of Serdika consisted in the fact that now, for the first time, what they meant by "Arianism" as a word of abuse, was clearly explained. It was by no means the doctrine of Arius alone, but any theology which recognized three hypostases in the godhead; or, to put it otherwise, ascribed a separate personal existence to the Logos as the Son of God. The effect was that war was declared against all who took their stand on the basis laid down by Origen.

The entire development of Greek speculative thought since the days of the Apologists was denied. What had been thought out in a lower degree by Tertullian and Novatian in the west, was left out of account, although it had been put forward in appropriately formulated doctrines. On the other hand, the influence of Marcellus's doctrines was quite clear; he had been declared orthodox, and was therefore to be protected. In contrast to the doctrine of the divine Trinity, there was set very insistently the belief in *one* hypostasis, i.e., the unity of the divine Being. In this sense, the old Monarchianism was re-affirmed, except that it was now extended by adding Biblical passages, making it unassailable. The theologians concerned did not trouble themselves with the question whether the structure they had made was, in itself, conceivable, for their whole interest was confined to the fundamental thesis of the *one* hypostasis.

Thus it came about that fronts which had been demarcated on the basis of church-policy were now further characterized and divided by theological terminology. Quite intentionally, neither the word *homousios* nor the Nicene Creed was mentioned either in the present encyclical or in any other official document of the synod. Of course both the word and the Creed had been discussed: inevitably so. The president at Serdika was Ossius, and he was the most eminent person present who had attended the Council of Nicea. His desire was intelligible that the synod should adopt that Creed as its standard; but it was rejected as inadequate. This was done rightly, for, at that time, there was no division of mind about this Creed. It was not the subject of controversy, and no one in either party really knew what to make of the term *homousios*.

Ossius conjointly with Protogenes of Serdika, wrote privately[1] to Julius of Rome, explaining what was to himself the un-welcome attitude of the synod, and assuring him that every bishop had after all assented to the Nicene confession, as was axiomatic. The letter has survived together with other writnigs issued at the same time from Serdika; they were afterwards brought together, and put in the archives of the Patriarch of Alexandria.[2] They all proclaim victory over the heretics, and record the deposition of the ringleaders.

Of greater importance are two other writings coming from the synod, and extant elsewhere. The first is an official letter, signed by the delegates taking part, addressed to Julius of Rome, and giving a short summary of the conclusions. In the

[1] In Leo Magn. *opera*, 3, 597 f. ed. Ballerini   cf. also Sozom. 3, 12, 6
[2] In the collection made by Theodosius Diaconus, printed in Leo, *opera*, 3, 597–614   cf. also E. Schwartz, *Gött. Nachr.* 1904, 379–381

beginning, incompletely preserved, they express their pleasure in having experienced the presence of the Holy Spirit, who had used the synod as His bodily organ of revelation; and they greet Julius as a member of the synod, physically absent but present in spirit. In the conclusion, they beg him, as did the delegates to the synod of Arles,[1] to publicize their conclusions in Sicily, Sardinia, and Italy. At the commencement of the letter, stands a sentence without context saying that it would be most appropriate if the Lord Bishops were to write from their several provinces to their head, viz., the Stool of the Apostle Peter. There is serious dispute whether this sentence is a later interpolation, or whether—as seems more likely to me—it is genuinely one of the extant fragments of the introduction to the letter.[2]

The second letter was sent to the Emperor Constantius asking for a command to be sent to all provincial governors to confine themselves to their political functions, and not to undertake anything attacking the Church's domain; in particular not to presume to act as judges in actions against clerics. Constantius must have been most interested in going on to read that it must be the highest principle of his rule that he should give all his subjects the pleasure of enjoying freedom, and that the preservation of free personal self-determination was the best means of abolishing unrest. In any case, he must make it possible for the orthodox to follow bishops possessing their own form of belief, and prevent the local authorities from favouring heretical machinations. Only so would the pest of Arianism vanish and true peace return home. Then they asked permission for the bishops still in exile to return, and concluded by threatening with the eternal pains of hell the Arians who had been condemned, and whose names they gave.[3]

The synod not only dealt with these high problems of the policy of Church and state, but also it used the opportunity afforded by the impressive assembly of western bishops, and went on to decide questions, still in suspense, regarding the inner life of the Church. The result has come down in thirteen

[1] *vide supra*, 88f.
[2] In Hilarius, 4, 126–139 E. Caspar, *Gesch. des Papsttums* 1, 587, believes the sentence is an interpolation
[3] Hilarius, 4, 181–184

canons. They are conceived in the style which had already become usual, and was also often employed later, viz., the proposal of the chairman of committee, the additional suggestions brought forward in the course of debate, together with the final conclusions of the synod, were given as part of the protocol of the session. The text has been preserved in both Latin and Greek, and for a long time it was uncertain which language represented the original. Now that the manuscript tradition has at length been completely recovered, thus giving a reliable basis for comparing the texts, there is no longer any doubt about the facts: the canons were composed in Latin, as were also most of the other official statements.[1] Latin was the official language of the western bishops in this assembly.

The content of these conclusions will be discussed in another connection, only one matter being significant at the present moment. In correspondence with the interests of the synod in building up the western province of the state also as an administrative unit of the Church—the East having already proceeded much further—the conditions were considered under which bishops might properly discuss the affairs of a neighbouring province in a way disallowed in general at present. Ossius, the president, declared that such a step should only be permitted on special application and for redressing an urgent exigency. But it should not be allowed if a bishop was merely in dispute with his provincial colleagues and wished to call in aid from the neighbouring province. Such differences must be resolved within the province concerned, or, if needs be, by the provincial synod's deposing the person in the wrong.

If the one thus condemned were not content, and believed he had been unfairly dealt with, he was not permitted without more ado to call in neighbours beyond the border of his own province, but he could require the synod pronouncing judgment—and if refusing to act, then colleagues from the neighbouring province—to write to the bishop of Rome, and so pay tribute in this form to the memory of Peter, the most holy Apostle. The Roman bishop was then to decide whether the

[1] Edited by C. H. Turner as *Ecclesiæ Occidentalis Monumenta Juris Antiquissima*, Tome 1, fasc. 2, pars 3 (1930), 452–486; Latin and Grk. 490–531 All earlier editions are out-of-date. Also cf. E. Schwartz, *ZNW.* 1931, 1–35

judgment was correct, or whether a re-examination was needed. In the latter case, he was to set up a court of justice consisting of bishops from the neighbouring province, and he could, if it were so desired, and he himself regarded it as necessary, delegate a Roman presbyter to that court.

This meant nothing less than that the Roman bishop was to be vested with the highest powers as a judge for the entire west, and for the explicit reason that he was the successor of Peter, a fact which could not be disputed. The Greek translator of the Serdikan canons, who was probably working in Thessalonika under the instructions of his bishop, attempted to transform this general ascription of authority into a personal privilege of Julius, in order to lessen what he felt to be its uncomfortably wide scope.[1]

The synod itself unanimously agreed to Ossius's proposal—and with the same unanimity silently undertook to neglect this stipulation: nor did they use it throughout the whole of the fourth century. The time for the legal confirmation of the Roman bishop's primacy had not yet come. The canon was complete in A.D. 342; it was not merely a demonstration of a complete union of the west as over against the east, but also a tribute paid to Julius, who had been the leader in the struggle. Athanasius's party, and especially the majority of the Egyptian bishops went, naturally, with Rome. A notice in the Alexandrian records[2] informs us that, at Serdika, agreement was also reached between Rome and Alexandria about the dating of Easter.

The eastern bishops, in their document,[3] explained once more in detail, their reasons for deposing Marcellus and Athanasius, enumerated the wrongs done by Paul of Constantinople, Asklepas of Gaza, and Lucius of Adrianople, and pointed out angrily that Protogenes of Serdika and Cyriacus of Naissus (Nish) had formerly shared in deposing Marcellus by signing the decree; and that, similarly, Athanasius had at an earlier date condemned Asklepas, as Paul had also condemned Athanasius. They raised the old objection in regard to the conclusions of Serdika, that a judgment pronounced by western

---

[1] The name "Julius" occurs only in the Greek and not in the Latin text, as first noticed by Turner
[2] Ath. *ep.* pref. p. 31 Larsow
[3] In Hilarius, 4, 48–67; the copy in Latin sent to Africa is extant

bishops concerning the valid conclusions of eastern councils, was an unheard of innovation. They then added the list of the names of those whom they themselves' had condemned: Julius, Ossius, Protogenes, Maximin of Trèves, and Gaudentius, the impious successor of Cyriacus in the see of Nish.

Like the western bishops, they accompanied their encyclical with a confession of faith. This was identical with the Antiochene formula[1] shortly before sent to Constans, with its theses directed against Marcellus; and at the end, a few clauses were added going still further. A curse was laid on (a) those "teaching three gods"—naturally no Christian did this, but it was a biased inference which certain opponents drew from the eastern doctrine of three hypostases; (b) those who declared Father, Son, and Spirit were identical—that was the sharpened "Sabellian" form of the doctrine of one hypostasis which the west had now accepted in defending Marcellus; (c) those who taught the temporal birth of the Son—an attack on Arianism— or denied that it originated in an act of will of the Father—as Marcellus[2] had denied in opposing Asterius. Finally, this synod, for the better execution of the Nicene decisions regarding Easter, issued an encyclical rooted in the Jewish mode of reckoning the Passover, but seeking to be independent of it.[3]

So it came about that the synod which had been called as representing the whole Empire, fell asunder from the first, breaking into two halves, each of which condemned and deposed the leader of the other. Then each party returned home, the question now being which of the two would be able to carry out its will. Schism had become fact. For the first time in the history of the Church, east and west separated from each other by formal decision. It was not merely differences in church-politics that found expression in the present division; there were also differences both in theological thought beneath the ambiguous formulas, as well as in many aspects of religious feeling, as between eastern and western Christianity. A straight line runs from Serdika to the final separation in A.D. 1054.

In the east, it seemed at first as if Constantius would support

---

[1] *vide supra*, 199

[2] cf. Fragm. of Marcellus no. 34 in Eus. p. 190, 18 ed. Klostermann. The formula *Makrostichos* is a valuable commentary, Athan. *de synod.* 26 c. 8

[3] E. Schwartz, *Jüdische u. Christl. Ostertafeln*, 122f.

the conclusions of his own bishops. An uproar in Adrianople directed against the synod-delegates who were passing through, was anticipated in time, and suppressed by force; he exiled the local bishop, who belonged to the opposition. Several other decrees of banishment were issued, and the illicit return of exiled persons was made punishable with death.[1] But the Emperor Constans regarded the party whom he least liked as by no means lost as a result of the failure at Serdika. At Easter, A.D. 343, he sent one of his generals, with bishops Vincentius of Capua and Euphrates of Cologne, to state the case, to his brother's Court at Antioch. This delegation brought a letter written by Constans, a letter about whose contents the writers of the surviving records could only make a variety of guesses.[2] Nevertheless it was so impressive that Constantius's policy in regard to the Church gradually changed thence forward.

The change was facilitated by Stephen, bishop of Antioch, who started a scandal which was as gross as it was foolish. He sent a public prostitute into the bedroom of the aged bishop of Cologne, with the idea of being then able to destroy his moral reputation. The girl, however, was insufficiently informed of the plot, raised an alarm at the wrong time, and the game was up. The general felt that he himself was included in the insult, and demanded searching inquiries. The result was a case in the courts, issuing unavoidably at last in the deposition of the bishop of Antioch.[3]

The first indication of a change in Constantius occurred in the autumn of A.D. 344, when he issued a decree of clemency to some of the clerics exiled from Alexandria, and instructed the local officials not to give further trouble to the clerics faithful to Athanasius. Then he began seriously to think of recalling Athanasius, and the way was opened when Gregory died on June 26, 345. He wrote to Constans on the subject, and invited Athanasius to come to his court. But Athanasius was suspicious, and remained in Aquileia, his former refuge. The only consequence of a second letter from Constantius was that Athanasius sent a few trusted clerics to the Court at Edessa there to open negotiations. Only when the Emperor wrote for the

---

[1] Athan. *hist. Ar.* 18. 19   [2] Socrates, 2, 22. Theodoret *H.E.* 2, 8, 54–57
[3] Athan. *hist. Ar.* 20   Theodoret, *H.E.* 2, 9, 1–10, 1

third time, did he make a move.[1] He went from Aquileia to Rome, apparently to take leave of Julius, who gave him a charming letter to the church at Alexandria.

Then at last he was received in audience in Antioch,[2] where a royal document was handed to him. It granted his return to his church, and removed all the legal disabilities weighing on his adherents. When he was passing through Jerusalem, a synod of sixteen Palestine bishops greeted him, and then, on October 21, 346, he once more entered Alexandria like a victor after a great battle. Other exiles, whom the Serdikan council had accepted, were recommended by Constantius to his brother's good will and were recalled, including, at last, Paul of Constantinople[3] who had suffered severely.[4]

Constantius's change of tone became clearly evident in the course of the year 344, and was quickly noticed by the eastern bishops. It brought them to the view that it would be advisable to modify their curtness to the western churches. They saw, moreover, that diplomatic relations had really been broken off by the decisions reached at Serdika, and therefore they sent a delegation of three bishops to Italy in order that "the entire west might understand that the heretics were shameless slanderers, whereas eastern views were orthodox". It would appear that the points in question in the west were set forth in detail and sent to Antioch about Easter, A.D. 343.[5]

The deputies, in their reply, proposed a long formula (*formula makrostichos*) which had been composed in Antioch, and which made no attempt to judge questions in dispute, but set forth the symbol of Serdika itself plus a detailed commentary. Here the charge of Arianism, which had been raised in the western confession of Serdika, was very cleverly refuted; and it was proved that belief in three natures or persons in the Trinity in no way implied a doctrine of three gods. Care was taken to avoid using the term "three hypostases" which gave the west very serious offence; neither was the word *ousia* employed in any place. All the greater was the emphasis on

---

[1] The document and the story are given in Athan. *apol.* 51–52; cf. also *hist. Ar.* 21; *apol. ad Const.* 4
[2] Athan. *apol.* 5   [3] *vide supra*, 193, 198
[4] Socrates, 2, 23, 39–43   Schwartz, *ZNW.* 1935, 148
[5] Synod of Ancyra, in Epiph. 73, 2, 3 p. 269, 10 ed. Holl.

repudiating the doctrines of Paul of Samosata and Marcellus of Ancyra, and on drawing up a battle line against Sabellianism. Along with the mention of Marcellus, occurs the name of his former deacon for the first time, Photinus having meanwhile been promoted bishop of Sermium (Mitrovitza) where he reproduced his master's teaching naïvely and in a dry way.[1]

The delegation was received in Milan by a synod in which legates of the pope of Rome also shared.[2] They immediately had the satisfaction of Photinus's being declared a heretic. Then the two Pannonian bishops, Ursacius and Valens, who had sided with the east in Serdika, confessed themselves nought but sinners, having been branded by name as guilty of Arianism in the western confession of faith.[3] In accordance with the way matters had proceeded, no halt could be called in the present situation in the realm of Constans; on the contrary the delegation laid a recantation before the synod of Milan, and condemned Arius and his adherents.

But that did not satisfy the assembled bishops. Indeed, the deputation from the east had to undergo the painful experience of seeing their carefully formulated articles found unacceptable to their judges at Milan. The latter required the condemnation of the doctrines of three hypostases, which appeared to them to be the fundamental error. Those who held this belief were regarded by them as Arians; this fact had been unmistakably set forth by them in their confession at Serdika. To agree on this point was an impossibility for the east—so it was to remain. The deputation therefore departed with their commission undischarged, and the division in the Church was continued.

By defending Marcellus of Ancyra, and accepting Athanasius's strategy of declaring Eusebians to be Arians, the synod of Serdika had transferred the contest to the theological realm. This proved now to be a serious difficulty in the way of peace, though peace might have been reached if church policy had been the only issue after Constantius had decided to recall Athanasius, and his bishops were prepared to let the matter drop. Photinus was compelled to pay the price for the change of front in the battle. Athanasius made use of an Apology

---

[1] Athan. *de synod.* 26   Hahn, *Bibl. d. Symbole* §159
[2] Synod. Arim., in Hilarius, 4, 80, 9   [3] *vide supra*, 200

written and published by Marcellus on behalf of Photinus; it afforded Athanasius an opportunity to rid himself of a man who at one time had been a fellow-sufferer. But he accorded church-fellowship to Marcellus[1] and that is the last we hear of him. Perhaps he remained quietly in Ancyra. At any rate, Epiphanius says that he died in A.D. 374, but does not mention his place of banishment. He remarks, however, that once, when he inquired of Athanasius about Marcellus, Athanasius only smiled ironically over the unfortunate man.[2]

This source of theological difficulties was thus side-tracked, and there would have been no further obstacle to agreement had not the new thesis been put forward. It was now declared that the doctrine of three hypostases was Arian in character. All unexpectedly, a further wall of partition had been raised, and it threw an ominous shadow into the future. True, Photinus was now condemned as a heretic, but he remained quietly in Sirmium, supported by adherents from his church; and the Emperor left him undisturbed. In A.D. 347, his judges assembled again, this time in his own city, and once more condemned him as a heretic.[3] But even then, he did not depart.

It must have accorded with the Emperor's wishes, when the synod of Milan had communicated their verdict of condemnation to the eastern bishops in a written document. It was also intended to be a gesture of reconciliation, and it was an un-friendly act when, in reply, the eastern bishops referred to Photinus's teacher as the wicked Marcellus, with whom Athanasius had now broken.[4] Meanwhile, Ursacius and Valens had turned to Julius of Rome, and had retracted their earlier attack on Athanasius in every form, professing they had been deceived by forged documents. They also condemned Arius after referring to a creed which had already been proposed in Milan.

Julius received them again into the fellowship of his church, while they wrote to Athanasius a corresponding letter from Aquileia.[5] Thus peace was restored in this quarter. But dealings with the eastern church were completely held up; three years passed, and still nothing happened. Then the great problem suddenly changed, and in a way no one had expected.

[1] Hilarius, 4, 146, 8–15   [2] Epiph. *haer.* 72, 4, 4
[3] Hilarius, 4, 142, 17ff.   146, 5–8. 22   147, 6–9
[4] *ibid.* 4, 146, 26   147,10   [5] *ibid.* 4, 143–145

Chapter Eight

CONSTANTIUS AS SOLE EMPEROR

ON JANUARY 18, 350, MAGNENTIUS, A GENERAL OF GERMANIC race, proclaimed himself emperor at Autun, and was accepted with astonishing alacrity by the entire west. Constans fled and was assassinated in a village of the Pyrenees. His sister, Constantia, the widow of Hannibalianus, saved Illyricum from the usurper by persuading Vetranio, the general in command there, to proclaim himself emperor, and so forestall worse events. A *Putsch* in Rome on behalf of the Constantine line was quickly suppressed. Magnentius sought to come to an understanding with Vetranio and so gain the time he needed.

When Constantius appeared on the scene, Vetranio combined his troops with those of the eastern empire, and, on December 25, 350, in Nish, surrendered to Constantius the crown which he had only pretended to assume. Meanwhile Magnentius had strengthened his position. Constans had been hated both by the populace and the army, and so the new master really seemed to many to be the "Liberator of the Roman Empire, the new founder of freedom and the state, the Protector of the soldiers and the subjects", and as such he was lauded on inscriptions.[1] Although he himself was a pagan,[2] and also immediately issued a decree permitting sacrifices, he minted coins bearing the symbol of Christ, and above all else, he sought to effect a union with Athanasius as the most influential person in Egypt. To this end he had an opportunity when he sent envoys *via* Alexandria to Constantius. Athanasius, for his part, wrote to the usurper a letter with his own hand; but later when fate placed him in Constantius's power, he volubly denied having written, and described the letter as a forgery.[3] But at that time he was being wooed, and Constantius assured him by letter of his immutable royal regard; he also confirmed him in his office.[4] Magnentius had to defend himself on the Rhine

---

[1] Dessau, *insc. lat. sel.* n. 742

[2] *Cod. Theod.* 16, 10, 5   Philostorgios, 3, 26. p. 52, 7, ed. Bidez

[3] Athan. *apol. ad Const.* 6–11

[4] *ibid.* 23, and Athan. *hist. Ar.* 24 in two different translations. Moreover, cf. *ep.*, Pref. to 350 (p. 33 Larsow) and the complaint in *hist. Ar.* 51

frontier against the Alemanni whom Constantius had roused, and he passed this task on to his brother, Decentius, whom he styled Cæsar at the beginning of A.D. 351.

Constantius himself now took steps to ensure the succession of his dynasty. In March, 351, he raised Gallus, his nephew, to the rank of Cæsar, married him to his own sister Constantia, who had just proved herself politically loyal, and directed him to Antioch as his residence. His political problems also included protecting the frontier against the Persians; and the Emperor knew from many years' experience how little glory was to be gained here.

Meanwhile, preparations were in process for the main struggle, for Constantius steadfastly refused all the usurper's proposals. His army advanced from the low lying plains of Roumania, up the Danube and towards the west. The advance-guard suffered a setback near Laibach, but on September 28, at Mursa (Essig), near to the mouth of the Drava, there was a severe battle ending in the defeat of Magnentius. The latter did not regard his case as hopeless, not even when the victor again refused to enter into peace negotiations. He abandoned Italy, and marched into Gaul, which was still loyal to him, although Sicily, Africa, and Spain had been won over by Constantius's fleets.

In the middle of the summer of A.D. 353, the imperial army won a victory which opened the way to Arles through the valley of the Durance. When now the firmness of the Gallic troops began to waver, Magnentius committed suicide in Lyons, the date being August 10, 353. His brother, Decentius, who had just defeated the Alemanni, followed his example. The son of the great Constantine had inherited his father's good fortune; he who at first was the least regarded and the weakest of the three Cæsars, outlived his brothers, and became the sole ruler of the whole empire.

The decisive day also gave a certain churchman his great opportunity. While the armies were wrestling together near Mursa, Constantius did not follow the example of his father, and dash among the enemy at the head of his knights; rather he awaited the outcome of the battle in a church on the outskirts of the town, receiving spiritual comfort from Bishop

Valens. That cunning cleric had taken good care that he should be the first to receive news of the victory. He took it in to the Emperor saying that an angel from heaven was his authority. Constantius never forgot his services, and from that moment made Valens his confidant.[1] The history of the Church during the next ten years tells how he and his inseparable friend, Ursacius of Belgrade, made use of their influence.

Firstly, an end was put to the enormity that the heretical Photinus still remained undisturbed as bishop of Sirmium. The Emperor ordered a synod in which now the eastern bishops took part, and which condemned Photinus after he had been worsted by Basil of Ancyra in a theological disputation arranged according to rule.[2] The symbol proposed on this occasion[3] was only another form of that which was contained in the long redaction of Antioch. This time, when the Emperor himself was residing in the city, the stubborn bishop was actually cast out of his see, never to return during Constantius's lifetime.

Then the storm-clouds gathered over Athanasius's head. His recall had only been effected by pressure from Constans, and the delay in responding to Constantius, as distrustful as it was disrespectful, still remained in count against the self-confident pope of Egypt. In addition there was the proof of his more than dubious attitude to Magnentius. It was decided to cite him to appear at the royal court, which had been transferred to Milan from autumn, A.D. 352. Athanasius heard about this, and attempted to meet the storm by sending a number of bishops and presbyters to Milan, but did not obey the demand for his personal presence. He asserted afterwards that a forged letter had played an important part here.[4]

Moreover, in the previous year, the eastern forces of the Church had again taken the field against him. The east, under political pressure, had only borne it silently that a bishop, lawfully deposed by their synod at Tyre, should have returned to Alexandria. After the death of Constans, there came the opportunity of again making good the verdict reached at Tyre,

[1] Sulpicius Severus, *chron.* 2, 38, 5–7

[2] Socrates, 2, 29, 1–2   30, 44   Epiph. *haer.* 71, 1, 4–8

[3] Athan. *de synod.* 27   Hahn, *Bibl.* §160

[4] *Hist. Athanasii*, 3 (p. 7of. ed. Fromen)=Sozom. 4, 9, 6–7 *Ep.* Preface (p. 34 ed. Larsow)   Athan. *apol. ad Const.* 19–21

but vainly defended in Serdika. Now, however, the eastern bishops proceeded more cautiously, and no longer spoke of the independence of the east. In view of the outer change in the sphere of politics, Constantius's interests were no longer confined to the east, and his particularism was not now to be reckoned with. It might even be possible, by skilfully restoring the former situation, to win the Roman bishop's co-operation.

So they wrote to Julius, repeated the old complaints, and suggested he might well take the lead in a new examination of Athanasius's case. In so doing, they came up against the claim, which Julius had made explicitly,[1] that the special rights of Rome as concerning Alexandria should receive recognition. The effects of their letter were seen surprisingly soon. Pope Julius was not able to answer himself, for he died on April 12, 352. Liberius, his successor, however, immediately sent a deputation to Alexandria, roughly cited Athanasius to appear before him for judgment, and threatened him with excommunication, should he refuse.[2] Athanasius naturally set the demand aside. In its present form, it was to him, of course, an administrative error, revealing an unskilled use of the reins in new hands. Liberius saw that he had placed himself between two stools. So he sent legates to the royal court at Arles, requesting the Emperor to call a council at Aquileia, and presenting him at the same time with all the relevant documents.[3]

By this time, Magnentius being dead, the Emperor was in the mood of a conqueror, and had no desire for prolonged discussions. Already a number of Italian bishops, conforming with the pressure exercised by the throne, had agreed to the condemnation of Athanasius. Now the same assent was required of the papal legates, and they agreed. To make certain, they also stipulated the condemnation of Arianism, though nothing more was heard of this point.[4]

Liberius took umbrage at the independent act, which robbed him of the prospect of the council he had desired. He therefore sent Lucifer, bishop of Cagliari (in Sardinia) with a letter to Constantius so as to bring it about, in spite of all, that

---

[1] *vide supra*, 194   [2] Liberius, *ep.* 18, *studens paci*, (Hilarius 4, 155)
[3] Liberius, *ep.* 4, 2. *obsecro* (Hilarius, 4, 90   cf. p. 167, 7)
[4] Liberius, *ep.* 4, 2. 5. *obsecro*, and 1, 1–2. *inter haec* (Hilarius, 4, 90. 92. 167)

an assembly of the Church should be called. He declared with emphasis, that he was himself in favour of universal peace, but this did not depend merely on a correct solution of the Athanasius affair, for the question of the true faith was still not cleared up between himself and the east. He then referred to the Nicene creed, which had been unanimously agreed to under Constantine, and which must remain as a model for the future. Then the Saviour Himself would rejoice that the Emperor put political requirements behind matters of faith and of peace in the Church.[1]

Taken as a whole, the position did not seem unfavourable to Constantius's intentions, and it must have seemed desirable to him to have the support of a decision reached by a synod. Hence in the summer of A.D. 355 a council was called to Milan where the court was in residence, a council consisting of more than 300 delegates, predominantly from the west. But the question of faith was not now the bone of contention, and when Eusebius of Vercelli required subscription to the Nicene creed, the Emperor's confidant intervened with a demurrer. The sittings were transferred from the church to the palace[2] and, hidden behind a curtain, Constantius secretly listened to the speeches.[3] He increased the pressure on the bishops in order to attain his end of condemning Athanasius. He roundly refused to allow the question of the faith to be introduced in this connection.[4] On the whole, he got his way, and the majority submitted. Only the actual leaders of the west offered resistance, above all Paul of Trèves, secondly Eusebius of Vercelli, then Dionysius of Alba, and Lucifer of Cagliari. Dionysius of Milan and Rhodanus of Toulouse had been inclined to agree at first. But all were sent into banishment.[5]

Lengthy negotiations were carried on with Liberius, but at the end, he had to appear in Milan, and because he could not comply with the Emperor's wishes, into exile he went. He was ordered to go to Beroea (Verria) in Thrace. Impressive accounts of his conversations with officials and the Emperor himself

---

[1] Liberius, *ep.* 4 (Hilarius, 4, 89–93)   [2] Hilarius, 4, 186f.
[3] Lucifer, *moriendum esse pro dei filio* 1. 4 (p. 285, 29; 291, 20, ed. Hartel)
[4] Significantly, Sulpicius Severus, *chron.* 2, 39, 7
[5] Record in Socrates, 2, 36; Sozom. 4, 9, 1–4   Hilarius, 4, 186f.   Sulp. Sev. 2, 39   Athan. *hist. Ar.* 31, 76   Letter to Eus. Verc. in Labbe, *Conc.* 2, 773f.

circulated among the people.[1] Athanasius quoted him indeed
as having asked for a purely church council, independent of
state influences.[2] Letters were rained on Ossius now nearly a
hundred years old, but to no purpose. Finally, the Emperor
ordered him to Sirmium, held him there a whole year, till he
became weary. Then he agreed to church fellowship with
Ursacius and Valens, but refused to condemn Athanasius now
as ever.[3] In Gaul, Hilary of Poitiers organized opposition to
the church policy of Constantius, and was consequently
deposed by a church synod at Biterrae (Béziers), and banished.
He was ordered to go to Phrygia and to stay there four years.[4]

Constantius had forced his will on the whole Church, and he
could regard himself as a worthy successor to his father. But
victory had been attained only after a far longer struggle, and
had been very dearly bought. Moreover, the Emperor had
been able to send all the deposed bishops into exile without
more ado, except one. The whole affair turned on Athanasius,
who remained unattacked in Alexandria, and who ordered the
Emperor's commissar to go home with nothing accomplished.
That made painfully obvious what were the limits of Constantius's power, and how well justified was the state in its
contest with this "pope".

As soon as the synod of Milan had arranged to issue the
necessary ecclesiastical authority a new envoy appeared in
Alexandria and tried to expel Athanasius. The envoy called
in the police and even broke into a church. But the people
offered stubborn resistance, and after a month he had to depart
crestfallen. Then the Emperor seized his final weapon. The
legions quartered in Egypt and Libya marched under the
command of General Syrianus into Alexandria; a month later,
during the night of February 8 to 9, 356, the church of Theonas
was besieged by armed forces, and Athanasius disappeared
without a trace.

Then, from a safe hiding-place, he wrote the *Apology to
Constantius*, in which he informed the Emperor that, with all

---

[1] Athan. *hist. Ar.* 35–39   Theod. *H.E.* 2, 16   Amm. Marc. 15, 7, 6–10   Sozom.
4, 11
[2] Athan. *ibid.* 36   [3] *ibid.* 42–45 and *infra*, p. 221 n. 1
[4] Hilarius, *c. Const.* 2 (2, 562f. Ben.)   Jerome, *vir. inl.* 100

due respect to His Imperial Majesty, he had fled, and was keeping himself in hiding. He had intended to journey to the Court, but while on the way had received such terrible news of acts of violence in Egypt and elsewhere, that he had turned back. For Syrianus's arbitrary power was all there was to trust in, and so he had no alternative to hiding himself. It would have been surely very grievous to the Emperor if he had suffered some evil while on his way to the royal residence. A summary of the events on that stormy night was placarded in Alexandria, and the people no longer left their churches empty, for fear of losing possession.

This state of affairs lasted four months, when the military put in another appearance, cleared the churches, and gave them over to the opposite party; these only received a bishop eight months later—George of Cappadocia. Not only had Athanasius many hard things to say, but even Ammianus Marcellinus described him as a noxious person of a common sort.[1] His entry into Alexandria was accompanied by various acts of violence. In Whitsuntide week, A.D. 356, an Athanasian congregation was cruelly ill-treated while holding a separate service in their own churchyard. Many were severely wounded or killed. Egyptian bishops and clerics began to be persecuted, if they refused fellowship to the new bishop, in a way reminiscent of Diocletian's times.[2] The city endured these plagues for nine months, when the people took the church of Dionysius by storm. The bishop was successfully saved from the raging mob, but a month later, he had to flee, the date being October 2, 358. During this period Athanasius lay hidden in Alexandria, and it is hardly likely that he remained a passive spectator.[3]

Apart from church problems, Constantius had not been able peacefully to enjoy his newly won sole-rulership. Gallus,[4] his Cæsar, did not get on well in Antioch, and he found his consort, Constantia, only too similar to him in sadistic tastes. His arbitrary rule was supported by a hateful espionage. He had no military ability, and the Isaurians plundered southern Asia Minor without restraint. Luckily for him, the Persians were

---

[1] Athan. *hist. Ar.* 75; Amm. Marc. 22, 11, 4
[2] Athan. *op. cit.* 59–72 *apol. de fuga*, 6–7
[3] *Hist. Athan.* 5. 6. (p. 52f. Fromen). *Epist.* preface p. 36 Larsow.
[4] *vide supra*, 212, and Seeck, *Gesch. des Untergangs*, 4, 121ff.

otherwise engaged, and gave him no trouble. At length, Constantius deprived him of the military command, as he had become quite incapable of it; and after he had committed further bloody outrages even against persons of the greatest eminence, Constantius commanded him to come to the court to justify his conduct. Constantia journeyed ahead to break the storm, but she died on the way. He himself only reached Istria, where he was tried and beheaded (A.D. 354). Naturally those who had shared his doings, shared his death. His brother Julian had satisfied in Pergamon and Ephesus his passion for building ever since A.D. 351. Now even he came under suspicion, and was examined. However, thanks to the warm support of the Empress Eusebia, he was allowed to go, and was able to continue his studies in Athens.

Trouble broke out on the Rhine following these worries in the east. Silvanus, the general in command, rebelled in Cologne in August, 355. He was killed only four weeks later, but soon afterwards Cologne was conquered by the Franks, who together with the Alemanni broke far and wide into the territory of the Empire. Nor was all in good order on the upper Rhine, in spite of the campaign in the spring of the same year. So Constantius reluctantly decided to raise the last surviving member of his dynasty to the rank of Crown Prince, and send him to the Rhine. Julian was called from Athens. On November 6, 355, he was made Cæsar in Milan, and married to Helena, the Emperor's sister.

He joined his army as early as December 1, and astonished the whole world. The philosophical dreamer and recluse became an exemplary soldier in the field. The hindrances placed in his way by the generals seconded to him could not prevent his marvellous success. He defeated the Alemanni near Strassburg, and in the following years, frequently crossed the Rhine. He drove the Franks back, and liberated Gaul from the invaders. But the greater his success, the more his youthful fame darkened the face of Constantius. At last no danger was in sight, and the Emperor could celebrate the twentieth anniversary of his reign, inaugurating the proceedings with a magnificent entry into Rome.

The same autumn he was in Sirmium, where he was

approached by his theological advisers, Valens and Ursacius, together with the local bishop, Germinius, who was therefore successor to the deposed Photinus. They proposed a theological formula which was to dissolve all difficulties conformably to the Emperor's own mind, and establish peace throughout the Empire.[1] This formula boldly seized the main issue, and spoke unambiguously. It declared there was only one God, and not two gods. No sermon was to be delivered and no question was to be raised, about *substantia*, called *ousia* by the Greeks. The same was to hold good about both *homousios* and *homoiousios*, for there was nothing about either of them in the Bible, and both went beyond human understanding. The Father and the Son were two persons, and moreover the Father was superior, and the Son inferior, as was made clear in John 14: 28. The Holy Spirit was sent to believers by the Son, and the Trinity was proved from Matthew 28: 19. The formula pleased the Emperor, as is understandable. How Ossius, a centenarian, was brought to sign[2] after a year's imprisonment during which he obstinately refused to condemn Athanasius, cannot be explained by saying his health was frail. The same question will shortly be raised as regards Liberius. The formula was sent round for signing, and Hilary from exile exhorted the Gallic bishops to refuse steadfastly.[3]

Theology had not been at a standstill in the east while all these contests were proceeding. In many respects much had been done to explain theological key words which had been brought into the sphere of power-politics. Antioch became the centre of a movement when the clever and ambitious Eudoxios left his small provincial bishopric, and, in A.D. 358, procured his own installation in succession to Leontius who had suddenly died. He succeeded, by the way, without the agreement of the leading eastern bishops, but in collusion with the chamberlain of the Court at Constantinople. Eudoxios had already taken part in several synods, including that of Antioch in A.D. 341,

---

[1] Hahn, *Bibl.* §161, following Hilar. *de synod.* 11 (2, 464 Ben.) J. Gummerus, *Die homöusianische Partei*, 52–57 For the date, cf. Loofs in Herzog-Hauck, *Realencl.* 2, 33, 27ff.

[2] Athan. *apol. de fuga*, 5 *hist. Ar.* 45 Socr. 2, 31 Sozom. 4, 12, 6 Marcell. et Faust. *liber precum*, 32, in *Coll. Avell.* 1, p. 15, Gunther Hilarius, *de synod.* 27 (2. 513 Ben.)

[3] Hil. *de synod.* 2 (2, 459)

and of Serdika. He had recently come forward in Sirmium and Milan,[1] so that the Court might well regard him as a useful instrument in the important see at the capital of Syria. He took Aëtios with him to Antioch—a man known for his quick-witted mind. The latter had been ordained there years before by Bishop Leontios, and there he had pursued his first studies. With Aëtios went his pupils, of whom the most important was Eunomios, whom he had ordained as deacon.[2] A series of theses written by Aëtios are extant, in which he examines with acute logic, the ideas of contemporary theologians, takes them to pieces, and proves that they conceal mutual contradictions. He says that it is universally acknowledged, and properly so, that God the Father is unbegotten. The idea of God is so far above the very idea of causality that we cannot even say He is the cause of His own being. Hence each and every causal relation within the divine nature must be abolished, nor is it possible to speak of "begetting" within God's being. Accordingly, God remained for all eternity unbegotten in His nature. Similarly a begotten being was for all eternity something different in substance from God, and all talk of the *homousios* or *homoiousios* of the Son of God was vain.[3] Here was an inexorable criticism of all the well-meant essays which had been made hitherto; and seen with unprejudiced eyes, it was also a criticism of the great Origen. Aëtios could see more keenly than the half-forgotten Arius himself, and his radicalism meant something more than putting new life into an old heresy. He cut to the root of every sort of speculative Christology, and did so in the name of the philosophical idea of God. His pupil and friend, Eunomios of Cappadocia, took up his ideas, and expanded them in effective fugitive writings. It is easy to see how these neo-Arians, refuting the formulas *homousios* and *homoiousios* on theoretic or speculative grounds, would quickly find themselves at home with politicians of the Church like Valens and Ursacius, who hated the same terms as being the symbols of certain parties of much influence in the Church.

In the spring of A.D. 358, Eudoxios, the new bishop of

[1] Hil. 4, 170, 5   Labbe, *Conc.* 2, 773d.
[2] Letter of Georg. Laodic. in Sozom. 4, 13, 2   Philostorgios 4, 8   p. 62, 17. Bidez
[3] For the theses of Aëtios see Epiph. *haer.* 76, 11-12   basic thesis 1-5

Antioch, gathered his friends together, including Acacius of Cæsarea and Uranios of Tyre. The assembly sent its thanks to the men of Sirmium for having definitely set aside the entire body of speculations regarding the *ousia*. Now, and really for the first time now, the Nicene formula, with its crucial term *homousios*, came into the forefront of the dispute. Hilary of Poitiers declares unambiguously that never since he had become a bishop, by then a considerable time ago, had he heard mention of the Nicene symbol. Only after his banishment was discussed, i.e., after A.D. 355, did he first become acquainted with this formula.[1] The opponents at Milan had made it a point of honour to reinstate Athanasius. This transformed the political struggle for power between Alexandria and Constantinople into a struggle regarding the faith; that struggle was now deepened, and also made desperately serious. In these circumstances, when the bishops at Antioch assented to the peace declared by the Emperor and proclaimed by Valens, it appeared as if the bishops had confessed adherence to the newly revitalized Arianism, and thereby also declared war theologically against the whole school of Origen. George of Laodicea immediately put his opinions into words, and demanded that steps should be taken to protest.[2] Basil of Ancyra invited bishops who shared his views to meet at a time when a church was to be consecrated.

In A.D. 358, here in Ancyra, this party's theological programme was drawn up. The fairly detailed memorandum has survived,[3] and provides a clear answer to the question in dispute. Father and Son were "of similar substance", (*homoiousioi*, or *homoioi kat' ousian*) just as a human father and his son were of similar substance. It was wrong, with the Arians, to deny the similarity, but just as wrong, with Marcellus of Ancyra or Sabellios, to describe Father and Son as identical: the latter error attached to the formula *homousios* which was accordingly condemned and set aside. In the last analysis, this was nothing else than giving a new framework to the old Eusebian views: and these were also the terms in which the leading thinkers of the eastern church had always thought. But

[1] Hil. *de synod.* 91 (2, 518 Ben.)   [2] Letter in Sozom. 4, 13, 2–3
[3] Epiph. *haer.* 73, 2–11   cf. Sozom. 4, 13

now for the first time an attempt was made to do away with the Nicene terminology altogether. This terminology had hitherto been passed over in complete silence and so rendered harmless. As its opponents also had good grounds for not using it, these tactics had been successful. All this was ended at Milan.

Athanasius is traditionally regarded as the man who was from the very first a fiery defender and exponent of the Nicene creed. Yet in his early theological writings: *Against the Pagans* and *On the Incarnation*, Nicea and *homousios* are never mentioned at all in spite of the fact that these tractates were written implicitly as polemics against Eusebius's *Theophany*. The three great speeches *Against the Arians* were written when the battle had reached its greatest height and heat, but it is very remarkable and significant that while, in its opening, the work mentions the condemnation of Arius by the ecumenical synod, and cites the term *homousios*, the formula never appears again in the further course of the discussions. On the contrary, the Son is constantly described as like (*homoios*) the Father, or equal in all respects, or similar in essence or nature (*homoios kat' ousian*).[1] All the key words which were branded at a later date as characteristic of Arian, or semi-Arian, heresy are used in these early works of Athanasius in a friendly manner. Athanasius employs them to describe the true faith, although he is well aware that the dangerous term *homousios* was being used by contemporaries.

All was altered quite suddenly in the fifties of the fourth century. About the very time when Pope Liberius was explaining to the Emperor the significance of the Nicene symbol, Athanasius was at work writing *On the Nicene decrees*. In this writing he unfolded the banner of *homousios* against the Eusebians and Acacius of Cæsarea. He examined the opinions of Dionysios in a short tractate of that name, in order to forestall unfriendly references to the attitude of Dionysios of Alexandria in regard to the problem of *homousios*;[2] in this tractate everything turns once more on the meaning of the Nicene watchword. Athanasius makes it quite clear that he regards this

---

[1] Athan. *or. c. Ar.* 1, 7. 9. Loofs, *Dogmengeschichte*, 4th ed. 239f. The fourth speech is spurious

[2] *vide supra*, 97

term as an excellent expression of the characteristic difference between the two parties.

The customary phrase, "the Son is like the Father" (*homoios*) no longer satisfied him, for that would be true of a human filial relationship. God remained Father, but for ever inseparably conjoined with His Son—here the human analogy failed —Father and Son were one, as in John 10: 30, and, in order to express this oneness a stronger term was needed, i.e., one-in-being, or one-in-essence, *homousios*. This term meant nothing less than identity of substance. God is the substance of all existence. But whereas everything that exists was created out of nothing, the Son alone was born out of the substance of the Father. Moreover this was to be understood in the absolute sense, and was not to be conceived in terms of the physical analogy in which a part was separated from the substance of the Father. The scriptures (Hebrews 1: 3) call the Son the brightness of His glory: really the brightness and the glory are all one, and the glory is the sun, and whoever sees the one, also sees the other.[1] Athanasius's purpose was unmistakable, viz., to establish the full divinity of the Son; unmistakable, too, was his dislike of the subordination of the Son to the Father in any conceivable way. But with this theory of his, Athanasius had created a substantial identity, which was to be regarded as indivisible, and was outside the sphere of ideas which could be actually conceived. In so doing, he abandoned the ground on which alone theology could exist as a science; instead he launched out into the uncharted darkness of the logic of mystery in which word and idea part company. For a while, however, he was unaware of all this, although his enemies did not overlook it.

The announcement made at Antioch in support of the Sirmian formula of neutrality[2] must have given real pleasure to the Emperor, although he had been annoyed when Eudoxios arbitrarily seized the throne of the bishop. A deputation from the synod of Ancyra, headed by Basil, made remarks of great political importance on Eudoxios's action, and they also drew attention to the changes of a neo-Arian character which had

[1] Athan. *de decr.* 20, 2–5 22, 4 23, 1–3 24, 1–2 30, 3
[2] *vide supra*, 221

taken place in Antioch. The result was that the Emperor wrote[1] to the Antiochene church, severely reprimanded Eudoxios, and required him to expel Aëtios and his adherents. This was carried out. Aëtios and Eunomios had to go into banishment, and the bishops of the party of Ancyra seem to have played a new rôle as fellow-workers with the police. Even Eudoxios could not keep his place for long, but soon returned to his home in Armenia; about seventy other clergy were deposed from office.[2] Basil of Ancyra held the field in triumph, and boldly placed it on record that the Emperor had adhered to the formula of *homoiousios* when he issued his rescript.[3]

But that was a deceptive appearance. The Emperor returned to Sirmium in June, 358 after a short campaign against the Sarmatians, when a great movement towards unity began to arise. A memorandum[4] was drawn up which combined the Church's verdicts against Paul of Samosata and Photinus of Sirmium with the fourth formula of Antioch. This made it plain that Paul the heretic of Samosata was referred to because it was easy then to find a reason for rejecting the term *homousios* by pointing out that Paul had been condemned. Constantius ordered Liberius to come to Sirmium from Beroea, his place of exile. The Roman pope had long been plied hard by Fortunatian of Aquileia[5] and his local bishop Demophilus, and after two years of exile had grown weary. He collapsed completely. He wrote a complaining letter to the eastern bishops. In it he declared that he regarded Athanasius as excommunicated, and had really done so since A.D. 352.[6] Then he followed with a second letter in which he again asserted that he had condemned Athanasius; he also said that he recognized the standpoint of the eastern bishops, and added that he heartily agreed with the first formula[7] of Sirmium with its theological intent as explained to him by Demophilus.[8] He also wrote to Ursacius, Valens, and Germinius of Sirmium, claiming the whole Roman presbytery as witness that Athanasius had been condemned, and deploring the late publication of this explanation as due to a confused or misplaced record. A similar communication addressed to the

[1] Sozom. 4, 14
[3] Sozom. 4, 14, 4
[5] Jer. *vir. inl.* 97
[7] *vide supra*, 212

[2] Philostorgios, 4, 8
[4] *ibid.* 4, 15, 2
[6] Liber. *ep.* 18, *studens paci* (Hil. 4, 155)   cf. *supra*, p. 213
[8] Liber. *ep.* 10, *pro deifico* (Hil. 4, 168)

Emperor was placed by Fortunatian in the hands of the chamberlain Hilary.[1] Liberius even wrote in the same style to Vincentius of Capua, his legate whom he had at one time castigated unmercifully.[2] And in each of these letters, he implored the recipient to intervene on his behalf and secure his return from exile.

To such a pass had matters now come. The Emperor forced him also to sign the memorandum, and this caused him still more bitterness of heart since it contained a clause condemning the *homousios* of Samosata. He got some poor comfort in being allowed to sign a creed containing a *homoiousios* clause, drawn up by the theologians at Ancyra: but that was accounted evil unto him even by contemporaries.[3] Also, a delegation of African bishops who intervened on behalf of Liberius, had to sign the Sirmian formula. These four men found no difficulty in complying, for all these questions were entirely beyond them.

The Sirmian synod now wrote to the Romans that they were permitted to reinstall Liberius as bishop, but that Felix, who had been functioning as bishop in his place, should retain his status; with the result that two bishops were to officiate in Rome at the same time.[4] This impossible situation was due to the Emperor's orders, and so had to be tolerated for a while. Naturally, disturbances arose and downright resistance. But Felix had not much support in the church, and soon had to quit. He left the city, and went to reside on his private estate in the south-west of Campagna, where he died a few years afterwards. Liberius lived a year longer, September 24, 366 being recorded as the day of his death.[5] He had always been beloved in Rome, but he bore no political influence. He had no longer any importance as the opposite number to the Emperor and the leader of the west. Others now took over this rôle from the hands of the pope of Rome.

Basil of Ancyra still remained the leading bishop in the east, and he kept the Emperor informed both orally and in writing as to the progress of the work of pacification. A great imperial

---

[1] Liber. *ep.* 11, 2, *quia scio* (Hil. 4, 171)

[2] *vide supra*, 214f. Liber. *ep.* 12 *non doceo* (Hil. 4, 172)

[3] Sozom. 4, 15   [4] *ibid.* 4, 15

[5] Theodoret, *H.E.* 2, 17   *Liber Pontif.* 37, 5   *Coll. Avell.* 1, 3–4 (1 p. 2 Günther) Mommsen, *Ges. Schriften* 6, 570–581

synod was to be called: but where? The name Nicea was
mentioned, but it raised doubts on account of the memories it
recalled. Nicomedia was projected, but in the midst of the
preparations came the news that the city had been destroyed
by an earthquake and a subsequent fire, on August 24, 358.
The synod had to be postponed to the spring of A.D. 359 when
it was to sit in two assemblies: the western bishops were invited
to meet in Rimini, while those of the east met in Isaurian
Seleucia. Preliminary discussions took place at the royal court
in Sirmium, and the Emperor drew up the main heads to be
discussed. Basil then noticed with a shock that, though his
position as leader was outwardly acknowledged, the Emperor's
decisions were determined in substance by the counsels of his
old confidants, Valens and Ursacius. On the Saturday before
Whit-Sunday, May 22, 359, a confession of faith was agreed
on[1] in the presence of His Majesty. This confession was on the
lines customary in the east, and concluded by prohibiting any
future mention of the term *ousia*. The final sentence runs, "We
declare the Son like (*homoios*) the Father in everything, as also
the Holy Scriptures say and teach." Mark of Arethusa, who
had rejected the first formula[2] of Sirmium, was given as the
editor of the text.[3] The court bishops had attained their goal;
the word *ousia* had been set aside, and it was poor comfort for
the Ancyrans that at least they had carried the phrase "like
in everything" instead of the mere "like" or "similar" as
desired by Valens.[4] Soon afterwards they drew up a memorandum[5] in which they explained the phrase "like or similar
in everything" as intended to rebut the neo-Arianism for
which the court bishops wanted to open up the way into the
church, and thus to develop a doctrine of the Trinity exactly
corresponding to the proposals[6] put forward in Ancyra, viz.,
one Godhead in three persons, i.e., *hypostases*. The purpose of
the memorandum was to show that this could be done in
conformity with the formula "like in everything" and without
using the term *ousia*. That was true, but the formula itself did

[1] Athan. *de synod.* 8   Hahn, *Bibl.* §163   Lietzmann, *Symbole*, 2nd ed. 31
[2] *vide supra*, 213   [3] Germinius in Hil. 4, 163, 18
[4] Epiph. *haer.* 73, 22, 5–8
[5] *ibid.* 73, 12–22   and remarks in Gummerus, *Die homöusian. Partei*, 121–133
[6] *vide supra*, 223f.

not say so. They had the word *hypostasis* for the Trinity—but for the Unity they lacked the term *ousia* which had just been propounded in Ancyra, and they lacked it because it was now forbidden. In such a situation, it was useless to prove that it corresponded to Scripture.

Meanwhile, the bishops gathered in the chosen cities. On May 28, an imperial decree[1] reached Rimini describing the purpose of the synod as to discuss faith and unity, and to regulate church affairs. Moreover it impressed sharply on the worthy gentlemen that they must not attempt to reach any decisions regarding the eastern bishops. When the sittings had ended, ten bishops were to report the results to the imperial court where they might discuss matters with the corresponding eastern deputation. It is a pity that the parallel decree[2] which was sent to Seleucia is not extant, for it would be instructive to compare the two. Four hundred western delegates gathered in Rimini,[3] and in accordance with the official character of this imperial synod, they lived as guests of the Emperor. The bishops of Gaul and Britain were alone in refusing this privilege, and lived at their own charges because it seemed to them more dignified to do so. The *praefectus praetorio* Taurus acted as Commissioner of State and was instructed not to permit the bishops to return home till they had reached harmony. He was promised the consulship in the following year for the successful performance of his duty: and he earned his reward.

At first affairs seemed most unpromising for the Emperor's plans. The differences were very marked when Valens and Ursacius appeared with the formula prepared in Sirmium, and began to argue about signing it. The great majority of the bishops declared that they could not depart from the old and traditional Nicene creed, and that they must stand firmly by the term and the idea of "substance" as an inalienable part of the creed.[4] The parties soon began to separate, and a minority of eighty bishops who agreed with Valens, left the main body of the church, and transferred their sittings to an empty hall. On July 21, 359, Valens, Ursacius, Germinius of Sirmium, and an otherwise unknown Gaius, were condemned as heretics

[1] In Hil. 4, 93
[2] cf. Sozom. 4, 17, 1
[3] The best record is in Sulp. Sev. *chron.* 2, 41. 43. 44
[4] Hil. 4, 95–96

and enemies of the Nicene faith.[1] The required deputation of ten bishops was sent to the Emperor, but the opposition also sent ten bishops. Ursacius and Valens had already departed to make the necessary preparations. The document sent by the synod to the Emperor contained a clear confession of the Nicene creed, refused to discuss any of the proposals made by Valens, and asked for permission to return home.[2]

The Emperor's answer[3] was brief and said that His Majesty was not in a position to receive the deputation as he must set out in preparation for a campaign against Persia. But he had arranged that the delegates should wait in Adrianople for his return, when he would give them an answer to take back to the synod. That was hard to bear, for the men in Rimini were growing more and more impatient. They wrote asking that perhaps His Majesty would glance at their document and be convinced that they would never depart from their views. And perhaps for this reason he would allow them before winter to return to their sees where they were urgently required. The delegates meanwhile lodged in Nike, a poor little town near Adrianople and had to acquire the oriental virtue of waiting patiently.[4] In addition they were carefully instructed in the views of Valens until, at last, on October 10, they were ready to go back on their commission, recall the deposition of Valens and his associates, enter into communion with them, and subscribe to the propounded symbol.[5] The records contain fourteen names.

They were now permitted to return to Rimini, and give news of what they had learnt in theology and at the court. There it had filtered through that the High Commissioner of State had been instructed to keep the synod together till all had signed, but to send into exile any stubborn remnant of the opposition of not more than fifteen bishops. The situation was seen to be serious, and one after another perceived that he really had no occasion to become a martyr for the sake of the Nicene creed. It had become used as a watchword, but only in the last few years and only in the sphere of church politics. It played no part in church life in the west, and in any case, who

[1] *ibid.* 4, 96–97   [2] *ibid.* 4, 78–85   [3] Athan. *de synod.* 55   [4] Hil. 4, 85f.
[5] Theodoret, *H.E.* 2, 21   Lietzmann, *Symbole*, 2nd ed. 33   Hahn, *Bibliothek* §164

could make anything of these Greek speculations? Ossius and Liberius finally entered into conversation with each other; and the weather grew steadily colder; and it was a long way home. The majority of those on the side of Nicea broke away slowly at first, but ever more rapidly; then those who had become moderate changed over. Finally there remained a handful of twenty righteous, but at last even they yielded to Valens's exhortations. The result was transmitted to the Emperor in a document which conveyed the synod's thanks for their instruction in theology and assured him of their obedience. It definitely repudiated *homousios*, and, without the slightest suspicion of the true state of affairs, took pleasure in declaring itself in complete harmony with "the orientals" in matters of faith—and now would the Emperor allow them to go home? The collapse of the great synod could hardly be described in more undignified terms.[1]

The parallel synod in the east met for the first time on September 27, at Seleucia:[2] their State Commissioner was a *comes* named Leonas who was accompanied by the Commandant of the Isaurian forces in case the bishops needed it, as the sources say tartly. On the first day, there were long debates about the agenda, and the synod separated visibly into two parties: the one was led by Acacius of Cæsarea (in Palestine) and numbered about thirty-seven persons including Eudoxios of Antioch and George of Alexandria; the other party comprised the great majority, more than one hundred bishops, and gathered round George of Laodicea and the other principal "*homoiousianists*". Basil of Ancyra belonged to them, as well as Makedonios of Constantinople, both of whom had good reasons for keeping well in the background. Also Hilary of Poitiers, who had been banished into this neighbourhood, attended[3] and sided with the men of Ancyra. No one defended the term *homousios* seriously, for the major party rejected it, and the handful of Egyptians who were there on purpose to do so, was negligible. On the other hand, no attempt was made to defend the Ancyranian theology of *homoiousios*; in this regard it was

[1] Hil. 4, 87f.
[2] Extract from the protocols in Socrates 2, 39–40 (=Sozom. 4, 22)
[3] Hil. *c. Const.* 12–15

felt sufficient to lay formal stress on the ancient formula of the Church Consecration synod at Antioch, for which the Eusebians had formerly shown strong preference.

_ There were serious disturbances on the very first day, and Acacius and his followers left the meeting. On the second day, the majority remained together, while the opposition got into contact with the State Commissioners. On the third day, September 29, the Comes Leonas[1] propounded an explanation made by the followers of Acacius,[2] in which they expressed their assent to the old Antiochene creed, but defined more exactly their attitude to the questions in dispute at the moment: "We reject *homousios* and *homoiousios* as contrary to the Scriptures, we condemn *anhomoios*. Our formula runs 'the Son is similar to or like (*homoios*) the Father'." Then followed a creed related to that of Antioch. This was essentially the same as had been propounded by Valens in Rimini as the fourth formula of Sirmium, and it was also weakened in the same way by deleting the words[3] "in everything" (*kata panta*) after "similar" (*homoios*). The debate then passed vigorously to and fro, and was continued on the next day, for the advocates of *homoiousios* wished to re-introduce the phrase *kata panta* (in everything) and so at least to maintain a hint of their view that the Son was of like substance with the Father. Agreement could not be reached, and at last the Commissioner arose and declared the synod at an end.

On October 1, the majority desired one more meeting in common with their opponents in order to clear up the proper position of Cyril who had been deposed from the see of Jerusalem, but the followers of Acacius played the part of constitutional loyalists and did not appear. Then the other party alone held a purely church synod, dealt with the matters in doubt—as they had indeed been ordered by the Emperor— and incidentally deposed the leaders of Acacius's party; others were suspended from office provisionally until further examination. They chose a certain Anianos in room of Eudoxios whom they had deposed, but Anianos could not take over his bishopric, because the Comes Leonas immediately dispatched

---

[1] O. Seeck, *Die Briefe des Libanius* p. 194
[2] Socr. 2, 40, 8–17 and Epiph. *haer.* 73, 25–26 and footnotes   [3] cf. *supra*, 226

him over the frontier. Just as in Rimini, both parties sent their ten delegates to the Court in order to announce the outcome of their discussions, but the remaining participants in the synod were more fortunate than their western brethren, for they were not prevented from going home.

The Emperor was in Constantinople where the opponents were in collision with one another in the final struggle. It had been of no help to the *homoiousians* to paint the neo-Arianism of Aëtios and Eunomios to the Emperor in such dark tints that the latter ordered the city prefect Honoratus, who had been recently installed, on December 11, 359, to examine the case; for the result was that the supporters of the formula *"anhomoios"* were condemned at a meeting of the state council.[1] Nor was the Emperor willing to have anything to do with the formula *homoiousios* which Silvanus of Tarsus tried to defend. What he did insist on was that the creed should contain the term *homoios* as in the symbol to which the synod of Rimini had recently bowed. After a few efforts to protest, the delegates from Seleucia signed the required formula on New Year's Eve A.D. 360.[2]

At the same time, the struggle about the thrones of the bishops proceeded further, and it soon became plain that Acacius and his adherents stood in the Emperor's good books, and were able to use the entire weight of the state's authority to convey their answer to the theoretical decree of deposition passed in Seleucia. They held a synod of their own, at which all the leaders of the *homoiousian* party were deposed, Basil of Ancyra, Cyril of Jerusalem, and Makedonios of Constantinople being at their head. The episcopal throne in the capital was mounted by the Antiochene bishop Eudoxios[3] who celebrated his installation by consecrating the great church of the Hagia Sophia[4] on February 16, 360. Eustathios of Sebaste, of whom more will be said on a later page as favouring ascetic tendencies, fell a victim to the decision of Acacius's synod.[5]

---

[1] Letter in Hil. 4, 174f. Sozom. 4, 23, 3. 4 Theodoret, *H.E.* 2, 27, 4–18 where the wrong reading *homousios* must always be corrected to *homoiousios*; similarly Philost. 4, 12 p. 64, 21 Bidez

[2] Sozom. 4, 23, 8   [3] *vide supra*, p. 223

[4] Traces of the entrance lobby have been recently discovered cf. A. M. Schneider, *Forschungen u. Fortschritte*, 1935, no. 22, p. 282f. *Byzant. Zeitschr.* 1936, 85

[5] Socr. 2, 40, 48–43, 16; Records of the Synod in Theodoret, *H.E.* 2, 28

The victory was carried out along the whole line. The court bishops had fulfilled the Emperor's instructions with brilliant success, and, in full collaboration with the State Commissioners and the Court-officials, had subjected the entire episcopacy of east and west to the *homoios* formula. They might well boast; and Constantius might believe himself born equal to his father. Acacius esteemed himself as a leader of the church. When he became bishop of Cæsarea he became not only of metropolitan rank, but also he inherited the library assembled by his predecessor Eusebius; and he made good use of both. He was wily and wide awake, and had much practical ability.[1] As Athanasius had been turned out, there was no one of equal quality on the other side, and the Emperor's favour was well earned. It was possible to flatter oneself that Constantine's mistake at Nicea had now been made good again: the term *homousios* with its difficulties had been set aside. The whole of the speculation of Origen's school about *ousia* was forbidden, and, as the outcome of the entire dispute, an acceptable formula had been found once for all in the recognition of the term *homoios*. Surely these purely objective grounds offered the best security for peace.

The answer is that that was a false calculation. Thirty-five years had passed since Nicea, and even at that time, while it might have been possible to agree on a neutral formula, it would have been impossible to forbid theological speculation. Constantine's real mistake had been to lend the state's support to a particular theological formula which had no prospect in itself of winning the regard of churchmen. Meanwhile, theological science had developed further, and had led among the *homoiousians* to a fruitful growth of the traditions tracing back to Origen. In the west, on the other hand, either the ideas of Tertullian and Novatian, or a naïve Monarchianism, lived on, but without glow. All this was brought into a state of unrest and confusion by the policy of enforcing unity; and even the Emperor's formula, on which unity had been based, was now rejected once more,[2] but with far greater passion than the Nicene creed long before. What had been forgiven Constantine from a sense of an honourable dependence on him, was

[1] Sozom. 4, 23, 2   [2] cf. Hil. 4, 43–47

accounted an abuse in his son; and the constraining of so many consciences, the banishing of large numbers of eminent bishops, brought forth in every land a load of bitter hatred such as had been unknown in Constantine's age. The ecclesiastical triumphal Arch of Constantine stood on sandy ground—but, at first, it did stand. And the Emperor must have been relieved to be delivered of this anxiety for the moment; for the outlook over the eastern frontier was threatening.

The Persians, after a few years of peace, suddenly thought it good policy to enter on war-like enterprises. In the summer of A.D. 359, they attacked Mesopotamia. The region round about Nisibis was put to flames, and, in October, the city of Amida, on the Armenian border, was conquered and destroyed after a long resistance. While it was true that King Shapur had returned home with greatly weakened forces after this campaign, there was no doubt that the next spring would see further aggression. Constantius had to strengthen the army in the east if he wished to be safe in face of worse surprises. He therefore gave orders to his Cæsar, the young Julian, to place a large number of picked troops at his disposal.

It was not merely military considerations that brought about this order. Latterly, Constantius had been disturbed by fears of insurgents, and the precautionary executions which he had carried out, had brought him little sense of security. The personal success which Julian had enjoyed among the soldiers must, in these circumstances, have increased his natural distrust towards the Crown Prince: consequently he was very glad to seize the opportunity, without arousing suspicion, of depriving the dangerous young man of part of his troops.

Julian was guileless enough to obey the command, but the soldiers were unwilling. They had only enlisted for protecting the Rhine frontier, and had no desire to go to the east. They also feared, not without grounds, that the decrease of the troops would entice the Alemanni to attack, and all the miseries of war might be brought upon their homes and their dependents. As a result, two battalions mutinied while marching through the chief quarter of Paris, going so far indeed, that they proclaimed Julian as Augustus. This solution of the difficulty was taken up by others. The Prince at first honourably strove against them, but had to yield. Also, in the previous night, the genius of the Empire had appeared to him in a dream, and had prepared him for a crisis in his life.[1] The dice fell, and Julian had to enter on the struggle for the crown.

He wrote Constantius, asking only for recognition of his rank as Augustus in the area of the Gallic prefecture,[2] and maintained as polite an air as possible in all respects. The messengers reached the Emperor in Cappadocia (spring, A.D. 360) and made him furiously angry. He refused to enter on any discussion, and issued orders that the two highest official posts in Gaul should be changed.[3] Then, after a little hesitation, he marched once more against the Persians, who however arrived in advance of him, and then cleverly disappeared, having destroyed Singara and Bezabde (on the upper Tigris), but could not be brought to battle by the Roman army.

Julian, as far as he was concerned, remained at his post and fought against the Alemanni who had again become restive. He learned now[4] that Constantius himself had stirred them up against him. He therefore felt himself freed from the last hindrances, and, in summer A.D. 361, he marched from the upper Rhine to the Danube, and then downstream to the neighbourhood of Nish where he established his winter quarters. Italy fell to him, and the Balkan peninsula did him homage. As against this, Africa, with its cornfields, remained true to Constantius, and in Aquileia a few thousand men would not serve the usurper, but barricaded themselves in. Apparently he would not conquer easily.

Constantius passed the winter A.D. 360–361 in Antioch, and there married for the third time, after his second wife, Eusebia, had died in February, 360. In the spring, he marched to Edessa to wage war against the Persians. Then came the news of Julian's advance, and at the same time, Constantius began to feel certain that the Persians would keep the peace this year. Hence he could lead his troops against the insubordinate prince, and they marched without reluctance. But night-visions and evil premonitions in broad day terrified the

[1] Amm. Marc. 20, 5, 10   [2] Julian. *ep. ad Athen.* p. 285d.
[3] Amm. Marc. 20, 9, 3–5   [4] Seeck, *Gesch. d. Untergangs*, 4, 491

Emperor. When he reached the foot of the Taurus mountains, he was overcome by a fever. He got as far as Mopsukrene, where he died on November 3, 361, at the age of forty-four. Euzoïos, bishop of Antioch, baptized him on his death-bed.[1]

[1] Philostorg. 6, 5   Socrates, 2, 47, 4

Chapter Nine

THE SPIRIT OF THE AGE FOLLOWING CONSTANTINE

CONSTANTINE'S POLITICAL GENIUS WAS TO BE SEEN NOT only in the military conquests and in the advances of culture which he achieved, but also in those which he thought it better to avoid. No one could prevent him from increasing his attack against pagan cults; but he was well aware that such a programme would estrange very many whose good will he valued, and that an opportunist policy might be slower, but could be followed much more safely if he was to attain his desired objective of Christianizing the Empire. Such a change over could be carried through in any case only in the course of generations: therefore he would proceed warily.

His sons were less hesitant. In A.D. 341 a law was promulgated which sharply ordered "an end to the folly of sacrifices",[1] and indeed made reference to a prohibition against sacrifices issued by Constantine himself. That must have been limited to a specific case,[2] whereas now an end was to be made to the entire sacrificial system, once for all. No records have come down describing the effects of this decree. But we hear that, ten years later, Magnentius sought to make himself popular by permitting sacrifices at night, and that Constantius repealed the usurper's permission in November, 353.[3] In the course of the next year, a quite general decree ordered the temples to be closed "in every place and in all cities"; everywhere, sacrifices were forbidden, and certain types of lawbreakers threatened with the death penalty together with confiscation of their possessions. The provincial administrators were to expect reprimand if they were slack in punishing such crimes. In February, 356, the threat of the death penalty was briefly repeated against sacrifices, and explicitly extended against all "worshippers of idols".[4]

That must have been a terrific blow against the ancient

[1] *Cod. Theod.* 16, 10, 2   [2] *vide supra,* 149f.
[3] *Cod. Theod.* 16, 10, 5ff.
[4] *Cod. Theod.* 16, 10, 4 (of A.D. 354, or 346?)   16, 10, 6 (of the year 356)

forms of religious life, and, in many places, where the Christians were in the great majority or knew themselves well protected, there may have been acts of violence. In Baalbek, a deacon named Cyril caused many images to be destroyed; in Arethusa (Rastan near Homs) in Syria, Bishop Markus, well known in history, built a church on the ruins of a temple; in Cæsarea in Cappadocia, a temple of Zeus and Apollo was destroyed. In Egypt General Artemios made himself prominent by similar acts of violence, and the Comes Heraklios used the threat of like action as a means of suppressing unruly masses.[1] The account which Libanius[2] gave later of lamentable conditions under Constantius would largely apply here.

But it is just as certain that apart from a few officials making themselves awkward, the old cult went on quietly. Indeed Christian clerics reckoned nothing of paying their tribute to the Heroes—if anything was to be gained by it. Julian[3] writing a letter when he was a prince, spoke in matter-of-fact tones about such a case. In April, 357, Constantius visited the city of Rome for the first time, and received a deep impression of its splendour. The wonderful historic buildings seemed to him each more beautiful than the last, and the gigantic site of the forum of Trajan impressed him as reaching an incomparable height of human achievement. The senate of the city greeted him in the curia in solemn assembly, and the unrestrained chatter of the masses pleased him so greatly that he behaved with unusual friendliness. In gratitude, he let the obelisk, which his father had already destined for Rome, be fetched from Egypt and set up in the Circus Maximus. It still stands in the square of the Lateran.[4] Constantius's friendly feelings made him well-disposed to the sacred traditions of the city. He allowed the privileges of the Vestals to remain untouched, the priestly offices were filled by members of ancient families as accorded with custom, and the dues for the temple cult continued to be paid. The Christian feelings of the Emperor

---

[1] Theodoret, *H.E.* 3, 6, 3   3, 7, 6–10; Cappadocia: Sozom. 5, 4, 2   Egypt: Theodoret 3, 18   Athan. *hist. Ar.* 54

[2] Libanius, *or.* 17, 7 (2, 209 Förster) *or.* 18, 23 (2, 246), and often. cf. Amm. Marc. 22, 4, 3

[3] Julian, *ep.* 79 (Bidez, p. 85ff.)

[4] Amm. Marc. 16, 10, 13–17   17, 4, 12–23

demanded only one sacrifice of pagan Rome, viz., the altar of victory must be removed from the chamber of assembly in the curia—at any rate for a time. Under Julian it was naturally brought back again.[1] The prohibitions about sacrifices were falling into oblivion about this time, for literary records and surviving inscriptions of this period tell of sacrifices, founding of temples, and a flourishing cult of Mithras.[2]

Christianity and paganism lived side by side in the Rome of those days. A valuable testimony to this fact is given by the calendar of A.D. 354, which was published under the official patronage of the papal court bookseller Furius Dionysius Filocalus and which provides us with a document of the highest rank for the history of civilization in the ancient Silver Age.[3] It is a mixture of secular, pagan, and Christian officialdom. The book begins with the four greatest cities of the Empire: Rome, Constantinople, Alexandria are represented as female figures, Trèves as an armed man in the pose of a conqueror. Then comes a list of the officially celebrated birthdays of those rulers who had been apotheosized, from Augustus to Constantine the Great, and of Constantius who was then Emperor.

The calendar of days, which now follows, introduces the seven planets into the imagery together with a synoptical table showing the day they ruled and the hours of the night and the day. Saturn and Mars were harmful; Mercury, the moon and the sun propitious; Jupiter and Venus definitely favourable. Further details are given for each planet on its own table, e.g., the day of the sun and its hour by night or day were useful to know for beginning a journey by land or water. One born would be able to live; one lost would be found; one falling ill would recover; a theft would be discovered. The appended signs of the Zodiac gave notes about enterprises that would be successfully undertaken when the moon was in the corresponding sign.

The facts of astrology, when presented in this way, are very impressive and appear of the greatest importance for the

[1] Symmachus, *relat.* 3, 4–7 (281 ed. Seeck)

[2] J. Geffcken, *Ausgang d. Heidentums*, 101. 281f.   Amm. Marc. 19, 10, 4   Dessau, *inscr. lat. sel.* 3222. 4267

[3] Edited by Mommsen in *chron. min.* 1, 39–148   The Calendar of the Month *C.I.L.*, 1 (2nd ed.) 254ff.

business of life day by day. The calendar for the separate months is the next subject to be treated, and, as with the planets, so now each month has its own illustration, usually a nude youth represented as busy with something corresponding to the season. The series of days is accompanied by the letters for the Roman week of eight days, and close by are the signs of the planetary week of seven days. Such a week had been customary since the time of Augustus and had nothing to do with Christianity or Judaism.[1] The old usage of grouping the days according to temple customs in *fasti*, or days when citizens and state might transact business, and *nefasti*, which were days given over to worship of the gods,[2] had disappeared by now, and official sacrifices were no longer noted. The various games are listed, each with a careful note giving the names of the different gods to whose honour they are dedicated, or the particular temples whose consecration they commemorate. Ancient pagan festivals are also very numerous, e.g., the Carmentalia, Lupercalia, Quirinalia, Feralia, Caristia, Terminalia; the opening and closing of the Vestal temple in June are recorded, and also the days of Cybele in March, the feasts of Ibis in March and October as well as a feast of Sarapis on April 25 are duly noted. December 25 was marked by games in the circus to celebrate the "birthday of the unconquerable sun" (*Natalis solis invicti*) just as in the time before Constantine.

After a decorated page with pictures of the Emperor Constantius and his Cæsar Gallus, there follows a list which is indispensable for reckoning time in practical life. It gives the consuls for the years 510 B.C. to A.D. 354, and the city prefects from A.D. 254–354: but between these two lists a Christian feature is introduced, viz., a table of Easter Sundays from A.D. 312–354, these being reckoned after a cycle of eighty-four years. The interpolation is not accidental as can be seen from the fact that there is added to every year in the consul-list, a note saying on which day of the week January 1 fell, and how old the moon was on that day, these being data necessary for calculating Easter. The next tables also came from the papal secretariat and contained the calendar of the feasts of the martyrs, and the days on which the Roman bishops died. This

[1] Schürer in *ZNW.* 6 (1905) 26   [2] Wissowa, *Religion und Kultus*, 2nd ed. 435

list of Roman bishops, expanded by occasional notes, from Peter to Liberius, is the original form of the later *liber pontificalis* or Book of the Popes. That was the extent of the calendar of Filocalus in A.D. 354. In another copy of the work, there is also a Latin redaction of Hippolytus's *Chronicle of the World*[1] and a *Chronicle of the City of Rome* as well as a list of the provinces in the year 334. The particular manuscript shows very plainly how Christianity, now in the ascendant, was related to the body politic of Rome.

Rome embodied its own tradition, and that is why it had so profoundly affected Constantius. But Constantinople, the New Rome, was conceived as the source of new life, and Constantius took pains to make the idea effective, though without real success.[2] Themistios was, under him, the dominant spirit, a man of sound philosophical schooling, who is interesting to students of a later day for having made useful paraphrases of Aristotle's writings. His father, a cultured merchant of North Asia Minor, had taught him this method; and when Themistios delivered his funeral address over his eminent father, the son envisaged him in the world beyond, taking his place beside Socrates and Plato, and greeting his favourite Aristotle.[3] But the youthful Themistios was drawn to public life. He trained himself to be a teacher of rhetoric, and seized a suitable chance of being heard by the Emperor. That decided his career.

He became the acknowledged favourite of Constantius, and a few years later was nominated by him to the Senate. From that time on, he was the representative speaker on behalf of that body on ceremonial occasions. In addition, he continued teaching in the "Capitol", which had really been built for his use, with increasing numbers of pupils. He fought a bitter fight against rival teachers of rhetoric who disputed his claim to be at once a philosopher and a rhetorician. Because he lived like a *grand seigneur* and entertained eminent men as guests at his table, and also because he dispensed with the large fees he might have charged, his popularity rose far above that of the average run of rhetoricians and professors. These were not

[1] cf. Vol. 2, 245f.
[2] F. Schemmel *in Neue Jahrbücher f. d. klass. Altertum*, 11 (1908) 147–168
[3] Themist. *or.* 20 p. 287, 5 Dindorf

really at home in society in Constantinople, a city of officials and soldiers, with luxury appropriate to the Court, and with a motley, intermingled, constantly-changing upper class.

A man like Libanios, whose ability towered far above that of the many with average gifts, found, as a consequence, that Antioch, his native city, suited him much better. At the beginning of his career he had been drawn to Constantinople, but he soon felt that many in the capital were unfriendly and intolerant towards him. This was a disadvantage not counterbalanced by the tepid good will shown by the great Themistios. In the end, he was even ordered to quit by the police. He was no more at home when he stayed in Constantinople on a second visit, and it was with relief that he returned to Antioch in A.D. 354. Here he began labours which were both fruitful and satisfying to himself. The Emperor gave him many distinctions and would gladly have recalled him to the capital, but in the end Constantius agreed to his change of residence and remained friendly. The people of Antioch were proud of their fellow-citizen with his ever-increasing fame. There was no one in Alexandria who rivalled him, although the various branches of learning continued to be cultivated in spite of all the disputes in the Church, and other disturbing influences.[1]

Athens maintained its exceptional standing. By now it had dwindled into a small city, and was insignificant politically and economically; it lived on visitors who came to see the sights, and on students who came to study at the university. As a seat of learning its name had a kind of sanctity owing to the glory of a celebrated past. To thousands the name recalled golden, glad, and gleaming memories of youthful days. The result was that Athens was a word that resounded in Greek ears with the same overtones as Jena and Heidelberg, Oxford and Cambridge, Yale and Harvard echoed in the ears of nineteenth-century students of Germany, England, and the United States.[2]

Student societies used to be formed in Athens on a national basis. Each attached itself to some favoured teacher, crowding his class-room with ever-faithful hearers. On the other hand, there used to be sharp "differences" between the professors; these were taken up by the students with a zeal characteristic

[1] Amm Marc., 22, 16, 17   [2] Translation slightly deviates from the text

of youth, and fought out in wild brawls. The academic year began late in autumn. At commencement of term, all the student societies would send out their scouts in order to seize every freshman or "fox" long before he reached the gates. Every ship tying up in the harbour was stormed, the "foxes" among its passengers were laid hold of and carried reluctantly ashore. Ranks were closed round them as they were taken by the conquering party, brought into secure quarters, and duly enrolled with one of the teachers favoured by the group. Frequently, the precious captive had to be defended from rival attacks *en route*.

Anyone who had once been "wedged fast" in this way was no longer free to choose, but must stick to the teacher which the society concerned had found for him. He was only a "fox", still without any rights, teased and fooled by everybody, browbeaten and bullied in finer or coarser ways. Finally he was taken in solemn procession to the baths, there to be given a "foxes' baptism", and afterwards received into the circle of students as an equal and full member. Then he began his career as a student with all its spiritual and physical demands, joys, sufferings, and dangers. Some who were former students at Athens wrote pleasant accounts, which have come down to us, of life in the old days at the university there. It amused them to think that the time they had spent as foolish youths should turn out to have done them good after all.[1]

In Athens at the time of Constantius, the most celebrated person was Prohaeresios of Cappadocia. A few years after Constantine's death, he had succeeded his famous fellow-countryman Julian in his regius professorship. He had many attractive invitations to other cities, and he stayed in Rome and further west for a visit of several years, but he remained faithful to Athens. Even in extreme old age, he vigorously carried on as a brilliant rhetorician, until in fact he was over ninety years of age. He died in A.D. 376. That he was a Christian, and gave fearless expression to his faith, did as little to lessen the admiration of his pagan hearers, as the pagan beliefs of his colleagues, Himerios and Epiphanios, alienated the

[1] Liban. *or.* 1, 16–22 Greg. Naz. *or.* 43, 15–16 Eunapius p. 74–77 Notes thereon by F. Schemmel, *op. cit.* 11 (1908) 494–513

Christians.[1] Rhetoric—and to a large extent philosophy also—was neutral ground.

Rhetoric enjoyed a new popularity in the fourth century, a popularity of which contemporaries were proud. It was characteristic of the outlook of the period that, about A.D. 400, Eunapios should publish a little book of the biographies of its most eminent sophists. He included only those who found grace in his eyes, i.e., when looked at critically from a neo-Platonic standpoint. Accordingly, a man like Themistios was omitted. From Eunapios and other contemporaries we learn the names of numerous celebrated rhetoricians; and there were many cities which sought to win such men, and hold them in high honour. This "sophism" enjoyed a vigorous aftermath in the whole of the east, deep into Asia Minor, and along the entire coast of Syria. But its mental calibre was not equal to the extent of its literary output.

Even the speeches of a Themistios have a far lower content of thought than those of an Aristides, or, indeed, of a Dion of Prusa; his court speeches sedulously avoided any definite reference to concrete facts, but dwelt for preference in the sphere of general observations; these were linked up to the person who was the subject of the speech by circumlocutions and allusive hints. Passing from Themistios to Libanios, one feels refreshed after all the formality as by a breath of real life, which can be traced, in his case, through all his rhetorical flourishes. His panegyric over Antioch, or his lamentation over the ruins of Nicomedia, throb with the heartbeats of a real and deep affection. The fact that Libanios could put all this into words, raised him far above the dull and pedestrian writers about him, and also over those who were regarded as great men.

The philosophers of this age were primarily schoolmasters, and lectured in college on the lives and opinions of the ancients, and did so in the form of compendiums purposely watered down. Side by side with this, Plato and Aristotle were expounded in detail, and not a few commentaries dating from the post-Constantine period have survived the centuries. The only place that could properly be said to be alive was the school of

[1] Jerome, *chron. Ol.* 285, 3 p. 242, 24, Helm Socrates, 4, 26, 6 Sozom. 6, 25, 9–10

Plato, and here the tradition of Plotinus was maintained and developed. But those who traded with this last talent of the Hellenic spirit were foreigners with· oriental souls. The Phœnician Malchos, known as Porphyry has already been discussed;[1] he journeyed on, faithfully following the lines of Plotinus's thought, but would not forgo necromancy and magic as a lower path to the liberation of the soul.

Jamlicha the Syrian was his pupil, called Iamblichos[2] by the Greeks. He was born in the little town of Chalkis—half-way between Beyrout and Damascus, and between Lebanon and Anti-Lebanon. After his studentship, which reached its climax in Rome, he returned to his native land, where we find him as a celebrated teacher in Apamea.[3] He belonged entirely to Constantine's period and died before the Emperor in A.D. 337. He developed Plotinus's system with what seems to us a light-hearted scholasticism, for he divided the higher world and its multitude of divine and dæmonic beings according to the principles of Pythagoras, into threes, fives, and sevens; then he combined these again into groups of larger numbers till he reached the highest one which was excelled by still another, quite ineffable, Being.[4] A further scheme, which he carried through methodically, enabled him to take the Dialogues of Plato and to read out of them, with all the appearance of scientific truth, that which he required in order to give substance to his world of phantasy.

But when all is said and done, systematic knowledge is not the way of redemption which leads to the Godhead. Granted, our salvation includes knowledge and therefore "gnosis", but these terms must not be narrowed and understood in the sense of a life in accordance with reason. True gnosis arises from the nucleus of our soul, the *ousia* which unites us with every daemonic and divine being above, and which alone could bring to pass that union with God for which we yearn as the highest good. That was brought out far and wide in writings concerned with the mysteries, and the more we read the clearer it becomes that here was the point where Neoplatonism parted company

---

[1] *vide supra*, 38–47   [2] cf. E. Zeller, *Phil. der Griechen*, 3b⁵, 735–773

[3] Liban., *Or.*, 52, 21

[4] Damascius, *de princ.* 43   Procl. *in Tim.* 3, 197 ed. Diehl

with the spirit of Greek philosophy, and stretched out its arms towards the nebulous figures familiar in oriental gnosis. Dreams, predictions, sacrifices of all sorts, including the bloody slaughterings of traditional cults, but not philosophical thought or refined mental exercises, were the means by which the soul was to mount out of her imprisonment to the supreme bliss of union with God. The books of Hermes Trismegistos, as sources of knowledge,[1] were read side by side with, but felt superior to, Plato's writings. Iamblichos, the spiritual leader, no longer appeared in his philosopher's mantle, but in the fantastic guise of an Egyptian priest with the mysteries and all the apparatus of an oriental witch's kitchen standing at his disposal.[2]

This eerie descent of philosophy was not a unique event that happened once, but was characteristic of the spirit of the age, and this teaching brought forth much fruit among Constantine's sons. The "divine" Iamblichos bathed his excited votaries in a simply overwhelming light. His influence determined the further course of the Platonic school, a devoted disciple of his being the would-be philosopher Prince Julian.

Christian literature could not maintain the height reached in Constantine's lifetime. Like the Church's inner life, it was in transition from a past age to a completely new one. The middle decades of the fourth century saw a generation grow up to whom it was to be given to unfold the full flower of Christian literature.

Didymos, a scholar who had been blinded as a child, wrote in Alexandria a tractate against Arius.[3] He hesitatingly developed ideas at which Bishop Alexander[4] had already hinted, and he sought to reach that solution of the problem of the Trinity afterwards attained by the great Cappadocians. His Origenism made itself felt not only here, but also and particularly in his numerous commentaries on the Bible. These have only survived fragmentarily, but nevertheless they afford

---

[1] Jambl. *de myst.* p. 7–10 p. 218–219 233–234 289–291 292–293, Parthey. For the genuineness of the writing, now cf. Bidez in *Mélanges Desrousseaux*, 1937 p. 11–18

[2] Vivid description in J. Bidez, *Vie de l'empereur Julien*, 1930, 73–81

[3] K. Holl. *Ges. Schriften* 2, 298–309 J. Leipoldt, *Didymus d. Blinde* (*TU. NF* 14, 3) 1905

[4] *vide supra*, 110f.

us a clear picture of an allegory rooted in a detailed knowledge of the Bible, an allegory which gives a genuinely Alexandrine ring to the popular lectures of the blind scholar. He wrote also against the Manichaeans. This was almost to be assumed in the fourth century, and Titus, bishop of Bostra[1] was specially famous in this regard. Didymos's writing is lost, but that of Titus has survived to a large extent. It shows that the author was a well-educated apologist who did not dally on secondary issues, but seriously tackled the fundamental problem of the nature of evil, and found its solution in the divine foreknowledge which provided the adjustments needed between the phenomena that necessarily follow from the freedom of the will on the one hand, and God's final purposes on the other. Origen had taught him that truth, whereas in his Bible commentaries he stood closer to the method native to Antioch, and avoided allegorical explanations. Finally, we may note that the extant remains of his literary activity belong to the time after Julian's death.

About A.D. 350, Cyril, bishop of Jerusalem, published his catechisms, and these form nothing less than a quite unique piece of theological literature. Stenographers took down the doctrinal sermons which he delivered to his catechumens during the week before Easter in the Church of the Holy Sepulchre in Jerusalem. The copies made were published essentially without alteration. Granted they are sermons, and the oratory is unmistakable. But the oratory was restrained and did not prevent the bishop from expressing his ideas clearly and plainly. The form nowhere washed away the content, as was usual in that period. Cyril, a learned theologian and a knowledgeable pastor of souls, speaks in an intimate way about the deepest things to hearers who are not uneducated. This gives us, at last, a picture of what passed in the Church for Christianity, and makes it possible for us to estimate how much of the theological scholarship of the time was able to get beyond its own terminology into the understanding of the laity. That is what gives these very attractive pieces of writing their incomparable value, a value which we shall discover also in another connection. They reflect the Christianity of the time

[1] R. P. Casey in *Pauly-W.* 2nd series, 6, 1586–1591

excellently, the image is not distorted by their mirror. For the gallant author lacked sufficient creative power and depth of thought, as well as religious passion, although he had felt in his own body the hardships which church disputes could bring, for he was thrice banished. But his nature was not polemical and his Christian doctrine ran quietly in the traditional grooves. That becomes particularly clear if one passes from his calm environment in Jerusalem to Athanasius's place of exile.

The energetic pope of Egypt, like others in exile, had begun to publish theological writings while he was in Trèves. Then as a pugnacious bishop he published "occasional" writings which acted like the strokes of a whip in the disputes of the Church, nor did they spare His Majesty the Emperor. That old weapon, a polemic[1] which made use of source-documents, was now handled by an expert, and the author let himself go with strokes that told; he did not bother about balanced periods or a polished style of language: that was the secret of the great attractiveness of his writings. They breathe the hot atmosphere of the battle in the midst of which they first saw the light.

Athanasius's so-called dogmatic tractates, even the famous *Speeches against the Arians* are, by contrast, notably lacking in literary effect. They are immeasurably prolix and tautologous; they weary us with detailed discussions which constantly circle round the same ideas. They omit every attractive rhetorical device which contemporary readers were rightly accustomed to expect even in theological writings. Yet their influence both on their own times and afterwards was very great. This was due primarily to the subject matter. Arianism in every shape and form was fought here with an unheard of thoroughness, and mainly with Biblical proof-texts. Athanasius possessed an extensive knowledge of the Bible, and could quote suitable passages very appositely. He never failed to demand that an exegete should weigh both the context of a passage and the author's intention, and not stick stolidly to the letter.[2] Actually the point at issue was of such a kind that each party could cite passages which supported their case as far as mere words went, because the entire dispute in the fourth

---

[1] Ed. Schwartz, *Ges. Schriften* I, 123–125   [2] *or.* 1 *c. Ar.* 54. 55

century was remote from the writers of the New Testament, and especially of the Old Testament. Hence proofs drawn from the Bible could not be fully cogent. Accordingly this use of the Bible, in spite of all the mastery displayed, was not the secret of the power of the speeches against Arius. What gave them their special quality was the weighty fact that Athanasius was handling a real theology and also one which was his own.

His way of thought was not that of Origen's school as was the case with those who opposed him wholly or in part. Rather he looked at the problem for himself and in its entirety, and considered it from the standpoint of man's redemption from sin. Even as early as the time when he wrote *de incarnatione* he regarded the question of redemption as the kernel of Christianity. This conviction led him to his theology of the Logos. He did not regard the dispute about *ousia* as a contest about some abstract form of the knowledge of God, but an argument about the ultimate understanding of the possibility and actuality of human redemption. The incarnation of the Logos was not an incomprehensible act of God, but something which issued of necessity from His nature. Death was the penalty laid on mankind for Adam's sin by the divine law, and no remorse nor repentance could abolish God's unchangeable word: God could not deceive. On the other hand, God's long-suffering would not tolerate that His creature, whom He had endowed with reason and created after His own image, should be helplessly handed over and abandoned to the wiles of the Devil.

Therefore the Logos of God, that had formerly called the world and mankind into being out of nothing, began the work of winning back the lost image of God, and of imparting immortality again to one otherwise destined to die.[1] For this purpose, the Logos required a human body, like ours in all respects, including substance, *ousia*. This made it possible for Him to live as a man among men, and take on Himself a human lot.[2] When Athanasius spoke of "body" or "flesh", he meant full humanity with body and soul and reason. That was self-evident[3] to him, and it was only in later years, when it had become a problem in itself, that he laid emphasis on it. While in this body, which the Logos had received from the Virgin Mary,

<hr />

[1] *de incarn.* 6, 7   [2] *de incarn.* B.   [3] *ibid.* 14, 2. 4. 6 cf. 57, 1

He taught and preached; at the same time, He convinced men of His divinity by means of miracles, and brought them to know God.[1]

But afterwards He died in His body, and He could die only through the instrumentality of His body. Because it was a genuine human body in its substance, this death could be regarded as a dying of all mankind, and be accepted by God as a vicarious sacrifice. In this way all men in Him died the death decreed for them as sinners.[2] Meanwhile this body had been cleansed by its union with the Logos, then sanctified and raised to a new life.[3] Thus even in the grave it was not touched by corruption, and it rose again as a sign that now death had lost its power for ever.[4] Since the Lord's body was in substance like our own, the work of redemption which the Logos had exercised on it passed over to us in the same way as the act of grace seen in the atoning death had become ours. Our own flesh was sanctified, cleansed from evil qualities, and awakened to a new life in which we should no longer be led astray by the seductive arts of the Devil, but guided by the Logos. The change which the Logos had effected on His body, then began to comprise all mankind; and the fact that the Logos dwelt in the Christian gave him complete assurance of immortality; it would not only protect, like an asbestos garment, from the flames of death, but from the very fear of death, as numberless examples proved.[5] A simple command of God could not have brought all this about; an incarnation was needed, i.e., the most intimate contact with human nature.[6]

So far the doctrine of redemption in Athanasius's first work. We recognize the astonishing vitality of the world of Paul's ideas, and also the genuinely Greek quality of the effort to know. Athanasius seriously believed himself able to take the divine properties and to prove from them the unavoidable necessity of the Incarnation: he pointed out the way which Anselm of Canterbury followed to its logical conclusion. And he also saw plainly that the Redemption could only be effected by an elevation of the very stuff of which man was made; that the divine nature must penetrate fallen human nature, and at

[1] de incarn. 14–16   [2] ibid. 8, 4   9, 1–2   20, 6   [3] ibid. 17, 5. 7
[4] ibid. 22, 4   30, 2   44, 5   [5] ibid. 28, 3   44, 7   [6] ibid. 44, 1

the same time drench it with a soteriological substance that would give it protection against sin and death. Only on those terms could man reach the goal, not of a merely temporary, but an enduring, salvation. Sin had damaged the substance of humanity, and therefore salvation must lay hold on that substance.[1]

The *Speeches against the Arians* bring this doctrine of Redemption to bear on the very problem of the Logos. Everywhere we find the same conceptions and details, but more precisely discussed. In particular, Athanasius now prefers to describe the Redemption as the apotheosis of man, and calls the redeemed man a "temple of God", because the Logos dwells in him as He had dwelt in Jesus's body.[2] He describes the Redemption of mankind from the power of sin in close connection with a right understanding of the Pauline conception of the second Adam,[3] and he shows in detail how the Logos, by dwelling in the flesh, makes its defects His own and so destroys them, till Christians are no longer sinful and mortal, but reborn and immortal.[4]

In this connection he gives the long-desired explanation as to the way the miracle of transformation performed within the person of Christ was transferred to the rest of mankind. Just as in Paul's doctrine, so Athanasius describes baptism as the act of rebirth, through which "the flesh was endowed with the Logos". The model was offered when the Lord was baptized in the Jordan, and "our flesh, worn by Him", became the habitation of the Holy Spirit after descending on Him, the process being repeated in every man at his baptism. It is rather strange to find that the Lord's Supper is not mentioned here, for elsewhere are passages which show that of course Athanasius regarded it as a means of salvation to eternal life.[5]

That is the extent of Athanasius's thought when he was simply expanding those passages where he had discussed the doctrine of redemption in his earlier writings, i.e., those passages which contained the irreducible nucleus of his theological system of thought. What all this had to do with the Arian controversy is

[1] *ibid.* 7, 3   44, 4–8   cf. *or. c. Ar.* 2, 70   3, 33
[2] Apotheosis: *or. c. Ar.* 1, 39. 42. 45   2, 47   3, 23. 33, 34; Temple: 1, 43
[3] *or. c. Ar.* 1, 51   *vide* Vol. 1, 119. 126
[4] *or. c. Ar.* 3, 33. 34   [5] *ibid.* 1, 47   *ep.* 4   *ad Serap.* 19

made plain by his proposition: we should not have been redeemed from sin and from the flesh unless that which the Logos
had assumed had been the flesh proper to human nature:
otherwise we should have had nothing in common with a
substance strange to us. In the same way, but on the other
hand, man would not have been truly made divine, unless the
Logos who became flesh, had been "by nature from the
Father", and therefore really and truly God.[1] Thus Athanasius
had started from the standpoint of the theology of redemption,
and had clearly proved the necessity to believe in the Logos as
truly God in the fullest sense of the word.

He now argued this point in detail or illustrated it with
parallels. He was particularly fond of the illustration, coming
from Origen, of light and its radiance; the radiance pours out
continually from the light without causing any diminution of
the light. He insisted that the radiance was itself light and not
something of a minor nature as contrasted with the sun. In
the same way, while the Logos, as the Son, was different from
the Father, yet, as God, He was not merely like or similar
(*homoios*) to Him, but identical.[2] He and the Father were "one
in the identity of the one godhead". In other words: he identified Son and Father, seen in one as far as possible, and therefore
he proclaimed the oneness of substance (*ousia*) with emphasis.
Nay, Athanasius inferred the necessity of praying to the Son
from the fact that there is only one God who was worshipped
no less in the Son than in the Father.[3]

But in expressing the unity of God, and in using the terms
"one Godhead", "one substance", or "one nature", Athanasius
got into difficulty in trying to find a word to express the difference of the divine persons. This was the point on which his
enemies, understandingly enough, laid hold because they, on
their part, maintained the doctrine of three hypostases.
Athanasius set no value on these speculations, for he was only
concerned to defend his own doctrine of redemption. Yet he
belonged to Origen's school to the extent that he had to reject
the primitive solution of Monarchianism, even in the form
represented by Marcellus.[4]

[1] *or. c. Ar.* 2, 70
[3] *ibid.* 3, 6
[2] *ibid.* 2, 31. 33. 35   3, 4. 9
[4] *vide supra,* 190f.

The consequence of both standpoints was that his position was made still more uncertain in relation to the new theology springing up elsewhere in the east. It will shortly be shown that the recognized theology of the Empire did not develop along the lines prescribed by Athanasius. Yet his manner of thought exercised the strongest influence on the future theology of the patriarchate of Alexandria; it fertilized the rising monachism, and in both ways smoothed the road for Monophysitism later to become a dominant force.

Athanasius was certainly not a mere theological pedant, and only with reservations can he be regarded as an influential writer; but both as an unbendable politician and as a strong religious personality, he was the most eminent man of the post-Constantine period. The mark of his work was indelibly impressed on the political and theological development of the next era.

A few pagan writers appeared in the west in the time of Constantine's sons, although they could not compare in significance with their Greek contemporaries. Aurelius Victor's *Historia Imperatorum*, like all his work, is poor. The African Nonius Marcellus wrote rather a dull work, a hybrid between a dictionary and an encyclopædia; but it is of great value to-day for its numerous quotations from ancient Latin writers. The best-known man of the time was the grammarian Aelius Donatus, who lived in Rome as civic professor. He was held in high honour, and reached the rank of Senator. Jerome was proud of having heard him in A.D. 354.[1] His lectures explaining Terence and Virgil were used later as school-books. Thus they came to be handed down to our day, though much edited. But his Latin grammars for schools, for beginners and for advanced pupils, achieved the greatest popularity, and were at once chosen as the basis for teaching Latin; they retained their dominating position even in the time of the Reformation.

Side by side, and equally famous, with him in Rome was the rhetorician Marius Victorinus[2] who was honoured with a portrait-statue on the forum of Trajan. If Donatus was Rome's

[1] Jerome, *chron. Olymp.* 283, 2   p. 239 Helm
[2] Wessner in *Pauly-W.* 14, 1840–1848

philologue, so Victorinus could be called its philosopher. He not only wrote commentaries on Cicero's philosophical writings, but also translated Aristotle's *Categories* and *Syntax* into Latin. In particular, he was the vehicle of Neoplatonism to Latin readers. Large portions of his translation of Porphyry's introduction to the five Fundamental Principles have survived,[1] and it was used in both east and west as the classical text-book of logic. He also translated other Neoplatonic writings now lost. Augustine read these writings enthusiastically and found inspiration in the example of their translator's life and death,[2] but he never tells whether he had read Plotinus or Porphyry in the Latin made accessible to him by Victorinus.[3]

In any case, when studying Neoplatonism, Victorinus was struck by the close relation between this world of thought and the speculative theology of Christianity. He gradually came to agree with the Church's teaching and finally—probably soon after A.D. 354—he took the decisive step, and to the horror of Roman society and the joy of the Christian church, he was baptized with all publicity.[4] He then began to take part in the theological disputes of the time: first with a little tractate on the genesis of the Logos, then—immediately after[5] the synod in Rimini in A.D. 359—with four books against Arius, followed by a short appeal to unite under the banner of *homousios*. Later, he wrote commentaries on the Pauline epistles, of which those on Galatians, Philippians, and Ephesians, are extant. Three hymns to the Trinity have come down and form a valuable addition to his theological writings, but their rhythm is still a complete riddle, whose solution would be helpful in several ways.

It is not surprising that Marius Victorinus was neither canonized as saint nor regarded as one of the Fathers of the Church. In spite of being baptized, and of the emphatic Christian tone of his writings, on every hand we detect a philosopher who used Biblical and theological formulas in order to expound his Neoplatonic doctrine of the nature of God. He lived in a different world from that of the bishops of

[1] In Boethius *in Isagogen Porphyrii com.*, ed. S. Brandt (*Wiener Corpus* Vol.48) p. xivf.
[2] Aug. *Conf.* 8, 2, 3–5 cf. 7, 9, 13
[3] E. Benz, *Marius Victorinus*, (1932): Plotinus, W. Theiler in *Gnomon* 10 (1934), 493–99 pleads for Porphyry
[4] *vide* footnote 2   [5] Benz, p. 32

the east or the west who entered on the battlefield of church-politics at their own risk. His honoured Arian friend, Candidus, had shown him, in an elegant little essay starting from Plato's idea of God, that the unchangeable Godhead could not be conceived as begetting, because this idea included that of change. And God, who, as the first cause, was above substance, i.e., "unsubstantial," could not Himself be substance nor bring forth anything "consubstantial". Consequently the Logos son was to be conceived as created out of nothing.

Then Victorinus, as a good "Catholic", placed a few sayings from the Bible side by side with this process of pure thought, but immediately betook himself to similar depart-ments of pure philosophy. He seized on one of an opponent's ideas of God, and explained that God as the final cause was above existence; yet He included existence potentially in Him-self, and did actually beget. Thus it was correct to say that the Existence which did actually come into being sprang from God's will. This will was nothing else than thought, life, conduct, or otherwise, the Logos of God, His essential Exist-ence. Hence the Logos was in God, and by nature *homousios* with Him. In speaking of the genesis of the Logos, he did not mean an event in time but a logical relation.[1] Victorinus followed these ideas with the finest distinctions to the limit, and then linked them up with Christian theology by means of a few passages from the Bible.

The proof offered was of the same kind in his four books against Arius. The most noteworthy thing now was that he discussed not only the relation between Son and Father, but handled the problem of the Trinity fundamentally and in detail. Father, Son, and Spirit were one substance, they were *homousioi*. The human soul revealed an essential identity of being, life, and thought, and this provided[2] the key for under-standing the Trinity. The whole matter is discussed with unending repetition, constantly making fresh starts, with meticulously careful syllogistic proofs and wearisome detail, throughout the course of four books.[3]

[1] Mar. Vict. *de gener. div. verb*, 2. 3. 16. 21–27 (Migne, *Patr. lat.* 8. 1021. 1029–1033)
[2] Mar. Vict. *adv. Arium*, 1, 52–64 (Migne, *Patr. lat.* 8, 1080–1088)
[3] Detailed account in Benz 39–188

It is easy to understand that contemporary theologians would not relish this fare, especially as among the multitude of the propositions, phraseology was to be found of a very dubious import. And it is really strange that the manuscripts of these works should have been handed down at all, for they are representative of the Neoplatonic school of philosophy rather than the theology of their period. The explanation no doubt is that Augustine obtained not a few stones for his own use from Victorinus's quarries, and, in particular, owed to that writer's Latin translations of Neoplatonic works, his own introduction to the subject. It is a pity that these translations have been lost.

The work of an otherwise unknown Chalcidius has been more fortunate. This writer translated a good half of Plato's *Timaeus*, and added a commentary consisting of extracts from Neoplatonic works. The translator and author was a Christian, and was set to the work by Ossius, bishop of Cordova. In the Middle Ages, his book provided readers in the west with an example of Plato's philosophy.

Firmicus Maternus was a much more obscure person, but two works of his have been preserved.[1] The first is a lengthy text-book on astrology put together, though the author knew little of the subject himself, out of other sources no longer extant. It consists of snippets from older, miscellaneous writings. But Firmicus knew what he was doing when he presented the educated public of the fourth century with a book so much *à la mode*. About ten years later, *c.* A.D. 347, he became a Christian[2] and wrote a book *Against the Error of Pagan Religions*. Once more it consisted largely of numerous extracts from excellent sources, and dealt especially with the mystery-cults which still survived in his time. Thus he preserved, at the eleventh hour, information of the utmost value to us.

His polemic had the rather nasty flavour of a renegade fouling his former nest, and it issued in an urgent request to His Imperial Majesty to smite the splendid pagan temples into pieces with an axe; and, obedient to the Old Testament commandment, to use the sword to put an end to idol worship, even if whole cities had to be razed to the ground. Was it the

[1] F. Boll, in *Pauly-W.* 6, 2365–2379
[2] Wendland in *Gött. Nachr.* 1910, 330f. cf. Firm. *de errore*, 8, 4 p. 25, 2 ed. Ziegler

case that, perhaps, this senator of Syracuse, was driven by his exceeding zeal, and wished to appear before the Christian emperor, there to do penance for the time when he had been a pagan interested in astrology? In view of the prevailing sympathies, that was hardly necessary, which fact makes the fanaticism shown here all the more astonishing and raises some little doubt about its genuineness.

Hilary was born of good family in Poitiers, and there he married. About that time, he became a Christian, and, soon, bishop of his native town. Then his interest in literary work led him to write on theology. His writings became popular among his contemporaries, and gained him the honourable title of a holy Father of the Church. Many of his works have survived in manuscripts dating back to the beginning of the sixth century. His significance consists in his being the first to make the west acquainted with the theology current in the east, and he did so in elegant and sonorous language. His writings were read with enjoyment even though they were not always easy to follow. This was due to the fact that Hilary was rather a man of ready words than of profound thought, and also, in spite of having good intentions, he could never plan his material well. This weakness makes it hard work to study his chief theological writing on the Trinity, but the oldest work extant from his pen, a commentary on Matthew, has been preserved in very much simpler form, and follows the Biblical text verse by verse. It would be an advantage to know by what sources Hilary was guided in making his commentary on Matthew, but there is no known clue. Naturally he made abundant use of allegory.

His fame as a theologian rests on the twelve books *On the Faith*: they have been entitled "*De Trinitate*" since the sixth century, although the word "Trinity" is not used in them. They were written when he was held in exile in western Asia Minor between A.D. 356 and 360,[1] and show how he strove to explain the theological problems which pressed on him in his new surroundings. The work is conceived from the start on broad lines, and leads the reader, struggling to slough off the limitations of a mere life of the senses, to the source of genuine,

[1] *vide supra*, 216

i.e., Christian knowledge of God. He took the prologue to John's Gospel as his foundation, although this basis for presenting the evangel meant he had to beware of the two opposite heresies of Sabellius and Arius respectively. He divided the work into twelve books, and made his plan plain enough to the reader, but gave the impression that the path to be followed was an intricate one. He is always clear as to what must be rejected, but when it comes to what is to be accepted his statements are indefinite and hesitating.

He frequently emphasized that the genesis of the Son was a secret which could not be comprehended by the human intellect, and he preferred to pile up Biblical passages against heretical doctrines, rather than present a theology thought out by himself. Formulas frequently recur which are to be found in Tertullian and Novatian. *Homousios* is used once, is defended against the Arians by means of plentiful Biblical quotations, and finally explained to mean that God the Father, and God the Son, are one, not in the oneness of a person, but in the unity of the substance.[1] The one indivisible divine nature has the one name, God. But birth from the eternal Father did not estrange the Son from the true nature of the divine substance, but only gave Him a special existence which was designated by such names as Logos, Wisdom, and similar terms —names which, however, applied at the same time to the inner essence of the Father.[2] He sharply rejects the application of the idea of time to the Godhead, and proves the eternal process of the Son as over against the Arian doctrine of the birth of the Logos in time.

Hilary also tried to establish a doctrine of the Holy Spirit to whom he frequently referred by the title "Gift" (*donum*) in accordance with Acts 2: 28. In the Scriptures, the "Gift" is described both as the Spirit of God and the Spirit of Christ, and therefore would be more properly attributed to the one divine nature.[3] According to John, 15: 26, He came forth from the Father and was sent out by the Son. But Hilary did not reach a clear conception, and still less did he deal with such a problem as that of the separate personality of the Spirit.

All his writings rest upon facts and doctrines which he had

[1] Hilary, *de trin.* 4, 4. 41   [2] *ibid.* 7, 11   [3] *ibid.* 8, 26 cf. 2, 29–35

borrowed from others, and which were dutifully reproduced by him. But the whole of Hilary is not to be found expressed in this book. We make the acquaintance of the real Hilary, on reading his splendid polemics. Here, his elegant Latin aided by his practical temperament makes him a most attractive writer. In these polemics, he asked for his rights from the Emperor Constantius. He distinguished the standpoint of his new Nicene orthodoxy plainly and frankly—as he had learned to do by the example of Athanasius—from the intrigues of Ursacius and Valens. Thus he captured the hearts of his own people in the west to no less a degree than Athanasius had done in the case of Christians in the east.

He was able to afford his fellow-countrymen convincing proof that the term *homoiousios*, which was defended by Basil of Ancyra and his compilers, was unobjectionable, and in no way inferior to the Nicene *homousios*. He had set his heart on winning friends in the Latin west for this group of religious leaders among the eastern theologians. But he also addressed himself to his Greek friends, and urged that they should abandon their opposition to *homousios* and make the Nicene creed the common basis of an orthodox Christianity. He had the right sort of insight into church policy, enabling him to see what was essential, but not the systematic training which could have pointed the theologically accessible way to this goal.

He appeared uninvited at the synod of Rimini, and requested permission from the Emperor to meet his accuser personally— Saturninus of Arles. That was not granted, but, being regarded as a dangerous man who had disturbed the peace in the east, he was now sent off back home to Gaul.[1] He at once proclaimed a "closer battle" against the Emperor;[2] he wrote and urged the bishops of his homeland to relentless opposition against the prosecution of Christians, which he said the "Anti-Christ" Constantius was carrying on hypocritically as a wolf in sheep's clothing. Written after a long and well-considered silence, this document, and this document only, contains the charges which he made fearlessly against the royal person of the Emperor. We

[1] Hilary, *ad. Const.* 2, 3 (4, 198 Feder)   Sulp. Sev. *chron.* 2, 45, 3–4   Jerome, *chron. Ol.* 284, 3
[2] *Contra Constantium* (2, 561–583 cd. Bened.)

cannot read it without apprehension, for in speaking so boldly, he was taking his life in his hands.

But Constantius had no desire to present the opposition church with martyrs. Otherwise, he would long ago have made away with Lucifer, bishop of Cagliari (in Sardinia) who had used much grosser language about him. Lucifer was a wild fanatic; he directed a large number of polemics against the Emperor. In these, he repudiated the imputation of dealings with heretics, and with equal vigour defended himself from the charge of having judged an accused man—viz., Athanasius— unheard and in his absence. He used an overwhelmingly large number of quotations to show that such pretensions would be against the divine commands, and he warned the Emperor against vainly trusting that the divine favour would become manifest in his political successes. On the contrary he drew his attention to instructive instances in the history of the kings of Israel, and demanded of him to repent. He described the Emperor as an Arian and a heretic *passim*, one who had chosen the Anti-Christ in place of Christ; he flogged his dullness and perversity, and heaped on him Biblical terms of abuse as found in the Epistle of Jude.

Constantius of course banished this critic—the tractates were written in exile—but did him no further hurt in spite of his insults. The polemical bishop had the impudence to have a codex of his writings sent to the Emperor; the latter merely inquired of Lucifer politely through a courtier whether the parcel had really come from His Holiness. The answer was in the affirmative, and the author asserted that he was ready joyfully to suffer the death that awaited him.[1] Then he immediately wrote another tractate on this subject with increased shrillness of tone, against the *Thickhead of an Emperor*. Here he piled up the terms of abuse, and indeed quoted Cicero's *quousque tandem*[2]—but the Emperor did not punish him for it. He does not appear to have taken him seriously.

The Church would also have been better advised if she had shared the Emperor's estimate of him. We shall see on a later page how much harm the self-willed blusterer did afterwards,

---

[1] Lucifer, *ep.* 3. 4 p. 321f. ed. Hartel

[2] Lucifer, *moriendum esse*, 4. 12   p. 292, 20   310, 11

being in all respects the antithesis to the cultured Hilary with his diplomatic suavity. Lucifer was proud that he was not acquainted with pagan worship and stressed also the fact that his writing was colloquial.[1] This in its turn has made him more interesting to present-day philologists than are the more educated writers of his time. His significance as a theologian is negligible, because he was out of contact with any of the relevant problems—and not merely with those of his own age; he took his cue only from the watch-words "Nicea" and "Arianism". For the subject-matter of his proofs, he went to the Latin Bible, which he quoted endlessly. This is an important fact nowadays because it illustrates graphically how much alive the Scriptures were even in those sections of the Church which were untouched by theological learning.

[1] Lucifer, *ibid.* 11   p. 306, 19   and *de non parcendo*, 21   p. 256, 7

Chapter Ten

JULIAN

CONSTANTIUS'S UNEXPECTED DEATH SETTLED THE QUESTION of the succession to the throne without further ado, and perhaps, the Emperor, on his deathbed, had actually designated his enemy as heir to the crown. Julian marched from Nish to Constantinople, and was accorded a ceremonial reception on December 11, 361. He received the tributes of the foreign ambassadors who came from all sides to the new ruler of the world. When Constantius's body was brought by his troops to the capital, Julian descended with a large escort to the harbour, and took the dead Emperor to his resting place in the Church of the Apostles, near his great father. He granted him also the honour of a consecration. Then began the trial of those held responsible for Constantius's misconceptions and machinations against Julian. Under the presidency of Sallustius[1] who had been raised to the rank of *Praefectus Praetorio*, and who had been a faithful helper of Julian in hard times, an extraordinary assize of high statesmen and military officers was instituted; it pronounced a series of death penalties, and decreed a number of banishments. The worst desperadoes were burnt alive. Then at last it was possible to breathe freely, and now the way lay open for introducing a new epoch.

The speed and magnitude of recent events had almost taken Julian by surprise, and the letters written in the first days of his sole rulership hint as much to the reader. Julian felt the weight of the burden which the gods had laid on his shoulders: his gods, the gods in whom he believed and to whom his life was dedicated.[2] He had lost his mother, Basilina, when he was still a little child; and he was deprived of his father, when a boy of seven years old, in A.D. 337, by a dynastic murder. Thus he grew up in quiet seclusion in Nicomedia, brought up by a

[1] Seeck in *Pauly-W.* 2nd Series, 1, 2072–2075
[2] Throughout this chapter the biography of Julian by J. Bidez, *Vie de l'empereur Julien* (1930), is to be compared *passim*. It is written with excellent descriptive power, on the basis of research of fundamental importance. Further, cf. Borries in *Pauly-W.* 10, 26–91

faithful slave, who once used to read Homer and Hesiod aloud to his mother, and who was trusted by Eusebius, the local bishop, and a distant relative.[1]

Three years later, Julian was sent together with his brother Gallus into the interior of Cappadocia, where he passed six years in relative solitude on the royal domain of Macellum. Here he was instructed in the Christian religion and eagerly learned Biblical texts by heart, the teachers being astonished at the progress made by their pupil. He not only attended the services in church, but also joined the lower clergy as a "reader", and actually read the passages of the Bible as required by the liturgy.[2] During this period, he made the acquaintance of Gregory who later became bishop of Alexandria, but who at that time lived at his home in Cappadocia, where he possessed a good library. The youth, hungry for knowledge, often borrowed books from it, and copied them for himself; of course he could browse about in the whole contents as he wished; for, after the owner's death, he wrote "I know Gregory's books—a good many, if not all." He then gave orders to transfer them to Antioch. The library contained valuable Christian literature, also some philosophers and orators;[3] and it probably afforded the precocious prince his first acquaintance with the world of classical Greece.

When Gallus was called to the royal court in A.D. 347, Julian too left his exile in Macellum and betook himself to Constantinople. Here he studied, with great diligence and moderate pleasure, grammar and rhetoric in the traditional manner, until he was directed to Nicomedia: in this city his fate was decided. Although he was strictly forbidden to hear Libanius who was teaching there, he was successful in getting secret copies of his lectures.[4] These gave him something more than the dry teaching of his tutor in the capital. His spirit took fire from the spirit of Libanius, and he burned for the genuine classical Greece. Among Libanius's pupils, he acquired that knowledge which thenceforth determined his life: esoteric communion with the gods. Up to that point of time, he had

[1] Julian, *Misopogon* p. 352 a b   Amm. Marc. 22, 9, 4
[2] Julian, *ad Athen.* p. 271 c d   Sozom. 5, 2, 9–10   Eunapius, *vitae soph: Maximus*, p. 47
[3] Julian, *ep.* 106. 107 p. 184ff.   [4] Liban. *or.* 18, 14. 15

been a Christian by conviction, and had hated the gods. But now he heard their voices prophesying, and to do that became his form of religious experience.[1] It ousted Christian teaching, filled his heart and mingled with his studies to form a unity with the romance of Greece.

When his brother Gallus was raised to the rank of Cæsar in March, 351, Julian was granted still greater freedom in prosecuting his studies. It soon became plain that the mystical machinations of his philosophizing friends had made a deeper impression on his soul than had the Greek clarity of Libanius. Julian went to Pergamon to hear the aged Aidesios, whose lectures kept alive the priestly wisdom of Iamblichos. He used dark words, and recommended Julian to consult his disciples Eusebius and Chrysanthios, who, in their turn, finally directed him with still more mysterious hints to Maximos of Ephesus. Julian went, "hung on him, and fastened his teeth into his wisdom",[2] until at length he was initiated into the mysteries. This took place in a cave underneath the earth, and was solemnized to the accompaniment of spirit-voices, raising of ghosts, thunder, lightning, and fiery magic.[3]

From now onwards, he believed himself called by the sun god to save the Empire by restoring the ancient cult of the gods; Christianity appeared to him as the enemy that had to be overcome. But none except a few confidants dared pretend to know anything about it. Outwardly, he played the part of a true Christian, so long as it was required by his dependent position, and by respect for Christians amongst the soldiers; as late as January 6, 361, he took part in the celebration of the feast of the Epiphany in Paris.[4] But after he had decided to fight for the throne, he felt free. He granted his troops every cult they desired, and in his proclamation to the Athenians, he confessed his belief in Athena and her protective angels which descended from the sun and the moon.[5] Oracular sayings constantly renewed, and a multitude of initiations into mysteries, served to strengthen continually a voice which came from the gods, and which called for a resurrection of the

[1] Liban. or. 13, 11   [2] Eunap. vitae soph. p. 48–51
[3] Bidez, Vie, 79ff.   Greg. Naz. or. 4, 55 (1, 102 Bened.)
[4] Amm. Marc. 21, 2, 5   Zonaras, 13, 11, 6
[5] Zonaras, 13, 11, 6   Julian, ad Athen. p. 275 a, b, cf. d

ancient religion in all its magnificence and glory. All this gave him inner certainty till at last he overcame his natural timorousness, and began the great work of reform.

The first thing was a transformation of life at Court. The whole swarm of court parasites and eunuchs disappeared, down to the head cook and the court barber: similarly, the numerous bureaux with their files, and also the officials and the whole secret service of Constantius.[1] He also set aside the Persian ceremonial and abolished the unapproachability of the most exalted person of His Majesty. Indeed the Emperor appeared on foot among the other dignitaries to congratulate the consul of A.D. 362 on entering office—but this was felt to be unsuitable. The senate at Constantinople attained undreamed of honour, and was presented with all sorts of privileges. What was hitherto unheard of, the Emperor often appeared in their chamber and took part in their discussions: his exemplar, Marcus Aurelius, had apparently also done the same.[2]

He was concerned to raise the leading circles of society in their self-respect, to awaken something like pride in their Hellenic heritage, and to lead them from the slavish feelings of the past into a consciousness of moral freedom. He had no desire to be narrow-minded, and therefore he attracted to his circle, not only his old philosopher-friends, but also men from the opposite camp, including Christians, and placed them in responsible positions. "We mix together, not with the polite hypocrisy with which you probably have hitherto been acquainted—in which a man speaks compliments to people whom he hates fiercely as his worst enemies—no! we upbraid one another with all due freedom, when it is needed, and blame one another, and in doing so, think no less of one another than of the best of friends." So wrote Julian to a former courtier of Constantius's, in order to win him to himself.[3] His purpose, really and with genuine conviction, was to be an enlightened sovereign, with free people about himself. He wished his empire to be modelled after Plato's ideal, and ruled by philosophers. When he entered on his great task, it was with hesitation and

[1] Amm. Marc. 22, 4, 9   22, 7, 5   Socrates, 3, 1, 50. 51   Liban. or. 2, 58
[2] Cod. Theod. 9, 2, 1   11, 23, 2. Liban. or. 18, 154   script. hist. Aug. M. Ant. 10, 7 and remarks by N. H. Baynes, The Historia Augusta (1926)
[3] Julian, ep. 32   p. 60   Thereon, Bidez, Vie, 217f.

serious concern;[1] soon he grasped it firmly and with growing courage; more and more he was forwarded not only by the encouragement of friends but especially by the gods themselves, for these accompanied him step by step with their revelations.

What happened in the capital was followed by similar events in the provinces. Here, too, Greek city life was to be re-established, and the councillors (*decuriones*) constitute a college of worthy senators. Julian reduced the exemptions from serving in municipal offices, made a point of depriving Christian clerics and monks of them, and so strengthened both the number and financial ability of the city authorities. He also lightened their duties and so opened up new possibilities for this moribund class. At the same time, he brought greater order into the system of taxation and, in many spheres, introduced a thrifty economy. He considerably reduced the abuse of the imperial post. In this way, he brought a sensible improvement into various departments of public life.

The decisive change took place in the field of religion. He ordered the restoration of the old cultus to its full extent. That implied the reopening of closed temples and the rebuilding of those that had been destroyed; it meant that the confiscated temple revenues would be paid again, together with support for the priests and others who served the cult; the granting of the sums required for the sacrifices, and the reviving of the publicly celebrated feasts, and much else would be effected.[1]

When Constantine had formerly decreed that Christians should receive compensation for their losses, the return of estreated goods caused not a few difficulties, although the confiscations concerned had been made during the persecutions not more than ten years earlier. But under Julian, the period was to date back fifty years: this was simply impracticable, and could only be realized in a minority of cases, and with good will on the part of all concerned. Julian's short reign did not give enough time to bring all the complications of this business to light, to say nothing of finding solutions for the problems raised. Libanius tells proudly of pilfered columns brought back by ship or heavy waggon, and replaced in their old

[1] cf. his *ep. ad Themist.* p. 253a–267b
[2] Amm. Marc. 22, 5, 2   Liban. *or.* 18, 126   Sozom. 5, 3, 1–2   Socrat. 3, 1, 48

positions[1]—in fact the majority remained where they were; and who would find much satisfaction in spending money or taking trouble to build temples which had become a matter of indifference to the people?

It was different in isolated places. Especially in Syria did the pagan population seize the chance of avenging themselves with bloody violence for the destruction of their ancient shrines; exact records have survived about events in Baalbek (Heliopolis), Arethusa, and Bostra. The worst scenes took place in Alexandria where the multitudes rioted, killed Bishop George, who was not generally popular, and murdered cruelly two high state officials. But those were destructive outbreaks of mob-passion, and not constructive efforts made on behalf of the old faith. In this respect, Julian, the idealist, had to face bitter disillusionments.[2]

The Emperor wished to be entirely impartial towards the Christians or, as he always called them, the Galileans. In the first place, he recalled all exiled bishops to their homes—naturally not to their offices about which he did not trouble—and they even received back their confiscated goods.[3] Then he assembled in his palace the heads of opposing parties and exhorted them urgently to unity—for he knew from experience "that Christians are more dangerous enemies to one another than are wild beasts".[4] Contrary to his expectations, the Church remained quite calm for the immediately following period, and the parties used the inevitable armed truce to consolidate themselves and to prepare for future action.

Aëtios, now provided with landed property,[5] appeared in Constantinople, having been invited to the Court by Julian. After him came his friend Eunomios, who had left his bishopric of Kyzikos in the lurch; and a group who agreed on *anhomoios*, and who, with Eudoxios as their patron,[6] were preparing to play a part in church politics. Athanasius returned to

[1] Liban. *or.* 18, 126 cf. Zonaras 13, 12, 30. 31
[2] Sozom. 5, 9–10 Philostorg. p. 228, Bidez, together with footnote Theodoret, *H.E.* 3, 7, 1–10 Greg. Naz. *or.* 4, 88–91 Liban. *ep.* 763, 3 Amm. Marc. 22, 11, 3–10 Bidez, *Vie*, 230–235
[3] Julian, *ep.* 110 p. 187, 19f. *ep.* 46, p. 65f. *ep.* 114, p. 193, 11
[4] Amm. Marc. 22, 5, 4
[5] Julian, *ep.* 46, p. 65f. Philostorg. 9, 4 p. 117 7, 6 p. 84 Bidez
[6] *vide supra*, 231

Alexandria on February 21, 362, and was able to resumé office without let or hindrance, since, as already noted, George had fallen a victim in a riot. Julian seems to have borne this violent act with remarkable patience, although it had involved state officials; he wrote a polite letter[1] with moral exhortations to the people of Alexandria. The Arian church in the city could not tolerate Athanasius's control, and chose a bishop of their own called Lucius: everyone could do what he liked unhindered. Two exiled bishops came from Upper Egypt into the Delta in order to go home from there; they were Eusebius of Vercelli and Lucifer of Cagliari.

Athanasius discussed the situation with Eusebius, and called a synod, in order to prepare a broad basis for the union of all who accepted the Nicene way of thought. This was specially needed in reference to Antioch where matters were quite out of hand and required regularizing. Lucifer believed himself capable of this, and set off to go there: we shall see what he did. Yet another person, Asterios of Petra, on his way home joined Eusebius in Alexandria. Lucifer sent two of his deacons from Antioch and the church of that city did the same. A few monks came from Laodicea in Syria commissioned by Bishop Apollinaris.

The result of taking counsel was a carefully thought-out proposal for peace of far-reaching significance, going far beyond the special local occasion. It was set down in a document of the synod[2] and confided the ordering of the church at Antioch to a commission of five bishops with Eusebius, Lucifer, and Asterios at its head.

The church of the capital of Anatolia had always been pursued by ill-fortune, and, after the departure of Eudoxios, only received a new bishop in the person of the Armenian Meletios in A.D. 360.[3] He commended himself to the Court by subscribing to the formula of Seleucia, and, in an extant sermon delivered before the Emperor on the familiar text in Proverbs 8: 22, "The Lord possessed me in the beginning of

[1] Julian, *ep.* 60, 69ff.=Soc. 3, 3, 5–25
[2] *Tomus ad Antiochenos* in Athan. *op.* 1, 2, p. 770–775, ed. Montf.
[3] *vide supra*, 224 cf. E. Schwartz, *ZNW.* 34 (1935), 162f. F. Cavallera, *Le Schisme d'Antioche*, 1905, 71ff.
[4] Epiph. *haer.* 73, 29–33

His way", he could not be accused of doing any violence to the confession of *homoios*. He did not trouble about "substance" or "hypostasis", although closer inspection reveals that the germs of a *homoiousian* theology were unmistakably there. And as he immediately made his peace with the clergy led by Eudoxios, but came into conflict with others, he became so suspect to those who had stood for him till then that, only a month later, he was deprived of office and sent back to Armenia.[1]

His place was taken by Euzoïos, whom we already know to have been a friend of Arius in his earlier days,[2] and who had worked in Alexandria till now under George. His name was sufficient to give widespread alarm, and therefore a large part of the church separated from him, and regarded Meletios, who had been expelled, as their true bishop now as before. At first, the "Meletians" held their services outside the city; afterwards they took possession of the church, restored[3] after the persecutions, "in the old town". Theologically they were inclined to the *homousians*, and so it was easy for them to unite with the other separate church, the Eustathians already thirty years old[4] who had the Nicene creed as their hall-mark! Their spiritual leader at that time was a presbyter named Paulinos.

It is much to the credit of the synod of Alexandria, and thus in the first instance to Athanasius, but also to Eusebius of Vercelli, a westerner, that they understood the signs of the times, and overcame the narrow-mindedness characteristic of the most recent past. Peace and church-fellowship were held out to all men of good will who kept apart from the Arians and fulfilled three conditions: they must curse the Arian heresy, accept the Nicene confession, and, thirdly, curse those who declared the Holy Spirit a creature and separated Him from the nature (*ousia*) of Christ. There were to be no further requirements, in particular the "trash from Serdika"[5] was bluntly rejected. No objections were to be raised against confessing three hypostases, if not meant in the Arian sense,

[1] Epiph. *haer.* 73, 35   Jer. *chron. Ol.* 284, 4

[2] *vide supra*, 123   Soc. 2, 44   3, 9, 4   Sozom. 4, 28   5, 13, 3   Theodoret, *H.E.* 2, 31, 10–11

[3] Theodoret, *H.E.* 1, 3, 1   2, 31, 11   3, 4, 3   cf. *Soc.* 3, 9, 4   *chron. pasch.*, p. 548, Dindorf

[4] *vide supra*, 126   [5] *Tomus*, 5, p. 772e   *vide supra*, 201

any more than against one hypostasis, or *ousia*—which was the same thing—except in so far as these terms served as cloaks for Sabellianism.

That was a big step forward, and on this basis it should have been possible to establish peace between the Meletians and the Eustathians in Antioch, and so to exercise a decisive influence on the history of the church in the east. But when the commission arrived with the document at its destination, it was already too late. Lucifer of Calaris, the undeviating radical, had already consecrated Paulinus the leader of the Eustathians, and installed him as bishop. This was a favour to an old friend of Athanasius, but it made it impossible to enter into any negotiations with the much more numerous and important followers of Meletios; and that was what Lucifer wanted to prevent.

As a result, there were now three congregations in Antioch, and a fourth was already coming into being. This last consisted of the followers of Apollinaris of Laodicea. He was closely associated with Athanasius in theology and church politics, and had worked out a Christology logically, which raised new questions and conjured up new strife.

He regarded the *homousia* of God, Father and Son, as axiomatic, and the same view held good for the Holy Spirit. The godhead was a unity represented in the Father, whose Son, but not brother, was the Logos; and the Logos sent the spirit.[1] One godhead in three persons (*prosopa*) was Apollinaris's formula, although he occasionally spoke of *one ousia* or nature (*physis*), and of *hypostases* instead of persons.[2] But his interest concentrated on the Incarnation. Was it possible to picture how the second Person of the divine Triad became man? His view was that the godhead, which was perfect and unchangeable by nature, did not in any case combine a true human being with itself, for two beings already perfect produce no unity, but only a hybrid.

Some sort of diminution must take place as soon as two independent beings united in one hybrid if the new being was

---

[1] Text in Lietzmann, *Apollinaris*, 1, p. 173, 1. 24   175, 24f.

[2] *Apoll.* p. 167, 19   172, 3. 13   *ousia*, 170, 27   177, 1   180, 14   *physis*, 172, 6   *hypostases*, p. 171, 22   173, 6

to be a unity.[1] As the godhead is unchangeable, the loss can only take place on the human side. Scripture indicates the correct understanding by using the phrase "the Word became flesh". This means that the deity of the Logos united only with the corporeality of man, or expressed otherwise, the Logos dwelt as soul in the body received from the Virgin Mary. The unity of every human person arises when body and soul work together. In Christ, the Logos took the place of the soul and was this life-principle from the conception onwards. It was not true to say that the divine thought and will had combined with the human—that would produce two beings, and by no means a unity. Rather the divinity of the Logos constituted "one nature" with human corporeality; there was one being that willed and acted.[2]

Since the full Logos-nature, which was one in essence with the Father, was united in the above manner with human flesh, that flesh became truly divine in as far as it assumed the divine qualities. Our redemption was effected by the "sanctification" of the human element of Jesus, for His flesh is flesh of our flesh, one in nature with ours. The apotheosis effected in Him, which in principle did away with the passions, with sin, and with death, passed over to us if we took His flesh as food at the Lord's Supper;[3] for that was what was meant by the phrase "accepted in faith".

Here we have therefore a more precise exposition of the doctrine of redemption which Athanasius had already put forward.[4] The only difference is that a genuine explanation of the divinely human person of Christ is developed logically in a way that could be really envisaged. God dwelt in a human body which became the organ of a redemption conceived in physical terms. Christ had no "human soul"—so ran the negative formulation of one main principle,—the model for His body being Solomon's temple which also had neither soul, nor reason, nor will.[5]

[1] *ibid.* p. 234, fr. 113   p. 224, fr. 81   p. 214, fr. 42; cf. p. 228   fr. 91. 92
[2] *ibid.* p. 181, 1. 9f.   185, 5. 11   191, 7f. 204 fr. 2   206, 26f.   207, 2. 12. 27
[3] *ibid.* p. 168, 10–16   cf. 235, fr. 116 (Lord's Supper)   178, 13–17   179, 7–9   188, 9–18
[4] *vide supra*, 249
[5] *Apoll.* p. 204, fr. 2

This thesis was the new element in Apollinaris's doctrine, or what gave a clear graphic quality to his expositions of it, and gained a wide publicity for the pamphlets he wrote. It was also new as distinct from the questions hitherto discussed, these having dealt with the Logos problem in a rather one-sided manner. The Nicene *homousios* was recognized as a presupposition unchallenged and firmly established; then there was a further step in a direction still almost untried, and one that promised logically to enrich the religion of the Church. The Apollinarian preachers proclaimed the new doctrine zealously and successfully, and at the same time gained adherents to the Nicene creed, for that was the only ground on which such fine fruits could grow.

Soon there arose doubts, however. Athanasius had formerly preached something similar, but had made a halt short of the last logical consequences which Apollinarius boldly and confidently drew. For Athanasius, it was a full human nature to which the Logos was united.[1] But now the phrase "body without soul" sounded offensive in his ears—although that was the kernel of the solution—and other people were not less troubled by the daring theory. The result of these hesitations was a discussion with representatives of Apollinarius at the synod of Alexandria; a thesis was formulated and sent forth, maintaining that "the Saviour did not possess a body without a soul, sense-perception, and understanding. Since the Lord became man for our sakes, it was impossible that His body should be without understanding (*nous*). Moreover, not only the body but also the soul were redeemed by the Logos."

The Apollinarians agreed, but had a rather different opinion from Athanasius. The latter believed, as the second clause shows plainly, that there must have been in Christ a soul originating in the human order.

Only so might the human soul be redeemed by contact with the godhead, and apotheosized. Salvation would then be brought not only to the bodies, but also to the souls of the rest of mankind. The Apollinarians[2] let this last clause melt away in their consciousness, but agreed emphatically with the proposition that Christ had not a soulless and reasonless body—

[1] *vide supra*, 248   [2] *Apoll*. p. 256, 7–15

just because (and then they spoke softly) the Logos was the soul and the reason of that body. Before they could be pinned down, they would have had to speak more clearly of a "human" soul or a "human" rationality in Christ; but that was what they did not do and for the very good reason that a certain Vitalis, an enthusiastic supporter of Apollinaris,[1] was also one of the leaders of Meletios's party in Antioch. The discussions in Alexandria were concerned with overcoming the differences among those believers at Antioch who inclined to Nicea, therefore the tendency was to be as accommodating as possible. So far, no success had been gained and we shall see in the sequel what a mighty blaze sprang in time from these first sparks.

The document drawn up by the synod at Alexandria required the confession of the Nicene creed, and added that the Holy Spirit must be included in the divine *ousia*, i.e., that the formula *homousios* held good of the Spirit also. Athanasius had defended this thesis not long before in letters he wrote to Serapion of Thmuis from the wilderness. The thesis became all the more important, when among *homoiousians*, a closer approximation to the Nicene doctrine of the Son had led to a more definite subordination of the Spirit.[2] This was due to the fact that those circles which kept close to the tradition of theological thought that went back to Origen, sought to develop the doctrine of the Logos, and correspondingly gave their attention almost exclusively to the relation of the Son to the Father; as a consequence, they did not touch the question as to the essential nature of the Holy Spirit, or did so only in passing. But the theologians, who were rooted in the Church's faith, thought in thoroughly trinitarian terms, and it was only due to the pressure exercised by their opponents that they put stronger emphasis on the second person in the Trinity. Hence it is easy to understand that it lay very near to their hearts to develop the doctrine of the persons in the Trinity, and consequently that of the right place of the Holy Spirit; and when a good opportunity came they put that doctrine well in the foreground. We can observe this fact in the case of Athanasius, but equally with Apollinaris. The same tendency had been

---

[1] *chron. pasch.* p. 548 Dindorf   [2] cf. Loofs in Hauck's *Realencycl.* 12, 46f.

adopted and maintained in the west from as early as Tertullian. But only now, about A.D. 360, did the differences come out plainly, and the thesis of the synod at Alexandria was the first rumble of a coming storm.

Athanasius's council, in the summer of A.D. 362, had not solved its primary problem of uniting the Antiochene church under the Nicene creed, but the synod had a much greater significance for the history of the Church than the delegates to it could have dreamt at the time. It meant the conclusion of that period of theological disputes which began with Nicea, and opened a new chapter with a programme clearly set out: work in the future was to be concerned with reaching unity under the Nicene creed, the development of the doctrine of the Trinity, the doctrine of the person of Christ, i.e., the incarnation of God. The period when Julian was emperor, gave to all who were to take part time for meditating upon these matters.

It was comprehensible that the Emperor should particularly wish to attract to his Court those men who had led him to a knowledge of the truth, and whom he therefore must regard as the true guides of his time. The most important of them was the great Maximos of Ephesus, who after some hesitation decided to go to the capital. He travelled like a conqueror through Asia Minor, and, on arriving in Constantinople, was immediately brought into the Senate by the Emperor, and there welcomed. Priscus also let himself be persuaded to come from Athens, whereas Chrysanthios remained in Sardes.[1] Whether it was the influence of these men, or the fruit of his own experiences, that drew Julian aside from his first programme of tolerance, cannot be determined.

The worship of the sun as the religion of the Empire had been a political necessity till Diocletian's time, but Christianity had been the ideological factor unifying the Empire since Constantine. These two religions, together with the old cults of the gods, could not now live peaceably side by side under the slogan of tolerance. That would have meant ceasing to

[1] Eunap., *Vitae*, p. 55f. Amm. Marc. 22, 7, 3

work at the religious sub-structure of the unity of the Empire, a sub-structure with which the imperium could no more dispense now than at an earlier date. Nor were the religions at all inclined to harmonious relations, but wrestled in a life and death struggle without any wish for an armistice. Thus, when once Julian had decided to separate himself from Christianity, he had to attack it, and make sun-worship the religion of the state: and from the beginning of A.D. 362 this was the road he took, though very reluctantly.

He had no desire to introduce a persecution on Diocletian's lines, and he knew also that anything of the sort could not even be considered in view of the advanced stage reached in Christianizing the Empire. But he trusted in the inherent superiority of his programme, and he hoped to cut off Christians from access to higher education, and thus to deprive Christianity of the roots of its power to attract. This was put very cleverly into operation. On June 17, 362, a law was promulgated which made the giving of instruction in school everywhere dependent on the permission of the city authorities; and these were directed to test more particularly the character of the applicants.[1] The permission was then to be laid before the Emperor for confirmation. We observe at once that the idea of permission being necessary expresses the important truth that teaching is always of significance in the education of public opinion and therefore deserves the attention of the state. That was something entirely new, and although philosophers had long declared that character training was more important than learned exercises, it was now for the first time put into legal form.

The city authorities throughout the Empire must have read the Emperor's decree with some head-shaking, for—what is character? And how determine whether an applicant fulfils the requirement? Ought philosophers to be put to the test? Which of the city-fathers could say, even of himself, that he possessed this rare quality in sufficient degree? But it soon became publicly known that the matter was not all that difficult. In a detailed proclamation,[2] Julian explained that the decisive trait of character in a teacher lay in the harmony

---

[1] *Cod. Theod.* 13, 3, 5   Julian *ep.* 61 p. 72   [2] Julian, *ep.* 61c, 73–75

between his teaching and his real opinions, and that it showed a contemptible and mercenary mind to praise something really held to be bad. This was the case, however, among the teachers who were Galileans. They presumed to teach Homer and Hesiod, Demosthenes, Herodotus, Thucydides, Isocrates and Lysias. For the opinions expressed by these classics rested on faith in the gods and these the Christians derided. In all honour then, they ought to cease expounding the ancients and stick to their Matthew and Luke. Young people ought to have unhindered access to the truth, but no Christians ought to give lessons in classical literature. All was now clear and the *decuriones* of all the cities knew where they were. The defect of character that would exclude a person from office consisted solely and simply in the Christian faith.

The decree caused tremendous excitement. It was a heavy blow against the Christians and was also felt to be a mean one. The Christians themselves reckoned the attack on their spiritual armoury as Julian's worst and most shameful act. Even non-Christians were estranged, and Ammianus[1] called the law "intolerable, and worthy of being cloaked with eternal silence". Christians of strong character, like Marius Victorinus and Prohaeresios, retired from teaching, although the Emperor was inclined to grant exceptions in the case of famous men.[2] The Apollinaris already mentioned, and his father, did something else: they manufactured antique literature with a Christian content, i.e., they took Biblical material and made of it comedies modelled on Menander, tragedies on Euripides, Pindaric odes and Homeric epics; indeed Platonic dialogues were fabricated out of gospel material.[3] These productions were admired at the time, though soon laid aside. Happily most have been lost, but a Psalter in hexameters has come down to our own day.

Julian did not remain content with mere negative action. He proceeded to draw up a regular scheme, a well-considered reconstruction of the ancient religion. His self-confidence rose higher on account of certain divine revelations, mediated to him by his teacher Maximus, which convinced him that he

---

[1] Amm. Marc. 22, 10, 7   [2] Aug. *Conf.* 8, 5, 10 Jer. *chron. Ol*, 285, 3
[3] Soc. 3, 16, 1–5 Sozom. 5, 18, 3–4

was a re-incarnation of Alexander the Great.[1] This may have also influenced him, early in A.D. 362, to put forth a plan for an important Persian campaign conceived on a grand scale. To make fuller preparations for it, he went to Antioch, but not without offering worship *en route* to the Great Mother Kybele of Pessinus. The desires and hopes with which the educated "Hellenes" greeted him in Antioch, may be gathered from the speech[2] with which his old teacher, Libanius, welcomed him there on his arrival. The Emperor honestly tried to fulfil them.

In Antioch, Julian had had his most valuable experiences of contemporary religious life, and made his plans accordingly. When he entered the city soon after the middle of July, he would have noticed that the festival of Adonis was still a living custom among the populace of the capital of the east, for wailing for the death of Aphrodite's lover would sound in his ears from all sides. But when soon afterwards, in August, he hurried to Daphne, one of the suburbs, in order to join in celebrating the great annual feast of Apollo there, it must have been painful for him to acknowledge that no preparations had been made, and instead of hecatombs of oxen, only a single goose was sacrificed. He traced that back to the fact that the government of the city lay in Christian hands,[3] but he could not hide from himself that no one had been prevented from offering voluntary sacrifices. He himself now did what he could, and the sacrificial cult bloomed as far as his influence extended.

But he laboured with restless haste, and with a diligence which seemed comic to people who were long hardened to such things. When, for the sake of making a good example, he bore a piece of sacred furniture in solemn procession to the temple, and patiently put up with a following of the poorer women, the scene struck the Antiochenes as worthless farce. And the measureless waste, with hundreds of slaughtered oxen, unnumbered flocks of sheep and birds to correspond, could only appear senseless at a time when people had grown quite unaccustomed to it. The acceptable duty of eating all this sacrificial meat was laid on the soldiers; and when they had

---

[1] Soc. 3, 21, 6–7   [2] Liban. *or*. 13 cf. especially §47
[3] Amm. Marc. 22, 9, 15   Julian, *Misopogon*, p. 361 d–363a

eaten to repletion, and then consumed much liquor, and finally had to be carried into the barracks dead-drunk—that was something which did not tend to gain converts for the religion preached by the Emperor.[1]

Nothing of this escaped Julian, but he bit his teeth together and looked undauntedly towards his high goal. Well did he know that this religion of his was not purely and simply that of the ancients, but he held it was identical in essence. He looked at the myths and the cult-ceremonies through Neoplatonic spectacles; and he had learned from Porphyry, still more from Iamblichos and Maximus, that the sacred texts were allegorical, and that the secrets of the old mysteries were to be found in the theurgy of the modern prophets. His speeches on Kybele, the mother of gods, or on King Helios, were filled with graphic details regarding this philosophical theology of myths, a theology which was, in the end, nothing more than the monotheism of the silver age of the ancient world pressed into forms modelled on Plato. King Helios is Aurelian's empire-god elevated into the world of Plato's ideas. Julian confided his life and plans to this god's care.

Such speculative philosophizings were only intended for the small circle of the educated; for the masses there were the visible symbols and the traditional cults with rites having theurgic efficiency. These cults had to be brought into closer correspondence with popular feeling. It was soon seen that it could not be done by simply restoring the old forms; indeed this first difficulty could not be easily overcome. A new road must be followed, and Julian discovered it. Two writings[2] of his are extant, in which he sketches proposals for revitalizing the ancestral religion; the first gives short prescriptions, the second an outline in the style of a sermon. Both pieces of writing were essays preparatory to the issue of an official memorandum.

Julian took his dignity seriously as Chief Priest of the Empire, as *pontifex maximus*, and organized a reform of the priesthood. To each province was sent a High Priest who controlled the entire public worship, and whose special duty it was to visit

---

[1] Amm. Marc. 22, 14, 3   22, 12, 6–7

[2] Julian, *ep.* 84, to Arsakios, High Priest of Galatia; and *ep.* 89 to High Priest Theodoros

and inspect the officials entrusted with the care of the cultus. Those were to be deposed who were not equal to the requirements which the dignity of their office laid on them. It was held desirable that the whole family of a priest should take part in the ceremonial, and not (say) that some of its members or servants should confess Christianity. Neither the priest nor his family was permitted to go to the theatre, or visit pot-houses or carry on a low business.[1] The priest must be continent, not only in act, but also in words and thoughts. That would be noticeable not only in his conversation, but also in what he read. The verses of the ancient iambic poets and comic writers as well as modern erotic romances were beyond the pale for him. He was to read philosophers—except Epicurus and Pyrrhus the sceptic—learn by heart the hymns to the gods, and pray thrice daily to the gods.[2] In harmony with this, candidates for the high office of priest were to be selected from the best and most religious citizens without regard to poverty or wealth.[3] The priest in his temple must be filled with the dignity of his position; and outside, see to it that public officials paid due respect to his office.[4]

Over and above all an important rôle was prescribed for him, viz., by word and act to promote human love. "The Jews do not allow any of their own people to become beggars, and the Christians support not only their own but also our poor; but we leave ours unhelped." Those of Greek sympathy, therefore, must be trained to similar acts and even on this plane bring sacrifices to the gods. "It is matters like this which have contributed most to the spread of Christianity: mercy to strangers, care for burying the dead, and the obvious honourableness of their conduct." Therefore numerous hostels for pilgrims should be established in all cities, and strangers and beggars fed at the expense of the state. The Emperor placed annually at the disposal of the province of Galatia 30,000 bushels of corn and 10,000 gallons of wine, 20 per cent. being handed over to the priests for use in their work of caring for the poor.[5] "And the people must learn to give part of their

---

[1] Julian, *ep.* 89, p. 153, 6ff.; *ep.* 84, p. 144, 18ff.   *ep.* 89, p. 170, 20ff.   173, 3
[2] *ep.* 89, p. 168, 10ff.   169, 6ff.   170, 2ff.   [3] *ep.* 89, p. 173, 5ff.
[4] *ep.* 89, p. 146, 12–20   [5] *ep.* 84, p. 144, 13–16   145, 17–20

possessions to others; to the better placed—generously, to the indigent and the poor—sufficient to ward off distress; and, strange though it sounds to give food and clothing to one's enemies is a pious duty, for we give to men as men, not to particular persons"—said Julian.[1]

He wanted to smite the Galileans with their own weapons, wanted to build up an organization of pagan clergy on the Christian pattern, wanted to train his priests on principles and for tasks which he had learned among the Christians—but men looked at him and were estranged, for their hearts did not re-echo to such tones.[2] He was, and he remained, an enigma to the people. What he introduced was quite new; it was not a revitalization of ancient cults and folk practices, but a philosophical religion of humaneness with moral prescriptions and "awkward" demands, but without any heart-conquering purpose. There was lacking that exalted fervour which, in Christianity, seized and compelled even the simplest soul.

Julian could not understand it. He thought he would make progress if he took new measures against the Christians. So he dismissed them from the higher ranks of officers in the army, and the higher posts in the administration and justiciary,[3] and retarded their promotion in every way. He went so far as to write to the city of Nisibis when it was threatened by the Persians. It had become predominantly Christian and had abolished the temple cultus, but he declared he would not come to their help till they turned over to "Greece".[4] The city of Constantia in Palestine was on like grounds deprived of the self-government, granted to it by Constantine, and made subordinate to Gaza.[5] Cæsarea, capital of Cappadocia, was struck from the list of cities, its church property confiscated, the clergy subordinated to the military authority, and the rest of the Christian inhabitants oppressed with malicious taxation. The reason was that here, the last existing temple, that of Tyche, had been destroyed even after Julian's accession: the

---

[1] ep. 89, p. 158   [2] Sozom. 5, 16, 2

[3] Soc. 3, 13, 1–2   cf. Julian, epistulae et leges, ed. Bidez et Cumont (1922), n. 50, p. 57   Julian, ep. 83, p. 143f.   ep. 88, p. 150, 12

[4] Sozom. 5, 3, 5   cf. Julian, ep. et leg. n. 91

[4][5]Sozom 5, .3, 6. 7   Julian, ep. et leg.   no. 56; cf. supra, 150 n. 4

persons directly concerned, together with Bishop Eupsychios, were immediately executed.[1]

He had also a special hatred for Edessa on account of its Christian population. When a dispute in this city between the Arian church and the gnostic Valentinians developed into a riot, he ordered the confiscation of the entire property owned by the church, in order that poverty might teach moderation to all Christian people, and that, in accordance with the Christian commandment (Matthew 19: 21ff.) they might more easily get to heaven—and he would gladly lend a hand to help them. The decree began, as Julian loved to have it, with an assurance that he sincerely wished to exercise every clemency to the Galileans, and not to compel anyone against his will:[2] it is difficult to say whether that was honest self-deception, or contempt replete with hate. The Christians said of him that his words were mild enough, but that he was not sorry when his directions were exceeded by acts of violence.[3] Only they must not go too far; and even the Christian writers do not ascribe the bloody martyrdoms they tell of, to the Emperor himself.

His method was rather to use some trickery which looked harmless, but that operated painfully. He might order certain ruined temples to be rebuilt. Often that was impossible and foolish in practice; then the corresponding value must be paid in gold—that always happened.[4] Under Constantine, it had been customary to support the clergy, also the widows and holy virgins, with money paid from the city revenues. Julian abolished this law, and demanded repayment of the sums even from the helpless women: who naturally raised a loud outcry.[5] Bishop Eleusios of Kyzikos had to rebuild out of his own resources a Novatian church which he had destroyed, although the Emperor could have had no other concern for this sect than that they were hostile to the church catholic. Later, that very Eleusios had to leave the city because, it was alleged, his conduct caused excitement; outside Christians whom he had attracted were expelled with him.[6]

---

[1] Sozom. 5, 4, 1–6　5, 11, 8　Julian, *ep. et leg.* n. 125

[2] Julian, *ep.* 115, p. 196　Sozom. 6, 1, 1　*re* tolerance, cf. footnote by Bidez to *ep.* p. 196, 1

[3] Sozom. 5, 15, 13　cf. 5, 9, 13　　　　　[4] Sozom. 5, 5, 5　5, 10, 9

[5] Sozom. 5, 5, 2–3　　　　　　　　　　[6] Sozom. 5, 5, 10　5, 15, 5–7

It was easy to put the blame on the Christians if unrest broke out, and Bishop Titus of Bostra once presented an address to the Emperor, on this subject, and drew attention to the tense situation, which was only kept peacefully in hand by the bishop's exhortations. It cannot be held to have been an act of wise statesmanship when Julian immediately responded by sending word to the population—urging them to throw the bishop out of the city because he had spoken ill of them.[1] It was genuine mockery to begin this communication by declaring that the bishops ought really to be grateful to the Emperor for not having sent them into exile like their predecessors, but had allowed them to return. Instead, they were angered because an end had been put to their tyranny and they had roused the people to resist the Emperor's humane laws. And he had not used any compulsion on them to "change over to Greece". On the contrary, all that was required from those who came voluntarily to offer sacrifice was a formal expiation before they were permitted to do so.

But it was a strange sort of voluntariness. For example, the soldiers received their usual pay in money in front of a statue of the Emperor surrounded by the heads of Zeus, Ares, and Hermes, but only after they had thrown incense on an altar-flame. Of course, the soldier could refuse to perform this pagan act, and at the same time refuse his pay. He would not be punished, and could please himself. But if he took the money, and afterwards repented, and wanted to give the money back, he was dismissed.[2] Was that honest tolerance, as Julian claimed? In addition, the Emperor made no secret of his hatred of the Galileans; he scoffed at them when he had the chance, and even wrote a polemic against them. Here he mixed the scholarship of Celsus and Porphyry with rather trivial thoughts of his own: remains have survived in the answer written by Cyril of Alexandria.[3]

But he wished to overthrow Christianity not only with words, but also with some monumental act. The temple at Jerusalem, the destruction of which was regarded as one of the fundamental

[1] *ibid.* 5, 15, 11. 12   Julian, *ep.* 114, p. 193–195
[2] Sozom. 5, 17, 3. 8–12
[3] *Juliani imp. libri c. Christianos*, rec. C. J. Neumann, 1880

proofs of the truth of Christianity,[1] must be rebuilt. He had a
certain preference for the Jews, on account of their very hatred
of Christianity; he esteemed them also on account of their
sacrificial worship and their ritual; and also because their god,
belonging exclusively to their race, fitted into his system.[2] He
now ordered the leaders of Judaism to appear before him, and
informed them of his purpose. He commissioned an official
called Alypios, of Antioch, who was standing near, with the
oversight of the work of building and placed large sums for it
at his disposal. Moreover, the Jews gathered with great zeal
for the work, and even themselves lent a hand. While they were
working at the foundations, an earthquake destroyed what had
been done so far, and buried a number of masons in the ruins.
Fire broke out and completed the destruction.[3] The plan was
not taken up again.

Julian had least success with the people of Antioch. Few
could tolerate him, no matter what their creed. This was only to
be expected among the Christians, and they showed him their
dislike in an effective way. In the paradise-like suburb of
Daphne stood the temple of Apollo already mentioned, at the
side of a waterfall which even to-day spouts beautifully. It was
then known as the "Castalian Spring" and once gave oracles.
But Julian could not get the spring to speak, and his theurgists
explained to him that it was due to the corpse of the martyr
Babylas which Cæsar Gallus had shortly before placed at rest
in a chapel near by. Julian immediately ordered the removal of
the coffin. The Christian multitude of Antioch were greatly
perturbed. They gained possession of the chapel and carried
the heavy stone coffin in procession, singing psalms, and
marching about six miles to the Christian cemetery.

During one of the following nights (on October 22, 362)
"fire fell from heaven" and burnt out the temple of Apollo to
the bare walls. Julian naturally guessed arson by the Christians,
and closed the "Great Church" by way of punishment; but he
was not certain, not even after torturing the priest of Apollo.
In the city, the rumour persisted that a dissipated professor of

<hr>

[1] *vide* vol. 1, 182f. 220 Sozom. 5, 22, 6 Philostorg. 7, 9 and p. 235f.

[2] Julian, *ep.* 89, p. 160, n. 2 *c. Galilaeos*, p. 115d, 306b

[3] Rufinus, *hist. eccl.* 10, 38–40 Amm. Marc. 23, 1, 2–3 Julian, *ep. et leg.* n. 134

philosophy used to spend time by night in the temple, and had forgotten to put the candles out when he went home: a flying spark had started the fire.[1] Regard for the Emperor was not increased by any of these events.

But on the whole and with all kindly feeling for him, it cannot be said that he enjoyed good luck in dealing with the people of Antioch. Whether it was a matter of parcelling out some fallow land, or of regulations to ward off a famine, he always missed the mark, and was blamed bitterly. When he fixed prices, he drove goods from the market, and when he ordered large quantities of corn from other places, the middle-men pushed in and took their profit. Nor were the Antiochenes content with bread alone, but complained of lack of meat, fish, and fowl.[2] That sort of thing would have been taken the wrong way even if the prince had been beloved. But Julian was explicitly not beloved, indeed he was a figure of fun to the people of Antioch.

The quick-witted town would have gladly forgiven him any hardship, but his parade of virtue aroused dislike and scorn. When the circus races were on, he remained at home, or came at most once on the festival day of a god, and went back again after a race or two. Nor did he attend the theatre; and there was no theatre at Court. Neither athletes, nor singers, nor dancers rejoiced his heart, and he was cool towards women. He had neither a harem nor mistresses—nor any love-children. He gave no magnificent banquets and never got drunk. Worst of all, he had no understanding of the fact that his dear Antiochenes saw in things of this kind all the joy of life and cultivated them day and night to excess. Instead, he preached them sermons on moral philosophy and urged them to attend diligently the temples of the gods. But when they complied with the last-mentioned wish, and crowded chattering noisily into the court of a temple—that was not right, and he complained of disorder. What did he look like? His hair was bristly, and as seldom cut as were his nails; his fingers were ink-marked and he never shaved. On his cheeks and chin

---

[1] Amm. Marc. 22, 12, 8–13, 3   Sozom. 5, 20, 5–6   Philostorg. 7, 8, p. 86–94 where there are other testimonies

[2] Julian, *Misopogon*, p. 350a–c, 368c–370a–d   *ep. et leg.* n. 100. 101

grew a fluttering appendage which he called a philosopher's
beard, on the model of Marcus Aurelius's; but in fact it looked
like a goat's beard and earned him the nickname of "Billy
goat".[1]

So the people mocked at him, and he heard, and worried,
and finally forgot that he was the Emperor. He sat at a table
and wrote, like any common scribbler, a work against the
"beard-hating" Antiochenes (the *Misopogon*), charged them
with impudence and ingratitude, explained and defended his
attitude, and finally announced that he would leave the city
and never return.[2] The Antiochenes must have serenely
rejoiced at his resolve when they read this document.

Julian was not immune from the contradictions, small and
great, to be found in men's hearts, and he had no sense of
dignity. The *Misopogon* proved it, and not less a second book,
the *Cæsares*, which he wrote for no obvious reason. Here he
describes a banquet in heaven at which the deceased Roman
emperors converse with each other at the table of the gods, and
finally with Alexander the Great who joins them. Almost all
are satirized with scornful criticisms, except only Marcus
Aurelius whom Julian sketched as his ideal. Whereas Constantine flees to Jesus who forgives sins, Julian proudly obeys
the commands of Mithra, his leader in life and death. But he
was not aware how paltry a thing it was to scoff at his own
predecessors, and he forgot that what might give a Lucian
pleasure was not permitted in an emperor.

Having finished all his preparations, Julian left Antioch
on March 5, 363. The crowds who assembled to watch his
departure wished him a successful campaign and a glorious
return. He answered ungraciously that they would not see him
again, for, after the end of the war, he intended going to Tarsus.
He kept his word, but in a sense different from what he intended. The army marched to Hierapolis (Membidj) and then
crossed the Euphrates at Carrhae (Harran) where he made his
final dispositions.

He divided an army of 30,000 élite troops as flank guards

[1] Julian, *Misopogon*, p. 338c–340a 342b–344c 345c–346d   [2] *ibid.* p. 364d. 370b

under the command of Generals Procopius and Sebastian, and ordered them to operate in northern Mesopotamia west of the Tigris. They were to combine with the Armenian troops of the allied King Arsakes, and then waste the land as they marched south to be at hand for the decisive battle.

He himself took the main army, marched south, and reached the Euphrates again near Kallinikum (Rakka) on March 27. He marched further along the left bank while a great fleet of transport vessels on the river accompanied the column. When they approached the desolate ruins of Dura (Salihiye)[1] on April 6, they saw the Persian troops for the first time in the far distance. They had disappeared by the next day, but the Roman army now marched in battle order. The fortress of Anatha (Anah) surrendered without opposition; other easy victories followed. The first collision with hostile troops occurred a short distance beyond Diacira (Hit); it ended favourably. Soon came evidence that serious fighting lay ahead. The fortress of Pirisabora (Ambar?) compelled him to use the greatest siege engines and there was heavy fighting to capture the strongly fortified Maiozomalcha.

The army were now between the Euphrates and the Tigris in the garden-land cut by numerous canals opposite the present-day Bagdad. Julian was approaching the enemy capital, Ctesiphon, which lay about twenty-six miles south-east of Bagdad on the left bank of the Tigris. The fleet was transferred to the Tigris by a canal, and, based on the ruins of ancient Seleucia, the army tried to force the crossing of the river. Success came after heavy fighting, and the Persians were thrown back into their capital after heavy losses. There could be no question of besieging the great city, fortified as it was in every way; and so the decision was taken to advance northwards up the left bank of the Tigris. Unfortunately the fleet could not sail upstream and would have required 20,000 men to drag it, and so it was burned.

Now, however, the troubles began. The enemy hindered provisioning by setting fire to the crops standing in the fields. Neither the army of Procopius and Sebastian, nor the Armenian auxiliaries, put in an appearance. In addition, the heat of

[1] vide Vol. 2, 46. 143

the summer oppressed and worried the troops with all the penetrating swarms of flies and midges. Sacrifices were offered to the gods, and they were questioned, but no propitious answers came. On June 16, Julian finally made the decision to retreat, and on the next morning, the Romans made contact with the Persian king's vanguard, and a few days later there was battle with the main army. The Roman legions maintained their reputation, and forced the splendidly accoutred ranks of Persian lancers, bowmen, cavalry, and elephant riders to retreat. An armistice of three days followed.

Then, during one of the nights, as once before in Gaul, the *Genius* of the Roman people appeared to Julian; but this time it left the tent sorrowfully and with veiled head. As the Emperor went out into the night, a star fell with a streak of light from the sky. Next morning, the march proceeded; it was June 26. The Persians refrained from provoking the Roman fighting formations, but they accompanied the army with a swarm of cavalry which threatened action here and there, and, indeed, gave no respite. The Roman rearguard was attacked and fell into confusion.

Julian hastened there, without mail, protected only with a shield. He sprang into the mêlée, and restored order to the ranks. Then came word from the vanguard: the same story; the Emperor rushed here also, and again sprang into the tumult, without concern for himself. At this moment, Persian armoured cavalry supported by elephants, flung themselves on the left wing of the centre, and made it give ground. Julian hastened to the threatened position, and dragged his troops forwards. Then a cavalry spear caught him in the side. He was taken into a tent. When his wound was dressed, he wanted to return to the battle. But, weakened by loss of blood, he sank back.

He knew that all was over when he learned that he was at a place called Phrygia: according to an old prophecy, that was to be the name of the place where he would die. His friends stood round while he took leave of them, and of life. The news of the death of a friend brought him his last sorrow. Now, he remained alone with his trusted friends, Maximus and Priscus, and talked with them of the sublimity of the soul. His wound opened again, and blood streamed out. His breath became laboured. It was midnight. A drink of water refreshed him, then he departed from life.

Next morning, after some hesitation, Jovian, General of the Guards, was chosen Emperor. It was he who, two years earlier, had provided the guard of honour for the body of Constantius. He now led the army further upstream. On the far side of Dura (Dor) he crossed the Tigris, and passing Hatra, Ur, and Nisibis, reached the Roman frontier proper. He concluded a shameful peace with the Persians before crossing the Tigris; the terms gave them the eastern provinces on the upper Tigris, and also Singara and Nisibis: and it contained a cruel provision that the Roman population of these cities might, or rather must, depart. Ammian who lived through this campaign, and described it,[1] speaks of this provision with deep indignation. In addition Jovian had to surrender the allied king of Armenia to Persian vengeance. The northern army was discovered in the neighbourhood of Singara, and one of its commanders brought the dead Emperor to Tarsus, where he was buried in accordance with his desire. His friends would have preferred the Eternal City in which to build a memorial to him and his fame.

[1] Ammianus is the principal source for all the above narrative: 23, 2–5. 24 and 25. *Re* the legend about Julian's death, *vide* N. H. Baynes in *Journal of Roman Studies* 27 (1937), 22–29

Chapter Eleven

WORSHIP

THE FOREGOING CHAPTERS HAVE DEALT WITH THE LAST struggle and final victory of Christianity in the Roman world. Much has also been said about church politics and academic theology, so much perhaps as to give the reader the impression that, in the fourth century, the essence of the life and work of the Church consisted of nothing else. It is therefore high time that we turned to the inner life of Christendom, and inquired after the spirit which was the soul and the source of the power of this world-embracing organism; that spirit was to be found, at its purest, in the public worship of the Church.

A Roman formulary, the Church Order of Hippolytus, has come down to us from the beginning of the third century, but for the middle and second-half of the fourth century several Greek sources have survived, affording plenty of material for examination. On the other hand, our knowledge of the forms of worship of the west has to be laboriously pieced together out of small fragmentary remains. A detailed description of the service of Communion in the Lord's Supper is extant from Jerusalem in Bishop Cyril's catechisms[1] which were taught about A.D. 350 in the Church of the Holy Sepulchre built by Constantine. The "Apostolic Constitutions", in the second book, gives a short description of Sunday worship, and, in the eighth book, a complete Order of Service with all the prayers. If we added incidental remarks in the Church Fathers[2] there is good reason for speaking of plentiful material. The "Constitutions" are a symposium of Orders and can be dated confidently about A.D. 380, although put together out of earlier documents. That it was composed in Antioch is not so certain as was once thought; signs multiply which point to Constantinople as at least the place of redaction.[3] The texts of prayers have been handed down in Egypt from the middle of the fourth century; they are connected with the name of

[1] vide supra, 246
[2] Passages assembled by F. E. Brightman, Liturgies, Eastern and Western, I. 467–1, 481   506–509   518–534
[3] E. Schwartz, Die Pseudapostolischen Kirchenordnungen, 1910, 27

Serapion of Thmuis, Athanasius's friend, and are being multiplied by discoveries among the papyri.[1]

About this time a standard style of church building had been developed which was to be found everywhere in east and west, though with many variations depending on local and provincial circumstances. The church was an oblong chamber with a space extending beyond the short east wall, and mostly an apse of semicircular shape. This was for the cleric and the Elements which he consecrated. Here, at the centre of the semicircle, sat the bishop on his throne, surrounded on both sides by presbyters, while deacons stood at the ends to preserve order.

The congregation filled the chamber, not merely as a general assembly, but rather in groups or companies. The two sexes were separated, and the young people were apart from the elders, whilst little children remained standing in charge of their parents. A deacon maintained proper order in the chamber, and silenced disturbing chatter or laughter. There were separate entrances for men and women, and doorkeepers and deaconesses watched that the regulations were observed. Not every member of the church was permitted to enter: any ordered by the church to do penance must remain outside the door, and they often used to ask arriving worshippers for their intercessory prayers: that was in accordance with a deep sense of repentance.

The essential element of the first part of the service was the reading of scripture and the sermon. The Constitutions prescribe a regular series of Bible readings. At the start of the service there were two Old Testament lessons, one from the historical books, the other from the Prophets or the doctrinal books. Then a singer rose, and intoned a Psalm: the congregation listened thoughtfully, and responded with the alternate verse if such there was, or with the final Hallelujah; it is conceivable and can sometimes be proved,[2] that there were other forms, including fully antiphonal singing between psalm-singer and congregation. There followed a lesson from the Pauline letters or the Acts. Then the congregation rose, and

[1] Wilcken, *Mitteil. a. d. Würzburger Papyrus-sammlung* (1933 no. 6), p. 31–36
[2] *Const. Apost.* 2, 57, 6   cf. Eus. *H.E.* 2, 17, 2   22 Philo, *vita contemp.* 80 (6, 68); Refrain verse e.g., Ps. 42, 5. 11   43, 5   46, 7. 11 57, 5, 11   80, 3. 7. 19, Ps. 136 is different

instead of the reader (*anagnostes*), a deacon or even a presbyter went to the reading-desk in order to read a passage from the Gospels with increased solemnity. It would be interesting to know to what extent even at this time the choice of texts was determined by the Church-year, but research in this respect has only just begun.[1] Our knowledge is more plentiful regarding the fifth century than for the fourth, when these matters had plainly only just begun to crystallize into definite shapes. In any case, certain Biblical passages were fixed for the festivals of the Church and for the weekdays in times of fasting; while on ordinary Sundays and weekdays the readings varied according to the bishop's choice. Doubtless also at first it was only at the great centres of the Church that such a system of readings was worked out, and the surrounding province only gradually followed the example of the capital. We shall have to go into greater detail on this point.

The sermon, or rather the sermons, followed the readings, for "the presbyters, one after the other, but not all, the bishop coming last, shall exhort the people". So runs the preface to the *Constitutions*, and it can be proved to correspond with fact. For in the sermons of John Chrysostom, presbyter of Antioch, there are frequent references to sermons to follow by other presbyters, and especially by the bishop. A similar custom can be proved to hold good for Jerusalem at about that period:[2] The Greek church always liked to hear well-polished addresses —the result of centuries of education in rhetoric—and so a series of sermons can be credited to such a congregation which would have frightened others away. It would happen not infrequently that excited speakers would go beyond the two hours[3] usual for a preaching service, but they could count on being pardoned by their hearers if they could combine the attraction of artistic form with interesting content. They might expect expressions of agreement and even loud assent from the congregation, although these were tabooed and sometimes denounced by serious preachers.[4]

[1] A. Rahlfs, *Die altest. Lektionen d. griech. Kirche. Gött. Nachr*, 1915, 28–136
A. Baumstark, *Nichtevang. syr. Perikopenordnungen*, 1921 (*Liturgie-gesch. Forschungen.* Heft 3)

[2] John Chrys. 2, p. 531b, 316c, 362d, 622a, etc.　　　[3] *ibid.* 2, 368b　3, 53b　73c

[4] John Chrys. 2, 25a　7, 232d　10, 33a, 239c

The public part of the service, i.e., the part open to all, ended with the conclusion of the last sermon. A deacon then invited the unbaptized in groups to a final prayer and pronounced a benediction over them, to the individual clauses of which the congregation responded with the *kyrie eleison*. Thereon the catechumens, followed by those making ready for baptism (*photizomenoi*), left the church; then the sick, and lastly the penitents who had been waiting inside the chamber near the door. The doors were now closed and the "believers", i.e., the congregation of the baptized, kneeled down for prayer.

A deacon recited the clauses of the general prayer of the church, and the congregation responded to each petition with the *kyrie eleison*. Then the bishop prayed for the congregation, and gave them his blessing of peace. The deacon cried "Greet one another with the holy kiss", whereupon the clergy kissed the bishop, and the congregation followed this example: the men kissed each other, and similarly the women; the Christian fellowship of love was now in being and ready to celebrate the "mystery". The deacon cried the warning: "No catechumens! No unbaptized! No unbelievers! No heretics! No one who hates another! No hypocrites! Let us stand uprightly before the Lord with fear and trembling!"

Meanwhile, a subdeacon had handed a bowl of water to the bishop and the presbyters, who performed the ceremony of symbolic washing of hands. The congregation looked on in silence as the sacrificial gifts, the bread and wine, were brought by the deacons to the altar, and there received by the bishop surrounded by the presbyters. The former engaged in silent prayer, and was then dressed in a gorgeous robe ready for the very solemn act in which he was to take part. Standing at the altar, he pronounced the trinitarian blessing of the grace of God, the love of Christ, and the fellowship of the Holy Spirit. The congregation responded with the ancient prayer:

> R⁊. *And with thy spirit.*
> ℣. *Lift up your hearts.*
> R⁊. *We have them in the Lord.*
> ℣. *Let us thank the Lord.*
> R⁊. *That is worthy and right.*

The "main eucharistic prayer" began with the ancient, traditional repetition of the response, "Worthy is it and right to sing praise to Thee before all, Thou who art truly God."— And now with a voice quietened to half-tone, he recited the long prayer of thanks. This began with praise to God and His only begotten Son, extolled the creation, and the miraculously purposeful ordering of the world, and was mindful of the man who entered into life as a citizen of this world (*kosmopolites*), and as a microcosm after the image of God. In his soul, he carried the seed-corns of the knowledge of God and of power leading to immortality; but through the deceitfulness of the serpent and of the woman, he fell, lost Paradise, but not the merciful care of God, who gave him the rulership over nature, and promised him rebirth and resurrection. The petitioner would wander through the entire Old Testament story of salvation as far as Joshua and the collapse of the walls of Jericho; then he would suddenly break off, and his voice gradually rise to full power: "For all this, honour be to Thee, Lord, Almighty. Unnumbered hosts of angels pray to thee— archangels, thrones, governments, powers, authorities, the might of eternal hosts, cherubim and six-winged seraphim, who with two wings cover their feet, with two their head, with two fly; and sing in chorus with a thousand thousand arch-angels, and ten-thousand times ten-thousand angels who cry ceaselessly and are never silent." The congregation, thrilled, joined in the triumphant chorus of the angels, and sang:

> Holy, holy, holy is the Lord of Hosts: Heaven and earth are full of His glory, blessed be He for ever. Amen.

Heaven was open, and the congregation passed beyond the confines of time and space into the fellowship of the higher world. In awed silence, they looked towards the altar, where the lips of the bishop quietly praised the redemptive counsel of the Holy God, by which the Creator of man became man, born of a virgin, and lived among the people, and performed miracles, and revealed God's name to them who knew nothing of Him. And when He had truly done all things, He com-pleted the Father's will, gave Himself into the hands of the unrighteous, suffered death on the cross under Pontius Pilate, and was buried, in order that He might liberate his own from suffering and snatch them from death, and break the bonds of the Devil, and set men free from his deceit. He rose on the third day and ascended to heaven, and sat down on the right hand of God, His Father. We are mindful of all that He suffered for us, and we thank Thee, Almighty God, not as we should, but as well as we are able, and we fulfil His will: for in the night when He was betrayed, He took bread—and now the mysterious words of institution hovered over the plate holding the bread, and over the cup with the wine, and the words about the body and blood were pronounced aloud to the "Amen" of the congregation.

The memorial of the suffering, the death, and the resurrection was proclaimed, and the prayer rose to heaven. "May God send His Holy Spirit upon this sacrifice and transform the bread into the body, and the cup into the blood, of His Christ, in order that all who partake thereof may be strengthened in piety, and receive forgiveness of sins. May they be liberated from the Devil and his deceit, filled with the Holy Spirit, made worthy of Christ, and win eternal life, for the Almighty Father is reconciled to them." The miracle then took place, the Spirit of God came down from the heights of heaven into the elements —in later centuries, those who were specially blessed were able to see it with their own eyes[1]—and changed them to life-giving, spiritual food.

The "bloodless sacrifice" of Christian faith had been made once more, for in the Eucharist, the body of Christ had been broken for us in death, His blood poured out in forgiveness of sins, the sacrifice on Golgotha had become real again by a divine miracle. At the moment when the words of institution were pronounced over bread and wine, what they said took place anew; anew was the Almighty Ruler reconciled with mankind through the self-surrender of His Son.[2] The Christian sacrifice of the eucharist was a genuine mystery, a divine act in earthly symbols—and the congregation felt the horror of death, and the tremor of eternity, and the victorious power of

[1] John Moschos, *Pratum spirituale*, c. 25
[2] Lietzmann, *Messe u. Herrenmahl*, 191f. O. Casel in *Jahrb. f. Liturgiewiss.* 6 (1926), 114ff. 13 (1936), 99–171

the incomprehensible miracle of life given by Christ to those who were his own.

The sacrifice had been completed; Christ, the lamb of God had again been slain[1]—but it was also a sacrifice of the congregation's, one which they brought to God, and which, like all sacrifices, they might accompany with their prayers. The bishop would bring a long series of the church's petitions before God's face and a deacon would recite aloud a shorter prayer followed by the *kyrie eleison* of the congregation.

Then the curtains were opened, which till then had prevented the altar from being seen. The bishop carried the sacrifice to the congregation,[2] and the distribution of the Lord's Supper began. "What is holy to the holy" cried the bishop, and the congregation sang in response: "One is holy, One is the Lord; Jesus Christ be Thou praised to the glory of the Father for ever. Glory be to God in the highest, peace on earth, and good will towards men. Hosanna to the Son of David. Blessed be He who comes in the name of the Lord. God is the Lord, and has appeared among us. Hosanna in the highest." The bishop now partook of the holy Elements, gave them to the clergy, and then to the congregation who came up in long succession to the altar. The bishop handed out the bread with the words "Body of Christ", and a deacon the wine saying "Blood of Christ". Each time, the communicant responded "Amen". During the whole communion, Psalm 34 was sung, the key words being in the ninth verse: "O taste and see how gracious the Lord is; blessed is the man that trusteth in Him". At the end of the ceremony, deacon and bishop offered a thanksgiving, and, with the bishop's benediction, the congregation departed.

Even the fourth century records reveal many variations in the provinces of the Church, and closer inspection shows that forms of prayer were exchanged and there was mutual influence. In Syria, a unique form was built up closely related to the Great Liturgy of the *Constitutions* described above, and the standard liturgies of the Middle Ages grew in Byzantium out of this root, and were named after St. Basil and St. Chrysostom. What is known as the Liturgy of St. James took shape in Jerusalem, but it is only a variant of the same original form,

[1] John Chrys. 11, 23d   [2] *ibid.* 11, 23d, 577f. 10, 340e

and betrays many closer contacts with the Liturgy of St. Basil. The national church of Syria built its liturgies upon it.

On the other hand, in Egypt, as is to be expected, a large element of original independence and of radical individuality can be traced, which, however, by the fourth century, had been extensively affected by influences from Syria. The Liturgy of St. Mark which became dominant there at a later date, requires very close analysis before traces of ancient Egyptian usage can be discovered. The quite peculiar Liturgy of Serapion expresses very clearly the character of the service as a mystery in which the sacrifice in Golgotha is repeated. Less clear, but ancient and widespread, is the view expressed in the "*Constitutions*"[1] that Christ had offered a spiritual sacrifice to his God and Father *before* His passion: and this is now occasionally repeated in the service in such a way that the Mass becomes an imitation of the act of institution: the priest does what Christ did. But it is difficult to see clearly how what Christ did on Maundy-Thursday evening can be a sacrifice: hence, here again, one must assume a mystical anticipation of Good Friday.

As distinct from the plenitude of records in the east, there is a grievous lack of western authorities enabling us to sketch the liturgy of the principal service. We are there almost entirely dependent on inferences drawn from the conditions obtaining at a later date; and, for the fourth century, we can only suppose that both the outer form and the religious content must have been on the whole the same.

A short writing was current under the name of Ambrose which dealt with the central act of consecration with startling frankness. Literary critics have hesitated greatly as to its place, but recently[2] strong reasons have been put forward for regarding it as a stenographer's copy of a catechism by Ambrose; thus it would belong to Milan in the time between A.D. 374 and 397. The speaker lays stress on the harmony between his rite and that of Rome, and in fact the prayers, given *in extenso*, agree to a great extent with the texts of the Roman canon in use to-day.

[1] *Const. Apost.* 8, 46, 14

[2] G. Morin in *Jahrb. f. Liturgiewiss,* 8, 86–106   Text of "*de sacramentis*" in Rauschen, *Florileg. patrist.* no. 7, *Monumenta eucharistica*

As tested by the parallels[1] the original form,[2] acknowledged to be in Hippolytus's Order, is seen to have been much altered by the introduction of Egyptian forms which, on their part, have been affected by Syrian influences. In this way, suggestions for the liturgy flowed from the east *via* Alexandria to Rome, and we shall not be in error if we regard Athanasius as the mediator.

But then it is quite striking that Rome lacks the invocation, which was still plainly present in Hippolytus, and which prays for the descent of the Holy Spirit in the way still customary everywhere in the east. In its place is a prayer for the gracious acceptance of this spotless, spiritual, bloodless sacrifice, which would then be borne by angels up to the heavenly altar. A new and very significant formula precedes the opening words. It reads: "Let this sacrifice be accounted unto us, sufficient, spiritual, acceptable, because it is the likeness of the body and blood of our Lord, Jesus Christ." The choice of words is none too skilful and betrays a mixture of older elements of various origins; but it is at least clear that the person engaging in prayer did not regard the Eucharist simply as a sacrifice made by the church, but rather as the actual offering of the body and blood of Christ, whose propitiatory effect may be accounted to the benefit of the church: and it was precisely to this end that he offered prayer.

This conception was dislodging into the background the older view, according to which the bread and wine, when consecrated, became heavenly food for the believers. When this older view was displaced the invocation appropriate to it disappeared at the same time. The Eucharist conceived as the cult-sacrifice of Christ gave rise to the Eucharistic prayer, whereas communion conceived as the Lord's Supper of the church give rise to the invocation. Both conceptions now lived side by side through the centuries to the present day, but their effect on the development of the liturgical forms differed according to place and time.

Weighty opinions have favoured the view that the sacrifice of Christ in the Eucharist is the older interpretation of the rite,

[1] Lietzmann, *Messe u. Herrenmahl*, 43–47   58–60   117–122   cf. 97
[2] *vide* Vol. 2, 127

and, correspondingly, that the western sacrificial prayers to be found in large numbers and great variety in the liturgical documents belonging to the early Middle Ages have been handed down from the earliest times.[1] This theory will be especially convincing to those scholars who, fresh from the study of the ancient mysteries, now approach the Christian liturgies; from that standpoint the theory carries a certain inner probability. But if one keeps fast to the existing texts and observes their chronological sequence, one is driven to the opposite result.[2] It must be granted as a principle that at the time of their origin, the prayers expressed simply the thought of the petitioner, and it was only later generations who introduced new interests into the traditional material of the liturgy.

The outer form of divine worship was enriched in the course of the fourth century. The favourable atmosphere of the times made the church wealthy, and enabled it to build splendid edifices. This fact of itself affected the decoration of the articles used in worship, including the material, the style of writing, and the binding of the Bibles. It particularly affected the raiment of the officiating clergy. Their vestments were obliged to assume a corresponding magnificence, and had also to be differentiated even in form from clothing generally worn. In the earliest centuries, clerics wore at service the garments generally in use at festivals; but from now on, they gradually adopted a special liturgical dress, which at the same time gave visible expression to the special rank of the cleric. But it is only in the succeeding centuries that we gain a glimpse of this process; for the times of Constantine and immediately afterwards, we are confined almost exclusively to conjecture.

The separate actions in the communion service were now given ever greater, even dramatic, solemnity. There were two opportunities which spontaneously provided for such further developments, viz., the reading of the gospel, and the carrying of the offerings to the altar. Both acts grew into processions which effectively enlivened the course of the service. Right and left of the space of the apse were usually the two vestries with doors opening on to the side aisles. The first was called the

---

[1] O. Casel in *Jahrb. f. Liturgiewiss.* 6 (1926), 113–204, 209–217
Lietzmann, *Messe u. Herrenmahl*, 116, n. 1

diakonikon, and contained the priestly garments and the articles used in worship: it was sometimes connected to the apse by a small side door, the other was the *prothesis* and served for preparing the sacred ceremonial. For the communion of catechumens, the clerics came out of it dressed in the prescribed vestments. They carried lighted candles and the books of the Bible from which the lessons were to be read, placing them on the reading desk or *ambon*. Again, at believers' communion, the procession of clergy issued from this door into the nave, and carried the sacrificial elements solemnly to the altar.

These two processions have been characteristic of all eastern liturgies down to the present day. The great Church Fathers of the fourth century do not mention them expressly, but an archæological observation makes it probable that the custom took its rise about the end of that century. A number of churches dating from the fifth century, indeed as early as A.D. 401, have one of the two sacristies with a widely opened door, often distinguished by a Roman arch and certain ornamentation, to show that it possessed special importance. This fact suggests that it was out of this door that the procession of clergy issued.[1]

The service of the Eucharist described so far, naturally, took place each Sunday, but was also celebrated on other days. Among the large number of eucharistic services from early times, and even in late centuries, we meet with a confusing variety to which even the Church Fathers refer.[2] In the west, from as early as Cyprian,[3] it was customary to offer the Eucharistic sacrifice daily and to take the Lord's Supper; and attention was drawn to this custom with a certain pride as contrasted with the east: in fact the Eucharist became identified with the "daily bread" asked for in the Lord's Prayer.[4] But Eusebius, too, says that the rite of the body and blood of Christ was observed "daily"; and in Antioch, in the ninth decade of the fourth century, Chrysostom complained that no communicant was present and the church was empty when the daily sacrifice was offered.[5] But perhaps in the east that was only a bit of

[1] H. W. Beyer, *Der syrische Kirchenbau*, 1925, 34. 40. 43
[2] Aug. *ep.* 54, 2   *tract.* 26, 15   *in John. de serm. in monte*, 2, 7, 25. 26   Ambrose, *de sacr.* 5, 4, 25   [3] Cypr. *orat. dom.* 18   [4] See footnote 2
[5] Eus. *dem. ev.* 1, 10 (p. 46, 13)   John Chrys. *hom.* 3, 4   *in Eph.* (11, 23a, Montf); *hom.* 3, 6.   *de incompreh.* (1, 469a)

rhetoric, for in another passage, the same preacher declares that "so to say" the holy mysteries are celebrated each day,[1] and in one place he mentions three days expressly, viz., Friday, Saturday and Sunday as distinguished liturgically by celebration of the Eucharist.[2]

There was on the whole a great difference in the eastern churches in this respect. Many held firmly to observing the Eucharist once, on Sundays, as in Alexandria and Jerusalem. According to the testimony of Epiphanius, the two weekly fast days, Wednesday and Friday, were distinguished in Cyprus by services of the Lord's Supper. They were held after the end of the day's fasting, at the ninth hour (*none*), i.e., 3 p.m.; whereas on Sunday, the Eucharist was in the early morning. In Alexandria, a preaching service without the Lord's Supper was held on the two fast days.[3] In Cappadocia, Saturday was added to Sunday, Wednesday, and Friday, presumably because there, as often, particularly in the west, Saturday was a fast day. Hence there was a full Divine Service four times in the week.[4]

As has already been noted, Antioch attended the service of Holy Communion thrice, Friday, Saturday, and Sunday; it would thus appear that in this city fasting was losing its obligatory character on Wednesdays. On the other hand, the *Apostolic Constitutions*[5] make no reference to fast days, but follow another tradition which approximates Saturday, as the Biblical sabbath and day of rest, to Sunday; and thus restricts the celebration of the Eucharist to these two days. If we add the days of the martyrs, which of course required an offering of the eucharistic sacrifice; and in every province, indeed in every town, were differently attended according to the local martyr's birthplace, we shall find a considerable multiplicity. Add a small number of regular week-day observances and the result will be very frequent usage of the liturgy of the Eucharist. It is easy to understand how Chrysostom came to speak of the "so to say" daily observance. But when we are told of the

[1] John Chrys. *hom.* 50, 3 *in Matt* (7, 517d)

[2] John Chrys. *hom.* 5, 3 *in 1 Tim.* (11, 577e) cf. *hom.* 3, 4 *adv. Jud.* (1, 611a)

[3] Soc. 5, 22, 45.55 Epiph. *de fide* 22 1 (3, 522f. Holl.) Carl Schmidt in *N.T. Studien f. G. Heinrici*, 1914, 66–78

[4] Basil, *ep.* 93 (3, 186f.)   [5] *Const. ap.* 8, 33

daily communion of church-members, what is meant is not always the receiving of the Eucharist in church. Basil[1] as early as A.D. 370 was acquainted with the custom of taking several hosts home and there communicating daily alone.

Besides these principal services, there were, almost universally in the fourth century, two others which had become customary, viz., purely devotional liturgies, one in early morning at sunrise, and a corresponding evening service. In present-day liturgical language in the western church, these services are called "Lauds" and "Vespers". The first begins with the morning Psalm 63, and the second with the Psalm of evening sacrifice, 141, when on each occasion, the catechumens and the other incompletely prepared persons were dismissed with prayer—as at the Eucharist. Then came the customary general congregational prayer of the "believers", i.e., the baptized, and finally the bishop's intercession and blessing.[2] These devotional services really transferred into the church the customary morning and evening prayers which were originally the duty of each individual at home. The same observation holds good to no less a degree in regard to the other "canonical hours": owing to the ever growing influence of monachism, these were passed on and became the duty of the company of "secular clergy" who officiated in church.

Thrice daily, viz., morning, afternoon, and evening, the Jews[3] were accustomed to repeat the "*Shemone Esre*". The Christians preserved this custom *mutatis mutandis*, and therefore the *Didache* (8: 3) prescribed the Lord's Prayer three times a day. Tertullian[4] recommended, *c.* A.D. 200, two further times of prayer, at the third and sixth hour (*tierce*, at 9 a.m. and *sext*, at noon), so that the day was divided up by five prayers following each other at intervals of three hours. His contemporary, Clement of Alexandria, knew of this arrangement of prayer, but recommended the Christian gnostic to pray frequently during the night as well. Hippolytus of Rome, about A.D. 220, pre-

[1] Basil, *ep.* 93 (3, 186f.)
[2] *Const. Apost.* 2, 59 8, 35–39 Hil. *tract. in Ps.* 64. 12 (p. 244 Zingerle) cf. S. Bäumer, *Gesch. d. Breviers*, 1895, 91–94 on Chrysostom
[3] E. Schürer. *Gesch. d. jüd. Volkes* 2 (4th ed.) 539 Mishna, *Berachot*, 4, 1
[4] Tert. *orat.* 25 (p. 197f. Wissowa)

scribed, beside prayer five times during the day, also prayer at midnight and at first cock-crow (i.e., 3 a.m.)[1] so that the seven canonical hours were in use early in the third century. These directions for prayer must be taken into account if one is to understand the spiritual quality of the separatist churches of Hippolytus. Knowledge of the customs of Clement of Alexandria throws fresh light on the way his circle kept its traditional relations with Egypt. And, on the other hand, it is clear that this discipline, which includes even the night in the system of prayer, could only be prescribed for a church with a marked ascetic tone, and not made a general rule for Christendom as such. Origen[2] declared it was obligatory to pray thrice daily, at dawn, midday, and evening, and added a fourth, at midnight, as indispensable.

For the great bulk of Christians, prayer thrice daily remained the rule even in the fourth century; but with the increasing influence of a growing monachism, efforts were multiplied to persuade the laity to be more diligent in private prayer—all three hours—and to get them into the habit of regularly attending "lauds" and "vespers" in church.[3] These services were often extended with the addition of prayers and hymns and, in the case of vespers, even with a sermon.[4]

In regard to church poetry, tradition affords scarcely any information, yet a few hymns have survived from the fourth century: particularly the evening hymn "Kindly light" still in use in the Greek church. Even in that early century, however, it was known and used as an ancient hymn.[5] Ambrose's night hymns came into use in the west, and the monkish poet, Ephraim of Edessa, began to write in Syria.

But wherever the monks were in a position to exercise direct influence in church life, they insisted on the rest of the canonical hours being observed in the daily liturgy, and soon they were

[1] Clem. *Strom.* 7, 40, 3 49, 4 *Paed.* 2, 79, 2 Hippol. *Chu. Ord.* 32 (p. 116–118 Funk)

[2] Orig. *de orat.* 12, 2

[3] John Chrys. *hom.* 4, 5 *de S. Anna* (4, 737c) *hom.* 18, 5 *in Acta* (9, 150d) *hom.* 6, 1 *in* 1 *Tim.* (11, 579a, b)

[4] Epiph. *de fide*, 23, 1 Socrates, 5, 22, 55

[5] Basil, *spir. sanct.* 29, 73 (3, 62b) Smothers, in *Récherches de science relig.* 19 (1929), 266–283 Other hymns in *Const. Apost.* 7, 47–49 Greg. Naz. *Carm.* 1a, n. 32 (2, 290)

calling the clergy into church during the night: and the people followed, to the extent that they were obedient to the monastic idea of religiosity. The influence of the monks continually increased in strength. This was particularly evident in Cappadocian Cæsarea, which was dominated by Basil, and the pilgrim city of Jerusalem.[1] Here also, towards the end of the fourth century, there grew up the monastic custom of keeping watch during the entire night in preparation for church-festivals, especially on Holy Days. The laity showed a growing zeal in sharing these "vigils" or "pannychia" with the clergy and in singing the psalms.[2] The people of the church were gripped to an extent hitherto unknown by the liturgical activities of the church and of the monks behind.

At this point, there are special reasons for noticing a pious custom which began in the fourth century, and became of crucial importance ever after, viz., pilgrimages to the Holy Land. As early as the third century, Origen initiated that kind of scriptural knowledge which covers the identification of the traditional sites, traditions which clung to all parts of Palestine and the bordering regions; Eusebius made a Biblical gazetteer summarizing the result of his researches. The queen-mother Helena came as a highly-honoured pilgrim to the Holy Land during Eusebius's lifetime and she inspired the building of churches in Bethlehem and on the Mount of Olives. This, and the erection of churches by Constantine's direct orders on sites consecrated by Biblical associations, gave a powerful impulse to the custom of making pilgrimages, and soon to writing records of them.

The traveller's diary of a man of Bordeaux has survived from as early as A.D. 333.[3] In it he carefully describes all the stopping places of a journey which took him through North Italy, the Balkan peninsula, Constantinople, Asia Minor, and Syria. He adds also a few notes on the things worth seeing which

---

[1] For Basil see Bäumer, *Gesch. d. Breviers*, 79–84　Jerusalem is described by Aetheria (cf. pp. 105–119)

[2] Athan. *apol. de fuga*, 24, 3　*hist. Ar.* 81　Basil, *hom. in Ps.* 114, 1 (1, 199b) Greg. Naz. *or.* 5, 25 (1, 163a)　*carm.* 1b, 10, 920 (2, 460)　2a, 50, 41 (2, 944) Hilar. *tract. in Ps.* 118　*lit.* 7, 6 (1, 322a)　Aetheria, *peregr.* 27, 7　29, 2　36　38 Amm. Marc. 28, 6, 27

[3] *Itinera Hierosolymitana*, ed. Geyer (*corp. script. eccl. lat.* 39) 3–33

he visited in Jerusalem and certain other places mentioned in the Bible.

About fifty years later[1] a record was made which constitutes one of the most attractive documents coming down to us from the early Christian era. It was written by a lady named Aetheria, whose home was a nunnery in the west; but whether in southern France or in Spain cannot be determined with certainty. She was evidently a wealthy pilgrim, and was received everywhere with manifest respect. She took her task very seriously, and studied the land of the Bible with a detail that would have done honour to a scholar. She lived for three whole years in Jerusalem, and, from there as centre, undertook systematic journeys in all directions in order to gain a complete impression. Then she journeyed through Antioch and Asia Minor to Constantinople, where she wrote for her sisters in the nunnery at home the detailed travel-narrative which has come down. This record is not in artificial and rhetorical language, but in colloquial Latin just as the pleasant gossip came to her lips, and it has a splendid graphic quality. She had really seen much, and had visited all the places mentioned in the Bible. What her guide had not pointed out on his own initiative, she herself inquired after—"as I am rather curious to know" she adds.[2] At the end of her story, she gives a detailed description of the liturgical customs of the church in Jerusalem. This account is an invaluable historical document, and shows that the Holy City, in the fourth century, was the centre of a special tradition of worship, and that its influence came to spread through the entire church by the instrumentality of the crowds of pilgrims.

The buildings which Constantine had erected over the Holy Sepulchre, naturally gave the greatest impulse in this direction. After the burial cave had been discovered and freed of the ruins of a temple to Aphrodite which had desecrated it, Bishop Makarios, acting on the Emperor's orders, began building; he completed the work in A.D. 335.[3] Over the grave

---

[1] But before A.D. 394 (chron. Edess. n. 38) when the relics of St. Thomas were transferred from the "Martyrium" into the great new church in Edessa: peregrin. 17, 1 19, 2 (p. 60, 14f. 61, 25 Geyer)

[2] Aetheria, peregr. 16, 3

[3] vide supra, 133 Eus. vita Const. 3, 25–40

(the same as is to be seen to-day) there stood a circular building surmounted by a dome, the present rotunda of the Church of the Holy Sepulchre being its successor. It was known as the Chapel of the Resurrection (*Anastasis*). In front of it, towards the east, on the site of the present Greek cathedral, was a portico surrounding an almost square court, in the south east corner of which rose the rock of Golgotha surmounted by a cross. During the course of clearing operations in this neighbourhood, wood must have been found which was declared to be remains of Christ's cross. Rufinus reports, about A.D. 375, what the guides used to say about the discovery of three crosses —of Christ and the two thieves—by the Empress Helena, and the miraculous identification of the true cross of Christ by the pilgrims.[1] Pieces of the relic must have been sent to the Emperor in Constantinople, as well as to Rome, and to many another place;[2] but most was kept in Jerusalem, preserved in the Church of the Holy Sepulchre enclosed in a silver casket.

The main church was contiguous to the east side of the court, a tremendous five-naved basilica with galleries over the rows of columns of the side aisles beneath. It began about the place where to-day the Greek church ends, stretched over what is known as the Crypt of Queen Helena some distance eastwards, near to the place where the present complex of buildings of the Abyssinian cloister begins. The apse of the church was to the west, i.e., turned to the *Anastasis*. The entrances faced east and opened into a court surrounded by pillars. The splendidly designed entrance façade of this court looked on the main thoroughfare of Jerusalem running north and south. The line of that thoroughfare is marked to-day by the row of shops of the Chan-es-Zet, the street which runs straight as a die from the Muristan to the Damascus gate. This great and splendid church building was the centre of the then recently instituted liturgical activity of which Aetheria wrote the extant account.

On ordinary weekdays, service began while it was still dark. "Before the first cockcrow", i.e., about 3 a.m., all the doors of the *Anastasis* rotunda were opened, and the monks and nuns waiting at the doors, together with the crowd of pious laity of both sexes who accompanied them, filled the space and began

[1] Rufinus, *hist. eccl.* 10, 7–8   [2] Cyril *cat.* 4, 10 10, 19 13, 4

the early service while still night, (the Matutin, or Mattins). In this service, as in all the "canonical hours", the singing of psalms and hymns alternated with prayers which were offered by two or three presbyters or deacons. At sunrise, "lauds" began with the singing of the usual hymns. While this was proceeding, the bishop appeared, accompanied by his chaplain. He entered the space enclosed by a lattice round the cave of the Sepulchre, and from there offered the general prayer of the Church, the same as that offered at the main service on Sunday, but adding any names which he had specially in mind. Then, just as in the communion service for catechumens, there came prayer and blessing, first over the catechumens, then over the baptized and the "believers". Afterwards, all crowded round the bishop to kiss his hand as he went out, and to obtain his blessing. The services conducted by the bishop at mid-day (*sext*) and at 3 p.m. (*none*) had the same form.

The vespers, beginning "about the tenth hour", i.e., about 4 p.m. and known as the *lychnikon* or *lucernare*, partook of a more elaborate character. The whole rotunda of the *Anastasis* was brilliant with the light of candles ignited at the eternal lamp burning in the Sepulchre. This time, the service began with a longer period of singing. The bishop then rose from his throne, and a deacon recited an almost endless series of names of those who desired intercession, and after each name the choir-boys broke in with *kyrie eleison*. The bishop again pronounced the Church's general prayer, accompanied aloud this time by the whole congregation. Then, as always, came prayer, benediction, and dismissal of catechumens and believers. But now the bishop, together with the whole congregation of worshippers, moved, singing hymns, from the *Anastasis*, across the court to the rock of Golgotha and the cross, now illuminated by candles and lamps. He offered prayer and gave his blessing, first "before the cross", then "behind the cross", i.e., in the space between the rock and the west wall of the basilica. As darkness came on, the service ended, those who had the chance kissed the bishop's hand, and all went home.

That is what took place each day throughout the week, but on Sunday the scene changed. Then while it was still night the multitudes coming in from the main street, crowded in the court of the basilica and waited. Lamps were burning and a few priests and deacons conducted a service for the people which consisted as usual of alternate singing and prayer. On this occasion, the doors leading to the *Anastasis* were not opened before the first cockcrow, but as soon as this signal was given, everything was thrown open. The crowds flowing in found the bishop already seated on his throne in the brightly lighted *Anastasis*. Thrice there followed in succession the recitation of a psalm, the congregation's antiphony, a prayer, and at last the roll call. Censers were now introduced, clouds of incense rose from the cave of the Sepulchre, and filled the whole space of the *Anastasis*. The bishop rose and read the story of the Resurrection from the book of the Gospels. When he began it the whole multitude of people broke into loud and tearful lamentation over the sufferings of Christ. There followed a procession to the cross, where the service was concluded with prayer and benediction. The bishop now went home, and most of the laity followed his example, and rested awhile. But the zealous, and especially all the monks, returned to the *Anastasis*, and, led by priests and deacons, prayed and sang there till break of day.

At sunrise, all went into the great basilica where the main service with the Eucharistic sacrifice and the communion took place. It lasted three to four hours because several presbyters, and finally the bishop, delivered sermons, a custom which, as we have seen,[1] prevailed elsewhere in the east. But that did not suffice. At the end of this service, the monks, singing, accompanied the bishop, with a train of pious lay folk, to the *Anastasis*, whose doors were this time open only to the baptized. Here were offered a prayer of thanksgiving, the general prayer of the Church, and the benediction. This formed the conclusion of Sunday worship, which might have lasted in this way till approaching mid-day. Late in the afternoon Vespers was observed as on all days.

The worship of the church followed these rules throughout the year. Changes took place only on festal days, the most important of which was Easter. Its approach was announced by the great fast, which, in accordance with Matthew 4: 2,

---

[1] *vide supra*, 290

took forty days. In the east, fasting is not allowed on Saturdays and Sundays, and therefore it was needful to begin eight weeks before Easter to complete the prescribed number. In this instance, fasting meant complete abstention from all usual foods, even bread and oil being forbidden; those who were fasting lived on gruel and water.

During the weeks of fasting, the services were increased in that an "hour" of prayer was held each morning at nine o'clock, and each Friday after Vespers, a watch night service (*vigilia, pannychis*) followed and lasted till dawn. In the seventh week, on Saturday at noon, a procession went to Bethany and celebrated the memory of Lazarus and the anointing of the Lord (John 12).

With Palm Sunday began Holy Week. On this day, service was held on the Mount of Olives immediately after noon, and from 5 p.m. a procession waving palm and olive branches moved down the hill and arrived at dusk in the *Anastasis* for Vespers.

Maundy Thursday was distinguished in that, from early afternoon, from 2 p.m. till 5 p.m., the sacrifice of the Eucharist was offered three times, first in the basilica, then before and behind the cross, when the whole people communicated. Then one returned home and prepared for the approaching exertions. The night service began at 7 p.m. in the church on the Mount of Olives. Hymns and antiphonies alternated with prayers and Bible lessons till near midnight, when all went to the place of the Ascension at the summit, and continued the service there "till the first cockcrow". Then more than two hundred candles were lighted, by whose flickering light, the congregation descended, singing and praying, to the olive plantation of Gethsemane. There, they listened to the reading of the Biblical records of the Lord's wrestling in prayer, of the sleeping disciples, the kiss of Judas, and the arrest of Jesus: and away down, as far as inside the city, the people's loud cries of woe re-echoed. Slowly the procession continued, through the city gate to the Church of the Holy Sepulchre, and to the Cross. Meantime daylight had come and it was a weary people that listened to the last lesson, the record of the trial before Pilate. Then the bishop exhorted the congregation to unwearied further endurance in meditation, and dismissed them home to rest.

It was Good Friday, and anyone who had not been on Olivet, had at least attended a service in the church of Zion (near the present-day *Dormitio Mariae*) in memory of the scourging of Jesus. At 7 a.m. the bishop entered the great court of the Church of the Holy Sepulchre: his throne had been placed in the space between the cross and the basilica, and a procession of priests laid the silver casket with the relics of the Cross on the altar erected in front of it. When the receptacle was opened, the wood and the superscription could be seen; the bishop then took the Holy Cross into his hands, and the people made a long procession past the altar. Each kneeled down and kissed the relic—and the deacons watched closely that none took the opportunity afforded by the kiss to bite off a splinter from the Most Holy Cross, and take it home as an amulet of miraculous power. Hence one was only allowed to kiss the Cross, not to touch it with one's hands. After the Cross, reverence was paid to the ring of Solomon, and to the horn used for the oil which once anointed the Israelitish kings: these were held by a deacon.

The procession of worshippers lasted till mid-day, when the memorial of the Passion began "before the cross", the reading of the last episode in the Passion story, its prediction in the Old Testament, its preaching by the Apostles, and the record of it by the four evangelists: the whole was embedded in prayers and hymns, and also accompanied by the loud weeping and lamentations of the people. This swelled to a great outcry when at 3 p.m. the word of the Gospel announced, "Then when Jesus had received the vinegar, He said, It is finished: and He bowed His head, and gave up His spirit". The multitude now crowded into the great church, where *none* and *vesper* were held till evening. As night came on, the day of mourning for Christian believers closed with reading, in the *Anastasis*, the gospel record of the burial of Jesus. The exhausted crowds went home, and only the stronger and younger of the laity or clergy watched through this night also.

On Good Friday, attention was chiefly directed towards preparing for the Easter vigil, during which those catechumens were baptized of whom notice had been given, and who had been prepared by the Bishop's teaching. The lady who wrote these accounts is content with a brief remark here that this was done in Jerusalem "as amongst us". But the gap in her narrative can be filled out completely from Bishop Cyril's catechisms.[1]

The candidates for baptism were led into the forecourt of the baptismal chapel and placed facing west—the land of darkness. They stretched out their hands, and cried out to the Devil, "I deny thee, Satan, and all thy works, and all thy company, and all thy service". Then they turned to the east, to the land of light, and confessed, "I believe in the Father, and in the Son, and in the Holy Spirit and in one baptism for repentance". The door of the chapel of the baptistry opened, and the group entered the inner space. All immediately undressed and stood there as naked "as Adam in paradise, without being ashamed". They were now anointed from head to foot with consecrated oil, which had power to blot out all traces of sin, and to ward off all invisible attacks of the Evil One. They entered one by one into the baptistry sunk into the ground, uttered the baptismal confession, and were immersed three times—as Christ was three days in the grave—and arose again—as Christ arose again: the imitative symbolism was something real in itself, and possessed saving power; they were born again to a new life. When Christ came up out of the water after being baptized in the Jordan, the Holy Spirit came down from heaven upon Him: hence the "new-born" were now anointed on forehead, ears, nose, and breast with holy oil, and so endowed with the Holy Spirit: at last they were really "Christians", i.e., anointed.

They put on white clothing and went with the bishop to the *Anastasis*[2] where the latter prayed for them. Then, under his direction, they went into the basilica which was gay with the greatest amount of decoration; the Eucharistic service of Easter evening began, in which they took part for the first time as guests at the Lord's Supper. In the early morning of Easter Sunday, as on all Sundays, there was service in the

[1] Cyril, *cat. myst.* 1–4   cf. *Kleine Texte*, n. 5, 10–14   also Vol. 2, 133
[2] Again according to Aetheria, *peregrin.* 38

Anastasis with the gospel record of the Resurrection as the lesson; following on this was the eucharistic sacrifice; but the rite was shortened in order that those who had watched through the night, might be allowed to go early. When the congregation poured out of the doors of the church into the street, the church part of the Easter festival was at an end—and with it also the fasting. The pleasure in eating and drinking as felt by natural and starving people entered—then as now in the eastern church—into its normal place.

The Easter fast began about this time to play an increasingly important part in church life. Originally the only fast-day was Good Friday as prescribed in the Gospel (Matthew 9: 15), for that was the day when "the bridegroom was taken from them", and this long remained the custom. Then the Saturday after Good Friday was added, this was in any case a week-day for fasting, but this meant two days of fasting before Easter.[1] Others went further and added other days. Some records tell of a forty-hour fast, beginning on Maundy Thursday about mid-day and ending "about cockcrow" in Easter-night. In the course of the third century, it became customary in Syria and Egypt to fast throughout the whole of Holy Week, and even Athanasius observed it in this way in the first years of his episcopate. But when an exile in Trèves, he became acquainted with the western custom of fasting forty days at Easter, and introduced it in A.D. 337 into Egypt: the extant Pastoral Epistles of Easter make it possible to fix the date exactly; and in addition is the letter in which Athanasius begged his friend, Serapion of Thmuis, to use his personal influence to introduce this new custom of fasting.[2] The data that have come down, show that the period of the fast began on the Monday following the sixth Sunday (*Invocavit*) before Easter, and therefore comprised six weeks, each of six days, and thus came not exactly to forty but only to thirty-six fast days. But if the four Sundays in the time of repentance were added, the result was a total duration of forty-one days for the preparation.

---

[1] Tert. *de jejun.* 2. 13. p. 275, 17–19   291, 16 (Reifferscheid)   Irenaeus in Eus. *H.E.* 5, 24, 12   Epiph. *haer.* 50, 1, 5   2, 4   Hippolyt. *Chu. Ord.* c. 55 p. 115 ed. Funk   Diony. Alex. *ep. ad Basilid.* p. 102, 8 Feltoe

[2] Most recently, E. Schwartz, *ZNW.* 34 (1935), 129–137   Athan. *Ep.* p. 127 de-Larsow.

It appears, therefore, that the idea of the "time of the forty days" (Tessarakoste, Quadragesima) was familiar enough in the fourth century. It was mentioned at the Council of Nicea (can. 5), and occurs in Eusebius; and afterwards in many places, e.g., in Jerusalem[1] about the middle of the century: the "time" comprised six weeks, including Holy Week. But in the east, there was opposition towards any fasting on Saturdays just in proportion as this day, the Biblical sabbath, was assimilated to the Christian Sunday. As a result, fasting in Quadragesima was confined to five week-days. But the appellation "Period of forty" had by now become firmly fixed to a period of six weeks. The custom was, therefore, to fast on five days a week for six weeks, and to call this period the Quadragesima, although it now comprised only thirty fast-days; but to this was added Holy Week with its six fast-days— for Good Friday was observed as a fast-day everywhere without opposition. The result was, once more, that the same total of thirty-six fast-days was secured in seven weeks, as elsewhere, and above all in the west, in six.

The seven-weeks' Preparation for Easter is to be found in the second half of the fourth century in the region led by Antioch and Byzantium, and in Cappadocia.[2] We have already noticed that Aetheria, the pilgrim, recorded that the church in Jerusalem was stricter, and fasted eight weeks in all in order truly to include forty days—but then Easter Saturday brought the total to forty-one days. Bishop Epiphanius in Cyprus, who had no objection to fasting on Saturdays, allowed fasting for only seven weeks but on six days per week, and a total of forty-two days was reached.[3]

Elsewhere there was greater restraint and the fast lasted only three weeks, or was observed quite strictly only for the last three weeks before Easter. For a long time, big differences had existed[4] in both east and west, about which further details are

---

[1] Eus. *de paschale* 4, in Migne, *Patr. gr.* 24, 697c   Cyril, *Procatech.* 4   *cat. ill.* 4, 3 cf. 18, 32   *conc. Laod.* can. 45. 49–52
[2] John Chrys. *hom.* 30, 1, *in Gen* (4, 293f.)   *Const. Ap.* 5, 13   Ps.-Ignat, *ad Phil.* 13, 3   Basil, *hom.* 14, 1 *in Ebrios.* (2, 122e)   See also *supra*, 299f.
[3] *vide supra*, 306f.   Epiph. *de fide* 22, 9 (3, 523) and remarks by K. Holl, *Ges. Schr.* 2, 370–377   On the whole subject, cf. F. X. Funk, *Kircheng. Abhand. u. Untersu.* 1 (1897), 241–278
[4] Socrates, 5, 22, 32–41

scarcely known. In addition to differences in time were also those of the manner of fasting. The full strictness of the monastic discipline at Jerusalem[1] can have been only rarely imposed elsewhere. Frequently, fruit and eggs might be eaten, in many places, one might have fish and even fowl; but everywhere meat was forbidden unconditionally. Then as now, the east must have outdone the west in strictness of observance.

The period of fasting at Easter was at the same time the favourite preaching season. The bishop instructed his catechumens in the morning hours, and any baptized person was free to come into the church and listen to the addresses. Similarly in the evenings, series of sermons were frequently delivered, and the people used to gather round the desks of popular speakers. Several sermon series by the great John Chrysostom have survived from Antioch, delivered during the fasting period. All of them are based on Genesis, and other evidence shows explicitly that the first book of the Bible was read chapter by chapter at Vespers during these weeks of fasting.[2]

It was about this time that the first schemes of Bible reading were laid out, and it became a universal habit always to read the whole of certain books at certain parts of the church year. The reading of Genesis during the fasting period became an established custom at an early date in both east and west. Acts was used for the lessons between Easter and Whitsuntide in Jerusalem, Antioch, and Constantinople. Other books, like Isaiah, Job, and the Proverbs of Solomon, were also accorded a fixed place in the system of lessons for the church year.[3] Able pastors based exegetical sermons thereon. Sometimes these sermons grew into detailed commentaries and continued occasionally long after the set reading had ended, and might cover almost the whole church year. For example, John Chrysostom, each Saturday and Sunday for 44 weeks, delivered 88 morning sermons on John's gospel; a series of 90 sermons on Matthew has survived, 55 on Acts, 32 on Romans, 67 on

[1] *vide supra*, p. 307

[2] A. Rahlfs, *Die altest. Lekt. d. griech. Kirche* (*Gött. Nachr.* 1915) 114–122

[3] On the whole subject, see A. Baumstark, *Nichtevang. syrische Pericopenordnungen*, 1912

Genesis. The church provided in this way for instruction in the Bible and training its own members, and it could rely on it that in many homes, and not only those of the well-to-do, there were Bibles, or at least New Testaments or Gospels, in which the passages expounded in church could be read over, or one could prepare for what was coming. Hence the frequent exhortations to study the Bible daily may well have applied largely to reading it at home.[1]

About this time, greater use was made of art to teach the people Biblical history. The panels of sarcophagi were much limited by tradition and by the laws of space in the choice of subjects, but church walls could be decorated by a whole series of pictures, and gave free play to the artists' powers of portrayal. Such series of pictures have naturally not survived in the original from the fourth century,[2] but descriptions have come down giving details of the subjects; and it is very probable that, in this sphere, much of the inspiration came from Jerusalem.[3]

A few couplets, probably written by Ambrose, have been preserved. Originally they stood underneath a series of Bible pictures and served to describe them. The majority concern Old Testament subjects but there are also four from the New Testament—probably the whole of the series is not extant. Forty-eight quatrains by Prudentius afford a better example, twenty-four being on the Old Testament and twenty-four on the New Testament. They filled both the walls of the nave of a basilica, whereas the forty-ninth, depicting the twenty-four elders of Revelation, decorated the semicircle of the apse. Paulinus of Nola used to speak very definitely about the educational value of such pictures for illiterate people, and in the course of his remarks, he described an Old Testament series in the local basilica of St. Felix.[4] Such a series of pictures, dating from the fifth century, may still be seen to-day in

---

[1] John Chrys. *hom.* 11, 1 and 32, 3 *in John* (8, 62f. 188a, b) *hom.* 9, 1 *in Col.* (11, 391c) cf. Cyril, *cat. ill.* 4, 33. 35.36 9, 13 17, 54 Ambrose *in Ps.* 118 *expos.* 12, 28 22, 19 Aug. *Conf.* 8, 6, 14 *in Ps.* 36 *sermo*, 1, 2 (4, 259d. Bened) cf. A. Harnack, *D. private Gebrauch d. hl. Schriften*, 1912, 67ff.

[2] Wilpert's dating of the mosaics in the nave of S. Maria Maggiore in Rome has not been confirmed

[3] Baumstark in *Byz. Zeitschr.* 1911, 177–196

[4] S. Merkle, *Die Ambrosianischen Tituli*, 1890 Prudentius, *tituli hist.* (Dittochaeum) p. 435–447 Bergmann; Paulinus Nol. *carm.* 27, 511–536 580–595

their full beauty in Rome, and from the same century is a portion of the earliest existing illustrated Bible on parchment, known as the "Vienna Genesis". In the west, the very fragmentary remains of the "Quedlinburg Itala"[1] have survived from the fourth century and are the oldest portions of an illustrated Bible of any sort.

Aetheria when a pilgrim in Jerusalem described the mode of celebrating Easter, the oldest and, originally, the only, yearly festival observed by Christians. Of necessity it was followed by Whitsuntide. During the fourth century two new principal festivals were added, Epiphany and Christmas. The first of these is referred to rather uncertainly in the second century, when Clement of Alexandria says[2] that the gnostic sect of the Basilidians celebrated the baptism of Christ in a certain night, either the 15th or the 6th of the month of January. No further references are to be found anywhere until the fourth century, when it is again mentioned, and at once raises a whole series of problems. For about the same time the festival of Christmas is recorded for the first time. There was a certain rivalry between their claims, and this fact together with the final combination of the two festivals gave rise to extraordinary complications. So much is this the case that to clear up and explain the facts presents one of the most alluring problems offered to students of the history of the liturgy. It is over half a century since the founder of the modern school of historico-religious criticism first used the method for throwing light upon the ancient church. New starts have constantly been made until the most recent date. A final solution has often seemed to be in sight, but new pieces of information have equally often caused further revision, and at the same time brought to view a new complex of problems.[3] Hence the account given below is offered, with due caution, as a summary of the present state of knowledge of the subject.

As its name is plainly intended to declare, the festival of

[1] Byvanck in *Mnemosyne*, 1938, 241–251   [2] Clem. *Strom.* 1, 146, 1–2
[3] H. Usener, *D. Weihnachtsfest*, 1889   K. Holl, *D. Ursprung des Epiphanienfestes* (=*Ges. Schr.* 2, 123–154) Lietzmann, *Petr. u. Paul.* 1927, 2nd ed. 103–109 E. Caspar, in *Zeitschr. f. Kirchenges.* 46 (1928), 346–355   B. Botte, *Les Origines de la Noël et de l'Epiph.* (Löwen 1932) etc.

Epiphany on January 6, was first celebrated in the east as the time of God's appearance on earth, i.e., the birth of Christ. This is the sense in which it was observed in Egypt until some date in the fifth century. But in the year 431 there occurs for the first time a record to the effect that in Alexandria, the birth of Christ, i.e., Christmas, was celebrated on December 25.[1] The leading place for observing Epiphany was naturally Jerusalem, or, more exactly, Bethlehem. Here, Queen Helena had erected a basilica over the cave where Jesus was born, traces of the very building having quite recently come to light.[2] The bishop and people of Jerusalem used to come here in procession in the night of January 6 for a rite by night, as Aetheria the Pilgrim tells, and a sermon delivered on one of these occasions has been preserved. That same sermon says that about this season, the baptism of Jesus was celebrated at the Jordan, and the rites were combined with the baptism of new members of the church, although nothing of this came to Aetheria's notice. The rites of the Armenian church, which were governed by those of Jerusalem, rejects to the present day the festival of Christmas, and celebrates the birth of Christ as Epiphany on January 6. Epiphanius followed the same custom in Cyprus in A.D. 380. The Syrian church did likewise, in the fourth century; and when preaching on Whit-Sunday A.D. 386 in Antioch, John Chrysostom mentions only three Christian festivals: Epiphany, Easter, and Whitsuntide; and he expressly describes Epiphany as the festival of the appearance of God on earth, i.e., the festival of Christ's birth.[3] But in the very same year on December 25, in the cathedral church at Antioch, he delivered the sermon introducing the Christmas festival, and said that the festival had been familiar in the city for ten years. Possibly it was observed only in the schismatic church of Paulinus.[4] The new festival enjoyed an immediate triumph.

[1] Cassian, *coll.* 10, 2, 1 (2, 286 Petschenig); *Acta conc. Ephes.* 1, 4 p. 9 ed. Schwartz
[2] Richmond in *Palestine Quarterly*, 6 (1938), 63–66   Vincent in *Revue Biblique* 45 (1936)   544–574   46 (1937), 93–121
[3] Aetheria, *peregr*, 25, 6–12   26, 1   Ps-Chrysost. *hom in S. Theophania* 13, 246f., 247a, b (preached in Bethlehem)   Conybeare, *Rituale Armen.*, 1905, p. 517 Epiph. *haer.* 51, 22, 4–7   Eph. Syr. in Usener, *Weihn.* 2nd ed. 202–208   John Chrys. *hom.* 1, 1. 2, *in Pentecost.* (2, 458d, 459b)   *Test. domini Syr.* c. 28, p. 67 c. 42, p. 101, ed. Rahmani
[4] *vide supra*, 269

The great Basil introduced it into Cæsarea in Cappadocia; his friend Gregory of Nazianzus into Constantinople in A.D. 379; his brother Gregory did the same in little Nyssa in A.D. 382; Amphilochios likewise in Iconium about the same time. Hitherto the festival of Christ's birth, Epiphany was everywhere deprived of half its meaning, and now continued to be observed only as the festival of Christ's baptism.[1] Jerusalem with its dependents, and Egypt refused to admit the festival for a long time, Jerusalem indeed till the middle of the sixth century.

The festival of Christmas on December 25 originated in the west, and undoubtedly Rome was its cradle. Here it was observed as early as A.D. 336 under Constantine. From that date onwards, it is mentioned wherever we are justified in expecting it. Epiphany was unknown in Rome throughout the whole of the fourth century, being observed for the first time about A.D. 450, when it was mentioned by Leo the Great as the festival of the "Magi", i.e., the wise men from the east. It was said to be eight days after Christmas, i.e., on January 6(!), that they visited Mary and Joseph to pay homage to the new-born Child. All Leo's Epiphany sermons speak of it in this way. In another passage, he emphatically disapproves of the Sicilian custom of baptizing on Epiphany, and thus indirectly Leo repudiated solemnizing this day as the festival of Christ's baptism.[2] Pope Gelasius,[3] in A.D. 494, named Easter-time, the festival of the Apostles, and Epiphany as proper days for the consecration of nuns. From this year, Epiphany became a fixed item in the church calendar of Rome.

In Milan, on the other hand, Epiphany and Christmas were equally familiar towards the end of the fourth century. Ambrose devoted hymns to both days. These hymns are undoubtedly authentic, and a sermon he preached in A.D. 385 confirms the fact that he used to solemnize Epiphany as the festival of Christ's baptism.[4] Close by, in Brescia, about the same time,

[1] References in Usener, *Weihn.* (2nd ed.) 221–268 with corrections by Holl, *Amphilochius von Iconium*, 107–110, and E. Schwartz, *Christl. u. jüd. Ostertafeln*, 169–184
[2] Leo Magnus, *sermo* 31–38; *ep.* 16, 1.3
[3] Gelasius, *ep.* 14, 12 (1, 369 ed. Thiel)
[4] Ambrose, the hymns "Intende qui regis" and "Illuminans altissimus", (Kleine Texte 47–49, p. 9. 11) and *expos. in Luc.* 4, 76 (177 Schenkl)

Bishop Filastrius characterized it as nothing less than heresy to observe Christmas only, and reject Epiphany. He regarded the latter, in the Roman fashion, as the memorial day of the Magi from the east, and refused to recognize it as commemorating the baptism of Jesus.[1] In Africa, the Donatists refused to celebrate Epiphany, a fact which Augustine held against them. As he says nothing about Christmas, one is inclined to suppose that the Donatists regarded it as the older festival, and had observed it at the time when they separated from the church catholic about A.D. 311.[2] In any case, Augustine observed both festivals, and celebrated Epiphany in memory of the Magi, the same view being held by later African authorities. In Gaul, on the other hand, as early as A.D. 361 we find that Epiphany was solemnized on January 6, for Julian went to church in Paris on this day. But we are not told what was the precise meaning of the ceremony. A Byzantine chronicler explained it as referring to the birth of Christ, but this is quite uncertain.[3] In both north and south Italy, but above all, far and wide in Gaul and Spain, passages dating from the beginning of the fifth century speak of celebrating Epiphany as the festival of the "three miracles", viz., the visit of the Magi, the baptism of Christ, and the marriage of Cana; whereas naturally Christmas was observed as celebrating Christ's birth.

This state of affairs admits of a simple and direct explanation. The eastern festival of the Saviour's birth was Epiphany on January 6. This was perhaps first celebrated early in the fourth century in Egypt, and, by way of Jerusalem, spread rapidly from there all over the east. About the same time, Rome began to observe the feast of Christmas on December 25, likewise commemorating the birth of Christ. This was immediately adopted in Africa, where Roman influence was always very strong, but it caught on only slowly in the rest of the western church. There, especially in Gaul as centre, Epiphany had become widespread and gained firm hold before claims began to be made for Christmas. The question as to how Epiphany reached Gaul without touching Rome may be answered by a very likely theory. Athanasius was banished

---

[1] Filastrius, *haeres.* 140 (p. 111 Marx)   [2] Aug. *sermo.* 202, 2 (5, 915c) cf. *supra*, 84f.
[3] Amm. Marc. 21, 2, 5   and also Zonaras, 13, 11 (p. 206, 31 Dindorf)

to Trèves in A.D. 336, and he must have told the church there of the Epiphany festival they observed in Egypt and recommended its introduction. He must have spoken of it as commemorating Christ's birth, a point which would settle the character of the ceremonial which Julian attended in A.D. 361.

Documents from the fifth and later centuries, however, help to explain considerably what has so far come to light. The festival introduced by Athanasius celebrated not only the birth of the Lord, including naturally the homage of the Magi, but also covered the Baptism and the marriage in Cana. In the last decades of the fourth century, when the Roman festival of Christmas penetrated Gaul and Spain, it was used only for the commemoration of the birth, the "three miracles" being reserved for celebration on the sixth of January. It seems possible that in this way the liturgy of Spain and Gaul will help us to reconstruct hypothetically the elements originally contained in the Alexandrian form of Epiphany, for which no direct evidence has come down. It is easy to understand that Jerusalem would accept only the first two of the three festival elements—birth, baptism, and marriage in Cana—because it possessed the key points for them in the holy places of Bethlehem and the Jordan. The marriage of Cana was rejected and remained unimportant in the east because the observation of Epiphany really spread from Jerusalem. Here the festival of January 6 comprised the birth and baptism of Christ. But after A.D. 386 Christmas began to spread from Antioch throughout the east and what had hitherto been confined to Epiphany was now shared between the two festivals, the birth celebrations being transferred to December 25, while those of the baptism remained true to January 6. In this way, by A.D. 400, both halves of the Empire had changed their birth festivals, and the result was a uniformity everywhere. Nevertheless the details of the festival of Epiphany as still observed, showed clear traces of its preceding history.

In some such way, the results of present-day inquiry may be summed up in broad outline, and made to give a tolerably clear picture. But it should be noted that this theory does not really explain how Epiphany came to be observed in the city of Rome. Unfortunately it is not absolutely certain that Epiphany was first celebrated in Rome only in the fifth century. The Roman bishop Liberius (A.D. 352–366) preached a sermon on an occasion when nuns were being consecrated, including Marcellina, sister of Ambrose. The latter passed a remark[1] about the sermon, and in spite of all the various attempts to explain that remark, the most likely still remains that it referred to Epiphany, i.e., to the day which Gelasius regarded as traditional for the consecration of nuns. But Liberius described the day as that of the festival of the birth of Christ, which meant that Epiphany bore that character as far as he was concerned, and therefore was so regarded in Rome, where the ceremony took place. And that theory could be immediately accepted, were it not for the fact that the official festal calendar of Rome,[2] published in the time of Liberius, mentions Christmas but not Epiphany. This difficulty has not been resolved.

Further, the Roman missals of the early middle-ages contain prayers for mass at Christmas, December 25, and also prayers for the feast of Epiphany on January 6, prayers which show that Epiphany was quite unmistakably spoken of and solemnized as the festival of the birth of Christ. It is possible to trace in the manuscripts how the earlier Epiphany texts have been altered and "corrected" in the course of time till Epiphany became the day commemorating the Magi.[3] It is hard to explain this state of affairs by saying that the prayers penetrated at a late date into the Roman liturgy. Here again we are faced with an unresolved problem which will give work to future scholars. But the preceding sketch is correct on the whole.

The question remains to be answered, how the two festivals arose, i.e., how did the Church come to observe the birth of Christ and why were just these days chosen? There was no lack of calculations at quite an early period, both as to the year and the day of the Saviour's birth. Even Clement of Alexandria[4] tells of scholars who dated the event May 20, 2 B.C., whereas a Latin writer of the third century put it on March 28 of the

[1] Ambrose, *de virginibus*, 3, 1; and cf. remarks by Frank, *Jahrb. f. Liturgiewiss*, 12, 145–155

[2] *vide supra*, 239f.

[3] Lietzmann, *Petrus u. Paulus*, 2nd ed. 103–109 Botte, *Origines*, 34ff.

[4] Clem. *Strom.* 1, 145, 6 cf. Epiph. *haer.* 51, 29, 1–2 Thereon, Usener, *Weihn.* 2nd ed. 4–9

same year. But no festival was ever celebrated on either of these days, the dates being nothing more than the outcome of laborious scholarship confined to the study. Against that, January 6 was familiar as a festival day. We have already seen[1] that, as early as the beginning of the second century, the Basilidean gnostics of Alexandria solemnized the baptism of Christ on it. How did they come to fix on this day? Because it had already for a long time played an important part in pagan religion: in particular the night of January 5 and 6 was regarded as sacred.

A night ceremonial was observed in Alexandria in the temple of Kore with flutes and singing, reaching its height "at cockcrow" early on January 6. Those taking part then went by the light of torches into an underground sanctuary whence they fetched the images of a god carved in wood and adorned with golden circlets on forehead, hands, and feet. This was carried seven times out of the inner temple in solemn procession during which exciting hymns were sung, and then hidden from view again in its underground chamber. The point of the mystery was joy that "to-day at this hour the virgin (*kore*) has given birth to the Aeon". Epiphanius, our authority here, appears to have heard of a similar birth-ceremonial during the same night in Petra and Elusa in northern Arabia.[2] The "Aeon" was the personification of eternity, and was held in high honour in the Hellenistic period. He appears to have been brought in some way into connection with Osiris in Alexandria, so that his birth was celebrated on the day of Osiris.[3] The birth of Aeon from a virgin was transformed in Christian circles into the celebration of the birth of the Lord from the Virgin Mary.

On the same night, there was another mystery: in it the waters of the Nile gained miracle-working power. These waters were drawn in pitchers by the Egyptians, and kept in the house as a defence against every evil. Christians held that their Lord and Master performed this miracle, and so January 6 became the day on which Christ sanctified the water. The Biblical record would seem to require us to understand that the baptism

---

[1] *vide supra*, 314   [2] Epiphan. *haer*. 51, 22, 8–11

[3] Holl, *Ges. Schriften*, 2, 148–153   E. Norden, *Geburt des Kindes*, 33–38

of the Lord took place by day, yet the custom of the pagan rite, when taken over, was strong enough to keep the celebration to the night. The Christian priest offered the prayer, consecrating the water at midnight—and then all rushed with their pitchers to the particular river in order to obtain the holy water for their own salutary use, just as the pagan Egyptians used to do at the Nile. Naturally, the Jordan was, for Christians, the classical place for this ceremonial, but it was observed throughout the east wherever a sufficient stream of water afforded the opportunity.[1] In this way, Epiphany became the festival of the baptism of Christ.

January 6 had a third significance for the pagan world. During the previous night, Dionysos appeared on earth and, in many places dear to him, changed water into wine. We do not intend to raise the question as to the nature of the links which originally connected the day of Osiris with that of Dionysos. The fact of the connection is undoubted, and is sufficient for our purpose. No explanation is needed to show how this very day came to be adopted for commemorating the marriage at Cana when Jesus himself performed the miracle which used to be performed by Dionysos. The Christians of the fourth century took over the day and also the miracle, and the sainted Epiphanius[2] tells us of springs which even in his time (*circa* A.D. 374), at the hour when Jesus ordered the water to be taken to the master of the feast (John 2: 8) changed their water into wine "as a testimony to the unbelievers." He insists that he himself had drunk of one such spring, but omits to say whether of water or wine.

The Christmas festival of December 25 developed out of the sun-feast observed on this day. In the fourth century B.C., the day marked the exact date of the winter solstice, and at that period, the "birthday of the sun" must have been fixed, in eastern sun-cults, on December 25. When the *Sol Invictus* became the protective deity of the Roman empire, his birthday grew into a festival of the first rank, and it is as such that it occurs under the title of *Natalis Invicti* in the Roman

[1] Holl, *op. cit.* 2, 124f

[2] Epiph. *haer.* 51, 29, 7–30, 3   p. 301 Holl, with further references. Arnold Meyer, *Das Weihnachtsfest,* 1913, 15–19

city calendar[1] of A.D. 354. When the church of Rome selected the same day for celebrating the birthday of Christ, who was the true "Sun of Righteousness" proclaimed by the Prophet Malachi (4: 24), they thereby gave a very plain expression to their sense of triumph. The last and the loftiest image of God in the ancient nature-religion, hitherto the protective deity of the Empire, had been vanquished. Christ had set his foot on the neck of the *invictus* and his conquering sign promised prosperity as it shone on Emperor and Empire. The Christmas festival is the liturgical form of thanksgiving for Constantine's victory.

Besides these two great feasts, the Church introduced an ever-growing number of sacred festivals into her calendar in the course of the fourth century, and, since the ceremonials were local in character as a rule, the life of the Church became quite varied. The earliest local church calendar has been preserved by Rome in the Calendar Book, frequently[2] mentioned above, and dating from A.D. 354. Here the church year begins with Christmas, and, on the average, one or two days each month are distinguished by observances in memory of some martyr. At the same time, mention is made of the catacomb where he lay buried and where, consequently, the rite would take place. In August there were four, and September five martyr-days. All the martyrs belong to the third century as far as it is now possible to fix the time of their death with certainty or even probability. The best known are Pope Xystus II with his deacons, and St. Laurence the archdeacon who followed him in death on August 10. They suffered in the persecution under Valerian in A.D. 258. Two Roman women, Agnes and Basilla, were also commemorated, but nothing is known about their martyrdom. The brotherly association with the African church is exhibited by the memorial of the martyrs' death suffered by Bishop Cyprian (September 14, 258) and the highly celebrated women, Perpetua and Felicitas (March 7, 203). Parthenius and Calocerus were both commemorated, on May 19 and September 22 of the year 304, but whether these were the dates of their martyrdom or those of the solemn

---

[1] *vide supra*, 239

[2] *vide supra*, 239   Text in Lietzmann, *Die drei ältesten Martyrologien* (Kleine Texte, 2) 2–4

transferring of their bones to another resting place, remains a difficult problem. Again, no one knows what really happened on June 29, 258. This day is assigned to commemorating the Apostle Peter and Paul, and a further note says the ceremonial would be observed on the Vatican hill (where the church of St. Peter stands), on the road towards Ostia (i.e., in St. Paul's church) and "by the catacombs" (the present-day church of St. Sebastian). The most likely supposition would seem to be that the relics of both apostles were transferred to the catacombs of St. Sebastian on June 29, 258; it can be proved that honour was paid to them there in A.D. 300;[1] but doubts about the truth of this solution will remain until a more satisfactory answer is suggested.

A festival is registered for February 22 and is quite outside the limits of the martyr-days—the feast of Peter's Stool. It serves to commemorate the day on which the Apostle Peter took up office as the first bishop of Rome. On the last decades of the third century in Rome, a custom had arisen of marking annually the day of the ordination of the then bishop by means of a church celebration. Since Peter was regarded as the first to hold this office, about A.D. 300 the feast of Peter's Stool was ordained as the liturgical pattern of the rite dedicated to his successor then alive.

But why on February 22? On this day the people of Rome used to celebrate the "caristia", the memorial of those who had died in each separate family, when meals were eaten on the graves of dead relatives. Even the Christians faithfully maintained this custom into the sixth and seventh centuries. At these memorial meals, a chair (*cathedra*) for the dead used to be left vacant at the table, and therefore the festival of the dead came to be called the festival of the *cathedra*, probably by those who spoke Greek. Then this word *cathedra* came to be a bridge from the pagan to the Christian festival. It was the *cathedra* of the dead person round which the family gathered at the grave. But in church, the Roman congregation stood before the altar in order to bring their thank-offering for the setting up of the *cathedra* of the Apostle Peter, who had founded the Roman bishopric when he ascended his stool.[2] The pagan festival

[1] Lietzmann, *Petrus u. Paulus*, 2nd ed. 167.   [2] *ibid.* 18–21

afforded a purely outward starting point for giving the day a Christian consecration. But there lacked an inner connection between the meanings of the festivals such as gave convincing authority to the triumph of the feast of Christmas over that of the *Natalis Invicti*. Hence the new feast of St. Peter might succeed in becoming an official festival of the Church, but it was not successful in ousting the old-established meals for the dead.

Besides this calendar, the Roman list of memorial days of the Church, there was a list of the days on which the popes died, from Lucius in A.D. 254, to Silvester in A.D. 335, arranged according to the church year. An appendix was added to the list, giving the dates of the death of Marcus in A.D. 336 and Julius in A.D. 352. Since the first calendar contained only the dates of the festivals of the martyrs, the Apostles, and of the birth of Christ, the existence of the second list shows that it was beginning to be customary to pay the bishop who had just died, the highest honours of the Church, and give him a place in the liturgy equal to that of a martyr. This was undoubtedly an after-effect of the struggle which the bishops maintained in the third century to assert and confirm their authority in face of the claims of the confessors and of those who honoured the martyrs.

A record has also been preserved in the east which makes it possible for us to study the growth of the calendar of saints in these provinces. A manuscript has come down written in Edessa in Syriac in A.D. 411 which includes a number of Greek writings dealing with the Church. It also includes a Syriac translation of works by Eusebius of Cæsarea, and finally an extensive calendar of martyrs. This calendar is not confined to one city, but sets down the festival days of all the great centres of the Church in the east as well as many smaller places.[1] The Greek original, which can be restored by retranslation and critical revision, was composed in Nicomedia—perhaps a reminder of the fact that this city, when it was the imperial residence, expected to become also the principal city of the Church in the east.

[1] German translation in Lietzmann, *Kleine Texte* 2, 7–15; Examination by H. Achelis, *Die Martyrologien* (*Abh. d. Gött. Ges. d. Wiss., N.F., Bd.* 3, no. 3), 1900, 30–71

At any rate, the document was written about the middle of the century, for the few entries of martyrs of Julian's time[1] prove to be later additions. Moreover, contemporary politics in the Church are clearly reflected in the lists; thus on July 6, the presbyter Arius was memorialized in Alexandria, and May 30 was devoted in Cæsarea to Eusebius the church historian, and the Eusebius recorded on November 8 was none other than the famous bishop of Nicomedia, the leader of the Eusebians. None of these three died as a martyr, but the fact that their deaths were recorded shows that the effort, already noticed in Rome,[2] to put leading bishops and churchmen on an equal footing with the martyrs, was also operative in the east. When the calendar came into use in Antioch at a later date, a whole series of Antiochene bishops was added.

If the scattered notices in regard to any single town are put together, lists are produced which correspond completely to the catalogue in the Roman calendar, and afford an account of the form of the services, in memory of the martyrs, as held in the various provinces of the eastern part of the Empire. In Antioch, John Chrysostom's sermons, in the ninth decade of the fourth century, provide a very instructive means of testing, and filling out, the data furnished by the lists. The relations between the churches among themselves were made concrete by adopting martyr-memorial services of other cities. The famous Lucian of Antioch suffered in Nicomedia, and the day of his death, January 7, was commemorated there, but his name was remembered also in Heliopolis, and Cæsarea of Cappadocia, although on different days: in Heliopolis, he was commemorated on January 6 and in Cappadocia on November 19, together with the native saints whose day this was. In other places also, the custom occurred of putting an alien on the same day as a native martyr.[3] The eastern calendar of Nicomedia did not extend its contacts beyond the Balkan province; and so, from the entire west, Africa was represented only by the martyrdom of Perpetua (March 7), and Rome only by that of Xystus (August 1).

Mention has been made of Peter and Paul for a special

---

[1] January 22; July 15, 19, 30, Achelis, p. 35
[2] *vide supra*, 324   [3] Achelis 52–54

purpose. Once the festival of Christmas had been adopted, efforts were made in the east, not only to give it the leading place in the church's year—as had been done in Rome before A.D. 336—but also to follow it up with a worthy series of secondary festivals. Clear testimony to this effect has survived in regard to Antioch and Cappadocia, but the Syriac catalogue of martyrs expresses the notion most clearly. It puts Christmas, the 25th of December, at the beginning of the church's year, follows it on December 26 by opening the list of martyrs with the "first martyr" Stephen; the 27th is dedicated to the brother-apostles to the east, James and John, the sons of Zebedee; and December 28 is given to the corresponding two who were apostles to the west, viz., Peter and Paul.

Plainly this is a thought-out liturgical system, and the œcumenical character of the Church's worship is revealed in the way the services for the year are arranged. And it was equally intentional that to the "first martyr" Stephen there should correspond the "last martyr" Peter of Alexandria at the end of the church year. He died on November 24, 311, and was often given that title of honour. The person who arranged the calendar drew the consequences required by his system, and put no martyr-day after November 24, although we may imagine that more than one date was at his disposal between November 24 and December 25. This is an example of the free arrangement of festivals which lacked an historical tradition; and they were assigned dates, with the same freedom as the Biblical festivals. All the remaining dates in the calendar rest upon historical tradition, as is true also of the commemoration of the Maccabean children and their mother, for the day assigned to them, August 1, was that on which their bones were interred in Keration, a suburb of Antioch.

It is true that it is unknown how these relics were discovered or recognized, and equally unknown whether the grave of John the Baptist near Sebaste in Palestine, and destroyed by Julian, was the actual grave. The records say that the bones of the Forerunner of Christ were burned and scattered although not by the Emperor's wish. But faithful Christians were successful in collecting a good proportion of the precious treasure, and in bringing it to Alexandria where Athanasius took care of it.[1] Aetheria's record shows how the persistent curiosity of pilgrims could not do otherwise than gradually lead the guardians of the sacred places in Palestine to add imaginary items to their information. Her record also shows how the prevailing eagerness for objects connected with Biblical history, produced the relics themselves in increasing numbers.

During Constantine's reign the coats and cloaks of Luke the Evangelist and of the Apostle Andrew were discovered, besides other articles of clothing worthy of respect, and placed with all due ceremonial on June 20, 336 in the Church of the Apostles in Constantinople, a city which still had but few relics. Twenty-one years later, the bodies of the two saints came to light, and were placed in the same church on March 3, 357.[2] That was the first important "translation" of relics in the capital. About the same time in Antioch, Cæsar Gallus transferred the body of St. Babylas to Daphne where it was to rest in a chapel erected to the honour of this martyr. It has already been said that Julian disturbed that rest,[3] and, without intending it, brought about a new translation, and even this was not final.

The cult of martyrs became even more important to, and prominent in, the life of the Church in the second half of the fourth century, and towns which could not boast of any martyrs of their own, began to feel a strong desire to possess relics, a desire which was met by gifts of small portions of the treasures of more fortunate places. Notice has already been taken of the fact that fragments of the wood of the sacred cross were widely distributed.[4] Now were added not only remains of the ashes of the saints and drops of their blood, but also some of their bones. Churches everywhere became well supplied with such relics.[5] But the more Biblical they were said to be in origin, the more doubtful was their authenticity.

Martyr-worship began to lose the historical and religious foundation which it had possessed hitherto, and was no longer confined to the intimate circles within which a church formerly expressed its religious faith. It entered a larger sphere, and grew

[1] Rufinus, *hist. eccl.* 11, 28

[2] Lietzmann in *Quantulacumque*, a presentation to Kirsopp Lake, 1937, 347f.

[3] *vide supra*, 282   [4] *vide supra*, 304

[5] H. Delehaye, *Les origines du culte des martyrs*, 2nd ed., 1933, 50ff.

into the worship of the saints as found in the world-embracing Church of the Empire; it made a place for itself whose limits have scarcely been defined even yet, but a place where the ancient nature-religion, which had been conquered by the Christianity of the militant period, took on new forms, but under ecclesiastical names. We shall see how the Church, as a great community, came to terms with this further development, and how the religion of the individual both accepted and refused the new allurements of the world.

Literature

In addition to the lists given in the same author's *The Beginnings of the Christian Church* (cited as Vol. 1) and *The Founding of the Church Universal* (cited as Vol. 2), the following require special mention:

Acts of the Martyrs. See *Märtyrerakten.*

Aetheria is quoted in Geyer's edition, *vide* p. 302, footnote *supra.*

Ambrose, quoted from the Vienna corpus as far as published; otherwise from the Benedictine edition, Paris 1686–90.

Athanasius, in general, the Montfaucon edition, Paris 1698. The edition published by the Berlin Academy, edited by H. G. Opitz, is used where available, Valuable material is afforded by the notes. In three volumes, it contains the "documents relative to the history of the Arian controversy," cited as *Doc.* by their number. *Apol.*, without qualification, refers to the *"Apologia contra Arianos"* which is described by Opitz as *apologia secunda.*

Augustine, usually the Vienna corpus; where not available, the Benedictine edition, Paris 1679–1700 is used.

Chronicon paschale, ed. L. Dindorf, Bonn, 1832.

Chrysostom, John, ed. Montfaucon, Paris, 1718–38 (13 vols.).

Collectio Avellana, Vienna edition: *epistolae imperatorum, pontificum, aliorum, rec.* O. Guenther 1895–98 (2 vols.).

Eunapius, ed. I. F. Boissonade, Amsterdam, 1822.

Hermetica, ed. Scott (*vide* p. 49, footnote 1, *supra*); and Parthey's edition, 1854, unfortunately still has to be used.

Hilary, *ed. Benedictinorum*, Verona, 1730 (2 vols.). The important "historical fragments" in Vol. 4, Vienna edition, ed. A. Feder, 1916.

Julian, *epist.* ed. J. Bidez, *L'empereur Julian, œuvres complètes*, tome 1, 2. (Paris, Belles Lettres, 1924). The numbers are the same as those of *Imp. Caes. Flavii, Claudii Juliani epistulae, leges, poematia, fragmenta rivaa, coll. et rec.* J. Bidez et F. Cumont (Paris, Belles Lettres.

1922). This work is cited as *epist. et leges*. The speeches and other writings cited from Bidez tome 1, 1 (Paris, 1932), or from the edition by Hertlein (Leipzig, 1875–76), but according to Spanheim's pagination. The writing *against the Christians*, according to Neumann's edition, *vide* p. 281, footnote 3, *supra*.

Libanii opera, rec. R. Foerster. Leipzig (1903–22).

Malalas, *Chronographia*, rec. L. Dindorf, Bonn, 1831.

Märtyrerakten (Acts of the Martyrs) selected and edited by R. Knopf, 3rd edition by G. Krüger, 1929.

Panegyrici latini iterum rec. G. Baehrens, 1911.

Plotinus is cited by the pagination of Porphyry's *Enneads*.

Seeck, Otto, *Geschichte des Untergangs der antiken Welt* (1–3 Aufl.), Berlin 1910–20; the earlier volumes are cited from the first edition.

Seeck, Otto, *Regesten der Kaiser und Päpste für die Jahre*, 311–476, Stuttgart, 1919.

Socratis eccl. hist., ed. R. Hussey, Oxford, 1853 (3 vols.). Cited as "Soc.," or "Soc., *H.E.*"

v. Soden. *Urkunden zur Entstehung des Donatismus*, 1913 (Kleine Texte, No. 122).

Sozomeni eccl. hist., ed. R. Hussey. Oxford, 1860 (3 vols.). Cited as "*Sozom.*"

Themistii orationes, ed. G. Dindorf, Leipzig, 1832.

A Short Bibliography

by The Rev. H. Chadwick M.A.,
Fellow of Queens' College, Cambridge

THE following list of books is intended only to provide the beginner who has not much Greek or Latin with information about those books in which he can find reliable historical studies and translations into English of some of the original sources.

The period in general is studied by L. Duchesne, *Early History of the Christian Church*, vol. ii. (London, 1922), and by B. J. Kidd, *A History of the Church to A.D. 461*, vol. ii (Oxford, 1922). See also J. B. Bury's edition of Gibbon, *Decline and Fall of the Roman Empire*.

CHAPTER I

Plotinus may be read in the English translation by Stephen Mackenn aand B. S. Page (5 vols., Medici Society, 1926-30); Porphyry's Life of Plotinus is translated in the first volume. Porphyry's letter to Marcella is translated by Alice Zimmern (London, Priory Press, 1910). The Hermetic writings may be read in W. Scott's translation (Oxford, 1925), though this edition has now been superseded by that of A. D. Nock and A. J. Festugière, *Hermès Trismégiste*, Collection Budé (text and French translation, with notes; Paris, 1945).

See also W. R. Inge, *The Philosophy of Plotinus* (Gifford Lectures 1917-18); T. Whittaker, *The Neoplatonists* (Cambridge, 1918); E. R. Dodds, *Select Passages Illustrating Neoplatonism* (S.P.C.K., 1923). For the Hermetica, C. H. Dodd, *The Bible and the Greeks* (London, 1935).

CHAPTER 2

On the great persecution see N. H. Baynes in *Cambridge Ancient History*, vol. xii, pp. 646-77, with his bibliography to this chapter. Lactantius is translated in the Ante-Nicene Christian Library. Eusebius' Church History is well translated by H. J. Lawlor and J. E. L. Oulton (2 vols. S.P.C.K., 1927-8). There are also translations of Eusebius' Life of Constantine, of his Oration at Constantine's jubilee, and of Constantine's Address to the Assembly of saints, in vol. i of the Nicene and Post-Nicene Fathers, *Eusebius* (Oxford and New York, 1890).

CHAPTER 3

Donatism: There is a translation of Optatus by O. R. Vassall-Phillips (Longmans, 1917).

CHAPTER 4

Dionysius of Alexandria: C. L. Feltoe has translated some of the,
more important works (S.P.C.K., 1918).

Melitian Schism: A translation of some of the sources is
printed in B. J. Kidd, *Documents Illustrative of the History of the
Church*, vol. i pp. 224-7.

Arianism: H. M. Gwatkin's *Studies of Arianism* (2nd ed., 1900)
remains the most important work. Many of Athanasius' writings
are translated by A. Robertson in the Nicene and Post-Nicene
Fathers (1892), with a useful introduction. In the same serie.
there are translations of Socrates, Sozomen, and Theodoret,
F. L. Cross, in *Church Quarterly Review* vol. 128 (1939), has
translated the recently discovered synodal letter of the Council
held at Antioch early in 325, together with Constantine's
letter summoning the Council of Nicaea.

CHAPTER 5

Constantine: The fundamental study in English is N. H. Baynes,
Constantine the Great and the Christian Church: Proceedings of the
British Academy XV, 1929. A. Alföldi's *The Conversion of
Constantine and Pagan Rome* has been translated by Harold
Mattingly, Oxford, 1948. A. H. M. Jones, *Constantine and the
Conversion of Europe*, E.U.P., 1948.

CHAPTER 6

Eusebius: *Praeparatio Evangelica* is edited with a translation by
E. H. Gifford (Oxford, 1903). *Demonstratio Evangelica* is translated by W. J. Ferrar: *Eusebius, the Proof of the Gospel* (S.P.C.K.,
1920).

For modern studies of Eusebius see H. J. Lawlor, *Eusebiana*
(Oxford, 1912); J. Stevenson, *Studies in Eusebius* (Cambridge,
1929); F. J. Foakes Jackson, *Eusebius Pamphili* (Cambridge,
1933).

For his apologetic cf. the *Theophania*, of which there is an
English translation from the Syriac by S. Lee (Cambridge,
1843).

Gregory Thaumaturgus: The Panegyric on Origen and other
works are translated in the Ante-Nicene Christian Librarys
vol. 20. Methodius' Symposium is in the same series, vol. 14
and Arnobius in vol. 19. The *Scriptores Historiae Augustae* are
translated in the Loeb Classical Library by D. Magie.

CHAPTER 9

The Catechetical Lectures of Cyril of Jerusalem are well translated by E. H. Gifford in the Nicene and Post-Nicene Fathers

(1894). Athanasius may be read in Robertson's translation (see above on chapter IV). See also F. L. Cross, *The Study of Athanasius*, with a review by N. H. Baynes in *Journal of Roman Studies* XXXV (1945), pp. 121-4. There is a good translation of some works of Hilary of Poitiers in the Nicene and Post-Nicene Fathers (1899).

CHAPTER 10

Julian's works are translated by W. C. Wright in the Loeb Classical Library. In the same edition there is a translation of Ammianus Marcellinus. The theology of Apollinaris of Laodicea is treated by C. E. Raven, *Apollinarianism* (Cambridge, 1924).

CHAPTER 11

For an introduction to liturgical study see J. H. Srawley, *The Early History of the Liturgy* (2nd ed., Cambridge, 1947); L. Duchesne, *Christian Worship* (5th ed., S.P.C.K., 1919).

Ambrose, *de Sacramentis*, is translated by T. Thompson and J. H. Srawley (S.P.C.K., 1919); the Apostolic Constitutions in the Ante-Nicene Christian Library vol. 17; the Pilgrimage of Etheria by M. L. McClure and C. L. Feltoe (S.P.C.K.); Bishop Sarapion's Prayer Book by J. Wordsworth (S.P.C.K.)

Select Index

(This contains the more important items often not mentioned in Table of Contents.)

The Era of the Church Fathers

Volume IV of

A HISTORY OF THE EARLY CHURCH

NIGELLO

THE ERA OF THE CHURCH FATHERS

CONTENTS

Chronological Table

A.D.
about 320 Pachomius founds a monastery
  „   350 Cyril of Jerusalem's "Lectures"
     356 Antony dies, aged 105

363–364 JOVIAN

West	East
364–375 VALENTINIAN I	364–378 VALENS
367–383 GRATIAN	

366–384 Damasus of Rome
373 Death of Athanasius
379 Death of Basil
373–380 Peter II of Alexandria
374–397 Ambrose of Milan

375–392 VALENTINIAN II   379 THEODOSIUS I
383–388 Maximus
392–394 Eugenius

(388) 392–395 THEODOSIUS I. Sole Emperor

381 Council of Constantinople
386 John Chrysostom ordained as priest in Antioch
389 Jerome, a monk in Bethlehem
389 Death of Gregory of Nazianzus
399 Death of Euagrius Ponticus
about 400 Publication of Histories of monasticism by Rufinus and by Palladius

Translator's Note

THE PRESENT VOLUME CONTINUES THE HISTORY OF THE early Church which Professor Lietzmann projected in five volumes. The earlier volumes were written in a way in which the mastery of the material was only rivalled by the clarity of the exposition. Dr. Lietzmann did not live to carry out his plans; but the present volume, like its predecessors, is complete in itself, and its account of the beginnings of Christian monasticism will surely rank as classic for many years. Nevertheless, it would have been enriched by the projected chapters on Civilization in the Fourth Century, and on the Beginnings of Christian Art. Even more valuable would have been a new, and much-needed, first-hand assessment of Jerome and Augustine, like the chapter on Origen in Volume II.

The Select Bibliography for English Readers has again been prepared by the Rev. H. Chadwick, M.A., Fellow of Queens' College, Cambridge, and kindly placed at the disposal of the publishers.

Mr. and Mrs. Andre Szanto of Chorley Wood, formerly of Vienna, have helped with the translation of many difficult passages; Mr. Harry Cowlishaw has again placed his skill freely at my disposal and has made innumerable happy suggestions, especially of English phraseology and in revising the proofs; my wife has given ungrudging help in every page of the MS. and the proofs, and not least in preparing the Index; the Rev. G. H. Gordon Hewitt, M.A., editor of the Lutterworth Press, has never failed in helping with his knowledge and his skill; I wish to put on record my profound gratitude to them all. And I hope that this volume, which is perforce the last, will be regarded in its English form as worthy of that scholar whose *magnum opus* is complete in every chapter, although it must forever remain unfinished.

B. L. W.

BEACONSFIELD.
August 21, 1950.

Chapter One

JOVIAN, VALENTINIAN, AND VALENS

WHEN JOVIAN ASCENDED THE THRONE, THE DEATH-KNELL was sounded for Julian's policy regarding Christianity. The new emperor was a Christian. Even as early as the middle of September, 363, a decree was issued that "only God Almighty and Christ were to be worshipped, and the people to assemble in the churches for worship". The former legal status and system, the former sources of income, and the former privileges were restored to the churches and the clergy, and pagan sacrifices were forbidden. A small temple still stands on the island of Corfu which is held to have been transformed by Jovian into a church.[1] Tolerance was proclaimed after a while, and worship permitted in the temples as long as it was free from magic and deception: Themistius extolled the new freedom as giving the possibility of approaching God in more than one way. Naturally also, Christian teaching was no longer prohibited.[2]

Immediately the state again granted recognition to the church, however, the issue arose once more as to which was correct among the many forms of its organization. The old parties of the pre-Julian era sprang up again, and plunged into the struggle for winning the recognition of the new lord. Even while he was still in Edessa, he received the first deputation of Arianizing bishops; they wished to get him on their own side as against Athanasius. But Athanasius himself was on the alert, and he waited on Jovian immediately afterwards in Baalbek. Then, when the emperor arrived in Antioch, he had to receive a deputation of the Alexandrian opposition party, who, on several occasions, had passionately objected to the restoration of Athanasius to his see. An amusing description of these audiences is still extant among the writings of

[1] hist. aceph. 12 p. 76 Fromen   Sozom. 6, 3, 3–4   Socr. 3, 24, 5   Kaibel Epigr. graeca n. 1060
[2] Themistius or. 5 p. 80–83 Dindorf   Cod. Theod. 13, 3, 6   cf. Vol 3, 274f.

Athanasius himself.[1] Jovian had brought Athanasius to Antioch, and now confirmed him in office. This man of many enemies had been sent once more into banishment by Julian in spite of a favourable start.[2] The excuse was incompetence, but the real reason probably was that his activities in Alexandria were awkward for the emperor: at any rate, we know that he complained of the conversion to Christianity of certain eminent ladies. Athanasius left the city on October 24, 362, but comforted his people by saying, "It is only a little cloud that will soon blow over". In fact, he returned after his successful journey to Jovian's court, and reached home again on February 14, 364.[3]

Here he called a synod of the Egyptian bishops, whom he induced to approve a statement of the true faith. He sent this statement to the emperor. It described the Nicene Creed as the only rule of faith, claimed that this creed was everywhere recognized as such throughout the empire, and required the co-equality of the Holy Spirit in accordance with the conclusions reached[4] in 362. It firmly set aside the attempts "of a small number of the friends of Arius" in the east to do away with the doctrine of *homoousios*, or even to introduce that of *homoios*, and to do this by means of the plausible acceptance of a false explanation.[5] This was aimed at the decision which the "Macedonians", Basil of Ancyra and his friends in the *homoiousian* camp,[6] had laid before the emperor. This decision required either the recognition of the *homoios* of Ariminum and Seleukia, or else freedom to form theological parties. With this Jovian was much displeased.[7]

More in harmony with the views of the emperor were those men who had gathered in Antioch round Meletius and Eusebius of Samosata, and who had been joined by the adaptable Acacius of Caesarea. The decrees[8] of their synod accepted the Nicene Creed, but on a certain explicit interpretation thereof

---

1 Edessa: Philostorg. 8, 6   Baalbek: Ath. *ep*. Pref. 35 p. 40   Larsow   Antioch Athan. *op*. 2, 334–36 Opitz. Addenda to the *Epist. ad Jovianum*
2 Vol. 3, 266f.
3 Julian *Epist*., 110–12   *hist. aceph*. 11. 13   Rufin. *H.E.* 10, 35   Jov. *ep. ad Ath* (*Ath*. 2, 330 Opitz)
4 cf. Vol. 3, 271f.   5 Athan. *Epist. ad Jov*. 2, 330–33, Opit
6 Vol. 3, 229   7 Sozom. 6, 4, 3–5   Socr. 3, 25, 1–
8 Socr. 3, 25, 10–7=Sozom. 6, 4, 7–10

They insisted that the term *homoousios* was to be understood in the sense of the "fathers"—meaning the old followers of Origen of the stamp of Eusebius. According to this interpretation, *homoousios* meant "similar in nature" (ὅμοιος κατ' οὐσίαν) and implied a denial of Arianism in either the old or the new form. In substance, this was the old standpoint of the proposals at Ancyra (A.D. 358),[1] except that the synod were now willing to accept the Nicene Creed. This accommodation seemed likely to serve the interests of the unity of the church, because it drew near to the requirements of the synod of Alexandria in 362. But the insistence on their own theology and the lack of any pronouncement about the Holy Spirit emphasized the division; and Athanasius felt this situation was too painful.[2] Even Apollinaris of Laodicea was obliged to expound his Christology to Jovian.[3] It would appear that, in trying to bridge the gaps, the emperor had requested the different parties to set out their views in writing.[4] But he had not time to reach a decision before he was overtaken by death in a village of Bithynia on February 17, 364, while he was still in his twenty-third year. He had been poisoned by the fumes of a charcoal fire, after having reigned less than eight complete months.

His successor was Valentinian, an officer of the Guards, just turned thirty-nine, a big, handsome man, with fair hair and blue eyes. His father, originally a private soldier of foreign blood, perhaps German, had forced his way up to the rank of general. In the end, however, he was brought to ruin, and he lost all his rather ill-gotten gains. A cunning old politician nominated the son, and the soldiers accepted the advice: Valentinian was proclaimed Augustus on February 26, 364. But the army immediately demanded a second emperor, and Valentinian could think of no one better than his own younger brother, Valens. Valens was actually serving as a private in the Guards, and did not possess a single one of the advantages of his elder brother. Both emperors were barbarians in the

---

[1] cf. Vol. 3, 221f.
[2] cf. Basilius *ep.* 89, 2 and the unnamed critic of the Antiochene synodal letter in Ath. *op.* 2, 31–33 Montf.
[3] Lietzmann, *Apoll.* 1, 250–53
[4] Athan. *ep. ad Jov.* 1, 2 (2, 331, 3 Opitz)   cf. Socr. 3, 25, 19

fullest sense of the term. The only difference was that Valentinian had acquired the veneer of cultured manners, and had a genuine regard for the arts and sciences; whereas Valens had remained more faithful to the conditions of his birth. The period during which the two brothers reigned was full of frontier affrays, which swung to and fro without any definite results. On the Rhine and the Danube, Valentinian made unsuccessful attempts to restore the old *limes* at least in the form of a series of blockhouses. In the east, too, the struggle with the Persians to gain predominant influence in Armenia and Iberia (Georgia), only led to an unsatisfactory outcome. Both in the court and the administration, many abuses reappeared which had previously been set aside by Julian; moreover, nepotism was a burden on the provinces. The treasury imposed taxes ruthlessly, and in a manner which was often out of harmony with serious efforts to economize, or with an attempt to ameliorate the condition of the lower classes. Finally, the smooth and accustomed running of the machine of government was interrupted from time to time by tempests of passion in the highest quarters, to the extent of bloodshed.

In regard to the affairs of the church, Valentinian exercised much restraint. This was possible because the entire west, after the lifting of the measures of compulsion imposed by Constantius, was united in accepting the Nicene Creed. No serious attack was being made for the moment on the special position taken up by the "Arian" Auxentius of Milan, and those who agreed with him, i.e., the Illyrian bishops who remained true to the creed of Rimini.[1] A decree is even said to have been issued, in which Valentinian expressly recognized that the church was competent freely to make its own laws on questions of faith, and to deal with cases where charges were made against the clergy.[2] His accession took place in Nicea, immediately after which he set out to the west. Hypatian of Heraklea-Perinthus, commissioned by the local bishops, obtained an audience with him, and requested the calling of a synod for the purpose of settling the question of the creed.[3] Valentinian replied stiffly, "I am a layman, and have no need to bother

[1] cf. Vol. 3, 228   [2] Ambrose, *ep.* 21, 2, 5   [3] Sozom. 6, 7, 2

myself about such matters. It concerns the priests, who must arrange their own assemblies where they like."

This they proceeded to do; and the place chosen was important on account of the change of the geographical centre of gravity in ecclesiastical politics: the synod took place at Lampsacus on the southern shore of the Dardanelles.[1] Valens granted his permission.[2] The deliberations lasted for two months; and an agreement was reached which expressly repudiated the *homoios* formula which had been imposed at Constantinople and Nike, and which affirmed the standpoint of the former majority at Seleukia (A.D. 359).[3] The synod therefore agreed on the validity of the old symbol of the "church dedication" synod at Antioch (A.D. 341), which had been interpreted in the sense of *homoiousios*. Moreover, those who had been deposed by the *anhomoians*, i.e., the followers of Acacius and, particularly, Eudoxius were to be recognized as the rightful incumbents of the episcopal offices. Eudoxius and his supporters were called upon to repent and submit. But these men never thought of submitting; rather they made vigorous and immediate use of their influence at the imperial court. When the delegates from the synod at Lampsacus arrived, Valens sent them word that the emperor required them to come to terms with Eudoxius, the bishop resident at court; those who refused were to go into exile. And that is in fact what happened: all who persisted in hostility to the man who had the emperor's confidence, were deposed, including Meletius of Antioch. There were exceptions, especially those who made a favourable personal impression on Valens; but, in general, the rule held that the bishops who had been deposed by Constantius in the year 360, and who had returned to their sees under Julian, were once more compelled to depart.

This applied also to Athanasius.[4] After fruitless discussions with the prefect, he left the city on October 5, 365, but returned on the 1st of the following February by permission of an imperial rescript. It was said that his enemies would rather put up with him in office than again provoke his skill as an

---

[1] Record in Sozom. 6, 7, 3–10   [2] Socr. 4, 2, 3   [3] Vol. 3, 229f.
[4] *hist. aceph.* 15. 16   Sozom. 6, 12, 5–16

agitator. From that time till his death, they left him in peace. The Arian bishop, Lucius,[1] tried to take charge again of his schismatic church in Alexandria (September, 367), but was quickly repulsed with the help of the civic authorities.[2] In the years 365 and 366, the emperor was in danger of losing his throne; for Procopius,[3] well-known in the Persian war under Julian, had had himself proclaimed emperor in Constantinople, and gained possession of the district of Bithynia, at the time when he was on the march to Antioch. The insurrection was not suppressed, nor the leaders executed, till May 366. It is at least possible that the striking clemency of Valens towards Athanasius was occasioned by his desire, in such a critical period, to keep this troublesome person in a friendly mood, and maintain peace in Alexandria.[4]

Otherwise, throughout the entire orient, Valens's "persecution" of the true faith was much bemoaned. Synods held at Lampsacus, Smyrna, and other places, discussed the matter anxiously. At last, they conceived the idea of sending a deputation to Valentinian, the elder brother, asking his intervention. Eustathius of Sebaste in Armenia, Silvanus of Tarsus in Cilicia, and Theophilus of Kastabala also in Cilicia, were commissioned and sent to Italy. But they did not meet the emperor, for, in the January of that year (366), he had gone away to Rheims. There was no point in following him, because it was necessary in any case first to be clear as to relations with the leaders of the western church. The three delegates, therefore, wrote[5] to Liberius of Rome. They declared that they recognized the Nicene Creed as the unshakeable rule of faith for the church catholic together with the formula *homoousios*, thus solemnly and piously repudiating Arius. They expressly cursed the formula of Rimini which had only been imposed by trick and perfidy. They stressed, by underlining, that they were taking this step in the name of the synod which had commissioned them, and they begged Liberius to write that he recognized them. Liberius at first regarded the deputation

---

[1] cf. Vol. 3, 267
[2] *hist. aceph.* 18   cf. 14 and Sozom. 6, 5, 2 (where he is only described as a presbyter)   Athan. *op.* 2, 334, 1 Opitz. He is called bishop in Sozom. 5, 7, 1
[3] cf. Vol. 3, 285f.   [4] Socr. 4, 13, 5f.
[5] *ibid.* 4, 12, 9–20   cf. Sozom. 6, 11, 1–3

with a mistrust for which there were grounds, for, from his personal knowledge, he was acquainted with the attitude of the east.[1] But he also knew the pressure that the emperor could bring to bear, and he had good reason, personally, to keep an open door for repentant sinners. In answer to their request, therefore, he sent them a detailed document addressed to the eastern bishops, of whom 64 were mentioned by name. This document expressed satisfaction that the east and the west had now agreed in recognizing the Nicene Creed, and in rejecting the conclusions reach at Rimini.[2] Armed with this proof of the fellowship of the church, the three delegates now went back to Sicily, where analogous conclusions were drawn up by a synod. Documents expressing agreement were also sent in from Africa and Gaul.[3] The delegates could make their way home feeling that they had been successful beyond all expectation.

They were received in the east with great joy. Some of the bishops who stood fast by the conclusions reached at Antioch in 364,[4] came together at Tyana in Cappadocia, in order to prepare for a great ceremony of union on the foundation that was now assured. Their intention was to proclaim the alliance of east and west at a gathering in Tarsus in the spring of 367, under the sign of the Nicene Creed. Only some 34 obstinate reactionaries held a synod in Antioch of Caria, and once more repudiated the Nicene Creed and re-asserted the fourth symbol of Antioch as defined by the conclusions reached at Lampsacus. But they were just as unsuccessful as the men of Tyana. Acting on the advice of Eudoxius, Valens forbade the council planned for Tarsus, and the rebels continued to be punished.[5] The gesture made by Liberius and his colleagues in the west left Eudoxius entirely unmoved.

After his defeat of Procopius, Valens undertook a campaign against the Goths on the lower Danube. This lasted "three full years", and so ended in the summer of 370.[6] He then gave his attention to the east with an increased eagerness to get on with things. He marched towards Antioch in order to join

[1] cf. Vol. 3, 223–25 [2] Socr. 4, 12, 21–37
[3] ibid. 4, 12, 38 Sozom. 6, 12, 3 [4] vide supra, p. 14 [5] Sozom. 6, 12, 2–5
[6] Am. Marc. 27, 5, 6. 7 Themistius or. 10 p. 166, 11 Dind.

issue again with the Persians in the war which had been broken off by Julian's death. He intended also to take advantage of this opportunity to arrange the affairs of the church to his liking, and, with this idea in mind, he sent on in advance Modestus, the Praefect of the Praetorians. The regulations fell like a hailstorm on Bithynia, and also on Galatia. The officials then appeared in Cappadocia,[1] from where at an earlier date they had had to depart without having effected their purpose.[2]

Eusebius, the bishop, had died in old age; and after lengthy negotiations, Basil the presbyter had taken his place. This Basil had been the soul of the opposition on the earlier occasion. Modestus and other people at the court, including Demosthenes the chef, used threats and promises in striving to make the new bishop acknowledge the emperor's policy for the church; but all in vain. Basil remained firm, even when dealing with the emperor himself, who treated him with respect. Although the decree of banishment had been written out, it was never signed; and the brave bishop suffered no further attacks.

The consequence of this attitude and conduct on the part of Valens had a far greater significance than anyone at all could have dreamed of at that time. For when Basil was elevated there was at last again to be found among the eastern bishops a man with a genuine gift for leadership. He was a man also of towering personality and great diplomatic skill, and he immediately set about the task, with burning zeal, of combining all the available forces. The Neo-Arianism of Eunomius did not prove able to attract adherents, but rather roused opposition on all hands. The theological neutrality of the *homoios* party, who received official support in every way for the time being, had been outmoded by the development of the last ten years. In addition, it was burdened by its responsibility for numerous acts of violence in both east and west. The generation which had grown to manhood during the struggles of the sixth decade of the century, strove eagerly to

[1] Greg. Nyssa *c. Eunom.* 1, 127f.
[2] cf. Greg. Naz. *or.* 43, 31, 33
[3] Greg. Naz. *or.* 43, 44–5   The other sources have legendary additions of Theodoret *H.E.* 4, 18–19; the parallel passages are given in Parmentier, 242–4

attain clarity in their theology; they set their minds against the attempts of the officials to reach appeasement.

During this period, men belonging to the centre of Asia Minor rose to prominence in increasing numbers. Cappadocia in particular appears, again and again, as the native land of bishops in prominent sees and even those which were contested. George and Gregory, the two bishops who had been the opponents of Athanasius, came from this region; similarly, Auxentius who had been installed by Constantius in Milan in 355.[1] Meletius of Antioch came from Armenia, a neighbouring province. It was at this stage that a triad of stars began to shine in the history of the church: Basil of Caesarea; his brother, Gregory of Nyssa; and his friend, Gregory of Nazianzus. The Greek world, with its culture and its theology, was a new revelation to this hinterland of Asia Minor, where the populace still spoke their traditional languages.[2] The new ideas were accepted gladly, and had remarkable effects. The two friends, Basil and Gregory, bear impressive witness to the exalted enthusiasm with which, in their district, classical Greek subjects were studied, and to the high esteem in which the life-work of Origen was held. All this meant that men were at hand with the spiritual capacity for a further development of theology, a development which was needed if a clear and self-consistent solution was to be found to the problem of the Trinity, after all the confusion of the past.

The frontier-guards who had taken up their post on the issue of the Nicene Creed still maintained their mutual hostility. On the one side was the Egyptian party with their theses of A.D. 362. These were a compromise, but did not make for a clear theology. They also required the recognition of the doctrine of the *homoousia* of the Holy Spirit, which meant the raising of new difficulties before they had been prepared for by systematic thought. On the other side were the *homoiousians*, who, since the synod of Ancyra (358), had advanced in that they had adopted the tactical advantage of recognizing the Nicene formula.[3] They had secured a certain success in the west, but had not gained the assent of Athanasius. Nay,

[1] Athan. *hist. Ar.* 75, 1   [2] K. Holl, *Ges. Aufsätze*, 2, 238–48
[3] cf. *supra*, p. 15

indeed, even in the ranks of the old comrades-in-arms, opposing camps were to be found, as the synod in Caria proved.

Basil set to work at this stage of affairs. His task was far from easy in itself, and it was rendered considerably more difficult by personal hostilities. Quite apart from the question of the natural antagonism between a pope of Alexandria and one of Antioch, Athanasius was out of humour about Meletius (as already explained), and even spoke of unfulfilled promises.[1] Moreover, once on a day, when Eustathius of Sebaste in Armenia had been deposed, Meletius had taken his place to the great displeasure of the local church. So much had this been the case that he had not been able to remain, but had had to retire to Beroea (Aleppo). He held out there until he was called to the see of Antioch.[2] There is no difficulty in understanding that Eustathius hated him. This feeling was aggravated when at length Meletius accommodated himself to the court policy of Acacius and the formula *homoios*;[3] and then further when, with surprising speed, he joined sympathy with the Niceans, and, in company with Acacius, solemnly acclaimed at Antioch that hotly debated formula. By contrast, Eustathius had remained faithful for a long time to the *homoiousian* standpoint. Only by reason of extreme necessity had he felt obliged to make that journey of repentance to the west, by which he had gained for himself and his group the recognition of Liberius. And it is only too easy to understand that the circle round Meletius, and now Athanasius besides, would have less than complete confidence in this new orthodoxy. In Egypt, since the synod of 362, the confession of the *homoousia* of the Holy Spirit had been required. The *pneumatomachoi* had repudiated this with all their strength: these included the old *homoiousians*, particularly Eustathius. Meletius and his friends gave way on this point also in 370.[4]

Basil set about boldly to create unity. It was plain to him that the personal and factual oppositions could only be got over if they were all lifted out of the narrow circles of local churches and their policies, and considered from the view of the church universal. He therefore wished to bring in the

[1] Basil *ep*. 89, 2   [2] Tillemont, 8, 343   [3] cf. Vol. 3, 267
[4] Epiph. *haer*. 73, 34, 2–5

church of the west, but not in the manner preferred in 366 by Eustathius and his adherents; for this had been the special action of a particular group, and without practical value. He aimed at a plenipotentiary delegation of western churchmen sent out from Rome to the east, where they would be entirely free to reach whatever conclusions the subject-matter itself required. He felt confident that a meeting of this importance and authority would be able to effect what the east had been unable to do out of its own resources. He was aware also that Athanasius was the ideal person to induce the bishop of Rome to take such a step; and this, firstly, on account of his close relations with the people at Rome, and, secondly, on account of the traditional connection of his episcopal throne with that at the old capital of the empire.

He therefore wrote in the most flattering terms to the aged bishop in Alexandria, and asked him to crown his life's work by a great act of reconciliation. It would be in point if he were to send a few of his most trustworthy people to the west in order to petition for support by the despatch of a delegation. In the first instance, however, he was to establish his own authority with a view to bringing about, in Antioch, a union of the three parties who favoured the Nicene Creed. Athanasius, however, was rather deaf in that ear, and sent no representatives to Rome. What he did, on the other hand, was to send a cleric to Basil, Peter by name, who was one of his helpers, and who, indeed, at a later date became his own successor. Basil then drew back somewhat, and now by way of a countermove, he sent a certain deacon of Antioch, named Dorotheus, to Alexandria with letters addressed to Rome. Athanasius was only asked to give his endorsement to these letters. Basil then came out into the open, and declared that, in Antioch, Meletius ought of course to be recognized as bishop, and that the heads of the small sects[1] must be made subordinate to him after suitable compromise. It was to be remembered, too, that Meletius had been recognized as orthodox by the west, a fact testified to by the document sent by Silvanus.[2] The Egyptian bishop required no further reasons for dropping the whole enterprise. Athanasius regarded Paulinus, the head of a sect,

[1] cf. Vol. 3, 268f.   [2] Basil *ep*. 66. 69. 67, and also the plans in *ep*. 70. 242

as the only rightful bishop of Antioch; and he hated Meletius. No letter of recommendation was given to Dorotheus, and he had no excuse for going on to Rome. Meletius had foreseen this outcome, and had never had the slightest confidence in Basil's plan, in spite of the fact that the latter had sent Dorotheus to him with an urgent letter. Basil did not allow himself to be put out of temper. He wrote again and again to Athanasius. He besought him to take the initiative himself, and address a letter to him (Basil) as a person of trust, and so do something towards reconciliation with "those whose faith was sound", i.e., of course, the group centring on Meletius.[1] Athanasius said never a word. When soon afterwards Basil sent a request to Meletius to abandon his reluctance, which was doing harm, and stretch out a friendly hand to the Alexandrians,[2] he met with no better success.

Meanwhile, several requests came in, from North Italy as well as from Egypt, for Rome to take action against the remnants, still in being, of "Arianism", i.e. against those who held to the council of Rimini. First of all, Ursacius of Singidunum (Belgrade) and Valens of Mursa (Esseg) were condemned by Pope Damasus at a synod in Rome; then after a further warning,[3] Auxentius of Milan was included. This last decree of condemnation was issued by a synod which had assembled in 372 on Valentinian's orders; its conclusions therefore received added significance as part of the emperor's policy for the church—at least as regards theology. Valentinian was less inclined than his brother to execute those he condemned; and Auxentius, though condemned and declared to be deposed, remained undisturbed in office; he died, still in possession, in the year 374. The eastern delegates had once received testimony as to their orthodoxy on the ground that they had accepted the Nicene Creed.[4] Athanasius must have been averse to this, because his synod of 362 had required in addition the recognition of the *homoousia* of the Holy Spirit. The Roman synod called by Damasus used the opportunity, occasioned by the condemnation of Auxentius and the conclusions of Rimini, to testify to the eastern bishops that Rome

---

[1] Basil *ep.* 80. 82   [2] *ibid. ep.* 89   [3] Athan. *ep. ad Afros*, 10, 3
[4] cf. *supra*, p. 19

accepted the *homoousia* of all the Trinity, as this doctrine was implied in the Nicene Creed. Anyone not accepting this view was to be regarded as outside their communion.[1]

The document was carried to Athanasius by Sabinus, a deacon at Milan; and Athanasius immediately sent this messenger on to Basil.[2] This gave Basil a fresh opening for trying to put his favourite scheme into operation. This time he was joined by Meletius, because there was now no need to go round by Alexandria, although Basil even yet strongly recommended it.[3] Meletius drew up a document in the name of 32 bishops and addressed it to their peers in Italy and Gaul. He went over the ground of Basil's earlier draft and described the deplorable state of things in the east. He requested that a commission should be sent, consisting of as many as possible, with the object of uniting under the sign of the Nicene Creed all those now separated who were of like mind. The document from the synod called by Damasus was accepted and agreed.[4] Basil also wrote himself in his own name, and addressed a note to Valerian of Aquileia as well.[5] Then Sabinus, armed with his important commission, once again set out for the west: it was probably round about Easter, 373.

He went in high hope . . . but was grievously disappointed. As before, Rome obtained tidings about the east from Alexandria, and, in Alexandria, the feeling towards Meletius and his adherents had if possible worsened. Athanasius had died on May 3, 373. On his death-bed, he had consecrated Peter, the presbyter, as his successor.[6] At this point, too, the other side took a hand. Euzoius of Antioch made contact with the court, which was resident in that city, and accompanied by Magnus, the minister of finance, made his journey to Alexandria. They carried to the prefect of Egypt a rescript jo the emperor's. It ordered the installation of the Arian bishop, Lucius,[7] and, if it should be necessary, sanctioned the use of force. Peter took flight to Rome,[8] where his dislike for Meletius

---

[1] Damasus's *Confidimus*, Coustant *epist. pont.* p. 487, now in Schwartz, *ZNW* 1936, 19   cf. 1935, 179, n. 120
[2] Basil *ep.* 90, 1   [3] cf. *ibid. ep.* 89
[4] *ibid. ep.* 92   The draft, *ep.* 242   cf. Lietzmann, *Apoll.* 52
[5] *ibid. ep.* 90. 91   [6] *hist. aceph.* 19   [7] *vide supra*, p. 18, and Vol. 3, 267
[8] Socr. 4, 21. 22   Sozom. 6, 19

and his distrust of Basil determined the decisions that Damasus made. A certain priest belonging to Antioch, Euagrius by name, had been resident in Italy for the last ten years, and now wished to return home. He was chosen as the messenger of the church at Rome. He took back to Basil the letters with which Sabinus had been entrusted, and said they were not acceptable. Euagrius then placed before Basil a document for signature. This document had been drawn up in Rome; and when Basil had signed, it was to be returned to Rome by the hands of important eastern representatives. Thus a suitable occasion would be provided for a return visit.[1] Euagrius went on to Antioch, where, in spite of the desires for peace which he had expressed orally to Basil, he denied church-fellowship to Dorotheus, a confidant of Basil's, on the ground that the former was one of Meletius's deacons. Two letters from Basil then arrived at Antioch putting an end to this way of going on. The first letter was addressed to the people of the church, and laid it down once more that the Nicene Creed, with the added clause regarding the Holy Spirit, was the only valid and sufficient confessional basis. The formulas propounded by others—meaning Rome—were set aside.[2] Euagrius himself received a letter, couched in cuttingly polite terms, repudiating all the Roman requirements, and containing a censure for his hostile attitude to Dorotheus.[3] It had become clear to Basil that Damasus was under Peter's influence, and had no desire for union with the east.

But Basil was tenacious, and was not prepared to let himself be discouraged by unfriendly acts, even some of the basest kind. Basil's friend, Eusebius of Samosata, was arrested in the spring of 374 and banished to Thrace. Thereupon Basil wrote once more to "the bishops of Gaul and Italy", described the hardships in pressing terms, and repeated his request that they should approach Valentinian by diplomatic means. If this were impossible, would they send a special delegation?[4] Dorotheus, who had meantime been consecrated priest, took the letter to Rome, and brought back the answer, of which a large portion has survived.[5] In regard to lending help, it said

<hr/>

[1] cf. Basil *ep.* 138, 2   [2] *ibid. ep.* 140   [3] *ibid. ep.* 156   [4] *ibid. ep.* 243
[5] Fragment *"ea gratia"*, Coustant, p. 495   Schwartz *ZNW* 1936, 20

no more than that they had discussed the question, as Dorotheus would testify. Then came lengthy dogmatic arguments. These had to do with an *ousia* and three "persons" in the Trinity, the phrase "three hypostases", which Meletius had accepted, being expressly avoided; confession of the complete humanity of the Son of God, and *homoousia* of the Holy Spirit. It was plain that now in Rome Meletius and his adherents were once again regarded as heretical on account of their doctrine of three hypostases. It also followed that Peter had in practice repudiated the broadminded viewpoint of the synod of 362. The document, moreover, contained an unexpected passage. This passage said that when bishops and priests were being consecrated, the canonical regulations must not go unobserved, and mistakes in this respect were not light matters. This phraseology made it clear to the reader that Meletius was going to be repudiated again; for, contrary to the custom of the early church, a custom re-affirmed at Nicea,[1] he had changed his first see, that at Sebaste, for the see of Antioch. Of course, translations of this kind had grown in time to be customary, and to prohibit them would mean that it was impossible to move a bishop who had made good, to a more important office. Nevertheless, the law laid down in the canon remained unchanged. Consequently, in the manœuvres for position that took place in the course of church politics, it gave an enemy a valuable weapon for use against any bishop who had risen to power and influence in the way described. And, in fact, frequent use was made of this stratagem. It was turned in the present instance against Meletius; and so, for the third time, Basil was frustrated.

In spite of all, however, he wrote to Rome in the same sense three years later (377); by now the situation was very different. The Apollinarians had, in the meantime, really separated from Meletius's church in Antioch,[2] and had consecrated their spiritual leader, Vitalis, to the office of bishop. Apollinaris himself had visited Antioch in 373–74 and had delivered theological lectures. When Epiphanius of Cyprus came on a visit, discussions arose which showed up the dubious character of the Apollinarian doctrine of the Incarnation; and

[1] *can. Nic.* 15   *can. Ant.* 21   *can. Apost.* 14   [2] cf. Vol. 3, 269, 271f.

this cast doubt on the orthodoxy of Vitalis.[1] Then, in the year 375, Vitalis took the course then fashionable; he set off to Rome, and returned happily with a letter from Damasus, which recognized him as orthodox, and commended him to Paulinus for further negotiations. But soon afterwards, Damasus must have received more exact particulars, for he hastened to follow up the first letter with a second in which[2] Paulinus was advised to require Vitalis to sign the Nicene Creed, and to add a clause acknowledging that the Son of God had had a human body, a human soul, and a human spirit; and not, e.g., the divine logos in the place of the human spirit. Vitalis was unable to grant this point, and so was compelled to dispense with an alliance with Paulinus. But Vitalis made good use of Damasus's first letter, which testified to his orthodoxy.[3] Paulinus, on the other hand, had better reasons for exultation, for both these letters from the pope of Rome testified to his own orthodoxy, a view which was by no means unquestioned by the other eastern bishops. The letters also brought out the important fact that Rome recognized him alone as the bishop of Antioch. He too, therefore, made no delay, but imparted this information to Terentius, the newly appointed *Comes Orientis*; and he requested him, quite logically, to put the pastorless flock of the exiled Meletius under his care. All this made a great impression on His Excellency, with the result that Basil saw all his plans endangered. Fortunately, Basil was already well acquainted with Terentius, whom he now seriously warned against Paulinus, the "Sabellian", and whom he had to instruct in matters under discussion in theology, especially the difference between *ousia* and *hypostasis*.[4]

Dorotheus, the confidant of Basil, set out once more for Rome in the spring of 377, in spite of the express misgivings of his senior. On this occasion, he was directly commissioned by Eusebius, the exiled bishop of Samosata, and was accompanied by a certain Sanctissimus, otherwise unknown, who had no official status in travelling from one bishop to another in the east, but whom even Basil had employed as a messenger.[5]

---

[1] Epiph. *haer.* 77, 20–24   Lietzmann, *Apoll.* 1, 16ff.
[2] Damasus *epist.* "*per filium*"   Coustant, p. 507
[3] Greg. Naz. *epist.* 102 (2, 94c)   [4] Basil *ep.* 214   cf. 215. 216
[5] *ibid. ep.* 239, 2   cf. *ep.* 120. 121. 129, 3   132. 254. 255

Once again, even this journey proved fruitless. Once more, Peter of Alexandria stood in the way of an agreement. There was, indeed, a heated argument, in the presence of Damasus, in which Peter described both Eusebius of Samosata and also Meletius as Arian heretics. This provoked Dorotheus to heated and unfriendly replies.[1] The two messengers had answers placed in their hands, from which Basil politely said he had drawn encouragement,[2] but it is not possible for us to say on what grounds. Perhaps the answers contained a fairly pointed remark about tolerating Apollinarian heresies on the part of the eastern bishops.[3]

At this point, Basil decided to abandon the reserve which he had concealed under vague phraseology, and proclaim clearly what were the requirements of the east. In the new call to a synod,[4] which was probably forwarded to Rome in the spring of 377 by the hands of Dorotheus and Sanctissimus, the west were requested, if they did not wish to attend personally, to lend their aid in a positive manner and in writing. Would they, at a representative synod, single out and condemn the mischief-makers in the east, with explicit mention of names? For the main danger was not constituted by the Arians whom all repudiated, but, rather, the wolves in sheep's clothing who had come forward out of the ranks of the orthodox. Examples were Eustathius of Sebaste with his denial of the *homoousia* of the Holy Spirit; Apollinaris of Laodicea with his doctrine of the Incarnation, together with many other philosophical speculations and Judaizing doctrines; and Paulinus of Antioch, who had once more shown his leaning towards the heresies of Marcellus of Ancyra (who had recently died) by recognizing his church in Galatia.

It is unlikely that Basil had any doubt that the west would refuse to accede to his request. At any rate, as long as Peter had the ear of Damasus, Paulinus would be regarded with favour in Rome. This was more particularly the case since that same Peter had taken an active part in what happened

---

[1] Basil *ep.* 266, 2   [2] *ibid. ep.* 263, 1
[3] If the fragment *"illud sane"* is part of this answer At the beginning the correct reading is *"vestros"* (Coustant, p. 498 Schwartz *ZNW*, 1936, 21, No. 3 cf. *ZNW*, 1935, 186, No. 138)
[4] Basil *ep.* 263

to the church in Galatia.[1] Nothing, therefore, came of the whole business that would have accorded with Basil's wishes. True, a synod was held in Rome, and it reached conclusions[2] on those doctrines which were troubling the east, decisions, indeed, which were all to Basil's mind. But as regards the question of personalities, which was Basil's principal concern, the synod was quite silent, or even worse. Although it solemnly anathematized the heresies which Basil had cited— and many others—there was no mention of any of the names which were debated in the east. Instead, there was an observation touching the canon law, and repudiating fellowship with people who moved across from one church to another—Meletius was meant. Such persons ought to return to their former office; and, should it turn out that they had been ordained there in the place of someone who was still alive, they should quietly stand aside till the death of their predecessor, before they exercised episcopal functions. This phraseology had been chosen so as to suit the case of Meletius, and demanded nothing less than that Meletius should return to Sebaste, and become subordinate to the very Eustathius for whose condemnation Basil had asked. A covering letter assured Basil that unfortunately it had not been possible to be of the smallest assistance to the eastern bishops; but it only confirmed that they had refused to meet his wishes. Damasus remained completely loyal to the traditional policy of co-operation with Alexandria, and he left the east to its own devices. At the same time, it became clear that he did not grant that the men of the east stood on the same level as himself; that explains the offensive form in which he expressed his refusals.

The various approaches had cost Basil the greatest self-command, and he used bitter words to characterize the arrogance and the superciliousness of the west, an arrogance which had increased with his own politeness.[3] Moreover, his last letter to Damasus was itself the result of much bitter experience. Basil regarded Eustathius,[4] in his sixties, as a

---

[1] Basil *ep.* 266, 1

[2] The document is given in Turner, *Mon.* 1, 283–94; discussion by Schwartz, *ZNW*, 1935, 189–92   For Damasus's writing, "*non nobis*", cf. *ZNW*, 1936, 22f. Coustant, p. 499

[3] Basil *ep.* 239, 2   [4] F. Loofs, *Eustathius v. Sebaste*, 1898, 68ff.

highly revered friend, and one who inspired him with his ascetic ideal of life. It was only after differences regarding the theology of the Holy Spirit had led to their being on opposite sides in regard to church policy, and after Eustathius had publicly attacked his old friend in certain indiscreet published writings, that they parted altogether. Basil's letters reflect the wrath of an insulted man; and it was an official announcement of an irreconcilable breach, when Basil wrote Damasus and charged Eustathius with heresy. Apollinaris was another person whom Basil had once held in high esteem, an esteem which the new doctrine of the Incarnation had done little to disturb. But in the "seventies" of that century, the Apollinarians began a powerful propaganda. They were self-confident; they installed their own bishops; they declared those who differed from them to be heretics; and they endangered the unity of the church which, in any case, was in rather a delicate state. Thus it could not appear otherwise to Basil, who had always been the protagonist of peace and reconciliation, than that Apollinaris was a pernicious person.[1] That Paulinus should have been recognized, in Rome and Alexandria, as the bishop of Antioch was the greatest hindrance to that unity of the east which had been sought under Meletius. Thus it would not seem to Basil to be altogether regrettable when the church at Ancyra, which, under Marcellus, had been more than suspected of heresy, was so rapidly recognized by Paulinus. Towards this event, effective assistance[2] had been given by eleven Egyptian bishops who had been banished to Diocaesarea in Palestine (Sepphoris near Nazareth) on account of their hostility to Lucius the Arian bishop of Alexandria. This assistance had given much offence, but it offered the opportunity to accuse Paulinus of leaning towards the heresy of Marcellus, and thus to assail him with threats from the standpoint of theology. But what purpose was being served? Rome continued in refusing to bend, Alexandria remained obstinate, and Paulinus felt himself beyond attack. Basil had been unsuccessful in striving for the olive branch in this world, and only found peace at last beyond the grave. He died on January 1, 379—shortly before the victory of the cause he had espoused.

[1] Lietzmann, *Apoll.*, 1, 20–24   [2] Basil *ep.* 265, 3   Facundus *pro def. trium cap.* 4, 2

Meanwhile further events had taken place in the outside world which paid little attention to the conflicts and concerns of ecclesiastics. Weightier matters were afoot: the racial migrations had begun. Since the time of the victory won by Constantius in 332,[1] the Goths settled north of the Danube had kept the terms of the peace treaty, and entered into a friendly relation with the Roman Empire; they had rendered the services for which they were asked: protected the frontier and supplied auxiliaries. Even before this period, Christianity had penetrated among them—and of this we shall speak in another connection—but was regarded with mistrust from many sides, just because it had come from the Roman Empire. As early as the year 348, Athanarich, the "judge" of the West Goths, had persecuted the Christians among his people, and had compelled Wulfila, their bishop, to flee across the Danube with his adherents, and put himself and them under Roman protection. They settled in the region between Svistov and Trnovo in modern Bulgaria.[2]

The war which Valens fought with the Goths,[3] and which cannot be called unavoidable, put an end to the peace which had lasted more than thirty years, and added fuel to the fires of racial hatred.

The first result of the tension was the wild outbreak of a passion for persecuting the Goths who had become Christian in the area ruled by Athanarich; but it met with unexpected resistance. Frithigern became the first leader of the oppressed section of the people, and, in alliance with the Romans, won their independence from Athanarich. This did not mean peace, however. The Huns, who were Mongolian horsemen from the region of the Ural mountains, began to press westwards; they conquered the Alans, a tribe related to the Sarmatians, and drove the East Goths into Bessarabia, except those whom they made their subjects. Their assault fell at this stage on the West Goths and broke them to pieces. Athanarich retired towards Transylvania, but the greater part of the people appeared across the Danube under Frithigern, and asked to be accepted

---

[1] cf. Vol. 3, 137   For further details, cf. Seeck, *Untergang*, 5, 84–121, and compare with the sources cited on pp. 461–77

[2] Jordanes, *Getica*, 267   cf. Philostorg. 2, 5, p. 18, 10 Parm.

[3] *vide supra*, p. 19

into the Roman confines. Their object was to settle in Thrace, i.e. eastern Bulgaria.

Valens, resident at that time in Antioch, gladly agreed to have such warlike Germanic frontierguards encamped where they would protect the capital of his empire, and gave orders accordingly. But the generals in command of the military forces of the southern region of the Danube delayed in giving effect to these orders, and used the distress of the famished people for their own personal advantage. The delay was long enough to cause hesitation on the part of these people who were essentially high-spirited and agreeable. Added to it all, the East Goths now appeared on the banks of the Danube and forced a crossing. A final piece of malice on the part of Lupicinus, the *comes*, set off the explosion. At the beginning of 377, Frithigern opened the racial war, defeated the troops of Lupicinus, and gave rein to the savage plundering of Thrace. The army which Valens sent managed to drive the Goths over the Balkan mountains into the region by the estuary of the Danube, and afterwards. to render at least the passes in the Balkans secure. Frithigern's reply, however, consisted of taking the most extreme measures: he came to terms with the Huns and the Alans, and sent hordes of their wild horsemen against the Roman rear. The passes had to be evacuated, and came again into possession of the Goths. Thrace was flooded anew with masses out for loot. Once and for all, the Roman frontier on the Danube had been broken open, and the folk-migration poured through the breach.

When the war in Thrace had lasted more than a year, with the situation continually worsening for the empire, it was high time for Valens to gather together all his forces for defence. Another thing of which he now perceived the importance was a church at peace; towards the end of 377, therefore, he abolished the pains and penalties imposed on the opposing clergy.[1] In May, A.D. 378, he withdrew into Constantinople with the eastern army, which had been fighting against the Persians. He negotiated with Gratian, the youthful son and successor of Valentinian, who had died in 375, and found him

[1] Rufin. *H.E.* 11, 13   Jerome, *Chron. Ol.* 289, 2   *Chron. Edess.* 33   Socr. *H.E.* 4, 38

willing to help. Battles on the Rhine delayed the despatch of the promised troops, but they arrived, nevertheless, during the summer. Meanwhile, Valens had grown impatient, and on August 9, 378, he went into the attack at Nike[1] near Adrianople. But it was to Frithigern's good fortune, for his West Goths had been strengthened by East Goths and Alans. The Romans were completely defeated and put to flight. The two commanding generals fell in battle, and Valens received a mortal wound from an arrow. His body was never found.

[1] cf. Vol. 3, 228

Chapter Two

THEODOSIUS I AND THE END OF THE ARIAN CONTROVERSY

WHEN GRATIAN RECEIVED NEWS OF THE SERIOUS MILITARY situation, and then of the death of his uncle the emperor, he began to advance, taking the direction towards Sirmium (Mitrovitza, to the west of Belgrade). Remaining there for the autumn and winter, and till March of the following year, he strove with all his might to ward off the threatening calamity. The commander-in-chief in the east was also anxious to help, and, on a certain day, killed off all the Goths serving in the eastern regiments. This weakened considerably the striking power of the army, but the act was regarded with indifference by the free Goths. Gratian saw at once that he could not do anything in this connection without neglecting dangers threatening other quarters in his own share of the empire. He therefore called Theodosius to court, a young man who had already made a brilliant reputation as a regimental commander, and made him supreme commander. Theodosius was then sent by Gratian on a military expedition in the region to the south of the Danube, and was most successful. After this test, Gratian raised him, on January 19, 379, to be the Augustus of the east; and gave him the necessary plenipotentiary authority to wage war independently in that part of the Balkan peninsula which belonged to the western empire.

Theodosius was a Spaniard by birth. His father, of the same name,[1] had been a successful general in wars in Britain and Africa, and regarded by Valentinian with the highest esteem. But he became the victim of spite at court, and was executed at Carthage in the beginning of 376. The son thereupon took his departure, and retired to the family estate in Spain. Now, at the age of thirty-three, he had returned to the centre of affairs, and found himself face to face with an extraordinarily difficult, indeed really insoluble problem. For it was impossible to re-establish the frontier on the Danube, and the gap here

[1] Pauly-Wissowa-Kroll, II, 5, 1937, No. 9

remained wide open to the racial migrations. An attempt might be made, however, to settle the Goths in the lower Danube basin, arrange favourable terms, and appoint them as guards in the service of the empire.[1] Theodosius carried out this plan successfully; the way was then open to continue the policy which had been largely followed since Constantine, viz. to enlist the excess forces of the barbarians, and make them available for filling the complement of the Roman army; and this project, again, was abundantly successful. In particular, about this time, Egypt was full of Germanic and Sarmatian regiments, and, in exchange, trustworthy Egyptian troops were transferred to the Danube.[2] Negotiations were entered into with Frithigern's Goths, who had seeped through and penetrated into the middle of Greece; by the end of October an agreement was reached. Athanarich, even as early as January 381, had gone to Constantinople, but had died in that very month. He received a splendid funeral after the Roman manner,[3] a fact which gave graphic expression to the emperor's political objectives.

If we take the overwhelming circumstances into account, we can see that this was the only possible outcome. The great racial migration was brought to a standstill, for the last time and for a space of thirteen years, i.e. till the death of Theodosius. It is probably true to say that the emperor and the inhabitants of the eastern empire made good use of this interval. Gratian's first concern at that time, even after the catastrophe of Valens,[4] had been for the church. He was well aware how his uncle had oppressed the Christians in the east; and therefore, even before promoting Theodosius, he issued a decree from Sirmium. This decree permitted all exiled bishops to return home, proclaimed complete freedom of worship for all except the Manicheans and the adherents of Photinus[5] and of Eunomius,[6] i.e. Sabellians and Arians.[7]

The effect, however, was not to overcome but to sanction

---

[1] Mommsen, *Ges. Schr.* 6, 227–30

[2] Zosim. 4, 30 References in Seeck, *Untergang*, 5, 482f. Mommsen, *Ges. Schr.* 6, 281f.

[3] Am. Marc. 27, 5, 10 Zosim. 4, 34, 5 [4] *vide supra*, p. 32ff.

[5] Vol. 3, 209f. [6] Vol. 3, 218f.

[7] Socr., 5, 2, 1 Sozom. 7, 1, 3 cf. *Cod. Theod.* 16, 5, 5 line 11, Mommsen

the divisions in the eastern church; and this fact was apparent immediately in the proclamations of the various synods.[1] This created an impossible state of affairs if ever the idea of a united established church were to gain ground in the east, such as was already an actuality in the west, except for the Donatists in Africa. Moreover, such an idea was of importance to the state no less than to the church. Basil had perceived that its own resources were not sufficient to enable the eastern church to reach unity, and had therefore turned for help to the west. His efforts had been in vain. At this juncture, Theodosius solved the problem, and did so in ways closely related to those advocated by Basil. He ordained,[2] probably as early as February 28, 380, that all his subjects should adhere to the religion preached by the Apostle Peter to the Romans; in particular, the form confessed by Pope Damasus and by Peter, bishop of Alexandria. This form declared, "We believe in one Godhead, and in the equal majesty of the Trinity: Father, Son, and Holy Spirit." All who held other beliefs were branded as heretics, and threatened with punishments by the state as well as those of a supernatural kind. Since the time when Eustathius had made his journey to Rome,[3] the eastern bishops had grown accustomed to regard the bishop of Rome as an impartial and authoritative arbitrator in matters of faith. Theodosius could therefore count on assent when he named Damasus. He took the western standpoint when considering the issue of the church, and regarded the Nicene Creed and the apostolic authority of Rome as axiomatic. And when he looked at the east it was from the standpoint of the west, as is plain when he named Bishop Peter as the second guarantor of the faith, for Peter had been the greatest stumbling block in the way of all efforts to attain unity. In fact, during the time of the war with the Goths, he had returned home to Alexandria[4] with a testimonial from Damasus, and had immediately decided on a vigorous prosecution of his own special policy.

The situation was genuinely dangerous, but the danger was nipped in the bud by the clever way in which Meletius

[1] *vide infra*, 59f.
[2] *Cod. Theod.* 16, 1, 2   Sozom. 7, 4, 5. 6   Schwartz, *ZNW*, 1935, 196, prefers a different date
[3] *vide supra*, p. 18f.   [4] Socr. 4, 37, 1. Sozom. 6, 39, 1

immediately intervened. Gratian's edict of tolerance had enabled him to return home to Antioch, where the "orthodox" church at once accepted his leadership. Sapor, the imperial commissioner, and the one responsible for the oversight of church affairs, recognized him as the legitimate bishop. Paulinus then had no alternative to accepting the arrangement proposed by Meletius. Retaining the title of bishop, he became the pastor of his own church and congregation, and recognized Meletius as bishop of the see of Antioch. He attempted to enlist the intermediation of Rome, however, in order to ensure at least his claim to the succession in case of Meletius's death.[1] In the meantime, Meletius was very much alive, and proceeded to take in hand the leadership of church affairs, not only in Antioch, but also the entire east. Even by autumn, A.D. 379, he had gathered a synod which was attended by 153 bishops. This synod documented the agreement of the bishops with the western faith as represented by Damasus; and did so by re-asserting the decree,[2] *Confidimus*, of the synod at Rome in the year 372, which had once been sent by Athanasius to Basil. They also re-asserted a few later pronouncements. All this was the best that could be done at first to meet the requirements of the emperor's rescript of February, 380. When the Nicene Creed was accepted together with the *homoousia* of the Holy Spirit, the importance for theology was that all Arian and semi-Arian formulas, together with Apollinarianism, had been repudiated.

In this way, the affairs of two of the great dioceses—later called patriarchates—were properly constituted; the third, that of Constantinople, the capital of the empire, still remained unaffected. Here, for 40 years, the emperor's direction of church policy had been determinative for the bishop and his people. Demophilus, the bishop now in office, had previously acted for Constantius as bishop of Beroea in Macedonia.[3] It was plain that he would be unable to join in the new approach to the Nicene Creed. In view of coming events, the Neo-Niceneans chose their best theologian and orator, Gregory of

---

[1] cf. Ambrose, *ep.* 12, 6
[2] *vide supra*, 24   The text is given by Schwartz, *ZNW*, 1936, 19–23; compare 15–16   Probably *ZNW*, 1935, 199 is more nearly correct
[3] Vol. 3, 224   cf. Philostorg. 9, 14

Nazianzus, a friend of Basil's, and sent him to the capital commissioned to build up a church; as the head of this church he would be able to claim the bishopric when it became vacant. He accepted the mission; but, in his case, we are probably justified in believing his assurances that he did so unwillingly.[1] Unlike Basil, he was not given to public life. Once on a time, when in the throes of the struggle for metropolitan authority in Cappadocia, Basil had ordained him as bishop of a tiny place called Sasima. Tempers rose seriously. Angered by the suggestion, he refused the task, did not enter on office, but fled and sought solitude in the mountains. At a later date, he had come to the assistance of his father in Nazianzus, where he was bishop. After his father's death, he managed to evade the appointment as successor, and withdrew to Seleukia in Cilicia. The call to Constantinople faced him anew with the question whether to abandon his life of leisure as a contemplative; and, on this occasion, the task ahead seemed so suited to his brilliant abilities that he overcame his hesitation and agreed.

In that great city, only a diminutive, out-of-the-way church could be placed at his disposal. This was the Anastasia, or Church of the Resurrection, which only at a later date was rebuilt in splendid proportions.[2] Naturally, too, the congregation which held to the Nicene Creed was, at first, very small.[3] As a consequence, the first stages were not easy. The great city-congregation remained loyal to Demophilus, their bishop; and on a certain day, Gregory had a dire experience. A rabble of monks and beggars, who depended on the bishop for their livelihood, attacked him while he was conducting service, and a hail of stones, flung by the incensed defenders of the faith, fell beyond him upon the altar and the sacred vessels and ornaments. Insult was added to injury when he was blamed for the entire disturbance; and, in fact, he needed all his well-trained readiness in speech to defend himself before the police authorities.[4] Matters went so far that the baser women, in a

---

[1] Greg. carm. de vita sua, v. 596. 607 (2, 704. 706 ed. Bened.)
[2] Alfons Maria Schneider, Byzanz (1936), 51f.   To-day the mosque of Mehmed Sakollu Pasha, near to the round end of the hippodrome, stands on its ruins
[3] Greg. or. 33, 1   42, 2   carm de vita, v. 587–89, p. 704
[4] ibid. carm. de vita, v. 652–78 (2, 710)   epist. 77, 1 (2, 66)

rage of fanaticism, broke into actual attacks on him.[1] It
scarcely requires to be said that Gregory was thoroughly
despised for his obvious defects: his unimpressive personal
appearance, his shabby clothes, his provincial bearing, and
his poverty.[2]

But all this was to count as nothing compared with his
astonishing powers of speech, which drew even his critics into
his church, and steadily increased the number of his hearers.
In dark days later on, the memory of his success as a preacher
in the Church of the Resurrection was a comfort and a consolation.[3] Of the addresses which he delivered during that period,
a large number have survived. They reveal splendour in
phraseology, rhythm in construction, as well as great care in
the theology and even in the philosophy of the argument. Most
worthy of note are the famous five "Theological Addresses"
against the Arians. They are skilfully planned; the problem of
the Trinity is developed in an orderly manner; the reader is
stirred by the graphic character of the sermon on the innate
idea of God; and by the penetrating dialectic with which he
discusses the doctrine of the Logos . . . all these features supply
unrivalled examples of an oratory which made the highest
effects on the hearers. Moreover, this was the very thing that
could be appreciated in Constantinople. Now, and for more
than 50 years, the best speakers had trained the people and
made them highly expectant. On the other hand, questions
of dogma had become the favourite topics of conversation,
not only in the salons of the upper classes, but also in the
shops of the bakers and the money-changers, and in the baths
and the bazaars.[4] Gregory was happy in his increasing success.
He could reckon it a certainty that his position would be
ultimately confirmed and that he would be promoted to become
bishop of Constantinople. This would take place as soon as
Theodosius had come into residence and the general position
of the eastern church had been made clear.

In the meantime, a Christian philosopher, Maximus by

[1] Greg. *or.* 35, 3–4   33, 5   [2] *ibid. or.* 33, 7. 8

[3] *ibid.. carm. hist.*, No. 16, *somnium de Anastasia* 1–47, p. 842–46   cf. *carm de vita*, 1079ff., 1126ff., p. 730–32   *or.* 23, 5

[4] Greg. Nyssa, *or. de deitate filii et spir. sanct.*   3, 466, ed. Paris

name, had arrived in Constantinople.[1] He had formerly been a member of the Nicene party in Alexandria, his birthplace, and had suffered exile as a consequence. He now joined himself to Gregory. The latter regarded the conceited coxcomb as a person of some consequence, with his coloured hair, his mantle and stick of cynic fashion, and his smooth way of speaking. Gregory went so far, indeed, as to commend him to his church, in a panegyric one Holy day,[2] as the pattern of a complete philosopher and a martyr of the true faith. And then, to Gregory's pained astonishment, a certain Egyptian who had unexpectedly come to the city suddenly, one evening, consecrated this man bishop of Constantinople. At the back of the malicious bit of work was Peter of Alexandria, who had been enviously observing Gregory's growing prestige. Peter preferred a creature indebted to himself on the episcopal throne of the capital, rather than that it should go to a supporter of the hateful Meletius. The coup created a great sensation, and Maximus left the city with all haste; but he only went as far as Thessalonica, there to beg the emperor to recognize his installation; naturally, in vain. The disillusioned pretender then went to Alexandria to his sponsor, and there were stormy scenes. In the end the prefect, taking precautions, expelled him from the city as a disturber of the peace. For Gregory, the whole episode was extremely painful, especially seeing that his own rhetorical commendation of Maximus was still fresh in popular memory. At the first shock, he wanted to resign his position, but the pressing requests of his church proved to him that he had not lost the confidence of his own people.[3]

At this point, the great change took place in Constantinople itself. Theodosius entered the capital on November 24, 380. Bishop Demophilus was confronted with the question whether he would submit to the emperor's decree regarding the faith; and he gave a negative answer. He left the city on November 26, followed, among others, by that Lucius who had once been bishop of Alexandria.[4] The emperor graciously received Gregory in audience, and appointed him to the cathedral

[1] Gregory's record in *carm, de vita*, v. 750–1056
[2] Greg. *or.* 25   cf. Jerome *vir inl.*, 117
[3] *Or.* 26 dates from this period   [4] *vide supra*, p. 25

church of the city, the Church of the Apostles,[1] in place of his modest chapel. Theodosius went so far as to accompany him personally in solemn procession to the sacred building. The Nicene party, which had assembled there in congregation, demanded the bishop's throne for Gregory in scenes of tumultuous acclaim. Outside, however, the populace surged in front of the ranks of soldiers protecting the church and the procession, and shouted their disappointment at the deposition of Demophilus; all the streets and squares re-echoed with complaints at the loss of the old customs of the church. Hatred for Gregory was so fierce that plans were seriously made to assassinate him.[2] Theodosius, on the other hand, continued on his way unruffled; Gregory kept discreetly in the background, and took pains to make friends even among the opposite party.

Meletius came to Constantinople in the meantime. Having ridded Antioch of the schism, he was the most influential person in the east, and was now making vigorous use of his opportunities. He felt that the neo-orthodoxy of the east had been compelled long enough to bow to the west and to bear with the whims of Peter of Alexandria. Already the movement was a force which had to be reckoned with in its own right, and was able to arrange its affairs according to its own will. A new law, promulgated on January 10, 381, declared that all dioceses, without exception, were to be handed over to orthodox bishops, and that heretics were no longer to be allowed to conduct public worship. A person was defined as orthodox if he confessed God and Christ according to the Nicene formula, and did not offend by denying the Holy Spirit; in addition he must accept, in the right sense, the undivided nature, *ousia*, of the Trinity. Less than twelve months before this date, Theodosius had regarded the popes of Rome and Alexandria as the guarantors of orthodoxy; but, by now, he had learned to look at questions of faith from the eastern standpoint, Meletius having been his mentor and guide.

Round about this time, the emperor sent out summonses to

---

[1] Greg. *or.* 42, 26   *carm. in somn. de Anast.* (*hist.* 16) v. 58–59 p. 846   C. Ullmann, *Greg. Naz.* (2nd ed., 1867) 153f.
[2] *ibid. carm. de vita*, 1441–72 p. 750

a council of the empire in Constantinople, which was intended to bring the whole of the confusions of the past once for all to an end. But, in order to make quite sure, only trustworthy persons were invited. This principle was now interpreted in the sense favourable to those who belonged to the circle of Meletius, or at least, those who, at an earlier date, had stood by him. The latter conditions applied to those who were known as the "Macedonians", 36 of whose bishops from the region of the Dardanelles accepted the invitation. When these bishops had examined the emperor's requirements more closely, they insisted, to the dismay of Meletius, on denying the *homoousios*, and walked out of the council. Because of their former attitude to Meletius, none of the bishops from Egypt or from Macedonia had been invited to the council, which therefore consisted essentially of bishops from the provinces of Asia Minor, Syria, and Palestine; according to a later official tradition, they numbered 150 delegates.[1] The minutes of this synod are not extant, so that we have to depend on the accounts of the church historians, incidental records, and canons preserved in law-books.[2]

The first question requiring attention was that of the appointment to the see of Constantinople. Under the chairmanship of Meletius, the synod declared the ordination of Maximus to be void;[3] Gregory of Nazianzus was then elected. He accepted, but with many misgivings, in the hope of being able to bridge the gulf, which was very obvious for all to see, between east and west.[4] But all hopes of agreement were dashed by the sudden death of Meletius shortly afterwards, a personal catastrophe, too, for Gregory. For good or ill, he had to take on the leadership of the synod, a synod whose passions could not be kept in bounds by brilliant oratory, but only by a firm hand, such as the sickly Gregory did not possess. The moment had arrived when the gesture of recognizing the aged Paulinus as the bishop of Antioch would have affected the

---

[1] Lists have been preserved in the Latin Canons (cf. Labbé, *Conc.* 2, 955ff.) but of doubtful value cf. Tillemont, *Mémoires*, 9, 716, No. 42.
[2] Accounts in Socr. 5, 8 Sozom. 7, 7–9 Theodoret 5, 6, 3–8, 9 Canons in Labbé, *Conc.* 2, 945ff.
[3] Can. 4, 1558–61 p. 754f.
[4] Greg. *carm. de vita* v. 1514ff. 1525ff. 1533 1538

whole of the east, including Egypt which had always been faithful to Nicea; and the gesture would have acted as a much needed glacis for fellowship with the west.[1] Gregory was anxious to seize the opportunity; instead, however, there was now seen, for the first time, the full measure of the profound embitterment occasioned by Rome's indifference to the necessities of the east during the seventh decade of the century. The result was that the hatred felt by the east poured in full flood on Paulinus when he was advanced by the west and by Egypt in concert. The gesture, which Gregory intended as an act of reconciliation, was indignantly swept aside, even though he threatened to resign otherwise.[2] He fell ill, was unable to leave the house, and had to abandon the raging tumult to its own devices.

The emperor wished to avoid any increase in the cleavage between east and west, and was therefore concerned about Gregory's policy. He now proceeded to enjoin the presence of "the Egyptians and Macedonians", and ordered them to attend the synod as soon as possible. Timothy of Alexandria appeared at the head of these messengers of peace, having succeeded his brother Peter on the latter's death in the previous February. Acholius of Thessalonica was associated with him in the leadership. In Gregory's phrase, they came with a raw west wind.[3] How raw it was he soon learned in his own person. For at a much earlier date, Acholius had received private instructions from Damasus. These were to the effect that, at the council, if the occasion arose, he should abandon Maximus as a fraud, but at the same time take care lest Gregory obtained the see of Constantinople.[4] The last remark did not mention any actual name, but its meaning was made no less clear by referring to the notorious canon 15 of Nicea.[5] Acholius acted accordingly.

The new peace-makers had scarcely arrived at the council when the storm blew up against Gregory. His consecration was declared irregular because he was the bishop of Sasima, and

---

[1] Greg. *carm. de vita* v. 1611–15 1636f. p. 758f.
[2] *ibid. carm. de vita* v. 1671 p. 762   [3] *ibid. carm. de vita* 1798–1802
[4] Damasus, *ep.* 8, *"decursis"* p. 535 and *ep.* 9 p. 539 Coustant   Also Ambros. *ep.* 13, 7 regarding the presence of Acholius
[5] *vide supra*, 26f. Greg. *carm. de vita* v. 1807–15 p. 770

could not transfer to another see. The attack was so unexpected and so violent that Gregory capitulated at once. He resigned his office, delivered a beautiful and touching farewell address to the assembled fathers,[1] and disappeared from church politics, for which he was indeed unsuited. The emperor nominated a certain Nektarius of Tarsus in Cilicia,[2] a jurist who was entirely remote from church affairs, and who in fact at that time had not even been baptized. He was baptized forthwith, and thereupon unanimously elected and installed. It may even be true that Timothy of Alexandria was among those who "laid hands on" him.[3] The bishops of the province of *Syria prima* and the eastern dioceses met together, paid no attention to the justifiable claims of Paulinus, but elected as bishop of Antioch a certain Flavian, one of the local presbyters. To this step Meletius's church agreed. The second synod of Constantinople, which met in A.D. 382, expressly subscribed to this election.[4]

Naturally this way of settling affairs at Antioch was intolerable to both Rome and Alexandria, and now both these bishops suffered further annoyance by the canons passed on July 9, 381, by the general council. Canon 3 accorded to the bishop of Constantinople precedence over all the other eastern bishops and second only to the bishop of Rome, "because the former city is the New Rome". This implied the repudiation of a claim long made by Alexandria. If the east really ought to have a pope, the synod, naturally in consonance with the emperor, wished to identify him with the bishop of Constantinople. On the other hand, the feeling in Rome was to accord the position of honour rather to Alexandria, on the basis of their long established relations—and utterly to repudiate the eastern principle of grading bishoprics according to their political importance.

The second canon had a clear reference to Alexandria. It repeated the prohibition against bishops meddling in other dioceses than their own; and it declared that the five eastern provinces of the empire, Egypt, Oriens, Asia, Pontus, and

---

[1] Greg. *or.* 42 p. 748–68   [2] Socr. 5, 8, 12 Sozom. 7, 8
[3] Marcellinus comes in *Chron. min.* 2, 61, 10
[4] Theodoret, 5, 9, 16 Sozom. 7, 11

Thrace, were independent administrative districts for ecclesiastical purposes. This was a further statement intended to clarify a rule (canon 9) which had been agreed at Antioch at an earlier date, but which only applied to the provinces;[1] it also affected the application of canon 6 of Nicea which accorded a more extended authority to Alexandria and Antioch.

These decisions were all unfriendly acts to the allies, Egypt and Rome, who, on their part, felt that the favourable decrees regarding the faith did not compensate them for the disabilities they suffered. This is borne out, in the first instance, by the details of the pronouncements of the synod,[2] although its actual minutes have not survived. Only a very brief extract has been preserved in the list of the heretics given in the first canon, and in the creed known as the Nicene-Constantinopolitan Symbol, which is still used in the Roman Mass. It is a confession of early-church type such as was used in Palestine, but adapted to the new situation by influences from two quarters, viz. the formulas of Nicea, and references hostile to Marcellus of Ancyra and to the *Pneumatomachoi*. Although doubts have been expressed in recent years, it may now be regarded as proved[3] that these pronouncements were officially decided upon at the present synod. A conclusive argument is the existence of the Greek collection of texts containing the canons of the church,[4] and preserving the covering letter sent to the emperor along with the canons of this synod. This letter requests that the conclusions be ratified because only when sealed by the emperor would they have the force of law. In so doing, the synod accepted the idea of a state-church with the emperor at its head. The emperor must have signified his consent towards the end of July, as is shown by a law bearing the date, July 30, 381.[5] This law gives universal validity to the synod's decrees on faith, as well as to its decisions regarding appointments to episcopal thrones. Moreover, at an earlier date, May 2 of the same year, the emperor had granted a unique privilege to his state-church: those members who

---

[1] cf. Vol. 3, 25f. and compare 204f.   Nicene canon, 4
[2] Theodoret, 5, 9, 13   [3] E. Schwartz in *ZNW*, 1926, 38–88
[4] Labbé, *Concilia* 2, 946   Beneschewitsch, *Syntagma* 14 *titulorum sec. vers. palaeosloven* (Petersburg 1906) 1, 94
[5] *Cod. Theod.* 16, 1, 3

became renegades into paganism were to be punished by
losing the right to make wills.[1] Christianity was now the
religion of the state in the full sense of that phrase.

From the theological standpoint, the synod of Constantinople
was important because the Arian controversy was now quite
at an end, and the doctrine of the Trinity had become an
accepted doctrine of the church. At Nicea, *homoousia* had only
been affirmed with reference to the Father and the Son; but
now, and for the first time, it was expressly asserted that prayer
could be addressed with equal propriety to the Holy Spirit;
this was one way of formulating the theology of the Trinity.
It had taken decades of contention and hard thinking before
the east had fought its way through to this conclusion, a
conclusion reached long before by the west by their religious
instinct, and without any particular difficulty. The step that
was crucial in the agreement reached at Constantinople was
taken by Basil; and what he had begun, his friend, Gregory
of Nazianzus, and his brother, Gregory of Nyssa, carried
further. In this way, the "Cappadocian Fathers" gave the
final shape to the Greek doctrine of the Trinity, in a form
which has proved normative for the theology of the eastern
church ever since.

We have already shown[2] how the synod held at Alexandria
in A.D. 362 smoothed the way for the union of the different
parties in the church. It decided that, granted certain pre-
suppositions, the doctrine of three hypostases should be
regarded as orthodox equally with the doctrine of one hypostasis or *ousia*. This was not a theological solution, but a
compromise reached in the interests of ecclesiastical policy.
A solution only became possible when the words, *hypostasis*
and *ousia*,[3] were no longer given the same fateful content.
The way was then open for expressing in a clear formula the
idea of the relation between unity and trinity.

It was Basil who took this step[4] when he made use of
Aristotelian categories, and declared that *ousia* meant the
general idea, the genus, but *hypostasis* the individual idea, the

[1] *Cod Theod.* 16, 7, 1 with explanatory articles 7, 2 and 7, 3   [2] Vol. 3, 268
[3] cf. the anathemas of the Nicene Creed
[4] Basil, *epist.* 38, 2   214, 4   236, 6   For a fundamental discussion of the whole
problem, cf. K Holl, *Amphilochius v. Iconium* (1909), 122ff.

species. He was fond of using as an illustration: "human" is a general idea connoting the *ousia*; whereas the specific idea differentiates the hypostases: Peter, Andrew, John; or Paul, Silvanus, Timothy. Each of these persons, considered from the standpoint of their *ousia*, is human, and therefore they are all *homoousioi*; each has his *ousia*. On the other hand, as individual persons (*hypostases*), they differ from each other, have their special traits and their individual characteristics which they alone possess, and which do not apply to the others. Peter is not Andrew, nor is he John. By this analogy, we can see that, from the standpoint of *ousia*, Father, Son, and Spirit, each is God; yet the Father is characterized by His Fatherhood, or, to put it negatively, by being "unbegotten", and therefore is not the Son or the Spirit; the specific quality of the Son is in being "begotten"; whereas the appropriate word for the Holy Spirit is "sanctified", or, as Gregory of Nazianzus in particular explained it, the Holy Spirit "proceeded" from the Father.

At first glance, all looked clear and acceptable, but closer examination laid bare the blot on the scutcheon. Peter, Andrew, and John were three men, and, by analogy, Father, Son, and Spirit are three gods. The opponents' criticism immediately fixed on this weak place, and the Cappadocians vied with them in taking pains to deliver their doctrine from the charge of tritheism.[1] This could only be done, of course, by calling in the help of all possible kinds of artificial devices, which in their turn robbed the fundamental idea of its original clarity; although it must be granted that the discussions produced much that was splendidly and profoundly conceived.

The fact is that these thinkers were struggling with a problem that was ultimately insoluble. They were successful in attaining their first objective, that there must be no whittling down of the doctrine[2] which rooted in the theology of Origen, and which had been clearly expressed as far back as the early Eusebians. This doctrine stated the independent existence of three persons in the godhead. But difficulties arose when the attempt was made to combine this doctrine with faith in the

---

[1] K. Holl, *Amphilochius*, 142–53, 173–78, 219–20   Important passages are to be found in Greg. Naz. *or*. 31, 19 (p. 568) and Greg. Nyssa, *quod non sint tres dii*
[2] *vide* Vol. 3, 196f.

entire oneness of the divine nature, a faith which was rooted in the old Monarchianism,[1] and which kept coming ever and again into the forefront with undiminished vigour. The dilemma forced the Cappadocians to adopt formulas and work out artificial theories which came to lack both clarity and logic.

Once on a day, the confession of the divine Triad had been a simple way of expressing the experience of Christian men and women: God had revealed Himself to them in creation as Father; in the redemptive purpose of Jesus Christ, as the Son; and in the life of the church, as the Holy Spirit. Theologians never ceased trying to restate this subjective experience of faith, and express it in objective terms borrowed from philosophy, in order to formulate pronouncements as to the nature of the godhead. In making this attempt, they were led by a genuine Greek confidence in the power of human reason to plumb the very deeps of the divine nature. But the spirit which, according to Paul (1 Cor. 2: 10), penetrates into these ultimate deeps, is not that of the inquiring philosopher, but of the Christian believer who has been laid hold of by God; it is not a human, but a divine spirit. The nature of God is incommensurable with human ways of thought; and, for this reason, the Greek theology of the Trinity was doomed to failure. Augustine tried to pave another road for the west.

[1] *vide* Vol. 2, 191f. Vol. 3, 95, 108

Chapter Three

THE CHURCH IN THE WEST HAD BEEN BADLY SHAKEN BY the policy of force adopted by Constantius. Peace was rapidly restored, however, when Jovian and, more effectively, Valentinian gave the sees back to their bishops, and granted the churches freedom to live their own lives. But scars still remained, in as far as it could not be denied that many bishops had been faithless; too many had bowed to the "Arian" decree of the emperor at Rimini, and had chosen to return home freely rather than to live in exile.

Lucifer of Calaris, at an earlier date, had effectively spoiled the whole policy of reconciliation.[1] When he now returned, he brought up accusations against Zosimus, bishop of Naples, and threatened him with divine judgment. From Sardinia as his headquarters, he organized resistance against the church catholic. Although this effort was insignificant, on the whole it produced a painful impression in some places. He mercilessly criticized Hilary, the head of the church in Gaul, although he had been the most important of those who had fought for the Nicene doctrine of the Trinity. Hilary thought it diplomatic to present him with a copy of his own principal work on theology, to which he had added explanatory glosses in the margin, and a copy of which has still survived.[2] At Cordova, Ossius, who was now in extreme old age, had great difficulty in defending himself from the attacks of Gregory of Elvira. Schismatic churches of "Luciferians" were constituted in several places: in Rome, under a bishop Ephesius; in Trèves, under the priest Bonosus; similarly also in Africa: in Oxyrhynchus (Egypt) and in Eleutheropolis (Palestine, west of Hebron) where Lucifer had lived in exile, opposition conventicles came into being. Naturally, if opportunity offered, they were persecuted by the catholic bishops with or without help

[1] Vol. 3, 269   [2] Karl Holl junr. in his unpublished studies of Hilary

from the state. In A.D. 384, two priests, Faustinus and Marcellinus, described the sufferings of the sect;[1] the record includes many miracles in which God showed His will as favourable to them. A copy was sent to the emperor, Theodosius, who issued an edict granting tolerance to the little movement, which died out with its own generation.

Nevertheless, Liberius of Rome had to bear the consequences of his own defection: the dispute with the opposition pope, Felix,[2] gave him grievous trouble, and the enmity between the two men had fateful effects even after the death of Liberius. Those adherents who remained faithful to him always defended themselves against Felix, asserting that he had been chosen in breach of oaths solemnly taken. And when Liberius died, they refused at first to enter into negotiations, but acted on their own responsibility; and, in the Basilica Juli (S. Maria in Trastevere), they chose Ursinus, a deacon, to be pope. At the same time, in the church of Lucina (S. Lorenzo in Lucina, near the Corso), the great majority elected the ambitious deacon, Damasus, to the throne. The latter was the son of a Roman cleric, well acquainted from his youth up with all the relations between city and church. He was also the favourite of the devout and very wealthy women of the upper classes, who, in the period after the death of Constantine, began to play an important part in the church of Rome.

Battle immediately broke out between the two sides in a manner unheard of before in Rome. The churches became the castles of the popes. First of all, a rabble retained by Damasus stormed the Basilica Juli and raged there for three days, while Damasus himself stayed in the Lateran protected by his guards; he persuaded Viventius, the city prefect, to expel Ursinus together with two deacons. But his further desires met with violent opposition of the crowds who barricaded themselves, together with the clerics who were endangered, in the church of Liberius (S. Maria Maggiore). A regular siege then began, with attack by storm; doors were burst in, and flaming torches thrown into the building. By the evening of October 26, 366, one hundred and sixty dead bodies of both sexes lay on the

[1] Known as the *Libellus precum* in the *Collectio Avellana*, 2 and 2a
[2] *vide* Vol. 3, 225f.

ground—the besiegers recorded no losses. Ammianus Marcellinus, who also gives an account of the occasion, speaks of 137 bodies. Yet he says, with a certain irony, that on the whole it was really worth while for people to act like that; for the victors in this struggle could assuredly reckon on the great generosity of the rich ladies, ride about in fine carriages, wear splendid clothes, and feast like kings. As compared with all this, the minor provincial bishops were to be regarded as fortunate; they had no cares, but lived modestly as pure and honourable worshippers of the eternal God.[1] The judgment has a bitter taste, but it is true. Even at that early date, i.e., less than a generation after the death of Constantine, we see how the secularized Christianity of the cities looked in the eyes of a pagan of good standing. The Christian church had triumphed politically, and thought it could dispense with further moral conquests. The struggle with Ursinus continued in ding dong fashion, but was now conducted to a greater extent through the official channels. It began to penetrate into many other departments; it ended, of course with the victory of Damasus who disposed of greater material resources, and who had better social contacts.

Towards the end of Liberius's lifetime, the after-effects of the anti-Nicene policy of Constantius were definitely traceable, in the west, only at Milan and in the "Illyrian" frontier districts of the northern Balkans. Records have survived telling of the discussions between the "semi-Arians", Ursacius, Valens, Gaius, Paul, et alii, with Germinius of Sirmium (Mitrovitza). The discussions took place at a synod meeting in December, A.D. 366, at Singidunum (Belgrade).[2] The court party in this district still felt itself strong. All this was very disagreeable to the "Nicene" bishops in the neighbourhood, especially in Venice and the alpine districts; and they seemed to have complained about the situation to the emperor, Valentinian. The emperor ordered that matters should be investigated at a synod to be held in Rome, with the result that 93 bishops gathered there under the chairmanship of Damasus; the precise year, however, cannot now be determined

[1] Coll. Avell. n. 1   and Am. Marc. 27, 3, 11–14
[2] Hilar. 4, 159–64

with certainty.[1] They sent a mild reproof to the Illyrians, in which they declared themselves unwilling to think that there was any serious intention of heresy; rather it must be that the true cause of a certain oscillation in holding the faith was either ignorance of the facts, or a simple-mindedness in understanding them. It was for such a reason, indeed, that, once on a time, even a person like Auxentius of Milan had been condemned. They went on to point out, on the other hand, that the Nicene creed, including the doctrine of the *homoousia* of the Holy Spirit, was the only criterion of faith; and they hoped that those bishops who were of another opinion would be excommunicated; they definitely repudiated the decrees of Rimini; and they also asked for a reply signifying agreement.

Of course these gentle phrases were of no avail; it had been similarly useless for those who made complaints about the condemnation of Auxentius. There was nothing else for it than that Damasus should "name" the delinquents. A new synod, therefore, declared the excommunication of Ursacius, Valens, and their associates. Athanasius sent congratulations to Damasus for what he had done, and this in the name of a synod in Egypt. At the same time, he deplored the fact that Auxentius still had unrestricted possession of the see of Milan. Athanasius sent word to the church in Africa, in an official letter from the synod, telling of what he had done.[2] We have pointed out, in a foregoing chapter,[3] that Valentinian refused to follow in the ways of Constantius, but allowed Auxentius to remain for life quietly in possession of his diocese, in spite of these theological pronouncements against him. When it came to a question of politics, this emperor brooked no interference on the part of the bishops.

There is room for some doubt whether Damasus was, in fact, greatly interested in affairs that went beyond his concerns in the city of Rome. He had plenty of anxieties of a domestic character at the beginning of his pontificate. His calm indifference, which we have already noted,[4] caused him to

---

[1] The document "*Confidimus*" (Schwartz in *ZNW*, 1936, 19–20), but the original address is given by Theodoret, *H.E.* 2, 22, 2=Soz. 6, 23, 7 *vide* E. Caspar, *Papsttum*, I (1930), 593
[2] Athanasius *epist. ad Afros*, 10, 3 p. 317, Opitz   [3] *vide supra*, 24f.
[4] *vide supra*, 26f., 30

disregard all requests coming from the eastern bishops. His attitude may well have been due to the fact that he did not feel himself firmly enough seated in the saddle to conduct a foreign policy in great style. He therefore contented himself with proud looks, by which he intended that his real weakness should be covered up. The fact is that both the Luciferians and the Donatists had active churches of their own in Rome, complete with bishops; a state of affairs which was very contrary to the mind of pope Damasus. Indeed the adherents of Ursinus tried to get at him during the street riots by indirect attacks. Records tell of a criminal charge by a Jew called Isaac which was due to be heard by the vicarius Maximinus.[1] This was the result of a plot, perhaps in A.D. 370, which originated among these people. The judge was known as a ruthless man of action; and he had in fact executed a fairly large number of the members of the upper class in Rome on a charge of practising magic. Even in the case of Damasus, he did not hesitate to act; he arrested and hanged numerous clerics. The proceedings might well have gone as far as to cost Damasus his life, if events had not suddenly taken another turn: for the emperor intervened in his favour. The blame then naturally rebounded on the heads of those who had brought the charges, with the result that Isaac had to go in exile to Spain.[2] Meanwhile, the pope's reputation suffered a severe blow.

It is not surprising that outsiders rather despised the authority of a bishop who was unable to assert himself unchallenged in his own see. We learn that the bishop of Parma defied the decree which had deposed him; that the bishop of Puteoli, who had been dealt with six years earlier, and, at that time, had vainly appealed to the emperor for help, now quietly returned and resumed office. The bishop of a see in Africa, ordered by the emperor to appear for trial before the bishop of Rome, simply withdrew from the process.

This state of affairs continued year after year until at length it became intolerable. Towards the end of A.D. 378, a synod[3]

---

[1] Seeck, *Untergang*, 5, 18, 17 and the note on p. 430
[2] Rufin, *hist. eccl.* 11, 10   Damasus, *epist.* 6, 9   *Coll. Avell.* n. 13, 5
[3] For the date, cf. Seeck, *Regesten*, p. 152, 30

was held in Rome attended by "almost innumerable" bishops "from various parts of Italy". Damasus submitted himself to their judgment, with success. Eight years earlier, he had been declared free from their jurisdiction in legal matters; and to this was now added, that he was not subject to the assembly of clerics, even in moral questions.[1] The synod itself then wrote at length to the emperor, Gratian, described the diminished respect in which Rome was held, and prayed the emperor's most gracious intervention. The assembly requested two decrees, and even went as far as to make suggestions regarding both suitable phraseology and the principles involved.[2] At an earlier date, as a consequence of the disturbances centring on Ursinus, it had been laid down by Valentinian[3] that "the bishop of Rome was to have the oversight of the priests of the church, to the extent that the pope and his councillors were to determine questions of religion". The principle is expressed by another ancient authority in the form: "in matters of faith and questions affecting their status, the clergy are to be judged by their own peers". On the other hand, it had never been possible to bring this imperial edict into satisfactory effect, because, as we have already pointed out, the bishops concerned were averse to it; and also because the administration betrayed little eagerness to give it validity by asserting the authority of the state.

But now, following a request from the Roman synod, the emperor issued orders to the vicarius Aquilinus; he expressed his displeasure, in vigorous language and without any polite and diplomatic phrases, that his commands had not been put into operation. After making one or two appropriate and intentional alterations, he now gave the force of law to the first proposal of the synod: a person deposed by Damasus and his synod, or by any other general synod, but refusing to obey, was to be expelled from office by the state. Accused persons refusing to obey a summons to appear before the

---

[1] Damasus, *epist.* 6, 10
[2] Dam. *epist.* 6 ("*et hoc gloriae*", p. 523 Coustant and the answer, *epist.* 7 p. 530=*Coll. Avell.* n. 13 p. 54–58 Günther, discussed by Caspar, *Zeitschr. f. Kirchengesch.* 47 (1928), 178–202
[3] Damasus, *ep.* 6, 2 Ambrose, *ep.* 21, 2

Roman court, were to be compelled to do so by forces at the disposal of the state. In the more distant provinces, the metropolitan was to try his own clerics; but he himself was subject to the jurisdiction of Rome or of some court appointed by the pope. A provincial cleric might appeal against the verdict either to the pope, or to fifteen bishops of a neighbouring province. It is known expressly that the praetorian prefects of Italy and Gaul were entrusted with enforcing this decree; and it follows, therefore, that it applies to the whole of the western empire, including Britain, Spain, and Africa. The consequence was that the celebrated canon of Serdika,[1] which had hitherto lacked practical effect, was now brought into sharper focus; and the status of the bishop of Rome was considerably enhanced. Of course, the Roman synod was well aware of the implications when it made the proposal to Gratian, and the proclamation promulgated in the form of an imperial rescript would now ensure in actual practice that the supreme court was the pope's. Moreover, it is obvious why the emperor gave his blessing to the synod's desire; for it could be nothing but agreeable to the state, either to have a clearer definition of the competence of the church, or that its organization should now be made visible at a glance. Nevertheless, it was a vain hope, for once again we hear nothing further of the results which the synod had sought.

The synod made a second request, however, a request illumined by the scandal of the trial of Isaac.[2] The senators had the privilege that, when they were tried on capital charges, their depositions must be laid before the emperor for a final verdict: the *relatio ad principem*.[3] In practice, this privilege was also granted to bishops—at least in important cases—and it had served to deliver Damasus from the blood-stained hands of Maximinus.[4] The synod now proposed that charges against the pope, which, of course, exceeded the competence of the spiritual courts, should be possible only if initiated by the emperor, and should be decided only by him. Although Gratian did not agree to this proposal, he comforted those

---

[1] cf. Vol. 3, 204f.   [2] *vide supra*, p. 54
[3] Mommsen, *Rom. Strafrecht*, 205   *Cod. Theod.* 9, 1, 13   2, 2   40, 10
[4] Dam. *ep.* 6, 9   The opposite in the case of Priscillian,   Sulp. Sever. *Chron.* 2, 50, 8

who put it forward by drawing attention to his natural sense of justice, and he gave assurances that he would himself see to the defence of a bishop against charges brought by malicious persons. Damasus had to be content with this reply; but he took care that the particular instance in mind did not recur in his case.

Meanwhile, when Theodosius came to the throne, ecclesiastical politics in the eastern empire entered upon a new phase. After a promising start had been made, the dubious consequences began to appear which followed on the policy of indifference and arrogance adopted by Damasus. Moreover, a leaf was now taken from his book by an incomparably stronger personality, by one, moreover, who, as the personal adviser of Gratian, stood close to the throne: Ambrose had come upon the scene. When Auxentius died in Milan in A.D. 374, there was naturally a severe contest for the succession; Ambrose, who was resident in Milan as the governor of the province of Liguria-Aemilia, entered the church to settle the uproar. He was an energetic governor, honoured and loved by the people; and he was now chosen bishop amid tumultuous acclamation. Already a catechumen, he was speedily baptized; on December 7, 374, he was installed.[1] This was the first time in the west that a member of the upper class of high officials— for the father of Ambrose had been the *praefectus praetorio* of Gaul—had accepted the office of bishop. This fact alone made a deep impression, but it must be granted that the impression made by the personality of Ambrose himself was still deeper.

On an earlier page, we have already seen how, while Auxentius was still alive, the orthodox bishops of northern Italy tried to persuade the emperor, Valentinian, to deal sharply with the Arianism which was dominant in Illyria. Their efforts were unsuccessful, and resulted in nothing more than an ecclesiastical condemnation pronounced by the Roman synod.[2] But now, with the accession of Ambrose, the Nicene party had found a young and vigorous leader, who carried the war into the enemy's camp. He gathered in Sirmium a synod of like-minded delegates, who accepted and

[1] The year is confirmed by Jerome, *Chron.* p. 247, 16 and 21f., Helm.
[2] *vide supra*, 25f., 52f.

underlined the articles recently formulated in Rome. They also condemned certain bishops, and informed the brethren in Asia, Phrygia, and Caria, of their decisions. Why it should have been these brethren in particular, remains obscure; but we do know that, in those parts, the opponents of Nicea were specially active. A further observation to be made is that our information in regard to the circumstances of the period is far from complete, and is also dependent, to some extent, on documents which have been preserved by accident. Even as regards the synod at Sirmium, our information is derived partly from the work of Theodoret, a church-historian of the following century,[1] who reproduces the minutes, many of which, by the way, are now incomprehensible; and partly from the incidental remark of a contemporary writer, Maximinus,[2] who relates that Ambrose took a responsible part in the proceedings. The synod communicated its findings to the emperor, who immediately sent them to Asia Minor, covered by a letter of pains and penalties. The record declares that this emperor was Valentinian, but the assertion is scarcely credible. Rather the probability is that the decree was promulgated by Gratian at a later time; it would be more comprehensible at a time when Valens had changed his point of view;[3] a date about A.D. 377 seems likely.

Valentinian died on November 17, 375, of an apoplectic seizure occasioned by an ungoverned outburst of temper. A few days later, his little four-year-old son of the same name was acclaimed Augustus. The consequence was that Gratian, the elder brother, who had previously been nominated Augustus by their father in A.D. 367, became the guardian of the boy, and thus the ruler of the entire west, Illyria, Macedonia, and Greece being included. The new imperial master, Gratian, was then 16 years of age, and for spiritual guidance looked to Ausonius, a professor of Bordeaux, whom his father had appointed to be his tutor. Ausonius, as citizen, orator, poet, and Christian, conformed to the standards of the time; he was an educated man skilled in impressing on his young

---

[1] Theodoret, *H.E.* 4, 7, 6–11, 8   Also see Campenhausen, *Ambrosius*, 32–36, 93–95   J. Zeiller, *Les Origines Chrét. dans les prov. Danubiennes* (Bibl. des écoles franc. n. 102, 1918) pp. 310–327
[2] Maximinus, *dissertatio*, 128, p. 87, Kauffmann   [3] *vide supra*, 33f.

pupil the value of certain things which the royal father had lacked. The young emperor was in Trèves when the news of Valentinian's death arrived, and, in a speech composed by Ausonius, he assured the Roman senate of his goodwill.[1] Shortly afterwards, in the province of Gaul, salaries paid by the state were provided for professors of rhetoric and the classical languages.[2] About the same time also,[3] a law appears to have been promulgated, ordering the seizure of heretical places of worship; but this law was only half-heartedly administered by the authorities. It seemed as if a new period was opening in which educated interests and also the life of the church would receive encouragement and support, and when the harshness of Valentinian's rule would give place to clemency and humanity. The spirit breathed by Ausonius could be detected in the words and deeds of the emperor; his name glittered among those nominated as consuls for A.D. 379, side by side with that of a member of the aristocracy. Meantime also, his relatives, one and all, were advanced into desirable posts.

When Valens fell near Adrianople, Gratian issued certain preliminary measures. As we have already indicated,[4] he ordained peace for most of the parties in the restless church of the east; and, in extending the scope of the last pardon decreed by Valens,[5] he allowed the exiled bishops to return home. Theodosius added to this, and gave clear directions that his church should conform to the Nicene creed as sealed by the council of Constantinople in A.D. 381. But before the new ruler began his work, bishops of the former Macedonian party met in Antioch in Caria, a city from which, eleven years earlier, a proclamation of an anti-Nicene character had been issued.[6] These bishops spoke with all their old firmness against *homoousios* and in favour of *homoiousios*. And this was meant to be their response to the synod of Sirmium which Ambrose had inspired.

In the west, meantime, Ambrose, the new bishop of Milan, had tested his talents, and concluded that he was called to be

---

[1] Symmachus, *epist.* 1, 13
[3] *ibid.* 16, 5, 4 says "*olim*" in regard to the year 378
[5] *vide supra*, 33

[2] *Cod. Theod.* 13, 3, 11
[4] *vide supra*, 35
[6] *vide supra*, 19

a leader in the church's warfare. Ambrose waited on the emperor Gratian, when the latter was about to depart to the east in aid of Valens, and was honoured with a commission[1] to draw up for His Majesty a conspectus of the Christian faith. This document, which was sent to the emperor in the field, has come down to us as the first two books of *de fide*. It suggested, in the conclusion, that the incursion of the Goths into the country south of the Danube must be regarded as the divine punishment for the Arian heresy which prevailed there.[2] At the end of July, A.D. 379, Gratian returned again to Milan; and there can be no doubt that he granted audiences to Ambrose for the sake of theological discussions. The issue was a law, signed on August 3, which expressly repealed the edict of tolerance promulgated at Sirmium, and prohibited as heretical every form of worship to be found outside the church catholic.[3]

Even before this time, Ambrose had stood in the good graces of the emperor, and he was now protected from legal proceedings by a strong avowal of confidence.[4] He had gained the young ruler to the side of his policy for the church, and he could now use increased powers, with broadened prospects of success, to root out the Arian heresy in northern Italy and Illyria. This seemed to him to be entirely necessary, whether from the standpoint of the church or that of politics. For the hostility of the Arians to the established church, with its Nicene character, inevitably caused the Illyrians, i.e. the inhabitants of the region which, at that time, was most endangered, to clash with their fellow-believers among the Goths; and that is apparently what was frequently threatened.[5] We have already described what took place in the first instance in Sirmium. There now broke out a fierce literary quarrel with Palladius, bishop of Ratiaria (Artsher, on the bend of the Danube below Vidin in Bulgaria), a person whom Ambrose had mentioned by name, and described as an Arian leader, in that summary of the faith which he had presented to the emperor.[6] When attacked, Palladius defended himself; nor

---

[1] Ambr. *de fide* 1 *prol.* 3
[2] *ibid. de fide* 2, 16, 139–41
[3] *Cod. Theod.* 16, 5, 5
[4] Ambr. *ep.* 1, 2   Maxim. *diss.* 84
[5] Maxim. *diss.* 13 *Coll. Avell.* 39, 4   Ambr. *ep.* 10, 9f.   *de fide* 2, 16, 140–41
[6] Ambr. *de fide* 1, 6, 45

did he refrain from making personal aspersions.[1] Ambrose then sent to the emperor the next instalment of his polemic against Arianism, in the form of three more books (III—V) of his work, *de fide*.[2] Of greater consequence was the resistance offered by the bishops of northern Italy, led by Ambrose, to the decision of Damasus rehabilitating Leontius, the deposed bishop of Salona. They simply refused to agree, and, as far as the bishops of northern Italy were concerned, the bishop of Salona, because suspected of Arianism, remained a cursed heretic.[3]

The Arian bishop of Sirmium died about this time, and was succeeded by Anemius, a Nicenean, a candidate put forward by Ambrose; he was successful on account of the latter's personal intervention and in spite of the passionate resistance of Justina, the dowager empress.[4] But the party in the opposite camp were strong enough to cause Gratian concern, for the danger from the Goths was by no means overcome. He therefore decided to promise a general council of the empire to the threatened Illyrians, which the eastern bishops would also be invited to attend; Aquileia was fixed as the place of meeting. It would seem that Theodosius, too, thought it would be an advantage to hold a general council of the church in view of the contemporary conditions. The "Arians" of Illyria, headed by Palladius, felt quite happy at the proposal, for they could rightly count on support for their side from the numerous persons of similar views in the east, who favoured the formulas of Rimini and Seleukia, formulas regarded by them as the best and most satisfactory solution on account of their lack of theological precision on the question of union.

The leaders of the Nicene party, in both east and west, however, quickly scented danger, and exercised sufficient political influence to avoid it. Theodosius followed the advice of Meletius, and invited to his capital a council of his own consisting of eastern bishops of a pronounced Nicene character. Gratian, on his part, was persuaded by Ambrose to make the synod at Aquileia into a meeting confined to bishops of northern Italy, and not to issue invitations to those in other regions.

---

[1] fragments in Maxim. *diss*. 82. 84–87, esp. 84
[2] Ambr. *de fide* 3, 1, 1f.
[3] Maxim. *diss*. 125–28   *vide infra*, 63f.
[4] Paulinus, *vita Ambr*. 11

Palladius had a personal audience with Gratian in Sirmium, and was once again assured that the eastern bishops had been invited. Thereupon, he and his friend, Secundianus (who was perhaps bishop of Singidunum=Belgrade), travelled to Aquileia, where he perceived, with dismay, that he had been deceived. The only persons who attended were twelve from northern Italy, five from southern Gaul, with two deputies from Africa, and, from Illyria, four trustworthy Nicenean bishops led by the very Anemius of Sirmium whom Ambrose himself had but recently installed. The more wary Illyrians had stayed away. In spite of these circumstances, Palladius, who was somewhat simple in his sense of honour, ventured to take part in the proceedings; but, before he quite knew what was happening, he found himself in the role of defendant round whose neck Ambrose had placed the noose, with surpassing skill. A large number of the records have survived in which Ambrose reported the proceedings;[1] here we find a vivid picture of the revolting injustice of this heresy-hunt. In the end, and in spite of their protests against the proceedings, the two miscreants, Palladius and Secundianus, were solemnly condemned as Arians.

The council immediately informed the emperor, and used the most bombastic phraseology in doing so.[2] It asked for his support in carrying out the sentences of deposition, and in the installation of orthodox successors. The document then went on to denounce a particularly dangerous "Illyrian" bishop, Julianus Valens by name, who had been driven from his church at Pettau on a charge of high treason. He had fraternized with the Goths, and now, with Milan as his base, was carrying on Arian propaganda in Italy, consecrating likeminded persons as bishops contrary to the law, and so gathering a party round about his own person. The emperor was also requested to suppress in Sirmium a very persistent church which supported Photinus.

Following upon the emperor's assent, Syagrius, the *praefectus praetorio*, took energetic measures against the condemned

---

[1] In the works of Ambrose, after *ep.* 8 (opera, 2, 786–805) Labbé, *Concilia*, 2, 979–92   Also latterly, cf. Kauffmann, *diss. Maxim.* 39–63   The concluding portions of the minutes have been lost   The date is September 3, 381
[2] Ambr. *ep.* 19

Arians.[1] Palladius did himself no good by publishing a protest attacking Ambrose, and venturing to demand a public debate on religion which was to last forty days, and to be conducted in the Roman senate in the presence of Christian Biblical scholars, pagans, and Jews. Finally, the two Illyrians tried to use the Gothic bishop, Wulfila, as an intermediary in securing an audience of Theodosius in Constantinople.[2] Unfortunately, their patron died shortly after reaching the capital;[3] moreover, there was only disappointment for the hope that a synod would be assembled and opportunity given during the proceedings for an unfettered statement.[4] Nicea conquered all along the line in both east and west, and an otherwise unknown bishop, named Maximinus, wrote an indignant polemic; he could only bewail the facts, but not alter them.

Now it was not simply the Nicene Creed that had prevailed in Aquileia; the personality of Ambrose had been at least equally victorious. For yet another Illyrian, Leontius of Salona, was deposed at that synod once and for all from his office. Leontius had been condemned for defective theology at an earlier date by a council of northern Italy led by Ambrose, and it had been Damasus who had ordered him to appear before that spiritual court. But when condemned, Leontius had made his way again to Rome, where he was fortunate enough to be declared orthodox. He had therefore journeyed to Aquileia in a happy frame of mind with hopes that his earlier sentence of condemnation would be revised. Ambrose, however, was relentless in spite of the verdict passed by Damasus.[5] When it suited his purpose, he ascribed much credit to the authority of Rome, and went as far himself as to read out three of Damasus' letters to the assembly.[6] Nevertheless, he refused to be deflected by a hair's-breadth from his policy of conquering Illyria in the interests, both of the Nicene faith, and of his own authority as bishop of Milan. He made up for this to Damasus by doing him a pleasure in another respect; for he induced the synod to give detailed reasons for asking the emperor to take energetic measures against Ursinus

---

[1] Max. *diss.* 121
[2] Fragments in Max. *diss.* 81–140
[3] Max. *diss.* 41
[4] *ibid. diss.* 71–73   cf. Socr. 5, 10   Sozom. 7, 12
[5] Maxim. *diss.* 125–26
[6] *ibid. diss.* 122

who was a nuisance on account of his cabals.[1] It is in this connection, by the way, that the records tell of the opposition-bishop in Rome, and say that he had made common cause with the Julianus Valens in Milan who had proved himself dangerous to Ambrose.

The council of Aquileia took action in a third direction, and this proved to be the most important; for it gave Ambrose an opening for snatching from Damasus's hands the reins of eastern policy, and for making himself the spokesman of the west. An extraordinary, and not altogether welcome visitor appeared on one of the days in Aquileia, viz. Maximus, who had already been turned down by Damasus as an impossible person, and who had also since been expelled from Egypt.[2] It was the very man who, a year earlier, had played a part against Gregory of Nazianzus as a candidate for the see of Constantinople. His present scheme was to take advantage of the pretended invitation to Aquileia addressed to the eastern bishops, and to attend this "ecumenical council" to gain support there for his claims to the see of the capital. He proved that he was in fellowship with Peter of Alexandria, and that his ordination was all in order; he was therefore recognized by the council as an orthodox bishop.[3]

Meanwhile, fuller and more accurate details had arrived in Aquileia about the outcome of the council of Constantinople, whereupon Ambrose decided to take up the gage against the triumphant group of eastern bishops. A letter on behalf of the synod[4] was addressed to the emperor, i.e. in the first instance to Theodosius. This letter expressed the concern felt in the west about the unrest in the east among the "catholics" who were now agreed as regards the faith. The problem raised by the refusal to recognize Paulinus in Antioch disturbed the minds of the bishops assembled in Aquileia; they therefore proposed that a general synod of the empire should meet in Alexandria to settle the questions in dispute. The fact that gave occasion for sending out this letter was that the settlement had been undertaken one-sidedly during the preceding summer by the eastern church meeting in Constantinople. But not so

---

[1] Ambrose, *epist.* 11, "*provisum*"   [2] *vide supra*, p. 40f.   [3] Ambr. *ep.* 13, 3–5
[4] *ibid. ep.* 12 "*quamlibet*"

much as a single syllable was said about this fact, although what was felt about it can be deduced from a phrase to the effect that the synods which had met in the capital of the empire had in no way communicated their findings officially to the church in the west. In particular, the bishops in Aquileia explicitly requested that the emperor should confirm the conclusions of the proposed council, and bring them to the attention of the west. It was pointed out, in so many words, that even the churches of Africa and Gaul, through their delegates, shared in this desire. Not a word was said about the election of Flavian, nor even about that of Nektarius: they acted as if they had never heard of these events; moreover, no mention was made of Maximus.

Theodosius was, of course, under no illusion as to what was in their minds; in any case, where he felt doubtful about certain points, he could have them explained at any time by Nektarius. A council of the empire held in Alexandria was just about the last thing which the bishops in the east, which was under Theodosius, would have found agreeable. On the other hand, antagonism on the part of the western bishops was thoroughly undesirable, and exactly what would serve to postpone the work of uniting the east; something therefore had to be done. To meet this situation, Theodosius invited the delegates who had attended the council which had just ended, and asked them to come again to Constantinople[1] for the summer of A.D. 382.

Ambrose was then compelled to recognize that his hopes were in danger of disappointment, and decided to make a final, desperate blow. He arranged that a combined synod should meet in Rome, and that Damasus should collaborate whether he liked it or not. In their name, he wrote[2] to Theodosius expressing in forthright terms what they thought of the synod which was on the point of meeting in Constantinople; Paulinus was the rightful bishop of Antioch, not the person (whose name was not mentioned) who had been installed in disregard of the canons. The election of Nektarius

[1] Theod. *H.E.* 5, 8, 10 cf. Greg. Naz. *ep.* 130, 132 Letter of the synod of Constantinople cf. Theod. *H.E.* 5, 9, 9, p. 291, 9–12 Parmentier
[2] Ambr. *ep.* 13 *sanctum* The succession of the events has been explained by E. Schwartz, *ZNW*, 1935, 207–10

was described as invalid; and, in all seriousness, the impostor, Maximus, was declared to be the rightful incumbent of the see in the capital. The proposed general council had been decided on too hastily in the previous year; and the west had a right to express its opinion and to be considered in regard to Maximus. It now demanded, either that his candidature be recognized, or that the case be settled by the combined east and west at a council to be held in Rome. It was not possible to see in any other way how church fellowship could be maintained between the two halves of the empire.

That was an ultimatum which, in effect, demanded nothing more nor less than submission to Ambrose's dictation. The emperor laid the document before the council at Constantinople; the council replied in very calm tones.[1] The points in the letter sent by Ambrose were either turned by polite phrases, or met with ripostes. On the practical side, they said that, as a mark of goodwill, they would send a delegation of three bishops to Rome. The election of Nektarius to Constantinople and of Flavian to Antioch had been in accordance with the rules laid down by the canons of Nicea; had also been agreed by the council; and were not subject to question. The same held good of Cyril of Jerusalem—a matter to which the west was indifferent. The faith of the eastern church was perspicuously determined by the Nicene Creed: the confession of the three hypostases, the *homoousios* and the perfect manhood of the Lord—in short the whole was there to be read in detail in the creed of Antioch (drawn up by Meletius in A.D. 379[2]), and in that of the synod of Constantinople held in the previous year. Not a single mention was made of Paulinus and Maximus; the synod completely ignored any question of a breach between east and west; it was as if unity, love, and peace prevailed everywhere. In conclusion, the western bishops were even urged to rejoice that affairs in the east were all in excellent order, and they were reminded that the fear of the Lord was able to beat back all tendencies to schism in favour of the will for building up the church.

These soft, flute-like notes, with their scornful overtones, were accompanied by a thunderstorm of the utmost violence

---

[1] Theod. *H.E.* 5, 9, 1–18   [2] *vide supra*, 38

springing from the imperial cabinet-chamber of Theodosius.[1]
To invite the eastern bishops to Rome was not only an unreason-
able request, but also nothing less than insulting. It was an
attempt to remove from the ground the boundary-stones
between east and west which the forefathers had set up. It
would be to transgress beyond the rights that could be established by the traditional fellowship of the church, and would
be to the special advantage of the west.

Ambrose replied in the name of the Roman synod; he used
injured tones, and sang small.[2] In it, the emperor's objections
were described as beside the point: everything that had been
done was solely due to a love of unity; they had desired to
avoid a breach with the east, and did not regret the attempt
which they had made; in any case, it could no longer be said
that the west had no interest in the eastern bishops; above all
else, the essential purpose of the whole enterprise was an
inquisition into the case of Apollinaris, the heretic. It concluded:
"we pay to Your Majesty our due respects, and assure you of
our love of peace and quietness."

This put an end to the quarrel in the main, for neither of
the emperors had any inclination to make it the subject of a
political altercation. Yet the fires continued to smoulder, and,
when occasion arose, burst into flame again. Ambrose was a
protagonist of the claims of the west whose perseverance and
influence far exceeded those of Damasus. He was skilled also
in forming a true estimate of what could be done in the
political field. His present experience taught him to exercise
moderation in future in matters affecting the east. He perceived that it was impossible to gain a complete victory over
the east, and minor gains scarcely paid him for the risks
involved.

[1] As deduced from Ambr. *ep.* 14   [2] Ambr. *ep.* 14, "*fidei*"

Chapter Four

AMBROSE AND THEODOSIUS

GRATIAN, THE RULER OF THE WEST, ATTAINED THE AGE OF twenty years in A.D. 379; his splendid qualities of both body and soul were equally well developed. He could write poems, fence in the schools, deliver addresses, and show his skill with the bow. He was a devout Christian well acquainted with theological issues; he was polite; and moreover he honoured his marriage vow.[1] On the other hand, he was lazy, and without a sense of duty. He left the administration to the officials, and devoted himself to the sport of archery which he loved above all else, and which he practised with his body-guard of Alans. Thus it came about that spiritual concerns were entrusted to his old tutor, Ausonius, who rose from one office to another. Ambrose supplied the important fillips to policy in matters of religion and the church, a fact which clearly indicates their direction, in the manner we have already discussed.[2] Although the particular claims of the churches in the two halves of the empire were frequently opposed to each other, yet Gratian was satisfied that, if he followed the direction pointed out by Ambrose, he would maintain a common front with Theodosius against paganism.

Inscriptions support the testimony of the ancient historian, Zosimos,[3] that Gratian discarded the title, *pontifex maximus*, and in addition declared that he did so in common with Theodosius. From then onwards, the titles of the emperor omitted all reference to this office. The decision to do so was more than a mere formality; it meant the end of state responsibility for pagan worship and religion. Up to that date, and in spite of all prohibitions, even in Rome a large number of contributions were unchallenged by the state as according to ancient custom, and paid to actual persons or to bodies legally responsible for pagan (i.e. state) religion and worship.

[1] The sources are indicated by Seeck in Pauly-Wissowa 7, 1832
[2] *vide supra,* 59f.
[3] Zosimos 4, 36, 5

All this now came at once to an end,[1] and, at the same time, paganism was deprived of the last remnants of its splendour; henceforth it could only subsist as a private conviction, and no longer as a part of a public occasion.

A second piece of evidence showing that the new attitude was unfriendly toward any reminder of the old ways was to be found in the fact that, as formerly under Constantius,[2] so now, the altar of Victory was removed from the senate house. This action roused the aristocracy of Rome, who thought of sending a deputation to the emperor; but Damasus induced many Christian senators to sign a petition to the contrary, and Ambrose prevented the delegates from obtaining an audience.[3]

While the last bonds between the state and its old forms of worship were thus severed in Rome, the two emperors were acting in common to promote the privileges of the church. The decree issued in May, A.D. 383, prohibiting renunciation of the Christian faith, constituted a further step towards according a monopoly for the state-church.[4] A month later, Theodosius went as far as to propose a debate with the heretics, a proposal not without its comic aspects, and which he carried out in a minor form; naturally the Nicene Creed alone was sanctioned. At the same time, it served a useful purpose by demonstrating to the bishops that the emperor laid claim for himself, *ex officio*, to the last word on theological issues.[5] This claim was the obverse to the fact that, in the east, there existed a dominant state-church.

Meantime, and since the spring of A.D. 383, a storm had been brewing in the west, which was to put a violent end to the game played light-heartedly by Gratian. The troops in Britain, who had been neglected by their emperor, rose in rebellion; they took their general, Maximus,[6] a Spaniard by birth and perhaps a distant relative of Theodosius, and declared him emperor. Gaul joined in the movement; Gratian tried to defend his crown, but was deserted by his troops near

---

[1] The individual regulations have been enumerated by Seeck, *Untergang*, 5, 186. 508 and Pauly-Wissowa 7, 1838 following Ambr. *ep.* 17. 18 and Symmachus, *relatio* 3
[2] *vide* Vol. III, 238   [3] Ambr. *ep.* 17, 10 and Symmachus, *relatio* 3, 1. 20
[4] *vide supra*, 46f.   [5] Socr. 5, 10   [6] Ensslin in Pauly-Wissowa 14, 2546–2555

Paris, and left in the lurch. He was murdered in Lyons on August 25, 383, by Andragathius, the *magister equitum*.

Maximus was now master as far as the west was concerned; but Valentinian II, a younger brother of the late emperor, was ensconced in Milan; he was twelve years old, and his inheritance was defended by Bauto, a Frankish general. Bauto had taken steps in good time to man the passes of the Alps and defend Italy against any incursion of the usurper. Both sides found it convenient to enter into negotiations. In Milan, Victor, the *comes*, tried to induce Valentinian to make the journey to Trèves; but Ambrose, at the court of Maximus, put forth efforts to obtain for the young emperor he was representing, tolerable terms of peace. A provisional agreement was reached with which Valentinian had to be content, if only because Theodosius hung back, and even recognized Maximus. The arrangements once made were gradually confirmed and established in the next year or two, especially after Valentinian decided on closer relations with Theodosius, to the chagrin of Maximus. This was because the lad had begun to look on the former as the guardian of his interests, as in fact he proved to be. Maximus would have greatly preferred it if Valentinian had placed himself under his protection like a dutiful son.[1] It is certainly the case that Ambrose had taken an active part in giving this eastern trend to Italian policy; at any rate, it was just about this time[2] that he dedicated to the emperor, Theodosius, a theological apologetic he had written called *David*. There were now five years of peace enjoyed between the three parts of the empire; but in the sphere of the church various important events took place.

The first phase of Priscillianism came to a tragic conclusion in Spain under Maximus. At that time, and indeed for many succeeding centuries, Spain was aloof from the theology of the remainder of the west. It was very conservative, and neither the bishops nor the churches cared to disturb their quietude by entering into the world at large and making public either the questions it debated or the learning it enjoyed. Nevertheless, on one occasion, a single spark gave

[1] Ambr. *ep.* 24, 7
[2] For discussion of the date, cf. Campenhausen, *Ambrosius*, 183ff.

proof of vigour and burst into flame; and then there was a spectacle to behold!

There lived at that time not far from Cordova a man of good family and considerable wealth, Priscillian by name. He combined a good secular education with a profound religious conviction, which led him to forsake the world and adopt an ascetic mode of life.[1] In this way, he became the gifted and enthusiastic prophet of a religious revival. The church at that time was growing ever more worldly, and Priscillian's revival was an attempt to recover the tone of the earliest years of Christianity. It entered anew into the experience of the irreconcilable contrast between flesh and spirit, between life lived in the light of God, on the one hand, and, on the other, surrender to the powers of darkness. The letters of St. Paul were, for the Priscillianists, the inexhaustible sources of a thorough-going asceticism; and Priscillian wrote for his followers a compendium of Paul's leading ideas, which he drew up in 92 "canons", complete with references in each case to the original passages in the epistles. In order to facilitate quoting the epistles, he divided them throughout into sections —and Bibles are still in use which are provided with Priscillian's numbers for the paragraphs, and with his "canons".[2] For the last fifty years several of the smaller tracts written by him[3] have been available, making it possible to form a picture of his thought and aims such as is not provided by the brief remarks of the judges who condemned him as a heretic.

He was concerned to lay aside altogether this world and its sins; the "first man, of the earth or of clay" (1 Cor. 15: 47) was characterized by the "works of the flesh"; the "second man from heaven" revealed the "works of the spirit", and, by dwelling within, transformed us into the temple of God.[4] The re-creation of man is completed in three stages: (i)

---

[1] Sulp. Sev. *Chron.* 2, 46   Priscill. *tract.* 1, 2 1, 15   pp. 4, 9   14, 12, ed. Schepss
[2] *Novum Test. Lat.* ed. Wordsworth et White 2, 7–32, 45ff. and pp. 109–147, 169–174 ed. Schepss
[3] I would like to agree with G. Morin's thesis (*Rev. Bénéd.* 1913, 153–73), which regards Instantius as the author of the tractates. But, on pages 4, 8–14, a layman of eminent family and conscious of a good education, is speaking of his wholly personal conversion: that surely is Priscillian   cf. Sulp. Sev. *Chron.* 2, 46, 3
[4] Prisc. *tract.* 1, 24f.   p. 21 Sch.

continence tames the earthly passions dwelling in the flesh;
(ii) the soul re-assumes its divine character when it accepts the
teachings of the spirit about the idolatrous sins which condition
and surround it; and, (iii) God dwells within us, and is the daily
witness and judge of our conduct. Who would not recoil from
being condemned to death, and, instead, obtain a share in the
divine nature by repudiating the works of the flesh?[1] To win
the highest prize, we must follow the commandments of the
Bible, abandon parents and children, gifts and goods, even
our own souls, and love God more than anything else in the
world; yet God's pardoning mercy is not refused to those who
content themselves with living on the second or the third
level, under God's supervision and command.[2] All must fight
the realm of the flesh, of creatureliness, and of darkness: but
the perfect sons of God neither marry nor are given in marriage;
they neither beget nor are begotten, but are like the angels
of God.[3]

The language and phraseology employed are Biblical in
character; the same matter is repeated time after time in
sentences of seemingly interminable length. All sorts of theological applications are introduced, but by way of illustration,
rather than for the sake of detailed proof; with the result that
Priscillian's ideas are very rarely clear. The power of thought
which had been brought to bear in the east, and the plain, if
also rougher, phraseology which had been used in Africa
and Rome, were unattainable by this Spaniard, who was
essentially a preacher. He had gained no advantage, in this
respect, from reading Cyprian and Hilary. He toiled away
simply to shape phrases and ideas. Besides the Bible, he had
read a variety of apocryphal writings, which had excited his
curiosity, and from which, on suitable occasions, he borrowed
ornate passages to intertwine with his own sequences of
thought. He was on solid ground when he defended an
experienced Christian's right to read such books, especially as
some of them were cited in the Bible itself.[4]

Priscillian practised what he preached, and his personality

---

[1] Prisc. *tract.* 6, 92–93   p. 70f.   7, 113   p. 83   [2] *ibid. tract.* 2, 43 p. 36
[3] *ibid. tract.* 6 p. 81, 14
[4] *ibid. tract.* 3 pp. 44–56   cf. the fragment p. 153, 11–18 and the report of
Orosius

was magnetic enough to win him the adherence of many followers, including some from the upper classes, who were won by the idea of asceticism. Two bishops, be it noted, Instantius and Salvian by name, joined the movement; later, Hyginus of Cordova followed their example; even Symposius of Astorga looked on sympathetically. Those who showed the greatest enthusiasm in devoting themselves to this way of salvation, reached by repudiating the world, were the women-folk.

The first attack, of which notice was given on a placard, was made by Ydacius, bishop of Merida, the capital city of the adjacent province. He "added fuel to the roaring furnace" in his "limitless desire for battle". He put forward his own estimate[1] of the way of life adopted by the Priscillianists, and for a long time the argument swung backwards and forwards. In the end, a synod was called at Saragossa (Caesaraugusta), and was attended by both Spanish and Aquitanian bishops. Their resolutions are extant,[2] bearing the date, October 4, A.D. 380, and showing what objections were raised. Priscillian himself believed that he was resuscitating the early Christian office of "teacher", and this was the appellation he adopted for himself.[3] In their acts of devotion, men and women gathered in common. During the three weeks of preparation for Epiphany and in the "Quadragesima" before Easter, i.e. Lent, the members of the community either withdrew into isolation in their homes, or in the countryside, or even the mountains. They fasted, held their own services for devotional purposes, but did not attend church. All this brought down the condemnation of the synod, but no anathemas were pronounced either on individual persons or on any heretical doctrines. Priscillian and his adherents did not put in an appearance; and Damasus of Rome, after being asked to declare his attitude, warned the synod about proceedings against absent persons, and without a due hearing.[4]

It then came to a closer battle. Hitherto, Priscillian had been a layman, but his friends now consecrated him bishop of

---

[1] Prisc. *tract.* 2   p. 35, 20
[2] Bruns, *Canones*, 2, 13   Lauchert, p. 175, where, however, the year is not given
[3] *Conc. can.* 7   cf. Prisc. *can.* 39. 48
[4] Prisc. *tract.* 2 p. 35, 17. 23   40, 7 against Sulp. Sev. *Chron.* 2, 47, 2f.

Avila,[1] in the province of Lusitania. His enemies immediately
raised the charge of heresy. Ithacius, bishop of Ossonoba
(to-day called Faro, to the east of Cape St. Vincent), did all
that could be done in proving them guilty of horrible heresies;
charging them, in particular, with astrological practices, the
gnostic kind of belief in demons, and Manichaeism.[2] The last
accusation was the most ominous, although, at the same time,
it was very trifling. The doctrine, which Priscillian preached
with much passion, was one found in both St. Paul and St.
John, viz. that of the contrast between the spirit of God and
worldly-mindedness; but if this contrariety were presented
from the metaphysical standpoint as the antagonism between
two "principles", you were at once face to face with the
fundamental thesis of Manichaeism. This is the excuse which
has been used times without number, in the course of the
church's history, to pillory preachers of repentance who were
causing a stir.

Those who stood in the forefront against Priscillian were the
least reputable of the Spanish bishops. Ithacius is said to have
been a shameless and morally worthless twaddler; whilst
Ydacius had to face charges preferred by his own presbytery,
his conduct having an evil notoriety far and wide in the land.[3]
The defence made by Priscillian in his writings[4] was, naturally,
not of the slightest use against enemies of this kind. It was not
long before he discovered that, on account of steps taken by
Ydacius, an anti-Manichaean decree of Gratian's was used by
the governors of the province against himself and the bishops
friendly with him. They were compelled to abandon their sees.
After making their way to Italy, they sought to obtain from
Damasus and Ambrose some protection from the blow delivered
by the secular arm.[5] It was all in vain; both of these princes
of the church turned the cold shoulder to the suspect suppliants.
Their next move was to apply to Macedonius, the minister of
police, from whom they had no difficulty in securing the

---

[1] Between Madrid and Salamanca
[2] According to Priscillian's Apology, *tract.* 1　　cf. pp. 23, 24　　Collected by E. Ch.
Babut, *Priscillien* (Paris, 1909) p. 144
[3] Sulp. Sev. *Chron.* 2, 50, 2　　Prisc *tract.* 2 p. 39, 24ff.
[4] Prisc. *tract.* 1　　*tract.* 2 is the memorandum presented to Damasus
[5] *ibid. tract.* 2 p. 41, 16

cancellation of the political order which had been made against them. They returned home, and re-assumed office; in fact, Volventius, the Spanish proconsul, was ordered to take action against their accusers as disturbers of the peace of the church. Ithacius took flight to Gaul; and then the question of the competence of the different administrators broke out into a lively quarrel, which lasted until the elevation of Maximus completely altered the situation.

The usurper considered it important to show that, in churchmanship, he was orthodox; and he ordered that the Priscillian affair should be examined by a synod at Bordeaux. Here, Instantius was deposed, but Priscillian withdrew from the proceedings and appealed to the emperor. Both accusers and accused then journeyed to Trèves, and St. Martin of Tours, himself castigated at the same time by the Spanish heresy-hunters as an ascetic, vainly tried to put an end to the scandal, and have the issue referred for judgment to a court of the church. Maximus allowed himself to be persuaded by the instigators. Euodius, the prefect, with his inquisitorial technique, was successful in seeing that Priscillian and his adherents were condemned for the crime of practising magic, and for organized immorality. The majority were executed by the sword; a few escaped with a sentence of exile. These acts of bloodshed turned out ill for the accusers, who fell into general disfavour; neither Ithacius nor Ydacius were able to retain their dioceses for very long. When visiting Trèves, Ambrose[1] gave unmistakable evidence of his dislike for the bishops of this group; and Rome, too, showed so much dissatisfaction, that Maximus, in self-defence, sent the records of the trial to the pope.[2] Martin of Tours had to bear other painful consequences, and from that time retired altogether from the stage of ecclesiastical politics.[3] It was the first time that authorities in the church had used the secular arm to carry the verdict of guilty, in a trial for heresy, to the length of a capital punishment. The nasty taste remained for a long time, and brought about a violent reaction a few years later. Of this something will be said in the sequel.

The most famous, as well as the most refined member of

[1] Ambr. *ep.* 24, 12   [2] *Coll. Avell.* 40, 4   [3] Sulp. Sev. *dial.* 3, 13, 5–6

the old aristocracy was Symmachus, who became the city prefect of Rome in A.D. 384. When this event took place, it appeared to be an appropriate opportunity for bringing up again to the new ruler, Valentinian II, a request which had been refused by Gratian; the request was that the state should make grants in support of the ancient religious ceremonial of Rome; and, further, it was asked that the altar of Victory should be re-erected in the court as a corresponding practical symbol. Symmachus, who had taken a leading part in the former application, used all his skill and artistry in drawing up the petition.[1] It is a marvellous example of the dignified Roman manner, a document full of the *maiestas populi Romani*. No ornate and complicated sentences, no chains of superlatives, and none of the magic of euphony and rhythm is used to gain assent by flattery. The simple construction which he was accustomed to employ in his private letters he also used on this occasion; and he was able to rise to classic heights, and produce the greatest impression. Each and every word is carefully weighed, put into the position where it really belongs, and makes its resonance fully felt in our ears.

He brought Roma herself, as it were, into the emperor's presence. She asked for the restitution of the old rights she had enjoyed for 1000 years, rights which harmed nobody, and which were worthy of respect even by those who denied their religious content. The old, traditional ceremonials had given laws wherever Rome held sway, driven Hannibal from her walls, and the Gauls from her capitol; they belonged to the common heritage, like the stars, the skies, and the earth, behind which a divine secret lay hidden, a secret which, though perhaps in different ways, we all sought to uncover. It was not without reason that a poor harvest and a time of famine had been the hard lot of the provinces; the lean year was due to wickedness. A livelihood refused to the priests will be denied to the whole population. O emperor, exercise your obligations to do justice, and render to each his due—*suum cuique*.

Ever since it was written, this address has been admired and its terms re-echoed, just as on the occasion when it was

[1] Symmachus, *relatio* 3 p. 280–83 ed. Seeck

first read in the emperor's consistory. Pagans and Christians alike were stirred by the solemn earnestness of an admonition[1] which called all men of goodwill to the aid of a glorious history, to render all worthy honour to a world that was fading away. It seemed safe to count on the emperor's assent.

Then Ambrose intervened. He had no need to adopt the ceremonial forms of the court, because his position afforded him direct intercourse with the ruler. He was the young man's father-confessor. He wrote[2] that the emperor was a soldier of God in duty bound to serve the faith; in no circumstances or shape must he agree to promote the worship of idols. His brother, Gratian, had always been faithful to duty in refusing any such request: the commandment of God ranked far in advance of consideration for the wishes even of persons who had rendered great service. In any case, these persons consisted of only a small group, and were opposed by the greater majority of the senators who were Christians. The plea needed no answer. Valentinian might, of course, mention it to Theodosius, his trustworthy councillor: the issue was indeed important enough. Ambrose concluded: "If the matter were to be settled in any other sense than that suggested, it would be impossible for us bishops to regard it with indifference, or let it pass without comment. Thou mayest go to church—but thou wilt find no clergy there; or if thou dost find them there, they will offer thee resistance." That was an unambiguous threat of excommunication should the emperor disobey.

In view of a situation where the state-church was a privileged institution, Ambrose made certain deductions of which no emperor had ever so much as dreamed. The thesis was that the ruler belonged to the church otherwise than as a private person only; he was also, by virtue of his very office, a "soldier of God", or, in later phraseology, the "advocatus ecclesiae". This, again, implied, not only that it was his duty to protect the church, but also that he was committed to the divine commandments in his political activity. If he ever felt himself in doubt as to his course, who else than the teachers in the church could tell him what was the will of Almighty God? If he did not avail himself of authoritative advice in this way,

[1] Ambr. *de obitu Valent.* 19, *ep.* 17, 8   [2] *ibid. ep.* 17

he would be liable to the means of correction of which the church disposed.

No one in the east had seriously dared to make a demand of that order. It revealed a mode of thought native to the west, embodied in a person like Ambrose who was on intimate terms with the head of the state; that special combination is what led to the development of this new article in the constitution of the Christian state-church. A claim like this, once it had been made by an eminent person in an important post, entered into the blood-stream of Latin Catholicism. It may have been relegated in practice to the background at the present day, but it has never been abandoned in principle. This was not the only occasion when Ambrose seized the opportunity of using it successfully. In the instance just described, it was not a matter of great importance. Ambrose secured the support of Bauto and Rumoridus, both of whom were generals, and the second of whom was a pagan.[1] He then composed a refutation of Symmachus's *relatio*, in very matter-of-fact terms, and supported by undeniable facts; he had it read out to the consistory together with his letter to Valentinian. In this way, he settled the matter. The youthful emperor bowed to the will of his spiritual adviser.

Near Easter in the next year, A.D. 385, a new clash occurred which gave Ambrose a chance of defending his conception of the church's rights. The dowager empress, who was the mother of the youthful Valentinian, the ruler on the throne, repudiated the Nicene Creed, and, at an earlier date, had even given support to the "Arians" of Illyria.[2] At the moment in question, she expressed a wish to be granted a certain church in the suburbs of the city, and asked that it should be assigned to her attendants and her bodyguard of Goths.[3] Her son was quite willing, and gladly granted what seemed a reasonable request, but Ambrose flatly refused the suggestion. When the objection was raised that the emperor would be only exercising a right that pertained to him, since everything was in his power of disposal, Ambrose answered,[4] that this principle might be granted in all cases of private property, and even of the lives of the emperor's subjects; but it was limited where it

[1] Ambr. *ep.* 57, 3   [2] *vide supra*, 17   [3] Ambr. *ep.* 20, 12   [4] *ibid. ep.* 20, 8. 61

touched on the possessions of the church: "What belongs to God, is outside the emperor's power."

It was an ancient principle of Roman law that any temple which had been solemnly set apart, either by a resolution of the Roman people, or by the emperor's orders, became the property of the relevant god; and *ipso facto* it was no longer available in any way for any man to use for secular purposes. It retained this character even when it existed only as a heap of ruins. Only if the god himself surrendered it, i.e., if he allowed it to fall into enemy hands, did it lose its sanctity; but this sanctity was immediately and automatically regained when the conqueror again vacated it, or otherwise set it free.[1] Ambrose applied this legal principle to the buildings belonging to the Christian churches, and deduced the utmost logical consequences. When a building had been dedicated to God by being consecrated, the act could not be undone by any decision on man's part, not even by the emperor with his over-riding orders. Further, the bishop, as the organ of the church, was the authority installed by God Himself, and the guardian of His property.

In this way, the issue was reduced to a sheer question of principle, and Ambrose was not prepared to give way an inch. He wrote a graphic account in a letter to his sister, Marcellina.[2] It appears that on Palm Sunday, April 6, 385, while Ambrose was celebrating mass in the city, the empress's men, after fruitless negotiations, had taken forcible possession of the little *Basilica Porciana* at the foregate,[3] and hedged it round with the royal pennons. Street riots broke out at once, developing into demonstrations in front of the royal palace.[4] Punishments were inflicted on the citizens immediately afterwards, while officials and military officers entered into negotiations with Ambrose. They urged that he should at least calm the people down. He replied: "I did not stir them up; I have done my part—only God can assuage their anger." The crisis was reached on the Wednesday: the emperor placed soldiers round the *Basilica Porciana*; the two churches in the city were

[1] Gaius, *Instit.* 2, 4–5   *Digest*, 1, 8, 6, 3   1, 8, 9, 1; 11, 7, 36
[2] Ambr. *ep.* 20   [3] *re* these *decani*, cf. Seeck in Pauly-Wissowa 4, 2246
[4] Ambr. *sermo c. Auxent.* 29

full of excited crowds weeping aloud; Ambrose delivered a very arresting sermon in the "old" church.[1] The sermon was based on the lesson for the day, a passage from the book of Job, and exhorted the people to Christian long-suffering and passive resistance; it also drew attention to the harmful parts women had played from time to time, starting from Eve, and going on to Jezebel and Herodias. While he was actually preaching, the church filled with soldiers forcing their way in; they had been tormented with anxiety by Ambrose's threats of excommunication, and they now assured him of their fidelity to the orthodox faith. They had come out of the ranks of the soldiers surrounding the church and cutting it off, and they now mingled with the weeping congregation. About the same time, the bishop was told that the imperial pennons had been removed from the *Basilica Porciana*, apparently with violence, for the children afterwards tore them to shreds. Ambrose continued refusing to surrender the Basilica, and sent sharp answers back by the emperor's intermediaries who were full of reproaches. Soldiers remained on guard over the churches throughout the night. At length, on Low Thursday, the emperor gave in. The military were withdrawn, the threatened penalties suspended, and, in the name of his troops, the general prayed the emperor to attend church in state. It betrays the atmosphere when we learn that Valentinian answered furiously, "Soon, if Ambrose gives the orders, you will be sending me to him in chains." There is no room for doubt that the issue had finally been forced by the attitude of the soldiers. Ambrose had good cause for fearing that the court would take its revenge for the insult, even if the Lord Chamberlain had not threatened to cut his head off.[2]

It was but in accordance with human nature that Justina, the dowager-empress, who was really at the bottom of the

[1] i.e. the church of St. Thecla (Cabrol-Leclercq, *Dict.* i, 1383 Fig. 317 n. 2) on the west side of the present-day cathedral square, but no longer existing. The Basilica Nova (minor) is the S. Maria Maggiore (*ibid.* n. 1), on whose site the present cathedral stands: both churches are mentioned in the Liturgy of Ambrose as Summer and Winter cathedrals. The Basilica Porciana is S. Victor ad corpus, to the west of S. Ambrogio, beyond the ancient line of the wall as marked by the Via Vittoria and the Via Garducci (Cabrol 1, 1443, Fig. 318 n. 9)

[2] Ambr. *ep.* 20, 28

whole affair, found it hard to accept defeat; nor will any one find it astonishing that the emperor, who was scarcely fifteen years of age, turned against his spiritual adviser with a heat consonant with his youth. But the manner in which both the royal persons concerned aired their grievances shows much room for doubt whether they possessed any sense of political proportion.

The year 385 was marked throughout with various hostile acts by the court party and Justina's Illyrian supporters; until at last the intentions of this group came to the light of day: to make one of their own persuasion bishop of Milan instead of Ambrose. With this end in view, they chose a certain Mercurius, who was bishop in one of the frontier districts. He took the name of Auxentius, and it is at least possible[1] that he is to be identified with an Auxentius of Durostorum (Silistria) who wrote a biography of Wulfila. The struggle issued into the open when the year 386 began. A decree was promulgated on January 23 granting freedom of worship to all who held to the creed of Rimini, "which had been drawn up with a view to complete permanence". The decree protected the *homoians*, and threatened heavy penalties against those members of the church, hitherto privileged, who had strongly opposed these liberties until now.[2] Soon afterwards, severer orders were issued, which made it obligatory on the whole of the western empire to hand over the churches to *homoian* bishops; these orders caused a genuine storm of excitement.[3]

Ambrose remained at his post, and let the tempest break upon him, although he was urged by the court to make no commotion and to disappear from sight. The emperor's own wish was that a debate on religion should be arranged between Ambrose and Auxentius, and held in the presence of the consistory. Auxentius readily agreed, but Ambrose refused to attend. He laid his ideas before the emperor in a document of fundamental importance. This document reached its climax in the claim that, in questions of faith, it was for the bishops to pronounce judgment on Christian emperors, not emperors

---

[1] A conjecture by L. Duchesne, *Histoire ancienne de l'église* 2, 552
[2] *Cod. Theod.* 16, 1, 4; only the innocuous section, 16, 4, 1 was published in the east
[3] Ambr. *ep.* 21, 11 *sermo c. Auxent* 16 Maximus in *Coll. Avell.* 39, 3

on bishops.[1] He went as far as to remind the youthful Valentinian that he had never been baptized, and that he seemed likely to transgress the principles which had been carefully weighed by his father, when he was already a grown man. Then he preached a thrilling sermon to the populace who crowded into the cathedral while it was still surrounded by a guard of soldiers; he assured them of the unbendable firmness of their bishop; he hammered home the words: "Give to Caesar what belongs to Caesar, and to God what belongs to God. Caesar is a son of the church; he is part of the church, not superior to the church." This sermon[2] was delivered on Palm Sunday, March 29, 386. It was soon published as a pamphlet, and became part of t e foundation underlying the western interpretation of the legal constitution of the state-church.

Ambrose had gained the suffrage of the masses, not only on account of his arrangements for using gold to provide alms in support of the poor and the beggars, but also because he exercised his gifts and composed new hymns to serve them as battle-songs in the war for the faith[3]—above all, because his towering personality exercised a powerful spell even over the cultured people in the city. Augustine's testimony is entirely convincing here. Once more, the fearless bishop came off victor, and the *Basilica Ambrosiana*, consecrated by him at this period, remains as a memorial of this triumph; for, on June 19, 386, he interred there the bones of the martyrs, Gervase and Protasius, which he had discovered two days earlier in the Basilica of Saints Felix and Nabor.[4] How he chanced upon these ancient and long-forgotten martyrs, and happened to look for them in exactly the right place, is not evident from the account[5] which Ambrose sent to his sister, Marcellina, although that record is very clear and precise in other respects. The time when the bones were transferred was made into a public holiday; and a miracle occurred to show the divine approval: Severus, a blind butcher well-known to

[1] Ambr. *ep.* 21, 4
[2] *ibid. sermo contra Auxentium* In the collected Works, the sermon follows *epist.* 21. The date is to be deduced from §19
[3] *ibid. sermo c. Aux.* 33, 34
[4] Near the S. Ambrogio; the site is now occupied by the Garibaldi barracks *vide* Cabrol, *Dict.* 1, 1443 Fig. 318 n. 3
[5] Ambr. *ep.* 22 and also Augustine, *confess.* 9, 7, 15–16

the whole city, touched the fringe of the shroud, and received his sight. Afterwards, he did not resume his gory trade, but became one of the servants in the Church of St. Ambrose.[1] There was then a series of cures, including exorcisms of demons; the rejoicings of the populace silenced any unkindly criticisms made by the "Arians".

Because of his child-like habit of complying with the wishes of his mother, who was, moreover, both little-minded and high-tempered, Valentinian had lost a great deal of the respect of his people. Furthermore, he was soon compelled to see that he had made a very serious political error. He received a genuinely paternal letter[2] on a certain occasion from Maximus, his fellow-emperor, a man whom he disliked in that position. This letter pointed out the catastrophic effects of his policy regarding the Arians, which was shaking the whole of the western empire; and urged him, out of the heartfelt feelings of a friend, to abandon the road which he had mistakenly been following. Maximus also wrote Siricius, the pope of Rome, with the assurance that, now and always, he was determined to keep watch and ward over the catholic faith.[3] What else lay in the background behind this correspondence remains hidden from us. However, in the autumn of 387, Maximus marched into Italy, and Valentinian had no alternative but to flee. He met with Theodosius in Salonika, whose straightforward policy he had renounced, to his own undoing. Theodosius had no alternative but to offer him asylum, and would have had none, even if he had not married Galla, Justina's lovely daughter, and had not Valentinian thus been his own brother-in-law. At no time in the east had Maximus ceased being regarded as a usurper, and the recognition accorded him was always felt to be in the nature of an armistice.

The occupation of Italy made it impossible to avoid the arbitrament of war. Theodosius made careful preparations, and advanced westwards in June, A.D. 388. He was successful in inflicting a decisive defeat on Maximus's troops at Siszeg on the Sau, and again, near Pettau in Steiermark. Maximus was taken prisoner near Aquileia and put to death. Theodosius

---

[1] Ambr. *ep.* 22, 2. 17   Paulinus, *vita Ambr.* 14 (Plate 2, facing p. 10 ed. Bened.)
[2] *Coll. Avell.* n. 39 (1, 88 Guenther)   [3] *ibid.* n. 40 (1, 90)

entered Milan as conqueror in October, A.D. 388, and in so
doing took over in fact the rule of the west. Valentinian,
having shown himself lacking in practical ability, remained
from now onwards a purely ornamental figure. He was dismissed to Vienne, and commended to the care of the Frankish
general, Arbogast, who treated the young weakling with such
brutality that the latter, in his doubts, finally committed
suicide (May 15, 392).[1] After Justina died in A.D. 388, he had
become reconciled with Ambrose, and had even sharply
reproved the senate when it addressed to him a new request
regarding support for the cultus. In the distress which he
suffered during his last days, he begged Ambrose to come and
baptize him. His former father-confessor arrived too late; but,
afterwards, during the mourning ceremonial in Milan, Ambrose
delivered a splendid funeral oration over him.[2]

When Theodosius took on his own shoulders the rulership
of the west, he had already decided henceforward to rule the
whole empire by himself, and then to bequeath it as a heritage
to his two sons. Arcadius, then eleven years of age, was designated for the east, and remained behind in Constantinople.
Honorius, then five years of age, was to follow his father, to
the west, and was later taken by him to Rome when he visited
the city in June, A.D. 389. Theodosius entered in a stately
procession, and presented his little son to the Romans unmistakably as their crown-prince.[3] He remained in Rome till
the end of August, and was greeted with a series of banquets
in his honour as a victorious emperor, and he, in turn, made
every effort to please the Romans. Leaving his military body-
guard behind, he entered into conversation with people in the
streets, took all pleasantries in good part, condescended so far as
to visit private persons in their homes; in short, he showed that
all he wanted was to be a "Roman citizen". He addressed the
people from the speaker's platform in the forum; he addressed
the senate in their house, and, while there, he permitted the
Gallic rhetorician, Pacatus, to deliver a long panegyric in

[1] So Seeck, *Untergang* 5, 242. 537. The ancient records oscillate between murder
and suicide.
[2] Ambr. *de obitu Valent.* 19. 23–27   cf. *ep.* 53, 2
[3] *Chron. min.* 1, 245, 298   Instructive records in Claudian, *de sexto cons. Honorii*
54–76   Pacatus *paneg.* 47, 3

his honour. The address is still extant, and the speaker was given a princely reward; he was appointed proconsul of Africa for the following year, and afterwards he rose to be Keeper of the Privy Purse,[1] in spite of his not being a Christian. The sun of grace came from behind the storm-clouds and shone also on Symmachus. During the critical days, he had held to Maximus, and even delivered a speech in his honour; now he was driven to seek asylum in the Church of Novatian in Rome. Yet he was pardoned by Theodosius, and was even permitted to present him with an address.[2] He became consul for the year 391. The honour was shared by Tatian, the *praefectus praetorio* of the east;[3] nor must it be overlooked that neither of these men, who had become prominent in this way, were well-disposed to Christianity. It is true that Theodosius had been moved by a desire to win the aristocracy of Rome, and this had outweighed certain doubts on the part of the church about giving any honour to Symmachus; nevertheless, the general conditions in the west, particularly in the city of Rome, made it imperative to adopt a cautious policy towards pagans and pagan institutions.

The situation in the east was rather different. Granted that Theodosius had prohibited recusancy from Christianity to paganism in this region, yet he had not promulgated any decrees hostile to pagans. His edicts had been confined to the practice of fortune-telling which was linked with animal sacrifices, and he had expressly permitted resort to the temples, which, on their part, were kept open as monuments of art;[4] indeed a Christian was not permitted an appointment as chief priest of a city, because his responsibilities regarding the temple were proper to a member of the ancient faith.[5] Kynegius,[6] the eastern Praefectus, was commissioned in A.D. 385 to journey to Egypt for the purpose of damping down the paganism which enjoyed there a dubious kind of life—but he was to act within the limits set by his commission. None-the-less, he appears to have exceeded his terms of reference and, not only in Egypt, but throughout the east, to have closed the temples and

[1] Seeck, *Symmachus*, p. CXCIII   [2] Socrates, *H.E.* 5, 14, 5–10
[3] Ensslin in Pauly-Wissowa, 2nd Series, 4, 2463 n. 3
[4] *Cod. Theod.* 16, 10, 8   *re* Nov. 30, A.D. 382
[5] *ibid.* 12, 1, 112   *re* June 16, A.D. 386   [6] Seeck in Pauly-Wissowa 11, 2527

stopped the sacrifices.[1] He seems to have been responsible fo having destroyed the splendid temple at Edessa; and he wa probably urged on by his wife, Acanthia, a devout Christian but under the influence of fanatical monks.[2] There are also good grounds for regarding Kynegius as the official who afforded military protection when Bishop Marcellus went to the extreme of brutality while reducing the temple at Apamea. Parallel to the destruction of temples initiated by responsible officials, were the campaigns of hosts of excited monks who went hither and thither in the countryside, destroyed the little shrines of the peasants, dealt roughly with their priests, or even killed them.[4] Kynégius died while still promoting thi kind of action, and Theodosius, recognizing that he had blundered, appointed a pagan, Tatian, as successor. Libaniu immediately sent a petition to the emperor on behalf of the temples.[5] In this petition, he drew pointed attention to the in consistency between what the emperor had ordered, and the excesses to which Kynegius had gone, as well as to those of the dissolute hordes of monks; nor did he omit suggesting that a policy of tolerance would be wise. He said: "If men could be converted by attacks on temples, the temples would have been destroyed long ago on your orders, for it is a long time since you began to desire men to be converted. But you were aware that you would not reach your goal, and therefore did not lay hands on these temples." At the very least, it can be said about this phraseology that it was not a piece of court flattery But Libanius disposed of much skill on other occasions in taking advantage of the psychological moment when the emperor, who tended to be cautious by nature, had already changed his mind sufficiently to bear being told the truth without getting angry. It was such an opportunity that Libanius cleverly seized when he addressed the emperor as counsel for public opinion. He could also count on being graciously received on the present occasion, because the nomination of Tatian had itself revealed that the emperor was not pleased with Kynegius's policy affecting religion, and

[1] Zosimos 4, 37, 3　　　　　　　　　　[2] Libanius, *or.* 30, 44–4
[3] Theodoret, *H.E.* 5, 21, 6–11　Gothofredus on *Cod. Theod.* 16, 10, 8
[4] Libanius, *or.* 30, 8–9　　　　[5] *ibid., or.* 30; in §53 Tatian is the "new man"

because even already, Libanius himself had been given the title of Praefectus, and thus elevated to the highest rank of governorships.

A synagogue at Kallinikum on the Euphrates had been set on fire by the Christians, and in a village to the east, a church of the Valentinian sect had been stormed by the monks. The local military commandant had sent a report, and Theodosius had responded by ordering severe punishment and due compensation. Word of all this immediately reached Ambrose, and a contest of historical importance began between the two men: a struggle between a priest on the one hand, and, on the other, a secular ruler. Ambrose addressed himself in writing to the emperor, for he had often found before that oral negotiations failed his purpose.[1] In his letter, he asked that the Christian rioters should be entirely pardoned as a tribute of respect to the church. On the next occasion when the emperor attended service, Ambrose preached on the necessity of forgiving, on the splendour of the church, and on the perversity of the synagogue; and he appealed directly to the emperor to forgive the wrong-doers as a favour to the church. When he left the pulpit, the emperor spoke to him on the subject, and promised to mitigate the penalties. Ambrose refused to be content, and demanded more, "in order that he might make the sacrifice (of the mass) with a good conscience on the emperor's behalf"—and in fact, he only proceeded to the altar, and began the sacrificial liturgy after the emperor had promised complete pardon.[2] Publicly, and in the presence of the congregation, he had compelled the emperor to give way. It had only been possible to do so because Theodosius was exactly like Ambrose in the great importance he attached to the arguments affecting the church, and in the high seriousness with which he conceived his duties as a Christian. He felt himself bound, as a Christian ruler, to observe the divine commands; and he acknowledged that, in Ambrose, there was a great and candid bishop, clothed with proper authority to expound those commands.

A little later, a deputation of the senate of Rome sought an

---

[1] The letter=Ambr. *ep.* 40   cf. *ep.* 41, 1
[2] The information is given in a letter to his sister, *ep.* 41

audience and made the old request for a renewal of the supplementary allowances given by the state to the shrines which were sanctified by tradition. Having in mind his experiences when visiting Rome, the emperor felt the position at least worth considering. Ambrose then expressed his own opinion plainly to his face, and noticeably avoided the court for a few days, until Theodosius took his side, and refused the request.[1] Ambrose was really acting as the voice of the emperor's conscience, but it is human nature to silence that voice, and prevent it speaking too often. Theodosius therefore gave instructions that, as far as this active and interfering bishop was concerned, the decisions reached by the imperial consistory were to be kept strictly private. Ambrose took this very bitterly, and complained that he was being robbed of his natural right of hearing, and this made it impossible for him to speak. But there were certain things which he was unable to pretend that he had never heard, and the silence imposed on him caused him serious dilemmas of conscience.[2]

This condition of affairs lasted for a while, till an event which he could not ignore compelled Ambrose to break through his self-restraint. Owing to the excitement engendered at the hippodrome at Thessalonika, an uproar had broken out, with the result that the officer commanding the province of Illyria had been killed. Theodosius, in his boundless wrath, ordered that the populace should be gathered in the hippodrome without raising their suspicions, and that there should be a massacre by the soldiers. News of it reached Milan at the very time when a synod of Gallic bishops was in session. All were deeply moved, and Ambrose decided to act forthwith. He left Milan shortly before the emperor's arrival, sent him a lengthy and detailed letter, with a concluding paragraph in his own hand intended only for Theodosius's eyes. The letter demanded that he should do penance in the same fashion as David, a king who had sinned and then repented; meanwhile, Ambrose himself would refuse to celebrate mass in the emperor's presence. The tone in which he addressed the emperor was as if he were speaking movingly and seriously to his godson with whom he had long been on intimate

[1] Ambr. *ep.* 57, 4   [2] *ibid. ep.* 56, 2–4

terms.[1] Theodosius had already shown often enough that he was not obstinate, and indeed, though he might strike hard when first aroused, further thought inclined him to clemency. Three years before, the people of Antioch had broken out into a wild riot, during which the statues of the emperors were smashed; as a consequence they were in terror, fearing the worst. But Bishop Flavian set off to the court, and was successful in obtaining a full pardon. In Thessalonika, the punishment had followed disorder only too quickly—but once more the emperor softened. He submitted to the penance demanded by Ambrose, went as far as to lay aside the royal insignia for a time, and confessed his sin publicly in the presence of the congregation. Ambrose then allowed him to partake of the sacraments once again.

Everyone now saw that in God's assize, and in the utterances of His earthly messenger no deference was paid to rank. The church was in a position to triumph as a moral force, and to congratulate itself on such a bishop and such an emperor. A straight line runs from Milan to Canossa, and it shows the interpretation placed by the west on the unity of state and church. The interpretation is that even the bearer of the highest office in the state is subject to the ethical commandments of the church, just because he is a Christian; in this way, by God's will, he becomes the instrument and the force needed to build up a Christian order of society. The practical implications of this interpretation were not apparent to either of the two chief actors at Milan; at Canossa, both the pope and the emperor were aware of the tragic difficulties involved. The earnestness with which Theodosius felt it, is shown by an extraordinary edict[2] promulgated on August 18, A.D. 390, which ordered the postponement of an execution for thirty days, "lest, contrary to our custom, we have pronounced a sentence unduly harsh, after duly considering the case". But the most important consequence of the shock felt in Theodosius's soul during these weeks was surely the law[3] regarding

---

[1] Ambr. *ep.* 51   also, *de obitu Theod.* 34   Rufin. *H.E.* 11, 18   elaborated by Sozom. 5, 25   greatly expanded by Theodoret, *H.E.* 5, 17–18   a bare record in Paulinus, *vita Ambr.* 24   cf. also Augustine, *conf.* 5, 26
[2] *Cod. Theod.* 9, 40, 13   Rufin. *H.E.* 11, 21   For the dating cf. Seeck, *Regesten.* p. 92, 44f.
[3] *ibid.* 16, 10, 10   addressed to Albinus P.U. (not P.P.)

religion, and bearing the date, February 24, A.D. 391, flatly prohibiting all forms of pagan worship, all kinds of sacrifices, and even every form of prayer in temples; and it imposed heavy fines on any office-holders who dared to transgress. The law was aimed at the city prefect of Rome and was unmistakably intended to affect the religious attitude of its aristocracy, who, it will be remembered, had been treated considerately when Theodosius visited the city as recently as the summer of A.D. 389. A similar edict[1] was addressed on June 16, A.D. 391, to the civil and military authorities in Egypt.

Until the beginning of the year 388, Kynegius had been working energetically against paganism in this country, and his departure was actually the signal for a closer battle; the Serapeum at Alexandria[2] was destroyed in A.D. 389. Certain caves used for pagan worship had been discovered by the Christians, and certain symbols used in the mysteries were profaned by them; all this led to tumultuous reprisals by the pagans. People were killed, and several Christians were actually slaughtered like sacrificial animals before some of the altars of the gods. The authorities became alarmed, and informed the emperor; he refrained from punishing the murderers, but declared the slaughtered Christians to be glorious martyrs, and demanded that idol-worship should be torn out, root and branch. The emperor's orders were read out to the people— and then the Christian part of the populace set about the most splendid temple in Alexandria, the Serapeum, which proudly crowned a high terrace. A soldier wielding a sledge-hammer, smashed the head of a certain statue of a god; and, in spite of all prophecies and predictions, the skies did not fall in. The judgment of God fell in full fury on the horrified pagans among the population. The remaining temples and shrines in Alexandria were treated in the same way, and the storms of destruction raged through all the towns and villages, over the ploughed fields, and even the desert places; the fanes of the old gods were wiped out. The bishops led the attack, and hosts of black-skinned monks formed the vanguard. A church was built on the ruins of the temple of Serapis, together with a martyr's chapel enshrining the bones of John the Baptist,

[1] *Cod. Theod.* 16, 10, 11   [2] The chief record is given by Rufin. *H.E.* 11, 22–30

which had been discovered by Athanasius in Julian's time. The sacred Nilometer, which was venerated with superstitious awe by the entire people, remained unharmed, and was accorded a place in the Christian basilica.

Theodosius is said to have thanked God that the great change had been effected without serious damage being suffered in Alexandria. He saw what could be done in the east if one did not hesitate to take the bull by the horns. The law of 391, regarding sacrifices, could be relied on to be effective in the east. In the autumn of 392, he promulgates, a new decree forbidding sacrifices,[1] and sent it to Rufinud the principal minister in the east. This decree was much more precise, entered into the smallest details, and placed any and every form of pagan worship under penalty. The pagan chancellor, Tatian, was dismissed in June, A.D. 392, and fell into deep disfavour. His place was taken by Rufinus, a Christian. After a period of doubt, the sterner measures proved successful. Even as late as September, A.D. 390, monks had not been allowed to make their residence in towns, as their public demonstrations, often accompanied by violence, created various difficulties for the authorities.[2] In April, A.D. 392, however, the emperor repealed this regulation, representing it to the authorities as being the result of unwarranted accusations.[3] This action showed plainly the emperor's change of heart, and be it remembered, after the summer of A.D. 391, he was once again in harmony with the church at Constantinople. These facts explain why a whole series of laws were enacted about this period, and were intended to give greater consequence in public life to the orthodox church and all it stood for.[4] But it can scarcely be the case that Ambrose was responsible for all the details.

Meanwhile, a new danger began to threaten the empire in the west. The death of Valentinian II, in May, A.D. 392, was in itself enough to give one pause as being a sign of the independent sovereignty of Arbogast, the Frankish king, especially as he was universally held to have murdered the young emperor.

---

[1] *Cod. Theod.* 16, 10, 12 of November, 392   [2] *ibid.* 16, 3, 1
[3] *ibid.* 16, 3, 2   and compare with Gothofredus
[4] Lists are given by Seeck, *Untergang*, 5, 234, and Rauschen, *Jahrbücher*, 372–76

Theodosius quietly awaited the inevitable developments, and set about his preparations for the fateful battle, but without drawing attention to his actions. Time dragged on till August, before Arbogast decided to act: he then promoted his friend, Eugenius, the imperial treasurer, and made him the Augustus of the west. An embassy, joined by a deputation of bishops from Gaul,[1] set off for Constantinople; the men of religion were commissioned, and they themselves desired, to bear testimony that Arbogast was innocent of Valentinian's death. Theodosius received the deputation very politely, but sent them back without a definite answer.

Eugenius approached Ambrose, too, by writing to him twice, but received no answer in either case.[2] The bishop of Milan had become a person of the first importance in the church, and therefore in politics. Consequently, he kept in the background during the present lull. There was a delay of fully two months after the death of Valentinian II, before Theodosius wrote to the princesses, the sisters of Valentinian, who were waiting in fear and trembling in Milan, and ordered interment near Gratian's tomb. Ambrose also took advantage of the opportunity and wrote to the emperor for the first time.[3] He spoke of his sorrow for the departed, and said that a worthy sarcophagus was being prepared. His funeral sermon, again, mentioned only the fine, human and Christian qualities of the dead man, and of the brother who had preceded him. Only when at length the usurper's forces began to threaten the safety of many persons, did Ambrose write to him and intervene on behalf of those in danger. This was a course he frequently took;[4] but even then he made no mention of the letters written by Eugenius.

Eugenius had no other course open than to admit that Ambrose, the prince of the western church, had no intention of taking his side, but he was bitterly disillusioned. Up to this point, he had entertained the hope that, by giving prominence to his Christian inclinations, he would win the support of the church; and, in fact, his policy seems to have

---

[1] Zosimos, 4, 55, 57   Rufin. H.E. 11, 31   [2] Ambr. ep. 57, 11
[3] ibid. ep. 53 cf. pars. 4–5, and de obitu Valent. 49
[4] ibid. ep. 57, 12 and notes by Campenhausen, Ambrosius 249, n. 1

succeeded in Gaul. The senate of Rome, on the other hand, which had just been faced with Theodosius's decree forbidding sacrifices, were relying on Eugenius's support and blessing, in view of the fact that he had formerly been a professor in Rome, and a representative of ancient and traditional culture. The senate therefore confidently drew his attention to their old request for a renewed grant of moneys in support of the temple worship—but were rebuffed. The effort was repeated, and again turned down. It was obvious that Eugenius had learned the lesson which his predecessors had been taught, viz., that this question was a point of honour in the public policy of the church as represented by Ambrose. The Romans, however, stubbornly maintained their position; moreover their supporters were of such a strength that their influence was by no means negligible. Eugenius conceived a plan which, he thought, would steer him between Scylla and Charybdis: he himself made a present of the sum needed, and sent it to the right honourable gentlemen of the pagan persuasion.

Ambrose seized on this as the occasion for an open declaration of war. When Eugenius was approaching Milan in the spring of A.D. 393, the bishop left the city, and made his way, first to Bologna, and then via Faenza to Florence.[1] He sent Eugenius a formal letter of protest,[2] in which he detailed the whole business of the petitions that had been preferred by the senate, and characterized the conduct of the new ruler as disobedience to God and betrayal of Christ. He added that he had expected this kind of attitude in Eugenius from the start, and had consequently left his letters unanswered. In writing like this, he spoke and acted in an entirely unfriendly manner; it could not be otherwise than clear, from now onwards, that Ambrose had adopted precisely the same policy to the usurper as Theodosius had done, and was now carrying that policy to its logical conclusion.

Eugenius could no longer depend on any semblance of sympathetic support from the churches of Italy. He therefore began to play another suit: he nominated Virius Nicomachus Flavianus[3] as chancellor of Italy; this man was related to the family of Symmachus, and had twice been a prefect under

[1] Paulinus, *vita Ambr.* 27   [2] Ambr. *ep.* 57   [3] Seeck in Pauly-Wissowa, 6, 2506, n. 14

Theodosius; he also enjoyed a distinguished reputation as a writer. His taste for the occult learning of the ancients, and for theology of a Platonic kind, marked him out as an appropriate leader of those reactionary pagans who were striving for the kind of ideals for which Julian had stood. A reactionary movement of this kind was now initiated with the greatest zeal. Flames once again flickered on the altars, and the entrails of sacrificial animals were read as showing signs favourable to Eugenius's victory.[1] A Greek oracle was in circulation to the effect that the worship of Christ would die out after 365 years, i.e. *circa* A.D. 395.[2] A poem is extant composed by a Christian, expressing his indignation at the new lease of life given to paganism by Flavian, and interpreting his early death as a retribution.[3] When Arbogast and Flavian left Milan in order to march against Theodosius, they threatened, on returning victorious, to turn the churches into stables and make the clergy into soldiers.[4]

The policy that had been followed in the struggle for power had led, thanks to the conduct of Ambrose, to a war of religion. The decisive battle was fought on the Wippach (Frigidus) in the Karst, when Eugenius's troops carried standards of Jupiter and Hercules.[5] Theodosius, on the other hand, felt himself to be a warrior of Christ; he marched on to the field after being blessed and promised the victory in a prophecy uttered by a hermit held in high respect, who lived in the Theban desert. Before this utterance, Theodosius, accompanied by clergy and people, had offered intercessory prayers at the graves of the Apostles and martyrs. And, indeed, the victory he gained seemed to him to be miraculous, and to have been brought about by the sudden onset of an Alpine hurricane which defeated and destroyed the enemy. Eugenius was taken prisoner in flight, and was immediately beheaded (September 6, A.D. 394); so also, both Arbogast and Flavian perished.[6]

Immediately after Eugenius had left Milan, Ambrose returned to his episcopal throne: it was at the beginning of

---

[1] Rufin. *H.E.* 11, 33   Sozom. 7, 22, 4–5   [2] Augustine *civ. dei* 18, 53
[3] Mommsen, *Ges. Schr.* 7, 485–98; O. Barkowski, *de carmine adv. Flavianum.* Diss. Königsberg, 1912
[4] Paulinus, *vita Ambr.* 31   [5] Augustine, *civ. dei* 5, 26   Theod. *H.E.* 5, 24, 4. 17
[6] Rufin. *H.E.* 11, 32, 33

August. The decisive blow fell about five weeks later. Theodosius sent word to Ambrose of the judgment that God had awarded. Ambrose took the emperor's letter and kept it in his hand while celebrating mass, in order to combine the king's thanks in the sacrament with that of the priest. Both men, in taking up this attitude, were of the deepest earnestness and reverence, and each was aware of the hold that he had on the other. The emperor supposed the bishop to be still far away, because he had not assured him of complete confidence in the victory of the eastern army—he had not even had it himself. But now Ambrose was in a position proudly to inform him that he had been certain of the happy issue. True to his duty as a bishop, when he offered his congratulations, he added a petition for mercy on any of the enemy who had repented and fled for protection to the church.[1] The bishop himself followed in the wake of his letters, and went as far as Aquileia. When they met, the emperor threw himself on the ground at his feet, and declared that he owed the victory to the bishop's merits and the bishop's prayer—at least, that is what Paulinus says in his biography of Ambrose.[2] Nor is it inconceivable. The lesson that the bishop had once read him had sunk in so far that, even after the battle on the Wippach, Theodosius withheld from partaking of the sacrament, on account of the blood that had been shed; but when his sons returned in safety, he regarded this happy issue as a sign of divine pardon.[3]

There seems to have been a certain amount of hesitation in the emperor's character in glaring contrast with the forthrightness of Ambrose; but no one can deny the emperor's honesty of heart in trying to do his duty as a Christian. At the very beginning of the campaign, he received a shattering *memento mori*: his consort, Galla, to whom he was passionately devoted, died in childbirth; and the child itself was still-born. He himself suffered from diabetes, and succumbed to this disease on January 17, A.D. 395. Severe earthquakes had shaken Europe in the preceding autumn, and were universally regarded as omens of his death.[4] Ambrose began by referring

---

[1] Ambr. *ep.* 61. 62   [2] Paulinus, *vita Ambro.* 31   [3] Ambr. *de obitu Theod.* 34   [4] Zosimos 4, 57, 3   Philostorgius 11, 2   Socrates 5, 26, 4   Ambr. *de obitu Theod.* 1   *Chron. min.* 2, 64

to this fact when preaching at the memorial service in Milan; he depicted the emperor, who had gone home to heaven, as the pattern of a Christian ruler. His life could be summed up in his dying words, "I have loved", understood in the sense of Paul's saying, "Love is the fulfilment of the law" (Rom. 3: 10). Ambrose spoke of his readiness to forgive, his merciful spirit, his humility before God; and then went on to depict him in heaven; how he greeted those of his children who had died before him, his father, and finally the Emperor Constantine. This was followed by a panegyric on Helena, who had found Christ's cross, and who had the sacred nails made into a bridle and a diadem: crown jewels which ever after were the insignia of the Christian emperors. The solemn service was attended by Honorius, who was ten years old, and his guardian, Stilicho, who was both generalissimo and brother-in-law; and Ambrose did not forget to urge them to carry out the last political decrees issued by Theodosius. Ambrose stressed this point in a matter-of-fact way that seems repellant at first blush, but that certainly issued from the core of his personality. He was a born statesman, and a statesman by the tradition of his family. He was certainly one of the great men of human history, even before he became a bishop, and he by no means regarded his office as a sinecure when he was the pastor and the political confidant of three emperors. That was also a fact of which the emperors themselves were very conscious. Theodosius was not wrong in giving way to this man, in whom the classical dignity proper to the Roman sense of what the state demands was combined with a profoundly earnest, Christian conception of the meaning of life. His funeral oration on Theodosius was, in a certain sense, Ambrose's own testament on church and politics. He left at once the scene where statesmanship played the grand role, and devoted himself exclusively to his episcopal duties and to literary work. In rather more than two years, on April 4, A.D. 397, he followed Theodosius to the other side. His age is not certain in tradition; but it appears most probable that he had begun his sixty-fourth year.[1] He had been a bishop for 23 years.

[1] Rauschen, *Jahrbücher*, 273 n. 7

Chapter Five

POPULAR CHRISTIANITY IN THE FOURTH CENTURY

THE FOURTH CENTURY WAS THE CRITICAL PERIOD FOR introducing those changes which shaped the Christian church and determined the character of its relation to the western type of civilization. Up to the time of Constantine, the church had been a voluntary fellowship of Christian believers who were held together by forces born in their own hearts. The forms in which it was organized, and the spirit with which it breathed, were a consequence of its own nature; this was the case even as regards those elements which it adopted from the world round about. Although on all formal grounds the church was subject to the authority of the state, yet it preserved a feeling of being different. This was the cause on account of which it suffered persecutions from time to time, and lay under a general interdict of illegality. A person joining the church did so at the risk of his position in life, sometimes even of his physical survival. In addition, he had to relinquish many of the pleasures which could be indulged when morals were not a consideration, and he had to adopt instead a strict self-discipline. This sort of thing repelled the man in the street, and attracted only persons of a greater depth of character. To become a Christian included and required taking a decision of a genuinely ethical kind, and the churches had much justification for regarding themselves as a company of the elect.

From the moment when Constantine changed the course of the ship of state, and not only recognized the church, but gave it public favour; and, in particular, from the time when Theodosius made Christianity the sole religion of the state, the entire situation was radically altered. Up to then, it had required courage to join the church; but from now onwards, this quality was needed, rather, in refusing to join. To profess the Christian faith began to serve as a testimonial to one's suitability for worldly affairs, and for an official career. Large numbers in good society laid emphasis on church activity—in short, the church grew into an essential element of public life, an element forming part of the very world which she had combated obstinately up to that point.

The change could not continue for very long without affecting the spiritual life of the church itself; the great crowds now streamed into its fellowship, and they, by the sheer weight of their numbers, moulded her spiritual endowment to meet their own needs, needs which arose from feelings rooted in nature-religions. The sacraments were held in higher esteem than ever before as the church's chief means of salvation; the consequence being that the gulf was widened which separated the baptized, fully-accepted Christians from the populace, and from the great numbers of catechumens waiting to be received as members. It had always been the practice that only baptized persons were admitted to the service of the Lord's Supper; this service was now invested with secrecy, and the secrecy was systematically extended to include further elements. Preachers adopted the habit of using the phrase, "The initiated will understand my meaning", when referring in public to matters connected with the sacraments. Even the rite of baptism came to be shrouded in mystery, and candidates under instruction were warned not to impart to catechumens anything that they were taught.[1] It was insisted, in particular, that the baptismal confession of faith should not be written down but committed to memory.[2] Learning this symbol by heart was a custom practised in the first epoch of the church, and is paedogogically sound. It gave rise, during the ceremony itself, to a special act, known as the *Traditio Symboli*, in which the creed was solemnly recited to the hearers for them to memorize the wording. A week later, came the *Redditio Symboli*, when the text was repeated aloud by each in turn.[3]

The secret character of the sacrifice of the mass and of the Lord's Supper was emphasized, with considerable psycho-

---

[1] Cyril of Jerusalem, *prokatechesis* 12
[2] Cyril, *Katech.* 5, 12   cf. Jerome, *c. Joh. Hieros.* 28   Rufin. *expl. symboli* 2 p. 54, Vallarsi   and even Iren. 3, 4, 1–2   Augustine, *sermo* 212, 2   214, 1
[3] Ritual in *sacramentarium Gelasianum* n. 35 (p. 53, ed. H. A. Wilson   1, 539 Muratori), and *missale Gallicanum vetus* n. 11 (2, 710 Muratori)   cf. Rufin. *explic. symb.* 3 p. 55 Vall.   Augustine, *conf.* 8, 2, 5   Conc. Laodic. *canon* 46

logical effect, by the custom, now being introduced, of veiling the altar behind a curtain. A subordinate item in this tendency was that the Lord's Prayer, which was used in the rite of the mass, was withdrawn from use by the generality of Christians. It was reserved for the use of baptized persons, on the ground that they alone[1] had the right to call God Father. In many places, it came about that the Lord's Prayer, together with the creed, formed the substance of the *Traditio* and the *Redditio*.[2] That fact makes it perfectly obvious that the whole business of secrecy was only a superficial device, a mere matter of outer form. Of course, the Lord's Prayer, at all times and in all places, was known to everyone, including catechumens; and it was expounded in complete detail by preachers in fully-attended public worship—which was never done with the creed. But every chance was eagerly seized of displaying the character of the "initiated", who attended the sacrament, as something distinct from the masses of merely mundane persons whose due place was among the catechumens; and there was a tendency to demand that, though the unbaptized might indeed know the Lord's Prayer, yet they were not to repeat it themselves.[3]

All phenomena of this kind are to be understood partly by reference to the prevailing air which favoured mysticism; and, more importantly, as a device of the church when seeking a means of self-defence against the incoming floods of people who wished for nothing more than a formal conversion to Christianity. If this last was in fact all they wanted, they could be content with remaining catechumens; but even as such, they were subject to the church's ethical discipline which, on occasion, was stringent enough.

The underlying cause of separation into two groups like this was that a certain early Christian principle continued to operate in full force, viz., that only those adults should be baptized who had received catechetical instruction in advance, and who, of their own free will, desired to receive the sacrament. Since the power of baptism to annul sin was universally

[1] Joh. Chrys. *in Mat. hom.* 19, 5 (7, 252c Montf.) Theodoret, *haeret. fabul.* 5, 28 (4, 479 Schulze)

[2] Augustine, *sermo* 56, 1   57, 1. 2   58, 1   59, 1

[3] see footnote 1, above, and very emphatically, *const. Apost.* 8, 34, 11

insisted on most emphatically, it seemed advisable to delay this crucial act to the last possible moment. Those who, like the Emperor Constantine, received the sacrament of baptism on their death-bed, might hope to enter heaven without sin— if only because they had no chance of sinning again. That is how the majority felt; with the result that preachers continually uttered warnings against playing in this dangerous way on God's patience; and they never wearied of rebutting the various excuses made by people who kept on delaying to accept the duties of the fully Christian state.[1] Infant baptism was, it is true, recommended as the safest means of sanctifying the body and soul of those who were growing up,[2] but the advice was seldom followed. Augustine, as a little boy, was once taken seriously ill, and he was immediately prepared for baptism; when however the danger passed with equal suddenness, the sacred rite was again deferred.[3] Numberless are the inscriptions telling of the administration of baptism immediately before death took place,[4] at all ages from the first to the fortieth year. Junius Bassus, prefect of the city of Rome, whose beautiful sarcophagus is well known, received baptism on his death-bed at the age of 42 in A.D. 359.[5] Throughout the early centuries, adult baptism was the rule; children were not usually baptized unless they fell ill.

In this way a new possibility was afforded the church. The preaching services were available for the people in general, but now it was feasible to give further and more detailed instruction to those few, more earnest Christians who were being prepared for baptism. We can draw on these very instructions as fruitful source-documents revealing the kind of religion which the church wished to bring to life in the souls of believers; they enable us to complete essential details of the pictures which can be deduced from the sermons. Records made by laymen themselves would have been of the greatest interest and importance, but practically all have been lost.

---

[1] Basil. *hom.* 13, 5–7 (2, 117ff. Garnier) Greg. Naz. *or.* 40, 11–12, 20–21 (1, 698f. 706f. Bened.) Joh. Chrys. *ad illum. catech.* 1, 1 (2, 226d)
[2] Greg. Naz. *or.* 40, 28 (1, 713f.) [3] Aug. *conf.* 1, 11, 17 cf. the story in 4, 4, 8
[4] Brought together by Diehl, *Inscr. lat. christ.* cap. 7, Nos. 1477–1509, and Nos. 1523–43 C. Wessel, *Inscr. graec. christ.* Nos. 359ff.
[5] Diehl, No. 90

It might be thought that inscriptions would be promising sources of information, but on account of their brevity and of their formal and stilted language, little can be gained from them. We must be content with making inferences from what preachers taught and from the forms in which worship was cast, and deduce what must have been the spiritual qualities of church-going people. If the hints drawn from various sources combine into a self-consistent whole, the likelihood is that we have got somewhere near the facts.

We shall turn in the first instance to the source which is at once the oldest and at the same time the richest and most instructive authority: the catechisms or "catechetical lectures" of Cyril of Jerusalem, dating from the middle of the fourth century, and used, about A.D. 350, in the Church of the Holy Sepulchre.[1] The bishop was well aware that by no means all his candidates for baptism were impelled by the purest motives. Many attended out of sheer curiosity; some were influenced by others, and desired to please either a friend, or in the case of slaves, their masters; others were brought into this circle by the hope of a marriage which they desired. None of these things threw dust into the preacher's eyes. But no matter what the bait was, he cast his line in the hope that even the superficial would be caught by the seriousness of the times of instruction. For the presumption that took precedence of all else was that anyone who had made up his mind to use the forty days of fasting in Lent for ousting his usual failings and sins, and who took himself seriously to task, was ready to do penance. Baptism was a rite performed but once in a Christian's life-time; its only pre-supposition was the right desire, but this was needed unconditionally. Therefore, from now onwards, avoid every evil deed, including those of the tongue and the eye.[2] In this way, the period of instruction in the catechism would be one of moral self-discipline. But this again was accompanied by the mystic allure of the ritual. Every period of instruction was preceded by the exorcism of each individual: his head was veiled in a cloth; formulas of adjuration, drawn from the Bible, were pronounced; the bishop breathed on him. Then the demon fled away, sin yielded, and the Holy

[1] vide Vol. 3, 246   [2] Cyril, procatech. 1–8

Spirit came, bringing salvation and the hope of eternal life.[1]

The mystic acts and the efforts of the inner self were combined into a unity: that was a characteristic feature of this form of religion as promoted by the church, and it was a form that adopted the idiom of nature-religion. This fact also explains why a warning was given against chattering about the esoteric experiences now about to be entered: "for we are handing on to thee a mystery, a hope of the Age to Come; guard the mystery from those who would waste this prize"— an exhortation aimed particularly at keeping the secret faithfully.[2] But the preacher's main purpose re-echoes again and again, no matter what the phrases employed: the strengthening of the will to moral endeavour.[3] That is what forms the entire content of the first catechism: it urges, go to confession without delay; avail yourself of the exorcisms always; lay aside all mundane concern; use the period of Lent just for striving for the salvation of your soul; forgive your personal enemies; and feed your soul by reading the Bible.[4] Sin is an evil thing that buds forth out of our own freedom of will; we bear full, personal responsibility for it, and this even when the devil leads us astray by the guile of his temptations.[5] We are challenged therefore to obtain forgiveness of sin by voluntary repentance. Forgiveness takes place during baptism, and salvation is impossible without baptism. Cyril expounded the sixth chapter of Romans in order to explain the rite: the sinner was submerged in the water just as Jesus was buried in the grave carved out of the rock; he left his own sins behind there, just as Jesus buried the world's sins there. Still following the example of the Lord, the baptized person came up out of the water, and began a new life. This life was lived in the power of the Holy Spirit, which enabled him always to gain the victory over the hostile forces. In the course of his struggles, the baptized Christian naturally can, and will, make progress, and will grow in grace.[6] It was in the course of the liturgy, and during the petitions to Christ and the Father, that the water received the power to perform this miracle. And the general context suggests that even a virtuous man would be

[1] Cyril, *Procatech.* 9   [2] *ibid.* 12   [3] *ibid.* 15   [4] *ibid.* 1, 5f.   [5] *ibid.* 2, 1–4
[6] *ibid.* 3, 12–14

unable to enter the Kingdom of Heaven without the seal of baptism.[1] The sacramental rite alone takes the moral impulse, which is proper to the will of the natural man and which it is the purpose of catechetical instruction to arouse, and transforms that impulse into a Christian effort which God rewards—but all depends on the man himself first exercising his own will. When he once belongs to the fellowship of those who have been baptized, the heavenly powers of sacramental grace will carry him forward step by step. Christians live on the religious teaching they have received and the good works they perform: the one without the other is worthless.[2]

The foundations having thus been laid down, we now begin on theological instruction in the church's articles of faith, given in the twelve catechisms that follow the Apostles' Creed. A summary statement of the subject-matter precedes the fourth article, and a discussion of the nature of faith precedes the fifth. The word faith, we are told, had a twofold connotation:[3] (i) on the side of dogma, it consisted of the believing acceptance of the gospel-message that Jesus Christ is Lord, and that God raised him from the dead. Accepting this teaching brings salvation and admits to paradise; and no doubts must be entertained whether this was possible. (ii) It means a gift of divine grace which can "move mountains", i.e. bring about superhuman events and work miracles. There is a solid basis here in the Bible. Moreover, the preacher went on to say that the baptismal creed contains, in summary form, "the whole dogma of the faith" as handed down by the church; nor did he forget to add that that dogma was confirmed by the whole of Scripture.[4]

The doctrine of God was defended, in accordance with the needs of the times, against heretics and Manichaean dualism; on the other hand, polytheism was given short shrift—it was nought but a foe that had long been vanquished. God, as creator and sustainer of the universe; God, the invisible, the perfect, the One who patiently bears with wickedness, is revealed to our eyes in the Bible and in nature.[5] But we must not forget that everything we say about Him is confined to the limits of our human nature and its weakness, and that no

[1] *catech.* 3, 3–4   [2] *ibid.* 4, 2   [3] *ibid.* 5, 10–11   [4] *ibid.* 5, 12   [5] *ibid.* 9

praise we can offer Him on earth is equal to the adoration which is His due.[1] Moreover, this inability of ours extends to our understanding of the relation between the Father and the Son: we can give no explanation as to how the Son was begotten, but can only say what it was not. From the standpoint of the Nicene Creed, it becomes clear that Cyril of Jerusalem was less than orthodox, in as far as he used the term *homoios*. Subsequently, he warned his hearers, on one occasion, not to tussle with and waste time over the concepts of *physis* and *hypostasis*, since never once were they mentioned in the Bible.[2]

It was Cyril's unremitting concern to base all his doctrines on the Bible, and he ended by plainly over-emphasizing what was good in itself, the result being that he wearied his readers.[3] But his exhortation to read the Scriptures diligently is well worth while noting as an indication of his conception of the pastoral office;[4] it shows, at the same time, that Bibles or at least portions of Scripture were not rare in the homes of the members of his church. With the same objective in mind, he also provided a list of the canonical books of the Bible, and uttered an earnest warning not to read uncanonical writings.[5] He answered the question, which could not help being raised: Why God became man, and, naturally, did so in terms of the Bible. God, the Logos, came here below to redeem sinful mankind. He changed His divine glory, and assumed a human form in order that we might be able to bear His glance. The body of flesh was the organ of which the devil made use against us; and the Lord assumed our flesh that it might learn to feel the power of the godhead, and that thus it might become the instrument of our salvation.[6] There is even a premonition of Anselm's dilemma in the statement that choice was confined to two courses: either God had to persist in His threats to punish sinners, and destroy them all; or else, He must show His mercy, and repeal His verdict.[7]

To people of that generation, Christ's death on the cross was no longer a scandalous thing; the cross had long become

---

[1] *catech.* 6, 3–4
[2] *ibid.* 11, 11   4, 7   16, 24
[3] *ibid.* 17, 1. 20. 30   16, 25. 32   18, 17. 30
[4] *ibid.* 9, 13 cf. 1, 5   17, 34
[5] *ibid.* 4, 33–36   [6] *ibid.* 12, 4. 14–15
[7] *ibid.* 13, 33

an emblem of salvation, an emblem which the very demons acknowledged with fear and trembling.[1] And now, particularly in Jerusalem, where the relics of the cross were treasured up, where all could see Golgotha, the house of Caiaphas, the judgment hall of Pilate, and the Holy Sepulchre; here, the story of the Passion, with its prophecy and its fulfilment in the Bible, was something that stood out before one's eyes; and moreover, all was penetrated by the fundamental confession: I confess the cross because I have had experience of the Resurrection.[2] Doubts had no place here, nor did even Christ's ascension imply that He was remote from the church. "He is here, in our midst; and He hears what we say about Him, and perceives what you think in private thought, and He tests heart and reins. He is ready, O you who want to be baptized, to bring you by the Holy Spirit into the presence of the Father, and to say, Lo, here I am, and the children God has given me".[3]

But at the last day, He would come to judge the living and all who had died since Adam; He would judge men and angels. They must refuse all inquisitive arts which attempted to determine when that day would come, for the Father had reserved the date to Himself alone. Scripture enumerated the signs of that time, and those who took a glance round about themselves would see with terror how that the foreshadowed declensions were taking place, and how invasions by pagans, schisms in churches, hatred between brethren, were proclaiming the approach of Antichrist.[4] When the signs had been completed according to the Scriptures, the incorruptible Judge would appear. "Thou hast no need to fear Him if thou hast bravely wrestled and laboured. Nothing of that effort is lost. In the Book is the record of every prayer, every psalm, every almsgiving, every fast, every true marriage, and every widowhood borne for God's sake; and virginity and continence are crowned with honour. But on the opposite page, the Book contains the record of all whoredom, all perjury, blasphemy, witchcraft, robbery, murder—these are things which annul the benefits of baptism: woe when wicked deeds return. Keep your eyes on the road that lies before you. It will lead you either

[1] *catech.* 13, 3. 36   cf. *ibid.* 17, 35   [2] *ibid.* 13, 4   [3] *ibid.* 14, 30   [4] *ibid.* 15, 18

to the Kingdom of Heaven, or else to the Everlasting Fire. Now is the time to live according to Christ's everlasting commandments."[1]

When the preacher came to the third article, he felt bound to deal with the living issues of his time: he entered into polemics against heretics, and discussed the Trinity. But he did this with much restraint, and soon turned to expound things said in the Bible, giving in great detail the passages of Scripture dealing with the Holy Spirit. In the course of these remarks, he made it quite plain to his hearers that spirit (*pneuma*) was an ambiguous word in itself: it meant every kind of thing that had no definite body, and therefore connoted wicked demons as well as human souls, the wind, also heavenly beings, and the Holy Spirit.[2] This passage shows how close his theology was to popular thought. We can see, and he himself discussed the point later, how it is possible for a person who possessed the Holy Spirit, to use the spiritual force within himself, overpower a demon by prayer, and banish him simply by breathing on him.[3] That was the bishop's own practice when exorcizing.

The hope of resurrection from the dead was felt to be something of which there could be no doubt; proofs were afforded by numerous examples drawn from nature; and then resurrection was demonstrated from Scripture. This hope also provided an incentive for living a good life; nay, it was "the root of good conduct", because it presented the soul with a concrete hope of reward. Moreover, it was the present body that was promised resurrection, and the believer would be careful not to defile it by immorality, or disfigure it by the scars of sin.[4] "The eternal life in which we believe is the guerdon of victory promised by the Lord to those who win in the Christian contest (*agōn*) on earth."[5] Here is an early Christian metaphor which had retained its force.

On the other hand, the inspired imagery of which the ancients had made use when paying their tributes to the church, had wilted in memory. True, she is described as a catholic, i.e. universal, institution for teaching and defending the articles of faith with which the people should be familiar;

[1] *catech.* 15, 23. 26   [2] *ibid.* 16, 15   [3] *ibid.* 16, 19   [4] *ibid.* 18, 1. 20   [5] *ibid.* 18, 28

she healed all sinners of their hurts in body and soul; she possessed in herself every kind of virtue, and this could find expression in deeds, words, and the gifts of spiritual grace;[1] lastly, the title "catholic" showed that she was different from each and every heretical institution. So the listeners were told, complete with illustrations drawn from the Bible; but it sounds unimpressive and dull as compared with the heartfelt paeans of praise offered in the past. Nor were solid reasons lacking: when the word, church, was used in the early days, the image called up was of a fellowship that had come down from heaven to earth, and that consisted of those who were united together in Christ. By contrast, when Cyril[2] thought about the church, it was the church which, though it had once been persecuted "now lived at peace and by God's grace; and also, as was her due, now enjoyed honours paid her by the emperor, by high officials, and by all races and peoples of mankind". It is plain that, here, the religious sense of the word had begun to pale. The decline of meaning did not take place at the same time in the west; rather, in that region, a classical doctrine of the church had been worked out in the period which began with Cyprian and extended to Augustine.

The theology expounded by Cyril to his baptismal candidates was one suitable for a simple laity of humble education. It put the whole force of early Christian discipline into an effort to gain improved ethical standards, and to induce ceaseless endeavours for attaining the highest levels of conduct. We are shown the dangers of the kind of seductions that sprang out of the former lives of the people and out of the pagan background. We can trace the high seriousness contained in the threats about the coming Day of Judgment with which Cyril, as a pastor of souls, enforced his warnings against sin. The whole of the period of the Forty Days (*tesserakostē*)[3] was to be a time of self-examination and of real repentance; and various external devices were adopted towards this end. In spite of all the emphasis on the fact that we enjoyed unlimited responsibility for our own selves, it was made quite indubitable that the ethical program could only be carried out with the help of the miracles experienced in the sacraments. Baptism

---

[1] *catech.* 18, 23   [2] *ibid.* 18, 27   [3] *vide* Vol. 3, 311

was needed in the first place to get rid of the accumulation of sins already there, and give a clean, new start. After that, the re-born human will would be able to walk in God's ways thanks to the Holy Spirit.

The "mystagogical" catechisms were used for instructing the newly-baptized between Easter Monday and the following Friday, and were the means of introducing them into the realm of the sacramental secrets. The ceremonies proper to the rite of baptism,[1] with their symbolism arising from nature-religions, were brought again to mind with the idea of giving a spiritual interpretation; and much was now said of all the temptations with which the devil lies in wait for the unarmed Christian. These included the seductive plays shown in the theatres and and low music halls, the blood-stained trade of the gladiators and the fighters with animals, the sheer break-neck madness of the horse-races. Even partaking in the foods that had been offered to idols might lead one into danger, for such foods were the resort of demons which had been exorcized in the temple. Woe to those who offered prayer in a pagan shrine, lighted candles or burned incense at holy wells in accordance with ancient custom, in order to get rid of some illness! A list of all the black arts was then provided: divination by birds, fortune-telling, necromancy, amulets, rings with magic stones, and all other kinds of witchcraft. This was the sort of thing that seethed round about and that was practised by people who were Christian only in name. The church's mysticism of the sacraments was now contrasted with these pagan practices; the ceremonies began with the rite of exorcism, which included breathing on the candidate and anointing him with holy oil. This oil, "when the name of God was invoked (*epiklesis*) and prayer offered, not only wiped out the traces of sin, but even abolished all the invisible effects brought about by the Evil One".[2] Moreover, myrrh (*chrisma*) was consecrated by *epiklesis* in the same way, and was smeared on the candidate's forehead, ears, nose, and chest when he came up out of the baptistry; and this myrrh was the material means used by the Holy Spirit for bringing heavenly gifts to the new-born. The bishop expressly taught that this oil, when given the *epiklesis* by the

[1] *vide* Vol. 3, 309   [2] *Cat. myst.* 2, 3

priest, became the vehicle of sacramental powers just as was the case with the bread and wine at the Lord's Supper.

The door is being pushed open, before our very eyes, through which the concrete, materialistic ideas of nature-religion penetrated into Christianity. Just because these materialistic conceptions satisfied the primitive needs of the natural man, they came in and took the places left vacant when the pagan ideas were ousted. The opening of the doors in this way facilitated the migration of the masses across to Christianity; but it involved, at the same time, a serious danger for that religion if it should be unsuccessful in leading the new converts from these low levels to the heights beyond. The best men of the fourth century had this objective in view, and they certainly did what they could even though they themselves were deeply involved in the toils of this very ritualism. The whole farrago of dedicating, anointing, breathing, crossing oneself, was really a low undergrowth, high above which grew the lofty and majestic rite of the Eucharist. But the hearers were instructed with emphasis that any man who did as the church taught, and devoutly entered into the spirit of a church service, with its dramatic structure crowned as it was by the mystery and the presence of the Lord in the elements; who partook of the miraculous food and drink in the communion service, and felt that he had become a vehicle of Christ (*Christophoros*); and had obtained a share in the divine nature;[1] that man was accoutred for a genuine Christian advance.

The Christianity of this order found its inspiration in the miraculous effects ascribed to the sacrament of the Eucharist. The teaching was quite independent of the rules of logic, but made direct appeals to men to use their freedom of will[2] for reaching complete self-mastery, and living heroically on the highest moral plane. At the same time it was firmly believed that this demand could only be met by apotheosizing human nature sacramentally. But he who entered on this warfare against sin and the devil could feel certain of a heavenly reward; and, from the first, he could be sure of being assisted by the miracle of the sacrament, the most precious jewel

[1] *Cat. myst.* 4, 3
[2] *catech.* 2, 1–2   4, 18–21; attacks on original sin 4, 19f.   12, 26

possessed by a Christian believer. His life as a whole, as well as every single "good work", would receive its reward.

The ideas expounded by Cyril in his catechisms correspond completely with the universal tenor of Christian teaching in the fourth century. They reappear everywhere, with variations which do not affect the substance; and the ideas were to be found also among writers in the west. For all its simplicity, Cyril's scholarship was somewhat pretentious; but if one allows for this fact, his sketch affords a picture of the essentials of Christianity as conceived by earnest and mature believers; it shows their concern to keep unsullied the grace received at baptism, and to earn the reward of a virtuous life. Some districts were more markedly affected by current theological controversies, and had polemical preachers for pastors; in these cases there would be relatively more of an amateurish discussion of theological and philosophical issues. In certain circumstances, some degree of fanaticism must be counted on.

The question arises as to the character of that level of Christianity which was to be met in the market-place and the side-streets, of which pagans made the actual acquaintance, and which the catechumens confessed as their faith. For answer, we must go to the preachers who held forth about it from the pulpits of the basilicas; and we must also inquire into the nature of the pastoral care which they exercised over the masses: all this, if we are to be in a position to grasp their objectives when they set about their task of training people to be Christian.

John Chrysostom, who used to preach in the city church of Antioch, is the earliest Greek bishop, a large number of whose sermons have come down to us; he did not write learned homilies complete with rhetorical phraseology, but, rather, sermons genuinely preached to the people themselves. From the first days after he entered on this office, in A.D. 386, a very large number, if not a complete set, of his sermons, are extant, written in shorthand. When we were listening, as it were, to Cyril, it was in the quiet surroundings of the Church of the Holy Sepulchre in Jerusalem, a city thronged by pilgrims; but Chrysostom introduces us to the centre of the gossipy life of a metropolis, and to a congregation who crowded a capacious church. Thus the preacher was used to good attendances; but one day, there were horse-races, and also there were empty spaces in his rows of hearers. John was annoyed, and decided to reprove the absentees when next they came; but he felt inclined to lenience when the day arrived, and so he merely suggested to them that they should get word from others about what he had said in their absence.[1]

The hearers used to follow the speaker with close attention. In a city which had been torn by quarrels over church and politics, he was glad to say that, although many among them had not yet agreed to the Nicene Creed, they liked to hear what he had to say about it; in fact they had ended by asking him to preach on the problem of *homoousios*. He promised to do so, but refused to indulge in bitter polemics; rather, his tone would be sympathetic, and his aim to win those who were against it. These remarks gained the approval of the congregation, and the preacher then urged his hearers to adopt the same principle in their daily lives.[2] The people present frequently signified their agreement with Chrysostom's pronouncements; but when it came to loud clapping, he reminded them that the church was not a theatre, and that the dignity of the sacred place must be duly observed.[3] Nor did he think it right that they should listen to him as they would to an opera-singer: for, after he had finished his sermon, off they went home, instead of staying for the continuation of the service, devoutly sharing in the main prayer offered by the church, and in the sacrifice of the Mass. He then spoke impressively about the significance and power of prayer in common, and against the evasive excuse: "I can pray quite as well at home".[4] That settled it, and the people remained for that occasion. But they talked during the sacred rite, and had to be admonished the next day.[5] The preacher sought to make them take things earnestly, and he pointed to certain pitiable persons possessed by demons, persons whom a deacon had brought in while the church was at prayer, in order that the

[1] Joh. Chrys. *c. anom. hom.* 7, 1 (1, 50:b–d)   8, 1 (1, 513e   514b)
[2] *c. Anom.* 1, 6–7 (1, 450–52)
[3] *ibid.* 4, 7 (1, 471a)   *de statuis*, 2, 4 (2, 25a)   *hom.* 17, 7   in Matth. (7, 232d) *hom.* 4, 6 in 1 Cor. (10, 33a)   *hom.* 26, 8 in 1 Cor. (10, 239e)
[4] *ibid.* 3, 6 (1, 469a)   [5] *ibid.* 4, 4–5 (1, 477)

intercessions of the people might be more definite. How was it possible to refrain from tears when faced with this lamentable sight? You chatter carelessly? Are you not afraid that a demon might possibly leap out of them and get into your unguarded soul? Yes, and do it at the very moment when the congregation are lifting up their hearts to join with the angels in heaven in singing the chorus, "Holy, holy, holy"![1]

Chrysostom had no grounds for complaining that his hearers lost interest even when he took wing and mounted the heights of speculative theology. The city congregation grew familiar with these subjects, and informed as to matters under discussion by the church. Ten sermons are extant, originally delivered in A.D. 386–87, attacking the opponents of *homoousios*. The sermons are a testimony to Chrysostom's marked ability as a teacher: he could take the problems at issue and reduce them to their simplest terms, avoiding abstract pedantry of all kinds. For instance, he would begin with the proposition that we are entirely ignorant of God's nature (*ousia*); and because of the finitude of human nature, we are quite incapable of comprehending it. Indeed, the very angels could not understand God's nature, nor would they ever be able to do so. That was what the Bible taught, but at the same time it taught quite plainly that the only begotten Son, who lies in the Father's bosom, knows Him as He is—because He is of a similar nature; and the same must be said of the Holy Spirit. Chrysostom based his argument on the Bible; and he took the Biblical passages cited by his opponents, explained them in detail, and turned their edge. All words used by Jesus, and all that was said about Jesus, were matters to be explained by the special circumstances relevant to each occasion; e.g. Jesus' prayer at the tomb of Lazarus[2] did not prove a position of subordination to, and dependence on, the Father; but that Jesus was concerned to use the occasion for giving proper instruction to the bystanders. The crucial passages were those in which Jesus condemns or commends, forgives sins or issues commandments, on His own authority and without addressing petitions to the Father: His purpose was to reveal his heavenly

---

[1] *c. Anom.* 4, 5 (1, 477)   cf. 3, 7 (1, 470c)   cf. Vol. 3, 292
[2] *ibid.* 9 (1, 525)   7, 5 (1, 507c)

origin to men.[1] Sometimes, in expounding Scripture, Chrysostom introduced quite artificial devices; but his sermons were always so vivid, and, at times, so striking and dramatic,[2] that it is easy to see how the congregation listened with rapt attention.

No preacher, either before or after him, has excelled Chrysostom in the degree to which he trained his hearers by systematic Biblical exegesis. During the twelve years of his ministry at Antioch, he preached several series of sermons, sermons in which he expounded Genesis, a selection of the Psalms, the gospels of Matthew and John, besides most of the Pauline letters. And, let it be said, this instruction, given by a preacher who was genuinely an exegete-born, must be taken into account in attempting to assess the religion of the church in Antioch; but this is a point to which we shall return.

Christians in Antioch were faced, on the one hand, with their relation to paganism, but, on the other, they had curious contacts with Judaism. Parallel phenomena have been recorded, too, by other authorities, and in other places. In particular, it was a usual practice to attend the synagogue, keep the Jewish fasts, and even make gifts of oil on taking part in the festivals celebrated in the synagogue. There were people in Spain who persuaded the Rabbi to pronounce a blessing over their fields; so, too, Africa seethed with the observance of Jewish customs and festivals.[3] And this sort of flirting with Judaism played a dubious role in Antioch. Jewish doctors were called in, and their ceremonial prescriptions, including even incubation in the synagogue, were accepted and complied with. When very important agreements were being made, people went to the synagogue to swear their oaths; it was firmly believed that oaths sworn in front of the coffer containing the Torah were more potent. And it is indubitable that those who joined in the Jewish fasts and festivals expected to gain advantages for themselves. The New Year's celebrations were felt to be particularly attractive, with their striking spectacle of blowing the trumpets; and many guileless people may have attended

[1] c. Anom. 10, 3 (1, 532d)   [2] e.g. c. Anom. 8, 4–6 (1, 518d   521a. d)
[3] Canon. apost. 64.   70. 71   Const. apost. 2, 61, 1   Conc. Laod. can. 37. 38
Conc. Elvira, can. 49, 50   Statuta eccl. Afric. 89 (Bruns, Canones Apost. et conc.
1, 149)

out of idle curiosity.[1] In any case, contacts of this sort with Judaism were not religious in essence, and not shaped by any kind of special leaning towards the religion of the Old Testament; rather they represented the overspill of the superstitious idea that, in special cases of need, help could be gained with greater certainty by going outside the familiar ways of their own religion, and taking to the by-paths.

The adherents of Christianity who were looking for help of a magical kind, divided themselves into two groups according as they resorted to paganism or to Judaism; and pastors acted not without reason when they called such renegades to account. Chrysostom was one of them, and he decided, in autumn A.D. 386, when the Jewish New Year was about to begin, to deal faithfully with this superstition, and to preach about it publicly in church—an experiment which he repeated the following year. It would seem, he said, that many people thought there was something specially valuable about the Jewish religion and its ceremonies; and even held the opinion that the Jews worshipped the true God. Nothing could be further from the truth; no Jew worshipped God, and the synagogue was the home of the devil and his demons; services held there were just cases of worshipping idols. Do you suggest that it must be a sacred place because the books of the Mosaic law and the prophets are kept there? But the sacred books are also kept in the temple-library of the Serapeum at Alexandria; Ptolemaeos Philadelphos had had a translation made for the very purpose; but did that make the Serapeum a sacred place? Not by any means: it is, and always will be, a place where idol-worshippers assemble. The same was true of the synagogue. There was nothing in common between us Christians and the Jews, for they did not obey the voice of the prophets, and they had come to be at the beck and call of demons. They did not recognize a God of punishment; they made gods of their bellies, and lived only for the joys of the present life. What they really appreciated was eating and drinking, and fighting about dancing girls and jockeys till blood flowed.[2]

[1] Joh. Chrys. c. Jud. hom. 1, 7 (1, 598b)   1, 6 (595d)   8, 5 (681c)   and remarks by H. Usener, Weihnachtsfest, 2nd ed. 235; 1, 3 (591a. c)   1, 8 (599c); 2, 1 (601b)   8, 5–6 (681c. 682e)
[2] c. Jud. 1, 4 (592a)

Was that the sort of people that a Christian should accompany to their synagogues, and expect to get help there? You ought to be ashamed of yourselves; they are just laughing at you, and cracking jokes about you in private.[1] That is how Chrysostom put Judaism in its place. Any and every contact with that religion was the subject of attack; it was plainly and simply condemned; and no ground was left to stand on for raising pleas about the Old Testament. In essence, it was the same position as Christianity had taken up from the first. The cry, "Crucify him, crucify him," shouted before Pilate's judgment seat, separated the disciples in principle from the people of the Talmud.

A great riot broke out in Antioch in January, A.D. 387 on account of the excessive burden of the taxes. All at once, alarming disturbances in the streets lent support to the complaints of the people with property; confused brawling took place during which the bronze statues of the royal family were demolished and trailed through the streets. In the end, a detachment of soldiers had to be called in, and the disorder was quelled. Dispatch-riders were sent at once to Constantinople to report to the emperor direct, and measures to punish the guilty were hastily taken in Antioch itself. The temper then suddenly changed; it was recognized with grave concern that the situation was of deadly seriousness, and it was feared that the emperor, in his wrath, would inflict the sort of vengeance which, three years later, in fact fell on the unhappy Thessalonika.[2] All those who were able to do so, either went away from the city, or lay hidden in the house; the streets and squares were left empty. Bishop Flavian, although crippled by age and illness, set out in spite of the wintry conditions, and made his way to the court in an attempt to get there before irremediable measures were decided on. He was passed on the road by a commission of inquiry furnished with the fullest authority. The commission ordered in the first instance the closing of the theatres and the baths, stopped the distribution of corn, and lowered the status of the city.

At that crisis of affairs, Chrysostom stood up in the pulpit and became the spiritual adviser of a distraught congregation.

[1] *c. Jud.* 8, 8 (687b)   [2] Joh. Chrys. *de statuis hom.* 2, 3 (2, 23e)

He dealt in his sermons with the events as they took place day by day, and his gospel message lifted their hopes, calmed their fears, and converted both moods into holy experiences. He declared that he had preserved silence for seven days, but now he would raise his voice in sorrow and in prayer, to inspire confidence: A Christian must show how he differed from an unbeliever by the courage with which he bore whatever happened.[1] Only a short time ago, he had urged them to put up a fight against those who talked too much. Would that they had listened. Woe had soon fallen on their city, but he would now call them back to their right senses.[2] The things that were of genuine value were becoming plain. Money by itself was not to be depended on, although it was not an evil as such; the important question had to do with the use to which it was put. A truly wealthy man not only possessed much, but also gave much away.[3] Christian virtues thrived on what was done for the needy. The real point in life was not to fill your homes with nice things, but to set up a tent in heaven, a tent that could not be destroyed, nor left empty, and that would not be lost even in death. God has given you money so that you can help the needy and, by your generosity, obtain forgiveness for your sins.[4]

The note which these sermons continually re-echoed was that of exhortation to regard the present troubles as a penance for one's own sins, and, by deepening one's own inner life in this way, to win forgiveness from God.[5] Moreover, since it was Lent, and a period of fasting before Easter, it was proper to repent; the season required us to put all our senses under discipline. We must work our passage through to an entirely new way of life; and this by abstinence, not just in matters of food, but in all the sins of the eye and the ear and the tongue and the hands and the feet. That was the important thing, and not merely to offer the prayers of the litany for two or three days, as usually happened if there was an earthquake or a famine: then for a short time, you would behave yourselves properly and be subdued; but afterwards, you would go back

[1] Joh. Chrys. de statuis hom. 2, 3 (2, 23e)   [2] ibid. 2, 1 (20d)
[3] ibid. 2, 5 (27c)   [4] de stat. 2, 7 (30d)
[5] ibid. 3, 7 (47b)   4, 2 (50e)   5, 4 (65d)   6, 1 (75a)   6, 4 (79b)   7, 1 (85a)
20, 1 (199b)

to your old habits. This time let it be different; cling to the better ways.[1]

Nor was Chrysostom content with general exhortations of this kind: the hearers must begin their self-discipline at once and, from now onwards, set themselves the aim of doing away with three things,[2] viz. back-biting, personal enmities, and the habit of cursing and swearing. Moreover, just as he had already done in the case of the sermons attacking the Jews, when he appealed to the people to teach each other, so in the present instance: he requested his hearers to do their part in spreading his advice; this would help the congregation to train and discipline their own selves. Should it come about that the head of a household heard either his wife, his children, or his slaves, cursing and swearing in spite of being forbidden, he should order them to bed without supper—but he must apply the same discipline to himself and his friends: hunger and thirst affect our senses and so impose restraint upon refractory tongues. Chrysostom's remarks evoked audible agreement from the church, and, after a few days, the preacher could count on it that the points he had made would have a good effect.[3]

Practical teachings of this kind were what Chrysostom hammered home to his congregations, and his sermons enable us to see how great was his sympathy for his hearers, and also, how the latter would agree with him. Besides urging the people in this way to follow a new mode of life, he dealt also very suggestively with Biblical passages, which had nothing to do with the problems of the moment, but which were chosen in agreement with the church's custom. Thus, e.g. in Lent, Genesis was appointed,[4] and accordingly, on the fifth day of his series of sermons dealing with it, he began expounding the story of creation; and this exposition, conjoined with Psalm 19(18) ran like a silken thread of Scripture through the following addresses. He said that it would be a sign of little-mindedness to want to be always harping on the difficulties of the present, and for this reason he would now turn and give his usual teaching-sermons: especially as all exposition of Scripture gave comfort and consolation.[5] But alarming days,

---

[1] de stat. 3, 3–7 (39e. 46c–e)   [2] ibid. 3, 7 (47d)   [3] ibid. 5, 7 (70d. e)   9, 1 (97a)
[4] vide Vol. 3, 312   [5] de stat. 7, 1 (85d)

full of anxiety, kept recurring, and people in their distress sought refuge in the church;[1] and Chrysostom always knew just what to say to stricken men and women. He lifted up their spirits and lent iron to their moral will; and then pagans would look at them and praise the God of the Christians because of the lives they lived.[2] That was also why he was quite offended when the mayor of Antioch appeared in the church one fine day, and gave a reassuring speech. He had meant well, but was it not a shameful thing that Christians, who ought to be an example to pagans, should have to submit to instruction by a pagan?[3] Chrysostom was familiar with the weaknesses of his people, and therefore gave the desirable didactic turn in exactly the right way when describing events, especially, e.g., the court inquiry; and, later, the audience which Bishop Flavian had of the emperor. He also took a peculiar pleasure in telling of hermits and monks, who, on the day when the court of inquiry was sitting, came down from the mountains and from the caves in Sipylos, and begged the royal commissioners to have mercy on the offenders. They only left the city again after having received a promise that a letter they had composed would be placed in the emperor's hands. Those were real Christian philosophers—but, in contrast, what had been done by the cynics who used to preach in the streets, and who, complete with their mantles and beards, were the pagan philosophers? They had all fled the city and crept into caves outside it.[4]

Meanwhile, both Bishop Flavian and Caesarius, the special commissioner who had returned to make his report, did what they could to incline the emperor to clemency. In the end, they succeeded in obtaining a full amnesty for the people of Antioch. Flavian returned in Holy Week bringing the news; and he celebrated Easter in the midst of a happy congregation. Chrysostom delivered the Easter sermon, and gave an account of the bishop's journey.[5] Both men had stood up well to the testing time of the dire distress of the church.

It is as well to add that the celebrated Libanius spoke about

---

[1] *de stat.* 4, 1 (49a. b)   12, 1 (124c)
[2] *ibid.* 9, 5 (104c)   3, 5 (42c)   cf. 21, 1 (215c)   21, 3 (220b)
[3] *ibid.* 16, 1 (160d)   [4] *ibid.* 17, 1–2 (172a–173b)   [5] *ibid.* 21 (21 3ff.)

the serious situation at Antioch. Five of his addresses on the subject are extant, including one composed for delivery in the presence of the emperor on behalf of the distressful city. Actually, however, Libanius stayed at home, and these addresses were only written after the danger was over—what is more, he made use of Chrysostom's sermons in doing so![1]

These sermons, just because of the pastoral concern they exhibit in times of danger, make it plain how closely the church was knit with the public life of the great city; and with what seriousness a man of Chrysostom's type felt his responsibilities for training his flock. Whatever the subject he may have chosen for his sermon, he always made it issue in exhortations and suggestions for bringing ethics to bear on the daily conduct of life. He displayed a noble earnestness in adopting the ambition which characterized the early church, viz. that Christians should be distinguished from pagans and Jews by their mode of life;[2] and we have already examined the way in which he took the faults and special failings of his hearers, and pursued them into their last recesses. Similarly, whenever he expounded Scripture, he brought it to a practical issue, with the idea of giving Christian people guidance for everyday living. It must be granted that he held the Eucharist and its sacramental mystery to be miraculous in nature and, as such, the source of the life which the church lived; but this was a subject that he spoke of very seldom and with much restraint,[3] but not because he hesitated to speak in the presence of persons other than those who were full members of the church. It appealed more to him to issue a direct challenge to the will of Christian people, and to strengthen the doubters and the hesitating. "Do not lose heart if you fail twice or thrice, or even as much as twenty times; take your courage in both hands anew, and begin again unwearied".[4] On the other hand, when addressing candidates for baptism, he would utter impressive

---

[1] Libanius, *or.* 19–23, and notes by R. Goebel, *de Joannis Chrys. et Libanii orationibus quae sunt de seditione Antiochensium*, Göttinger Diss. 1910
[2] *de stat.* 3, 5, (2, 42c) 9, 5 (104c) 16, 1 (160d. 162a) 21, 1. 3 (215c. 220b) *hom.* 15, 8 *in Matt.* (7, 198c) *hom.* 17, 7 *in Matt.* (232b) *hom.* 21, 4 *in Matt.* (274a)
[3] *ibid.* 2, 9 (2, 34b) *c. Anom.* 6, 4 (1, 499e) *de bapt. Christi* 4 (2, 373d. e) *de prod. Judae hom.* i, 6 (2, 384)
[4] *hom.* 17, 7 (7, 232c)

warnings against the danger of backsliding into sin, and therefore insist that they should test and prove their own firmness of character;[1] yet, on the other hand, when preaching in the course of public worship, he always spoke in glowing terms of God's mercy on all sinners, and of the purifying efficacy of repentance. Those who did really desire to lead better lives would find that God would respond and help them.[2] Those who had pure motives, who accepted the troubles and cares of life, and who bore them without murmuring; or those who imposed sacrifices on themselves if only to the extent of fasting and almsgiving—which the annual Easter fast might call for—all such people could throw off their sins by repentance of this kind, always granted that the first requirement was met by their living better lives. For[3] this purpose, it would be fitting to exercise self-denial for the sake of converting one's neighbour, and this would be accepted by God as a penitential act.[4] It is relevant to note in this connection, that Chrysostom, in the course of the duties of his pastoral office, saw many who needed advice, and heard their confessions in private; the unrepentant being punished, indeed, with exclusion from the sacraments.[5]

When Chrysostom preached a series of expositions of the Sermon on the Mount, he made it as plain as possible what he understood Christian morality to be. It was Christ's law—"in order that you may be like your Father in heaven"; the change that he made in the wording of Matt. 5: 45 is significant. The "peak of philosophy" was to be attained by ascending a ladder. It began with prohibiting wrong-doing; and then the increasing demands of the Sermon on the Mount were cleverly fitted in to a nine-fold scheme, in such a way that the seventh grade (loving one's enemy), the eighth (doing good to him), and then the ninth (praying to God for him), would reach the goal.

The exhortations of Jesus Himself are constantly interwoven

---

[1] ad illum. catech. 2, 2 (2, 237d)
[2] hom. 19, 5 in Matt. (7, 252b ff.)   22, 5 in Matt. (7, 281a. b)
[3] de stat. 4, 1. 2 (2, 50c. e)   5, 4 (65d. 66a)   6, 1 (74d. 75a)   6, 3 (77a. b)
6, 4 (79b)   7, 1 (85a);   fasts 3, 3ff. (39ff.)   20, 1 (199)
[4] c. Jud. 8, 4 (1, 6, 79a)
[5] de stat. 20, 9 (2, 213c)   hom. 17, 7 in Matt. (7, 232e)   cf. Cyril, catech. 1, 5

with references to various rewards which God gives to willing disciples; and, in so doing, Chrysostom reveals his skill as a teacher, a skill which, plainly, he was always trying to improve. He said that, taken on the whole, Jesus "did not really make exaggerated demands, but only a little more than that customary thing which was enough to satisfy pagans".[1] But Chrysostom went too far when he said that no one should regard these commandments as impossible, because, as a matter of fact, many Christians were already living the apostolic life that was required: he had in mind the monks who, by their continence, exemplified on earth what it was to live like the angels. The essence of Christian perfection was exhibited by their asceticism and their total repudiation of earthly cares.[2] But Chrysostom would not make demands on his hearers to this extent; he would be content if they merely learned to avoid dishonesty and to give to charity. That would represent a step forward, from which rapid progress to greater heights would be possible.[3] He kept insisting that this way was not difficult; nay, it was easy: for human nature was fitted for the moral life. Moreover, the grace of God, which is ultimately the source of all, comes to our aid when we pray, and assists our good intentions. But it remained true that we were responsible in the first instance for our own salvation or condemnation.[4]

The primary objective which Chrysostom tried to set before his church had three main aspects: i. moral conduct took first place, in the sense of ordinary law-abiding citizenship; ii. a forgiving spirit; iii. an increased willingness to exercise self-denial for the sake of the common good. He demanded that, in these respects, they should go beyond pagans and Jews in all circumstances and in every case. With that as a starting point, they might gradually rise to the spiritual kind of life characteristic of a full and rounded Christianity. A "life like that of angels" was the ultimate goal, a fact which led him to become celebrated for his praise of the martyrs, who, by

---

[1] *hom.* 18, 4–6 in Matt. (7, 238d. e 242b. d)
[2] *ibid.* 21, 4 in Matt. (7, 273)   angels: *hom.* 18, 6 (244a)   *hom.* 19, 5 (251d) *hom.* 26, 7 (321a)   cf. *hom.* 10, 4 (144b)
[3] *ibid.* 21, 4 (273c)
[4] *ibid.* 22, 5 (281b. c) *hom.* 23, 3 (288e–289a)   23, 5 (291ab)   21, 3 (273a)

dying heroically, had attained the status of angels, and had given Christians the noblest examples of supreme virtue.[1] He exercised his gifts by dwelling in all sorts of ways on their model character in this respect, and delivered numerous memorial addresses on their feast days. The religious esteem in which the martyrs were held was characteristic of all the early church, but in this respect, the tributes paid by Chrysostom went far beyond what was then customary.

For a long time, it had been a pious custom to honour the graves of martyrs with artistic adornments, and emperors entered into rivalry with each other in building martyrs' churches and chapels. The people used to visit these places frequently, and pay to the heroes of the church the kind of respect which, in pagan times, they had been accustomed to pay to the heroes of Greek mythology. Chrysostom gave high praise to the custom, and attributed quite a special efficacy to the tombs and their precious relics. He said that God had taken the souls of the martyrs to Himself, but left their bodies with us on earth; the sight of them would awaken in us a motive for striving towards the highest philosophy.[2] "I myself", he averred, "might threaten you, flatter, frighten, or urge you without effect. But when you enter a martyr's chapel, and just look at the sainted man's grave, your eyes stream with tears, and your heart warms with fervent prayer. Why is this? Because you envisage the figure of the martyr, and that evokes the thought of his achievement. Face to face with his grandeur, you become conscious of your beggarly poverty; you realize how great is the gulf between your own self and his: the martyrs are in a position to speak freely in God's presence, and to rejoice in His honour and glory."[3]

But there was more to be said. Just as a brave warrior was buried with his weapons, so also the bodies of the martyrs had their weapons at hand. These consisted of the power of Christ which resided in their wounds. These powers always continued to scare demons away, as you could prove each time you brought a possessed man to visit one of their tombs.[4]

[1] Joh. Chrys. *in s. Julianum* 4 (2, 676d)
[2] *in s. Julianum* 4 (2, 676f.)　*in s. Barlaam* 4 (2, 685e)　　[3] *de ss. martyribus* 2 (2, 653)
[4] *in s. Barlaam* 4 (2, 686b)　*in s. Julianum* 2 (2, 674d)　*de s. Droside* 2 (2, 691d)
de stat. 8, 2 (2, 93b)

It was therefore good and commendable to visit their tombs often. It brought down blessings, for the martyrs were very worthy in God's eyes. They were His friends, and had free access to Him at all times. Just as veteran soldiers might address the emperor boldly, when they showed him the wounds they had received in his service, so the martyrs could carry their decapitated heads in their hands, enter God's presence, and then ask for whatever they liked. We ought to try and gain the help of these powerful intercessors, so that, by their inter-mediation, we might draw God's mercy to our own selves.[1]

[1] *c. Jud.* 6 (1, 683b) *in Juventinum et Maximinum* 3 (2, 583c) *de s. Beronice et Prosdoce* 7 (2, 645d) Sources in E. Lucius, *Anfänge des Heiligenkults*, 1904, 125ff. H. Delehaye, *Les origines du culte des martyrs*, 2nd ed. (1933), 100ff.

Chapter Six

MONASTICISM

(1) The Preparatory Stages

JOHN THE BAPTIST WAS AN ASCETIC. HE LIVED IN SOLITUDE, wore a tunic woven of camel hair and a belt made of leather; his food was grasshoppers and the honey of wild-bees; his disciples undertook frequent fasts. An ancient tradition[1] describes the contrast offered by Jesus, who had no rules about food and drink, and imposed none on His disciples. While accustomed to seek the solitude of the mountains when He wished to pray, He did His work in the towns at the lakeside, and in the presence of large numbers of the public. He often had meals in the company of tax-collectors and sinners, but this did not lead Him to refuse invitations from well-to-do Pharisees.[2]

The contrast is striking, but it reveals merely a difference in way of life, not in essential attitude. Jesus shared the view that to enter the fellowship of the Kingdom of God, it was a necessary pre-supposition to disrupt all the bonds that bound men to the material world, including their own homes and their own parents. If the present world should offer hindrances and oppose God's call, then our seductive love for it must be met with an exalted hatred.[3] Possessions of a material kind lead our hearts away from God: "You cannot serve God and Mammon." It would be easier for a camel to go through the eye of a needle than for a rich man to enter the Kingdom of God. The rich young man was therefore told to go and sell his property in order that he might be unencumbered, and so follow the Master who had nowhere to lay His head. The church gratefully remembered the names of certain women who had placed their means at the disposal of the Lord and His disciples.[4] Not one of this band showed concern for the morrow; each was content to ask God for his daily bread.

---

[1] Matt. 11: 18. 19=Luke 7: 33. 34   cf. Mark 2: 18
[2] Luke 7: 35   cf. Luke 14: 7. 12   [3] *ibid.* 14: 26   cf. Vol. I, 33f.   [4] *ibid.* 8: 3. 3

Jesus regarded marriage as a divine institution, and therefore as a holy and unbreakable bond; but He denied it to Himself; the labour demanded by the Kingdom of God left no leisure for the happiness of family life. A tradition of doubtful authenticity ascribes to Jesus a saying[1] regarding those who had emasculated themselves for the sake of the Kingdom of God— "He who is able to receive this, let him receive it". Those who were ready to serve God unconditionally, would repudiate all the joys of earth untouched, and render obedience unto death, even on the cross. This attitude bore but an outward resemblance to asceticism, and was in fact only an unavoidable subsidiary phenomenon in a life entirely devoted to the goal set by God.

Christians of the earliest generations preserved similar feelings. Paul contrasted his own active, self-denying, itinerant, and solitary life with that of the "other apostles", including the Lord's brother and also Cephas whose wife shared his journeys.[2] Marriage was good and not sinful, but it distracted one's attention from perfect devotion to the Lord, and entangled one in the cares of the present world. To this extent the apostle's requirements kept to the principles laid down by Jesus. However, when Paul referred[3] to the approaching times of stress, "immediately impending"—a catastrophe in which "the present shape of things would disappear"—the exhortation to refrain from marriage may be regarded as a further application of the Lord's teaching.

On the other hand, it was in an entirely different note when he said, "It is good for a man not to touch a woman",[4] and declared that marriage was only a concession to human frailty for the sake of obviating something worse. Such a contention is based on the idea, associated with nature-religion, that sexual intercourse is a defilement in God's sight.[5] It also linked up with a primitive, lowly estimate of the status of woman, making her simply the object of physical desire; and so it is a foreign element in the system of Christian thought. Seen from this standpoint, to refrain from marriage was no longer

---

[1] Matt. 19: 12 and remarks by K. Heussi, *Ursprung d. Mönchtums* (1936), 27
[2] I Cor. 9: 5   [3] *ibid.* 7: 26, 29, 31   [4] *ibid.* 7: 1-2
[5] cf. also I Cor. 7: 5

incidental to an overriding purpose, but something to be held in esteem for its own sake. A further consequence was the fact, which is in itself incontestable, viz. that only a few are capable of making this heroic decision; and this, in turn, demanded and received respect. Thus it came about that whereas custom, law, and the words of Jesus Himself, sanctioned marriage by calling it "good", the word "better" was used to praise those who voluntarily denied themselves marriage.[1] Two degrees of morality were thus created, of which the first was regarded as normal and the second as superior.

The doctrines which Paul had taught the church at Corinth continued to play an active part in the thought of the churches, which distinguished between the usual run of Christians, on the one hand, who were concerned to do their best in keeping the divine commandments; and, on the other, the "perfect", who had no place for marriage and possessions, and ill-used their bodies.[2] The earliest documentary evidence is to be found in the change made in the record when Matthew borrowed Mark's account of the rich young man.[3] According to Mark, Jesus simply requested the young man to sell all his property; but Matthew added the prefatory clause, "If thou wilt be perfect"! The Roman church is fully justified in maintaining that this was not a commandment; it was an admonition for those who strove for a higher morality; the early Christians were of exactly the same view. Their thought, and, in the case of those who had sufficient strength of character, their conduct, were based on three principles, viz. a low estimate of personal property, of woman, and of the human body. From the standpoint of the Master, these had been nothing more than three forms of self-denial imposed by the necessity of fulfilling His mission; but they were now regarded as ideals with a philosophical basis, and as part of an ethic which consisted of striving to exceed the degree usually required. This change, however, transformed their essential character, and led them to find their inspiration in non-Christian sources.

From the time of Diogenes, and therefore now for several generations, Cynic philosophers had been preaching that the

[1] 1 Cor. 7: 1, 7, 8, 28, 38, 40   cf. also Rev. 14: 4
[2] *ibid.* 9: 27   [3] Matt. 19: 21   compare with Mark 10: 21

freedom and independence of the sage presupposed his repudiation of earthly possessions; and there had been thousands of
instances of men who had put this doctrine into practice.
Among the familiar sights during the first century of the
Roman empire were the Cynics wearing rough cloaks, carrying
begging bags and thorn-sticks. They used to wander from
town to town preaching to the people, and hammering in their
platitudes. When the apostles went preaching the gospel, they
travelled about in a similarly unencumbered manner.[1] Men
at large, and shortly also the churches themselves, regarded
these missionaries as exercising the same kind of calling and as
possessing the same variety of spiritual qualifications as were
to be obtained from the schools of philosophy. Thus it came
about that people living at that time combined the Christian
idea of denying the world for the sake of the kingdom of God,
with the Cynic idea of despising the world for the sake of
personal freedom.

The low esteem in which woman was held owed its origin
to oriental modes of thought, and has been preserved among
the Jews; what Paul had to say about their subordinate position in the services of worship of the church[2] breathes with the
spirit of the synagogue. The view that sexual intercourse
makes a person unfit to take part in public worship is to be
found in all nature-religions; in many of them, it has issued in
numerous regulations for sexual restraint on the part of persons
offering prayers or making sacrifices, as well as prescriptions
for the continence of priests of both sexes.[3] Rules of this kind
are in force in Judaism. Further, the belief that a girl was the
bride of a god, was in many cases extended to a lifelong
prohibition of any earthly love; and this, in turn, gave rise to
rules for the continence of priestesses and women dedicated to
the godhead when their services to public worship were affected.
Both these lines of thought led to the view that sexual continence brought men closer to the godhead and could compel the

---

[1] Mark 6: 7-11   Matt. 10: 5-16   *Didachē* 11: 3-6   12: 1-5
[2] 1 Cor. 11: 3-10   14: 34-35   and the Jewish records in Billerbeck, Vol.
III, *ad loc.*   cf. also Strathmann (compare the following footnote) 1,
18-21
[3] Details in H. Strathmann, *Geschichte d. frühchristlichen Askese* 1 (1914)   E.
Fehrle, *Die kultische Keuschheit im Altertum*, 1910

god to make revelations. In ancient times, therefore, prescriptions for the continence of men and women were a commonplace; sometimes, religious duty imposed denial for life.[1] Philosophers adopted ideas of this kind and gave them a mental content, either in sympathy with the Cynic sage's freedom from the bonds of the world and with the ethical necessity for mastering the passions and needs of the body; or, on the other hand, in continuation of the Orphic and Pythagorean ideal of purity as seen in the praise accorded to, if not in the requirement of, sexual continence.[2] Among the Jewish sects of the Essenes and the Therapeutae, intercourse with women was forbidden; and Philo supplied a theory for this mode of life, a theory which he based on the antithesis of soul and body as seen of old in Plato and, more recently, among the neo-Pythagoreans.[3]

A type of asceticism had developed as early as the first Orphics, and was seen in their negative attitude to life and their doctrine of a pitiless "wheel of re-births". Ascetics of this type regarded the body as the enemy of the soul, and refused to nourish it by eating any flesh, except that used as food during the rites of worshipping the dead.[4] Considerations of a philosophical character lent support to their abstention, which soon came to be widely adopted. The early Christians were among those who formed such circles within the churches, and held reasons of a religious character for regarding only vegetable foods as permissible.[5] In this way, a course of development took place without raising any suspicion as to what was happening: it began with the unencumbered manner of life adopted by the early Christian apostles, and issued in accepting asceticism as a principle. This principle then linked up with the surrounding pagan world, and established an agreement which had still further effects. Account must also be taken of the additional fact that, at an early date, the church adopted the Jewish custom of fasting twice each week, and came to regard it as an obligatory practice; and there

---

[1] vide Fehrle op. cit. 162   Hopfner in Pauly-Wissowa, Supplement 7, 50–64
[2] vide Diog. Laert. 8, 19 re Pythagoras   Philostratus, Vita Apollonii, 1, 13 Alexander Polyhistor in Clem. Alex. Strom. 3, 60, 4
[3] vide Vol. I, 34. 94f. 135f.   [4] E. Rohde, Psyche, 2, 125f.
[5] Rom. 14   cf. Handb. ad 14: 1

were numerous occasions when the practice was still further extended.[1] Considerations of this kind make it perfectly clear that, from the very beginning of the Christian movement, there were ample possibilities for the growth of ascetic practices in regard to food.

The further Christianity spread in countries with a Greek culture, the more vigorous were the churches in developing tendencies to go beyond the customary exercises of fasting and the usual practice of continence. A principle of general application was laid down in the *Didachē*, 6: 2, "If you are able to carry the entire yoke of the Lord, you will attain perfection; but if you are unable, then do as much as you can". The same sentiment is expressed in other words in the epistle of *Barnabas*, 19: 8, "Let your neighbour share in all that you possess, and refuse to call anything your own.[2] And, as far as you can, you must live continently for the sake of your soul". In fact, even by the early date of Paul's church in Corinth, there were "spiritual marriages" between ascetics of the two sexes.[3] Such persons were regarded for centuries by the official church with mistrust,[4] but the habit continued ineradicably as part of the practice of perfection. Those who became ascetics voluntarily were naturally held in high esteem, and it is significant that even Ignatius, early as was his date, had to warn them against spiritual pride. They claimed, indeed, that their self-control gave them insights, which were in the nature of divine revelations, and were superior to the authority of the bishop. In other words, these ascetics made pretensions to be persons spiritually endowed (*pneumatics*), and they felt themselves superior to the clergy. Other aspects of church-life at this early time called forth similar admonitions to humility, and such aspects multiplied rapidly.[5]

The Montanist movement was very revealing of the connection between ascetics, on the one hand, and the pneumatic prophets, on the other. Again, among the Marcionites, the world was repudiated on the basis of a dualistic philosophy,

---

[1] *vide* Vol. I, 65f.; Vol. 2, 197ff.   Vol. 3, 310ff.   [2] So also *Did.* 4: 7
[3] *vide* Vol. I, 136
[4] Ps.–Clem. *de virginitate*, ep. 2, in Wetstein's Ed. of N.T. 1751, Vol. II, Appendix, p. 15ff.   Aphrahat, *hom.* 6, 4, p. 260   *hom.* 6, 7, p. 271
[5] Ign. *ad Polyc.* 5: 2   1 Clem. 38, 2   Tert. *virg. vel.* 13

and this dualism made asceticism a binding duty for every member of the church.[1] Dualism was at the root of the asceticism of gnostic sects; records prove this in the case of Satornilus,[2] and it can be traced among the Valentinians.[3] Naturally, in all these different groups, asceticism was the hall-mark of perfect Christians, the *pneumatics*, and these were held up as models challenging the weakness of commonplace, married Christians, the "*psychics*".

The crucial test was always that of sexual continence. It was a widespread opinion in the church that a Christian "really" ought to practise it, and that marriage was only tolerated on account of the frailty of the flesh.[4] Further, it was held that one had to reckon with the fact that half-measures of this kind only served to delay the yearningly awaited parousia of the Lord. The only thing that could create the ideal conditions in harmony with the Kingdom of God as desired by the Lord, and bring about that Kingdom on earth,[5] was the complete elimination of the sex element among the members of the church. The apocryphal *Acts of the Apostles* written in the east make it appear, rather surprisingly, that the authors regarded celibacy as the principal requirement demanded by Christianity.[6] This idea was put into practice and observed for a long time in the churches of Mesopotamia. Even about the middle of the fourth century in that region, when a Christian was baptized, he "really" undertook the obligation of celibacy. This meant that baptized persons, as Christians in the full meaning of the term, constituted a church of "saints" in the sense of ascetics.[7]

The church catholic repudiated all radical views of this kind from an early date.[8] Although, according to these views,

---

[1] *vide* Vol. 2, 197   Vol. I, 260   [2] Iren. 1, 24, 2 (1, 198 Harvey)
[3] *ibid.* 1, 6, 3. 4 (1, 56f. Harvey)
[4] Thus Pinytos of Knossos in Euseb. *H.E.* 4, 23, 7.
[5] *Gosp. acc. to the Egypt.* fr. 2, Klostermann (Kl. Texte 8); M. R. James *Apocryph. N.T.*, p. 10ff. 2 Clem. 12, 2–5   cf. Mark 12: 25=Matt. 22: 30= Luke 20: 35
[6] *vide* Vol. 2, 86ff.
[7] Karl Müller, *Ehelosigkeit aller Getauften in der alten Kirche*, 1927   Aphrahat, *hom.* 7, 18. 20 (p. 341. 345 Parisot)
[8] 1 Tim. 4: 1f.   *Didache*, 11: 11   *re* resurrection, cf. *Acta Pauli et Theclae* 12 (1, 244 Lipsius)=*Acta Pauli*, ed. C. Schmidt, 2nd ed. (1905), p. 34=M. R. James, *op. cit.* 12, p. 275   cf. Luke 20: 35

celibacy was a presupposition of eternal salvation, and sometimes even of the resurrection, yet, taken on the whole, the church catholic gained the victory, though without being able to prevent hostile opinions like this from breaking into flame at frequent intervals. The church was accustomed to receive into her fellowship ascetics of a moderate type; they were regarded with respect as model Christians, and great pride was taken in their outstanding ethical achievements.[1] At the other end of the scale, a second marriage, after the death of the first partner, was usually felt by Christians to be of a dubious character, in spite of the fact that it was not actually forbidden.

The theologians of Alexandria thought out a complete theory regarding the relation between ascetics and other Christians, and their theory issued in very remarkable consequences. Clement vanquished the hostile, "heretical" gnosis by constructing a system of Christian gnosis. According to his system, truth was reached in a series of steps, the first being taken when the simple believer was held to have received the gift of the spirit; whereas the perfect gnostic was marked by the entire wealth of communion with God, and even became a means of conveying the divine love to the church.[2] Clement did not regard the ascetic mode of life as enjoined by divine commandment, but, in the individual persons who practised it, only as a testimony to the fact that they had broken with the world. It was only after this stage had been reached that Origen worked out a far-reaching system, in which asceticism appears as an element necessary for completing his doctrine about the soul mounting upwards to the comprehension of the logos. He himself, by example and preaching, sought to make converts to the practice of asceticism.[3] He described ascetics as the true philosophers of Christendom, and even gave them the title of "the philosophers". Educated writers on the new faith called theoretic asceticism, "philosophy", a name which it deserved on account of its principal source—and throughout

[1] Justin, *apol.* 15, 6 29, 1 Tatian, *or.* 32, 2 Athenagoras, *suppl.* 33, 1 Galen (*c.* A.D. 165) in Koch, *Quellen*, p. 63f.
[2] *vide* Vol. 2, 291ff.
[3] *vide* Vol. 2, 315f. Euseb. *H.E.* 6, 3, 9–13 Eusebius was an apt pupil of Origen's; cf. Vol. 3, 166f.

all the centuries since that time, the unlettered have followed the example of the educated in adopting the custom of calling the monks "philosophers".

The question of the beginning of monasticism only arises when ascetics, either as single individuals or in groups, separate themselves from the churches whose members take a normal share in the life of the world round about; their "apotaxis", or repudiation of the world, then becomes a matter of geography, and can be seen objectively. There were hardly any examples of this sort of thing either before the advent of Christianity or afterwards outside its borders.

Admittedly, records have survived, dating from the second century B.C., which tell of ascetics who immured themselves in the temple of Serapis at Memphis, and who lived wholly apart from the world: they were known as the *katochoi*.[1] The custom was perpetuated for centuries, and records testify that, even as late as *c*. A.D. 400, it was to be found in the Serapeum at Alexandria.[2] These facts call to mind also the legendary figure of the prophetess, Anna,[3] who "did not depart from the temple, worshipping with fasting and prayer night and day". Cases of this kind, however, are characterized, not so much by the fact of separating from the world, as by that of living close to God.

Josephus, describing his teacher, Ban(n)us,[4] sketched a genuine fore-runner of the anchorites. Bannus lived in the desert, wore garments of palm-hemp, ate wild fruits, and kept himself clean by bathing in cold water morning and night. Josephus lived with him for three years. A similar case is that of John the Baptist, who is to be reckoned among this class of Jewish anchorites, a genus of which, unfortunately, no other records have survived. The notices regarding the Jewish Essenes are so lacking in perspicuity[5] that it is quite uncertain whether their type of life-in-common also necessarily and regularly led to their living together in cloisters; moreover, there are no records at all to the effect that they actually cut themselves off from the rest of the world. If such records had

---

[1] Reitzenstein, *Hellen. Mysterienreligionen*, 3rd ed., 200–15
[2] Rufin. *hist. eccl.* 11, 23   [3] Luke 2: 37
[4] Jos. *vita*, 11, 12 (par. 2, Whiston's edition) cf. Vol. I, 40
[5] cf. Vol. I, 34ff., but present opinion is less assured of the data.

survived, the settlements near Engeddi, on the west shore of the Dead Sea, of whose existence excellent testimony has come down,[1] would have to be regarded as partaking of that character.

On the other hand, the sect of the Therapeutae, which Philo held in high esteem, had a settlement on Lake Mareotis in Egypt.[2] There can be little doubt, in this instance, that there was a definite intention to flee from the world. Even so, it would be a dubious and rash undertaking to use these poor instances for the foundations on which to build a theory as to the origin of Christian monasticism. It would be better, in view of the facts which can be actually envisaged, to propose another problem: whether the processes of development within the Christian movement itself did not compel the ascetics to separate themselves from the fellowship of the church catholic.

(2) Anchoritism and Monasticism

It was among the fellahin of Egypt, who were untouched by Greek ideas, that there were the first examples of Christian anchorites, i.e. ascetics who went to live in a place apart. Toward the end of the third century, it had become a custom in that country when an ascetic repudiated the world, that he should also abandon his native village and build a hermitage at some little distance from it. After a time, an old hermit would be joined by novices, who settled in his neighbourhood and learned the art of self-denial.[3] Unorganized settlements of this type were greatly influenced during the first quarter of the fourth century by two men who gave the movement its main character, and carried it further in two different ways: Antony was responsible for initiating the desert type of holy men; Pachomius organized the monastics.

The feature that was characteristic of Antony's type was that he went quite away from human dwellings. In his first period, he followed the customs and directions of an older man, and was content with merely increasing greatly his ascetic practices. Next, he betook himself to a cemetery lying remote from the village, and shut himself up in a tomb; an acquaintance brought him food at intervals. He was attacked

[1]3 Pliny, *nat. hist.* 5, 17   [2] Philo, *vita contempl.* 22 (6, 52)   [3] Athan. *vita Ant.*

there by demons, but managed to withstand them successfully; in this way he had tested his powers. He then took the final step, but one in which his old teacher refused to join: he wandered "across the river" into the boundless desert, and climbed into the mountains. He found there an abandoned fort which he converted into a dwelling. A stream supplied him with water, and for food he had some Theban biscuit which he had brought, and of which he received further supplies from his friends perhaps after six months.[1] He lived in this wild place for twenty years constantly battling with demons. No one caught actual sight of him throughout this period, although his friends sought out his habitation from time to time, and shouted to attract his attention.

Finally, when fifty-five years of age, he presented himself to pilgrims as a master and teacher of asceticism, and made converts to his way of repudiating the world. The desert became populated with monks, and numerous settlements were founded, all of which looked up to him as their father.[2] Maximin's persecution took place during this period of his activity, and he and his monks were carried off to Alexandria;[3] but the city prefect ordered the undesirable men of the desert out of the city. After Bishop Peter had been martyred on November 24, A.D. 311, Antony returned to the desert and resumed his solitary life, but he did not find the quietude which had formerly been his happy lot there. Visitors multiplied, and they disturbed him ever more seriously; the claim made by his miraculous powers drew innumerable needy persons, whom he could not deny. He then began to be afraid of fame and self-pride, and therefore decided to wander off into the upper Thebaid; but a voice from heaven commanded him to seek another goal. He joined a caravan of Bedouin travelling "into the interior desert ' and, after a journey of three days, came to a very high mountain group, where he found a level place with palm-trees and water. Here he remained in complete isolation, and soon made himself independent even of the dry biscuits sent by the brethren. By this means, he found at last the consummation of all that he had striven for; and it was here also that, in A.D. 356, he died in

[1] *vita Ant.* 8–12   [2] *ibid.* 14. 15   [3] *ibid.* 46

extreme old age, apparently 105 years.[1] The place remains till the present time a grateful monument of monasticism, and is marked by a cloister of the greatest antiquity. From Biad, a village on the Nile, or from Baiad-el-Nassara, near Beni-Suef, a journey eastwards of about 36 hours by camel (i.e. three days as cited above) is needed to reach the monastery of Antony in the mountains of Wadi-Araba, about 25 miles from the Red Sea.[2]

Our information about Antony is drawn from Athanasius's biography of the holy man. This work is markedly conventional in character, so strongly conventionalized indeed, that the summary given in the foregoing paragraphs may possibly not be strictly in accordance with the historical facts regarding the various stages in the process by which geographical separateness was established. Nevertheless the work written by Athanasius is of the greatest historical value, because it gives a clear picture of the extreme type of asceticism, and therefore of the goal sought by the movement. At the same time, it must be granted that Athanasius lifted it as it were to a higher plane, and transfigured it to a finer degree of spirituality.

Athanasius was only reflecting popular opinion when he held certain factors to be important in the process by which his hero developed into the perfect ascetic: these were that his increasingly severe acts of self-denial provoked the demons; and that, by going into the waste places and the deserts, he invaded their special preserves, and challenged them to battle to the death. He wrestled not only with those temptations which were due to the passions of the flesh, but, more particularly, with a thousand forms of physical torment; and it was his victories over those assailants and these difficulties that made him the "perfect" ascetic. As such, God graciously vouchsafed to him visions, foreknowledge, and the gift of miraculous healing; even wild beasts obeyed his commands and served him, just as they had once served Adam in the garden of Eden. As an ascetic, he regained the lost image of God.

Athanasius proceeds at this point to reproduce a whole host of popular traditions of his miracles; and the stories he recorded

[1] *vita Ant.* 49. 50. 89–92   [2] Baedeker, *Aegypten*, 8th ed. 211; plan at p. 392

provided what succeeding generations of readers have mostly found to be of absorbing interest. With these popular traditions as a basis, however, Athanasius went on to make fresh points which were of higher value. In the first place, he showed that the course of Antony's life as an ascetic followed the example of Pythagoras, as depicted in the legends of philosophy. So closely did he resemble his model, according to Athanasius, that not only isolated phrases which were characteristic of Pythagoras, but even whole sentences could be quoted verbatim and applied to him.[1] At first glance, anyone reading the biography of an ascetic might be confounded by the cost of gaining complete indifference to the claims of the body, involving self-denials practised over a period of twenty years; but the reader was made to understand how this cost was counterbalanced by the creation of an ethos entirely spiritual in quality and undisturbed by any passions. Thus Antony is described coming on to the public scene, "from the adytum, as a consecrated mystic filled with God". He then began to organise (*polizein*) his theocracy of monks in the same manner as, at an earlier date, the great Greek, Pythagoras, had shaped a philosophical "*polis*" in southern Italy for his own disciples.[2]

Athanasius puts a long speech into the mouth of Antony,[3] explaining to the monks the real art and manner of asceticism. Their whole life was to be conducted under the guidance of the dominant idea of the Last Judgment, and each day was to be to them as if it were their last. Their whole effort was to be concentrated on the "path of virtue"; and this included the virtues taught by the philosophers, such as wisdom, uprightness, temperance, courage, insight; and also the Christian virtues of love, meekness, faith in Christ, good temper, and hospitality. This goal lay within our own hearts, and we were to set our wills on it. Our souls were naturally good and in harmony with virtue; and these teachings were the means by which they were to be restored to health, and kept permanently in the state with which they had been endowed by God at creation.

---

[1] R. Reitzenstein, *Des Athanasius Werk über das Leben des Antonius*, 1914 (Sitzungsber. Heidelberg. Akad. 1914, Abh. 8) p. 14ff.
[2] *vita Ant.* 14   [3] *ibid.* 16–43

After having dwelt on matters on this high and philosophical level, the speech rapidly descends to lower ground, and discusses what even Athanasius appears to have regarded as the main practical problem of the monastic life, viz., wrestling with demons. Demons surrounded us on all hands, crowded in upon us in all kinds of forms, and exercised innumerable cunning devices, all in order to hinder the progress of an earnest devotee. Athanasius then goes into the minutest detail, instructing his readers about the nature of demons, their methods of attack, the dangers encountered by the soul through fear of demons or through self-deception; but then, further, about the effects of an unshakeable confidence in God, and about the serene superiority of the beleaguered soul. He utters many warnings against haughtiness and credulity, against the laziness of monks, and over-weening confidence in the gifts of God's grace; and he mingles these warnings with his teachings. In this way he portrays Antony from two sides: on the one hand, as the model of a genuine ascetic, and on the other, as preaching Athanasius's own ideals of the monastic life, ideals which combined crass belief in demons with high aims of a philosophical and Christian kind.

It is indeed this book on monasticism which reveals to us for the first time certain unexpected and deeply hidden roots in the personal religion of Athanasius. It is astonishing to gaze into the heart of a person like Athanasius, especially when we remember that he was one of the leading men at the beginning of the silver age of the Graeco-Roman world, and that his theological writings reveal a profound insight into the nature of Christian truth.[1] Yet, in spite of all this, there were at the basis of his thought crude ideas drawn from nature-religions, with thousands of devils and evil spirits roaming everywhere. Moreover his whole world of thought was shaped by forces and principles derived from an outworn Greek philosophy.

Antony, as a historical person, and the other ascetics of the Coptic tradition, were altogether lacking in the Greek element noticeable in Athanasius. That fact draws attention all the more definitely to their hostility to everything that

[1] *vide* Vol. 3, 247–52

belonged to the surrounding physical world, a world which was conceived by them to be full of devils possessing an objective reality. These devils devoured every human being who did not exercise the most ruthless self-denial to an extent, indeed, bordering on self-immolation; and who did not refuse all place to the claims of the senses, in their efforts to reach safety in a life "like that of the angels". Ideas of this kind were dominated by a soteriology in which redemption is attained by a voluntary act of one's own, in which Christ serves only as an example and the Bible only as a text-book, and in which church and sacrament were regarded merely as subsidiary aids.

Of the ascetics who lived in the desert, Antony is the first whose name is definitely known. This contention is supported, not only by Athanasius's biography, but also by the unanimous tradition of the monks in the succeeding period. Jerome attempted to dispute his priority in favour of the sainted Paul of Thebes, but this thesis was hopeless from the start; and, in spite of Jerome's prestige and his many writings, his fanciful ideas have rightly been refused acceptance. On the other hand, it is true enough that, shortly after Antony became a figure of historical importance, in another region a number of ascetics took to the desert and flourished there. They attracted far greater attention than Antony because, in spite of living apart from the world, these hermits exercised a mutual influence on each other, and thus facilitated one another's progress towards realizing the ideal of the ascetic life. The region chosen by them was the Natron Valley (Wadi Natrun), some 60 to 70 miles north-west of Cairo.[1] In ancient times, the monks were said to be congregated round three centres: Scetis, Nitria, and the Cellia. The founder of Nitria is reputed to be Amun who actually died before Antony;[2] Scetis owes its origin to Makarius of Alexandria, who was born c. A.D. 300, and who lived to be nearly one hundred years old. He also did some work of a preliminary character in the Cellia and in Nitria.[3]

These settlements were arranged in such a way that the

---

[1] Baedeker, *Aegypten*, 8th ed. 31, plan at p. 5; a light railway goes in that direction *via* El-Chatatba to Bir Hooker See also Butler, *Hist. Lausiaca*, 2, 187–90 Heussi, *Mönchtum*, 157, n. 1 Description: *Hist. mon.* 23, 3 cf. 30, 1 *Hist. Laus.* 7

[2] *Hist. Laus.* 18, p. 44, 5 51, 10. 12 56, 15   [3] *Hist. mon.* 30, 1

individual cells were so widely separated that the monks could neither see nor hear one another, and each was able to live a life of undisturbed meditation. But on Saturdays and Sundays, the members of the monastic community gathered together for worship; and these occasions afforded their only opportunity for mutual intercourse. It was therefore possible for a monk to lie dead in his cell for four days before the brethren were aware of his demise. Apart from these assemblies, the records tell of agapēs, i.e. common love-feasts, as an arrangement whereby the monks came into human and spiritual contact with each other.[1] A "sanhedrin" of the brethren punished serious transgressions of the regulations governing the ascetic life.[2] The hermits earned their subsistence by manual labour, mostly in the form of weaving mats from palm-leaves, the mats being sold in the city by merchant entrepreneurs.

The colonies of monks in the Natron Valley became very famous before the end of the fourth century; but, in the second decade of the fifth century, the colony at Scetis was looted and entirely destroyed by an attack of barbarians. A further consequence was a failure of courage from which this particular monastic world never recovered.[3] The first head of the colony of anchorites was Father Amun, and Antony is said to have seen his soul journey up to heaven. The person of the greatest importance among them was, however, his slightly younger contemporary, Makarius the "Egyptian", i.e. the Copt, a sobriquet used to distinguish him from Makarius of Alexandria who laboured nearby. Other outstanding names in this monastic paradise are Pambo, Paul the Simple, Poimen, and Sisoes. Arsenios, who had previously been a courtier, was among those who were present when Scetis was laid waste.

During the early, prosperous times in the Natron Valley, the beginnings were made of writing a document which came to be of unbounded significance for the whole monastic movement: the *Apophthegmata Patrum*, or *Sayings of the Fathers*. A monk was under the obligation of silence, and, if he spoke at all, he was to utter things of divine import, good for the

---

[1] *Apophth.* Joh. Kolobos 9, p. 205   Sisoes 2, p. 392
[2] *ibid.* Moses 2, p. 281   Pior 3, p. 373   [3] Heussi, *Mönchtum*, 138

soul. The more important men of advanced years observed the rule strictly, and they were regarded as having attained perfection; or at least, that is the opinion that ruled in their immediate neighbourhood. As a consequence they were held to possess the Holy Spirit, and their words to have more than a human validity and significance. Disciples would beg their master, and pilgrims would beseech a famous holy man, and say: "Grant me a word"; but they often had to wait a long time for an answer to their request. When at last the holy man broke silence, and either answered the question that had been put, or uttered some helpful sentence, what he said was received as a gift from heaven and gratefully stored up in the memory,[1] especially when it was in direct harmony with the rules of the monastic life, and was free from the dangerous ambiguity of Biblical passages.[2] A parable or a symbolical act might take the place of a mere saying—for the holy man of the desert, like the spirit-filled prophet of the church's earliest days, was the vehicle of divine revelations. And, just as had been done formerly in the case of the Montanists,[3] so now in the Natron Valley, care was taken to put the "Sayings of the Fathers" on record, and, in appropriate cases, to relate the particular circumstances.

An anthology of this kind was rapidly built up, of considerable historical trustworthiness even as to the names of the sages. It goes without saying that, in the first instance, the tradition was of an oral character and in the Coptic language. It was later translated into Greek and written down; then it was expanded by the addition of sayings from other areas;[4] possibly, even at an early date, the anthology was divided into several branches. Then, probably in the sixth century, some ingenious person gathered up everything he could lay hands on, and arranged the series in alphabetical order according to the names of the speakers, and in Greek; this series has survived in later redactions and various translations.[5]

---

[1] Bousset, *Apophthegmata*, 79f.　　[2] *Apophth. Amun. Nitr.* 2, p. 128
[3] *vide* Vol. 3, 193ff.　　[4] Heussi, *op. cit.* 145. 158
[5] Of fundamental importance is Bousset's examination of the whole of this literature, *Apophthegmata*, 1923; text in Cotelier, *Ecclesiae Graecae Monumenta*, 1, 338–712 (1677)=Migne, *Patr. Gr.* 65, 71–440 English trans. of the Syriac version by E. A. W. Budge, *The Wit and Wisdom of the Christian Fathers of Egypt*, Oxford, 1934

Springing as they do directly from life, these literary deposits are sources of a special value; they give a vivid picture of the monks in the Natron Valley as regards their habits of life and, more particularly, the character of their religion. We shall take the opportunity on a later page of returning to this subject. The influence which this book exercised on the future may be estimated from the fact that it was used in various languages for the devotional exercises of monks in both east and west.

During the time when anchoritism was in process of development in the northern provinces of Egypt, Pachomius the Copt was giving tentative shape to the monastic life properly so-called, in a situation near the loop of the Nile at Dendera in southern Egypt. He had been born in the upper Thebaid of pagan parents, and first came into contact with Christianity as a recruit in the army. With other fellow-sufferers in his levy, he was incarcerated in a village of the Thebaid, and experienced in his own person the sympathy and care of the local Christians. After regaining his freedom, he set off to Chenobaskeia (Shenesit, today El-Kaor wa's Saijad, at the western end of the loop), sought baptism, and then entered on the ascetic life. His teacher, Palamon, instructed him in fasting, prayer, and obedience. The two men wove sack-cloth to earn their necessary means of living and to give away as alms. At length, Pachomius heard a voice from heaven when he was at prayer in the village of Tabennisi, which lay a little further up-stream, and was commanded: "Stay here and build a monastery; for many will gather round you in order to become monks." He and Palamon immediately removed there and settled down, but the latter was already a sick man, and soon died. Pachomius was then joined by his brother John; and within a short time the promise was fulfilled: strangers came to him in order to share his way of life. After putting them to the proof, he let them don the monkish habit. The names of the first eight have been celebrated in the memory of a proud tradition.[1] That is how Pachomius's first monastery came into existence; the date was probably about A.D. 320.

[1] *Pachomii vita*, 25. 26, cf. 79

This was not the first of all the monasteries, nor even the first in that area. The records say expressly that when Pachomius's monastery began to flourish, two other monasteries of "aged brothers" requested that they might be strengthened with some of Pachomius's monks, and reconstituted on the model of his order. Moreover, a certain Aotas is explicitly mentioned as a predecessor, although it must be granted that he was not very successful.[1] The important characteristic in the case of Pachomius was that he put an end to the loose association of the earlier ascetics, who merely lived in the same neighbourhood as each other; he housed the community of monks together and made them into a fellowship; and he issued definite rules to govern their life.

It was with the matter of having "rules" that Pachomius introduced a new feature, and one that was to prove of unbounded significance for future ages; and a legend[2] that cropped up a few generations later, was not entirely baseless. But it was rhetorical in asserting that the holy man received his rules engraved on bronze and from the hands of an angel. In A.D. 404, Jerome translated the Greek version of these rules, with certain additions, into Latin; and there is every reason for regarding this translation, not only as the earliest form of the text now extant, but also as a reliable copy of Pachomius's regulations for his monasteries.[3] The very fact of the haphazard way in which the rules follow on one another is a sure sign that they were drawn up as a result of actual practice and experience; and there are many sections which are clearly due to the need for new addenda to the corpus of rules as it had previously existed. If we take these regulations and put them side by side with those explanations of, and comments on, the monastic tradition which are to be found both in the best Greek accounts of Pachomius's life,[4] and also in Jerome's preface to his translation, the principles behind the movement and its constitution become obvious.

A person wishing to become a monk applied to the porter, and, after orders had been received from the abbot, he was

[1] *Pachomii vita*, 54   cf. also 33. 120. p. 97, 35   [2] *Hist. Laus.* 32, p. 88, 4, Butler
[3] Edited by Amand Boon, *Pachomiana Latina* (Louvain, 1932)
[4] *S. Pachomii vitae Graecae*, ed. F. Halkin, Brussels, 1932 (*Subsidia Hagiographica* 19). *Vita prima*, §28, p. 18

lodged in the visitors' quarters close to the gate. While lodging there, he had to learn by heart the Lord's Prayer and certain Psalms; meantime inquiries were made into his character and general circumstances. If there proved to be no obstacle to his reception, he was taught the rules of the monastery; when his training was complete, he was given the monk's habit, his own secular garments being taken in charge by the relevant officers.

At a later date, these regulations were extended; and now, before being accepted, the novice was required to learn by heart twenty psalms and either two epistles from the New Testament, or some other equivalent part of the Bible. He had also to learn how to read and write: "and no one at all is to be admitted to the monastery who cannot read, and who does not know some part of the Bible by heart, at least from the New Testament and the Psalms". The requirement naturally meant that proper arrangements had to be made for loaning books of the Bible for study in the cells, and for their due return to the librarian. All these preliminaries only required a few days to fulfil, after which the novice was initiated into the fellowship of the monks. Nothing stands on record about taking a vow.[1] The first time the initiate was to join the community in worship, *ipso facto* on either a Saturday evening or on a Sunday, the porter led him through the gates of the cloister into the church, and ushered him into the last seat in the congregation; there he was to remain till he was appointed to a house. Then at last, he was in a position to become acquainted with his new home.

The monastery itself was constituted of a great complex of buildings shut off from the outside world by a surrounding wall.[2] The monks lived together in groups in houses, and each had his own cell there; the cell could not be locked; it was provided with the inmate's possessions, viz. two shirts (*lebiton*) properly so-called, as well as one worn at work; a linen cloth to protect the head and shoulders from the sun; a mantle of goat-skin (*melotes*), a pair of shoes, two caps, a girdle, and a stick. A small pointed instrument for extracting prickles and splinters from the skin hung for common use at a

[1] *Reg.* 49. 139. 140 *vide* loans: 25. 100. 101   [2] *Regula*, cap. 84, p. 38, 4, Boon

window.[1] But all concern for the well-being of the body, and all washing and bathing, were regarded as suspect in the genuine ascetic tradition.[2]

Each house had its own head, and three or four houses constituted a group (*tagma, tribus*). The inmates of any single house all performed the same kind of manual labour, especially the weaving of mats; but there were also linen weavers, fullers, tailors, shoemakers, waggon-makers;[3] and frequently all the members of the colony went out to work in the fields, in the desert, or in the low-lying, reedy lands on the banks of the Nile. The general affairs of the monastic community were assigned to three special houses, of which the first was responsible for the cooking, the second for the care of the sick, and the third for dealings with the outside world. The last lodged the guests, received and instructed the novices, and also arranged the dealings with entrepreneurs who supplied the monastery with all the goods it needed, and took in exchange the products of the monks' own labours.[4]

The three special houses carried out their duties for three weeks, at the end of which time they resumed their customary manual labour, and were replaced by monks belonging to another group.[5] It seems to have been a still earlier rule that each house took its turn weekly in serving, i.e. in giving out the materials and the tools for work, reciting the Biblical passages at worship, and singing in the choir.[6] All who lived in one house took their meals together, the first about midday, and the second towards evening: and this latter was the main meal. To go without the mid-day meal was regarded as a specially ascetic act, but not always as meritorious.[7] The

[1] *Reg.* 107. 81. 82   Orsiesius, 22   p. 123, Boon
[2] *ibid.* 67. 92f.   cf. *Hist. Laus.* 1, p. 15, 15   Athan. *vita Ant.* 60
[3] *Praef. Hier.* 6, p. 8, Boon   cf. *Hist. Laus.*, 32, p. 94, 7
[4] A group of American archaeologists in 1912–14 excavated a monastery in a valley near Thebes dating from the fifth to the seventh centuries, work that has afforded a very vivid glimpse of the life of the desert monks. The discoveries included buildings, furnishings, tools, and even the mummified bodies of the monks in their habits; also correspondence. A short study by W. E. Crum (Vol. I, 125–85) summarizes their conclusions regarding the lives of the hermits of the Thebaid   cf. *Publications of the Metropolitan Museum of Art: Egyptian Expedition*, ed. by Albert Morton Lythgoe   *The Monastery of Epiphanius at Thebes*, ed. by H. E. Winlock, W. E. Crum, H. E. Evelyn White, N.Y. 1926, 2 vols. folio   review in *Göttinger Gel. Anz.* 1928, 112–16
[5] *Pachomii vita*, I, 28, p. 18.   [6] *Reg.* 13. 15. 23. 24. 27   cf. 64. 111. 129
[7] *Pachom. vita*, 69, p. 46, 8   *Paralipom.* 29, p. 156, 25   Jerome, Praef. 5, p. 7

members of each house also met for worship twice in every twenty-four hours: once in the early morning before dawn, and again in the evening.[1] The service consisted of twelve psalms followed by a similar number of prayers and two readings. The psalms were read aloud by separate persons; they stood up in turn in the midst of the congregation, who remained seated on low hassocks.[2] These customs were observed in all the monasteries in Egypt; but a special feature of the rules laid down by Pachomius[3] was that, at the evening service, the number of psalms and consequently the number of prayers were reduced to six.[4]

The whole of the monks in the monastery met together for worship on Saturday evening and on Sunday,[5] and made use of the same order of service as in the daily devotional exercises.[6] But at the early morning service on Sunday, perhaps also on Saturday evening,[7] the eucharistic sacrifice was offered with an accompanying liturgy. For this purpose, it was arranged, in the earliest days, that a priest should come from one of the churches in the vicinity; and it gradually became usual for priests to enter the monastery themselves, but without claiming special privileges.[8] When these celebrations were ended, the abbot went on to deliver a doctrinal address: a "catechism". Wednesdays and Fridays were fast days, and then, at the early morning service, the head of each house used to give catechetical instruction to the members of his household.[9] Very often at these services, a monk would be plagued with sleepiness early and late in the day; but even so he was not allowed to get slack at work. Rather he had to ply the spindle and keep busy spinning thread for his mats.

All did the same kind of work between morning and evening prayer, and it was done by each monk in his own cell; the isolation of anchoritism was preserved to this extent even in

---

[1] vide Vol. 3, 300   [2] So Cassian, Instit. 2, 6. 7   [3] Pachom. vita, 58, p. 40, 14
[4] Reg. 23. 121. 125. 126. 155. 186; twelve evening prayers; so epist. Amunis, 22 p. 110, 33
[5] Pachom. vita, 29, p. 19, 8. 9   147, p. 93, 15   Epist. Amun. 22, p. 111, 5. 8
[6] Reg. 155   [7] Socrates, 5, 22, 43–44 cf. Pachom. vita, 29
[8] Pachom. vita, 27   Reg. 15–16. 18.
[9] ibid. 28, p. 19, 3–5 (should Reg. 20 be corrected to harmonize? Or is Reg. 20 an earlier phase?) For the early morning cf. Reg. 19. 22 cf. Paral. 19, p. 143f.

the cloister; indeed there were regulations specifically enjoining silence, forbidding the brethren to break it by visiting each other's cells, and discussing anything at all concerning the outside world. No conversation of any kind was permitted at meal times, and each monk had to keep his head concealed in his hood in order to maintain an outward separateness although the brothers were sitting side by side.[1] They did not sleep on bunks, but on chaise-longues.[2]

It was a very strenuous mode of life, and it was kept up by the quite voluntary assent of the monks; the punishments provided for in the regulations were insignificant and almost of a childish kind. The one that is most frequently mentioned, and that was used as punishment on ten successive occasions when a man transgressed by bad habits or ill-deeds, took the form of a reproof given by the abbot and received by the monk in a humble attitude, in front of the whole community.[3] Another punishment consisted of being made to stand while the other brothers sat, a punishment which could be very trying after, or even before, a hard day's work in the heat.[4] A different sort of punishment was the loss of status due to seniority, and degradation to a place among the new-comers; leaders might suffer a temporary suspension from office.[5] On rare occasions, an offender might be excluded from a meal, and even condemned to a more prolonged absence from the brethren, and to subsistence on "bread and water".[6] Thrashing is only mentioned once in the rules,[7] and was provided for a monk "who angers the brethren with his remarks, and seduces the souls of the simple".

The power of punishment was reserved entirely to the abbot (*abba*, father); indeed in his hands lay the whole responsibility for the life and prosperity of the monastery; like all office-bearers in a monastic community, he had a permanent deputy (*deuteros*), beside an assistant to attend to the domestic business (*oikonomos*). Some monasteries had a council of the leading monks, a kind of senate of the cloister.

All the monasteries were subject to Pachomius, the abbot-

---

[1] *Reg.* 112. 116. 122. 60. 31. 29   cf. *Hist. Laus.* 32, p. 92, 1
[2] *ibid.* 88   *Hist. Laus.* 32, p. 89, 7   [3] *ibid.* 8   [4] *ibid.* 21. 22. 31
[5] *ibid.* 161. 136. 137   [6] *ibid.* 32. 160. 163   [7] *ibid.* 163

general, and he resided in the senior cloister at Pabau (Fau-Kebli)[1] which was the seat of the central authority. Here, twice annually, at Easter and on August 13, the general assembly was convened; and not only the abbots, but also all the monks of all the monasteries, were due to attend. Spiritual and administrative questions were dealt with on these occasions; and also a statement of accounts to the end of July had to be presented by each monastery showing how it had discharged its stewardship.[2] The original monastery at Tabennisi had given rise in only two decades to a great association of monasteries, all founded by Pachomius, and all observing the same rules. They all lay in the region above the loop of the Nile between Dendera and Panopolis (Achmim) and only at Pichnum, near Latopolis (Esna), did they stretch an antenna into the upper Thebaid.[3]

Foundations of this kind were not invariably welcomed. The bishop of the city of Panopolis was anxious that a monastery should be founded there, but the inhabitants pulled down as much of the walls as had been built, and it required a miracle before the work could be successfully completed.[4] Taken on the whole, however, the monastics of the kind that lived under a "rule" flourished, and increased. This system was imitated elsewhere, and it attracted to Christianity mostly the pagan fellahin. Usually the inmates of Pachomius's monasteries were Copts; when, as was rarely the case, Greeks were to be found in them, they were grouped into their own "house" —e.g. in Pabau, there were twenty. The addresses delivered in Coptic by the abbot were translated for their benefit by an interpreter.[5]

Egypt was the classic land of monasticism even before the end of the fourth century,[6] and visitors went there to study the real nature and practice of asceticism at the feet of celebrated anchorites, and this in monasteries which were reputed to be models of their kind. The surviving *Itineraries* trace journeys

---

[1] Baedeker, 8th German ed., 224   [2] *Pachom. vita*, 83. 122   *Reg.* 27
[3] General map in Butler, *Hist. Laus.* 2, XCVIII   The *vita Pachomii*, 112, p. 73, 11 lists 9 monasteries, cf. 81. 83. and 54. Eleven were under Theodore, cf. *Epist. Amun.* 21, but later there were twelve, cf. *Pachom. vita*, 134
[4] *Pachom. vita*, 81   [5] *Amunis epist.* 7 cf. 27
[6] A list of the Egyptian monasteries is given in Cabrol, *Dict.* 2, 3129–36

through the whole of Egypt, from the Delta and the Natron Valley to as far south as Esna; and the town of Oxyrhynchos (Behnesa),[1] is depicted as a veritable paradise for monks. Neither pagans nor heretics were to be found there, and so the bishop could bestow his blessing while on the open street. The people gathered for worship in twelve churches, but the number of monks was greater than that of the laity. Monastery after monastery was huddled together within the city walls, each with its own chapel; but space became too limited, and a new town, consisting of nothing but monasteries, had to be built outside the walls in order to provide accommodation for 10,000 monks and 20,000 nuns. The spirit of the Christian religion was so greatly in the ascendant in the whole of public and social life, that the chief magistrate ordered the police under him to keep watch at the city gates for needy travellers, and bring them to the council house to receive alms. When painting this picture of the state of affairs, of course the writer had given it a very rosy hue; nevertheless, the underlying facts are clearly visible, viz., that c. A.D. 400, there were places in south Egypt in which monasteries dominated the life of the towns.

Trustworthy documents of an early date are extant, testifying to the very great increase of the number of monasteries of Pachomius's type. The adherents of Meletius, with their rigour conceived after the manner of the early church,[2] were inclined, naturally enough, to the practice of asceticism. Certain papyri, recently discovered, show that, as early as the year 335, monasteries with "regular" organization were to be found in central and upper Egypt. There is a *prima facie* probability that these monasteries were connected with the movement initiated by Pachomius,[3] an opinion supported by evidence that they, too, observed Pachomius's custom of praying in a standing position, with the body in the attitude of a crucifix.[4]

Contemporary with the adoption of rules governing the lives of men who became ascetics, there was a similar develop-

---

[1] *Hist. mon.* 5   [2] *vide* Vol. 3, 104f.   [3] K. Holl, *Ges. Aufsätze*, 2, 295f.
[4] H. Idris Bell, *Jews and Christians in Egypt* (1924), 81f. *Pap.* n. 1917, 6. 19
cf. *Pachom. vita*, 16, p. 10, 29   cf. 5, p. 3, 29   *vita altera*, 50, p. 219, 12

ment for the welfare of nuns. Antony introduced his sister to a nunnery (parthenon) which was already in existence, and Pachomius built one for his own sister, supplied it with a "rule", and put it under the supervision of an aged monk.[1] Theodore, who succeeded him next but one, founded two more nunneries.[2]

(3) The Religion of the Monastics

Thus it came about that countless thousands of simple Egyptian peasants were crowding their way into the cloisters; this fact in itself poses the question, "What was their conception of Christianity, and why did the majority of people regard Christianity as identical with the monastic life?" In as far as it was a matter of external things, entering a cloister meant that life became secure: the step guaranteed protection from hunger and gave one a home; and it got one into the habit of regular labour, even if that labour was usually very monotonous. The monasteries developed into factories producing woven goods of every kind, and carried on a steady trade with the capital in the Delta. If an abbot with well-developed business instincts was at the head of the monastery, vessels would be built on his own wharves, and the profits would go to the purchase of additional farm-lands and forests.[3] Granted that the more rigorous-minded brethren would voice their protests if commerce of this kind went beyond certain limits, nevertheless, in course of time, all the monasteries had adapted themselves in one way or another to the economic necessities of the situation. On the other hand, we must recognize that there were essential considerations besides those of an external kind. The training and discipline of the cloister could not do other than exercise an immediate and direct influence on the monk's inner life, and face him with a task which concerned his very soul. It is the nature of that task which now demands our investigation.

The problem of the specific religion of the Egyptian monks can be approached from various angles, because documents

[1] Athan. *vita Ant.* 3   *Pachom. vita altera*, 28, p. 196=*tertia*, 42, p. 278   similarly Theodore's mother, *Pachom. vita*, 33
[2] *Pachom. vita*, 134   [3] *ibid.* 127, 146

have come down whose very purpose was to give a vivid description of it. We have already mentioned the *Sayings of the Fathers*,[1] records which, in many respects, give precisely the details for which we are looking; they are coloured by theological and literary considerations only in isolated patches of a late date. The writings that tell of Pachomius preserve much valuable information. They were put together by Theodore, who came into control next but one after Pachomius; and they contain, in addition, numerous records having to do with Theodore himself. Thirdly, there is the account of monasticism written by Rufinus: it tells of a journey made by him in A.D. 394; and, in spite of all its conventionalism and tendentiousness, it provides the student with ample data for drawing inferences as to the real nature of the religion of the monks. The document was originally written in Greek, and a Greek text has survived; but the Latin translation of Rufinus has an independent worth because based, to a large extent, on a superior form of the Greek text.[2]

The above account by Rufinus was imitated, at a slightly later date, in a work ascribed to Palladius and known as *Historia Lausiaca*; Lausos, a Lord Chancellor, being the person to whom this account of monasticism was dedicated.[3] The scheme of the work is such that it goes beyond the confines of Egypt and the interests of the male anchorites; rather, it includes holy women, and gives a description of the monastic movement in Palestine, Syria, and Asia Minor. The same author, who had himself been for many years an ascetic in Egypt, was also responsible for the biography of John Chrysostom. He mingles his own experiences with all sorts of irrelevant information and romancing; nevertheless, the various items give the outlines of a self-consistent picture of the inner life of monks belonging to the early period, i.e. the fourth century.

The essentials are as follows: the world was full of demons,

---

[1] *vide supra*, p. 139　For assessment of this source, cf. Heussi, *Mönchtum*, 154–280
[2] The Greek text is edited by E. Preuschen, *Palladius und Rufinus* (1897), p. 1–130　Latin: cf. Migne, *Patrol. Lat.* 21, 387–462　Remarks thereon: E. Schwartz, *ZNW*, 36 (1937), 164, n. 6
[3] Ed. by C. Butler in *Texts and Studies*, 6, 2 (1904)　notes by Ed. Schwartz, *ZNW*, 36 (1937) 161ff.

who threatened mankind in both body and soul, and barred the way to God. They had this purchase over mankind on account of sin. Once the facts were firmly grasped, the person concerned yearned for liberation from these infernal dangers. Liberation was offered by the Christian religion; it guaranteed victory over sin and the peril of demons, if one would but repudiate the world. To do so, however, was no simple affair, but had to be slowly and painfully learned. Hence it turned out that the safest course was to consult a teacher of asceticism, and ask him for instruction; but it was simpler to enter a cloister, where the larger community helped one to learn how to avoid sin, and to practise the Christian virtues. It is easy to see why, in the earliest stages, the question was never raised whether the same goal could not be attained by the ordinary fellowship of the Christian church. The technique used by the ascetics in the warfare against demons was an elaborate affair; and when that fact was realized, it was also realized that it could simply not be carried out during one's ordinary life as a citizen, no matter if one were a member of the Christian church. Not to mention other considerations, the restlessness of ordinary everyday life and the innumerable contacts with persons of the opposite sex, disturbed that concentration of soul upon which all spiritual progress depended. True, the writers occasionally pointed out how God had recognized the virtues of certain members of the "laity",[1] but this was only done to reprove monkish pride, and as a kind of aside for paedagogical reasons. With this exception, it can be said that everyone in this part of the world regarded Christianity, conceived in terms of practical redemption, as a synonym for monasticism; demons could only be vanquished by asceticism, and asceticism could only be followed when the world had been repudiated.[2]

If the foregoing be accepted as giving the true state of affairs, it is obvious that the monks considered that, in essence, Christianity was an ethic; it consisted in disciplining the body and the soul till all the emotions were banished, till everything

[1] *Apophth. Antonius*, 24, p. 84 *Hist. mon.* 16 thereon, remarks by Reitzenstein, *Studie*, 34ff.
[2] *Apophth. Poimen*, 8, p. 324a

of a physical nature had been sacrificed in the highest degree. It also becomes plain why people of this standpoint were completely indifferent to speculative theology and questions of dogma; and this is the case in spite of the fact that their indifference was occasionally depicted as a humble attitude to heavenly verities too high for human kind. The fact remains that there was no essential connection between the ethic of asceticism and the careful discussion of Christian doctrine. A man like Origen was able to feel at home in both worlds at once, and reduce them to a unity; but the Egyptian monks had not the same capacity. Nay, they scarcely mentioned even the name of Jesus Himself; true, they did hold to the Sermon on the Mount, whose stern requirements they regarded as principles of asceticism to be kept in mind. Yet when the cross of Christ was mentioned by them, it was not to recall the story of the Passion and all the theological doctrines that had been drawn from it; but to speak of the sign of the cross, and its power in exorcizing demons.

In spite of all factors of this kind, however, the monks laid the greatest stress on orthodoxy, and were fanatically hostile to every form of heresy;[1] nevertheless, their attitude is to be understood as nothing more than an adherence to certain accepted forms, and not as due to any understanding of the issues themselves. They received a password, as it were, from the bishop of Alexandria,[2] and turned against everyone whom he characterized, for the time being, as a heretic. That is how it came about that the monks of the desert developed into a body of troops on whom the pope of Egypt could rely. There was a marked Meletian influence in the cloisters only during the initial stages of the movement; and also, round about A.D. 400 in the Natron Valley, a group of monks of Greek education stood in defence of Origen; apart from these cases, the monks in their multitudes were loyal to the policy of their patriarchate, and they attacked heretics fiercely. But it must be remembered at the same time, that they were acting in defence of a primitive conception of God and against

[1] *Amun. epist.* 2. 12. 32   cf. *Pachom. vita,* 31; *Paralip.* 7   *Apophth.* in Heussi, *Mönchtum,* 272ff.
[2] *Pachom. vita,* 94

the mental refinements of Greek thought—the monks in the Natron Valley naturally succumbed.

The Bible occupied a prominent place in the practical life of the monastics, in as far as it was a book to be learned by heart. We saw on an earlier page[1] how an applicant had to prove that he was a suitable candidate by learning by heart certain psalms and New Testament epistles; and a faithful monk would make every effort to increase the number of passages he knew in this way. There are plenty of instances where monks are said to have known the whole of the Bible by heart.[2] Doubtless many of such reports were exaggerated, but an actual performance was recorded by a witness who heard for himself.[3] It was the case of a certain Father Heron who, on a journey of some forty miles, recited the following by heart: fifteen psalms, the Epistle to the Hebrews, the book of Isaiah, a part of Jeremiah, the gospel according to St Luke, and, finally, the Proverbs of Solomon.

It should of course be understood that this learning by heart was nothing more than a superficial accomplishment, ascetic in character, a kind of weaving of mental matting. In spite of the English idiomatic expression, this mechanical memorization did not penetrate the heart; it gave indeed only the faintest Biblical tinge to the world of ideas in which the monks lived. A study of the *Sayings of the Fathers* reveals an astonishing paucity of citations from the Bible, and even these are quoted for their value as admonitions to the practice of asceticism. Very rarely is any mention made of the men and women of the Bible, and even when such mention is made, it is only to exhibit them as examples of a type of life or as ideals of virtue. The difference between these monks and the church's mode of thought was brought into sharp relief when a bishop like Epiphanius of Cyprus gave an address to a congregation of monastics: Epiphanius made use of a long series of passages quoted from the Bible, but he did this because they formed part of his own message.[4] There is also the witness of Father Amun's rule.[5] If the monks visited a neighbour in his cell,

---

[1] *vide supra*, p. 142f.   [2] *Hist. Laus.* 11. 26. 32. 37. 58.   [3] *ibid.* 26
[4] *Apophth. Epiphanius* 5–15, p. 164ff.   cf. also *Kronios* 1. 2. p. 248
[5] *Apophth. Amun.* 2, p. 128

they must, of course, not discuss anything "external", i.e. having to do with the outside world. A disciple then asked whether they were to use sayings from the Bible, or from the *Sayings of the Fathers* when they conversed. Father Amun replied, "It is preferable to use the *Sayings of the Fathers* and not passages from the Bible; it is very dangerous to quote the Bible." The incident gives an exact reflection of the way in which the Coptic monks used to think. They regarded the Bible as a book of divine origin, and for that reason it was to be held in high honour and respect, and learned by heart as a matter of duty; but, for the most part, it was incomprehensible and, in the last analysis, an eerie book. They therefore preferred to keep to the teachings of men whom they regarded as authentic messengers sent by God from their own flesh and blood, and who were therefore closer and more comprehensible.

Besides the reciting of the Psalms and other books of the Bible, prayer was in daily use to provide food for the soul. Naturally, prayer did not take the form of a spontaneous and personal talking with God, but that of repeating prayers previously formulated; in particular, the Lord's Prayer. How completely prayer was conceived as an ascetic exercise was apparent in a case like that of Father Paul of Scetis, who knew by heart more than 300 formulated prayers, and who recited them daily. He checked off the number by 300 small pebbles, letting one fall to the ground at the end of each petition. When he was informed, however, that a woman in a certain village was able to recite 700 prayers per day, he became very dejected. Makarius comforted him by advising that he should not repeat more than 100 in a day, and yet could retain a clear conscience. If Paul still felt scruples of conscience about the 300, the reason was that his heart was not pure while he prayed, or else because it was in fact possible for him to reach a higher total.[1]

One of these forms of prayer is extant as an isolated instance. Father Lucius of Enaton, a maker of sail-cloth, prayed without ceasing while at work, and used the formula: "Have mercy upon me, O God, according to Thy loving kindness: according

[1] *Hist. Laus.* 20

to the multitude of Thy tender mercies blot out my transgressions" (Ps. 51: 1), and repeated the formula all day till nightfall.[1] In this case, the explicit ground and reason for offering the prayer was the monk's consciousness of sin; but it must not be forgotten that that was the very element that lay at the root of whatever else expressed a monk's sense of need, or his humility. Awareness of sin constituted the chink in his armour which demons could use as a point of attack; and he found that prayer was the most powerful means of safety, a means of lifting the soul to God, and far above the sphere where the demons were active. Tradition has handed down a very significant saying by Father Agathon[2] to the effect: "On every occasion when a man has it in his heart to pray, the demons try to prevent him; they know that nothing is so dangerous to them as prayer to God. No matter what path a man chooses, if he follow it perseveringly, he will reach some goal. But prayer is needed up to the last effort he is called on to make". So too Father Makarius, who gave the plain advice:[3] "There is no need for a lot of babble; simply spread out your hands and say: Lord have mercy on me according to Thy will and wisdom. In times when you are beset, say: Lord, help me. God knows full well all that you need, and He is merciful."

This conviction, that sin separates us from God and that it can only be overcome by prayer to God in His mercy, is the only genuinely Christian element in monasticism; otherwise, it has nothing more than external relations with the Christian religion. It should also be remarked that this element lies at a great depth, and only rarely reaches the light of day; rather, as a general rule, far from being a part of life, prayer was a mechanical repetition which achieved its purpose if one was successful in keeping weariness at bay by an act of will. The technique concentrated everything, in fact, on a single focal point: by a monotonous regularity in habits of life, and by the utmost exertion of one's spiritual powers, to concentrate all the activities of the self on reaching the one and only goal, viz., to lay hold of the divine; and this, in its highest form,

---

[1] *Apophth. Lucius*, p. 253c   [2] *Apophth. Agathon*, 9, p. 112
[3] *Apophth. Makarius*, 19, p. 269

the contemplation of God, was granted to those rare souls who were blessed in the full sense.

No visions were granted to ordinary monks; but to one who was "perfect",[1] the spirit of God revealed things supernatural or future. The celebrated gift possessed by the early Christian prophets of reading the thoughts in the minds of others, was shared by outstanding ascetics, and they also had authority to proclaim forgiveness of sins in God's name.[2] They could foresee coming events, or those taking place at a distance; and they received an early intimation of the day of their own death;[3] if one of their number parted from this present world, they saw his soul borne to heaven by a choir of angels.[4] When Father Sisoes was on his death-bed, he spoke to the Fathers sitting round about, and told what his eyes beheld:[5] Father Antonius was coming to meet him, followed by a band of prophets, and then by the apostles. His face lit up more and more as the angels bore him upwards; the Lord Himself drew near and said: "Bring to me the chosen vessel of the desert." Then his face shone as brightly as the sun, and he gave up the ghost; there was a flash of lightning, and incense filled the whole house.

The world of the Bible came alive in the visions of the monks; and it is even on record that one of them stood at the foot of the cross at the side of Mary, the mother of God.[6] The Last Judgment was seen in vision, but it was not described in all the majesty of New Testament apocalyptic; rather, it was confined to hints and suggestions, and restricted to the monks themselves. Abbot Theodore of Pabau once shared in the worship offered at night by the angels in the church of his monastery, and he beheld the flashing splendour of the heavenly hosts. He had a very large number of visions granted to him—but on account of this very fact he became suspect to the church, and was called upon for his defence before the

---

[1] *Hist. mon.* 30, 1

[2] *Pachom. vita,* 106   *Amun. epist.* 3. 16. 17–23. 28   *Hist. mon.* 8, 25   13, 10   18, 1

[3] *Amun. epist.* 13. 31. 34   *Hist. Laus.* 4. 14   Athan. *vita Ant.* 82. 87.   *Hist. mon.* 1, 65   16, 23   19, 3; 32

[4] Athan. *vita Ant.* 60   *Amun. epist.* 25   *Paralip.* 13   *Hist. mon.* 16, 24

[5] *Apophth. Sisoes,* 14, p. 396   [6] *Apophth. Poimen,* 144, p. 357

synod at Latoplis. As a consequence, he preserved the strictest secrecy afterwards regarding his ecstatic experiences.[1]

There is only one recorded case of attaining the ultimate goal; Father Silvanus, the very person who saw the Last Judgment. He assured a disciple who had observed him in ecstasy,[2] and said: "I was carried up to heaven, and I beheld the glory of God." In other instances of the use of that lofty term, "vision of God" (*theoria*), it is in the connotation of "contemplativeness", the concentration of one's thoughts on God, i.e. the perception of God as the experience takes place in the heart. Those who were granted visions saw with their eyes only portions of the heavenly substance, and these in the form of flaming appearances.[3] But in the periods when they sank silently into their own selves, God touched their souls; and it depended on the general condition of the person concerned whether he would rise into ecstasy and gaze in vision on the heavenly world. Very little is said of this kind of experience in the records left behind by the monastics within our purview.[4]

Pachomius's ideal monk is described in a few words in one passage.[5] A disciple who had transgressed was assigned by Pachomius to an older brother for him to train. "So it came about that they wove their mats side by side, carried out their fasts and said their prayers in the proper way. The young man had been commanded to obey the senior, and he did so in every respect: he did not eat even a leaf of lettuce without being told. Moreover, he was so humble and modest that he never spoke; nor did he readily lift his eyes to look at another person. He practised asceticism consistently. He kept watch alone during the night; when he had prayed to the point of exhaustion and fatigue, he sat down in the middle of his cell, and took some rest in this attitude; he then carried on with his weaving throughout the night.[6] In short, he became a real monk." There is as little exaggeration and extravagance in this passage as in the hearts of the men among whom it was written,

---

[1] *Apophth. Silvanus*, 2, p. 408   *Pachom. vita*, 71. 102   Theodore: *Amun. epist.* 14 and *Pachom. vita*, 112. 135

[2] *Apophth. Silvanus*, 3, p. 408

[3] Heussi, *Mönchtum*, 267. 179

[4] e.g., *Hist. mon.* 11, 19–20   12, 7   cf. 28, 5–12   and remarks by Reitzenstein, *Studie*, 174f.

[5] *Pachom. vita*, 105

[6] cf. *Hist. Laus.* 2, p. 17, 10

and for that reason it gives a clear and trustworthy picture of the
way in which a simple disciple obeyed the phrase in the *Sayings
of the Fathers*[1] which declares, "A man will find no peace until
he says in his heart, I am alone with God in the world."

A monk had no need of his fellow-men. Strictly speaking,
he had no need of either church or sacrament, for his salvation
depended entirely on his own moral powers. Nevertheless,
service on Sunday was inconceivable without the eucharistic
sacrifice and the communion which followed. The sacrament
had therefore a place in the monk's life, if not in the monastic
system; it was something ineffably holy, something divine
that was projected into the earthly life of the monk; but there
is no record that it was preached as helping the soul forward,
or that this subject was ever discussed.

Still, there is a record to the effect that, on a certain occasion,
"an eminent exponent (of asceticism)[2] was relieved of his
doubts concerning the transubstantiation of the bread, and
converted to the orthodox belief of the church catholic"; and
he found salvation by this means, for otherwise all his efforts
"would have been in vain". When the priest took the bread
in his hands, the monk saw a child; then the angel of the Lord
came down from heaven with a sword, slew the child, and let
its blood run into the chalice. Then again, when the priest
broke the bread into small pieces, the angel hewed the child
into small pieces also. Then, when the bloody flesh was
offered as communion to the doubter, he drew back with a
shudder; but the incident taught him why God gave the
sacrament to our use, not in its true form, but in a form
acceptable to human sensibility.[3]

That was a graphic way of presenting the orthodox teaching
about the real nature of the events at the ceremony of the
sacrifice of the eucharist; that, and no more. All the efforts
of the monk "would have been in vain" if he had persisted
in a wrong opinion about the rite; he would have been nothing
more nor less than a heretic.

On the other hand, not a word is said, and no aspect of the
problem is discussed, showing in what way the sacrifice

---

[1] *Apophth. Alonios*, 1, p. 133   [2] See remarks by Reitzenstein, *Studie*, 129, n. 2
[3] *Apophth. Daniel*, 7, p. 156f.

benefited him, or why he stood in need of it. Light was thrown on the question, rather, by those records which describe the perfect ascetics as living for long periods, if not permanently, on the eucharist alone, to the exclusion of all earthly foods. In a case like this, the elements of the communion were obviously the bread of heaven belonging to the next world, and used as food by the angels themselves; in other words, it was the means of subsistence granted to believers while still on earth; their foretaste of eternal life. It must be said, however, that other accounts are of more frequent occurrence, which say that miraculous bread from heaven was given to the "perfect", apart from sharing in the eucharist.[1] On one occasion, this led a presumptuous ascetic, who had been blinded by demons, to declare that he had seen Jesus in vision, and that he therefore required the sacrament no more. As it stood, that was a quite logical consequence of monastic theory on its radical side,[2] but it was out of harmony with the monks' loyalty to the church in practice. The Fathers therefore went as far as to declare the man insane; they put him in irons for a year, till he regained his right senses.

The fact that communion was a necessity, and this without qualification, for every Christian, was driven home by Saint Makarius of Egypt in a sermon after he had restored to human form a woman who had been changed into a mare: the only reason why the magician had been able to get her into his power, was because she had not gone to sacrament for five weeks.[3] Father Apollos of Hermupolis used to teach that a good monk should take sacrament daily if possible.[4] Here is the explanation why priests were a matter of necessity even in the cloisters and in colonies of monks; and the priests in turn offered a possible means which bishops might use, with caution and tact, for establishing relations with various groups of ascetics. The first result was a really friendly relationship, characterized by mutual respect and politeness.[5] The next was that the monks themselves gradually came to enter the ranks of the clergy; this development was against the wishes

---

[1] *Hist. mon.* 15, 2   1, 47   2, 9   8, 5. 38–41   11, 6. 21   12, 5   13, 3. 4. 14 *Hist. Laus.* 18. 26
[2] cf. also *Apophth. Motios*, 1, p. 300   [3] *Hist. Laus.* 25, p. 80, 10   17, p. 46, 7
[4] *Hist. mon.* 8, 56   [5] *Pachom. vita*, 29. 30. 81. 143f.   *Hist. Laus.* 16

of Pachomius, but rendered inevitable by the practical requirements of the situation. A monk held in high esteem in the
district would be consecrated as priest, and therefore recognized
by the church as a legitimate person to offer the sacrifice of
the eucharist.[1] It then came to be regarded as unwarrantable
arrogance for a monk to assert[2] that "during last night he had
been consecrated presbyter by Christ"—yet, by so doing, he
was only re-asserting the ancient claim of the "pneumatics"
as distinct from the "regular" clergy. As a consequence of the
developments which had taken place in the monasteries by
about A.D. 400, public opinion among the monks was adverse
to recognizing these special forms of the operation of the
Holy Spirit. In certain circumstances, monks might be consecrated as bishops;[3] but since installation carried with it the
obligation to abandon the life of a hermit, and enter busily
into worldly affairs, the monks in every case made their
resistance quite outwardly and markedly evident: several
cases are on record where very determined ascetics would have
an ear cut off in order to evade consecration,[4] for a mutilated
person could not be ordained.

*

Miracle is a feature of monasticism to the present day.
The signs and wonders performed by the men of God in the
Old Testament, the "mighty works" of Christ and the apostles,
all had their counterparts performed by the "pneumatics"
of the early church; indeed greater miracles were worked by
them. The words of John 14: 12, "Verily, verily, I say unto
you, he that believeth on me, the works that I do shall he do
also; and greater works than these shall he do", were read
with a very definite interpretation. The "proof of the spirit
and of power" was furnished ever and again, in a variety of
different ways, by men and women who had been blessed
with a special endowment by God. The more the church
adopted and conformed to the kind of Christianity which
melted imperceptibly into the life of the people at large, the
more did it come about that unusual and unaccustomed

[1] e.g. *Hist. mon.* 14. 18. 20. 32   *Hist. Laus.* 7 (p. 26, 9)   9 (p. 31, 11). 44. 45.
47. 48. 49. 58   *Apophth. Matoe*, 9, p. 292
[2] *Hist. Laus.* 53   [3] *Apophth. Appho*, p. 133   *Nitra*, p. 312
[4] *Hist. Laus.* 11, p. 8   *Hist. mon.* 26, 2

features found their niches among anchorites, fanatics, schismatics, and finally the monastics. Here was a movement whose members felt themselves quite specially called upon to cultivate and produce men of the spirit in the full sense of the term. And what testimony other than that of miracles could be more convincing of the fact that the desired goal had indeed been reached?

It is therefore natural that miracle and monasticism should have been inseparably conjoined from the start, and that miracle-stories were an essential element in every record of monastic life. The biography of Antony written by Athanasius is in fact the classi example of this sort of element. It should be remembered, of course, that miracles and miracle-workers were by no means confined to the Christian movement; rather, they were frequent phenomena in every period of the ancient world. They seemed almost to sprout from the ground afresh daily in each and every nature-religion. It follows therefore that no one in the age of decline in the ancient world saw anything remarkable and strange in the claims of a monk to work miracles; such a monk would simply be reckoned to belong to the genus, "men of God", the *theioi andres*, a genus which had been very familiar for centuries as disposing of superhuman powers. And this is the reason, too, why ancient miracle-stories, widely recounted in various popular traditions, were ascribed, quite naïvely, to holy men of the Christian strain.[1]

We have already given some attention to their visions and predictions, and also to their prophet-like gifts of telepathy. But in quite an outstanding degree, a great ascetic was famed as a helper in time of stress, i.e. as physician; and people would make a pilgrimage to him, and be cured of lameness and blindness, of sores and snake-bites, of fevers and fits; people in any way possessed by demons would be set free from torment at a word spoken by the holy man. In rare cases, even death itself was proved to be not invincible.[2] The very animals readily obeyed such a monk's commands; they would avoid trampling on the herbs he had planted out, and abandon the places he had forbidden to them. Wild asses, snakes, and

[1] cf. Ludwig Bieler, *Theios Aner, Das Bild des "göttl. Menschen" in Spätantike und Frühchristentum*, 1935–36
[2] *Hist. mon.* 11, 8–9. 13–14. 15–17

crocodiles, would be called on to render useful services as messengers or guards; beasts of prey were killed at a word. There was even a case where a cunning hyena had brought its blind offspring to a holy man, who healed it; whereon the grateful dam brought a goatskin to her kind benefactor.[1] A further case was that of a holy man who might inflict miraculous punishments: an angry word on his part might cause an earthquake, kill men or toothsome animals;[2] and a milder form of the exercise of the same powers consisted of making a wrong-doer stand stock-still for hours on end rooted to the spot; stolen cabbage would not cook when boiled.[3]

In a time of famine, one such man of God was able to renew the contents of three large bread-baskets, and use them to feed the 500 monks of his own monastery and also the inhabitants of the neighbouring village; the narrator of this incident declares that, at the end of the meal, he had himself seen the baskets carried out already full again.[4] From this point it is but a short stage to the holy man who made corn grow out of the sand of the desert;[5] and again, to him who walked on the water, flew through the air, and ordered the setting sun to stand still long enough for him to reach the end of his journey.[6] It would be possible to recount many more legends of miracles that were performed in this magic garden, but other matters call for our attention; the inquiring student is referred to the documentary sources themselves, which give much space to this kind of record.[7] We must now return to church history properly so called.

---

[1] *Hist. mon.* 13, 5. 6–9; 9, 5–7. 8–10　Hyenas: 28, 15–16
[2] *ibid.* 8, 10–13　36–37　13, 5　　[3] *ibid.* 6, 2　*Hist. Laus.* 31　*Hist. mon.* 11, 32
[4] *ibid.* 8, 44–47
[5] *ibid.* 11, 25–27　cf. also *Das apokryphe Evangelienfragment, ZNW,* 34 (1935), 290
[6] *ibid.* 11, 18. 10–12
[7] Athan. *vita Antonii,* German translation by Hans Mertel in the Bibliothek der Kirchenväter, vol. 31, 1917 (Athanasius, vol. 2). The *vita Pachomi* is in the appendix of the same vol. Athanasius's *Vita Antonii* is translated into English in *The Nicene and Post-Nicene Fathers,* 2nd Series, vol. iv (1892), ed. A. Robertson.

The *Historia Lausiaca* is translated into German by S. Krottenthaler (Bibl. d. Kirchenv. vol. 5 (1912), where it follows the Greek liturgies) and is succeeded by the *Life of S. Melania.* W. K. L. Clarke has published an English translation, with notes, of *The Lausiac History of Palladius* (S.P.C.K. 1918).

The East-Syrian *Lives of the Monks according to Thomas of Marga* is translated into German by Oskar Braun (Bibl. d. Kirchenv. vol. 22, 1915) following the account of the Persian martyrs.

For later centuries see Lietzmann, *Byzantinische Legenden,* 1911

(4) The Geographical Distribution of Monasticism

Asceticism had come to be practised in many localities within the length and breadth of the territory that could be called Christian; and, in isolated cases, a form of monasticism might have been found which had a "prehistoric" character; nevertheless there can be no doubt of the Egyptian origin or inspiration of those forms of monasticism which were to prove really viable, and which had grown up under the general aegis of the church. It must be conceded, however, that even in Egypt itself it was possible to find elements originating elsewhere. The custom whereby a new-comer was put under the instruction of an older and trusted exponent, thus constituting the nucleus of an arrangement which gave shape to the ascetic kind of life, was a custom which came to Egypt in the first instance from Syria. In other words, it derives from an alien and "prehistoric" tradition of monasticism; and this origin is witnessed by the fact that all spiritual Fathers and Mothers, and accordingly all heads of cloisters of both sexes, were addressed with the Syriac titles of "Abba", father, and "Amma", mother,[1] and not with Egyptian names. The title of Abbot for the superior of a cloister was adapted from this nomenclature; its use spread from Egypt to every other country, and is customary to the present day. This isolated exception does not weaken the general principle.

Jerome traced back the origin of ascetic practice in Palestine to Hilarion of Thabata near Gaza. But the biography which Jerome wrote as a tribute to this holy man is interpolated with romantic and fabulous stories to such an extent that it is difficult to sort out those elements which can be safely used for historical purposes.[2] It would seem that Hilarion had been a disciple of Antony, that he afterwards settled near Gaza, and that in course of time he gathered a colony of eremites round him; he also laboured as a miracle-worker and an evangelist. Sozomen says[3] that his own grandfather's family were converted to Christianity by him. During the reign of Julian, he left the place where he had been settled, and took

---

[1] Amma, cf. *Hist. Laus.* 34, p. 99, 17   59, p. 153, 8 in the *apparatus criticus*
[2] Sozom. 3, 14. 26–28   and 5, 10, 1–4 based on Jerome   [3] *ibid.* 5, 15, 14f.

to a life of wandering. He went to Egypt, thence to Sicily, and then to Dalmatia; in the end, he made his way to Cyprus, where he died in A.D. 371 at about eighty years of age.[1] A few monastic colonies close to Gaza traced their foundation to him.[2]

Epiphanius, who counts among the Fathers of the church, had been one of the Palestinian ascetics of this early period. He was born in a village near Eleutheropolis (Beth-Djibrin, south-west of Jerusalem), spent a long time among the monks of Egypt, and afterwards, in his twenties, returned to his native place. Here he continued to practise his ascetic habits, until he was chosen, in A.D. 367, to be bishop of Salamis in Cyprus. His new office gave him the opportunity of fostering monasticism in the island.[3]

When Aetheria, with her inquiring mind, travelled to and fro in Palestine about A.D. 390,[4] she found hermits on mount Nebo and in the Hauran, besides a few here and there in places connected with the Biblical tradition. Monks used to come in troops to attend the services in Jerusalem. It is easy to understand how places in Palestine which had noteworthy mention in the records of Holy Scripture would exercise a magnetic attraction on settlers of the ascetic type;[5] there is something to be said for the hypothesis that it was from among these anchorites that the monks originated who were responsible for founding the monasteries on Mount Sinai, where God had spoken with Moses. When Aetheria visited the mountain-group, she found monastic settlements everywhere on the hills and in the valleys. Palladius knew monks who lived near to Jericho, and on the banks of the Jordan.[6] In the environs of Jerusalem, the Mount of Olives became a "mount of hermits" at an early date. A group who took a special interest in theology went to live there in the seventh decade of the fourth century.[7]

---

[1] Jerome, *vita Hilar.* 44   c . the statement in c. 25: in A.D. 356, he was 65 years of age.
[2] Sozom. 5, 32, 5–8   [3] *ibid.* 5, 32, 3–5   Epiphan. *Ancoratus* praef. p. 1, Holl
[4] *vide* Vol. 3, 303   Aeth., *peregr.* 10, 9   13, 1   3, 1ff.
[5] Lists of cloisters in Palestine are given in Cabrol, *Dict.* 2, 3165–75
[6] *Hist. Laus.* 48–51
[7] Basil, *ep.* 258, 2   259   cf. Athan. *ep. ad Palladium*, t. 1, p. 957   *Hist. mon.* prol. 2

Much about the same time, at the end of A.D. 373 or in the spring of A.D. 374, a lady of the name of Melanius,[1] an incredibly wealthy member of the aristocracy of Rome itself, came to Palestine after having completed a pilgrimage through the cloisters and monastic settlements of Egypt. She founded a cloister in Jerusalem for sixty nuns, and acted as its head for 27 years; her spiritual adviser was Rufinus, who was at that time on terms of intimate friendship with Jerome. So also Palladius belonged to her circle as a young man, the very person who afterwards wrote the *Historia Lausiaca*. He lived on the Mount of Olives as an accepted novice in the eighties of that century. It seems, too, that Jerome was very successful in proclaiming to the eminent ladies in Rome the advantages of the ascetic life; and when, for various reasons, he left the capital in August A.D. 385 in order to go to the Holy Land, he was followed by a wealthy lady, Paula, and her daughter, Eustochium. He accompanied both ladies on the customary journey through Egypt, and returned with them in the summer of A.D. 386 to Palestine, indeed to Bethlehem. In the year 389, Paula built there three nunneries, and also a monastery in which Jerome lived till his death in A.D. 420. There was at least one other monastery in Bethlehem, that in which Cassian when a youth received his first training as a monk.[2]

In the parts of Syria which bordered on Palestine, asceticism was regarded with favour at an early date, particularly the practice of celibacy. Tatian, the "apologist", a disciple of Justin Martyr in the second century, was known to be a supporter of that kind of self-discipline,[3] and was regarded by the orthodox of a later date as the founder of the sect of the "Encratites". How strong an influence he exercised can be judged from the fact that his *Diatessaron*, a harmony of the four canonical gospels, remained in use well into the fifth century as the official book of the gospels in the Syrian church. He himself was an instance illustrating the truth that the

---

[1] This apparently masculine form was used also for women, cf. E. Diehl, *Rhein. Mus.* 62 (1907), 415   Pauly-W., Series II, Vol. 2, 2450, etc.   The name Melania or Melanium is an adjustment to the customary forms,   cf. E. Schwartz, *ZNW*, 36 (1937), 165, n. 7
[2] E. Schwartz, *ZNW*, 38 (1939), 3   [3] Irenaeus, 1, 28, 1 (1, 220, Harvey)

non-Greek element of an eastern people was characterized by an eastern type of asceticism, very different from the forms that we have been describing hitherto; and this on account of its fanaticism, its fundamental one-sidedness, its tendency to extremism, and its exaggerated fondness for miracles. The church itself had often repudiated the special peculiarities of Syria, and excommunicated their protagonists as schismatics; but much remained in her bosom and was tolerated; nay, in the course of time, it was practised with increasing devotion.

Aphrahat was an ascetic who came from Persia about A.D. 340; he was a popular evangelist, and delivered a number of addresses in Syriac. The addresses reflect the kind of Christianity which was current at that time in and around Mosul,[1] and also throw a light on the kind of asceticism that was practised there. It would appear that Christianity was regarded as essentially a perpetual warfare between the believer and the devil. To carry on this warfare with full success, it was indispensable to be an ascetic, a hermit, a devotee; and as such to have repudiated the world in general, and marriage in particular; for woman was Satan's instrument.[2] Any person who decided to adopt the Christian life should seriously examine himself again before accepting baptism; if he traced any inclination for marriage, he should marry before being baptized. But anyone who did come to be baptized, by that very act took his place in the ranks making war against Satan. The water used in baptism put the test, like the brook at which, according to Judges 7: 4-7, Gideon was able to separate the true warriors from the weaklings. It was therefore the duty of priests, "when baptism had been administered, to look and see which were the strong and which the weak. They were to encourage the strong, but publicly to turn the frail and the weak away from the battle lest, when overtaken by war, they threw down their weapons, took to flight, and relapsed."[3]

The purport of such a passage is unmistakable: a person who was fully a Christian and who had received the seal of baptism, ought to become an ascetic; any dalliance in the society of one's fellows, or in marriage, was regarded as weak-

---

vide Vol. II, 266f. [2] Aphrahat, *hom.* 6,4. 6. 7, p. 26off. [3] *ibid.* 7, 21, 34 p.8

ness; and any backsliding from the life of a hermit into conformity to the ways of the world was felt to be treason to the
flag. At the same time, the words of the preacher show plainly
that to make celibacy or anchoritism a definite *sine qua non*,
was no longer practicable in every case of candidates for
baptism; and he had no alternative to coming to terms with
the "weak" Christians who constituted the churches. But he
preserved the principle intact; it was very much in the
atmosphere in this corner of the world, and was maintained
long afterwards by the Marcionite and the gnostic sects; it
also lent a tinge to Manichean ethics.

About the time when the ecumenical council was being held
in Nicea, a deacon named Audi was at work near Edessa
(Urfa), and afforded a typical example of those who criticized
the church and its clergy. He was felt to be a source of irritation, and attempts were made to get rid of him; but for a long
time in vain. As a result of violence and ill-treatment, he was
at length brought to the point of breaking with the church,
and large numbers of his sympathizers broke away with him.
They founded their own churches, either in the desert or in
the city-suburbs; they housed themselves in monastic establish-
ments, and earned their subsistence by manual labour. The
surviving information is too little to indicate precisely in what
way they adopted ascetic practices; but there is enough to
show clearly that they were loyal to the rigorousness of life
and to the idea of estrangement from the world; these features
were characteristic of the early Christian attitude, as opposed
to the changes through which the church was passing. Their
leader, Audi, was installed as bishop; and in the course of
time, they built up an organization headed by several bishops,
and stretching from the Taurus mountains and the desert
near Antioch in the north, through Palestine, to Arabia and
Mesopotamia in the south and east. Having suffered injury
to this extent, the church, helped by the emperor, was successful in exiling Audi to "Scythia". This strategy only meant,
however, that the attraction exercised by Christian asceticism
began to make itself felt among the Goths, and with considerable success. When Athanarich persecuted the Christians in
A.D. 372, many members of the Gothic churches of Audi's

communion crossed over the frontier into Roman territory.[1]

These were forms of asceticism which maintained closer or looser bonds with the world, either by work done, or by social intercourse. But there were other forms, radical in character, which can be discerned on the Syrian landscape about the year 300, and which about that time were systematically established by a man who had his own ideas and went his own way.[2] His key to the problem of salvation was a complete break with the world: a denial of literally every form of labour or activity that belonged to this Earth. One's whole confidence must be placed in the help of God, who would stir the pity of kindly persons, and through them give what was necessary to the hungry and shivering, "perfectly" holy men. This particular movement began to be of historical importance about A.D. 370, and the adherents were known by the Syriac word, "Messalians",[3] or Men of Prayer; for they had abandoned the world and all their possessions in order to give themselves entirely to a life of prayer, and this to such a complete extent that they would have nothing to do even with the pious practice of fasting. For the same reason, they did no work, but gathered by begging what they needed to live on; these principles meant that they did not resort to the desert, but remained in contact with the rest of the community. They had no homes of their own, and throughout the night both men and women might be seen asleep on the streets; in veritable fact, they had nothing on which to lay their heads. They believed that they lived in the world of the Risen Lord and were full of His spirit; they believed they were pneumatics in the same sense of the term as in the first church. Originating in Mesopotamia, the movement spread to the coastal region near Antioch and thence to Asia Minor, where it came into contact with similar opinions. Amphilochius, bishop of Iconium, sprang into the fray which had already been begun there by Basil,[4] carried the battle further, and at a synod in Side[5] on the gulf of Adalia, stigmatized the Messalians' practices as heresy; Flavian of Antioch became his ally.

---

[1] Epiphan. *haer.* 70, 1, 1–5; 14, 5–15, 5   further sources on p. 232
[2] *vide infra*, 183ff.   [3] Epiphan. *haer.* 80, 3, 2ff., p. 487f.   cf. note on p. 485
[4] Basil, *ep.* 188. 198   [5] Proceedings in Photius, *Bibl. cod.* 52

A short time earlier, i.e. in the years 381-83, imperial edicts had been promulgated[1] against the sects which Basil was attempting to suppress, calling them "strait-laced, world-repudiating, bag-carriers"; classing and prohibiting them along with the Manicheans. Amphilochius was anxious that the steps he had taken, should not only drive the Messalians out of the fellowship of the church, but also that they should be branded as heretics, and therefore as dangerous to the state. He hoped to be able by these means to keep the church free from dubious pneumatics of this kind, a problem which, as we shall show a little later on, was severe in Asia Minor also. In Syria the problem was quite insoluble; this was because the soil was so prolific of holy men who were marvelled at, that the church capitulated and made her peace with them.

Theodoret, bishop of Cyrrhus, a small city in a wild district between Antioch and the Euphrates, wrote a book, c. A.D. 440, on the ascetics of northern Syria. He wrote with reverence and awe of hermits who loaded themselves with chains, wore iron belts and collars, lived in cisterns, restricted their range of movement by having only a path the breadth of a span by which to go to church, or even had themselves walled up. Disciples gathered round the cells of the masters, and colonies of hermits came into being. At the same time, the monastic life made great headway, and it was not rare for cloisters of the same foundation to divide on the basis of language into Syrian and Greek branches. The descriptions given by Theodoret make it clear that, by the end of the fourth century, the monastic life was a highly developed institution in Syria, and full of vitality.[2]

About the year 375, Jerome went as a disciple among the ascetics in the desert near Aleppo; it will be remembered that, on an earlier page,[3] we described the hermits who lived in the mountains near Antioch, and discussed the important part played by them in A.D. 387.

Monasteries multiplied to an increasing extent in the fifth

[1] *Cod. Theod.* 16, 5, 7. 9. 10. 11 and discussion by K. Holl, *Amphiloch. v. Iconium*, 36f.
[2] Theodoret, *hist. relig.*: irons, cap. 4. 10. 11. 15 cisterns, 13 short journeys, 4 walling up, 18. 19 Greek and Syrian cloisters, 4. 5
[3] *vide supra*, 118

century, without putting an end to the practice of anchoritism; rather, its forms became even more remarkable and excessive. The masses of iron with which the strange holy men loaded themselves grew to be ever greater, until they could only walk bending under the weight. Baradatos walled himself up in the first instance, but later went to live in a crate of laths that was open alike to the sun and the rain; it was also too small for his body, and forced him into a bent posture. But he was outdone by Thalelaios, who made himself a cylinder of two wheels joined by laths, in which he lived with his knees drawn right up—he must have sat like a white mouse in its exercise-wheel—and then he had the whole apparatus hung from a structure like a gallows. Others chose the tops of mountains, where they were exposed to all the discomforts of wind and weather; sometimes the place where they came to a halt was surrounded by a wall to protect them from unwelcome visitors.[1] John had an almond-tree cut down because it gave him shade.

Symeon Stylites went through a whole gamut of mounting types of asceticism. By birth he belonged to a family of prosperous farmers. Before he was twenty, he began to wear a cord round his body which chafed his skin till the blood ran; he had himself "buried" for two years; he beat off sleep by continually standing. In February, A.D. 412, he abandoned the monastery where he had lived to that date, and removed to the mountain village of Telnechin between Antioch and Aleppo. He lived there in a cell, but had himself walled up for the forty days of Lent, a procedure which he repeated on two occasions. Later, he climbed a neighbouring mountain, and lived within an encircling wall under the open sky, at first fettered to the place by an iron chain. Soon afterwards, he climbed on a rock about three feet high, whose top gave him not more than two square yards for movement. He spent five years on this pedestal, then adopted higher and yet higher rocks, until he took to pillars properly so-called. In the end, he reached the goal of his desires on the top of a pillar about 70 feet high, where he stood for thirty years, till his

[1] Theodoret, *hist. relig.*: iron, 21. 23. 29   Baradatos, 27   Thalelaios, 28   mountain tops, 21. 22. 23. 29

death on September 2, A.D. 459. The platform on the top was at most only four square yards, and there he lived in continuous prayer accompanied by a rhythmical falling on his knees, and bowing his forehead to the platform. Theodoret gazed with astonishment at this method of practising prayer, and counted 1,244 obeisances before he gave up counting.[1]

The pillar-saints represented the extreme of localized ascetics, as is made clear by the history of the whole movement. It was not a case of copying pagan practices indigenous to Syria, as was formerly sometimes thought. Its unique character was appreciated by public opinion, and was regarded as the greatest ornament of eastern anchoritism.[2] A generation after the death of Symeon Stylites, a great building, comprising a church and a cloister, was erected round the pillar, a building which was one of the most splendid examples of architecture in the declining age of antiquity.[3] The church catholic was proud of the holy man.

Symeon embodied the Syrian ideal of a hermit in the highest degree. His opposite number among those that lived in cloisters was Alexander, the founder of the Acoimetai,[4] i.e. the unsleeping. By birth, he belonged to one of the leading families of the Prince Islands, received a good Greek education in the capital, but at an early age, entered a Syrian monastery whose fame had attracted him. Yet the monastic life did not satisfy his longing for a perfect and literal fulfilment of the requirements set down in the gospels; and he refused to admit that it was true, as was commonly said, that fulfilment was impossible. He abandoned the monastery, and went to live in the desert near the Euphrates as a typical Syrian hermit. Throughout the day, he stood on a hill; and crept at night into an earthenware vessel let into the ground. He followed that mode of life for twenty years, during which time a monastic community gathered round him, nearly 400 obedient disciples all told, comprising Romans and Greeks, Syrians and Egyptians. He divided them into choirs for singing psalms, adopting the

---

[1] Lietzmann, *Das Leben d. hl. Symeon Stylites* (Texte u. Unt. 32, 4, 1908), 238–45
[2] H. Delehaye, *Les Saints Stylites*, 1923
[3] Cabrol, *Dict.* 1, 2380ff. for further details. O. Krencker, *Die Wallfahrtskirche des Simeon St.*, Preuss. Akad. Abh. 1938, No. 4
[4] *Vie d'Alexandre l'Acém* Stoop, in *ète*, ed.Patrol. orientalis, Tome 6, fasc. 5 (1911)

seven canonical hours,[1] which he soon doubled in number.
By ceaselessly striving to perfect the liturgy on the model of
the Bible, he came at last to the idea of imitating on earth
the praises which the angels sang to God without intermission.
He therefore laid it on the monks to sing the *Gloria* each day
seventy times seven, and to kneel each time. Hence there were
490 occasions in the twenty-four hours, or roughly twenty
Glorias per hour. The consequence was that his monastery
resounded every three minutes, day and night, with the angels'
song of "Glory be to God in the highest, peace on earth, and
goodwill to men". The choirs of monks sang in rotation but
the chorus continued, always the same, without pause, breaking
out afresh every three minutes—for centuries.

At length, Alexander was drawn by the idea of going on
pilgrimage, as was common among ascetics. He selected a
number of his devotees as companions, and made his way
through the desert from fort to fort along the Persian frontier;[2]
he approached Palmyra, but the city refused entrance to the
singing monks; he arrived in A.D. 420 at Antioch, where the
reception was not very friendly. He and his band settled down
in the site of some ancient warm baths, and began to take part
in the public life of the city, both helpfully and with criticism
of a more negative kind, until expelled by the military authorities. After experiences of all sorts he arrived finally at Constantinople;[3] by this time, he had attracted 300 monks from other
monasteries, and enlisted them in his choirs; and, of course,
they sang the *Gloria*, by turns, ceaselessly. Unfortunately, he
was again opposed, being now charged with heresy—the
similarity with the Messalians was quite unmistakable—and
he and his followers ended with being ill-used and expelled.
They found refuge in the monastery of Hypatius on the west side
of the Bosphorus,[4] until the empress intervened in their defence,
and they were able to establish a monastery on the Asiatic shore
of the Bosphorus. But in the course of time, the strange phenomenon was successful even in the capital, and the Akoimete
Monastery played an important part in Byzantine history.

[1] *vide* Vol. 3, 301   [2] *vide* Vol. 3, 30
[3] The authority for this period is *Callinici, vita S. Hypatii,* ed Bonn. 82–84
[4] *vide infra,* 174f.

Mention has already been made[1] of the fact that there were various currents of radical asceticism also in central Asia Minor. Eustathius, who at a later date became bishop of Sebaste (Siwas), is said to have been the head of a movement of this kind, which was scattered through Lesser Armenia, Pontus, and Paphlagonia. His adherents laboured enthusiastically in the cause of repudiating the world, and declared all married persons and all possessing property as incapable of eternal salvation. They held aloof from the church, regarding it as a secularized institution; they despised its services and customs; and, exercising the privilege of pneumatics, they conducted their own services. They wore a special habit to distinguish themselves alike from the general public and the clergy; many women wore male garments and cut their hair short, because in the Kingdom of God there was no difference between the sexes. A synod was held in the early forties (343?) in Gangra (Kiangri) of Paphlagonia,[2] when the church put up resistance, but apparently without any real effect. Eustathius, who had an imposing personality, remained undisturbed; he later had a powerful influence on Basil as a young man.[3]

Basil was to become the leading organizer of monasticism and the chief instructor of the recluses, first in Asia Minor and then, in the course of time, in the whole of the Greek church. After completing his studies in Athens he travelled through Egypt, Palestine, Syria, and Mesopotamia, in order to study monasticism at the fountain-head.[4] About A.D. 360, he founded for himself a monastery[5] where he was joined by friends of a similar turn of mind, including in particular Gregory of Nazianzus. He built it close to his family property at Annesoi, where his mother and sister had already established a cloistered community among the women of.their household. He drew up an order for the manner of life in his monastery.[6] His order started from the psychological standpoint, and laid down rules in the first instance for the inner life, and then for

---

[1] *vide supra*, 168f.
[2] Our authorities are their minutes and canons (Lauchert, 79–83 Turner, *Monum.* 2 164–214) together with Sozom. 3, 14, 31–36 4, 24, 9=Socr. 2, 43, 3-7
[3] Basil, *ep.* 223, 3. 5 cf. 99, 3 212, 2 [4] *ibid. ep.* 223, 2
[5] Greg. Nyss. *vita Macrinae*, Migne gr. 46, 965b-c Basil, *ep.* 3, 2 223, 5 Greg. Naz. *ep.* 6 *or.* 43, 61 cf. Tillemont, 9, 31. 43ff.
[6] Basil, *ep.* 2 cf. *ep.* 22

the outer life, which depended on it but was on a lower plane; nor did he stop there, but proceeded to throw spiritual light on the problems of monasticism in every direction. In the sequel we shall discuss further the classical writings of this great teacher of the church. He had a personality full of elemental power for giving practical effect to his ideas, and he had set himself the task of spreading that form of monastic organization which had penetrated everywhere in the south; at the same time, of course, he impressed on it the stamp of his own spiritual quality.

Eustathius and his followers had brought a movement to birth which led to the formation of communities in certain towns and villages of Lesser Armenia, Cappadocia, and Pontus. Small settlements consisting of two or three members also made their appearance, but nothing was produced by way of anchoritism properly so-called; nor of cloisters to any great extent.[1] Basil took another direction: he organized his friends in Pontus and later, a monastic community of the Egyptian type in Caesarea, and developed them into a monastery; he travelled to and fro in Pontus with a view to furthering his ideas.[2] The vigorous opposition which he met in so doing, an opposition based on dislike for any kind of innovation, is recorded in a surviving letter (No. 207) which he wrote to the community at Neocaesarea (Niksar).

For a long time Constantinople refused to tolerate monasticism, and this must be said in spite of all legends to the contrary. In A.D. 378, the year when Valens died, there was in that city still "not a single sign of a monk";[3] and it was only in A.D. 381 that an ascetic of the Syrian desert, Isaac by name, who had become famous, came to a halt there at the request of two persons at the royal court; he made a hermitage in the suburbs outside the city wall.[4] His cell soon grew to be the centre of a monastic settlement into which Dalmatius, an officer of the Guards, entered in A.D. 383. It would appear to have been

---

[1] Sozom. 6, 34, 7   Cassian, *Coll.* 18, 7, 8   cf. the "brotherhoods" of Eustathius mentioned in Basil, *ep.* 223, 5

[2] Rufin. *H.E.* 11, 9, p. 1015, 4, Schwartz   Sozom. 6, 17, 4

[3] *Vita S. Isaaci, Acta Sanctorum*, May 7, p. 250e=257a

[4] In Psamathia: discussion by A. M. Schneider, *Byzanz* (1936) pp. 85 and 3, also his maps, B 8–9   Records *re* the cloister in *Callinici Vita S. Hypatii*, ed. Bonn, p. XIIIff.

this man that founded the monastery proper, and succeeded after Isaac's death to the leadership: the monastery being thenceforward known by his name. Following this example, and apparently under the same man's oversight, other cloisters were established afterwards in Constantinople itself.[1]

The second monastery of later renown was founded near the capital by Rufinus, the imperial chancellor; the site was three miles east of Chalcedon (Kadikoi) close to the beautiful Church of the Apostles which he had built. He induced some Egyptian monks to inhabit his foundation; but after he had died and had been buried in the Church of the Apostles, the Egyptians returned home, and the monastery fell vacant. Then it was that Hypatius, a native of Phrygia, and his adherents took up residence there; he had previously lived in a monastery of which Jonas (later canonized) was the head, and which lay in the suburbs of Constantinople on the Thracian side. This time, the occupation of the monastery proved to be permanent, and the leader was soon held in high honour among both the adherents of the church and the general community of the city.[2]

Attention has already been drawn[3] to the fact that Hypatius gave asylum to Alexander, the pilgrim monk, from the hatred of his enemies; and made it possible for him to found an Akoimete monastery "on a lonely site" fifteen miles from Kadikoi. The name of the place was Gomon, and it lay on the coast at the junction of the Black Sea and the Bosphorus.[4] John, who was Alexander's successor, transferred the site of the monastery, in the decade beginning with A.D. 430, to Irenaion (Tshibukle), half-way on the road to Scutari; with the help of a wealthy benefactor, he built there a new Akoimete monastery, the very institution which was later to be the place of origin of many a movement of importance in the history of the church.[5] Abbot Marcellus was of acknowledged authority in the disputes waged by the church in the decade from

[1] *Callinici, Vita S. Hypatii*, p. 23, 17–20   cf. p. 39, 11. 15
[2] See previous footnote and the records in Callinici, *Vita S. Hypatii*, p. XIff.
[3] *vide supra*, 172
[4] *Callinici vita S. Hypatii*, p. 84, 25–31   *vita S. Alexandri*, p. 700, 13   and *vita S. Marcelli*, 4 in Migne gr. 116, 709
[5] *vita S. Marcelli*, 6–7, Migne Gr. 116, 712. C.p. J. Pargoire, *Les débuts du monachisme à Constantinople* (1899), p. 73

A.D. 440. On his initiative, the monastery of Studios was founded at Constantinople in A.D. 463. A quiet and retiring kind of ascetic life had been practised in the west from an early date, and the ideals of asceticism were cultivated among a few groups of like-minded people. A group of devout clerics gathered round Jerome and Rufinus at Aquileia in A.D. 374;[1] and similarly, after being baptized (A.D. 387), Augustine became the centre of a group of disciples practising asceticism. The family of the elder Melanius was influenced by their nephew of the same name, and adopted the life of self-denial.[2] From A.D. 382 to 385, St. Jerome preached asceticism in Rome to upper-class ladies of Marcella's circle, and these had been receptive to such teachings for decades.[3] Anicius Paulinus, the Consular of Campania, together with his consort, Therasia, withdrew from the world in A.D. 394, and practised the ascetic life at Nola.[4] But the west only took slowly and haltingly to the complete repudiation of the world as understood in the east.

Then came St. Martin in the role of a pioneer. Born at Stein on the river Auger in Hungary, he grew up in Pavia; after a short career in the army under Julian, he took his departure and became a hermit. After a restless period of wandering, he settled down not far from Hilary of Poictiers, till he was elected bishop of Tours in A.D. 372. He discharged the duties of his office without surrendering his ascetic way of life. He built himself a cell in the suburbs, two miles from the city; disciples soon gathered round him, living in huts and caverns, until they formed a monastic community of about eighty members: the nucleus of the monastery of Marmoutier, which was very famous at a later date. It is diagnostic of the trend of the times that these monks included many members of the upper classes; later on, the church drew on the group for bishops.[5] In the early stages, however, the community only met with mistrust. The choice of Martin as bishop was vigorously attacked by the existing bishops, from whose standpoint the poverty of the monks seemed to be an undignified self-abasement. The bishops showed their distaste for the holy

---

[1] Jer. *Chron. Ol.* 288, 2, p. 247f., Helm   [2] *Hist. Laus.* 54. 61   [3] *vide supra,* 156
[4] Rauschen, *Jahrbücher,* 547ff.   [5] Sulp. Sev. *vita Martini,* 10

man throughout his official career; nor were they in any way mollified by his attitude to the persecution of the Priscillianists, with its violence and bloodshed.[1] He died on November 10, A.D. 400, revered by the populace as a great miracle-worker; a biography by Sulpicius presented him in that light, and enjoyed a wide public. The laudatory terms in which the work is written, should not be allowed to hide the fact that his bold and aggressive policy did much to put an end to pagan forms of religion, and to carry through the evangelization of the country.

About this time also, the west began to be influenced by Athanasius's *Life of Antony*, which had been translated about A.D. 380 by Euagrius, bishop of Antioch. Monks who lived outside the walls of Trèves came to possess a copy of the book, and they gave it to serious inquirers for their reading. It served to convert the laity: Augustine himself was deeply stirred by the accounts of the celebrated recluse and his scorn of the world. Brothers given to this type of piety were patronized by Ambrose, and they established a monastery outside the gates of Milan.[2] A monastery and also a nunnery were established at Marseilles in A.D. 404 by John Cassian on the eastern model, which he had studied for over seven years in Bethlehem and Egypt.[3] During the time that he spent in his wanderings, St. Martin once chose for a short period, as a site suitable for monastic seclusion, the small "Hen Island" opposite Albenga in the Riviera di Ponente. St. Honoratus stayed for a longer time and with greater practical results on the Isle of Lerinum near Cannes: he founded a monastery there at the beginning of the fifth century,[4] which soon flourished exceedingly and came to be held in great respect in Gaul. St. Eucherius settled on the neighbouring Isle of Lero, and lived there till he was elected bishop of Lyons in *c.* A.D. 435. Castor, who was bishop of Apt in the Vaucluse, established a monastery at his cathedral church; he requested Cassian to give him an account of the monastery rules and the ascetical principle accepted by the monks of Palestine and Egypt, so that they might serve as

[1] *vide supra,* 75 and *vita Mart.* 27   [2] Augustine, *conf.* 8, 6, 15   cf. 8, 12, 29
[3] Gennadius, *vir. inl.* 61   E. Schwartz, *ZNW*, 38 (1939), 8
[4] Hilar. Arelat. *vita S. Honorati*, Migne lat. 50, 1249b

models for cloisters in Gaul. The request gave rise shortly
before A.D. 430 to Cassian's two works: the *Institutes* and the
Collations; a few books of these works being dedicated to the
"brothers living on the Stoechad Islands (Iles d'Hyères)."[1]
In passing, we should remark that islands lying off the coast
in other parts of the world became favourite refuges for monks.
About A.D. 400 Jerome wrote in praise of the devout Fabiola
who, either personally or by means of trustworthy agents,
distributed her benefactions over the Islands, the Tyrrhenian
Sea, the region of the Volsci, and the hidden recesses of the
indented coastline, with its cliffs and chasms, where the
monks lived.[2] A colony of monks was founded in A.D. 398 on
Capraia, an island near the north point of Corsica; within
eighteen years, the monks had stamped their character on the
whole island.[3]

In Spain, it was through the instrumentality of Priscillian
and his friends that asceticism became a widespread movement, although it met with opposition of a most vigorous kind
on the part of the bishops, who had grown worldly. They were
able to gain the victory, though only by violence and bloodshed, over the leaders of the movement, and to brand as heretics
all who had similar tendencies.

In Africa, any and every kind of charismatic inclination
was regarded as a deviation from the ways of the church
universal, and therefore as suspect of Donatism; not till
Augustine made his weight felt was a change of attitude
possible. After his return to Tagaste, his native town, he began
by gathering his friends of Milan into a house-fellowship of
ascetics, of which he himself was the centre. When he was
ordained presbyter in Hippo, he established a "cloister within
the church" for the "servants of God", as he preferred to call
them. Here the case was different from that at Tagaste, in that
it was no longer merely a private group of ascetics. Augustine's
disciples soon began to be looked upon as desirable clerics,
and many of them were elevated to episcopal sees; nevertheless
they continued to be monks, and founded cloisters in their

---

[1] Cassian, *Coll.* 11, praef., p. 312, 9
[2] Jerome, *ep.* 77, 6
[3] Orosius, *hist.* 7, 36, 5   Rutil. Namat. *de red.* 1, 439f.

new bishoprics.[1] Nunneries, too, were established by virtue of Augustine's inspiration; one being founded in Hippo and directed by his sister.[2] After her death, certain irregularities took place, and Augustine wrote to the nuns the famous *epistle 211*; here he laid down the general principles governing the monastic life, and these at a later date were given the necessary alterations of literary form, and then known as the "Rule of St Augustine". This course of events was not contrary to Augustine's views, for he himself desired that the nuns should use the letter as a glass in which they could examine and test themselves; and he wanted it read aloud to them week by week. There were several cloisters in Carthage *c.* A.D. 400; and this was another place where quarrels and disputes occurred regarding the necessity for manual labour: Augustine, at the request of Aurelius, their bishop, had dedicated to them his book on the *Work of Monks*.[3] He was in the full sense of the term the founder and organizer of monasticism in North Africa.

In Italy, as far as can be made out, monasticism of the strict kind, i.e. confined to cloisters, only gained a foothold after the beginning of the fifth century. The monastery outside the gates of Milan to which Ambrose lent his support, and which we have already described,[4] appears to have been the first herald of the whole movement. There is no means of settling the question whether the *pinetum*, in which *c.* A.D. 400 Rufinus laboured and quietly meditated, corresponded to the Egyptian type or not.[5] Nevertheless, Italy felt the influence of the Latin form given by Rufinus to the *History of Monasticisife* of his translation of the Rules of Basil; of Jerome's writings on Pachomius; of the works of Cassian; and most of all, and constantly repeated, of Euagrius's Latin version of the *Lm*; *of Antony*. After A.D. 400, cloisters properly so-called began to increase slowly in Italy. As far as the extant records go, it would seem that Xystus I (A.D. 432-40) founded the first monastery in Rome, near San Sebastiano "*ad Catacombas*"; Leo I (A.D. 440-61) followed in his steps by founding a

[1] Possidius, *vita Aug.* 3. 5. 11   Selections in Cabrol, *Dict.* 11, 1849–58
[2] Possid. *vita Aug.* 26
[3] Aug. *de opere monachorum* and relevant remarks in *retractat.* 2, 47
[4] *vide supra*, 177   [5] Rufin. *de bened. patr. lib.* 2 praef., p. 22, Vallaris

monastery near St Peter's.[1] From this date onwards details, not always trustworthy, begin to multiply as to what was taking place in other cities;[2] and in the course of the fifth century, monasticism had become fully naturalized even in Italy.

When in the time of Pope Damasus (366–84) oriental forms of asceticism were beginning to make a great appeal, opposition to the innovation was expressed in various ways, including that of polemical writings. A certain Helvidius, of whom there is no other record, wrote a tract in which he asserted that, after the birth of Jesus, the Virgin Mary had lived conjugally with Joseph, and borne him children described in Scripture as the brothers and sisters of Jesus. "And why not, indeed? Are virgins in any way superior to Abraham, Isaac, and Jacob, who were married men?" That was an attack on the monks' ideal of Mary, and on the theory of the irrefragable superiority of celibacy which lay at the foundation of asceticism. Jerome attacked the bold scribe and drove him back with vitriolic language, and by an appeal to the support of St. Paul; Damasus rewarded Jerome with his approval.[3]

But in a short time a mightier warrior appeared in the arena. A monk named Jovinian aroused attention and gained respect at Rome, in that, by one and the same stroke, he abandoned the eastern strictness he had been practising, resumed forms of asceticism which were normal in the west, and which did not exclude outright all intercourse with the world.[4] He uttered a warning against the heresy of thinking that celibacy constituted a special merit in God's sight; he even urged men and women who had lived so far as monastics to enter into marriage.[5] He defended his teaching in a document that was widely read by the people of Rome. In it he declared that all who had been baptized, no matter whether they lived in continence, in the widowed or the married state, were equally meritorious, granted that the rest of their conduct was of equal quality. The power to repulse the temptations of the devil was afforded, not by asceticism, but by baptism received in real faith. His doctrine was that being born of

[1] *Lib. pontif.* 46, 7   47, 7   [2] Summary in Cabrol, *Dict.* 2, 3179–92   cf. 11, 1873
[3] Jer. *adv. Helv.* and *ep.* 49, 18, 2   [4] Jer. *adv. Jovinianum,* 1, 40   2, 21
[5] August. *de pecc. mer. et rem.* 3, 13, 7   *retract.* 2, 22   cf. Jer. *adv. Jov.* 2, 36

God as taught by 1 John 3: 9 and 5: 18, shielded us from sin. Similarly, as taught by 1 Tim. 4: 4, it was equally good whether one refrained from certain foods or ate them with a thankful heart; for in God's sight there were no degrees and grades of merit. One and the same reward in the Kingdom was promised to all who had been baptized, as was clearly proved by Matt. 20: 1-16, in the parable of the Workers in the Vineyard.[1]

The attack, made as it was from the gospel as its base, broke with full force on the egoistic motivation of asceticism, and raised a corresponding resentment among those who favoured monasticism; the latter proceeded to lay complaints before Bishop Siricius. The whole of the Roman clergy assembled in convention, defined their attitude to the "abominable document", consigned the initiators of the "new heresy", Jovinian and eight of his followers, to eternal damnation, and excommunicated them from the church. They reported their conclusions officially to a few bishops,[2] and the answer which was sent from Milan is still extant. The men against whom the pronouncement had been directed had made their way to this very place, closely followed by the official representatives of the Roman convention. These delegates were successful in persuading Ambrose to call a few bishops together, and these in turn pronounced sentence of condemnation on Jovinian and his friends. It is in this connection that we are told of certain points that the heretics had asserted: among other things, they had said that after the birth of Jesus, Mary was no longer a virgin in the accepted sense of the term; the predicate applied to her only before she had given birth to Jesus. This is a point, by the way, that brings out clearly the connection between asceticism and the worship of Mary. How serious a view was taken of the attack made by Jovinian is seen in the fact that the powers at the disposal of the state were invoked against him. The result was that the emperor, Honorius, promulgated a decree on March 6, A.D. 398, ordering him to be whipped and then to be banished to an island on the Dalmatian coast; his adherents were to be

[1] Jer. *adv Jov.* 1, 3 cf. 2, 1. 20
[2] Siricius, *ep. 7 Optarem semper* (Coustant, p. 663) Ambrose's answer follows as number 8 *Recognovimus* (Coustant, p. 669); both occur under the name of Ambrose as *ep.* 42

separated and interned on different islands.[1] Jovinian did not live very long, for he is known to have been dead by A.D. 406.[2]

Jerome responded to the request of friends in Rome by writing a refutation of Jovinian in two books. The work is not a judicious piece of writing, but full of perverse distortions and exaggerations so outrageous that his keenest supporters in the project felt ashamed. They recalled the copies which had arrived in Rome, and sent Jerome a list of the offensive passages, together with a request that he would re-write them; above all else he must avoid giving the appearance that praise and appreciation of the condition of virginity was necessarily conjoined with a low regard for, and even condemnation of, the married state:[3] for that would border on the Manichean way of thinking. Jerome felt rebuffed; but his critics were eminent persons, and hence to be dealt with politely. He therefore wrote an open letter, and did his best to meet their objections. Nevertheless what it all amounted to, in the end, was that he claimed the support of St. Paul, and adduced passages from the Bible agreeing with the view that marriage was a state of lower merit. It should be added that this contention of his was also the practical effect of his own experience of life: asceticism had been the one thing to give him a purchase on morality; he could only evaluate marriage in the light of the brothels he had known in his youth, and of the salacious images drawn from them, which only too often flickered in and out among the elements that constituted his religious life. This fact also explains why all his writings and letters which discuss the nature and value of asceticism betray a strong after-taste of abstract studies; they lack the freshness and the force given by genuinely religious experience.

(5) Monastic Theorists

The *Sayings of the Fathers* has frequently been referred to in the preceding pages; it is plainly an artless record portraying

[1] *Cod. Theod.* 16, 5, 53 for the date, cf. Tillemont, 10, 753 and Mommsen *ad loc.*
[2] Jer. *ad Vigilantium*, 1. 2   [3] *ibid. ep.* 49, 2, 50, 3   and *ep.* 48 for Jerome's apology

the feelings and the popular character of the ideas found among the monks in the Natron Valley. On the other hand, Athanasius was a trained thinker who used his literary gifts to commend the ideal of the hermit, and wrote a biography of one of these holy men which is indispensable for understanding the subject. In the seventies of the fourth century, Symeon of Mesopotamia came to the front as a theologian of the Messalian type of ascetics, although his name has only become known to modern scholars as the consequence of researches first published in 1941.[1] It is true that his writings, or at least a considerable selection of them, have for a long time been held in the highest esteem as part of the mystical literature of the Greek Church;[2] they bore the name of Makarius, the early Egyptian ascetic, a device which concealed the secret that the real author was a heretic, and made it possible for his writings to be included in the literature of the Greek Church. Such a camouflage was frequently adopted in those days: among other instances of the sort were certain writings of Apollinaris,[3] which were published as works of Athanasius, Julius of Rome, or Gregory Thaumaturgos, and thereby preserved for the use of the church catholic. Nor are further parallels lacking in the history of early Christian literature. Symeon wrote his works in Greek and they breathe the Greek spirit. The stern, root and branch character of the Messalian Syrians is left on one side; and of the blank refusal by an ascetic to do any kind of labour, or to have the least traffic with anything earthly, there is no mention. On the contrary: an active, practical concern for one's neighbour was a duty explicitly commanded, and not to be condemned.[4] Symeon wrote to encourage and instruct a group of brothers who had had a change of heart, and were making efforts to reach Christian perfection. He shared the view that there was need for completely dispensing with all earthly ties and all possessions, and for the literal fulfilment of the ascetic prescriptions in the Sermon on the Mount, if that perfection was to

---

[1] H. Dörries, *Symeon von Mesopotamien*, 1941 (Texte u. Unters. 55, 1), and other works by Dörries
[2] *Macarii Aegyptii opera*, especially the 50 homilies, ed. Floss, *Migne gr.* 34, 449–822   Also J. Stoffels, *Die mystische Theologie Makarius d. Aeg.* 1908
[3] *vide* Vol. 3, 269f.   [4] *hom.* 3, 2   8, 1. 4

be reached; for anything of an earthly character fettered one's thoughts once more to the earth, and gave Satan a purchase for bringing wickedness into effect.[1] When our Lord said, "Be not anxious", the words were to be obeyed quite literally; with the consequence that the true monk was forbidden to use curative herbs or medicines, or indeed take advantage of any kind of medical therapy. God had ordained such things only for people of the world and "all other outsiders", who were not yet able to surrender themselves to God in complete faith.[2] What was not forbidden was to prepare in a simple way for meeting the requirements of life on the morrow; nay, it was a duty in accordance with God's will that a "perfect" Christian should so prepare.[3]

In the meantime, it was necessary to recognize that outer austerities were of a preliminary nature, and might lead to that false conception of the monastic ideal which never shook itself free from the bonds of earth.[4] The crucial factor was that of a change of heart, for redemption proceeded from within outwards. Even after the fall of Adam, mankind could be said, on formal grounds, to have retained the image of God, in that man's will was still free.[5] But the higher aspect of our nature, due to the logos, had gone, having been replaced by the image of Cain; and the tempestuous nature of the passions tossed human thoughts pell-mell together, as if they were shaken in a sieve.[6] Ever since the days of Adam, Satan had shrouded every human soul in a finely-spun veil, which cut off the divine light, and consigned the soul to the empire of darkness.[7]

It was impossible for a man by his own resources to escape from this woeful state of sin; but God, by His grace, had provided a way of deliverance: Christ, by the death He died on the cross quite guiltlessly, had been too adroit for the devil, and had snatched from him any further claim on the descendants of Adam.[8]

Moreover, by becoming incarnate in man, Christ had restored the possibility of union between the spirit of God and

[1] hom. 11, 7   [2] ibid. 48, 5–6   [3] ibid. 8, 4   [4] ibid. 5, 4   17, 15   38, 1   43, 3
[5] ibid. 1, 7   15, 23   37, 10   [6] ibid. 5, 1–3   [7] ibid. 28, 4   32, 10   cf. 8, 3. 5
[8] ibid. 11, 9–10

human nature, and had smoothed the way along which our soul could again become the habitation of God.[1] The process came about in the individual person in the following manner: God knocked at the door of our heart, to be allowed in; when it came about that we opened to Him, He entered and presented us with the gifts proper to His spirit.[2] At this point, our soul became the scene of a struggle between God and the devil, light and darkness; and the issue depended on the strength of our will.[3] If a man surrendered himself in complete earnestness to the grace of God, his soul would be born anew of God; and the image of Christ, constituted of a fine, delicate, heavenly substance, would form in him and would cast out the aforesaid veil of darkness.[4] The process was not a sudden one, but took place slowly[5] with a continual struggle on the part of the will against sin, which used all its powers to defend its former habitation. In putting up the fight, the soul's most valuable means of aid was prayer, which should be offered up to God unceasingly, but with an evident calmness and quiet peace of heart.[6] Any man whose will could not be bent, and who drove himself forcibly to the practice of the virtues which he lacked, would find a hearing; the Lord would supply him with power such that, in the course of time, he would become habituated to virtue, and do willingly what he had formerly been able to achieve only despite the cravings of his heart. He would then be full of the fruits of the spirit; for the Lord Himself would live in him and fulfil His own commandments in him, with the result that it would be his nature to practise the Christian virtues.[7]

In some cases when a man was earnestly battling in prayer, God would grant his petition at once, even though he were living in the ordinary world; others, He would allow to wait in spite of having long been ascetics, and would test them to see whether their strength of will alone would enable them to bear this trial. But one could be assured of God's grace in the end, for He was One who unfailingly redeemed His promises: "Seek and ye shall find."[8] From another angle of approach,

[1] *hom.* 32, 6   cf. 1, 7   [2] *ibid.* 30, 9   cf. 15, 5   [3] *ibid.* 26, 24
[4] *ibid.* 1, 10   30, 2. 3   49, 4   4, 9. 11   11, 3   30, 4. 5   46, 4   [5] *ibid.* 15, 41. 42
[6] *ibid.* 6, 1–4   40, 2   Dörries, 24   [7] *ibid.* 19, 2–3. 5–7   [8] *ibid.* 29, 1–2   Dörries, 15

it must nevertheless be understood that even the holiest person
was not safe from falling back into sin; not even if, for a time,
he had attained the highest degree of perfection; Symeon
himself had never seen a Christian, free to follow his own
heart, who was in an enduring state of perfection.[1]

In spite of all the preceding, it must still be insisted that an
objective change came about when a man experienced the
divine re-birth. On the one hand, it was seen in his increasingly
effective repression of sin, his growing ease in practising
virtue, his joyful assimilation to the sufferings of Christ in
bearing the hatred of the world. Christians filled by the spirit
fulfilled the commandments of the Sermon on the Mount
joyfully, forgave every act of injustice, loved those who
persecuted them, and did not judge others, not even if they
were openly known to be sinners, and were universally
shunned.[2] On the other hand, the presence of the spirit in
the soul of the re-born was made manifest by the soul's
rapturous ardour of love for God, which was the blessing
given by Christ, the bridegroom, to the soul betrothed to
Him.[3] It was as a kind of heavenly fire that this love glowed
everywhere in the soul, purified her, fed her with heavenly
food, and clothed her in heavenly garments.[4] Her veil of
darkness fell to the ground, the light of heaven illumined the
eyes of her understanding; and those who were specially
blessed were enabled by this light to perceive their own souls
looking like angels, exactly as would be plain to all at the
general resurrection.[5] God in His goodness and mercy might
"abase" Himself, and form a body for Himself out of the most
delicate material, thus becoming similar to sainted souls
whose faith was worthy; and these latter would be able to
see Him, taste His sweetness, and enjoy the graciousness of
His ineffable light. In the same way, God might make His
epiphany in the form of the Heavenly Jerusalem, or incarnate
Himself at the Lord's Supper in the Bread of Life and the
Wine of Heaven; and that was indeed why it came about

[1] *hom.* 17, 6   29, 13   50, 4   8, 5   Dörries, 94
[2] *epist.* 2, p. 420b, c   437c, d   *hom.* 8, 6   37, 4   15. 8   32, 9
[3] *hom.* 4, 14   8, 1   9, 9   30, 4   31, 4   45, 7   46, 6
[4] *ibid.* 4, 14   14. 3. 4. 7   25, 10
[5] *ibid.* 46, 4. 5   7, 5–7   5, 9   11, 1

that He was seen in bodily form by the men of the Old Testament.[1]

The surviving corpus of Symeon's writings contains a few passages in which he spoke about himself, and related his experiences as a visionary; here he explained to the reader why all earthly joys were worthless and entirely of a negative character to a man who had once enjoyed the blessedness of the heavenly vision.[2]

On one occasion, a certain man came home from his day's work and began to pray in his little chamber; within a single hour the prayer laid hold of his veritable inner self, and translated him in rapture into the boundless depths of the world beyond; his thoughts forgot all that was earthly, and were filled with all that was Divine, Heavenly, Boundless, Incomprehensible, Miraculous—and, in the midst of that experience, he prayed and said, "Would that my soul might take wings with my prayer".

Grace was implanted in a man in his earliest youth, as if it were an element of his nature; but it operated by its own choice and with increasing effect. At one time, it would let the fire flame high and the light shine clear in intoxication; but then damp everything down and make it dark. In many cases, the light would imprint the sign of the cross on his inner self; many would be transported by prayer into ecstasy, find themselves in church standing at the altar, and eating bread which increased miraculously; many received a garment of light like John and Peter on the Mount of Transfiguration; or, again, the light which shone in the heart would reveal that other, inner, deeply-buried light, till the whole self sinks away in a sweet vision, and loses his earthly consciousness in the overflow of love and delight due to the hidden secrets.

When the right time came, the man would receive his freedom, reach the height of perfection, and be pure and free from sin. After that, grace withdraws, the veil of the hostile powers returns, and the man sinks down to a lower degree of perfection. There were twelve degrees, and there were blessed persons who spent day and night on the highest stage. But complete permanence was not accorded to that state, for the

---

[1] *hom.* 4, 9-13   [2] Combined from *hom.* 8 cf. 7, 1 and Dörries, 29ff.

one who was enjoying the experience sat in ecstasy and intoxication on one side, unable either to attend to his own needs, to those of his brethren, to the work of preaching the gospel, or to the cares of the morrow. It was therefore not granted that anyone should remain permanently in a state of perfection.

The disciples thereupon requested the master, "Tell us at what stage you yourself stand?" He replied that, first of all, he had received the sign of the cross; then grace began to operate, spreading a sense of peace throughout his body and into his heart until, on account of its intense joy, his soul seemed to be that of an innocent child. As far as he was concerned, he ceased to condemn anybody, whether pagan or Jew, sinner or worldling; rather his inner self surveyed them all with guileless eyes, and rejoiced at everything; he desired nothing else than to pray to God and to exercise love. He trusted as a king's son would trust in the Son of God: like trusting the king, his own father; and when he walked about in His Kingdom, with its numerous habitations (John 14: 2), hundreds upon hundreds of doors opened to him; he was the rich heir of possessions beyond human description. After that, he preached to men as one who had been sent by Christ, and spoke of the heavenly secrets, as far as mankind was able to grasp those incomprehensible elements which belonged to the higher world. The division between these worlds had been dissolved as far as he was concerned, and the heavenly light shone brightly on him day and night, although with varying intensity; sometimes indeed it was veiled in mist, and it was for this reason that Symeon referred to himself and said, "I do not enjoy perfect freedom". In the exegesis[1] that he gave of the well-known vision in which Ezekiel saw the chariot of God, it is possible to perceive the reflexion of a vision which Symeon had seen in ecstasy; and this in turn makes it possible to deduce how he transmuted events in the other world of experience, and used them to teach his disciples in his sermons.

In regard to the question as to the nature of this type of Christianity, the answer is unhesitating, just as in the case of the Egyptian form of asceticism: it was essentially a religion

[1] *hom.* 1   Dörries, 161

of self-redemption, depending on one's strength of will when supported by grace as given by God. Even granted that much emphasis was placed on the fact that it was God who took action in the first instance, and that it was only His grace which conferred any real value on the human will or on human works—nevertheless, the crucial factor was a man's own free will, and his own faithful continuance in steadfast prayer. The incarnation of Christ provided a metaphysical basis for the rehabilitation of the soul in pneumatic and ethical terms; yet it remained true that that rehabilitation was conceived materialistically; the sufferings of Christ were a model, and an inspiring example, for men striving to follow Him.

The church was scarcely mentioned at all, and the sacraments were only incidental matters: they were not the starting-points for the operation of grace. The situation is particularly clear in passages which declare that grace is present as a nucleus even in a child. Statements of this character show that Symeon was a faithful disciple of the Messalian school of ideas about religion. Moreover, he constantly put forward a kind of eschatological relativity, really interested only in the "perfect"; all the rest, whether Christians belonging to the church or pagans outside it, were graded according to their balance of rewards over penalties in the next world. "Many people declare that there is only one Kingdom of Heaven and one hell; our doctrine, however, is that there are many stages, and differences, and degrees, in both heaven and hell"; and he was quite explicit and emphatic in the way he carried these ideas beyond the frontiers of the church.[1] It is there, of course, that we find the very point at which asceticism of this type betrays clearly that it had some roots in soil external to Christianity; and however cautious the "men of prayer" might be, it was always a possibility that the church would set on foot some motion to repudiate them. Yet it must be said in their favour that the profound earnestness of the spirit in which they repudiated the world, and the blessedness of mystic love found in their souls, combined with the rapture of the vision of God, have exercised an irresistible compulsion

[1] *hom.* 40, 3f.

over the hearts of Christians in isolated cases, at all times and in every age, down to and including those who share the religious sensibilities of our own day. In spite of all this, however, we must insist that this type of religion derives not its substance, but only its modes of thought, its metaphors, and its similes, from Christianity.

In the case of Symeon, what had happened was that the Messalian movement had been refined by Greek influences. The fanaticism by which he was animated, with all its radical quality so characteristic of Syria, recurs in a series of thirty Syriac tractates, called the Book of Grades (*Liber Graduum*), discovered recently and first printed in 1926.[1] The tractates were written towards the end of the fourth century, but it is impossible to deduce from their language anything as to the place in which they were written. The anonymous author addresses himself to the brethren, fathers, and sisters in Christ; he urges them to search the Scriptures for the commandments of God, and to grasp their variety and their differences; granting, however, that it could only be done with the help of the Holy Spirit, and by a person who hated his own self, humbly took up his cross, and completely repudiated the world.

The ascetical doctrine of salvation is repeated a hundred times[2] throughout these addresses; it insists on the difference between the "righteous", i.e. those Christians who are members of the church and who live in the world in the ordinary way; and, on the other hand, the "perfect", who are of a different calibre. The "righteous" keep the commandments as to what is required of a citizen who is also a Christian: they avoid murder, theft, adultery; make their assertions only by saying Yes, or No; and they are not greedy of another's property. They are honest in business and do not accept interest on loans. They maintain the purity of the church, and banish from their midst any sinners who do not amend their ways—in accordance with Matt. 18: 16, 17. They had a "decalogue" which was not derived from the Old Testament, but ran as

---

[1] Edited with splendid introductions and provided with a translation by the discoverer, Michael Kmosko, and published in *Patrologia Syriaca*, pars, 1, tome 3, *Liber Graduum*, Paris, 1926 For the problem of the date, cf. Hausherr in *Orientalia Christiana periodica*, 1 (1935), 495–502

[2] Formulated with special clarity in sermons 14. 19. 20.

follows:[1] "Hear, O Israel, our Lord and God is One. Thou shalt love God thy Lord with all thy heart, with all thy strength, and with all thy soul. And thou shalt love thy neighbour as thyself. Thou shalt not kill, not commit adultery, not steal, not bear false witness"—in other words their commandments were compounded from Mark 12: 29-31 and Matt. 19: 18. At baptism, the church administered the sacrament which conveyed the Holy Spirit, and so made it possible to fulfil these commandments and depart this life without sin.[2] And further, a backsliding sinner could restore his purity by means of repentance, for the seal of baptism remained with a Christian till death; it persisted even through times of sinful weakness. All was lost only in the case of the man who stood out unrepentant till the last.[3]

Yet the truth was that the entire earthly church, complete with its sacraments, was only a symbol, like all other earthly things; it was a copy, comprehensible to man, of a supersensible reality: the "hidden church" with its redemptive powers.[4] It was to this church that the "perfect" belonged, i.e., those who had come to possess the Holy Spirit perfectly, and to whom the Paraclete imparted the entire fullness of His revelation.[5] The "perfect" climbed the steep grades which led up to the hidden city; and did not wander off into the easy ways followed by the "righteous".

Three things were indispensable for perfection:[6] humility, love of enemies, a spirit of reconciliation no matter what the circumstances; then the dispensing with all possessions, and even with labour for the means of subsistence; and, finally, continence, and a purity of heart such as Adam enjoyed before the Fall. It was there that one found the secret of redemption which Christ had brought as the Second Adam (1 Cor. 15: 45): we should follow His example, and conquer the sinfulness which had grown from the sensual passions.[7] The conquest would be achieved by repudiating anything and everything earthly, and thus that purity of heart would be gained by which one was enabled to see God.

---

[1] Sermo 22, 21   [2] *ibid.* 28, 8   12, 4   [3] *ibid.* 24, 2   [4] *ibid.* 28, 8
[5] *ibid.* 15, 16   [6] *ibid.* 20, 1, with remarks on p. CVIIIf.
[7] *ibid.* 15, 9   21, 4. 11   25, 2   Christ's Passion as example, cf. Sermo 17

Only the "perfect" had the possibility of fulfilling God's will, in following word for word the sternest of Jesus' sayings; they alone received their reward while yet on earth, for heaven was open to their gaze every day; they sang praises to the Lord as they confessed Him; they walked in the spirit from one stage of glory to the next; and they beheld the Lord in their hearts as if in a mirror.[1] After death, they and they alone, would enjoy the sight of the Lord Jesus Christ in His heavenly church, and join in His blessedness.[2] True, "in the Father's house were many mansions", and the "righteous" would also receive their reward and inherit the Kingdom of God; but their blessedness would be of a lower degree, not to be compared with the bliss of the "perfect".[3] Similarly, those who were only half-heartedly righteous would be found worthy of a reward suited to their good works, after they had suffered the punishment appropriate to their wicked ways.[4]

The point was, therefore, that there was only one course open for a man who meant to take the Christian life in earnest, and attain the goal indicated by the Lord: he must not dally at the preparatory stage characteristic of average churchgoers; but boldly decide to have done with the world altogether, and lay hold on perfection. All the thirty homilies re-echo this exhortation time and again; they were expressly written, indeed, for the purpose of hammering the doctrine home into the souls of the readers. It is insisted with the greatest emphasis that any and every type of asceticism was to be repudiated as just the deceit of the devil, if it clung to the world by manual labour, trade, or possessions of any kind whatsoever; or if it used these means, either for gaining subsistence, or for doing good to others.[5] All works of charity were denied to the "perfect"; all manual labour was forbidden him. What little he needed to live on, the "righteous" were to provide for him;[6] he himself was to concentrate entirely on the progress of his own soul. In other words, he was to give himself to unceasing praise, prayer, and chanting psalms.[7] Nor should he any longer have a home, neither any fixed place for rest; rather, if he have properly and adequately trained him-

---

[1] Sermo 14, 2   [2] ibid. 12, 7   16, 12   20, 14   [3] ibid. 3, 2. 3   15, 10   30, 27
[4] ibid. 15, 10   30, 27   [5] ibid. 25   [6] ibid. 25, 3. 8   [7] ibid. 3, 15   7, 20   14, 2   27, 5

self as an ascetic, he would roam from place to place as a wandering apostle and a living example of the gospel of Jesus Christ.[1]

The homilies betray no hostility of any sort to the church and her teaching; rather, the writer stresses his respect for the church, her bishops, and her doctrine. The significant difference was that he taught it to be the duty of the "perfect" to be friendly towards the "sects", and show pastoral concern for them—whereas the church was in the habit of persecuting heretics; occasionally, even the "perfect" were martyred as a bloody sacrifice to the hatred felt by the church, because they "had said something she thought enigmatic", i.e. some heresy was suspected.[2] Nothing else is required to complete our understanding of the movement: it was obviously a form of radical asceticism such as was characteristic of Syria; nay, the qualities specific to Messalianism are reflected in its repudiation of labour; its regard solely for singing praise or the psalms, and for the practice of prayer; and in its homelessness.

It was Euagrius Ponticus who worked out the theory of monasticism as practised in the desert of Scetis; and fuller records have survived regarding this person and the events of his life.[3] As his name shows, he was born in Pontus of Asia Minor, the actual place being the town of Ibora[4] which lay not far from the Cappadocian border. That may well have been how he became acquainted with Basil, whose monastery at Annesoi[5] was in the vicinity. He became one of the many monks under his supervision, and was installed as "reader" by him. But a monk's life of this kind failed to hold him permanently. After Basil's death, he abandoned the cloister; and he next comes to notice at Constantinople in A.D. 381 as a deacon, and an eager disciple of Gregory Nazianzus. He told a travelling companion of his good fortune in finding his ideal in Gregory, a great Christian orator, and a philosopher. One sign that he had really learned something from Basil was that he soon afterwards wrote a pamphlet on the essential

[1] Sermo 19, 31 27, 4–5 30, 2 [2] ibid. 27, 5 30, 4
[3] Hist. Laus. 38 Socr. 4, 23, 34–71 epist. 22, p. 581, ed. Frankenberg (cf. p. 21), and Bousset. Apophth. Patr. 336
[4] Pauly-W. 9, 816 [5] vide supra, 173

problems of the doctrine of the Trinity.[1] The pamphlet plainly
revealed a characteristic which was to be unmistakably
evident among writers of a later date, viz. that the two
Cappadocians had given him a thorough grounding in Origen's
theology, and that he had taken to it with enthusiasm. When
Gregory left Constantinople, Euagrius remained behind, and
lodged with Nektarius. He only tore himself away and went
to Jerusalem for his own soul's good, but with a bleeding
heart: he had fallen in love with an eminent lady, a love which
caused him severe distress of conscience. The sainted Melanius
was able to speak to him so impressively that she healed his
wounds. He then journeyed to Egypt, and after two years
made his way to the hills of Nitria, where he became a disciple
of Makarius of Alexandria and of Makarius the "Egyptian",[2]
and, eventually, the leading authority on monasticism. Those
monks of the Nitrian desert who were capable of more academic
thought, probably owed it to him that they brought the study
of Origen to full bloom—although, at a later date, the fruits
they garnered were very bitter.

It was while in this district that Euagrius composed those
writings which were soon to be studied as classical documents
and invaluable text-books by the monks of east and west
alike, and which were also translated into Syriac, Armenian,
and Latin. But the verdict of condemnation which the church
pronounced on Origen in the sixth century, applied also to
Euagrius; with the result that, except for small fragments, the
original Greek text of his works has disappeared. The translations were more fortunate, and almost everything he wrote
has survived in the Syriac version.[3] It comprises two major
writings and a number of smaller tracts. I have pointed out on
an earlier page that the Egyptian monks regarded the Bible
with a certain timorous awe as a "holy" book, and were unable
as a consequence to approach the problem of its meaning;[4]
but in the *Antirrhetikos*, Euagrius showed how to follow Christ's

---

[1] Extant in Syriac, cf. Frankenberg, 620–34 and in Greek, cf. Basil, *epist.* 8,
where it is therefore pseudonymous *vide* Bousset, *Apophth.* 335–41
[2] *vide supra*, 139
[3] Edited and translated by W. Frankenberg, *Euagrius Ponticus (Abh. Gött. Ges.*
N.F. 13, No. 2), 1912
[4] *vide supra*, 153

example (Matt. 4: 1-11), and use quotations from the Bible to overcome temptations offered by demons.[1]

There were eight evil spirits which kept a monk under constant attack: the demons of gluttony, adultery, avarice, despondency, irritability, weariness of being a monk, sloth, arrogance. For each of these eight vices, Euagrius indicated the causes and the devilish foundations; and then he gave a quotation from the Bible which would enable the monk to gain the victory. Thus the *Antirrhetikos* formed a useful *vade mecum* for what Euagrius called the "active" monk, i.e. one who was struggling and striving to get nearer heaven. For the "perfect", who had been granted a glimpse of the heavenly secrets, he then wrote *On the 600 gnostic problems*. The work was divided into six books, and as each book dealt with 100 propositions, it is customarily referred to as the *Centuries*.[2]

One feature which marked the *Antirrhetikos* is also very evident in the *Centuries*: Euagrius consciously adopted the literary form which was characteristic of the *Sayings of the Fathers*. He eschewed long discussions, and dispensed altogether with continuous and unbroken discourse—such as occurred in Symeon's writings—and aimed at simply setting forth a series of short and pithy sentences. Thus he presented his teaching in a vivid and effective form easy to remember. It may be added that the *Centuries*, in which speculation was free to move at pleasure, has survived in its Syriac form with a detailed commentary written *c.* A.D. 600 by the archimandrite, Babai. The commentary is of great help in revealing how the construction put on the *Centuries* had been expanded by the monks. Euagrius gave a short sketch of his doctrine of monasticism in a work of two parts called *The Monk*: here 100 sentences are devoted to the "*Praktikos*,"[3] and 50 more to the "*Gnostikos*",[4] and similarly 50 to the *Looking Glass for Monks and Nuns*.[5] A series of letters completes his literary remains.[6] The feature that makes a notable difference between the writings of Euagrius, on the one hand, and on the other, everything else of a cognate kind, was the fact that he owed to Origen the

---

[1] Frankenberg, 427–545   [2] *ibid.* 8–471
[3] Extant in Greek, *Migne gr.* 40, 1219–52   [4] Frankenberg, 546–53
[5] Greek text ed. H. Gressmann in *Texte u. Unters.* Vol. 39 part 4 (1913)
[6] Frankenberg, 554–635

air he breathed, and the idiom he employed; nay, indeed, he went back even earlier—to the tradition of Alexandria. The idea that the perfect monk was a gnostic can be traced back in a straight line to that ideal Christian gnostic whom Clement of Alexandria, in his own day, portrayed as the genuine alternative to the syncretistic gnostic.[1] The conception of heaven and earth, of ways of life here and hereafter, which Euagrius everywhere assumes, is neither more nor less than Origen's idea in all its breadth and depth. It was from the same master that Euagrius learned his Biblical exegesis; and he frequently imparts to his readers the mystical doctrines which he had found in Origen's commentary on the Psalms.[2] The very demons—not mentioned in the Messalian writings —reappear in the forefront of the monastic life in accordance with the Nitrian tradition; not now as mere desert wraiths, but sharing the traits of Origen's spiritual world. They constituted a graded hierarchy of their own; their powers of attack corresponded with their privileges. A person who knew what these were could play off their powers against each other—to his own advantage.[3]

Only a few words need be devoted to describing the graduated system in which the various stages were arranged. The *praktikos* began with faith and reverence, which were undergirded by asceticism, and made permanent by patience and hope. The goal of life was freedom from all emotion, *apatheia*, which gave birth to love. But love was the gateway to knowledge of things (physical gnosis), leading in turn to the praise of God (*theologia*) and supreme bliss.[4] Numerous sentences discuss methods for dealing with the attacks of subversive thoughts; and it is said emphatically that freedom from emotion cannot be gained without disregarding food, drink, reputation, and hygiene.[5] That was what constituted the pre-supposition for higher advance—to the stage of gnosis or *theoria*. The lower stage of knowledge was constituted by that grasp of the concrete or the abstract world which was gained

---

[1] *vide* Vol. 2, 291–95   [2] Bousset, *Apophth.* 287–321
[3] *Pract.* No. 43–46   *Migne* 40, 1244 and No. 58, 1248   No. 31f., p. 1250
[4] *Pract. init.* p. 1221c, No. 56, p. 1223c, d   cf. Bousset 316f.   Reitzenstein, *Hist. Monach.* 128ff.
[5] *Pract.* No. 63, p. 1236

by the use of rational and discursive thought—in other words, it consisted of those objects which Origen spoke of enthusiastically as the first goal of his desires when he began to strive for knowledge.[1] The first goal was succeeded and exceeded, according to Euagrius and also Origen his master, by the intuitive vision of the Holy Trinity, which vision, according to Matt. 5: 8, was reserved for those who were "pure in heart". And that, again, was the blessed condition of those persons who were exalted above all isolated phenomena, continuously engaged in prayer, and who enjoyed perfect communion with God.[2]

In conclusion, it should be said that, while everything that Euagrius had set down in his various writings had to do with the attainment of the final goal, yet it was only rarely and with great restraint that he spoke of the condition of blessedness itself. He frequently emphasized the fact that the blessed ecstasy was granted to the *nous* in time of prayer, and was accompanied by the phenomenon of light.[3] The light enabled the soul to gaze on its own self, "appearing like a sapphire" and see in it "God's place", where God dwells in the illumined *nous*.[4] The first commentator and his later followers, when dealing with the mystic experience of light, were very much more explicit, and loved to describe in detail what the soul might expect to see by virtue of the divine light. It will be recalled that Symeon gave expression to very similar ideas,[5] ideas which originated, not in theoretical considerations, but in the vivid experiences of an ascetic in times of ecstasy. Experiences of an entirely analogous kind are recorded in connection with extra-Christian mysticism: both Plotinus and Philo discussed them.[6]

Basil was another case in point, and was among those who had seen light of that kind;[7] although there would have been

[1] *vide* Vol. 2, 310ff.
[2] Letter 62, p. 611   *Cent.* 7, 23. 29. 30. 43, pp. 443, 53, 55, 59, ed. Frankenberg
[3] *Cent.* 7, 4, p. 427   7, 6, p. 429   7, 29, p. 453   7, 30, p. 455, Frankenberg
[4] *ibid.* 7, 28, p. 453, Frankenberg   *Pract.* No. 70. 71   Migne 40, 1244   ct No. 36, p. 1232   Further details in Bousset, *Apophth.* 318. 332   Holl, *Enthusiasmus u. Bussgewalt*, 38–40. 181. 211
[5] *vide supra*, 184ff.
[6] Plotinus, *Enn.* 4, 8, 16, 99   cf. Vol. 3, 36f.   *re* Philo, *vide* Bousset, *Apophth* 332f.
[7] Greg. Naz. *or.* 43   *Migne gr.* 46, 809c

no record of it except for Gregory of Nazianzus, who frequently discussed ecstasy and the vision of God,[1] and who described the kind of experience that his friend had had. Basil wrote about such matters with great restraint in his various works; his speeches and tracts on asceticism, of course, point out the way to the goal of perfection, and do so with a sober dignity of language; but they do not touch on the delicate secret of the highest phase of the inner life. Yet the cogency and clarity with which he wrote, and which reflected the strength of character of an outstanding leader, meant that what are known as the "Rules of Basil" afterwards became the text-book for the Greek monastics. If the objects sought were further and deeper experiences of a mystical character, they were always accessible in discussion by other writers.

Four addresses of fundamental importance have come down from Basil himself: on the nature, aim, and mode of organizing the ascetic life.[2] In addition are his *Detailed Rules* under 55 heads and his *Short Rules* under 313 heads. They are in the form of question and answer, but without any special arrangement; and they discuss in penetrating fashion, not only the basic problems of the monastic life, but also the numberless incidental questions which arise in the day-to-day life of a cloistered community, together with all the searchings of conscience and the minutiae of the practice of asceticism. The *Short Rules* are in fact based on notes of the pastoral conversations between Basil and the inmates of his monastery, held by night during the hours set aside for meditation.[3]

In the *Moralia*, it is as obvious as it is impressive that Basil was a Biblical scholar trained in the school of Origen. He presents a large number of the most varied questions of faith and practical morals, states his own position in a few words, and supports each instance with a quotation from Scripture. Although the writing was not specifically intended for monks, but was addressed to Christians as such, yet in effect it is a single, forceful admonition in support of the ascetic life. Basil did not adopt the current distinction between the ethics of a

[1] K. Holl, *Amphilochius*, 205–7
[2] For the problem of authenticity cf. Holl. *Enthusiasmus u. Bussgewalt*, 157, footnote 1; and regarding Basil, 156–70
[3] Bas. *reg. brev. proem.* p. 413c

Christian in the world, on the one hand, and, on the other, a higher type striving for perfection. God's commandments applied to all men, and were binding without exception. The words, "ye shall be perfect", applied to every individual; and no one was free to choose whether he would strive for perfection, or content himself with a lower degree of acceptable righteousness. His only choice was whether he would set himself the highest goal as a continent person, or live in the married state. That was the sole concession that God had made to human weakness: He "forgave" the physical emotions which arose in marriage. Once this was granted, all the rest of the requirements were identical for both conditions of life; and anyone who thought he could neglect certain commandments when carrying on the business of life in the world did so at his own peril, and the peril was great and fearful.[1]

It was possible to become perfect even in the world; but it was very difficult, so difficult that it could almost be described as impossible.[2] If a man would save his soul, let him lay hold of the ascetic life: it would train him in keeping God's commandments, all of which could and should be fulfilled.[3] Similarly to the first of Luther's Ninety-five Theses, there is a stern echo in the saying:[4] This world is the place for repentance, the next for retribution and reward. According to Matt. 22: 36-40, the first commandment had to do with our love for God, the second with that for one's neighbour; and in each case, the nucleus of the power necessary to keep it was planted in our own nature.[5] But consider the facts: to love God means to keep His likeness always in mind; to let the whole of one's thought be ruled by Him; and with this as a source of power, to march out and fulfil the commandments, which would imply breaking entirely free from the fetters welded on us by this life and its passions. A man who accomplished that would, *ipso facto*, enter into another world, and could no longer remain as a prisoner in this world below.[6] To love God meant to deny the world completely.

---

[1] *reg. fus. prooem.* 3. 4, p. 329–333   *de renunt. saec.* 1. 2, p. 202d–4a
[2] *reg. fus.* 6, p. 344d   *moralia* 2, 1, p. 236c   [3] *mor.* 8, 1, p. 240d
[4] *reg. fus. prooem.* p. 327d
[5] *reg. fus.* 1. 2, p. 335–36   natural state, 2, 1, p. 337a   and 3, 1, p. 340c
[6] *ibid.* 5, 2, p. 342b, c

That was not to be understood as meaning we should follow
the path that led to the isolation of anchoritism, for side by
side with the commandment to love God was that which bid
us love our neighbour; the two were inseparable, and each
had need of the other.[1] And it was a life lived in common
with other ascetics that first made it possible for us to combine
repudiation of the world with an active, neighbourly love;
and, by the submission of one's will to that of the spiritual
director, to develop the virtue of obedience; in one's attitude
to the brothers, humility, helpfulness, long-suffering, and all
the Christian virtues. Such a monastic community became
what Paul termed "a body", of which the head was Christ,
each member being aware of serving Him; and in which the
power of the Holy Spirit streamed out from a single person,
and enveloped all the others.[2] Such a cloister would also be a
source of blessing for those outside its circle; and many a man
in need of spiritual support or some word of wisdom would
knock on the door and be given a friendly welcome.[3]

In describing the ascetic way of life, Basil agreed with
the main lines which Athanasius's *Vita Antonii* had made
traditional. He also shared the view that the repudiation of
the world and the surrender of all possessions was the first
step in the warfare against every earthly passion; and that the
goal was the recovery of the lost image of God. Only by
recovering this image, and with it the original beauty of
creation, was it possible to attain eternal salvation. Those who
wanted to live the discarnate life of the angels and, like them,
see God continuously face to face, must march forth beyond
the common ruck of mankind.[4]

The directions for practical life begin by prescribing rules
for a novice's first steps under the guidance of an older
teacher;[5] they go on to a comprehensive set of regulations for
the whole of the monastic life, in both forms of the rules.
Basil set the greatest value on a president who acted as a
monarchical ruler in the strict sense of the term, and who thus
led the community; he was to function in God's place regarding

[1] *reg. fus.* 3, 1. 2, p. 340b–d   [2] *ibid.* 7, 2, p. 346c–e
[3] *ibid.* 45, 1, p. 392a   cf. *reg. brev.* 97, p. 449c
[4] *sermo ascet.* 1, 1, p. 318f.   1, 2, p. 320a, b   [5] *de renunt. saec.* 2–4, p. 204–5

both the outer and the inner details of the monks' lives; he would also be their example in every respect.[1] Common prayer at the stated hours was a duty. Basil reached the seven canonical hours in the following way: he adopted the six customary hours of matins, tierce, sext, nones, vespers, midnight, and divided the mid-day prayers (sext) into one portion before and one after the meal.[2] However, in another passage, he increased the number of hours to eight. In this case, there was but one prayer at mid-day, but a night prayer was introduced between midnight and dawn: the matutin, "at the first cockcrow", which is also recorded elsewhere;[3] then, in addition to vespers, which was observed on the completion of the day's work, another prayer was introduced at dusk and before retiring for the night, at which Psalm 91 was recited.[4] In the prescriptions which he laid down for the reception of novices, Basil showed that he had a clear understanding of the practical questions involved; and it is highly instructive to read how grave were the warnings he uttered against a hasty and unconsidered parting with one's earthly possessions; and how he points out the dangers to which it may lead, e.g. unedifying arguments and even lawsuits.[5] Runaway slaves were not received in,[6] nor was a married person unless he or she was in a position to testify before several witnesses that the other spouse was agreeable.[7] Children were to be received no matter what their age: orphans without more ado, but others only when given over by their parents in the presence of witnesses.

All children were to be looked after and trained apart from the adults, and even provided with a higher education. When they were old enough to reach decisions for themselves, they were to exercise their own freedom of choice whether to dedicate themselves to the monastic life, or go out into the world. In the latter case, they must make their choice in the presence of witnesses.[8] A monk who did not wish to return to the world, but who wished to leave the community in order

---

[1] *sermo ascet.* 1, 3, p. 320f.   2, 2, p. 324f.   *reg. fus.* 43, p. 389f.
[2] *de renunt. saec.* 8, p. 209e   *sermo ascet.* 1, 4, p. 321f.   [3] *vide* Vol. 3, 304f.
[4] *sermo ascet.* 1, 4, p. 321, reckons seven hours   *reg. fus.* 37, 3–5, p. 383f. reckons eight hours
[5] *reg. fus.* 9, 1–2, p. 351f.   [6] *ibid.* 11, p. 353   [7] *ibid.* 12, p. 354
[8] *ibid.* 15, p. 355–57

the better to be able to profit his own soul—of which Euagrius Ponticus was an example—must explain his reasons to the leading persons of the cloister, and then, with their agreement shown in front of witnesses, he could take his departure.[1] Considerable insight is shown by Basil in what he has to say about the supervision and administration of an ascetical community, and about the self-denials or the penalties which may be imposed. As compared with the radical character of many of the injunctions on which Symeon of Mesopotamia laid stress, there is much that is very satisfying in Basil's warm defence of the art of medicine with which he concluded his Detailed Rules.[2]

All these directions and discussions reveal the quality of Basil, and show that he was a man trained in the Greek tradition and in Origen's religious attitude. He showed the freshness of youth in his loyalty to his group; he seized with all his might on the revelation of God vouchsafed by the Greek tradition of Christianity, and he strove to preserve it in all its fullness. The Greek church, in her turn, showed her sense of obligation to him; for she adopted his Rules universally, and has preserved them to the present day as the main principles of monastic life in the Orthodox form of Christianity.

[1] *reg. fus.* 36, p. 381　　　　[2] *vide supra*, 184 *reg. fus.* 55, p. 397–401

Here ends the manuscript as Hans Lietzmann left it at his death on June 25, 1942.

Literature

and original authorities cited in abbreviated form in the foregoing pages; the lists given in the preceding volumes are not repeated here.

Aphrahat, cited in the edition by J. Parisot in the *Patrologia Syriaca*, 1, 1-2, Paris, 1894-1907.

Apophthegmata Patrum, vide supra, p. 140, footnote 5.

Athanasius: H. Fromen, *Athanasii historia acephala,* Phil. dissertation, Münster, 1915; F. Larsow, *Die Festbriefe d. hl. A., Bischofs v. Alex, aus dem Syrischen Übersetzt,* Leipzig, 1852; A.'s *vita Antonii,* ed. Montfaucon, Vol. 1, 2 (1698); *vide supra,* 162, footnote 7.

Augustine: The works cited are, *De opere monachorum, Retractationes, De peccatorum meritis et remissione,* as given in *Corp. Script. Eccl. Lat.:* Vols. 41, 36, and 60. The *Confessiones* are cited according to Skutella, Leipzig, 1934.

Basil is cited from the Benedictine edition by J. Garnier and Pr. Maran, Paris, 1721-30, 3 vols. (the letters in Vol. III, and the ascetical writings in Vol. II).

Campenhausen, Hans von, *Ambrosius von Mailand als Kirchenpolitiker,* Berlin, 1929 (*Arb. z. Kirchengesch.* 12).

Canons of the Councils, if Labbé is not cited (*vide* Vol. II, 318) then cf. H. Bruns, *Canones Apostolorum et Conciliorum,* Vol. I, Berlin, 1839; Fr. Lauchert, *Die Kanones der wichtigsten altkirchlichen Konzilien,* Leipzig, 1898.

Cassianus, John, ed. by Petschenig in *Corp. Script. Eccl. Lat.,* Vols. XIII and XVII, Vienna, 1886-88.

Chronicon Edessenum cited from Guidi's edition in *Corp. Script. Christ. Orientalium, script. Syri* III, Vol. IV, Paris, 1904.

Claudianus, ed. by Th. Wirt, Berlin, 1892 (*Monum. Germaniae, Auct. antiqu.* Vol. X).

Codex Theodosianus, ed. Th. Mommsen and P. M. Meyer, Berlin, 1905.

Coustant, Pierre, *Epistolae Romanorum Pontificum*, Paris, 1721.

Cyril of Jerusalem cited in the edition by W. Reischl and J. Rupp, Munich, 1848-60, 2 vols.

Digesta in the stereotype ed. of *Corpus Iuris*, by Th. Mommsen and P. Krüger, Vol. I, Berlin, 1911.

Epiphanius cited from edition by K. Holl, Leipzig, 1915ff. (In the *Berlin corpus*, Vols. 25, 31, 37.)

Facundus, *Pro defensione trium capitulorum*, ed. J. Sirmond, Paris, 1629 (followed by *Migne Lat.* 67, 527ff.).

Gaius, *Institutiones*, edd. P. Krüger and W. Studemund, Berlin, 1905 (*Collectio librorum juris antejustiniani*, Vol. I).

Gennadius, small edition by C. A. Bernoulli, *Hieronymus und Gennadius, De viris inlustribus*, Freiburg, 1895.

Gregory of Nazianzus, cited from the Benedictine edition, Vol. I (The speeches), Paris, 1778, Vol. II, 1840.

Gregory of Nyssa, *Contra Eunomium*, ed. W. Jaeger, Berlin, 1921, 2 vols.

Heussi, Karl, *Der Ursprung des Mönchtums*, Tübingen, 1936.

Holl, Karl, *Enthusiasmus und Bussgewalt beim Griechischen Mönchtum*, Leipzig, 1898.——*Amphilochius von Ikonium*, Tübingen, 1904.

Iordanis Romana et Getica, rec. Th. Mommsen, Berlin, 1882 (*Monum. Germaniae Auct. Antiqu.*, Vol. V, 1).

Jerome, complete edition, by D. Vallarsi, Verona, 1734ff., 11 vols. *Letters*, ed. J. Hilberg, in *Corp. Script. Eccl. Lat.*, 54-56, 1910ff. *The Chronicle*, ed. R. Helm in Vol. VII (2 parts) of the edition of Eusebius in the Berlin Corpus (Vol. XXIV and XXXIV), Leipzig, 1913-26.

Koch, Hugo, *Quellen zur Geschichte der Askese und des Mönchtums in der alten Kirche*, Tübingen, 1933.

Maximini dissertatio contra Ambrosium, ed. Fr. Kauffmann, *Aus der Schule des Wulfila*, Vol. I, Strassburg, 1899.

Namatianus, Rutilius Cl., *De reditu suo*, ed. L. Müller, Leipzig, 1870.

Pacatus in *Duodecim Panegyrici Latini*, ed. Guil. Baehrens, Leipzig, 1911.

Pachomius, *vide supra*, 142, footnotes 3 and 4.

Palladius, *Hist. Lausiaca*, *vide supra*, 150, footnote 3, and 162, footnote 7.

Paulinus, *Vita Ambrosii*, in the Benedictine edition of Ambrose, Vol. I, Paris, 1686.

Photius, *Bibliotheca*, ed. J. Bekker, Berlin, 1824.

Possidius, *Vita Augustini*, Benedictine edition of the works of Augustine, Vol. X (Paris, 1690), Appendix, 257ff.

Priscillian, edition by G. Schepss, in *Corp. Script. Eccl. Lat.*, Vol. XVIII, Vienna, 1889.

Rauschen, Gerhard, *Jahrbücher der Christlichen Kirche unter dem Kaiser Theodosius d. Grossen*, Freiburg, 1897.

Reitzenstein, Richard, *Historia Monachorum* und *Historia Lausiaca, eine Studie zur Geschichte des Mönchtums und der frühchristlichen Begriffe Gnostiker und Pneumatiker*, Göttingen, 1916. (Cited as *Studie*.)

Rufinus, *Church History*, ed. Th. Mommsen in the large edition of Eusebius's *Church History*, ed. E. Schwartz, Leipzig, 1903ff., 3 vols. (in the Berlin Corpus). The history of Monasticism (=Hist. mon.) *vide supra*, 150, footnote 2.

Seeck, Otto, edition of Qu. Aurelius Symmachus, Berlin, 1883, (*Monum. Germaniae Auct. Antiqu.*, Vol. VI, 1).

Sulpicius Severus, ed. C. Halm, Vienna (*Corp. Script. Eccl. Lat.*, Vol. I).

Theodoret, Complete edition, ed. Schulze-Noesselt, Halle, 1769-74, 5 vols. The *historia religiosa* in Vol. III.

Tillemont, Seb. Le Nain de, *Mémoires pour servir à l'Histoire ecclésiastique des six premiers siècles*, Paris, 1693ff., 16 vols.

Turner, C. H. *Ecclesiae occidentalis monumenta iuris antiquissimi*, 2 vols., Oxford, 1899-1939.

Wessel, Carolus, *Inscriptiones graecae christianae*, Berlin, 1950.

Zosimus, *Historia*, ed. L. Mendelssohn, Leipzig, 1887.

SUGGESTIONS FOR FURTHER READING

The following general works may be consulted: L. Duchesne, *Early History of the Christian Church*, vol. ii (1922); B. J. Kidd, *A History of the Church to A.D. 461*, vol. ii (1922); *Cambridge Medieval History*, vol. i *The Christian Empire* (1911), which has useful bibliographies of the older literature.

For theology and dogmatics, see J. F. Bethune-Baker, *An Introduction to the Early History of Christian Doctrine to the time of the Council of Chalcedon* (eighth edition, 1949); J. Tixeront, *History of Dogmas*, vol. ii (St. Louis, Mo., second edition, 1926); A. Harnack, *History of Dogma*, Eng. tr. vols. iv-v; G. L. Prestige, *Fathers and Heretics* (1940).

Good articles on many of the characters in this period are to be found in the *Dictionary of Christian Biography*, edited by W. Smith and H. Wace (1877-87).

For credal developments, see J. N. D. Kelly, *Early Christian Creeds* (1950); J. F. Bethune-Baker, *The Meaning of Homoousios in the Constantinopolitan Creed* (Texts and Studies, vii. 1, 1901).

On Ambrose, Chrysostom, and the problem of Church and State, see F. Homes Dudden, *The Life and Times of St. Ambrose* (1935); K. M. Setton, *The Christian Attitude to the Emperor in the Fourth Century* (New York, 1941); C. N. Cochrane, *Christianity and Classical Culture* (1940).

Monasticism

C. Butler, *The Lausiac History of Palladius* (Texts and Studies, vi. 1-2, 1898-1904); W. O. Chadwick, *John Cassian* (1950); W. K. L. Clarke, *St. Basil the Great* (1913); R. N. Flew, *The Idea of Perfection* (1934); J. O. Hannay, *The Spirit and Origin of Christian Monasticism* (1903); K. E. Kirk, *The Vision of God* (1931); E. F. Morison, *St. Basil and his Rule* (1912); E. White, *History of the Monasteries of Nitria and of Scete* (New York, 1932); H. B. Workman, *The Evolution of the Monastic Ideal* (1913).

Translations

A. J. Mason, *Fifty Spiritual Homilies of St. Macarius the Egyptian* (1921), translates the 'Messalian' homilies. W. K. L. Clarke has translated Gregory of Nyssa's *Life of St. Macrina* (1916), *The Lausiac History of Palladius* (1918), and *The Ascetic Works of St. Basil* (1925). Chrysostom's Homilies on the Statues and on the New Testament are in the Oxford *Library of the Fathers* (1841 ff.). Works of Ambrose, Basil, Gregory of Nazianzus, Gregory of Nyssa, Jerome, Rufinus, Cassian, Sulpicius Severus, Cyril of Jerusalem, and Athanasius, are translated in the *Nicene and Post-Nicene Fathers* (Oxford and New

York, second series, 1890 ff.). Basil's letters are also available in the Loeb *Classical Library*, translated by R. J. Deferrari; Athanasius's *Life of Antony* is also translated by R. T. Meyer (*Ancient Christian Writers*, vol. 10, Westminster, Maryland, 1950). Augustine's *de Opere Monachorum* is in the Oxford *Library of the Fathers*, vol. xxii (1847). Palladius' *Life of Chrysostom* is translated by H. Moore (1921).

The Byzantine World

On the culture and piety of the East Roman world see also N. H. Baynes, *The Hellenistic Civilization and East Rome* (1946), and *The Thought World of East Rome* (1947). Contemporary biographies of Byzantine saints are translated with notes by E. Dawes and N. H. Baynes, *Three Byzantine Saints* (1948). In general see N. H. Baynes and H. St. L. B. Moss, *Byzantium* (1948), with bibliographies there.

INDEX

Mostly of proper names and of important items not mentioned in the Table of Contents.